PRINCIPLES OF EQUITY

NATURAL LAW AND
ENLIGHTENMENT CLASSICS

Knud Haakonssen,
General Editor

Henry Home, Lord Kames

NATURAL LAW AND
ENLIGHTENMENT CLASSICS

Principles
of Equity

Henry Home, Lord Kames

The Third Edition

Edited and with an Introduction by
Michael Lobban

Major Works of Henry Home, Lord Kames

LIBERTY FUND
Indianapolis

Introduction, editorial apparatus, and index © 2014
by Liberty Fund, Inc.

Frontispiece and cover (detail): Portrait of Henry Home, Lord Kames, by David Martin. Reproduced with permission of the National Galleries of Scotland.

Library of Congress Cataloging-in-Publication Data

Kames, Henry Home, Lord, 1696–1782.
Principles of equity/Lord Henry Home Kames; edited and with an Introduction by Michael Lobban.—Third Edition.
pages cm.—(Natural law and enlightenment classics) (Major Works of Henry Home, Lord Kames) Includes bibliographical references and index.
ISBN 978-0-86597-615-3 (hardback)—ISBN 978-0-86597-616-0 (paperback)
1. Equity—Great Britain. I. Lobban, Michael. II. Title.
KD674.K36 2014
346.41′004—dc23   2013020012

LIBERTY FUND, INC.
8335 Allison Pointe Trail, Suite 300
Indianapolis, Indiana 46250-1684

CONTENTS

EDITOR'S INTRODUCTION

Henry Home was born in 1696 at Kames in the Scottish borders, the son of an indebted laird. Having been educated at home by private tutors, he was sent at the age of sixteen to train for the lower branch of the Scottish legal profession by studying in the chambers of a writer to the signet (attorney). Attracted by the riches promised by the bar, within two years he resolved to become an advocate (counsel) and began to study both Roman law and the classics. He attended James Craig's private College of Civil Law in Edinburgh, where he composed for himself a collection that identified errors made by civilian writers. He continued to study hard after his admission to the Faculty of Advocates in 1723, and nine years later he applied unsuccessfully to fill the vacant professorship of Roman law in Edinburgh. By now, he had obtained a good and lucrative legal practice, particularly in commercial matters. Coming from a family which had both Jacobite and Hanoverian connections, Kames had been a zealous Jacobite when a young man. Although by the 1730s he had become "quite disentangled from Jacobitism"[1] and was appointed an Advocate Depute (or crown prosecutor) in 1737, his early Jacobite connections may have contributed to his slow advancement to the bench. It was not until 1752 that he was appointed to Scotland's highest civil court, the Court of Session, whereupon he took the title of Lord Kames, after the modest family estate which he had inherited in 1741. His later wealth derived not from that estate, but from his wife Agatha Drummond's inheritance of her family's estate at Blair Drummond in Stirlingshire in 1766. In 1763, Kames secured an additional appointment to the High Court of Justiciary, dealing with criminal cases, and remained active on that court until his death in 1782.

---

1. Geoffrey Scott and Frederick A. Pottle, *Private Papers of James Boswell from Malahide Castle* (privately printed, 1932), vol. 15, p. 270.

Kames is well known as one of the leading figures of the Scottish Enlightenment. He was a friend (as well as a cousin) of David Hume and a mentor and patron to Adam Smith, John Millar, and Thomas Reid. His interests were broad and he wrote influential works in a number of fields. His *Principles of Morality and Natural Religion* (1751) was a work of moral philosophy, which helped establish the Scottish Common Sense philosophy developed more fully by Reid. His *Historical Law-Tracts* (1758) and *Sketches of the History of Man* (1774) were works of historical sociology, which discussed the well-known 'four-stage theory' of social development. His *Elements of Criticism* (1762) was an important work on aesthetics. Late in life, he even wrote a work on husbandry, *The Gentleman Farmer* (1776). Besides such works on history, philosophy, and aesthetics, Kames also produced a number of works on legal topics. These included his *Essays upon Several Subjects in Law* (1732), *Statute Law of Scotland, abridged with historical notes* (1757), and *Elucidations Respecting the Common and Statute Law of Scotland* (1777). But the most important of his law works was his *Principles of Equity*, first published in 1760. Kames continued to work on it in later life, producing a second edition in 1767 and a third in 1778.

The book brought together his philosophical interests and his knowledge of the detailed doctrines of Scots law. This knowledge derived not only from his experience as an advocate and judge, but also from his work as a reporter, for he was particularly influential in the development of systematic law reporting in Scotland. Decisions of the Court of Session had long been collected privately and circulated in manuscript, but it was not until the 1680s that any collection was put into print.[2] In the early eighteenth century, the Faculty of Advocates appointed a number of individuals to develop an official collection of decisions, and some of their work found its way into print. At the same time, unofficial collections which would contribute to the systematization of reporting were made by other lawyers,

---

2. The first to appear was Sir James Dalrymple of Stair, *The Decisions of the Lords of Council & Session in the Most Important Cases Debate before Them, with the Acts of Sederunt . . . from June 1661 to July 1681* (Edinburgh: Andrew Anderson, 1683), with a second volume following in 1687. On the history of law reports in Scotland, see David M. Walker, *A Legal History of Scotland,* vol. V: *The Eighteenth Century* (Edinburgh: T. & T. Clark, 1998), pp. 5–17.

including the young Henry Home. In 1728, he published a collection of *Remarkable Decisions of the Court of Session from 1716 to 1728*, in which he sought to illustrate new points of law which had developed since the publication of Lord Stair's *Institutions*. In 1766, he published a further set of *Remarkable Decisions,* covering the years 1730 to 1752; and shortly before his death, another collection of *Select Decisions* appeared. More influential still was his work in assembling a dictionary of decisions, the first volume of which was published in 1741.[3] In it, he gathered together and abridged material from eight printed and seventeen manuscript collections, arranging it in a way to illustrate particular principles. Kames's two volumes were supplemented by two further volumes by Alexander Fraser Tytler published in 1770 and 1797. Together, these works laid the foundation for William Maxwell Morison's definitive thirty-eight-volume *Dictionary.*

By the time *Principles of Equity* was published, Kames had been on the bench for eight years. As a judge, he acquired the reputation of wanting to get through business as quickly as possible, to leave time for his other pursuits. He was not always popular, since he could be blunt or coarse, having a "fretfulness and liveliness in his expressions as an Ordinary, which did not suit with the gravity and dignity of a judge."[4] At the same time, if the nature of the case was such as to encourage metaphysical speculation, he could engage in subtle and abstract reasoning which might go over the heads of the audience. Kames was also sometimes unpopular with his colleagues for seeking to make innovations both in substantive law and procedure, in line with his view that law was mutable and susceptible to improvement with the progress of society. The tension is well captured in Boswell's ditty:

> Alemoor the judgement as illegal blames,
> 'Tis equity, you bitch, replies my lord Kames.[5]

---

3. *Decisions of the Court of Session, from its first institution to the present time. Abridged and digested under heads in the form of a dictionary,* 2 vols. (Edinburgh: Richard Watkins, Alexander Kincaid and Robert Fleming, 1741).

4. John Ramsay of Ochtertyr, quoted by Ian Simpson Ross, *Lord Kames and the Scotland of His Day* (Oxford: Clarendon Press, 1972), p. 132.

5. James Boswell, *The Court of Session Garland,* quoted in Ross, *Lord Kames,* p. 222. Boswell's other judge is Andrew Pringle, Lord Alemoor, a judge of the Court of Session and High Court of Justiciary from 1759 to 1769.

Kames on Legal Development

Kames's legal and philosophical thought developed together. His view of law was informed by his ideas on the nature of human development and the influence of the moral sense. In turn, some of these ideas were developed in his elaboration of legal doctrines, both in his reports and in his treatises. For instance, in his first work, *Essays upon Several Subjects in Law,* he explained that an examination of human nature could show that rules of prescription were not merely the creature of positive law, but derived from natural feelings. Mankind, he argued, had an affection for property, which "leads us to bestow Care in preserving, Labour and Industry in improving what we thus consider as our own." This affection was "as much founded in Nature as that we bear to our Children, or any Affection whatever." Rules of prescription, according to which rights to land could be lost and gained over time, thus derived from the fact that the feelings of affection one had for one's property faded the more one was separated from it. Anyone who consulted "his own Heart about it" would find confirmation of this basis for prescriptive rights.[6]

Kames's theory of the moral sense, and its relation to law, was first set out in his *Principles of Morality and Natural Religion.* It was later restated in the preliminary discourse to the second edition of *Principles of Equity* and then included in the *Sketches.* According to his theory, the principles of morality—or the law of nature—were not to be found in abstract reason but in the facts of human nature. This nature "is made up of appetites and passions, which move us to action, and of the moral sense, by which these appetites and passions are governed."[7] Unlike animals, man was endued with a conscience "to check and control his principles of action, and to instruct him which of them he may indulge, and which of them he ought to restrain."[8]

6. "Observations upon Prescription," in *Essays upon Several Subjects in Law* (Edinburgh: R. Fleming & Co, 1732), pp. 101–3.

7. Henry Home, Lord Kames, *Essays on the Principles of Morality and Natural Religion* (3rd edition, Edinburgh: John Bell; London: John Murray, 1779; edited by Mary Catherine Moran, Indianapolis: Liberty Fund, 2005), p. 40.

8. Ibid., p. 41.

While Kames's view of the moral sense built on the work of Shaftesbury and Hutcheson, he considered that these writers had not fully explored the nature of duties and justice in a way that would provide principles to guide human actions. In Kames's view, the moral sense taught a distinction between duty and benevolence. The moral sense dictated—as a matter of fact confirmed by everyone's experience—that actions directed at harming others were wrong and that people were consequently under a duty not to perform them. Equally, it taught that people were under a duty to be grateful to their benefactors and to perform their engagements. These "primary virtues" were essential to society: since society could not subsist without them, they "are objects of the foregoing peculiar sense, to take away all shadow of liberty, and to put us under a necessity of performance." Kames argued, against Hume, that the sense of justice which taught these duties was naturally universal, not artificial as argued by his kinsman. Anyone who harmed another or invaded his property, or who failed to keep his positive promises, experienced remorse and felt that he merited punishment for breaching a duty. By contrast, the virtues of benevolence or generosity, which were not "so necessary to the support of society," were regarded by the moral sense as "secondary." They were a matter of choice rather than compulsion, and were "left upon the general footing of approbatory pleasure."[9] Against Shaftesbury, he argued that there was no principle of universal benevolence. While the principles of justice were enforced by effective natural sanctions, universal benevolence could not be made into a strict duty, since the limited abilities and capacities of man were unsuited to it. However, Kames also argued that benevolence could become a duty in certain circumstances. The stronger the connection between two parties, the greater was the impulse to benevolence. Where the connection was a close one—as between parent and child—benevolence could become a duty, since neglecting to act would be "attended with remorse and self-condemnation."[10] But the more distant the connection, the weaker the sense of duty.

Kames also argued that the moral sense developed with the progress

9. Ibid., pp. 33, 35–36.
10. Ibid., p. 57.

of society. The law of nature was not stationary, but "must vary with the nature of man, and consequently refine gradually as human nature refines."[11] The four-stage theory of human development played a prominent role in Kames's views of both social and legal development.[12] He argued that in his original state, man was ruled more by his appetites and passions than by general principles which could be derived from the moral sense. Hunter-gatherer societies had only the most limited notion of property— that a man who caught prey could use it—and no notion of contracting. But since man was not designed to be an animal of prey, this precarious life was not suitable to his nature, and he progressed naturally to the pastoral, agricultural, and finally commercial stages of society, where the respect for property and fidelity to promises which were part of the moral sense could become more cultivated. At the same time, as societies progressed, the legal concepts of property and contract became ever more refined.

With this social and moral advance, the number of duties enforced by law increased, as the boundary between duty and benevolence changed. Municipal law, he noted, was concerned only with whether a man transgressed the regulations necessary for the preservation of society; it was not concerned with whether or not he was virtuous. One reason for this was that municipal law had to be reducible to precise and clear rules, which could be applied in general. Only matters which could be reduced to rules could be regarded as duties which were enforced as a matter of justice. The duty to be benevolent could not usually be reduced to a rule, since the degree of benevolence called for depended too much on particular circumstances. Nonetheless, Kames argued, in some cases, the "duty of benevolence arising from certain peculiar connections among individuals" could be made into a precise rule. In such cases, "benevolence is also taken under the authority of the legislature, and enforced by rules passing commonly under the name of the law of equity."[13]

In the *Principles of Equity*, Kames aimed to explain how equity worked over time to convert what were duties of benevolence into duties of justice.

11. Ibid., p. 65.

12. See his exposition in *Historical Law-Tracts*, 2 vols. (Edinburgh: Millar, Kincaid and Bell, 1758), vol. I, pp. 77–79 (note).

13. *Essays on the Principles of Morality and Natural Religion* (Liberty Fund ed.), p. 61.

In it, he argued that as societies progressed, benevolence became "a matter of conscience in a thousand instances, formerly disregarded."[14] This was something to which a court of common law, which dealt with the ordinary duties of justice, was blind. However, a court of equity was able to recognize this development, and to intervene in "remarkable cases" when it perceived from the circumstances that the duty was "palpable." The court of equity thus worked to help convert the duty of benevolence which had refined over time into a duty of justice. It "commences at the limits of the common law, and enforces benevolence where the law of nature makes it our duty. And thus a court of equity, accompanying the law of nature in its gradual refinements, enforces every natural duty that is not provided for at common law."[15] Over time, as case law developed, judges in equity became more acute at making distinctions and developed these duties in a more systematic way. Once a rule in equity had become fully established in practice, it became part of the fixed rules of common law. This meant that the borderline between common law and equity was flexible: the task of a court of equity was to recognize, refine, and incorporate new rules recognized by the moral sense.

The Nature of Equity

The *Principles of Equity* was the fullest elaboration of Kames's theory of legal development. Yet it was not really a book of legal philosophy, but a practical work, aimed at an informed legal audience. Although a book primarily about Scottish law, it was written for a legal audience throughout Great Britain. In the preface to the *Historical Law-Tracts*, he stated that it was unfortunate that the different parts of the kingdom were ruled by different laws. "A regular institute of the common law of this island, deducing historically the changes which that law hath undergone in the two nations, would be a valuable present to the public," he noted, "because it would make the study of both laws a task easy and agreeable."[16] He added that one man could not do it alone, but that such a work would both help

14. *Principles of Equity*, below, p. 21.
15. Ibid., below, p. 23.
16. *Historical Law-Tracts*, vol. 1, p. xiv.

bring about a more effective union and improve Scots law. The *Principles of Equity* was in many ways his contribution to this project, for in it he aimed to treat one aspect of the law and set out a general treatise which drew on the case law of both countries.

The very project of writing a treatise on equity which would address legal audiences on both sides of the border was highly ambitious, since it raised questions about what was meant by *equity*. The classical definition was to be found in Aristotle's *Nicomachean Ethics,*[17] according to which it was sometimes necessary for the rules of law to be adapted or modified in particular cases where a strict adherence to a rule would lead to injustice. Yet neither English nor Scots lawyers argued that equity could be used simply to set aside unjust laws. In the words of Kames's contemporary Lord Bankton, the Court of Session had no equitable power to give relief "where the prescription of the law is clear, and yet happens to fall very hard in any particular case."[18] In such cases, it was for the legislature to intervene.

English writers generally saw equity in jurisdictional terms. It was associated with the Court of Chancery,[19] which had an equitable jurisdiction wholly denied to courts of common law. Although there had been a famous clash between the courts of common law and the Chancery in 1616,[20] writers on equity accepted Christopher St. German's sixteenth-century view that the Lord Chancellor's jurisdiction in equity did not stand in opposition to the common law and that his conscience should be guided by the law. The role of the Chancery was to provide a remedy where the common law courts could not do so, due to the nature of their procedure. In England, the procedure used in the common law courts was wholly

17. Aristotle, *The Nicomachean Ethics,* trans. D. Ross, rev. L. Brown (Oxford: Oxford University Press, 2009), pp. 98–99 (1137a–1138a).

18. Andrew McDouall, Lord Bankton, *An Institute of the Laws of Scotland in Civil Rights,* 3 vols. (Edinburgh: Fleming for Kincaid & Donaldson, 1751–53), vol. 3, p. 94.

19. The court of Exchequer had a jurisdiction over both common law and equitable matter, but the two sides of the court were distinct and operated with different procedures. See W. H. Bryson, *The Equity Side of the Exchequer* (Cambridge: Cambridge University Press, 1975), and H. Horwitz, *Exchequer Equity Records and Proceedings, 1649–1841* (London: Public Record Office, 2001).

20. On this, see especially J. H. Baker, "The Common Lawyers and the Chancery: 1616," in his *The Legal Profession and the Common Law: Historical Essays* (London: Hambledon Press, 1986), pp. 205–29.

different from that used in the Chancery. Common law procedure was an adversarial one, in which parties set out their disputes in pretrial pleadings which refined the matter to a single point. A jury would then find for one party or the other on the question put to them and award damages. By contrast, the procedure used in the Chancery was more inquisitorial. Cases were commenced with a bill explaining the plaintiff's claim and demanding an answer from the defendant. It was this procedure which gave the court its jurisdiction over matters of trust, fraud, and confidence. For the Chancery's procedure allowed it to probe the consciences—or knowledge—of the parties in a way not possible at common law. It also offered a more flexible and discretionary set of remedies. By the eighteenth century, the equitable jurisdiction of the Court of Chancery had become increasingly settled, with the court following rules and precedents which had created a body of doctrine over time.

By contrast, the Scottish Court of Session had both a "common law" and an "equitable" jurisdiction. Since this court used an inquisitorial procedure taken from the Romano-Canonical tradition, there was no need for a separate court to explore the parties' consciences and administer equity. At the same time, in Scotland, only the Court of Session had a jurisdiction over equity: inferior courts were limited to matters of common law. What, then, was this "equity" which the highest court applied? Scottish writers spoke of it as "the *nobile officium* of the judges," a power which was "inherent in the supreme judicatory of every state."[21] According to John Erskine, this power allowed the court "to proceed by the rules of conscience, in abating the rigour of the law, and in giving aid, in the actions brought before them, to those who can have no remedy in a court of law." The notion of the *nobile officium* derived from civilian teaching dating back to Bartolus of Sassoferrato (1313–57), who distinguished between the "mercenary office" (*officium mercenarium*) of a judge, by which was meant his ordinary power, and his "noble office" (*officium nobile*), which connoted his extraordinary power. When exercising the former power, the judge strictly followed the forms of the law.

---

21. John Erskine, *An Institute of the Law of Scotland*, 2 vols. (Edinburgh: John Bell, 1773), vol. 1, p. 44 (book I, tit. iii, sect. 22).

When exercising the latter, he acted on his own initiative and by his own authority.[22]

In the late seventeenth century, Sir George Mackenzie associated this power with "Arbitrary Actions wherein the Judge is tied to no particular Law." It operated "in opposition to that *officium ordinarium & mercenarium;* wherein he is obliged to follow the *will of the Contracters* precisely, *& hoc officium mercenarium Judex nunquam impertit nisi rogatus.*"[23] This discretionary power allowed the court to provide remedies which parties could not demand of right, but where the court's intervention was needed to prevent injustice. For instance, it was used by the Court of Session to allow creditors to attach a debtor's property to secure a debt not yet due, if the creditor was in danger of losing his money by the threatened flight of the debtor. It also allowed the court to set aside fixed procedural rules which operated at common law.[24] In the seventeenth century, the *nobile officium* was associated with the court's relaxation of its rules of procedure which required parties to obtain a decision on points of law raised by the alleged facts, before going to proof on those facts. In place of this procedure, the court used its discretion to allow mixed questions of fact and law to proceed, so that the court would pronounce the law subsequently on the basis of facts which had emerged in further investigation. This procedure allowed the court in effect to adapt the law to the particular circumstances of individual cases.[25]

22. See the discussion in J. D. Ford, *Law and Opinion in Scotland during the Seventeenth Century* (Oxford: Hart, 2007), p. 486.

23. Sir George Mackenzie, *The Institutions of the Laws of Scotland* (Edinburgh: John Reid, 1684), pp. 343–45 (part 4, tit. 1). [And the judge never exercises this mercenary office unless asked.]

24. For example, it might deviate from the standard rules of evidence. As Erskine put it, "they frequently ordain *ex officio* a party to be examined, though his adversary, who declines referring the matter in issue to his oath, has no title to insist for such examination." Erskine, *Institute,* vol. 1, p. 44 (book I, tit. iii, sect. 22). In his *Dictionary of Decisions,* Kames illustrated the exercise of the *nobile officium* by reporting a case where the judges, having pronounced an act before answer, admitted witnesses, otherwise exceptionable, to obtain as much evidence as possible of fraud, "reserving to themselves, at advising, what it should operate." Kames, *Dictionary,* vol. 1, p. 498 (citing *Scot* contra *Fowler,* 3 Dec. 1687, from Fountainhall, 487).

25. See Ford, *Law and Opinion,* p. 490. The normal procedure was for litigants to have questions of law settled on the supposition that the facts alleged by the pursuer

The court also had the power by its *nobile officium* to introduce new rules to overcome imperfections in the law. There was some debate over how far this extended. Lord Bankton illustrated the power by referring to "a memorable instance" in 1725 when the Court of Session made an act of sederunt[26] to order the brewers of Edinburgh, who had entered a resolution to give up their trade, to give a security that they would continue to brew beer, on pain of imprisonment.[27] Some critics found this legislative power of the court to be alarming. James Boswell wrote a *Letter to the People of Scotland* in 1785, in which he described the *nobile officium* of the court as an "undefined arbitrary jurisdiction."[28] He referred his readers to Gilbert Stuart, who had said that through its exercise, "the judicial powers usurp upon the legislative." "It is in a wild hostility with our constitution," Stuart added. "It is a Turkish jurisdiction in a country of liberty."[29] Another writer attacked the Court of Session's use of its *nobile officium* to make acts of sederunt which repealed or dispensed with statutes, or imposed taxes.[30] Yet if some pamphleteers found this power dubious, particularly when it was seen to usurp the role of legislation, most legal writers regarded it as a necessary means to allow new remedies to emerge to

---

were true. The decision—or "acts of litiscontestation"—was followed by the proof. However, the court also allowed a procedure known as "acts before answer" in cases where law and fact were mixed, allowing the facts to be settled before the law was ruled on. Swinton claimed that by the late eighteenth century acts before answer "have now come in fashion to be pronounced almost in every case": John, Lord Swinton, *Considerations concerning a proposal for dividing the court of session into classes or chambers; and for limiting litigation in small causes; and for the revival of jury-trial in certain civil actions* (Edinburgh: Peter Hill, 1789), p. 83.

26. See glossary, "act of sederunt."

27. Bankton, *Institute,* vol. 2, pp. 517–18. He noted that the act of sederunt "had the desired effect." The episode was mentioned by Kames in *Equity,* 3rd ed., vol. 2, p. 93. For the act of sederunt, see *AS,* 280.

28. James Boswell, *A Letter to the People of Scotland, on the alarming attempt to infringe upon the articles of union, and introduce a most pernicious innovation, by diminishing the number of the lords of session* (London: Charles Dilly, 1785), p. 5.

29. Gilbert Stuart, *The History of Scotland, from the establishment of the Reformation, till the death of Queen Mary, to which are annexed, Observations concerning the public law and the constitution of Scotland,* 2nd ed., 2 vols. (London: J. Murray, 1784), vol. 2, pp. 102, 104.

30. John Martin, *An Inquiry into the State of the Legal and Judicial Polity of Scotland* (London: J. Johnson, 1792).

deal with imperfections in the common law, in areas which attracted little legislative attention.[31]

Kames explained his own understanding of the *nobile officium* in the *Historical Law-Tracts*. He associated it with a power to redress wrongs of all kinds. It worked in a way to uncover principles for unsettled subjects on which men were apt to disagree and judge by sentiment. As he put it,

> Matters of law are ripened in the best manner, by warmth of debate at the bar, and coolness of judgment on the bench; and after many success-ful experiments of a bold interposition for the publick good, the court of session will clearly perceive the utility, of extending their jurisdiction to every sort of wrong, where the persons injured have no other means of obtaining redress.[32]

This meant that "all extraordinary actions, not founded on common law, but invented to redress any defect or wrong in the common law, are appro-priated to the court of session," exercising a jurisdiction denied to inferior courts.[33]

Kames himself explored this power of equity in his reports. For in-stance, in his report of the case of *Charles M'Kinnon* contra *Sir James M'Donald* in his *Select Decisions of the Court of Session from the Year 1752 to the Year 1758,* he commented on how a new rule regarding which heir could take charge of a deceased person's estate had emerged "in the fa-mous case of Sir George M'Kenzie's entail." The new rule developed by the judges, he commented, "was a new exertion of the *nobile officium* in order to remedy many hardships, and even injustice that must arise in this case, from the aforesaid rule of succession established at common law." Kames proceeded to explain to readers the reason for the rule, and to make a commentary on what he felt were the consequences of the rule.[34] In his

---

31. Bankton (*Institute,* vol. 2, p. 517), for instance, gave as an example "the case of ad-judications in implement, introduced by authority of the court of session, to complete a party's right to lands." For such adjudications, see glossary, "adjucation in implement."

32. *Historical Law-Tracts,* vol. 1, p. 324.

33. *Historical Law-Tracts,* vol. 1, p. 329.

34. *Select decisions of the Court of Session, from the Year 1752 to the Year 1768. Collected by the Honourable Henry Home of Kames,* 2nd ed. (Edinburgh: Bell and Bradfute, 1799), 298–304. The case was also discussed in the *Principles of Equity,* below, p. 303.

Elucidations Respecting the Common and Statute Law of Scotland, he also set out proposals on how the Court of Session could use its *nobile officium* to provide new remedies.[35]

Kames also discussed the nature of the *nobile officium* of the Court of Session in a letter he wrote in 1764 to Robert Dundas of Arniston, Lord President of the Court of Session, proposing an act of sederunt which would reform an aspect of Scottish bankruptcy law.[36] In an accompanying document on the jurisdiction of the court, Kames sought to persuade his colleague that the court did have this power, giving numerous examples of the court's use of its equitable powers, and arguing that the court must be taken to have inherited the powers of the Scottish Privy Council to redress injuries, after its abolition at the union.[37]

In the *Principles of Equity*, Kames did not discuss the *nobile officium* of the Court of Session as such, for in this book he was interested in exploring a wider concept of equity which would speak to English as well as Scots lawyers. Here he argued that equity intervened both when the settled rules of the common law acted in an unjust way and when they failed to fulfill the needs of justice. This occurred as societies progressed and the moral sense began to recognize connections between people which turned benevolence into a duty. Equity's intervention was not boundless, however: it was limited to those connections which related to interests in property. Equity could not concern itself with connections arising from personal circumstances, for it was only the former which could be made into a rule. The book was therefore primarily about property and civil obligations. In the body of the work, he accordingly spent much time exploring what constituted an unjustified enrichment—discussing the Roman law maxim *Nemo debet locupletari aliena jactura*[38]—and what principles lay behind the respective claims of different creditors on an indebted estate.

35. For example, *Elucidations Respecting the Common and Statute Law of Scotland* (Edinburgh: William Creech, 1777), 197–98.

36. Kames's proposal was to revive an earlier act of sederunt which made all creditors taking legal proceedings against a bankrupt rank *pari passu.*

37. The letter, which is in the Dundas of Arniston papers (and on microfilm in the National Archives of Scotland, ref. RH4/15/2) is published for the first time in the present volume.

38. "No one should be enriched at another's expense."

A further feature of equity identified by Kames was that it looked more closely at the intentions and motivations of parties, so that it could root out injustices to which the common law was blind. For instance, when dealing with contracts and deeds, the common law simply looked to the text, whereas equity could look at the real intentions of the parties. Hence, much of the book was concerned with showing how the court should interpret contracts, and at how it treated vitiating factors such as pre-contractual pressure or undue influence. Just as equity could go farther than common law with deeds, so it could intervene in other civil wrongs. For example, where the common law only looked at whether a man had exercised his rights, a court of equity could look at his intentions and intervene against a man who had exercised a right with the sole motive of harming another. Equity also intervened, he added, to prevent the common law acting in an unjust way, as where the wording of statutes went beyond their intended purpose and led to injustice in particular cases.

Much of the *Principles of Equity* was devoted to discussing how equity worked to secure justice when the common law failed to do so. But Kames added that a court of equity also intervened on the grounds of utility, by preventing acts which were not in themselves unjust, but which were mischievous and against the public interest. For the most part, the principle of justice (which looked only to the individual litigants) and the principle of utility (which looked to the interests of society) worked in harmony. But he noted that they might come into opposition. In such cases "[e]quity, when it regards the interest of a few individuals only, ought to yield to utility when it regards the whole society."[39] For example, the regulations which were designed to abridge lawsuits meant that the courts would refuse to listen to a claim which an individual might have in justice—as where he had accepted an unequal settlement of a lawsuit in error—simply because to do otherwise would be to encourage endless litigation. At first glance, it may be thought that Kames's stress on utility sat uneasily with his theory of justice, as derived from the moral sense. Yet the two were not in his view incompatible. For Kames's argument suggested that utility itself dictated the limits of equity. One might, he noted, be

39. *Principles of Equity,* below, p. 29.

able to do justice in individual cases, but without being able to formulate this into a rule. To allow judges nevertheless to give a remedy in such cases created the risk of making them arbitrary and often unjust, which would be harmful to society.[40] There were hence limits to equity's intervention to enforce just claims, though he added that it should never enforce unjust claims. The principle of utility confirmed that duties of justice had to be capable of being formulated as rules.

In the Introduction to the *Principles,* Kames added his views that it was better to have a single court with the power to administer both common law and equity (as in Scotland) and that the court of equity itself should follow rules. These were topics on which he had corresponded with the former Lord Chancellor of England, Lord Hardwicke, shortly before the publication of the first edition. Hardwicke disagreed on the first of these points, feeling that a union of the judicatures might allow a judge to alter the settled rules of property law at his discretion. Such an arbitrary power exercised in matters of property might then extend to matters of life and liberty. On the second point, Hardwicke admitted that there should be general rules which guided the court (such as those which related to trusts), yet he felt that the judge should not be absolutely and invariably bound by them. In his view, equity had grown in response to the luxuriant growth of fraud, and since fraud was infinite, the Lord Chancellor's powers had to be flexible.[41]

If Lord Hardwicke was sceptical about some of Kames's views, the Chief Justice of the King's Bench, Lord Mansfield, was enthusiastic. After the publication of the first edition of the work, he wrote to Kames,

> I read ev'ry thing yr L[ordshi]p writes with great Satisfaction. The best of our Judges are delighted with some of yr Law Pieces. You have taught Men to trace Law to its true noble Sources: Philosophy & History. Your Principles of Equity are very ingenious; but the Opposition of Equity to Law as now administered in England by different Courts, is not to be learnt from anything yet in Print & is not deducible from Reason. It can

40. Ibid., pp. 27, 312–13.
41. Alexander Fraser Tytler, *Memoirs of the Life and Writings of the Honourable Henry Home of Kames,* 2 vols. (Edinburgh: W. Creech, 1807), vol. 1, pp. 243–46.

only be explained positively & by Historical Deductions. I wish we had a Pen & Genius & Diligence like yr L[ordshi]ps to do it.[42]

Mansfield wrote to Kames again when the latter was preparing the second edition of the book. Reflecting on the work, the Chief Justice wrote,

> I was not single in wishing, you had considered Principles of Equity, not in opposition to, but as one Ground of Law absolutely necessary in the administration of justice the same at all times & in all places. Non alia lex Romae, alia Athenis[43] [. . .] To reduce principles of Equity into a System of Science, & to illustrate them by Examples from all times & Countrys is a lesson of Jurisprudence to the whole World; & worthy of your Ldsp. It equally suits the Parliament of Paris, the Court of Session, & the Courts in England whether called of law or Equity, but the plan of a distinct Court of Equity, upon natural or political Principles may embarrass the Subject; & any allusion to the Case in England, upon a supposed natural division of law and Equity into two Sciences can only lead to mistakes.[44]

Lord Mansfield was famously enthusiastic about introducing equitable principles into his court, and Kames's admiration for him was shown by the letter to Mansfield at the start of the second edition.[45] Although it cannot be denied that these two judges did not always agree even on some of the most important issues of their day—as can be seen from the contrary positions

42. Quoted in Ross, *Lord Kames and the Scotland of His Day*, pp. 237–38.

43. From Cicero, *De re publica*, Loeb Classical Library (Cambridge, Mass.: Harvard University Press, 1928), p. 210 (book III, sect. xxii): "nec erit alia lex Romae, alia lex Athaenis; alia nunc, alia posthac, sed et omnes gentes et omni tempore una lex et sempiterna et immutabilis continebit" [there will not be one law at Rome, another at Athens; one law now, another law hereafter; but one eternal and unchangeable law shall bind all nations and all times]. Mansfield also cited this maxim in *Luke* v. *Lyde* (1759), 2 Burrow 882 at 887, reprinted in *The English Reports*, vol. 97, p. 614 at 617, referring to maritime law as being part of the general law of nations.

44. Letter from Lord Mansfield to Kames, 26 May 1766, National Archives of Scotland, GD24/1/564, ff. 35v–36; quoted in part in Ross, *Lord Kames and the Scotland of His Day*, p. 242.

45. On seeing the second edition, Mansfield wrote to Kames in November 1766, "I am extreamly flattered with the letter you have done me the honour to prefix to it, & particularly pleased with the manner in which it is wrote." National Archives of Scotland, GD24/1/564, f. 38.

they took on the question whether there was a common law right to literary property[46]—Kames did, in at least one respect, modify his argument in the *Principles of Equity* to take a position closer to Mansfield's view. Between the first and second editions of the work, Kames modified the formulation of his argument concerning the principles behind the restitutionary *actio negotiorum gestio.*[47] Where in the earlier edition he rooted the obligation in an implied contract, in the later edition he rooted it in a broader notion of justice.[48] Soon after Kames had finished the first edition of the *Principles,* Mansfield decided the case of *Moses* v. *Macferlan,* in which he described the English restitutionary action of money had and received as "an equitable action, to recover back money, which ought not in justice to be kept." In so deciding, he rejected an argument that the remedy could only be brought in a case where an express or implied contract could be found, holding instead that "the defendant be under an obligation, from the ties of natural justice, to refund; the law implies a debt, and gives this action, founded in the equity of the plaintiff's case."[49] Kames did not mention this case in the *Principles*—nor any other case of Mansfield's[50]—but it may be assumed that England's chief justice would have approved of the modification.[51]

46. In *Millar* v. *Taylor* (1769), 4 Burrow 2303, reprinted in *The English Reports,* vol. 98, p. 201, Lord Mansfield (and the majority of the King's Bench) held that there was a common law right, a decision overruled by the House of Lords in *Donaldson* v. *Beckett* (1774), 2 Brown's Parliamentary Cases 129, reprinted in *The English Reports,* vol. 1, p. 837. In *Hinton* v. *Donaldson* (1773), Kames (and a majority of the Court of Session) held that there was no such right (see James Boswell, *The Decision of the Court of Session, upon the Question of Literary Property in the Cause John Hinton of London, Bookseller, Pursuer against Alexander Donaldson and John Wood, Booksellers in Edinburgh and James Meurose Bookseller in Kilmarnock, Defenders* [Edinburgh: Alexander Donaldson, 1774], pp. 18–21). See also Kames's comments on *Daniel Midwinter* contra *Gavin Hamilton* (1748) in *Remarkable Decisions* ii, pp. 154–61. See further T. Ross, "Copyright and the Invention of Tradition," *Eighteenth-Century Studies* 26 (Autumn 1992): 1–27.

47. See glossary, "actio negotiorum gestorum."

48. See further the discussion in the section on major variant readings between the first, second, and third editions.

49. *Moses* v. *Macferlan* (1760), 2 Burrow 1005 at 1012, 1008, reprinted in *The English Reports,* vol. 97, p. 676 at 680, 678.

50. All the English case law cited by Kames was from late seventeenth- or early eighteenth-century published reports.

51. In later years, Mansfield and Kames did correspond occasionally on legal matters. For instance, in 1773, Mansfield wrote a letter, correcting an error on English law in a

When the *Principles of Equity* was first published in 1760, Kames sought to use the text as a vehicle to gain promotion to the High Court of Justiciary.[52] But long after he had achieved his ambition to be a criminal judge, he continued to refine and revise a work which he clearly regarded as of considerable importance. In November 1777, he wrote to a friend,

> I have been busy at my Principles of Equity for a new edition ever since I returned from the Circuit; and I have never laboured harder upon any subject. That book I always considered as my chief performance; and the advance of ten years of my life since the last publication made me doubtful whether I would be able to make any improvement. It delighted me to find my mental faculties still entire, even so much as to be able to detect several errors that had escaped in the former edition. You cannot conceive my satisfaction in detecting these errors myself, instead of having my reputation wounded by their being detected after my death.[53]

A Note to the Reader

The pagination of the third edition is indicated in the text with page numbers placed within angular brackets (<1>). Readers should bear in mind that the original work was published in two octavo volumes, and that the material of volume 2 commences at p. 243 below.

Kames's own notes, as in the original, are indicated by asterisks, daggers, and other symbols or by the letter (a), while the editor's annotations of Kames's notes appear within brackets. The editor's own notes are indicated by arabic numerals.

---

commentary Kames had sent him on the law of entails (which may well have been the "Commentary on act 22 parliament 1685, concerning entails" in Kames's *Elucidations Respecting the Common and Statute Law of Scotland* of 1777), National Archives of Scotland GD24/1/564, f. 43. However, no letters have been found between these judges on the topic of unjust enrichment.

52. When sending a copy of the work to Charles Townshend, Kames complained of "being allowed to rust as it were in a Corner and having daily younger people advanced above me." National Archives of Scotland, GD224/295/3/16. He also complained to Hardwicke that he had been neglected when it came to appointment to the criminal bench.

53. *The Scots Magazine and Edinburgh Literary Miscellany*, n.s., 5 (1819): 542.

A NOTE ON LEGAL SOURCES
AND CITATIONS

Kames's *Principles of Equity* is replete with a large range of technical terms from Scots, Roman, and English law. To assist the reader, I have appended my own glossary to the text of terms used (p. 543), to serve as an addition to Kames's brief "Explanation of Some Scotch Law Terms Used in This Work" (p. 15). Some of the language of Scots law uses terms which might at first glance appear to bear no specific meaning, but which in fact have a particular legal connotation. The glossary and notes seek to explain them as simply as possible. Latin tags and phrases are in general translated in the body of the text, but the glossary also contains terms used repeatedly.

The work also makes extensive reference to Scottish and English statutes and case law and to Roman law. What follows is a brief introduction to the citation of this material.

Scottish Legislation

At the time when Kames was writing, the standard printed collection of statutes was that produced by Sir Thomas Murray of Glendook, the lord clerk register from 1677 to 1681.[1] It was produced in a folio edition in 1681 and a two-volume duodecimo edition in 1682 (taking the statutes to 1681), and was subsequently supplemented by another volume taking the collection to 1707. The duodecimo edition was the one most commonly cited in courts. In Kames's day, the method used to refer to statutes was

1. Sir Thomas Murray of Glendook, *The Laws and Acts of Parliament made by King James the First and His Royal Successors, Kings and Queens of Scotland*, 2 vols. (Edinburgh: D. Lindsay, 1682).

by reference to the year and chapter number given in Glendook's edition (and not by name).[2] It is this method which Kames uses in his text and footnotes.

In the nineteenth century, a new definitive printed edition of the statutes was compiled by Thomas Thomson and Cosmo Innes. Their edition of *The Acts of the Parliament of Scotland* was published between 1814 and 1875 in Edinburgh in twelve folio volumes and became the standard point of reference for historians. This edition is also flawed, and a new digital, on-line edition of the Scottish parliamentary material, entitled *The Records of the Parliament of Scotland to 1707* has been produced by the Scottish Parliament Project at the University of St. Andrews. The database of statutes can be accessed via: http://www.rps.ac.uk/. Readers wishing to follow up the references are recommended to consult the database, where translations are given into modern English.

In the footnotes, I have used both these forms of citation, giving the Glendook reference in the notes (where Kames omits to do so in the text), followed by the citation and title given in the *Acts of the Parliament of Scotland.* Scottish statutes were only given short titles as a result of legislation passed in 1892, 1896, and 1964, which assigned short titles to un-repealed public acts of the Scottish parliament passed between 1424 and 1707. Where such a short title exists, I have also given it.

Scottish Case Law

In Kames's time, a number of manuscript collections of law reports existed, which were kept in the Faculty of Advocates' Library in Edinburgh and used by practitioners in the court. In addition, a number of these had been published by the time Kames composed the *Principles of Equity.* Kames himself published a number of collections of law reports, the most important of which was his *Dictionary* (first published in 1741 in two volumes), which, when supplemented later by Alexander Fraser Tytler, Lord Woodhouselee, was referred to as the Folio Collection.

The majority of these reports were subsequently collated and published

---

2. The citation is in the following form: *act 83. parl. 1579.*

in the forty-two-volume collection edited by William Maxwell Morison, *The Decisions of the Court of Session from its institution until the separation of the Court into two divisions in the year 1808, digested under proper heads in the form of a dictionary* (Edinburgh: Archibald Constable & Co., 1811). This became the standard reference work for earlier cases for Scottish lawyers.

Most of the cases cited by Kames were included in Morison's *Dictionary of Decisions:* and I have therefore given the reference to Morison in the footnotes. Morison's *Dictionary* is continuously paginated, and so a reference such as M 9505 indicates that the case cited is in Morison's collection, p. 9505.

Where Kames himself reported a case referred to (either digesting an earlier report or reporting it for the first time himself), a reference is given to Kames's report. Cases discussed by Kames without any citation (beyond a date) are unpublished cases.

Kames's own footnotes frequently name the reporters whose work he is referring to: for example, *Fountainhall, July 29, 1708, Rag contra Brown.* The following is a list of the published collections which are cited by Kames; many are now available in electronic form on databases of seventeenth- and eighteenth-century literature.

Bruce   Alexander Bruce, *The Decisions of the Lords of Council and Session, in most cases of importance, for the months of November and December 1714, and January, February, June and July 1715* (Edinburgh: James McEuen, 1720).

Dalrymple   *Decisions of the Court of Session from 1698 to 1718, collected by the Right Honourable Sir Hew Dalrymple* (Edinburgh: G. Hamilton and J. Balfour, 1758).

Dirleton   *Some Doubts and Questions in the Law, especially of Scotland. As also, some decisions of the Lords of Council and Session: collected and observ'd by Sir John Nisbet of Dirleton* (Edinburgh: G. Mosman, 1698).

Durie   Sir Alexander Gibson of Durie, *The Decisions of the Lords of Council and Session . . . from July 1621 to July 1642* (Edinburgh: George Mosman, 1690).

Falconer	David Falconer, *The Decisions of the Court of Session. From the Month of November 1744,* 2 vols. (Edinburgh: W. & T. Ruddimans).
Forbes	William Forbes, *A Journal of the Session. Containing the Decisions of the Lords of Council and Session . . . from February 1705 till November 1713* (Edinburgh: for the author, 1713).
Fountainhall	*The Decisions of the Lords of Council and Session from June 6th 1678 to July 12th 1712. Collected by Sir John Lauder of Fountainhall,* 2 vols. (Edinburgh: G. Hamilton and J. Balfour, 1759–61).
Gilmour	*A Collection of Decisions of the Lords of Council and Session in two parts. The first contains decisions from July 1661 to July 1666. Observ'd by Sir John Gilmour of Craigmiller* (Edinburgh: John Vallange, 1701).
Harcase	*Decisions of the Court of Session, collected by Sir Roger Hog of Harcase . . . from 1681 to 1691* (Edinburgh: G. Hamilton and J. Gilmour, 1757).
Home	Henry Home, Lord Kames, *Remarkable Decisions of the Court of Session from 1716 to 1728* (Edinburgh: T. Ruddiman, 1728).
Kilkerran	*Decisions of the Court of Session, from the year 1738 to the year 1752. Collected and digested into the form of a dictionary. By Sir James Fergusson of Kilkerran* (Edinburgh: J. Bell and W. Creech, 1775).
Stair	Sir James Dalrymple of Stair, *The Decisions of the Lords of Council & Session in the most Important Cases debate before them, with the Acts of Sederunt . . . from June 1661 to July 1681* (Edinburgh: Andrew Anderson, 1683).

England

Kames also refers to cases reported in manuscript by the following authors, whose works were digested by both Morison and Kames in their printed collections:

Haddington	Thomas Hamilton, Earl of Haddington
Hope	Sir Thomas Hope of Kerse

Gosford   Sir Peter Wedderburn of Gosford

Nicolson   Sir Thomas Nicolson of Carnock

Spottiswoode   Sir Robert Spottiswoode of Pentland

Statutes passed by the English Parliament, and by the British Parliament after 1707, are generally cited by Kames according to the regnal year, chapter, and section number (for example, 29 Car. II, c. 3, s. 1); I have added the date and title (for example, An Act for Prevention of Frauds and Perjuries, 1677).

At the time Kames was writing, reports of English cases were published under the name of the reporter who compiled them, and Kames refers to these "nominate" law reports (for example, "Salkeld," "Vernon"). Full references for these reports are given in the list of abbreviations (p. xxxiii). The reports he cites were subsequently reprinted in *The English Reports,* 176 vols. (London: Stevens & Sons, 1900–1930). Where Kames refers to an English case, I have given both the original reference and the reference to where it can be found in *The English Reports* reprint.

Roman Law

In *Principles of Equity,* Kames makes frequent reference to the Roman *Corpus Iuris Civilis* (Body of Civil Law) compiled on the orders of Emperor Justinian between the years 530 and 534. Three principal works made up this body of law: the *Institutes,* the *Code,* and the *Digest.* Where Kames quotes or cites from these sources, I have given the modern form of citation, which is as follows:

Inst   *Institutes.* References are given to the book, title (that is, chapter) and *lex* (that is, section). Thus, Inst. 2.23.1 refers to Justinian's *Institutes,* book 2, title 23, *lex* 1.

C   *Code.* References are given to the book, title, and *lex.* Thus, C 8.34.3 refers to Justinian's *Code,* book 8, title 34, *lex* 3.

D   *Digest.* References are given to the book, title, *lex,* and subsection of the *lex.* Thus D 9.2.29.3 refers to Justinian's *Digest,* book 9, title 2, *lex* 29, and section 3.

pr.   *prooemium* (preface). Many of the titles and *leges* have an introductory preface. Thus, D 9.2.2.pr. refers to the introductory preface to book 9, title 2, *lex* 2 of the *Digest* of Justinian.

For quotations from the *Digest* of Justinian, I have relied on the translation in *The Digest of Justinian,* ed. Theodor Mommsen and Paul Krueger, ed. and trans. Alan Watson, 4 vols. (Philadelphia: University of Pennsylvania Press, 1985), and referred the reader to volume and page numbers in that edition, as well as giving the standard citation for the source. For translations of quotations from the *Institutes,* I have relied on the edition of Peter Birks and Grant McLeod: *Justinian's Institutes* (London: Duckworth, 1987), and similarly given page references and standard citations. Other translations are my own.

ABBREVIATIONS

APS

The Acts of the Parliament of Scotland, 12 vols., ed. T. Thomson and C. Innes (Edinburgh, 1814–75).

AS

The Acts of Sederunt of the Lords of Council and Session, from the 15th of January 1553 to the 11th of July 1790 (Edinburgh: Elphinstone Balfour, 1790).

C

Codex Iustinianus (The Code of Justinian), ed. Paul Krueger (Berlin: Weidmann, 1877).

1 Chancery Cases

Cases Argued and Decreed in the High Court of Chancery, 2nd ed. (London: Atkyns for Walthoe, 1707).

2 Chancery Cases

The Second Part of Cases Argued and Decreed in the High Court of Chancery continued from the 30th Year of King Charles II to the 4th Year of King James II (London: Atkyns for Walthoe, 1701).

D

The Digest of Justinian, ed. Theodor Mommsen and Paul Krueger, trans. and ed. Alan Watson, 4 vols. (Philadelphia: University of Pennsylvania Press, 1985).

Eq. Cas. Abr.

A General Abridgment of Cases in Equity, 2 vols., 4th ed. (London: Lintot, 1756).

Inst

Justinian's Institutes, trans. and ed. Peter Birks and Grant McLeod (London: Duckworth, 1987).

Kames, *Dictionary*

(Kames, Henry Home, Lord), *The Decisions of the Court of Session from its first institution to the present time. Abridged, and digested under proper heads in the form of a Dictionary,* 2 vols. (Edinburgh: Richard Watkins, Alexander Kincaid and Robert Fleming, 1741).

Kames, *Remarkable* (Kames, Henry Home, Lord), *Remarkable Decisions of*
Decisions i   *the Court of Session from 1716 to 1728* (2nd ed., Edin-
                   burgh: Bell & Bradfute, 1790, 1st ed. 1728).

Kames, *Remarkable* (Kames, Henry Home, Lord), *Remarkable Decisions of*
Decisions ii   *the Court of Session from 1730 to 1752* (2nd ed., Edin-
                   burgh: Bell & Bradfute, 1799, 1st ed. 1766).

Kames, *Select*   (Kames, Henry Home, Lord), *Select Decisions of the*
Decisions   *Court of Session, from the year 1752 to the year 1768. Col-*
                   lected by a member of the Court (2nd ed., Edinburgh:
                   Bell & Bradfute, 1799, 1st ed. 1780).

M   William Maxwell Morison, *The Decisions of the Court*
                   of Session from its institution until the separation of the
                   Court into two divisions in the year 1808, digested under
                   proper heads in the form of a dictionary, 42 vols. (Edin-
                   burgh: Archibald Constable & Co., 1811).

Salkeld   William Salkeld, *Reports of Cases Adjudg'd in the Court*
                   of King's Bench (London: Nutt & Gosling for Walthoe,
                   1717).

Sid.   Thomas Siderfin, *Les reports des divers special cases argue*
                   & adjudge en le Court del Bank le Roy, 2nd ed., 2 vols.
                   (London: Nutt for Keble, Browne, Ward, Mears and
                   Browne, 1714).

Vernon   *Cases Argued and Adjudged in the High Court of Chan-*
                   cery Published from the Manuscripts of Thomas Vernon, 2
                   vols. (Dublin: Watts, 1726–29).

Watson   *The Digest of Justinian,* ed. Theodor Mommsen and
                   Paul Krueger, trans. Alan Watson et al., 4 vols., Phila-
                   delphia: University of Pennsylvania Press, 1985.

PRELIMINARY DISCOURSE

BEING

An Investigation of the Moral Laws of Society.

The science of morality hath for its subject, human actions, with their effects; and its end or purpose is, to regulate these actions.

To act by instinct signifies, to act by blind impulse, without having any end in view. The brute creatures act generally by instinct: the instinct of hunger prompts them to eat, and of cold to take shelter, without considering what these actions may produce. The same must be the condition of infants: for infants are not capable of any consideration: they apply to the nipple, without foreseeing that this action will relieve them from hunger; and they cry when pained, without having any view of procuring relief. But as soon as our ripened faculties unfold to us the connection between our actions and their effects, then it is that we begin to act with an intention to produce certain effects; and our actions, in that case, are means employed to bring about the effects intended.

Intention and *will,* though generally reckoned synonymous terms, signify different operations of the mind: will is relative to the external action; for we never act without a will to act: intention is relative to the effect; for we act in order to bring about the effect intended. It is my intention, for example, to relieve a certain person from distress by giving money: as soon as I see that person, it is my will to deliver the money: the external act of delivery follows: and the person is relieved; which is the effect intended. <2>

Some effects proceed necessarily from the action. A wound is an ef-

This essay was included in the second edition only. The page break signs which follow in this section (<>) refer to the pagination of the second edition.

xxxv

fect necessarily connected with the action of stabbing a man with a sharp weapon: death is the necessary effect of throwing a person downward from the battlements of a high tower. Some effects are probable only: I labour, for example, in order to provide for my family; fight for my country, in order to repel its enemies; take physic, in order to restore my health. In such cases, the event intended does not necessarily nor always follow.

A man, when he wills to act, must at the same time intend to produce the effect that he knows to be necessarily connected with the action. But where the effect is probable only, a man may proceed to act without intending to produce the effect that follows. For example, a stone I throw at random into the market-place, may wound a man without my intending that effect.

Instinctive actions, from their very definition, exclude intention: actions that necessarily produce their effects, must imply intention: effects that are probable only, not necessary, are sometimes intended, sometimes not.

A *right* and a *wrong,* in such actions as are done intentionally to produce some effect, are universally acknowledged; and yet philosophers have been much difficulted to assign the cause of this eminent distinction. The various opinions that have been entertained about it, would be a delicate historical morsel; but come not within the compass of this short inquiry. I shall only observe, negatively, that the science of morals cannot be founded on any truths that may be discovered by reasoning: which will thus appear. As the faculty of reason is confined to the investigation of unknown truths by means of truths that are known, it is clear, that in no science can we even begin to reason, till we be provided with some *data* to found our reasonings upon: even in mathematics, there are certain principles or axioms perceived intuitively to be true, upon which all its demonstrations are founded. Reason is indeed of great use in morality, as well as in other sciences; but morality, like mathematics, is and must be provided with certain axioms or intuitive propositions, without which we cannot make a single step in our reasonings upon that subject; and to trace these with care and caution is the chief purpose of the present inquiry. <3>

CHAPTER I

The Moral Sense.

When we reflect upon the different branches of science, it might seem, that of all subjects human nature should be the best understood; because every man has daily opportunities to study it in his own passions, and in his own actions. But human nature, an interesting subject, is seldom left to the cool investigations of philosophy. Writers of a sweet disposition, inflamed with a warm imagination, compose man mostly or wholly of benevolent principles: others, of a cold temperament and narrow views, bring him down to be an animal entirely selfish. These systems are equally distant from truth: man is of a complex nature, endued with various principles, some selfish some social; and it is highly expedient that man should be so framed, in order to act the part that is allotted him in this life. The unhappy progress of selfishness, especially among commercial nations, is a favourite topic of declamation; and facts are accumulated without end to inforce that topic. It would be no difficult task to produce instances, not less numerous, of benevolence, generosity, and disinterestedness. In the midst of these opposite instances, what can any sensible person fairly conclude, but that the social and selfish principles are, by divine wisdom, so blended as to fit man for his present state? But supposing selfishness to prevail in action, it certainly prevails not in sentiment, nor in affection: all men equally conspire to put a high estimation upon generosity, benevolence, and other social qualities; while even the most selfish are disgusted with selfishness in others, and can scarce be reconciled to it in themselves. Another fact, equally worthy of attention, proceeds from the same cause with the former. Laying aside particular prejudices arising from love or hatred, good fortune happening to any one is agreeable to all, and bad fortune happening to any one is disagreeable to all. Hence effects or events, whether produced by the operation of the laws of matter, or by the actions of self-motive beings, may be distinguished into three kinds, *viz.* agreeable, disagreeable, and indifferent. Beneficial effects or events are agreeable: hurtful effects or events are disagreeable: and those that are neither beneficial nor hurtful, are indifferent.

These preliminaries lead directly to the true foundation of mora- <4> lity, which foundation is discovered upon taking under consideration effects or events produced by human actions. An agreeable effect or event produced intentionally by acting, is perceived by all to be *good:** a disagreeable effect or event produced intentionally by acting, is perceived by all to be *ill:* and an indifferent effect or event is not in our perception either good or ill. These perceptions of good and of ill are the primary moral perceptions, with which, as will be seen afterward, every other moral perception is intimately connected.

In an attempt to investigate the true foundation of morality, an effect or event, being the end for which we act, presents itself first to the mind as its capital object: an action is only a mean employ'd to produce some effect or event, and means are always subordinate to the end. For this reason, I thought it necessary to vary from other writers upon moral philosophy, who begin with actions as the capital object, without giving due attention to the ends for which we act.

Good and *ill,* like agreeable and disagreeable, bitter and sweet, hard and soft, are simple qualities, incapable of a definition; and, like these, and all other qualities, are objects of perception, independent of consequences, and independent of reasoning or reflection. I illustrate this doctrine by the following examples: We require no argument to prove, that children of the poor bred to useful employments by means of a charitable endowment, an infant rescued from the jaws of a lion, a sick person restored to health, the hungry fed, and the naked clothed, are good effects; they are perceived to be such intuitively: an argument is as little necessary to prove, that an old man abandoned to poverty by his favourite son in opulent circumstances, a virtuous young woman corrupted by artifice, are ill effects; and that breach of engagement, and harm done to one who dreads

---

* Hence the intimate connection between morality and the fine arts. "It has always been my opinion," says a celebrated writer, "that the good and the agreeable are nearly related; and that a mind sensible to the charms of virtue, must equally be sensible to those of beauty" [Jean-Jacques Rousseau, *Lettres de deux amans habitans d'une petite ville au pied des Alpes* (*La Nouvelle Heloïse;* Amsterdam: Rey, 1761), 42: "J'ai toujours cru que le bon n'étoit que le beau mis en action, que l'un tenoit intimement à l'autre . . . & qu'une ame bien touchée des charmes de la vertu doit à proportion être aussi sensible à tous les autres genres de beautés"].

no harm from us, are equally so: these effects are perceived intuitively to be ill.

Next as to actions considered as means productive of effects. To the qualities of good and ill in effects, correspond the qualities of *right* and *wrong* in actions: An agreeable effect produced intentionally, is perceived to be good; and the action by which it is produced, is perceived to be right: a disagreeable effect produced intentionally <5> is perceived to be ill; and the action by which it is produced, is perceived to be wrong.* And as it will be seen afterward, that some effects are perceived to be ill without being intended; it will also be seen, that the actions by which such effects are produced, are perceived to be wrong.

An action is perceived to be right or wrong according to the effect intended, whether the effect follow or not. Thus, if to save my friend from being drowned, I plunge into a river, the action is right though I come too late: and if I aim a stroke at a man behind his back, the action is wrong though I happen not to touch him.

It holds in actions as in effects: good effects are a species of agreeable effects, and right actions a species of agreeable actions: ill effects are a species of disagreeable effects, and wrong actions a species of disagreeable actions.

Thus, right and wrong, like good and ill, and all other qualities, are objects of perception or intuition; and supposing them hid from our perception, an attempt to discover them by reasoning would be absurd; not less so, than such an attempt with respect to beauty or colour, or with respect to the external objects to which these qualities belong.

For the sake of perspicuity, the foregoing observations are confined to the simplest case, that of an effect or event produced intentionally. When we afterward descend to particulars, there will be occasion to show, first, That if in acting we foresee the probability of a disagreeable effect, though

---

* The sense we have that an action is right when intended to produce a good effect, and wrong when intended to produce an ill effect, may seem to be the result of reasoning, not merely of perception. But it is not so in reality: for though by the power of abstraction an action may be considered singly, without joining it either to its cause, or to its effect; yet when we do not abstract, we consider it in its natural appearance as connected with both; and in this view we perceive, at the first glance, without reasoning, an action connected by intention with a good effect to be right, and an action connected by intention with an ill effect to be wrong.

without intending it, the effect in that case is perceived to be ill, and the action to be wrong; but not in such a degree as when intended: and, next, That if the disagreeable effect, though not foreseen, might have been foreseen, it is also perceived to be ill, and the action wrong, though in a still lower degree.

As instinctive actions are caused by blind instinct, without the least view to consequences, they are not perceived to be right or <6> wrong, but indifferent: and the effects produced by them may be agreeable or disagreeable; but they are not perceived to be good or ill; they are also indifferent.

Right actions are distinguishable into two kinds, *viz.* what *ought* to be done, and what *may* be done or left undone. Wrong actions are all of one sort, *viz.* what ought not to be done. Right actions that may be done or left undone, are, from our very conception of them, a matter of choice: they are right when done; but it is not a wrong to leave them undone. Thus, to remit a just debt for the sake of a growing family; to yield a subject in controversy, rather than go to law with a neighbour; generously to return good for ill, are right actions, universally approved: yet every man is sensible, that such actions are left to his free will, and that he is not bound to perform any of them.

Actions that *ought* to be done, as well as actions that *ought not* to be done, merit peculiar attention; because they give occasion to the moral terms *duty* and *obligation;* which come next in order. To say that an action ought to be done, means that we have no liberty nor choice, but are necessarily tied or obliged to perform: and to say that an action ought not to be done, means that we are necessarily restrained from doing it. Though this necessity be moral only, not physical; yet we conceive ourselves deprived by it of liberty and choice, and bound to act, or to forbear acting, in opposition to every other motive. The necessity here described is termed *duty:* the abstaining from harming the innocent is a proper example; which the moral sense makes an indispensable duty, without leaving a single article of it to our own free will.

If I be bound in duty to perform or to forbear any particular action, there must be a *title* or *right* in some person to exact that duty from me; and accordingly a *duty* or *obligation* necessarily implies a *title* or *right.*

Thus, the duty of abstaining from mischief implies a right in others to be secured against mischief: the man who does an injury, perceives that he has done wrong by violating the right of the person injured; and that person hath a perception of suffering wrong by having his right violated.

Our duty is two-fold; duty to others, and duty to ourselves. With respect to others, an action that we ought to do is termed *just;* an action that we ought not to do is termed *unjust;* and the omission of what we ought to do is also termed *unjust.* With respect to ourselves, an action that we ought to do is termed *proper;* and an action that <7> we ought not to do, as well as the omission of what we ought to do, are termed *improper.*

Thus, *right,* signifying a quality of certain actions, is a genus, of which *just* and *proper* are species: and *wrong,* signifying a quality of other actions, is a genus, of which *unjust* and *improper* are species.

The sense by which we perceive the qualities of *good* and *ill* in effects, of *right* and *wrong* in actions, and the other moral qualities mentioned and to be mentioned, is termed the MORAL SENSE or CONSCIENCE.*

There is no cause for doubting the existence of the moral sense, more than for doubting the existence of the sense of beauty, of the sense of seeing, of hearing, or of any other sense. In fact, the perception of right and wrong as qualities of actions, is not less distinct and clear than that of beauty, of colour, or of any other quality; and as every perception is an act of sense, the sense of beauty is not with greater certainty evinced from the perception of beauty, than the moral sense is from the perception of right and wrong.

This is the corner-stone of morality: for, abstracting from the moral sense, the qualities of good and ill in effects, and of right and wrong in

---

* Every perception, being an act of the mind, must proceed from some faculty or power of perception, termed *sense.* Whether the moral sense, by which we perceive a right and a wrong in actions, and a good and an ill in effects, be a sense distinct from all others, or whether it make a branch of the sense by which we perceive the actions themselves, and their effects, appears an arbitrary question: the senses by which objects are perceived, are not separated from each other by distinct boundaries; and the sorting or classing them, seems to depend more on taste and fancy than on nature. For this reason, I have followed the plan laid down by former writers; which is, to consider the moral sense as a sense distinct from others, because it is the easiest and clearest manner of conceiving it.

actions, would be altogether inexplicable. We find this sense distributed among individuals in different degrees of perfection: but there perhaps never existed any one above the condition of an idiot, who possessed it not in some degree; and were any man entirely destitute of it, the terms *right* and *wrong* would to him be not less unintelligible than the term *colour* is to one born blind.

That every individual is endued with a sense of right and wrong, more or less distinct, will readily be granted; but whether there be among men what may be termed a COMMON SENSE of right and wrong, producing uniformity of opinion as to what actions are right and what wrong, is not so evident. There appears nothing absurd in supposing the opinions of men about right and wrong to be as various as their faces; and the history of mankind leads us to suspect, that this supposition is not destitute of foundation. For from <8> that history it appears, that among different nations, and even in the same nation at different periods, the opinions publicly espoused with regard to right and wrong are extremely various; that among some nations it was held lawful for a man to sell his children as slaves, and in their infancy to abandon them to wild beasts; that it was held equally lawful to punish children, even capitally, for the crime of their parent; that the murdering an enemy in cold blood, was once a common practice; that human sacrifices, impious not less than immoral according to our notions, were of old universal; that even in later times, it has been held meritorious to inflict cruel torments for the slightest devia-tions from the religious creed of the plurality; and that among the most enlightened nations, there are considerable differences with respect to the rules of morality.

These facts, however well founded, tend not to disprove the reality of a common sense as to morals: they only evince, that the moral sense has not been equally perfect at all times, and in all countries: which is not surprising, being the case of all our more refined senses and faculties; witness, in particular, the sense of beauty, of elegance, of propriety. And with regard to this point, the following observation may give satisfaction. In the order of Providence, the progress of our species toward perfection resembles that of an individual: we may observe an infancy in both; and in both a gradual progress toward maturity: nor is the resemblance the less perfect, that certain tribes, like certain individuals, ripen faster than others. The savage state is the infancy of man; during which the more delicate senses lie dormant, abandoning nations to the authority of custom, of imitation, and of passion, without any just taste of morals more than of the fine arts. But nations, like individuals, ripen gradually, and acquire in time a refined taste in morals, as well as in the fine arts; after which we find great uniformity of opinion about the rules of right and wrong, with few exceptions but what may proceed from imbecillity, or corrupted education. There may be found, it is true, even in the most enlightened ages, some men who have singular notions upon some points of morality; and there may be found the like singularity upon many other subjects: which affords no argument against a common sense or standard of right and wrong, more than a monster doth against the standard that regulates our external form, nor more than an exception doth against the truth of a general proposition.

That there is in mankind a common sense of what is right and wrong, and an uniformity of opinion, is a matter of fact, of which <9> the only infallible proof is observation and experience: and to that proof I appeal; entering only one caveat, That, for the reason above given, the inquiry be confined to nations of polished manners. In the mean time I take the liberty to suggest an argument from analogy, That if there be great uniformity among the different tribes of men in seeing and hearing, in truth and falsehood, in pleasure and pain, &c. what cause can we have for suspecting that right and wrong are an exception from the general rule? Whatever minute differences there may be to distinguish one person from another; yet in the general principles that constitute our nature, internal and external, there is wonderful uniformity.

That man is by nature a social being, is evident from many of his principles and faculties, calculated chiefly or solely to qualify him for the social state. This is eminently the case of the moral sense; the very purpose of which is, to regulate our conduct in society. That the uniformity of this sense among the different tribes of men, intitling it to be termed *the common sense of mankind,* must be calculated for the further improvement of society, is highly probable; and yet does not appear altogether so clear at first view. For may it not be urged, that we are bound notwithstanding to regulate our conduct by our own sense or private conviction; and that to act otherwise would be to act against conscience? This argument is at least plausible; and if it hold true, society, it must be yielded, cannot be benefited by a standard that is not calculated to regulate any branch of our conduct. But the Almighty leaves no imperfection in his works: he intended man for society; he endued him with a sense of right and wrong; he made the perceptions of that sense uniform in all men; and to complete us for society, he has moulded our nature so admirably, as that even the man who has the most correct sense of morals, is not better qualified for society, than they are who deviate the farthest from it. The contrivance, simple and beautiful, is, to bind us by a law in our nature to regulate our conduct by the common sense of mankind, even in op-position to what otherwise would be our own sense or private conviction. And that this truly is the system of nature, I endeavour to make out as follows.

We have an innate sense or conviction of a common nature, not only in our own species, but in every species of animals: and our conviction is verified by experience; for there appears a remarkable uniformity among creatures of the same kind, and a disformity, not less remarkable, among creatures of different kinds. This common <10> nature is conceived to be a model or standard for each individual of the kind. Hence it is a matter of wonder, to find an individual deviating from the common nature of the species, whether in its internal or external structure: a child born with aversion to its mother's milk, is a wonder, not less than if born without a mouth, or with more than one.

Secondly, With respect to the common nature of man in particular, we have an innate conviction, that it is invariable not less than universal; that it will be the same hereafter as at present, and as it was in time past; the same among all nations, and in all corners of the earth. Nor are we de-ceived; because giving allowance for the difference of culture, and gradual refinement of manners, the fact corresponds to our conviction.

Thirdly, We have an innate conviction, that this common nature or standard is PERFECT and RIGHT; and that every individual OUGHT to be framed according to it. Every remarkable deviation from the standard, makes an impression upon us of imperfection, irregularity, or disorder;

and raises a painful emotion: monstrous births, exciting the curiosity of a philosopher, fail not at the same time to excite aversion in a high degree.

This conviction of perfection in the common nature of man, reaches every branch of his nature; and particularly his sense of the morality and immorality of actions, termed the *moral sense.* This sense accordingly, considered as a branch of the common nature of man, is admitted by all to be perfect; and, consequently, to be the ultimate and unerring standard of morals; to which all are bound to submit, even in opposition to their own private sense of right and wrong. At the same time, as this standard, through infirmity or prejudice, is not conspicuous to every individual, we find instances, not few in number, of persons deluded into erroneous moral opinions, by mistaking a false standard for that of nature. And hence, with respect to individuals, a distinction between a right and a wrong sense in morals; a distinction which, from the conviction of a moral standard, is obvious to the meanest capacity; but of which distinction we could not otherwise have the slightest conception.

The final cause of this branch of our constitution is illustrious. Were there no standard of right and wrong for determining our endless controversies about matters of interest, the strong would have recourse to open violence; the weak to cunning, deceit, and treachery; and society would be altogether intolerable. Courts of law could afford no resource: for without a standard of morals, their de- <11> cisions must be arbitrary, and consequently have no authority nor influence.

Happy it is for men, that in all their disputes about right and wrong, they have this standard to appeal to: it is necessary, that in society the actions of individuals be uniform with respect to right and wrong; and in order to uniformity of action, it is necessary that their perceptions of right and wrong be uniform: to produce such uniformity, a standard of morals is indispensable; which is daily applied by judges with great success.

To complete this theory, it must be added, that, independent of the author's opinion, it is the goodness or illness of the effect intended which qualifies an action to be right or wrong. Thus, when a man impelled by friendship or pity, rescues from the flames one condemned to be burnt for heresy, the action is right, even though the man, convinced that heretics ought to be destroy'd, be of opinion that the action is wrong.

But with respect to the author of the action, nature leads us to judge of him by a different rule. He is approved, and held to be INNOCENT, when he does what he himself thinks right: he is disapproved, and held to be GUILTY, when he does what he himself thinks wrong. Thus, to assassinate an Atheist for the sake of religion, is a wrong action: and yet the enthusiast who commits that wrong may be innocent: and one is guilty who, contrary to conscience, eats meat in Lent, though the action is not wrong. Upon the whole, an action is perceived to be right or wrong independent of the author's own opinion: but he is approved or disapproved, held to be innocent or guilty, according to his own opinion.

We learn from experience, as above, that every right action is agreeable, and every wrong action disagreeable. But the author appears to us in a different light: he is agreeable when he acts according to conscience, though the action be wrong; and disagreeable when he acts against conscience, though the action be right. He is, however, more agreeable, when he does a right action according to conscience; and more disagreeable, when he does a wrong action against conscience: in which light he must always appear to himself; for when he acts according to conscience, he must think the action right; and when he acts against conscience, he must think the action wrong. <12>

CHAPTER II

Laws of Nature that regulate our conduct in Society.

Having thus established a standard for morals, which lays a solid foundation for the science of morality, the regular progress is, to investigate the laws that are derived from this standard: and these laws may be shortly defined, "Rules of conduct that are declared to be such by the common sense of mankind, which is the moral standard."

When we endeavour to investigate the laws of nature, those regularly take the lead that concern our duty: and as duty is of two kinds, duty to others, and duty to ourselves, we begin with the former. Of the duties we owe to others, some tend to action, some to restraint; and before entering into particulars, it may be proper to present them in a general view.

There is one duty so general as to comprehend all mankind for its object, all at least that are innocent; and that is the duty of forbearing to hurt others, whether externally or internally. A man may be hurt externally in his goods, in his person and relations, and in his reputation. Hence the laws, Thou must not steal, Thou must not defraud others, Thou must not kill nor wound, Thou must not be guilty of defamation.

A man may be hurt internally by an action that occasions to him distress of mind; and he may be hurt internally by receiving false notions of men and things. Therefore in dealing or conversing with others, conscience dictates that we ought not to treat them disrespectfully; that we ought not causelessly to alienate their affections from others, nor the affections of others from them; and, in general, that we ought to forbear whatever may tend to break their peace of mind, or tend to unqualify them for being good men and good citizens.

Our active duties regard particular persons, such as our relations, our friends, our benefactors, our masters, our servants, &c.; and these duties are more or less extensive, in proportion to the degree connection. We ought to honour and obey our parents; be affectionate to our children, and endeavour to establish them in the world with all advantages, internal and external: we ought to be faithful to our friends, grateful to our benefactors, submissive to our masters, and kind to our servants: and, according to our ability, <13> we ought to relieve the distresses of each of them. To be obliged to do good to others beyond these bounds, must depend on positive engagement: for, as will appear afterward, universal benevolence is a virtue only, not a duty.

Being prepared for particulars by this general sketch, the first duty that comes in view, is that which restrains us from harming the innocent; and to it corresponds a right in the innocent to be safe from harm. This is the great law preparatory to society; because without it society could never have existed. In this duty, the inflexibility of the moral sense is peculiarly remarkable; for it dictates, that we ought to submit to any distress, even death itself, rather than procure our own safety by laying violent hands upon an innocent person. And we are under the same restraint with respect to the property of another; for robbery and theft are never upon any pretext indulged. It is true, that a man in extreme hunger may lawfully take food where he can find it; and may freely lay hold of his neighbour's horse, to carry him from an enemy who threatens death. But the reason is, that the proprietor's consent may justly be presumed in such cases, upon our submitting to make up the loss: it is the duty of the proprietor, as a fellow-creature, to assist me in distress; and I may lawfully take what he ought to offer, and what I reasonably presume he would offer were he present. For the same reason, if in a storm my ship be drove among the anchor-ropes of another ship, which ropes I am forced to cut in order to get free, the act is lawful, provided I be willing to pay the value. This provision is equitable: for if, on the one hand, my neighbour be bound to aid me in distress, reason and conscience bind me, on the other, to make up his loss, as far as in my power.* <14>

The prohibition of hurting others internally, is perhaps not essential to the formation of societies, because the transgression of that law doth not much alarm plain people: but among people of manners and refined senti-

---

* This doctrine is founded on the principle of justice; and yet there are in the Roman law two passages which deny any recompence in such cases. "Item Labeo scribit, si cum vi ventorum navis impulsa esset in funes anchorarum alterius, et nautae funes praecidissent, si nullo alio modo, nisi praecisis funibus, explicare se potuit, nullam actionem dandam"; *l.* 29. §3, *ad legem Aquiliam* [the *Lex Aquilia,* D 9.2.29.3: Watson i: 287: "Furthermore, Labeo writes that when a ship was blown by the force of the wind into the anchor ropes of another vessel and the sailors cut the ropes, no action should be allowed if the vessel could be extricated in no other way than by severing the ropes"]. "Quod dicitur, *damnum injuria datum Aquilia persequi,* sic erit accipiendum, ut videatur damnum injuria datum quod cum damno injuriam attulerit: nisi, magna vi cogente, fuerit factum. Ut Celsus scribit circa eum, qui incendii arcendi gratia vicinas aedes intercidit: et sive pervenit ignis, sive ante extinctus est, existimat, legis Aquilae actionem cessare"; *l.* 49. §1. *eod.* [the *Lex Aquilia,* D 9.2.49.1: Watson i: 291: "What is said about suing under the *lex Aquilia* for damage done wrongfully must be taken as meaning that damage is done wrongfully when it inflicts wrong together with the damage, and this is inflicted, except where it is done under compulsion of overwhelming necessity, as Celsus writes about the man who pulled down his neighbour's house to keep a fire off his own: he also thinks that there is no action under the *lex,* regardless of whether the fire would actually have reached him or been put out first"]. These opinions are obviously erroneous; and it is not difficult to say what has occasioned the error: the cases mentioned are treated as belonging to the *lex Aquilia;* which being confined to the reparation of wrongs, lays it justly down for a rule, that no action for reparation can lie where there is no *culpa* [fault]. But had Labeo and Celsus adverted, that these cases belong to a different head, *viz.* the duty of recompence where one suffers loss by benefiting another, they themselves would have had no difficulty of sustaining a claim for that loss.

ments, the mind is susceptible of more grievous wounds than the body; and therefore without that law a polished society could have no long endurance.

By adultery mischief is done both external and internal. Each sex is so constituted as to require strict fidelity and attachment in their mates; and the breach of this fidelity is the greatest external mischief that can befal them. It is also a hurt internally, by breaking their peace of mind. It has indeed been urged, That this hurt will be avoided if the adultery be kept secret; and therefore that there can be no crime where there is no discovery. But they who reason thus do not advert, that to declare secret adultery to be lawful is in effect to overturn every foundation of mutual trust and fidelity in the married state.*

Veracity is commonly ranked among the active duties: but erroneously; for if a man be not bound to speak, he cannot be bound to speak truth. It is therefore only a restraining duty, importing that we ought not to deceive others by affirming what is not true. Among the many corresponding principles in the human mind, a principle of veracity,† and a principle that leads us to believe what is said to us, are two: without the latter, the former would be an useless principle; and without the former, the latter would be a dangerous one, laying us open to fraud and deceit. The moral sense accordingly dictates, that we ought to adhere strictly to truth, without regard to consequences.

From this it must not be inferred, that we are bound to explain our thoughts when the truth is demanded from us by unlawful force. Words uttered voluntarily are naturally relied on as expressing the speaker's mind;

---

* It is clear beyond all doubt, says a reputable writer, that no man is permitted to violate his faith; and that the man is unjust and barbarous who deprives his wife of the only reward she has for adhering to the austere duties of her sex. But an unfaithful wife is still more criminal, by dissolving the whole ties of nature: in giving to her husband children that are not his, she betrays both, and joins perfidy to infidelity; *Emile, liv.* 5 [Jean-Jacques Rousseau, *Émile, ou de l'éducation,* 4 vols. (Frankfurt, 1762), vol. 4, pp. 8–9].

† Truth is always uppermost, being the natural issue of the mind: it requires no art nor training, no inducement nor temptation, but only that we yield to a natural impulse. Lying, on the contrary, is doing violence to our nature; and is never practised, even by the worst men, without some temptation. Speaking truth is like using our natural food, which we would do from appetite, although it answered no end: lying is like taking physic, which is nauseous to the taste, and which no man takes but for some end which he cannot otherwise attain; *Dr Reid's Inquiry into the human mind* [Thomas Reid, *An Inquiry into the Human Mind, on Principles of Common Sense* (Edinburgh: Millar, Kincaid & Bell, 1764), p. 475].

and if he falsify their meaning, he tells a lie, <15> and is guilty of deceit. But words drawn from a man by unlawful force, are no evidence of his mind; and therefore, to save his life in such circumstances, it is no infringement of duty to utter whatever words may be agreeable, however alien from his thoughts: there is no reason to presume, in this case, any correspondence between his words and his mind; and if the author of the unlawful violence suffer himself to be deceived, he must blame himself, not the speaker.

It need scarce be mentioned, that the duty of veracity excludes not fable, nor any liberty of speech intended for amusement, and not to be a voucher of truth.

The first active duty I shall mention in particular, is that which subsists between parents and children. The relation of parent and child, being one of the strongest that can exist among individuals, makes mutual benevolence between these persons an indispensable duty. Benevolence among other blood-relations is also a duty; though inferior in degree, for it wears away gradually as the relation becomes more distant.

Gratitude is a duty directed to a particular object; and the object of gratitude is one whose kindness and good offices require suitable returns. But though gratitude is strictly a duty, the measure of performance, and the kind, are left mostly to our own choice. It is scarce necessary to add, that the active duties now mentioned are acknowledged by all to be absolutely inflexible; perhaps more so than the restraining duties: many find excuses for doing harm; but no one hears with patience an excuse for deviating from friendship or gratitude.

Distress tends vigorously to convert the virtue of benevolence into a duty. But distress alone is not sufficient, without other concurring circumstances; for to relieve the distressed in general, would be a duty far beyond the reach of the most powerful prince that ever existed. Our relations in distress claim this duty from us, and even our neighbours; but distant distress, where there is no particular connection, scarce rouses our sympathy, and never is an object of duty. Many other connections, too numerous for this short essay, extend the duty of relieving others from distress; and these naturally make a large branch in every treatise upon equity.

One great advantage of society is, the co-operation of many to accomplish some useful end, for which a single hand would be insufficient. All the arts, manufactures, and commercial dealings, require many hands, which cannot be depended on if there be no en- <16> gagement; and therefore the performance of promises and covenants is in society a capital *duty*. In their original occupations of hunting and fishing, men, living scattered and dispersed, had seldom opportunity to aid and benefit each other; and in that situation covenants, being of little use, were little regarded. But husbandry, being favourable to population, and requiring the co-operation of many hands, drew men together for mutual assistance; and then covenants began to make a figure: arts and commerce made them more and more necessary; and by the improvement of man's nature in society, the utmost regard at present is had to them.

But contracts and promises are not confined to commercial dealings: they serve also to make benevolence a duty, independent of any pecuniary interest. They are even extended so far, as to connect the living with the dead. A man would die with regret, if he thought his friends were not bound by the promises they make to fulfil his will after his death: and to quiet the minds of men with respect to futurity, the moral sense makes the performing such promises our duty. Thus, if I promise to my friend to erect a monument for him after his death, conscience binds me, even though no person alive be intitled to demand performance: every one holds this to be my duty; and I must lay my account to suffer reproach and blame, if I neglect my engagement.

To fulfil a rational promise or covenant deliberately made, is a duty not less inflexible than those duties are which arise independent of consent. But as man is fallible, liable to fraud and imposition, and to be misled by ignorance or error, his case would be deplorable, were he compelled by the moral sense to fulfil every engagement, however imprudent or irrational. Here the moral sense, bending to circumstances, is accommodated to the fallible nature of man: it relieves him from deceit, from imposition, from ignorance, and from error; and binds him to no engagement but what fairly answers the end proposed by it.

The other branch of duties, comprehending those we owe to ourselves, may be discussed in a few words. The sense of propriety, a branch of the moral sense, regulates our conduct with respect to ourselves; as the sense of justice, another branch of the moral sense, regulates our conduct with respect to others. The sense of propriety dictates, that we ought to act suitably to the dignity of our nature, and to the station allotted us by Providence; and, in particular, that temperance, prudence, modesty, and regularity of conduct, are self-duties. These duties contribute greatly to private happiness, by <17> preserving health, peace of mind, and a justly founded self-esteem; which are great blessings: they contribute not less to happiness in society, by procuring love and esteem, and consequently aid and support in time of need.

Upon reviewing the foregoing duties respecting others, we find them more or less extensive; but none of them so extensive as to have for their object the good of mankind in general. The most extensive duty is that of restraint, prohibiting us to harm others: but even this duty suffers an exception respecting those who merit punishment. The active duties of doing good are circumscribed within much narrower bounds; requiring an intimate relation for their object, such as what we bear to our parents, our children, our friends, our benefactors. The slighter relations are not an object, unless with the addition of peculiar circumstances: neighbourhood, for example, does not alone make benevolence a duty; but supposing a neighbour to be in distress, we become bound to relieve him in proportion to our ability. For it is remarkable in human nature, that though we always sympathise with our relations, and with those under our eye, the distress of persons remote and unknown affects us very little. Pactions and agreements become necessary, where the purpose is to extend the duty of benevolence, in any particular, beyond the bounds mentioned. Men, it is true, are sometimes capable of doing more good than is prescribed to them as a duty; but every such good must be voluntary.

And this leads to moral acts that are left to our own will to be done or left undone; which is the second general branch of moral actions mentioned above. Writers differ strangely about the benevolence of man. Some hold him to be merely a selfish being, incapable of any motive to action but what ultimately respects himself: this is too bold an assertion, being contradictory to the experience of all ages, which affords the clearest conviction, that men frequently act for the good of others, without regard to their own good, and sometimes in direct opposition to it. Other writers, running to the opposite extreme, advance benevolence to be a duty, maintaining that every one of the human race is intitled to all the good we can possibly do them: which banishes every consideration of self-interest, other than what we owe to ourselves as a part of the general society of men. This doctrine is not less contradictory to experience than the former: for we find that men generally are disposed to prefer their own interest before that of those with whom they have no particu- <18> lar connection: nor do we find such bias controlled by the moral sense.

With respect to the actions that belong to the present branch, the moral sense imposes no laws upon us, leaving us at freedom to act or not according to our own inclination. Taking, accordingly, under consideration any single benevolent act by itself, it is approved when done, but not condemned when left undone. But considering the whole of our conduct, the moral sense appears to vary a little. As the nature of man is complex, partly social, partly selfish, reason dictates that our conduct ought to be conformable to our nature; and that, in advancing our own interest, we ought not altogether to neglect that of others. The man accordingly who confines his whole time and thoughts within his own little sphere, is condemned by all the world as guilty of wrong conduct; and the man himself, if his moral perceptions be not blunted by selfishness, must be sensible that he deserves to be condemned. On the other hand, it is possible that voluntary benevolence may be extended beyond proper bounds. The true balance of the mind consists in a subordination of benevolence to self-love; and therefore, where that balance is so varied as to give superior weight to the former, a man thus constituted will be excessive in his benevolence: he will sacrifice a great interest of his own to a small interest of others; and the moral sense dictates that such conduct is wrong.

With respect to the subject of this chapter in general, we have reason to presume from the uniformity of our moral perceptions, that there must be some general character distinguishing right actions, and their good effects, from wrong actions, and their ill effects. And from the deduction above given it will appear, that the general tendency of the former is, to promote the good of society; and of the latter, to obstruct that good. Universal benevolence, as a duty, is indeed not required of man; for an evident reason, that the performance is beyond the reach of his utmost abilities: but for promoting the general good, every duty is required of him that he can accomplish; which will appear from the slightest review of the foregoing duties. The prohibition of harming others is an easy task, and therefore is made universal. Our active duties are in a very different condition: man is circumscribed both in his capacity and powers; he cannot do good but in a slow succession; and therefore it is wisely ordered, that the obligation he is under to do good should be confined to his relations, his friends, his benefactors. Even distress cannot make benevolence a general duty: all a man can readily do, and <19> all he is bound to do, is to relieve those at hand; and accordingly we hear of distant misfortunes with very little or no concern.

At the same time, let us not misapprehend the moral system, as if it were our duty, or even lawful, to prosecute what, upon the whole, we reckon the most beneficial to society, balancing ill with good. In the moral system, it is not permitted to violate the most trivial right of any one, however beneficial it may be to others. For example, a man in low circumstances, by denying a debt he owes to a rich miser, saves himself and a hopeful family from ruin. In this case the good effect far outweighs the ill: but the moral sense admits no balancing between good and ill, and gives no quarter to injustice, whatever benefit it may produce. And hence a maxim in which all moralists agree, That we must not do evil even to bring about good. This doctrine, at the same time, is nicely correspondent to the nature of man: were it a rule in society, That a greater benefit to others would make it just to deprive me of my life, of my reputation, or of my effects, I should follow the advice of a celebrated philosopher, renounce society, and take refuge among the savages.[1]

CHAPTER III

Principles of Duty and of Benevolence.

Having thus shortly delineated the laws of nature, we proceed to a very important article; which is, to inquire into the means provided by the author of our nature for compelling obedience to these laws. The moral

---

1. See Anthony Ashley Cooper, Earl of Shaftesbury, *Soliloquy: or, Advice to an Author* (London: J. Morphew, 1710), p. 184.

sense is an excellent guide; but the most expert guide will avail nothing to those who are not disposed to follow him. Intuitive knowledge of what is right, cannot of itself be a motive to act righteously, more than intuitive knowledge of what is wrong can be a motive to act unrighteously. From this single consideration, it must be evident, that, to complete the moral system, there ought to be some principle or propensity in our nature, some impelling power, to be a motive for acting when the moral sense says we ought to act, and to restrain us from acting when the moral sense says we ought not to act.

The author of our nature leaves none of his works imperfect. In order to render us obsequious to the moral sense, as our guide, he hath implanted in our nature the three great principles, of duty, of voluntary benevolence, and of rewards and punishments. <20>

It may possibly be thought that rewards and punishments, of which afterward, are sufficient of themselves to enforce the laws of our nature, without necessity of any other principle. Human laws, it is true, are inforc'd by these means, because no higher sanction is under the command of a terrestrial legislator: but the celestial legislator, with power that knows no control, and benevolence that knows no limits, has inforc'd his laws by means not less remarkable for their mildness than for their efficacy: he employs no external compulsion; but in order to engage our will on the side of moral conduct, has in the breast of every individual established the principles mentioned, which efficaciously excite us to obey the dictates of the moral sense. Other principles may solicit and allure; but the principle of duty assumes authority, commands, and must be obey'd.

As one great advantage of society is, the furnishing opportunities without end of mutual aid and assistance, beyond what is strictly our duty; nature hath disposed us to do good by the principle of benevolence, which is a powerful incitement to be kindly, beneficent, and generous. Nor is this principle, as will afterward appear, too sparingly distributed: its strength is so nicely proportioned to our situation in this world, as better to answer its destination, than if it were an over-match for self-interest, and for every other principle.

Thus, moral actions are divided into two classes: the first regards our duty, containing actions that ought to be done, and actions that ought not to be done: the other regards actions left to ourselves, containing actions that are right when done, but not wrong when left undone. It will appear afterward, that the well-being of society depends more on the first class than on the second; that society is indeed promoted by the latter; but that it can scarce subsist unless the former be made our duty. Hence it is, that actions only of the first class are made indispensable, actions of the second class being left to our own free will. And hence also it is, that the various principles or propensities that dispose us to actions of the first sort, are distinguished by the name of *primary virtues,* giving the name of *secondary virtues* to those principles or propensities which dispose us to actions of the other sort.* <21>

CHAPTER IV

Rewards and Punishments.

Reflecting upon the moral branch of our nature qualifying us for society in the most perfect manner, we cannot overlook the hand of our maker; for means so finely prepared to accomplish an important end, never happen by chance. At the same time it must be acknowledged, that in many men the principle of duty has not vigour nor authority sufficient to stem every tide of unruly passion: by the vigilance of some passions we are taken unprepared, deluded by the sly insinuations of others, or overwhelmed with the stormy impetuosity of a third sort. Moral evil thus gains ground, and much wrong is done. This new scene makes it evident, that there must be some article wanting to complete the present undertaking. The means provided for directing us in the road of duty are indeed explained; but as in deviating from the road wrongs are committed, there is hitherto nothing said of redressing these wrongs, nor of preventing the reiteration of them. To accomplish these valuable ends, there are added to the moral system the principle of rewards and punishments, and that of reparation; of which in their order.

Such animals as are governed entirely by instinct, may be qualified for

---

* Virtue in general signifies that disposition of mind which gives the ascendant to moral principles. Vice in general signifies that disposition of mind which gives little or no ascendant to moral principles.

society; which, among quadrupeds, is the case of the beavers; and, among winged animals, of the bees, of the crows, and of some other kinds. But very few of the human actions are instinctive: they are generally prompted by passions, of which there is an endless variety, social and selfish, benevolent and malevolent: and were every passion equally intitled to gratification, man would be utterly incapable of society; he would be a ship without a rudder, obedient to every wind, and moving at random, without any destination. The faculty of reason would make no opposition; for were there no sense of wrong, it would be reasonable to gratify every desire that harms not ourselves: and to talk of punishment would be absurd; for the very idea of punishment implies some wrong that ought to be repressed. Hence the necessity of the moral sense to qualify us for society, and to make us accountable beings: by teaching us what is our duty, it renders us accountable for our actions, and makes us fit objects of rewards and punishments. The moral sense fulfils another valuable purpose: it <22> forms in our minds an unerring standard, directing the application and the measure of rewards and punishments.

But to complete the system of rewards and punishments, it is necessary, that not only power, but also inclination, be conferred upon one, or upon many, to reward and to punish. The author of our nature has provided amply for the first, by intitling every individual to exercise that power as his native privilege. And he has equally provided for the other, by a noted principle implanted in our nature, prompting us to reward the virtuous, and to punish the vicious. Every act of duty is rewarded with our approbation: a benevolent act is rewarded with our esteem: a generous act commands our affection. These, and other virtuous actions, have a still reward; which is, the consciousness of merit in the author himself.

As to punishment, it would be inconsistent to punish any defect in benevolence, considered as a virtue left to our own free will. But an action done intentionally to produce mischief is criminal, and merits punishment: such an action being disagreeable, raises any resentment, even though I have no connection with the person injured; and being impelled, by the principle under consideration, to punish vice, as well as to reward virtue, I must chastise the delinquent by indignation, at least, and hatred. An injury done to myself raises my resentment to a higher pitch: I am not satisfied with so slight a punishment as indignation or hatred; the author must by my hand suffer mischief as great as he has done me.

Even the most secret crime escapes not punishment; for, though hid from others, it cannot be hid from the delinquent himself. It raises in him the painful passion of remorse: this passion, in its stronger fits, makes him wish to be punished; and, in extreme, frequently impels him to be his own executioner. There cannot be imagined a contrivance more effectual to deter us from vice; for remorse is itself a severe punishment. But this is not the whole of self-punishment: every criminal, sensible that he ought to be punished, dreads punishment from others; and this painful feeling, however smothered during prosperity, becomes extremely severe in adversity, or in any depression of mind. Then it is that his crime stares him in the face, and that every accidental misfortune is, in his disturbed imagination, converted into a real punishment: "And they said one to another, We are verily guilty concerning our brother, in that we saw the anguish of his soul, when he besought us; and we would not hear: therefore is this distress come upon us. And Reuben answered them, saying, Spake I not unto you, saying, <23> Do not sin against the child; and ye would not hear? therefore behold also his blood is required"; *Genesis,* xlii, 21, 22.

No transgression of the duty we owe to ourselves escapes punishment, more than the transgression of the duty we owe to others. The punishments, though not the same are nearly allied; and differ in degree more than in kind. Injustice is punished by the delinquent himself with remorse; impropriety with shame, which is remorse in a lower degree. Injustice raises indignation in the beholder, and so doth every flagrant impropriety: slighter improprieties receive a milder punishment, being rebuked with some degree of contempt, and frequently with derision.

So far have we been carried in a beaten track: but in attempting to proceed, we are intangled in several intricacies and obstructions. Doth an action well intended, though it fall short of its aim, intitle the author to a reward; or an action ill-intended, though it happen to produce no mischief, subject him to punishment? The moral sense, in some individuals, is known to be so perverted, as to differ, perhaps widely, from the common sense of mankind; must the former or the latter be the rule for punishing or rewarding such persons? At first there will be little hesitation in affirming, that the common sense of mankind must be the standard for rewards and punishments, as well as for civil claims: but these questions suggest some doubts, which, after due examination, lead to an important discovery, That rewards and punishments are regulated by a different standard.

It is the common sense of mankind that determines actions to be right or wrong, just or unjust, proper or improper. By this standard, all pecuniary claims are judged, all claims of property, and, in a word, every demand founded upon interest; not excepting reparation, as will afterward appear. But with respect to the moral characters of men, and with respect to rewards and punishments, a standard is established far less rigid; which is, the opinion that men form of their own actions: and accordingly, as mentioned above, a man is held to be innocent when he does what he himself thinks right; and is held to be guilty when he does what he himself thinks wrong. Thus we are led, by a natural principle, to judge of others as we believe they judge of themselves; and by that rule we pronounce them virtuous or vicious, innocent or guilty; and we approve or disapprove, praise or blame them accordingly.* Some, <24> it is true, are so perverted by bad education, or by superstition, as to espouse numberless absurd tenets, flatly contradicting the common standard of right and wrong; and yet even these make no exception from the rule: if they act according to conscience, they are innocent, however wrong the action may be; and if they act against conscience, they are guilty, however right the action may be. Here then is a conspicuous standard for rewards and punishments: it is a man's own conscience that declares him innocent or guilty, and consequently fit to be rewarded or punished; for it is abhorrent to every natural perception, that a guilty person be rewarded, or an innocent person punished. Further, in order that personal merit and demerit may not in any measure depend upon chance, we are so constituted as to place innocence and guilt, not on the event, but on the intention of doing right or wrong; and accordingly, whatever be the event, a man will be praised for an action well intended, and condemned for an action ill intended.

But what if a man intending a wrong, happen by accident to do a

---

* Virtuous and vicious, innocent and guilty, signify qualities both of men and of their actions. Approbation and disapprobation, praise and blame, do not signify qualities; but signify certain feelings or sentiments of those who see or consider men and their actions.

wrong he did not intend; as, for example, intending to rob a warren by shooting the rabbits, he accidentally wound a child unseen behind a bush? The delinquent ought to be punished for intending to rob; and he is also subjected to repair the hurt done to the child: but he cannot be punished for this accidental wound; because the law of nature regulates punishment by the intention, and not by the event.* <25>

The transgression of the primary virtues is attended with severe and never-failing punishments, which are much more effectual than any that have been invented to inforce municipal laws: on the other hand, there is very little merit ascribed even to the strictest observance of them. The secondary virtues are directly opposite, with respect to their rewards and punishments: the neglect of them is not attended with any punishment;

---

* During the infancy of nations, pecuniary compositions for crimes obtained universally; and during that long period very little weight was laid upon intention. This proceeded from the grossness and obscurity of moral perceptions, joined with the resemblance of a pecuniary punishment to reparation: where a man does mischief intentionally, or is *versans in illicito* [engaged in unlawful activity], as expressed in the Roman law, he may justly be bound to repair all the harm that ensues, however accidentally; and from the resemblance of pecuniary punishment to reparation, the rule was inadvertently extended to punishment. But this rule, so gross, and so little consistent with moral principles, could not long subsist after pecuniary compositions gave place to corporal punishment; and accordingly, among civilized nations, the law of nature was restored, which prohibits punishment for any mischief that is not intentional. The English must be excepted, who, remarkably tenacious of their original laws and customs, preserve in force, even as to capital punishment, the above-mentioned rule that obtained when pecuniary compositions were in vigour. The following passage is from Hale's Pleas of the crown, *ch.* 39. "Regularly he that voluntarily and knowingly intends hurt to the person of a man, as for example to beat him, though he intend not death; yet if death ensues, it excuseth not from the guilt of murder, or manslaughter at least, as the circumstances of the case happen" [Matthew Hale, *The History of the Pleas of the Crown*, 2 vols. (London: Nutt and Gosling, 1736), vol. 1, p. 472]. And Foster, in his Crown-law, though a judicious and accurate writer, lays down the same doctrine, without even suspecting in it the least deviation from moral principles: "A shooteth at the poultry of B, and by accident killeth a man; if his intention was to steal the poultry, which must be collected from circumstances, it will be murder, by reason of that felonious intent; but if it was done wantonly, and without that intention, it will be barely manslaughter"; *p.* 259 [Sir Michael Foster, *A Report of Some Proceedings on the Commission of Oyer and Terminer and Gaol Delivery for the Trial of the Rebels in the Year 1746 in the County of Surry, and of Other Crown Cases to which are added Discourses upon a few Branches of the Crown Law* (Oxford: Clarendon Press, 1762), pp. 258–59].

but the practice of them is attended with the highest degree of approbation. Offices of undeserved kindness, returns of good for evil, generous toils and sufferings for our friends, or for our country, come under this class: to perform actions of this kind, there is no motive that, in a proper sense, can be termed a law; but there are the strongest motives that can consist with freedom, the performance being rewarded with a consciousness of self-merit, and with universal praise and admiration, the highest rewards human nature is susceptible of.

From what is said, the following observation will occur: The pain of transgressing justice, fidelity, or any primary virtue, is much greater than the pleasure of performance; but the pain of neglecting a generous action, or any secondary virtue, is as nothing, compared with the pleasure of performance. Among the vices opposite to the primary virtues, the most striking moral deformity is found: among the secondary virtues, the most striking moral beauty.

CHAPTER V

Reparation.

Reparation, a capital part of the moral system, promotes two ends of great importance: it represses wrongs that are not criminal; and it also makes up the loss sustained by wrongs of whatever kind. With respect to the former, reparation is a species of punishment; and with respect to the latter, it is a branch of justice. These ends will be better understood, after ascertaining the nature and true foundation of reparation. Every claim for reparation supposes a wrong action done by one, and loss or mischief thereby occasioned to another: And hence, 1mo, There can be no claim for repa- <26> ration if the action was innocent, whatever be the mischief; 2do, Nor can there be any claim unless mischief have happened, however wrong, or even criminal, the action may be. That the reparation to be awarded must correspond to the extent of the loss or mischief, is self-evident. The single difficulty is, to separate, by precise boundaries, actions that are wrong from those that are innocent. In order to explain the qualities of right and wrong, it was sufficient at first to lay down in general, That an action done

intentionally to produce an agreeable effect, is right; and done intentionally to produce a disagreeable effect, is wrong. But upon examining this
subject more narrowly, certain actions are discovered to be wrong, though
the mischief they have produced was not intended; and certain actions are
discovered to be innocent, though they have produced mischief. And these
I shall endeavour to explain, as follows.

The moral sense dictates, that in acting we ought carefully to avoid
doing mischief: the only difficulty is, to determine what degree of care
is requisite. An action may produce mischief that was foreseen, but not
intended; and it may produce mischief that was neither intended nor foreseen. The former is not criminal; because no action has that character,
without an intention to produce mischief: but it is CULPABLE or FAULTY,
because the moral sense prohibits every action that may probably do
mischief; and if we do mischief by transgressing that prohibition, we are
blamed by others, and even by ourselves. Thus, a man who throws a large
stone into the marketplace among a crowd of people, is highly culpable;
because he foresaw that mischief would probably ensue, though he had no
intention to hurt any person. With respect to the latter, though the mischief was neither intended nor foreseen, yet if it *might* have been foreseen,
the action so far is rash or incautious, and consequently culpable or faulty
in some degree. Thus, if a man, in pulling down an old house adjacent to
a frequented place, happen to wound a passenger, without calling aloud
that people may keep out of the way, the action is in some degree culpable,
because the mischief might have been foreseen. But though harm ensue,
an action is not culpable or faulty, if all reasonable precaution have been
adhibited: the moral sense declares the author to be innocent: the effect
is perceived to be accidental; and the action may be termed *unlucky* or
unfortunate, but cannot be said to be either right or wrong.* <27>

---

* Si putator, ex arbore ramum cum dejecerit, vel machinarius, hominem praetere-
untem occidit: ita tenetur, si is in publicum decidat, nec ille proclamavit, ut casus ejus
evitari posset. Quod si nullum iter erit, dolum dumtaxat praestare debet, ne immittat
in eum, quem viderit transeuntum: nam culpa ab eo exigenda non est; cum divinare
non potuerit, an per eum locum aliquis transiturus sit; *l.* 31, *ad legem Aquiliam* [the
Lex Aquilia, D 9.2.31: Watson i: 288: "If a pruner threw down a branch from a tree and
killed a slave passing underneath (the same applies to a man working on a scaffold), he
is liable only if it falls down in a public place and he failed to shout a warning so that

With respect to rash or incautious actions, where the mischief might have been foreseen, though neither intended nor actually foreseen, it is not sufficient to escape blame, that a man naturally rash or inattentive acts according to his character: a degree of precaution is required of him, both by himself and by others, such as is natural to the generality of men. The author, in particular, perceives, that he might and ought to have acted more cautiously; and his conscience reproaches him for his inattention, not less than if he were naturally more cool and attentive. Thus the circumspection natural to man in general, is applied as a standard to every individual; and if they fall short of that standard, they are culpable and blameable, however unforeseen by them the mischief may have been. This rule is distinctly laid down in the Roman law: "Culpam autem esse, quod, cum a diligente provideri poterit, non esset provisum."* Here the person's ordinary diligence is not referred to as the standard, but the ordinary diligence of mankind. Aristotle, in his Rhetoric, has evidently the same rule in view: "Reason teacheth us to distinguish between an injury and a fault, and between a fault and a mere accident. A mere accident can neither be foreseen nor prevented: a fault is where the mischief *might* have been foreseen, but where the action was done without evil intention: an injury is that which is done with an evil intention."[2]

What is said upon culpable actions is equally applicable to culpable omissions; for by these also mischief may be occasioned, intitling the sufferer to reparation. If we forbear to do our duty with an intention to occasion mischief, the forbearance is criminal. The only nice point is, how far forbearance without such intention is culpable. If the probability of mischief was foreseen, though not intended, the omission is highly culpable; and though neither intended nor foreseen, yet the omission is culpable, in

---

the accident could be avoided. But if there is no path, the defendant should be liable only for positive wrongdoing, so he should not throw anything at someone he sees passing by; but, on the other hand, he is not to be deemed blameworthy when he could not have guessed that someone was about to pass through that place"].

* l. 31, *ad legem Aquiliam* [the *Lex Aquilia*, D 9.2.31: Watson i: 288: "there is a fault, when what could have been foreseen by a diligent man was not foreseen"].

2. Not a direct quotation, but Kames's elaboration of the arguments of book 1.10 of Aristotle's *Rhetoric* (1368^b–1369^b).

a lower degree, if there have been less care and attention than are proper for performing the duty required. But supposing all due care, the omission of extreme care and diligence is not culpable.

Upon ascertaining what acts and omissions are culpable or faulty, every intricacy with respect to reparation vanishes; for it may be laid down as a rule, without an exception, That every culpable act, and every culpable omission, binds us in conscience to repair the mischief <28> occasioned by it. The moral sense binds us no farther; for it loads not with reparation the man who is innocent, though he have done harm: the harm is accidental; and we are so constituted as not to be responsible in conscience for what happens by accident. But here it is requisite that the man be in every respect innocent; for if he intend harm of any sort, he will find himself bound in conscience to repair the harm he has done, even accidentally: as, for example, when aiming a blow unjustly at one in the dark, he happens to wound another whom he did not suspect to be there. And hence it is a rule in all municipal laws, That one *versans in illicito*[3] is liable for every consequence. That these particulars are wisely ordered by the author of our nature for the good of society, will appear afterward.

We are now prepared for a more particular inspection of the two ends of reparation above mentioned, *viz.* the repressing wrongs that are not criminal, and the making up what loss is sustained by wrongs of whatever kind. With respect to the first, it is clear, that punishment, in its proper sense, cannot be inflicted for a wrong that is culpable only; and if nature did not provide some means for repressing such wrongs, society would scarce be a comfortable state: without a pecuniary reparation, there would be no compulsion, other than that of conscience merely, to prevent culpable omissions: and with respect to culpable commissions, the necessity of reparation is still more apparent; for conscience alone, without the sanction of reparation, would seldom have authority sufficient to restrain us from acting rashly or incautiously, even where the possibility of mischief is foreseen, and far less where it is not foreseen.

---

3. "Engaged in unlawful activity."

With respect to the second end of reparation, my conscience dictates to me, that if a man suffer by my fault, whether the mischief was foreseen or not foreseen, it is my duty to make up his loss; and I perceive intuitively, that the loss ought to rest ultimately upon me, and not upon the sufferer, who has done no wrong.

In every case where the mischief done can be estimated by a pecuniary compensation, the two ends of reparation coincide. The sum is taken from the one as a sort of punishment for his fault, and is bestowed on the other to relieve him from the loss he has sustained. But there are numberless instances, where the mischief done admits not an equivalent in money; and in such instances, there is no place for reparation except with relation to its first end. Defamation, contemptuous treatment, personal restraint, the breaking one's peace of mind, are injuries that cannot be repaired by money; and <29> the pecuniary reparation that the wrong-doer is decreed to make, can only be as a sort of punishment, in order to deter him from a reiteration of such injuries: the sum, it is true, is awarded to the person injured; but this cannot be to make up his loss, which money cannot do, but only as a *solatium*[4] for what he has suffered.

Hitherto it is supposed, that the man who intends an ill effect is at the same time conscious of its being ill. But a man may intend an ill effect, thinking, erroneously, that it is good; or a good effect, thinking, erroneously, that it is ill: and the question is, What should be the consequence of such error with respect to reparation? The latter case is clear: if the effect be good, the action that produced it is right, whatever be the author's opinion; and no person who occasionally suffers loss by a right action is intitled to complain. On the other hand, if the effect be ill, and the action consequently wrong, the innocence of the author, for which he is indebted to an error in judgment, will not relieve him from reparation. When he is made sensible of his error, he perceives himself bound in conscience to repair the harm he has done by a wrong action: and all others, sensible from the beginning of his error, perceive that he is so bound; for to them it must appear obvious, that a man's errors ought ultimately to affect

---

4. "Solace"; compensation for grief (Scots law).

himself only, and not the person who has not erred. Hence, in general, reparation always follows wrong or injustice; and is not in the least affected by an erroneous opinion of a right action being wrong, or a wrong action right.

But this doctrine suffers an exception with respect to a man who, having undertaken a trust, is bound in duty to act: as where an officer of the revenue, upon a doubtful clause in a statute, makes a seizure of goods, as forfeited to the crown, which afterward in the proper court are found not to be seizable. The officer, in this case, ought not to be subjected to reparation, if he have acted to the best of his judgment. This rule, however, must be taken with a limitation: a gross error will not excuse a public officer, who ought to know better.

It is scarce necessary to observe, that a man is not accountable for any harm he does by an involuntary act. A mason, for example, tumbling from a scaffold, happens in falling to wound one below: his conscience blames him not for what he could not help; and there is nothing in his conduct to lay hold of, for subjecting him to reparation. But it is not sufficient that one of several connected actions be involuntary; for reparation may be claimed, though the immediate act be involuntary, provided it be connected with a preceding <30> voluntary act. Example: "If A ride an unruly horse in Lincolns-inn-fields to tame him, and the horse breaking from A run over B, and grievously hurt him; B shall have an action against A. For though the mischief was done against the will of A, yet since it was his fault to bring a wild horse into a frequented place where mischief might ensue, he must answer for the consequences."[5] Gaius seems to carry this rule still further, holding in general, that if a horse, by the weakness or unskilfulness of the rider, break away and do mischief, the rider is liable.* But Gaius probably had in his eye a frequented place, where the mischief might have been foreseen. Thus, in general, a man is made liable for the mischief occasioned

---

5. Kames's reference is to the English case of *Mitchell* v. *Alestree* (1676); the quotation is taken from Matthew Bacon, *A New Abridgment of the Law* (London: Nutt and Gosling for Lintot, 1736), vol. 1, p. 53. The case was reported in numerous places: see *The English Reports,* vol. 83, p. 504; vol. 84, p. 932; and vol. 86, p. 190.

* L 8. §1. ad legem Aquiliam [the *Lex Aquilia* D 9.2.8.1: Watson i: 277].

by his voluntary act, though the immediate cause of the mischief be involuntary.

CHAPTER V[I]⁶

The Laws of Society considered
with respect to their final causes.

By our senses, external and internal, we are made acquainted with objects external and internal, and with their qualities: knowledge so acquired is termed *intuitive,* because we acquire more knowledge by sight or intuition than by any other of our senses. The reasoning faculty investigates truth by a regular progress from premises to consequences; and, upon that account, knowledge so acquired may be termed *discursive.* Thus certain properties of a triangle, and of a square, are laid open to us by reasoning; and the knowledge we thereby acquire is discursive. Of the different degrees of conviction, the very highest belongs to intuitive knowledge: and it ought to be so, because this species of knowledge is acquired by perception alone; which is not only a single mental act, but is also complete in itself, having no dependence on any thing antecedent: whereas discursive knowledge requires, not only a plurality of mental acts, but also one or more intuitive propositions to found upon. We accordingly rely more upon intuitive knowledge than upon the strictest reasoning: witness external objects, of whose existence we have a more solid conviction than of any proposition in Euclid. The application of this doctrine to morality, will be obvious at first view. <31>

By perception alone, without reasoning, we acquire the knowledge of right and of wrong, of what we may do, of what we ought to do, and of what we ought to abstain from: and considering that we have thus a greater certainty of the moral laws than of any proposition discovered by reasoning, man may well be deemed the favourite of Heaven, when such wisdom is employ'd in qualifying him to act a right part in life: the moral sense or conscience may well be held the voice of God within us,

---

6. The 1767 edition misprints this as Chapter V.

constantly admonishing us of our duty; and requiring on our part no exercise of our faculties but attention merely. The celebrated Locke ventured what he thought a bold conjecture, that the moral duties may be capable of demonstration:[7] how great his surprise to have been told, that they are capable of much higher evidence!

It would be losing time to indicate the final cause of establishing morality upon intuitive knowledge. Let us only consider what must have been our condition, had we been left to the glimmering light of reason. This faculty is distributed among men in portions so unequal, as to bar all hopes from it of uniformity, either in opinion or in action. Reason, it is true, aided by experience, may support morality, by convincing us that we cannot be happy if we abandon our duty for any other interest: but reason, even with experience, seldom weighs much against passion; and to restrain its impetuosity, nothing less is requisite than the vigorous and commanding principle of duty, directed by the shining light of intuition.

A second final cause respecting also morality in general, results from the connection above mentioned between right and agreeable in human actions, and between wrong and disagreeable. Were our duty disagreeable, man would be an inconsistent being; for his inclination would be constantly in opposition to his duty. To mislead us from our duty, even though agreeable, there are so many temptations, that it is no easy task to keep the straight road: would we persevere in it if our duty were disagreeable?

As the moral duties above mentioned are obviously calculated for the good of society, it might be thought, that, instead of particular duties, all should be reduced to a single general rule, that of doing every thing in our power for the good of society. But I shall endeavour to evince, that this imagined system, however plausible, is neither suited to the end proposed by it, nor to the nature of man; and in the course of the argument it will be seen, with what superior wisdom the true system of morality is contrived, which will set its final cause in a conspicuous light. It has been shown how essential in- <32> tuitive knowledge is to the performance of our duty: and I begin with examining what place there might be for intui-

---

7. John Locke, *An Essay Concerning Human Understanding*, 15th ed., 2 vols. (London: D. Browne et al., 1760), vol. 1, p. 30.

tive knowledge in the proposed system. As the general good of mankind results from many and various circumstances intricately combined, that good may be a subject for reasoning, but never can be an object of intuitive knowledge. But reason employ'd in weighing an endless number and variety of circumstances, seldom affords any solid conviction; and upon the proposed system we would be often left in the dark about our duty, however upright our intentions might be. At the same time, we would in vain expect from such faint conviction, authority sufficient to counterbalance the influence of passion: our duty would vanish from our sight in a maze of subtilties; and self-partiality would always suggest plausible reasons, for slight transgressions at first, and afterward for the very boldest. It is therefore ordered with consummate wisdom, even for the general good, that, avoiding general and complex objects, the moral sense should be directed to certain particular acts, and their effects; which, being plain and simple, can be made our duty by intuitive perception.

In the next place, to make universal benevolence our duty, without distinction of persons or circumstances, would in effect subject us to the absurd and impracticable duty, of serving at the same instant an endless number and variety of persons; which, instead of promoting the general good, would evidently be detrimental, by unqualifying us to perform any part.

The true system of morality, that which is display'd above, is better suited to the limited powers of man; and yet is contrived in the most perfect manner for promoting the general good. There is no occasion to lose time in demonstrating, that a man entirely selfish is ill fitted for society; and we have seen, that universal benevolence, considered as a duty, would contribute to the general good perhaps less than absolute selfishness. Man is much better fitted for society, by having in his constitution the principles of self-love and of benevolence duly proportioned. Benevolence, as far as a duty, takes place of self-love; which is wisely ordered, because so far it is essential to the very constitution of society. Benevolence, again, as a virtue not a duty, gives place to self-love; which is ordered with equal wisdom, because every man has more power, knowledge, and opportunity, to promote his own good, than that of others: by which means more good is actually produced, than if we were entirely surrendered to benevolence. At the same time, the principle of benevolence is as extensive as can consist

with the limited capa- <33> city of man: the chief objects of his affection
are his relations, his friends, his benefactors, to serve whom he is bound in
duty: some share of benevolence is reserved for his neighbours, and even
for those he is barely acquainted with; and to make benevolence more
extensive, would be entirely fruitless, because here are objects in plenty to
fill the most capacious mind. But though there is not room for a greater
variety of particular objects, yet the faculty we have of uniting numberless
individuals into one complex object, enlarges greatly the sphere of our
benevolence: for by this power, our country, our religion, our constitution, become objects of the most vigorous affection and public spirit. The
individuals that compose the group, considered apart, may be too minute,
or too distant, for our benevolence; but when comprehended under one
view, they become a complex object that warms and dilates the heart. By
that wonderful faculty, the limited capacity of our nature is remedied;
distant objects, otherwise invisible, are rendered conspicuous; accumula-
tion makes them great; greatness brings them near the eye; and affection,
preserved entire, is bestow'd upon a complex object, as upon one that is
single and visible; but with much greater force in proportion to its superior importance.

We now proceed to particulars; and the first that meets us is the great
law of restraint. Man is evidently framed for society; and because there
can be no society among creatures who prey upon each other, it was necessary, in the first place, to provide against mutual injuries; which is effectually done by this law. Its necessity with respect to personal security is
self-evident; and its necessity with respect to matters of property, will be
evident from what follows. There is in the nature of man a propensity to
hoard or store up the means of subsistence; a propensity essential to our
well-being, by prompting us to provide for ourselves, and for those who
depend on us. But this natural propensity would be rendered ineffectual,
were we not secured in the possession of what we thus store up; for a man
will never toil to accumulate what he cannot securely possess. This security is afforded by the moral sense; which dictates to all men, that goods
stored up by individuals are their *property,* and that property ought to be
inviolable. Thus, by the great law of restraint, men have a protection for
their goods, as well as for their persons or reputation; and have not less

security in society than if they were separated from each other by impregnable fortresses.

If the law of restraint be essential to the existence of society, several other duties are not less so. Mutual trust and confidence, with- <34> out which there can be no society, enter into the character of the human species; corresponding to which are the duties of veracity and fidelity: the latter would be of no significancy without the former; and the former without the latter would be hurtful, by laying men open to fraud and deceit.

With respect to veracity, in particular, such is our situation in this world, as to be indebted to the information of others for almost every thing that can benefit or hurt us; and if we could not depend upon information, society would be very little beneficial. Further, it is wisely ordered, that we should adhere strictly to truth, even where we perceive no harm in transgressing that duty; for it is sufficient that harm may possibly ensue, though not foreseen. At the same time, falsehood always does mischief; for if it happen not to injure us externally in our reputation, or in our goods, it never fails to injure us internally; which will thus appear. Men were made for society; and one great blessing of that state is a candid intercourse of hearts in conversation, in communication of sentiments, of opinions, of desires, and of wishes; and to admit any falsehood or deceit into such intercourse, would poison the most refined pleasures of life.

Because man, is the weakest of all animals separately, and the very strongest in society, mutual assistance is one great end in the social state; to which end it is necessary that covenants and promises be binding, and that favours received be thankfully repaid.

The final cause of the law of propriety, which enforces the duty we owe to ourselves, comes next in order. In a discourse upon those laws of nature which concern society, we have no occasion to mention any self-duty but what is connected with society; such as prudence, temperance, industry, firmness of mind, &c. And that these should be made our duty, is wisely ordered in a double respect; first as qualifying us to act our part in society; and next as intitling us to the good-will of others. It is the interest, no doubt, of every man to suit his behaviour to the dignity of his nature, and to the station allotted him by Providence; for such rational conduct contributes to happiness, by preserving health, by procuring plenty, by gaining the esteem of others, and, which of all is the greatest blessing, by gaining a justly founded self-esteem. But here even self-interest is not relied on: the powerful authority of duty is superadded to the motive of interest, that in a matter of the utmost importance both to ourselves and to the society we live in, our conduct may be steady and regular. These duties tend not only to make a man happy in <35> himself, but also, by gaining the good-will and esteem of others, to command their help and assistance in time of need.

I proceed to the final causes of natural rewards and punishments. And what at first will occur to every one is, that right and wrong ought to be the rule for distributing rewards and punishments, as well as for determining civil claims; for does it not seem rational that a right action should be rewarded, and a wrong action punished? But, upon more mature reflection, we are forced to abandon that opinion. All civil claims, and all controversies about things, must be adjusted by the standard of right and wrong; for where parties differ about *meum et tuum*,[8] the plaintiff's opinion cannot be the rule, and as little the defendant's: there must be an appeal to a judge; and what rule has a judge for determining the controversy, other than the common sense of mankind about right and wrong? But to bring rewards and punishments under the same standard, without regarding private conscience, would be a system unworthy of our maker; it being extremely clear, that to reward one who is not conscious of merit, or to punish one who is not conscious of guilt, can never answer any good end; and, in particular, cannot tend either to improvement, or reformation of manners. How much more like the Deity is the plan of nature; which rewards no man who is not conscious that he ought to be rewarded, and punishes no man who is not conscious that he ought to be punished! By these means, and by these only, rewards and punishments attain every good end that can be proposed by them. Here is a final cause most illustrious!

The rewards and punishments that attend the primary and secondary virtues, are finely adjusted for supporting the distinction between them set forth above. Punishment must be confined to the transgression of primary

8. "Mine and yours": property.

virtues, it being the intention of nature that the secondary virtues should be entirely voluntary. On the other hand, the secondary virtues are more highly rewarded than the primary: generosity, for example, makes a greater figure than justice; and undaunted courage, magnanimity, heroism, rise still higher in our esteem. One would imagine at first view, that the primary virtues, being more essential, should be intitled to the first place in our esteem, and be more amply rewarded than the secondary; and yet nature, in elevating the latter above the former, hath taken her measures with peculiar wisdom and foresight. Punishment is reserved to inforce the primary virtues; and if these virtues were also accompanied with the higher rewards, the secondary virtues, brought down <36> to a lower rank, would lose entirely that warm enthusiastic admiration which is their chief support: self-interest would universally prevail over benevolence, and sap the very foundation of those numberless favours we receive from each other in society; favours, not only beneficial in point of interest, but a solid foundation for affection and friendship.

In our progress through final causes, we come at last to reparation, one of the principles destined by Providence, for redressing wrongs committed, and for preventing the reiteration of them. The final cause of the principle of reparation, when the mischief arises from intention, is self-evident: for, to afford security to individuals in society, it is not sufficient that the man who does intentional mischief be punished; it is necessary that he also be bound to repair the mischief. Secondly, Where the act is wrong or unjust, though not understood by the author to be so, it is wisely ordered that reparation should follow; and, in general, that no error, whether in law or in fact, should avail against this claim; which will thus appear. Considering the fallibility of man, it would be too severe to permit advantage to be taken of error in every case. On the other hand, to make it a law in our nature, never to take advantage of error in any case, would be giving too much indulgence to indolence and remission of mind, tending to make us neglect the improvement of our rational faculties. Our nature is so happily framed as to avoid these extremes, by distinguishing between gain and loss. No man is conscious of wrong, when he takes advantage of an error committed by another to save himself from loss: if there must be a loss, common sense dictates, that it ought to rest upon the person who has erred, however innocently, rather than upon him who has not erred. Thus, in a competition among creditors about the estate of their bankrupt debtor, every one is at liberty to avail himself of even the slightest defects in the titles of his competitors, in order to save himself from loss. But, *in lucro captando*,[9] the moral sense teacheth a different lesson; which is, that no man ought to take advantage of another's error to make gain by it. Thus, an heir finding a brute diamond in the repositories of his ancestor, sells the same for a trifle, mistaking it for a common pebble: the purchaser is, in conscience and in equity, bound to restore the same, or to pay a just price. Thirdly, The following considerations tend to unfold a final cause, not less beautiful than the foregoing, of what the moral sense dictates with respect to mischief done without intention. Society could not subsist in any tolerable manner, were full scope given to rashness and negli- <37> gence, and to every action that is not strictly criminal: whence it is a maxim, founded not less upon utility than upon justice, That men living in society ought to be extremely circumspect as to every action that may possibly do harm. On the other hand, it is also a maxim, That as the prosperity and happiness of man depend on action, activity ought to be encouraged, instead of being discouraged by the dread of consequences. These maxims, seemingly in opposition, have natural limits that prevent their incroaching upon each other; which limits, at the same time, produce the most good to society of all that can be contrived by the most consummate lawgiver. There is a certain degree of attention and circumspection that men generally bestow upon affairs, proportioned to their importance: if that degree were not sufficient to defend against a claim of reparation, individuals would be too much cramped in action; which would lead to indolence instead of activity: if a less degree were sufficient, there would be too great scope for rash or remiss conduct; which would prove the bane of society. These remarks concerning the good of society, coincide entirely with what the moral sense dictates, as above mentioned, that the man who acts with foresight of the probability of mischief, or acts rashly and incautiously without such foresight, ought to be liable for the consequences; but that the man who acts cautiously, without foreseeing

9. "In seeking a profit."

or suspecting that any mischief will ensue, and who therefore is entirely innocent, ought not to be liable for the consequences.

And upon this subject I add the final cause of what is explained above, *viz*. That the moral sense requires from every man, not his own degree of vigilance and attention, which may be very small, but that which belongs to the common nature of the species. That this is a wise regulation, will appear upon considering, that were reparation to depend upon personal circumstances, there would be a necessity of inquiring into the characters of men, their education, their manner of living, and the extent of their understanding; which would render judges arbitrary, and such law-suits inextricable. But by assuming the common nature of the species as a standard, by which every man in conscience judges of his own actions, law-suits about reparation are rendered easy and expeditious.

NOTANDUM BENE[10]

Among the many divisions of human actions in the preliminary discourse, there is one all along supposed, but not brought out into a clear light. It is what follows: 1. Actions that we are bound to perform. 2. Actions that we perform in prosecution of our rights or privileges. 3. Actions that are entirely voluntary or arbitrary; such as are done for amusement, or from an impulse to act without having any end in view. Thus one leaps, runs, throws stone, merely to exert strength or activity; which therefore are in the strictest sense voluntary.

In the preliminary discourse, p. <lxii>. we have the following proposition, That the moral sense prohibits every action that may probably do mischief; and therefore, that if the probability of mischief be foreseen, or may be foreseen, the action is culpable or faulty. In stating this proposition no actions were in view but the last in the foregoing division; and it was an omission not to confine the proposition to these; for it holds not with respect to actions done in prosecution of our rights or privileges. Such actions are governed by a different principle, mentioned p. <41>, That the

---

10. This note was appended to the end of the text of the second (1767) edition of the *Principles of Equity*.

probability of mischief, even foreseen, prohibits me not from following out my rights or privileges. And it is happily so ordered by nature. When we act merely for amusement, it is a salutary and just regulation, that we should be answerable for what harm we do that either is foreseen or may be foreseen. But our rights and privileges would be very little beneficial to us, were we put under the same restraint in making these effectual. What actions may be lawfully done in prosecuting our rights and privileges, are handled in book 1. part 1. chap 1. sect 1. What actions may be lawfully done without having in view to prosecute any right or privilege, are handled in the section immediately subsequent.

PRINCIPLES

OF

EQUITY.

THE THIRD EDITION.

IN TWO VOLUMES.

VOL. I.

EDINBURGH:

Printed for J. Bell, and W. Creech, *Edinburgh*;
and T. Cadell, *London*.

MDCCLXXVIII.

LETTER

TO

Lord MANSFIELD

An author, not more illustrious by birth than by genius, says, in a letter concerning enthusiasm, "That he had so much need of some considerable presence or company to raise his thoughts on any occasion, that when alone he endeavoured to supply that want by fancying some great man of superior genius, whose imagined presence might inspire him with more than what he felt at ordinary hours."[1] To judge from his Lordship's writings, this receipt must be a good one. It naturally ought to be so; and I imagine that I have more than once felt its enlivening influence. With respect to the first edition of this treatise in particular, I can affirm with great truth, that *a great man of superior genius* was never out of my view: Will Lord Mansfield relish this passage—How would he have expressed it—were my constant questions.

But though by this means I commanded more vigour of mind, and a keener exertion of thought, than I am capable of *at ordinary hours;* yet I had not courage to mention this to his Lordship, nor to the world. The subject I had undertaken was new: I could not hope to avoid errors, perhaps gross ones; and the absurdity appeared glaring, of acknowledging a sort of inspiration in a performance that might not exhibit the least spark of it.

No trouble has been declined upon the present edition; and yet that the work, even in its improved state, deserves his Lordship's patronage, I am far from being confident. But however that be, it is no longer in my power

1. Anthony Ashley Cooper, Earl of Shaftesbury, *A Letter Concerning Enthusiasm* (London: J. Morphew, 1711), p. 13.

to conceal, that the ambition of gaining Lord Mansfield's approbation has been my chief support in this work. Never to reveal that secret would be to border on ingratitude.

Will your Lordship permit me to subscribe myself, with heart-satisfaction,

Your zealous friend,

HENRY HOME

August 1766

PREFACE to the Second Edition

An author who exerts his talents and industry upon a new subject, without hope of assistance from others, is too apt to flatter himself; because he finds no other work of the kind to humble him by comparison. The attempt to digest equity into a regular system, was not only new, but difficult; and for these reasons, the author hopes he may be excused for not discovering more early several imperfections in the first edition of this book. These imperfections he the more regretted, because they concerned chiefly the arrangement, in which every mistake must be attended with some degree of obscurity. No labour has been spared to improve the present edition: and yet, after all his endeavours, the author dare not hope that every imperfection is cured: that the arrangement is considerably improved, is all that with assurance he can take upon him to say.

For an interim gratification of the reader's curiosity before entering upon the work, a few particulars shall here be mentioned. The defects of common law seemed to the author so distinct from its excesses, that he thought it proper to handle these articles separately. But almost as soon as the printing was finished, the author observed that he had been obliged to handle the same subject in different parts of the book, or at least to refer from one part to another; which he holds to be an infallible mark of an unskilful distribution. This led him to reflect, that these defects and excesses proceed both of them equally from the very constitution of a court of common law, too limited in its power of doing justice; whence it appeared evident that they ought to be handled promiscuously as so many examples of imperfection in common law, which ought to be supplied by a court of equity. This is so evident, that even in the same case we find common law sometimes defective, sometimes excessive, according to occasional or accidental circumstances, without any fundamental difference. For example, many claims, good at common law, are reprobated in equity because of some incidental wrong that comes not under the cognisance of common law. A claim of this kind must be sustained by a court of common law, which cannot regard the incidental wrong; and in such instances common law is excessive, by transgressing the bounds of justice. On the other hand, where a claim for reparation is brought by the person who suffered the wrong, a court of common law can give no redress; and in such instances common law is defective. And yet the *ratio decidendi*[1] is precisely the same in both cases, namely, the limited power of a court of common law.

The transgression of a deed or covenant is a wrong that ought to be distinguished from a wrong that misleads a man to make a covenant or to grant a deed. The former only belongs to the chapter *Of Covenants;* the latter, to the chapter *Of the powers of a court of equity to protect individuals from injuries.* For example, a man is fraudulently induced to enter into a contract: the reparation of this wrong, which is antecedent to the contract, cannot arise from the contract; and for that reason it is put under the chapter last mentioned.

---

1. "The reason for deciding"; that is, the principle or rule on which the decision is grounded.

PREFACE to the Present [Third] Edition

An useful book ought not to be a costly book.

To bring this edition within a moderate price, not only the size is smaller, but the preliminary discourse on the principles of morality is left out, being published more complete in *Sketches of the History of Man*.

To mould the principles of equity into a regular system, was a bold undertaking. The pleasure of novelty gave it a lustre, and made every article appear to be in its proper place. The subject being more familiar in labouring upon a second edition, the many errors I discovered produced an arrangement differing considerably from the former. My satisfaction however in the new arrangement, was not entire: the errors I had fallen into produced a degree of diffidence and a suspicion of more. And now, after an interval of no fewer than ten years, I find the suspicion but too well founded, chiefly with respect to the extensive chapter of deeds and covenants. The many divisions and subdivisions of that chapter, I judged at the time to be necessary; but after pondering long and frequently upon them, I became sensible that they tend to darken rather than to enlighten the subject. That chapter is now divided into fewer and more distinct heads; which I expect will be found a considerable improvement. In an institute of law or of any other science, the analyzing it into its constituent parts, and the arranging every article properly, is of supreme importance. One could not conceive, without experience, how greatly accurate distribution contributes to clear conception. Before I was far advanced in the present edition, the many errors I found in the distribution surprised and vexed me. I have bestowed much pains in correcting these errors; and yet I will not answer that there are none left. Many escaped me before; and some may again escape me. No work of man is perfect: it is good however to be on the mending hand; and in every new attempt, to approach nearer and nearer to perfection. To compile a body of law, the parts intimately connected and every link hanging on a former, requires the utmost effort of the human genius. Have I not reason to think so, considering how imperfect in that respect the far greater part of law-books are; witness in particular the famous body of Roman law compiled under the auspices of the Emperor Justinian,[1] remarkable even among law-books for defective arrangement? Let the candid reader keep this in view, and he will be indulgent to the errors of arrangement in this edition, if after my utmost application, any remain.

But imperfect arrangement in the former editions, is not the only thing that requires an apology. Frequent and serious reflection on a favourite subject, have unfolded to me several errors, still more material, as they concern the reasoning branch of my subject. These I blush for; and yet, to acknowledge an erroneous opinion, sits lighter on my mind than to persevere in it.

1. The reference is to the *Digest, Code,* and *Institutes* of Roman law, compiled under the orders of the Emperor Justinian between 530 and 534.

CONTENTS

CONTENTS.

VOLUME II.

BOOK II.

BOOK III.

Explanation of Some Scotch Law Terms Used in This Work

Adjudication, is a judicial conveyance of the debtor's land for the creditor's security and payment. It corresponds to the English *Elegit*.

Arrestment, defined, book 3, chap. 4.

Cautioner, a surety for a debt.

Cedent, assignor.

Contravention, an act of contravention signifies the breaking through any restraint imposed by deed, by covenant, or by a court.

Decree of forthcoming, defined, book 3, chap. 4.

Fiar, he that has the fee or feu; and the proprietor is termed *fiar*, in contra-distinction to the liferenter.

Gratuitous, *see* Voluntary.

Heritor, a proprietor of land.

Inhibition, defined, book 3, chap. 4.

Lesion, loss, damage.

Pursuer, plaintiff.

Propone, to propone a defence, is to state or move a defence.

Reduction, is a process for voiding or setting aside any consensual or judicial right.

Tercer, a widow that possesses the third part of her husband's land as her legal jointure.

Voluntary, in the law of Scotland bears its proper sense as opposed to involuntary. A deed in the English law is said to be voluntary when it is granted without a valuable consideration. In this sense it is the same with *gratuitous* in our law.

Wadset, answers to a mortgage in the English law. A proper wadset is where the creditor in possession of the land takes the rents in place of the interest of the sum lent. An improper wadset is where the rents are applied for payment, first of the interest, and next of the capital.

Writer, scrivener.

INTRODUCTION

Equity, scarce known to our forefathers, makes at present a great figure. It has, like a plant, been tending to maturity, slowly indeed, but constantly; and at what distance of time it shall arrive at perfection, is perhaps not easy to foretell. Courts of equity have already acquired such an extent of jurisdiction, as to obscure in a great measure courts of law.[1] A revolution so signal, will move every curious enquirer to attempt, or to wish at least, a discovery of the cause. But vain will be the attempt, till first a clear idea be formed of the difference between a court of law and a court of equity. The former we know follows precise rules: but does the latter act by conscience solely without any rule? This would be unsafe while men are the judges, liable no less to partiality than to error: nor could a court without rules ever have attained that height of favour, and extent <2> of jurisdiction, which courts of equity enjoy. But if a court of equity be governed by rules, why are not these brought to light in a system? One would imagine, that such a system should not be useful only, but necessary; and yet writers, far from aiming at a system, have not even defined with any accuracy what equity is, nor what are its limits and extent. One operation of equity, universally acknowledged, is, to remedy imperfections in the common law, which sometimes is defective, and sometimes exceeds just bounds; and as equity is constantly opposed to common law, a just idea of the latter may prob-

---

The text which follows is from the third edition of the work. Page break signs refer to the pagination of the third edition.

1. In England, courts of common law (which grew in the late twelfth and thirteenth centuries as the judicial business of the king's court was given over to technical specialists) were distinct from courts of equity (especially the Court of Chancery, which first evolved as a court presided over by the Lord Chancellor in the late fourteenth and fifteenth centuries). In Scotland, the Court of Session was both a court of common law and a court of equity.

ably lead to the former. In order to ascertain what is meant by common law, a historical deduction is necessary; which I the more chearfully undertake, because the subject seems not to be put in a clear light by any writer.

After states were formed and government established, courts of law were invented to compel individuals to do their duty. This innovation, as commonly happens, was at first confined within narrow bounds. To these courts power was given to enforce duties essential to the <3> existence of society; such as that of forbearing to do harm or mischief. Power was also given to enforce duties derived from covenants and promises, such of them at least as tend more peculiarly to the well-being of society: which was an improvement so great, as to leave no thought of proceeding farther; for to extend the authority of a court to natural duties of every sort, would, in a new experiment, have been reckoned too bold. Thus, among the Romans, many pactions were left upon conscience, without receiving any aid from courts of law: buying and selling only, with a few other covenants essential to commercial dealing, were regarded.[2] Our courts of law in Britain were originally confined within still narrower bounds: no covenant whatever was by our forefathers countenanced with an action: a contract of buying and selling was not;* and as buying and selling is of all covenants the most useful in ordinary life, we are not at liberty to suppose that any other was more privileged.[†] <4>

But when the great advantages of a court of law were experienced, its jurisdiction was gradually extended, with universal approbation: it was extended, with very few exceptions, to every covenant and every promise: it was extended also to other matters, till it embraced every obvious duty

2. In Roman law, informal bargains, or "naked pacts," could not be sued on (hence the maxim from D 2.14.7.4, "nuda pactio obligationem non parit, sed parit exceptionem": "a naked pact gives rise not to an obligation, but to a defence"). However, Roman law did enforce four defined "consensual" contracts, where the obligation was incurred by simple consent: sale, hire, partnership, and agency.

* Reg. Maj. lib. 3. cap. 10. [T. M. Cooper (ed.), *Regiam majestatem* (Edinburgh: Stair Society, 1947), vol. II, pp. 202–3], Fleta, lib. 2. cap. 58. §3. and 5. [H. G. Richardson and G. O. Sayles (eds.), *Fleta* (London: Selden Society, vol. 72 for 1953; London, 1955), pp. 194–96].

† See Historical Law-tracts, tract 2 [Henry Home, Lord Kames, "History of Promises and Covenants" in *Historical Law-Tracts*, 2 vols. (Edinburgh: Millar, Kincaid and Bell, 1758), pp. 91–121, at p. 99].

arising in ordinary dealings between man and man. But it was extended no farther; experience having discovered limits, beyond which it was deemed hazardous to stretch this jurisdiction. Causes of an extraordinary nature, requiring some singular remedy, could not be safely trusted with the ordinary courts, because no rules were established to direct their proceedings in such matters; and upon that account, such causes were appropriated to the king and council, being the paramount court.[a] Of this nature <5> were actions for proving the tenor or contents of a lost writ; extraordinary removings against tenants possessing by lease; the causes of pupils, orphans, and foreigners; complaints against judges and officers of law,[*] and the more atrocious crimes, termed, *Pleas of the crown.* Such extraordinary causes, multiplying greatly by complex and intricate connections among individuals, became a burden too great for the king and council. In order therefore to relieve this court, extraordinary causes of a civil nature, were in England devolved upon the court of chancery; a measure the more necessary, that the king, occupied with the momentous affairs of government, and with foreign as well as domestic transactions, had not leisure for private causes. In Scotland, more remote, and therefore less interested in foreign affairs, there was not the same necessity for this innovation: our kings, however, addicted to action more than to contemplation, neglected in a great measure their privilege of being judges, and suffered causes peculiar to the king and <6> council to be gradually assumed by other sovereign courts. The establishment of the court of chancery in England, made it necessary to give a name to the more ordinary branch of law that is the province of the common or ordinary courts: it is termed, *the Common Law:* and in opposition to it, the extraordinary branch devolved on the court of chancery is termed *Equity;* the name being derived from the nature of the jurisdiction, directed less by precise rules, than *secundum aequum et bonum,*[3] or according to what the judge in conscience thinks

a. We find the same regulation among the Jews: "And Moses chose able men out of all Israel, and made them heads over the people, rulers of thousands, rulers of hundreds, rulers of fifties, and rulers of tens. And they judged the people at all seasons: the hard causes they brought unto Moses, but every small matter they judged themselves." *Exodus,* xviii, 25. 26.

* See act 105, parl. 1487 [*APS* ii: 177: 1487, c. 10: Of jurisdictioun and process in civile accionis questionis and pleyis].

3. "According to what is just and good."

right.[a] Thus equity, in its proper sense, comprehends every matter of law that by the common law is left without remedy; and supposing the boundaries of the common law to be ascertained, there can no longer remain any difficulty about the powers of a court of equity. But as these boundaries are <7> not ascertained by any natural rule, the jurisdiction of common law must depend in a great measure upon accident and arbitrary practice; and accordingly the boundaries of common law and equity, vary in different countries, and at different times in the same country. We have seen, that the common law of Britain[4] was originally not so extensive as at present; and instances will be mentioned afterward, which evince, that the common law is in Scotland farther extended than in England. Its limits are perhaps not accurately ascertained in any country; which is to be regretted, because of the uncertainty that must follow in the practice of law. It is lucky, however, that the disease is not incurable: a good understanding between the judges of the different courts, with just notions of law, may, in time, ascertain these limits with sufficient accuracy.[5]

Among a plain people, strangers to refinement and subtilties, law-suits may be frequent, but never are intricate. Regulations to restrain individuals from doing mischief, and to enforce performance of covenants, composed originally the bulk <8> of the common law; and these two branches, among our rude ancestors, seemed to comprehend every subject of law. The more refined duties of morality were, in that early period, little felt, and less regarded. But law, in this simple form, cannot long continue sta-

---

a. At curiae sunto et jurisdictiones, quae statuant ex arbitrio boni viri et discretione sana, ubi legis norma deficit. Lex enim non sufficit casibus, sed ad ea quae plerumque accidunt aptatur: sapientissima autem res tempus, (ut ab antiquis dictum est), et novorum casuum quotidie author et inventor. *Bacon de Aug*[*mentis*] *Scien*[*tiarum*] *lib.* 8. *cap.* 3, *aphor.* 32 [Bacon, *Works*, vol. 1, p. 252: "But let there be courts and jurisdictions, to determine according to the judgment and sound discretion of a good man, where a legal rule is lacking. For the law does not provide for all cases, but is adapted to those which happen for the most part: and indeed time is the wisest thing (as has been said by the ancients) and is every day the author and inventor of new cases"].

4. Kames's reference here is to the customary legal rules followed in England and Scotland, rather than to the distinct technical systems of "common law" developed by professional lawyers in England and Scotland.

5. In place of this sentence, the first edition has the text to be found in Appendix, p. 485, Extract [1st: iv–v].

tionary: for in the social state under regular discipline, law ripens gradually with the human faculties; and by ripeness of discernment and delicacy of sentiment, many duties, formerly neglected, are found to be binding in conscience. Such duties can no longer be neglected by courts of justice; and as they made no part of the common law, they come naturally under the jurisdiction of a court of equity.

The chief objects of benevolence considered as a duty, are our relations, our benefactors, our masters, our servants, &c.; and these duties, or the most obvious of them, come under the cognisance of common law. But there are other connections, which, though more transitory, produce a sense of duty. Two persons shut up in the same prison, though no way connected but by contiguity and resemblance of condition, are sensible, however, <9> that to aid and comfort each other is a duty incumbent on them. Two persons, shipwrecked upon the same desert island, are sensible of the like mutual duty. And there is even some sense of this kind, among a number of persons in the same ship, or under the same military command.

Thus mutual duties among individuals multiply by variety of connections; and in the progress of society, benevolence becomes a matter of conscience in a thousand instances, formerly disregarded. The duties that arise from connections so slender, are taken under the jurisdiction of a court of equity; which at first exercises its jurisdiction with great reserve, interposing in remarkable cases only, where the duty is palpable. But, gathering courage from success, it ventures to enforce this duty in more delicate circumstances: one case throws light upon another: men, by the reasoning of the judges, become gradually more acute in discerning their duty: the judges become more and more acute in distinguishing cases; and this branch of law is imperceptibly moulded into a <10> system.[a] In rude

---

a. At curiae illae uni viro ne committantur, sed ex pluribus constent. Nec decreta exeant cum silentio: sed judices sententiae suae rationes adducant, idque palam, atque adstante corona; ut quod ipsa potestate sit liberum, fama tamen et existimatione sit circumscriptum. *Bacon de Aug[mentis] Scient[iarum]*, *lib.* 8, *cap.* 3, *aphor.* 38 [Bacon, *Works*, vol. 1, p. 252: "But do not let those courts be entrusted to one man, but let them be composed of several. And do not let their decrees issue in silence: but let the judges give the reasons for their opinion, and that publicly, and in open court; so that that which is free in terms of power, may nevertheless be restrained by publicity and public opinion"].

ages, acts of benevolence, however peculiar the connection may be, are but faintly perceived to be our duty: such perceptions become gradually more firm and clear by custom and reflection; and when men are so far enlightened, it is the duty as well as honour of judges to interpose.*

This branch of equitable jurisdiction shall be illustrated by various examples. When goods by labour, and perhaps with danger, are recovered from the sea after a shipwreck, every one perceives it to be the duty of the proprietor to pay salvage. A man ventures his life to save a house from fire, and is successful; no mortal can doubt that he is intitled to a recompence from the proprietor, who is benefited. If a man's affairs by his absence be in <11> disorder, ought not the friend who undertakes the management to be kept *indemnis,*[6] though the subject upon which his money was usefully bestowed may have afterward perished casually?[7] Who can doubt of the following proposition, That I am in the wrong to demand money from my debtor, while I with-hold the sum I owe him, which perhaps may be his only resource for doing me justice? Such a proceeding must, in the common sense of mankind, appear partial and oppressive. By the common law, however, no remedy is afforded in this case, nor in the others mentioned. But equity affords a remedy, by enforcing what in such circumstances every man perceives to be his duty. I shall add but one example more: In a violent storm, the heaviest goods are thrown overboard, in order to disburden the ship: the proprietors of the goods preserved by this means from the sea, must be sensible that it is their duty to repair the loss; for the man who has thus abandoned his goods for the common safety, ought to be in no worse condition than themselves. Equity dictates this to be their duty; and <12> if they be refractory, a court of equity will interpose in behalf of the sufferer.

It appears now clearly, that a court of equity commences at the limits of

---

* See Essays on morality and natural religion, second edition, p. 108 [Henry Home, Lord Kames, *Essays on the Principles of Morality and Natural Religion,* 2nd ed. (London: C. Hitch & L. Hawes, R. & J. Dodsley, J. Rivington & J. Fletcher, and J. Richardson, 1758); cf. Liberty Fund ed., p. 64].

6. "Free from loss or damage."

7. Kames's allusion here is to the civilian remedy offered by the *actio negotiorum gestorum,* which was a part of Scottish but not of English law (see glossary, *"actio negotiorum gestorum"*).

the common law, and enforces benevolence where the law of nature makes it our duty. And thus a court of equity, accompanying the law of nature in its gradual refinements, enforces every natural duty that is not provided for at common law.

The duties hitherto mentioned arise from connections independent altogether of consent. Covenants and promises also, are the source of various duties. The most obvious of these duties, being commonly declared in words, belong to common law. But every incident that can possibly occur in fulfilling a covenant, is seldom foreseen; and yet a court of common law, in giving judgment upon covenants, considers nothing but declared will, neglecting incidents that would have been provided for, had they been foreseen. Further, the inductive motive for making a covenant, and its ultimate purpose and intendment, are circumstances disregarded at common law: these, however, are capital circumstances; and justice, where they are <13> neglected, cannot be fulfilled. Hence the powers of a court of equity with respect to engagements. It supplies imperfections in common law, by taking under consideration every material circumstance, in order that justice may be distributed in the most perfect manner. It supplies a defect in words, where will is evidently more extensive: it rejects words that unwarily go beyond will; and it gives aid to will where it happens to be obscurely or imperfectly expressed.[8] By taking such liberty, a covenant is made effectual according to the aim and purpose of the contractors; and without such liberty, seldom it happens that justice can be accurately distributed.

In handling this branch of the subject, it is not easy to suppress a thought that comes cross the mind. The jurisdiction of a court of common law, with respect to covenants, appears to me odd and unaccountable. To find the jurisdiction of this court limited, as above mentioned, to certain duties of the law of nature, without comprehending the whole, is not singular nor anomalous. But with respect to the circumstances that occur in the same <14> cause, it cannot fail to appear singular, that a court

8. The first edition (p. vii) and second edition (p. 43) have the following in place of this sentence: "It sometimes supplies a defect in words, where will is evidently more extensive; and sometimes supplies a defect even in will, according to what probably would have been the will of the parties, had they foreseen the event."

should be confined to a few of these circumstances, neglecting others no less material in point of justice. This reflection will be set in a clear light by a single example. Every one knows, that an English double bond[9] was a contrivance to evade the old law of this island, which prohibited the taking interest for money: the professed purpose of this bond is, to provide for interest and costs, beyond which the penal part ought not to be exacted; and yet a court of common law, confined strictly to the words or declared will, is necessitated knowingly to commit injustice. The moment the term of payment is past, when there cannot be either costs or interest, this court, instead of pronouncing sentence for what is really due, namely, the sum borrowed, must follow the words of the bond, and give judgment for the double. This defect in the constitution of a court, is too remarkable to have been overlooked: a remedy accordingly is provided, though far from being of the most perfect kind; and that is, a privilege to apply to the court of equity for redress. Far better had it been, either to withdraw <15> covenants altogether from the common law, or to impower the judges of that law to determine according to the principles of justice.[a] I need scarce observe, that the present reflection regards England only, where equity and common law are appropriated to different courts. In Scotland, and other countries where both belong to the same court, the inconvenience mentioned cannot happen.—But to return to the gradual extension of equity, which is our present theme:

A court of equity, by long and various practice, finding its own strength and utility, and impelled by the principle of justice, boldly undertakes a matter still more arduous; and that is, to correct or mitigate the rigour, and

9. A *double bond,* or *conditional bond* was a sealed bond granted by a debtor, which obliged him to pay a penal sum if he did not fulfill a condition stated in the bond. The usual practice was for a borrower to grant a bond for double the sum borrowed, with a condition that the bond would be void if he repaid the sum actually borrowed by a certain date. The English Court of Chancery gave relief against penalties, requiring the debtor only to pay the sum really due; and legislation in 1697 and 1705 (8 & 9 W 3, c. 11, s. 8; 4 & 5 Anne, c. 16, s. 13) enacted that the common law would also require the debtor to pay only the sum really due.

a. And accordingly, by 4° Annae, cap. 16. §13 [an Act for the amendment of the law, and the better administration of justice, 1705,] the defendant, pending action on a double bond, offering payment of principal, interest, and costs, shall be discharged by the court.

what even in a proper sense may be termed the *injustice* of common law. It is not in human foresight to establish any general rule, that, however salutary in the main, may not be oppressive and unjust in its application to some singular cases. Every work of man <16> must partake of the imperfection of its author; sometimes falling short of its purpose, and sometimes going beyond it. If with respect to the former a court of equity be useful, it may be pronounced necessary with respect to the latter; for, in society, it is certainly a greater object to prevent legal oppression, which alarms every individual, than to supply legal defects, scarce regarded but by those immediately concerned. The illustrious Bacon, upon this subject, expresses himself with great propriety: "Habeant curiae praetoriae potestatem tam subveniendi contra rigorem legis, quam supplendi defectum legis. Si enim porregi debet remedium ei quem lex praeteriit, multo magis ei quem vulneravit."*

All the variety of matter hitherto mentioned, is regulated by the principle of justice solely. It may, at first view, be thought, that this takes in the whole compass of law, and that there is no remaining field to be occupied by a court of equity. But, upon more narrow inspection, we find a number of law-cases into <17> which justice enters not, but only utility. Expediency requires that these be brought under the cognisance of a court; and the court of equity, gaining daily more weight and authority, takes naturally such matters under its jurisdiction. I shall give a few examples. A lavish man submits to have his son made his interdictor:[10] this agreement is not unjust; but, tending to the corruption of manners, by reversing the order of nature, it is reprobated by a court of equity, as *contra bonos mores.*[11] This court goes farther: it discountenances many things in themselves indifferent, merely because of their bad tendency. A *pactum de*

---

* *De Aug. Scient.* lib. 8, cap. 3, aphor. 35 [Bacon, *Works,* vol. 1, p. 252: "Let the praetorian courts have the power both to give relief against the rigour of the law and to make good the deficiency in the law. For if a remedy ought to be given to someone whom the law has overlooked, much more should it be given to someone whom it has wounded"].

10. In Scots law, a person could lay himself under a voluntary restraint, called a *voluntary interdiction.* This interdiction was in the form of a bond, whereby the grantor obliged himself to do nothing which might affect his estate without the consent of a person or persons named in the grant, who were known as *interdictors.*

11. "Against good morals."

quota litis[12] is in itself innocent, and may be beneficial to the client as well as to the advocate: but to remove the temptation that advocates are under to take advantage of their clients instead of serving them faithfully, this court declares against such pactions. A court of equity goes still farther, by consulting the public interest with relation to matters not otherwise bad but by occasioning unnecessary trouble and vexation to individuals. Hence the origin of regulations tending to abridge law-suits. <18>

A mischief that affects the whole community, figures in the imagination, and naturally moves judges to stretch out a preventive hand. But what shall we say of a mischief that affects one person only, or but a few? An estate, for example, real or personal, is left entirely without management, by the infancy of the proprietor, or by his absence in a remote country: he has no friends, or they are unwilling to interpose. It is natural, in this case, to apply for public authority. A court of common law, confined within certain precise limits, can give no aid; and therefore it is necessary that a court of equity should undertake cases of this kind; and the preventive remedy is easy, by naming an administrator, or, as termed in the Roman law, *curator bonorum*.[13] A similar example is, where a court of equity gives authority to sell the land of one under age, where the sale is necessary for payment of debt: to decline interposing, would be ruinous to the proprietor; for without authority of the court no man will venture to purchase from one under age. Here the motive is humanity to a single individual: but it would be an <19> imperfection in law, to abandon an innocent person to ruin, when the remedy is so easy. In the cases governed by the motive of public utility, a court of equity interposes as court properly, giving or denying action, in order to answer the end purposed: but in the cases now mentioned, and in others similar, there is seldom occasion for a process; the court acts by magisterial powers.

The powers above set forth assumed by our courts of equity, are, in effect, the same that were assumed by the Roman Praetor,[14] from neces-

---

12. "An agreement about a portion of the amount in issue"; that is, a contract by which a client agrees to pay his advocate a part of the sum he wishes to recover in litigation, in exchange for services in recovering it.

13. The administrator of the estate of an insolvent debtor.

14. An annually appointed magistrate in the Roman Republic, who was responsible for civil law and who had control over the formulary system of Roman civil litigation.

sity, without any express authority. "Jus praetorium est quod praetores introduxerunt, adjuvandi vel supplendi vel corrigendi juris Civilis gratia, propter utilitatem publicam."*

Having given a historical view of a court of equity, from its origin to its present extent of power and jurisdiction, I proceed to some other matters, which must be premised before entering into particulars. The first I shall insist on is of the greatest moment, namely, Whether a court of <20> equity be, or ought to be, governed by any general rules? To determine every particular case according to what is just, equal, and salutary, taking in all circumstances, is undoubtedly the idea of a court of equity in its perfection; and had we angels for judges, such would be their method of proceeding, without regarding any rules: but men are liable to prejudice and error, and for that reason cannot safely be trusted with unlimited powers. Hence the necessity of establishing rules, to preserve uniformity of judgment in matters of equity as well as of common law: the necessity is perhaps greater in the former, because of the variety and intricacy of equitable circumstances. Thus, though a particular case may require the interposition of equity to correct a wrong or supply a defect; yet the judge ought not to interpose, unless he can found his decree upon some rule that is equally applicable to all cases of the kind. If he be under no limitation, his decrees will appear arbitrary, though substantially just: and, which is worse, will often be arbitrary, and substantially unjust; for such too frequently are human proceedings <21> when subjected to no control. General rules, it is true, must often produce decrees that are materially unjust; for no rule can be equally just in its application to a whole class of cases that are far from being the same in every circumstance: but this inconvenience must be tolerated, to avoid a greater, that of making judges arbitrary. A court of equity is a happy invention to remedy the errors of common law: but this remedy must stop somewhere; for courts cannot be established without end, to be checks one upon another. And hence it is,

---

Each praetor could issue a new edict for his year in office, setting out what actions he would countenance; this led to the development of a body of praetorian law.

* l. 7. §1. De justitia et jure [On justice and law, D 1.1.7.1: Watson i: 2: "Praetorian law is that which in the public interest the Praetors have introduced in aid or supplementation or correction of the *jus civile* (civil law)"].

that, in the nature of things, there cannot be any other check upon a court of equity but general rules. Bacon expresses himself upon this subject with his usual elegance and perspicuity: "Non sine causa in usum venerat apud Romanos album praetoris, in quo praescripsit et publicavit quomodo ipse jus dicturus esset. Quo exemplo judices in curiis praetoriis, regulas sibi certas (quantum fieri potest) proponere, easque publice affigere, debent. Etenim optima est lex, quae minimum relinquit arbitrio <22> judicis, optimus judex qui minimum sibi."*

In perusing the following treatise, it will be discovered, that the connections regarded by a court of equity seldom arise from personal circumstances, such as birth, resemblance of condition, or even blood, but generally from subjects that in common language are denominated *goods*. Why should a court, actuated by the spirit of refined justice, overlook more substantial ties, to apply itself solely to the grosser connections of interest? doth any connection founded on property make an impression equally strong with that of friendship, or blood-relation, or of country? doth not the law of nature form duties on the latter, more binding in conscience than on the former? Yet the more conscientious duties are left commonly to shift for themselves, while the duties founded on interest are supported and enforced by courts of equity. This, at first view, looks like a prevailing attachment to riches; but it is not so in reality. The duties arising from the connection last <23> mentioned, are commonly ascertained and circumscribed, so as to be susceptible of a general rule to govern all cases of the kind. This is seldom the case of the other natural duties; which, for that reason, must be left upon conscience, without receiving any aid from a court of equity. There are, for example, not many duties more firmly rooted in our nature than that of charity; and, upon that account, a court of equity will naturally be tempted to interpose in its behalf. But the extent of this duty depends on such a variety of circumstances, that the

---

* *De aug*[*mentis*] *scient*[*iarum,*] l. 8. cap. 3. aph. 46 [Bacon, *Works,* vol. i, p. 253: "It was not without good reason that the white tablet of the Praetor, on which he set down and made known in what way he would administer justice, came into use in Rome. And following this example, judges in praetorian courts ought (as far as possible) to set out fixed rules for themselves and set them up in a public place. For the law is best, which leaves the least discretion to the judge, and the judge is best, who leaves the least to himself"].

wisest heads would in vain labour to bring it under general rules: to trust, therefore, with any court, a power to direct the charity of individuals, is a remedy which to society would be more hurtful than the disease; for instead of enforcing this duty in any regular manner, it would open a wide door to legal tyranny and oppression. Viewing the matter in this light, it will appear, that such duties are left upon conscience, not from neglect or insensibility, but from the difficulty of a proper remedy. And when such duties can be brought under a general rule, I except not even <24> gratitude, though in the main little susceptible of circumscription, we shall see afterward, that a court of equity declines not to interpose.

In this work will be found several instances where equity and utility are in opposition; and when that happens, the question is, Which of them ought to prevail? Equity, when it regards the interest of a few individuals only, ought to yield to utility when it regards the whole society. It is for that very reason, that a court of equity is bound to form its decrees upon general rules; for this measure regards the whole society by preventing arbitrary proceedings.

It is commonly observed, that equitable rights are less steady and permanent than those of common law: the reason will appear from what follows. A right is permanent or fluctuating according to the circumstances upon which it is founded. The circumstances that found a right at common law, being always few and weighty, are not variable: a bond of borrowed money, for example, must subsist till it be paid. A claim in equity, on the contrary, seldom arises without a multipli- <25> city of circumstances; which make it less permanent, for if but a single circumstance be withdrawn, the claim is gone. Suppose, for example, that an infeftment of annualrent[15] is assigned to a creditor for his security: the creditor ought to draw his payment out of the interest before touching the capital; which is an equitable rule, because it is favourable to the assignor or cedent,[16] without hurting the assignee. But if the cedent have another creditor who arrests[17] the interest, the equitable rule now mentioned ceases, and gives

15. The grant of an annualrent-right, that is, a yearly rent of land, granted to a lender as security for a loan, redeemable on repayment of the loan (Scots law). See also glossary, "infeftment."

16. A person who assigns property to another; assignor.

17. See glossary, "arrestment and forthcoming."

place to another; which is, that the assignee ought to draw his payment out of the capital, leaving the interest to be drawn by the arrester. Let us next suppose, that the cedent hath a third creditor, who after the arrestment adjudges[18] the capital. This new circumstance varies again the rule of equity: for though the cedent's interest weighs not in opposition to that of his creditor arresting, the adjudging creditor and the arrester are upon a level as to every equitable consideration; and upon that account, the assignee, who is the preferable creditor,[19] ought to deal impartially between them: if he be not willing to take <26> payment out of both subjects proportionally, but only out of the capital, or out of the interest; he ought to make an assignment to the postponed creditor,[20] in order to redress the inequality; and if he refuse to do this act of justice, a court of equity will interpose.

This example shows the mutability of equitable claims: but there is a cause which makes them appear still more mutable than they are in reality. The strongest notion is entertained of the stability of a right of property; because no man can be deprived of his property but by his own deed. A claim of debt is understood to be stable, but in an inferior degree; because payment puts an end to it without the will of the creditor. But equitable rights, which commonly accrue to a man without any deed of his, are often lost in the same manner: and they will naturally be deemed transitory and fluctuating, when they depend so little on the will of the persons who are possessed of them.

In England, where the courts of equity and common law are different, the boundary between equity and common law, where the legislature doth not <27> interpose, will remain always the same. But in Scotland, and other countries where equity and common law are united in one court, the boundary varies imperceptibly; for what originally is a rule in equity, loses its character when it is fully established in practice; and then it is considered as common law: thus the *actio negotiorum gestorum*,[21] retention, salvage, &c. are in Scotland scarce now considered as depending on principles of equity. But by cultivation of society, and practice of law,

18. See glossary, "adjudication."
19. The creditor with a right to priority of payment.
20. A creditor whose claims rank behind those of another (preferable) creditor.
21. See glossary, "*actio negotiorum gestorum.*"

nicer and nicer cases in equity being daily unfolded, our notions of equity are preserved alive; and the additions made to that fund, supply what is withdrawn from it by common law.

What is now said suggests a question, no less intricate than important, Whether common law and equity ought to be committed to the same or to different courts. The profound Bacon gives his opinion in the following words: "Apud nonnullos receptum est, ut jurisdictio, quae decernit secundum aequum et bonum, atque illa altera, quae procedit secundum jus strictum, iisdem curiis deputentur: apud alios autem, ut diversis: omnino <28> placet curiarum separatio. Neque enim servabitur distinctio casuum, si fiat commixtio jurisdictionum: sed arbitrium legem tandem trahet."* Of all questions those which concern the constitution of a state, and its political interest, being the most involved in circumstances, are the most difficult to be brought under precise rules. I pretend not to deliver any opinion; and feeling in myself a bias against the great authority mentioned, I scarce venture to form an opinion. It may be not improper, however, to hazard a few observations, preparatory to a more accurate discussion. I feel the weight of the argument urged in the passage above quoted. In the science of jurisprudence, it is undoubtedly of great importance, that the boundary between equity and common law be clearly ascertained; without which we shall in vain hope for just decisions: a judge, who is uncertain whether the case belong to equity or to common law, cannot have a clear conception what judgment ought to be pronounced. But a court that judges of both, being <29> relieved from determining this preliminary point, will be apt to lose sight altogether of the distinction between common law and equity. On the other hand, may it not be urged, that the dividing among different courts things intimately connected, bears hard upon every one who has a claim to prosecute? Before bringing his action, he must at his peril determine an extreme nice point, Whether the case be governed by common

---

* *De aug[mentis] scient[iarum,]* l. 8. cap. 3. aph. 45 [Bacon, *Works,* vol. 1, p. 253: "Among some people it is established that the jurisdiction which determines according to equity, and that which determines according to strict law, should be given to the same courts; among others, however, they are separate: the separation of courts commends itself in every respect. For if there be a mixing of jurisdictions, the distinction between cases will not be observed, but discretion will in the end take over the law"].

law, or by equity. An error in that preliminary point, though not fatal to
the cause because a remedy is provided, is, however, productive of much
trouble and expence. Nor is the most profound knowledge of law sufficient always to prevent this evil; because it cannot always be foreseen what
plea will be put in for the defendant, whether a plea in equity or at common law. In the next place, to us in Scotland it appears extremely uncouth,
that a court should be so constituted, as to be tied down in many instances
to pronounce an iniquitous judgment. This not only happens frequently
with respect to covenants, as above mentioned, but will always happen
where a claim founded on common law, which <30> must be brought
before a court of common law, is opposed by an equitable defence, which
cannot be regarded by such a court. Weighing these different arguments
with some attention, the preponderancy seems to be on the side of an
united jurisdiction; so far at least, as that the court before which a claim
is regularly brought, should be empowered to judge of every defence that
is laid against it. The sole inconvenience of an united jurisdiction, that it
tends to blend common law with equity, may admit a remedy, by an institute distinguishing with accuracy their boundaries: but the inconvenience
of a divided jurisdiction admits not any effectual remedy. These hints are
suggested with the greatest diffidence; for I cannot be ignorant of the bias
that naturally is produced by custom and established practice.[22]

In Scotland, as well as in other civilized countries the King's council was
originally the only court that had power to remedy defects or redress injustice in common law. To this extraordinary power the court of session
naturally succeeded, as <31> being the supreme court in civil matters;[23] for
in every well-regulated society, some one court must be trusted with this
power, and no court more properly than that which is supreme. It may at
first sight appear surprising, that no mention is made of this extraordinary
power in any of the regulations concerning the court of session. It is prob-

22. Until 1875, English courts of equity (the Court of Chancery and the equitable side
of the Court of Exchequer) were distinct from the common law courts (the King's Bench,
Common Pleas, and Exchequer).

23. The Lords of Session, who had dealt with civil cases as part of the King's Council
in the later middle ages, were reconstituted as a distinct court (the College of Justice)
by legislation in 1532 (*APS* ii 335–36: 1532, c. 2).

able, that this power was not intended, nor early thought of; and that it was introduced by necessity. That the court itself had at first no notion of being possessed of this power, is evident from the act of sederunt,[24] November 27, 1592, declaring, "That in time coming they will judge and decide upon clauses irritant[25] contained in contracts, tacks,[26] infeftments,[27] bonds and obligations, precisely according to the words and meaning of the same;"[28] which in effect was declaring themselves a court of common law, not of equity. But the mistake was discovered: the act of sederunt wore out of use; and now, for more than a century, the court of session hath acted as a court of equity, as well as of common law. Nor is it rare to find powers unfolded in practice, that were not in view at the <32> institution of a court. When the Roman Praetor was created to be the supreme judge, in place of the consuls, there is no appearance that any instructions were given him concerning matters of equity. And even as to the English court of chancery, though originally a court of equity, there was not at first the least notion entertained of that extensive jurisdiction to which in later times it hath justly arrived.

In Scotland, the union of common law with equity in the supreme court, appears to have had an influence upon inferior courts, and to have regulated their powers with respect to equity. The rule in general is, That inferior courts are confined to common law: and hence it is that an action founded merely upon equity, such as a reduction upon minority and lesion,[29] upon fraud, &c. is not competent before an inferior court. But if against a process founded on common law an equitable defence be stated, it is the practice of inferior courts to judge of such defence. Imitation of the supreme court, which judges both of law and equity, and the inconvenience of removing to another court a process that has perhaps long depended, paved the <33> way to this enlargement of power. Another thing

24. See glossary, "act of sederunt."
25. Clauses in a deed specifying that if the holder performs an act specifically prohibited by the deed, the deed shall be voided.
26. Leases.
27. *Infeftment:* the act of transferring ownership of an estate in land; the act of giving symbolic possession of land or other heritable property (Scots law).
28. *AS* 19.
29. "Reduction upon minority and lesion": the setting aside of a deed granted by a minor (or his tutor) on the ground that it is "to his lesion," that is, to his damage.

already taken notice of, tends to enlarge the powers of our inferior courts more and more; which is, that many actions, founded originally on equity, have by long practice obtained an establishment so firm as to be reckoned branches of the common law. This is the case of the *actio negotiorum gestorum,* of recompence, and many others, which, for that reason, are now commonly sustained in inferior courts.

Our courts of equity have advanced far in seconding the laws of nature, but have not perfected their course. Every clear and palpable duty is countenanced with an action; but many of the more refined duties, as will be seen afterward, are left still without remedy. Until men, thoroughly humanized, be generally agreed about these more refined duties, it is perhaps the more prudent measure for a court of equity to leave them upon conscience. Neither doth this court profess to take under its protection every covenant and agreement. Many engagements of various sorts, the fruits of idleness, are too trifling, or too ludicrous, to merit the countenance of <34> law: a court, whether of common law or of equity, cannot preserve its dignity if it descend to such matters. Wagers of all sorts, whether upon horses, cocks, or accidental events, are of this sort. People may amuse themselves, and men of easy fortunes may pass their whole time in that manner, because there is no law against it; but pastime, contrary to its nature, ought not to be converted into a serious matter, by bringing the fruits of it into a court of justice. This doctrine seems not to have been thoroughly understood, when the court of session, in a case reported by Dirleton, sustained action upon what is called there a *sponsio ludicra.*[30] A man having taken a piece of gold, under condition to pay back a greater sum, in case he should be ever married, was after his marriage sued for performance. The court sustained process; though several of the judges were of opinion, that *sponsiones ludicrae* ought not to be authorised.* But, in the following remarkable case, the court judged better. In the year 1698, a bond was executed of the <35> following tenor. "I Mr William Cochran of Kilmaronock, for a certain sum of money delivered to me by Mr John Stewart younger of Blackhall, bind and oblige me, my heirs and succes-

---

30. A "laughable promise": that is, in Scots law, an obligation which is unenforceable in court; especially wagers and gambling agreements.

* February 9. 1676 [A against B: M 9505].

sors, to deliver to the said Mr John Stewart, his heirs, executors, and assignees, the sum of one hundred guineas in gold, and that so soon as I, or the heirs descending of my body, shall succeed to the dignity and estate of Dundonald." This sum being claimed from the heir of the obligor, now Earl of Dundonald, it was objected, That this being a *sponsio ludicra* ought not to be countenanced with an action. It was answered, That bargains like the present are not against law; for if purchasing the hope of succession from a remote heir be lawful,* it cannot be unlawful to give him a sum, on condition of receiving a greater when he shall succeed. If an heir pinched for money procure it upon disadvantageous terms, equity will relieve him: but in the present case there is no evidence, nor indeed suspicion, of inequality. It was replied, That it tends <36> not to the good of society to sustain action upon such bargains:[31] they do not advance commerce, nor contribute in any degree to the comforts of life; why then should a court be bound to support them? It is sufficient that they are not reprobated, but left upon conscience and private faith. The court refused to sustain action; reserving it to be considered, whether the pursuer, upon proving the extent of the sum given by him, be not intitled to demand it back.†

The multiplied combinations of individuals in society, suggest rules of equity so numerous and various, that in vain would any writer think of collecting all of them. From an undertaking which is in a good measure new, all that can be expected is a collection of some of the capital cases that occur the most frequently in law-proceedings. This collection will comprehend many rules of equity, some of them probably of the most extensive application. Nor will it be without profit, even as to subjects omitted; for by diligently observing the application of <37> equitable principles to a

---

* See Fountainhall, July 29. 1708, Rag *contra* Brown [M 9493].

31. In the first edition (p. xvii) and second edition (pp. 52–53), Kames wrote, "It was replied, That judges of equity must act by a general rule, and must either condemn by the lump such ludicrous bargains, or approve them by the lump. If they be indulged where they appear to be fair and equal, they must be indulged whatever their circumstances be; because no precise boundary can be fixed betwixt that degree of inequality which is permitted, and that which is condemned. In the next place, it tends not to the good of society to sustain action upon such bargains."

† Feb. 7. 1753, Sir Michael Stewart of Blackhall *contra* Earl of Dundonald [M 9514, from Kames, *Select Decisions*, p. 44].

number of leading cases, a habit is gradually formed of reasoning correctly
upon matters of equity, which will enable us to apply the same principles
to new cases as they occur.

Having thus given a general view of my subject, I shall finish with explaining my motive for appearing in print. Practising lawyers, to whom
the subject must already be familiar, require no instruction. This treatise
is dedicated to the studious in general, such as are fond to improve their
minds by every exercise of the rational faculties. Writers upon law are too
much confined in their views: their works, calculated for lawyers only,
are involved in a cloud of obscure words and terms of art, a language
perfectly unknown except to those of the profession. Thus it happens,
that the knowledge of law, like the hidden mysteries of some Pagan deity,
is confined to its votaries; as if others were in duty bound to blind and
implicit submission. But such superstition, whatever unhappy progress it
may have made in religion, never can prevail in law: men who have life or
fortune at stake, take the liberty to think for them- <38> selves; and are
no less ready to accuse judges for legal oppression, than others for private
violence or wrong. Ignorance of law hath in this respect a most unhappy
effect: we all regard with partiality our own interest; and it requires knowledge no less than candour, to resist the thought of being treated unjustly
when a court pronounceth against us. Thus peevishness and discontent
arise, and are vented against the judges of the land. This, in a free government, is a dangerous and infectious spirit, to remedy which we cannot be too solicitous. Knowledge of those rational principles upon which
law is founded I venture to suggest, as a remedy no less efficacious than
palatable. Were such knowledge universally spread, judges who adhere to
rational principles, and who, with superior understanding can reconcile
law to common sense, would be revered by the whole society. The fame
of their integrity, supported by men of parts and reading, would descend
to the lowest of the people; a thing devoutly to be wished! Nothing tends
more to sweeten the temper, than a conviction of impartiality in judges;
by which we hold ourselves se- <39> cure against every insult or wrong.
By that means, peace and concord in society are promoted; and individuals are finely disciplined to submit with the like deference to all other acts
of legal authority. Integrity is not the only duty required in a judge: to

behave so as to make every one rely upon his integrity, is a duty no less essential. Deeply impressed with these notions, I dedicate my work to every lover of science; having endeavoured to explain the subject in a manner that requires in the reader no particular knowledge of municipal law. In that view I have avoided terms of art; not indeed with a scrupulous nicety, which might look like affectation; but so as that with the help of a law-dictionary, what I say may easily be apprehended.

Order, a beauty in every composition, is essential in a treatise of equity, which comprehends an endless variety of matter. To avoid obscurity and confusion, we must, with the strictest accuracy, bring under one view things intimately connected, and handle separately things unconnected, or but slightly connected. Two <40> great principles, justice and utility, govern the proceedings of a court of equity; and every matter that belongs to that court, is regulated by one or other of these principles. Hence a division of the present work into two books, the first appropriated to justice, the second to utility; in which I have endeavoured to ascertain all the principles of equity that occurred to me. I thought it would benefit the reader to have these principles illustrated in a third book, where certain important subjects are selected to be regularly discussed from beginning to end; such as furnish the most frequent opportunities for applying the principles ascertained in the former part of the work. <41>

Powers of a Court of Equity derived from the Principle of Justice.

In the Introduction occasion was taken to show, that a court of equity is necessary, first, to supply the defects of common law, and, next, to correct its rigour or injustice. The necessity in the former case arises from a principle, That where there is a right, it ought to be made effectual; in the latter, from another prin- <42> ciple, That for every wrong there ought to be a remedy. In both, the object commonly is pecuniary interest. But there is a legal interest which is not pecuniary; and which, for the sake of perspicuity, ought to be handled separately. In that view, the present book is divided into two parts. In the first are treated, the powers of a court of equity to supply defects and to correct injustice in the common law, with respect to pecuniary interest; and in the second, the powers of a court of equity with respect to matters of justice that are not pecuniary.

Part I

Powers of a court of equity to remedy the imperfections of common law with respect to pecuniary interest, by supplying what is defective, and correcting what is wrong.

The imperfections of common law are so many and so various, that it will be difficult to bring them into any perfect <43> order. The following arrangement, if not the best, seems at least to be natural and easy. 1. Imperfections of common law in protecting men from being harmed by others. 2. In protecting the weak of mind from harming themselves. 3. Imperfections of common law with respect to the natural duty of benevolence. 4. Imperfections with respect to deeds and covenants. 5. With respect to statutes. 6. With respect to transactions between debtor and creditor. 7. With respect to actions at law. 8. With respect to legal execution. 9. Power of a court of equity to inflict punishment.

CHAPTER I

Powers of a court of equity to remedy what is imperfect
in common law, with respect to the protecting
individuals from harm.

The social state, however desirable, could never have taken place among men, were they not restrained from inju- <44> ring those of their own species. To abstain from injuring others, is accordingly the primary law of society, enforced by the most vigorous sanctions: every culpable transgression of that law, subjects the wrong-doer to reparation; and every intentional transgression, subjects him also to punishment.

The moral principle of abstaining from injuring others, naturally takes the lead in every institute of law; and as the enforcing that principle was a capital object in establishing courts of justice, it is proper to commence a treatise of equity with examining in what cases the interposition of a court of equity is required to make it effectual; which can only be where no remedy is provided at common law.

With respect to harm done intentionally, there is no imperfection in common law, and consequently no necessity for a court of equity. But that court may be necessary in the following cases. First, Harm done by one in exercising a right or privilege. Second, Harm done by one who has it not in view to exercise any right or privilege. Third, A man tempted or overawed by undue influence to act <45> knowingly against his interest. Fourth, A man moved to act unknowingly against his interest, by fraud, deceit, or other artificial means. I close the chapter with the remedies that are applied by a court of equity against the wrongs above stated. Of these in their order.

SECTION I

Harm done by a man in exercising a right or privilege.

The social state, which on the one hand is highly beneficial by affording mutual aid and support, is on the other attended with some inconveniences, as where a man cannot have the free exercise of a right or privilege without harming others. How far such exercise is authorised by the law of our nature, is a question of nice discussion. That men are born in a state of freedom and independence is an established truth; but whether that freedom and independence may not admit of some limitation from the collision of opposite rights and privileges, deserves to be examined. If the free exercise of my right <46> be indulged me without regarding the harm that may ensue to another, that other is so far under my power, and his interest so far subjected to mine. On the other side, if I be restrained from the exercise of my right in every case where harm may ensue to another, I am so far dependent upon that other, and my interest so far subjected to his. Here is a threatening appearance for civil society, that seems to admit no resource but force and violence. Cases there certainly are that admit no other resource; as where in a shipwreck two persons lay hold of the same plank, one of whom must be thrust off, otherwise both will go to the bottom. But upon the present supposition, we are not reduced to that deplorable dilemma; for nature has temper'd these opposite interests by a rule no less beautiful than salutary. This rule consists of two branches: the first is, That the exercising my right will not justify me in doing any action that directly harms another; and so far my interest yields to his: the second is, That in exercising my right I am not answerable for any indirect or consequential damage that another may suffer; and so far the <47> interest of others yields to mine: I am sorry if my neighbour happen thus to suffer; but I feel no check of conscience on that account. The first branch resolves into a principle of morality, That no interest of mine, not even the preservation of life itself, authorises me to do any mischief to an innocent person.* The other branch is founded on expediency in opposition to justice; for if the possibility of harming others, whether foreseen or not foreseen, were sufficient to restrain me from prosecuting my own rights and privileges, men would be too much cramped in action, or rather would be reduced to a state of absolute inactivity.[†]

This rule, which is far from being easy in its application, requires much illustration. I begin with the first branch. However profitable it may be to purge my field of water, yet it is universally admitted, that I cannot legally open a new passage for it into my neighbour's ground; because this is a direct damage to him: "Sic enim debere quem meliorem agrum <48> suum facere, ne vicini deteriorem faciat."[‡] Where a river is interjected between my property and that of my neighbour, it is not lawful for me to alter its natural course, whether by throwing it upon my neighbour's ground, or by depriving him of it; because these acts, both of them, are direct encroachments upon his property. Neratius puts the case of a lake which in a rainy season overflows the neighbouring fields, to prevent which on one side, a bulwark is erected. He is of opinion, that if this bulwark have the effect, in a rainy season, to throw a greater quantity of water than usual upon the opposite fields, it ought to be demolished.[§,1] As the damage here is only

* Sketches of the History of Man, vol. 4. p. 31. 32. [The reference is to the second edition of Kames's *Sketches of the History of Man*, 2nd ed. (Edinburgh: Strahan, Cadell and Creech, 1778), where he includes the passage from the Preliminary Discourse (above, p. xlvii) that the moral sense "dictates, that we ought to submit to any distress, even death itself, rather than procure our own safety by laying violent hands upon an innocent person." Cf. Henry Home, Lord Kames, *Sketches of the History of Man*, ed. James A. Harris (Indianapolis: Liberty Fund, 2007), p. 716.]

† Eod. p. 64. 65 [Kames, *Sketches* (1778), vol. 4, pp. 65–66 (Liberty Fund ed., p. 732) reproduces the text of these two sentences].

‡ De aqua, et aquae pluv[iae arcendae] l. 1. §4 [On water and the action to ward off rainwater, D 39.3.1.4: Watson iii: 395: "one must only improve one's field in such a way as not to reduce the quality of one's neighbour's field"].

§ De aqua, et aquae pluv[iae arcendae] l. 1. §2 [On water and the action to ward off rainwater, D 39.3.1.2: Watson iii: 395].

1. In the second edition (pp. 58–59), the corresponding paragraph up to this point ends with the following: "This opinion is undoubtedly well founded at common law; because by the supposition the bulwark is directly prejudicial to the neighbouring proprietor. But this rule strictly followed would bar many improvements; and for that

occasional or accidental, this opinion is not well founded. It has not even a plausible appearance. Is it not natural and common for a proprietor to fence his bank, in order to prevent the encroachments of a river or of a lake? The course of the river is not altered; and the proprietor on the opposite side may fence his bank, if he be afraid of encroachments. <49>

The foregoing examples, being all of the same kind, are governed by a practical rule, That we must not throw any thing into our neighbour's ground; *ne immittas in alienum,*[2] as expressed in the Roman law. But the principle of abstaining to hurt others regards persons as well as property. "It seems the better opinion, that a brew-house, glass-house, chandler's shop, or stie for swine, set up in such inconvenient parts of a town that they cannot but greatly incommode the neighbourhood, are common nuisances."* Neighbours in a town must submit to inconveniences from each other; but they must be protected from extraordinary disturbances that render life uncomfortable. Upon the same ground, the court of session was of opinion, that the working in the upper storey of a large tenement with weighty hammers upon an anvil, is a nuisance; and it was decreed that the blacksmith should remove at the next term.†

As to the second branch of the rule, it <50> is agreed by all, as above mentioned, that where a river gradually encroaches on my property, I may fence my bank in order to prevent further encroachments; for this work does not tend to produce even indirect or consequential damage: all the effect it can have is, to prevent my neighbour from gaining ground on his side.[3]

In matters of common property, the application of this second branch

---

reason there is room for the interposition of a court of equity to mitigate the common law upon the principle of utility. It will indulge me to raise a fence within my own property, to prevent my ground from being overflow'd by a river when in flood, or by a lake: if this work tend at times to throw a greater weight of water upon my neighbour, he may fence his ground as I did."

2. "Do not send anything into another's land."

* [M. Bacon,] A new abridgment of the law, vol. 3. [1740,] p. 686.

† Kinloch of Gilmerton against Robertson, Dec. 9. 1756 [M 13163, from Kames, *Select Decisions,* p. 175].

3. In the second edition (p. 59), Kames added: "A much narrower case is determined in the Roman law, That I may lawfully dig a pit in my own land for gathering water to my cattle, though it happens to intercept a spring that run under ground into my

is sometimes more intricate. A river or any running stream directs its course through the land of many proprietors; who are thereby connected by a common interest, being equally intitled to the water for useful purposes. Whence it follows, that the course of the river or running stream cannot be diverted by any one of the proprietors, so as to deprive others of it. Where there is plenty for all, there can be no interference: but many streams are so scanty, as to be exhausted by using the water too freely, leaving little or none to others. In such a case, there ought to be a rule for using it with discretion; though hitherto no rule has been laid down. To supply the defect in some measure, I venture to suggest the following particulars, which practice <51> may in time ripen to a precise rule. It will be granted me, that if there be not a sufficiency of water for every purpose, those purposes ought to be preferred that are the most essential to the well-being of the adjacent proprietors. The most essential use is drink for man and beast; because they cannot subsist without it. What is next essential, is water for washing; because cleanness contributes greatly to health. The third is water for a corn-mill, which saves labour, and cheapens bread. The fourth is watering land for enriching it. The fifth is water for a bleach-field. And the lowest I shall mention, is water for machinery, necessary for cheapening the productions of several arts. There may be more divisions; but these are sufficient in a general view. From this arrangement it follows, that one may use the water of a rivulet for drink, and for brewing and baking, however little be left to the inferior heritors.[4] But a proprietor cannot be deprived of that essential use by one above him, who wants to divert the water for a mill, for a bleachfield, or for watering his land. Nor can a proprietor divert the water for a bleachfield, or for <52> watering his land, unless he leave sufficient for a mill below. According to this doctrine, I may lawfully dig a pit in my own field for gathering water to my cattle, though it happens to intercept a spring that run under ground into my neighbour's field, and furnished him with water.*

---

neighbour's field, and furnished him with water" (citing D 39.3.1.2: Watson iii: 395). The next two paragraphs are new to the third edition.

4. Downstream riparian proprietors.

* l. 1. §12. De aqua [et aquae pluviae arcendae (On water and the action to ward off rainwater): D 39.3.1.12: Watson iii: 396].

Under this head comes a question that may be resolved by the principles above laid down, which is, How far the free use of a river in carrying goods can be prevented or impeded by a cruive for catching salmon. It is admitted, that a navigable river fit for sailing, ought to be free to all for the purposes of commerce; and that the navigation ought not to be hurt, or rendered difficult, by any work erected in the channel of the river. But supposing a river that can only admit the floating of timber, is it lawful to erect there a cruive with a dam-dike, so as to prevent that operation? A cruive for catching salmon is an extraordinary privilege, granted to a single proprietor, prejudicial to all above who have right to fish salmon. The floating of timber, on the contrary, <53> is profitable to the proprietor, and to every person who stands in need of that commodity. A cruive, therefore, ought to yield to the floating of timber, as far as these rights are incompatible. But will positive prescription[5] give no aid to the proprietor of a cruive in this case? This prescription regulates the competition among those who pretend right to the same subject; but protects not the possessor from burdens naturally affecting his property. Now it is a rule, That property, which is a private right, must yield to what is essential for the good of the nation. In order to defend a town besieged, a house standing in the way ought to be demolished. The right of property will not avail in this case, even admitting the proprietor and his predecessors to have been in possession for a century. Or suppose, that to repel a foreign enemy, my field is found to be an advantageous situation for the national troops, it is lawful to encamp upon it, though the consequence be to destroy the trees, and all it produces. Or, to come nearer the present case, a manufacturing village is erected on the brink of a rivulet, which is used for a mill below <54> that has been in constant exercise forty years and upward. The manufactures succeed, and the village becomes so populous as nearly to exhaust the water in drink for man and beast, in brewing, and in other purposes preferable to that of a mill. Yet I take it for granted, that positive prescription will not protect the proprietor of the mill; because here there is no competition, but only property subjected to the burdens that naturally attend it. The transition from this example to the case in hand is direct. The

---

5. See glossary, "prescription."

possession of a cruive for a hundred years, will not bar a superior heritor from planting trees, nor consequently from floating them down the river for sale; for evidently positive prescription can have no operation in this case. It can have no effect but to bestow upon the possessor the property of the cruive, which otherwise might have been doubtful. But such property must, like all other property, be subjected to its natural burdens; and cannot stand in the way of a right of greater importance to the public.

It is lawful for me to build a house upon my march,[6] though it intercept the light <55> from a neighbouring house; for this is consequential damage only: beside, that if my neighbour choose to build on his march, he must see that I am equally intitled.

With regard to this section in general, there is a limitation founded entirely upon equity; which is, That though a man may lawfully exercise his right for his own benefit where the harm that ensues is only consequential; yet that the exercise is unlawful if done intentionally to distress others, without any view of benefiting himself. Rights and privileges are bestowed on us for our own good, not for hurting others. Malevolence is condemned by all laws, natural and municipal: a malevolent act of the kind mentioned is condemned by the actor himself in his sedate moments; and he finds himself in conscience bound to repair the mischief he has thus done. The common law, it is true, overlooks intention, considering the act in no other view but as legal exercise of a right. But equity holds intention to be the capital part, being that which determines an action to be right or wrong; and affords reparation accordingly. Hence a general rule in e- <56> quity, That justice will not permit a man to exercise his right where his intention is solely to hurt another; which in law-language is termed the acting *in aemulationem vicini.*[7] In all cases of this nature, a court of equity will give redress by voiding the act, if that can be done; otherwise by awarding a sum in name of damages. We proceed to examples.

---

6. Boundary of land.

7. "In envy of the neighbour." In Scots law, it referred to the use of land in a way intentionally injurious to one's neighbor. It was taken by Scots writers from the medieval civilian writers who developed the *ius commune* tradition. Scots used the phrase to support the principle that one should not exercise a legitimate right with the sole aim of annoying one's neighbor, or "purely out of envy." See Bankton, *Institute,* vol. 1, p. 252.

A man may lawfully dig a pit in his own field in order to intercept a vein of water that runs below the surface into his neighbour's property, provided his purpose be to have water for his own use; but if his purpose be to hurt his neighbour without any view to benefit himself, the act is unlawful, as proceeding from a malevolent intention; and a court of equity will restrain him from this operation.*

Upon the same principle is founded the noted practice in a court of equity, of refusing to sustain an action at law, unless the plaintiff can show an interest; for if he can take no benefit by the action, the presumption must be, that it is calculated <57> to distress the defendant, and done *in aemulationem vicini.*

In order to establish the *jus crediti*[8] in an assignee, and totally to divest the cedent or assignor, the law of Scotland requires, that notification of the assignment be made to the debtor, verified by an instrument under the hand of a notary, termed *an intimation.* Before intimation the legal right is in the cedent, and the assignee has a claim in equity only. In this case, payment made to the cedent by the debtor ignorant of the assignment, is in all respects the same as if there were no assignment: it is payment made to the creditor, which in law must extinguish the debt. But what if the debtor, when he makes payment to the cedent before intimation, be in the knowledge of the assignment? The common law knows no creditor but him who is legally vested in the right; and therefore, disregarding the debtor's knowledge of the assignment, it will sustain the payment made to the cedent as made to the legal creditor. But equity teaches a different doctrine. It was wrong in the cedent to take payment after he conveyed his right to the assignee: and <58> though the debtor was only exercising his own right in making payment to the cedent, who is still the creditor; yet being in the knowledge of the assignment, the payment must have been made intentionally to distress the assignee, without benefiting himself. A court of equity, therefore, correcting what is imperfect in common law, will oblige the debtor to make payment over again to the assignee, as reparation of the wrong done him.

* De aqua, et aquae pluv[iae arcendae] l. 1. §12 [On water and the action to ward off rainwater, D 39.3.1.12: Watson iii: 396].

8. "The right of a creditor"; that is, the personal right vested in a creditor to the debt.

With respect to this matter, there is a wide difference between the solemnities that may be requisite for vesting in an assignee a complete right to the subject, and what are sufficient to bar the debtor from making payment to the cedent. In the former view, a regular intimation is necessary, or some solemn act equivalent to a regular intimation, a process for example. In the latter view, the private knowledge of the debtor is sufficient; and hence it is, that a promise of payment made to the assignee, though not equivalent to a regular intimation, is however sufficient to bar the debtor from making payment to the cedent. The court went farther: they were of opinion, that the assignee <59> having shown his assignment to the debtor, though without intimating the same by a notary, the debtor could not make payment to the cedent.* But historical knowledge of an assignment, where it falls short of ocular evidence, will scarce be sustained to put the debtor *in mala fide.*[9] And this rule is founded on utility: a debtor ought not to be furnished with pretexts against payment; and if private conviction of an assignment, without certain knowledge, were sufficient, private conviction would often be affected, to gain time, and to delay payment.

SECTION II

Harm done by one who has it not in view to exercise any right or privilege.

In tracing the history of courts of law with respect to this branch, one beforehand would conjecture, that common law should regard no acts injuring others in <60> their rights and privileges, but where mischief is intended; neglecting acts that are culpable only, as having a foundation too slight for that law. But upon examination we discover a very different plan; so different as that damage occasioned even by the slightest fault is, and always was, repaired in courts of common law. In the criminal law, very little distinction was originally made between a criminal and a culpable act, even with respect to punishment,† not to talk of reparation: the pas-

* Fountainhall, February 16. 1703, Leith contra Garden [M 865].
9. In bad faith.
† [Kames,] Historical law-tracts, tract 1 ["History of the Criminal Law," pp. 1–89 of the 1758 ed.].

sion of resentment, in a fierce and lawless people, is roused by the slightest harm; and is too violent for any deliberate distinction between intentional and culpable wrong. In fact, both were equally subjected to punishment, even after the power of punishment was transferred to the magistrate. Of this we have a notable example in the *lex Aquilia* among the Romans: "Qui servum alienum, quadrupedem vel pecudem, injuria occiderit; quanti id in eo anno plurimi fuit, tantum aes dare domino damnas esto."* Here the word *injuria*¹ is interpreted, "quod <61> non jure factum est; i.e. si culpa quis occiderit."† The retrospect here may happen to be a great punishment; for the obliging a man who kills a lame horse not worth fifty shillings, to pay fifty pounds because the horse was of that value some months before, is evidently a punishment. And as even a *culpa levissima*² subjects a man to the *lex Aquilia*,‡ it is clear, that the slightest fault by which damage ensues is punishable by that law. The *lex Aquilia* was accordingly held by all to be penal; and for that reason no action upon it was sustained against the heir.§ The only thing surprising is, to find this law continuing in force, without alteration or improvement, down to the reign of the Emperor Justinian. The Roman law was cultivated by men of great talents, and was celebrated all the world over for its equitable decisions: is it not amazing, that in an enlightened age such gross injustice should prevail, as to make even the slightest fault a ground for punishment?

---

* l. 2. p. ad leg[em] Aquil[iam (the *Lex Aquilia*), D 9.2.2.pr. Watson i: 277: "If anyone wrongfully kills a slave belonging to someone else or a four-footed beast of the class of cattle, let him be condemned to pay the owner the highest value that the property had attained in the preceding year"].

1. A wrongful or unlawful act.

† l. 5. §1. ad leg[em] Aquil[iam (the *Lex Aquilia*), D 9.2.5.1: Watson i: 278: "something done illegally, that is, if one kills wrongfully"].

2. "The slightest fault": jurists in the *ius commune* tradition categorized varying degrees of fault, distinguishing between *culpa levissima* (the lightest fault, or failure to use the greatest care); *culpa levis* (light fault, or the failure to use ordinary diligence); and *culpa lata* (extensive fault or gross negligence). The word *dolus* was used to connote intentional wrongdoing.

‡ l. 44. eod. [the *Lex Aquilia*: D 9.2.44: Watson i: 290].

§ l. 23. §8. ad leg[em] Aquil[iam (the *Lex Aquilia*), D 9.2.23.8: Watson i: 282: "It is settled that this action is given to heirs and other successors, but it will not be given against an heir or other successors because it is penal, unless perchance the heir has been made richer as a result of the damage done].

When such was the common law of the Romans with regard to punishment, there <62> can be no difficulty to assign a reason, why that law was
extended to reparation even for the slightest fault; and as little, to assign
a reason why the same obtains in the common law of most European
nations, the principles of which are borrowed from the Roman law. The
penal branch, it is true, of wrongs that are culpable only, not criminal,
has been long abolished; having given way to the gradual improvement
of the moral sense, which dictates, that where there is no intention to
do mischief, there ought to be no punishment; and that the person who
is hurt by a fault only, not by a crime, cannot justly demand more than
reparation. And as this is the present practice of all civilized nations, it is
clear, that the reparation of damage occasioned by acts of violence comes
under courts of common law, which consequently is so far a bar to a court
of equity.

And considering, that regulations restraining individuals from injuring others and compelling them to perform their engagements, composed
originally the bulk of common law,* it will not be surprising, <63> that
courts of common law took early under their cognisance every culpable
act that occasions mischief; which was the more necessary, in respect that,
punishment being laid aside, reparation is the only mean left for repressing a culpable act. Thus we find ample provision made by common law,
not only against intentional mischief, but also against mischief that is only
foreseen, not intended. And so far there is no occasion for a court of equity.

But for the security of individuals in society, it is not sufficient that a
man himself be prohibited from doing mischief: he ought over and above
to be careful and vigilant, that persons, animals, and things, under his
power, do no mischief; and if he neglect this branch of his duty, he is liable to repair the mischief that ensues, equally as if it had proceeded from
his own act. With respect to servants, it is the master's business to make a
right choice, and to keep them under proper discipline; and therefore, if
they do any mischief that might have been foreseen and prevented, he is
liable. Thus, if a passenger be hurt by my servant's throwing a stone out
of a <64> window in my house, or have his cloaths sullied by dirty water

* See Introduction.

poured down upon him, the damage must be repaired by me at the first instance; reserving to me relief against my servant. But if a man be killed or wounded by my servant in a scuffle, I am not liable; unless it can be specified, that I knew him to be quarrelsome, and consequently might have foreseen the mischief. With respect to animals, it is the proprietor's duty to keep them from doing harm; and if harm ensue that might have been foreseen, he is bound to repair it; as, for example, where he suffers his cattle to pasture in his neighbour's field; or where the mischief is done by a beast of a vicious kind; or even by an ox or a horse, which, contrary to its nature, he knows to be mischievous.* As to things, it is also the duty of the proprietor to keep them from doing harm. Thus both fiar[3] and liferenter[4] were made liable to repair the hurt occasioned to a neighbouring tenement by the fall of their house.† It is the duty of a man who carries stones in a waggon a- <65> long the highway, to pack them so as to prevent harm; and if by careless package a stone drop out and bruise a passenger, the man is liable. But as to cases of this kind, it is a good defence against a claim of reparation, that the claimant suffered by his own fault: "Si quis aliquem evitans, magistratum forte, in taberna proxima se immisisset, ibique a cane feroce laesus esset, non posse agi canis nomine quidam putant: at si solutus fuisset, contra."‡ If a fierce bull of mine get loose, and wound a person, I am liable; but if a man break down my fence, and is hurt by the bull in my enclosure, I am not liable; for by an unlawful act he himself was the occasion of the hurt he suffered.

Thus, with respect to matters falling under the present section, it appears, that faults come under common law as well as crimes, and omis-

---

* Exodus, chap. xxi. 29. 36.

3. The owner of an estate (or fee), in respect of which a liferent has been created. In Kames's definition "he that has the fee or feu; and the proprietor is termed *fiar,* in contradistinction to the liferenter." See also glossary, "fiar."

4. *Liferent:* the right to use and enjoy the property of another (the fiar) during one's life. The liferenter is the person in possession of the estate.

† Stair, 16th February 1666, Kay contra Littlejohn [M 13974: Hay contra Littlejohn].

‡ l. 2. §1. Si quadrupes pauperiem fecisse dicatur [If a four-footed animal is alleged to have committed *pauperis* (a legal mischief), D 9.1.2.1: Watson i: 277: "If someone is fleeing from somebody, perhaps from a magistrate and rushes into the nearest shop and is there injured by a ferocious dog, some authorities maintain that action cannot be brought in respect of the dog, though they think otherwise if the dog were at large"].

sions as well as commissions; and therefore so far the common law appears complete, leaving no gleanings to a court of equity. <66>

SECTION III

A man tempted or overawed by undue influence to act knowingly against his interest.

The imperfections of man are not confined to his corporeal part: he has weaknesses of mind as well as of body; and if the taking advantage of the latter to distress a person by acts of violence be a moral wrong, intitling the sufferer to reparation, it is no less so to take advantage of the former. Society could not subsist without such prohibition; and happy it is for man as a social being, that the prohibition with respect to both articles makes a branch of his nature.

For the sake of perspicuity, this section shall be split into two parts: the first, where a man, yielding to a temptation, acts knowingly against his interest: the next, where he is overawed to act knowingly against his interest. <67>

ARTICLE I. *Where a man, yielding to a temptation, acts knowingly against his interest.*

Jean Mackie, heiress of Maidland, having disponed several parcels of land, lying about the town of Wigton, to persons who were mostly innkeepers there, a reduction was brought upon the head of fraud and circumvention by her sister, next heir in virtue of a settlement. It came out upon proof, 1st, That Jean Mackie was a habitual drunkard; that she sold her very cloaths to purchase drink, scarce leaving herself a rag to cover her nakedness; and that, by tempting her with a few shillings, it was in the power of any one to make her accept a bill for a large sum, or to make her dispone any part of her land. 2dly, That the dispositions challenged were granted for no adequate cause. The court accordingly voided these dispositions.*

---

* November 24. 1752, Mackie contra Maxwell, &c. [M 4963, from Kames, *Select Decisions,* p. 25].

Upon this case it ought to be observed, that though fraud and circumvention <68> were specified as the foundation of this reduction, which is a common but slovenly practice in processes of that sort; yet there was not the least evidence, that Jean was imposed upon or circumvented in any manner. Nor was there any necessity for recurring to such artifice: a little drink, or a few shillings to purchase it, would have tempted her at any time, drunk or sober, to give away any of her subjects. And she herself, being called as a witness, deponed, that she granted these dispositions freely, knowing well what she did. Where then lies the ground of reduction? Plainly here: It is undoubtedly an immoral act, to take advantage of weak persons who are incapable to resist certain temptations, thereby to strip them of their goods. To justify such an act, the consent of the person injured is of no avail, more than the consent of a child. With respect to the end, it is no less pernicious than theft or robbery. <69>

ARTICLE II. *Where a man is overawed to act knowingly against his interest.*

If it be a moral wrong to tempt a weak man to act against his interest, extortion is a wrong still more flagrant, by its nearer approach to open violence. What therefore only remains upon this article, is to illustrate it by examples.

Every benefit taken indirectly by a creditor, for the granting of which no impulsive cause appears but the money lent, will be voided as extorted. Thus an assignment to a lease was voided, being granted of the same date with a bond of borrowed money, and acknowledged to have had no other cause.* At the time of granting an heritable bond of corroboration,[1] the debtor engaged by a separate writing, That in case he should have occasion to sell the land, the creditor should have it for a price named. The price appeared to be equal; and yet the paction was voided, as obtained by extortion.† <70> Upon the same ground, a bond for a sum taken from

---

* Fountainhall, June 20. 1696, Sutherland contra Sinclair [M 9460].

1. See glossary, "bond of corroboration."

† November 30. 1736, Brown [of Carsluith] contra Muir [of Craig. Patrick Grant of Elchies, *Decisions of the Court of Session from the Year 1733 to the Year 1754,* ed. W. M. Morison (Edinburgh: Printed for the Editor, 1813), vol. 2, p. 310].

the principal debtor by his cautioner[2] as a reward for lending his credit, was voided.*

Rigorous creditors go sometimes differently to work. If they dare not venture upon greater profit directly than is permitted by law, they aim at it indirectly, by stipulating severe irritancies upon failure of payment. One stipulation of that sort which makes a great figure in our law, is, That if the sum lent upon a wadset[3] or pledge be not repaid at the term covenanted, the property of the wadset or pledge shall *ipso facto* be transferred to the creditor in satisfaction of the debt. This paction is in the Roman law named *lex commissoria in pignoribus,*[4] and in that law seems to be absolutely reprobated.† With us it must be effectual at common law, because there is no statute against it. But then, as it is a hard and rigorous condition, extorted from a necessitous debtor, a court of equity will interpose to give relief. And this can be done by fol- <71> lowing a general rule applicable to all cases of the kind; which is, to admit the debtor to redeem his pledge by payment, at any time, till the creditor in a declaratory process[5] signify his will to hold the pledge in place of his money. This process affords the debtor an opportunity to purge his failure by payment; which is all that in fair dealing can be demanded by the creditor. And thus, the declarator serves a double purpose: it relieves the debtor from the hardship of a penal irritancy, by furnishing him an opportunity to pay the debt; and

2. Surety.

* Forbes 24. Fountainhall 27. January 1711, King contra Ker [M 9461 and 9462].

3. See glossary, "wadset."

4. *Lex commissoria in pignoribus:* agreements for strict foreclosure of pledges; the term applied to a clause inserted in a contract of pledge, stating that the pledge should be forfeited if the demand was not paid at the time agreed. It was outlawed by Emperor Constantine in A.D. 326: *Codex* of Justinian C 8.34.3: cf. the following note.

† l. ult. C. De pactis pignorum [On agreements of Pledge, C 8.34.3. The text of the *Codex* (referring to the outlawing of such agreements by the Emperor Constantine in A.D. 326) reads, "Quoniam inter alias captiones praecipue commissoriae pignorum legis crescit asperitas, placet infirmari eam et in posterum omnem eius memoriam aboleri": "Since, among other deceptions, the harshness of agreements for the strict foreclosure of pledges has particularly increased, it is resolved to render them void and to banish all memory of them in future"].

5. Declaratory actions: actions where the pursuer seeks to have a right judicially declared, but without making any claim on a defendant.

if he be silent, the extracted decree operates a transference of the property to the creditor, which extinguishes the debt.

Hence it follows, that the debtor can redeem the wadset or pledge, whether the bargain be lucrative or no. A declarator being necessary, the property is not transferred to the creditor, if the debtor be willing to redeem his pledge: and this option he must have, whether the creditor have made profit or no by possession of the pledge. Supposing a proper wadset granted, by which the creditor makes more than the interest of his money; justice requires, that the debtor <72> have an option to redeem even after the term limited, until the equity of redemption[6] be foreclosed by a declarator; and if a declarator be necessary, as is proved, the debtor must have his option, even where the creditor has drawn less than his interest.

In equity, however, there is a material difference between a proper wadset with a *pactum legis commissoriae,* and a proper wadset where the term of redemption is not limited. In the latter case, the parties stand upon an equal footing: the creditor may demand his money when he pleases; and he has no claim for interest, because of his agreement to accept the rents instead of interest: the debtor, on the other hand, may redeem his land when he pleases, upon repayment of the sum borrowed. But the matter turns out differently in equity, where the power of redemption is by paction limited to a certain term. There being no limitation upon the creditor, he may demand his money when he pleases; and he has no claim for interest, even tho' the rents have fallen short of the interest. But if the debtor insist upon the equity of redemption after the term to which the re- <73> demption is limited; he must, beside repaying the sum borrowed, make good the interest, as far as the rent of the land has proved deficient. For impartiality is essential to a court of equity: if the one party be relieved against the rigour of a covenant, the other has the same claim: after taking the land from the creditor contrary to paction, it would be gross injustice to hold the paction good against him, by limiting him to less interest than he is intitled to by law upon an ordinary loan.*

6. See glossary, "equity of redemption."

* To this case is applicable an English maxim of equity, "That he that demands equity must give equity."

From what is said it will be clear, that a power of redeeming within a limited time annexed to a proper sale for an adequate price, cannot be exercised after the term limited for the redemption. The purchaser, to whom the property was transferred from the beginning, has no occasion for a declarator; nor doth equity require the time for redemption to be enlarged contrary to paction, in a case where an adequate price is given for the subject. <74>

Many other hard and oppressive conditions in bonds of borrowed money, invented by rigorous creditors for their own conveniency, without the least regard to humanity or equity, were repressed by the act 140, parl. 1592.[7] And, by the authority of that statute, such pactions may be brought under challenge in courts of common law, against which otherwise no remedy was competent except in a court of equity.

It was perhaps the statute now mentioned that misled the court of session into an opinion, that it belongs to the legislature solely to repress such rigorous conditions in agreements as are stated above. One thing is certain, that immediately after the statute there is an act of sederunt, November 27, 1592, in which the court declares, "That, in time coming, they will judge and decide upon clauses irritant contained in contracts, tacks, infeftments, bonds, and obligations, precisely according to the words and meaning of the same."[8] Such a resolution, proper for a court of common law, is inconsistent with the nature of a court of equity. The mistake was soon discovered: <75> the act of sederunt wore out of observance; and now, for a long time, the court of session has acted as a court of equity in this as well as other matters.

It is usury by statute to bargain with a debtor for more than the legal interest;[9] but it is not usury to take a proper wadset, even where the rent of the land exceeds the interest of the money. For the creditor who accepts the rent instead of interest, takes upon himself the insolvency of the tenants; and the hazard of this insolvency, however small, saves from usury; which consists in stipulating a yearly sum certain above the legal interest.

---

7. *APS* iii: 571: 1592, c. 56, Aganis unlawfull condicionis in contractis or obligationis.
8. *AS* 19.
9. 13 Ann. c. 15 (An act to reduce the rate of interest without any prejudice to Parliamentary Securities, 1713).

But tho' such a bargain, where the rent exceeds the legal interest, is not, strictly speaking, usury; it is rigorous and oppressive, and plainly speaks out the want of credit in the person who submits to it; upon which account, it might be thought a proper subject for equity, did we not reflect that all wadsets are not lucrative. When such is the case, what shall be the judge's conduct? Must he give an opinion upon every wadset according to its peculiar circumstances? or ought he to follow some <76> rule that is applicable to all cases of the kind? The former opens a door to arbitrary proceedings: the latter, fettering a judge, forces him often to do what is materially unjust. Here equity, regarding individuals, weighs against utility, regarding the whole society. The latter being by far the more weighty consideration, must preponderate: and for that reason only are wadsets tolerated, even the most lucrative; for it is not safe to give any redress in equity.

This doctrine may be illustrated by a different case. A debtor standing personally bound for payment of the legal interest, is compelled to give an additional real security, by infefting the creditor in certain lands, the rent of which is paid in corn, with this proviso, "That the creditor, if he levy the rents for his payment, shall not be subjected to an account, but shall hold the rents in lieu of his interest." This, from what is observed above, is not usury; because the value of the corn, however much above the interest in common years, may possibly fall below it. But as the creditor is in all events secure of his interest by having his <77> debtor bound personally, and may often draw more than his interest by levying the rent when corn sells high; equity will relieve against the inequality of this bargain. For here the court may follow a general rule, applicable to all cases of the kind, affording a remedy equally complete in every case; which is, to oblige the creditor to account for what he receives more than his interest, and to impute the same into his capital. In the case of a proper wadset this rule would be unjust, because the creditor has a chance of getting less than his interest, which ought to be compensated with some benefit beyond the ordinary profit of money: and if the door be once opened to an extraordinary benefit, a precise boundary cannot be ascertained between more and less. But the covenant now mentioned is in its very conception oppressive; and the creditor may justly be deprived of the extraordinary benefit he draws from it, when he runs no chance of getting less than the legal interest.

Pacta contra fidem tabularum nuptialium[10] belong to this article. Such private pac- <78> tions between the bridegroom and his father, contrary to the marriage-articles openly agreed on, are hurtful to the wife and children; who will therefore be relieved upon the head of fraud. But the husband cannot be so relieved, because as to him there is no fraud: he is relieved upon the head of extortion. Every such private paction is, by construction of law, extorted from him: and the construction is just, considering his dependent situation; for the fear of losing his bride, leaves him not at liberty to refuse any hard terms that may be imposed by his father, who settles the estate upon him. The relief granted to the wife and children upon the head of fraud, comes properly under the following section; but for the sake of connection is introduced here. In a contract of marriage the estate was settled upon the bridegroom by his father; and the bride's portion was taken payable to the father, which he accepted for satisfaction of the debts he owed, and for provisions to his younger children. The son afterward having privately before the marriage granted bond for a certain sum to his father, it was voided at the wife's in- <79> stance, as *contra fidem tabularum nuptialium.** Hugh Campbell of Calder, in the marriage-articles of his son Sir Alexander, became bound to provide the family-estate to him and the heirs-male of the marriage, "free of all charge and burden." He at the same time privately obtained from his son a promise to grant him a faculty of burdening the estate with £2000 Sterling to his younger children; which promise Sir Alexander fulfilled after the marriage, by granting the faculty upon a narrative "of the promise, and that the marriage-articles were in compliance with the bride's friends, that there might be no stop to the marriage." In a suit against the heirs of the marriage for payment of the said sum, at the instance of Hugh's younger children, in whose favour the faculty was exercised, the defendants were assoilzied,[11] the deed granting the faculty being *in fraudem pactorum*

---

10. "Agreements against the provisions of the marriage settlement."
    * Stair, July 21. 1668, Paton contra Paton [M 9475].
11. Absolved.

nuptialium.[12,*] The following cases relate to the other branch, namely oppression, intitling the husband to reduce deeds granted by him- <80> self. A man, after settling his estate upon his eldest son in that son's contract of marriage, warranting it to be worth 8000 merks of yearly rent, did, before the marriage, take a discharge from his son of the said warrandice.[13] The estate settled on the son falling short of the rent warranted, he insisted in a process against his father's other representatives for voiding the discharge; and the same accordingly was voided, as *contra fidem.*[14,†] A discharge of part of the portion before solemnization of the marriage, was voided as *contra fidem,* at the instance of the granter himself, because it was taken from him privately, without the concurrence of the friends whom he had engaged to assist him in the marriage-treaty.[‡] In England the same rule of equity obtains. It is held, that where the son, without privity of the father or parent, treating the match, gives a bond to refund any part of the portion, it is voidable.[§] Thus the bridegroom's <81> mother surrenders part of her jointure[15] to enable her son to make a settlement upon the bride, and the bride's father agrees to give £3000 portion. The bridegroom, without privity of his mother, gives a bond to the bride's father, to pay back £1000 of the portion at the end of seven years. Decreed, That the bond shall be delivered up, as obtained in fraud of the marriage-agreement.[||] On the marriage of Sir Henry Chancey's son with Sir Richard Butler's daughter, it was agreed, that the young couple should have so much for

12. "In fraud of the marriage settlement."

* Feb. 8. 1718, Pollock contra Campbell of Calder [M 9448, from Kames, *Dictionary,* vol. 2, p. 18].

13. An obligation on a party conveying a right to land or goods to ensure that the right is effectual; binding him to indemnify the grantee in case it is not: a warranty.

14. "Against good faith."

† Forbes, Jan. 28. 1709, M'Guffock contra Blairs [M 9483].

‡ Home, Nov. 22. 1716, Viscount of Arbuthnot contra Morison of Prestongrange [M 9487, from Kames, *Remarkable Decisions* i: 1].

§ Abridg. cases in equity, chap. 13. sect. E, §1 [1 Eq. Cas. Abr. 88, reprinted in *The English Reports,* vol. 21, p. 900. The reference is to *Kemp* v. *Coleman* (1707), reported in Salkeld, vol. 1, p. 156, reprinted in *The English Reports,* vol. 91, p. 144].

15. See glossary, "jointure."

|| Abridg. cases in equity, chap. 13. sect. E, §2 [1 Eq. Cas. Abr. 88, reprinted in *The English Reports,* vol. 21, p. 900. The reference is to *Turton* v. *Benson* (1718) in 2 Vernon 764, reprinted in *The English Reports,* vol. 23, p. 1099].

present maintenance. The son privately agrees with his father to release part. The agreement was set aside, though the son, as was urged, gave nothing but his own, and might dispose of his present maintenance as he thought fit.*

I promise a man a sum not to rob me. Equity will relieve me, by denying action for payment, and by affording me an action for recalling the money, if paid. The latter action is, in the Roman law, styled, <82> *Condictio*[16] *ob injustam causam.*[17] To take money for doing what I am bound to do without it, must be extortion: I hold the money *sine justa causa*[18] and ought in conscience to restore it. Thus it is extortion for a tutor to take a sum from his pupil's mother for granting a factory to her.† And it was found extortion in a man to take a bond from one whose curator[19] he had been, before he would deliver up the family-writings.‡

A bargain of hazard with a young heir, to have double or treble the sum lent, after the death of his father or other contingency, is not always set aside in equity; for at that rate it would be difficult to deal with an heir during the life of his ancestor. But if such bargain appear very unequal, it is set aside, upon payment of what was really lent, with interest.§ One intitled to an estate after the death of two tenants for life, takes £350 to pay £700 when the lives should fall, and <83> mortgages the estate as a security. Tho' both the tenants for life died within two years, yet the bargain being equal, no relief was given against it.‖ A young man, presumptive heir to an

---

* Ibid. §3 [1 Eq. Cas. Abr. 88–89, reprinted in *The English Reports,* vol. 21, p. 900. The reference is to *Gifford* v. *Gifford* (1699)].

16. A personal action in Roman law used to demand the return of something, including money (from *condicere,* to demand back).

17. The *condictio* for immoral or illegal payments: D 12.5: De condictione ob turpem vel iniustam causam.

18. "Without just cause."

† Durie, penult. Feb. 1639, Mushet contra Dog [M 9456].

19. Guardian.

‡ Nicolson, (*turpis causa*), July 24. 1634, Rossie contra her curators [M 9456].

§ Abridg. cases in equity, ch. 13. sect. G, §1. note [1 Eq. Cas. Abr. 90, reprinted in *The English Reports,* vol. 21, p. 901].

‖ Abridg. cases in equity, chap. 32. sect. I, §2 [1 Eq. Cas. Abr. 275–76, reprinted in *The English Reports,* vol. 21, p. 1042. The reference is to *Batty* v. *Lloyd* (1682) 1 Vernon 141, reprinted in *The English Reports,* vol. 23, p. 374].

estate-tail[20] of £800 yearly, being cast off by his father, and destitute of all means of livelihood, made an absolute conveyance of his remainder in tail to I. S. and his heirs, upon consideration of £30 paid him in money, and a security for £20 yearly during the joint lives of him and his father. Though the father lived ten years after this transaction, and though I. S. would have lost his money had the heir died during his father's life, yet the heir was relieved against the conveyance.* The plaintiff, a young man, who had a narrow allowance from his father, on whose death a great estate was to descend to him in tail, having, in the year 1675, borrowed £1000 from the defendant, became bound, in case he survived his father, to pay the defendant £5000 within a month after his father's death, with interest; but that, <84> if he did not outlive his father, the money should not be repaid. After the father's death, which happened *anno* 1679, the plaintiff brought his bill upon the head of fraud and extortion, to be relieved of this bargain, upon repayment of the sum borrowed, with interest. The cause came first before the Lord Nottinghame, who decreed the bargain to be effectual. But, upon a rehearing before Lord Chancellor Jeffreys, it was insisted, That the clause freeing the plaintiff from the debt if he died before his father, made no difference; for in all such cases the debt is lost of course, upon predecease of the heir of entail; and therefore that this clause, evidently contrived to colour a bargain which to the defendant himself must have appeared unconscionable, was in reality a circumstance against him. Though in this case there was no proof of fraud, nor of any practice used to draw the plaintiff into the bargain; yet, because of the unconscionableness of the bargain, the plaintiff was relieved against it.† In the year 1730, the Earl of Peterborough, then Lord <85> Mordaunt, granted bond at London, after the English form, to Dr William Abercromby, bearing, "That £210 was then advanced to his Lordship; and that, if he should happen to survive the Earl of Peterborough his grandfather, he was to pay £840 to the Doctor, two months after the Earl's death; and if he, the Lord Mordaunt, died in the lifetime

---

20. See glossary, "entail."

   * Ibid, §1. [1 Eq. Cas. Abr. 275, reprinted in *The English Reports,* vol. 21, p. 1042. The reference is to *Nott* v. *Johnson* (1687) 2 Vernon 27, reprinted in *The English Reports,* vol. 23, p. 627].

   † 2. Vernon 14, Berny contra Pitt [reprinted in *The English Reports,* vol. 23, p. 620].

of the Earl, the obligation was to be void." Upon the death of the Earl of
Peterborough, which happened about five years after the date of the bond,
an action was brought in the court of session against the Lord Mordaunt,
now Earl of Peterborough, for payment; and the court, upon authority of
the case immediately foregoing, unanimously judged, that the bond should
only subsist for the sum actually borrowed, with the interest.* <86>

SECTION IV

*A man moved to act unknowingly against his interest, by fraud, deceit,
or other artificial means.*

It is thought, that a court of common law, seldom interposes in any of the
cases that come under the section immediately foregoing; and the reason is,
that whether a man be led against his own interest by a violent temptation
or by extortion, there is still left to him in appearance a free choice. But
with respect to the matters that belong to the present section, a man is led
blindly against his own interest, and has no choice. This species of wrong,
therefore, being more flagrant, is not neglected by courts of common law.
It is accordingly laid down as a general rule in the English law, "That without the express provision of any act of parliament, all deceitful practices
in defrauding another of his known right, by means of some artful device,
contrary <87> to the plain rules of common honesty, are condemned by the
common law, and punished according to the heinousness of the offence."†
Thus the causing an illiterate person to execute a deed to his prejudice,
by reading it to him in words different from those in the deed, is a fraud,
which a court of common law will redress, by setting the deed aside. The
same where a woman is deceived to subscribe a warrant of attorney for con-
fessing a judgment,[1] understanding the writing to be of a different import.‡

---

* July 13, 1745, Dr William Abercromby contra Earl of Peterborough [M 4894 and
16429; from Falconer, and Sir James Ferguson of Kilkerran].

† [M. Bacon,] New abridgement of the law, vol. 2 [1736,] p. 594.

1. By executing a warrant of attorney, a debtor authorized an attorney named by his
creditor to confess an action of debt on his behalf and to suffer a legal judgment to be
entered against him.

‡ 1. Sid. 431 [*Roy* v. *Parris* (1669), reprinted in *The English Reports,* vol. 82, p. 1200].

In selling a house, it being a lie to affirm that the rent is £30, instead of £20, by which the purchaser is moved to give a greater price than the house is worth; this loss will be repaired by a court of common law, though the purchaser, by being more circumspect, might have prevented the loss.

In general, every covenant procured by fraud will be set aside in a court of common law. But with regard to covenants or agreements disregarded at common law, there can be no relief but in a court of e- <88> quity. Thus a policy of insurance was set aside upon fraud by a bill in chancery.*

We next proceed to enquire, whether every deceitful practice to impose upon others comes under common law.[2] Fraud consists in my persuading a man who has confidence in me, to do an act as for his own interest, which I know will have the contrary effect. But in whatever manner a man may be deceived or misled, yet if he was not deceived by relying upon the friendship and integrity of another, it is not a fraud. Fraud therefore implies treachery, without which no artifice nor double dealing can be termed *fraud* in a proper sense. But there are double-fac'd circumstances without number, and other artful means, calculated to deceive, which do not involve any degree of treachery. Where a man is deceived by such artifice, it must in some measure be his own fault; and bystanders are more apt to make him the object of their ridicule than of their sorrow: for which reason, frauds of this inferior nature have been overlooked by common law. But as every attempt to <89> deceive another to his prejudice is criminal in conscience, it is the duty of a court of equity to repress such deceit, by awarding reparation to the person who suffers. Utility pleads for reparation as well as equity; for if law were not attentive to repress deceit in its bud, corruption would gain ground, and even the grossest frauds would become too stubborn for law. It is this species of deceit, excluding treachery, that Lord Coke probably had in his eye,[†] when he lays down the following doctrine, That all covins, frauds, and deceits, for which there is no remedy at common law, are and were always redressed in the court of chancery.

---

* 2. Vernon 206 [*Whittingham* v. *Thornburgh* (1690), reprinted in *The English Reports*, vol. 23, p. 734].

2. For the treatment of fraud in the first edition, see Appendix, p. 501, Extract [1st: 100–1].

† 4 Inst. 84 [Coke, 4 *Institutes*, p. 84].

It is mentioned above, that a covenant procured by fraud will be set aside in a court of common law; and I now give instances where a covenant procured by deceit that amounts not to fraud, is set aside in a court of equity. A man having failed in his trade, compounded with his creditors at so much per pound, to be paid at a time certain. Some of the creditors refusing to fulfil the agreement, a bill <90> was brought by the bankrupt to compel a specific performance. But it appearing that he had underhand agreed with some of his creditors to pay their whole debts, in order that they might draw in the rest to a composition,[3] the court would not decree the agreement, but dismissed the bill.* A purchase made by a merchant in the course of commerce will be effectual, however soon his bankruptcy follow, provided it was his intention by continuing in trade to pay the price. But if he had bankruptcy in view, and no prospect to pay the price, the bargain, brought about by a palpable cheat, will be reduced in a court of equity, and the subject be restored to the vender. The only thorny point is, to detect the *animus*[4] of the purchaser to defraud the vender. In the case of Joseph Cave,† the presumptive fraud was confined to three days before the *cessio bonorum;*[5] but in that case Cave the purchaser was in good credit, till he demanded a meeting of his creditors in order to surrender his effects to them.[6] Other circumstances may concur with in- <91> solvency to enlarge that period. Gilbert Barclay merchant in Cromarty was in labouring circumstances, and owed much more than he was worth, when he made a purchase of salmon from Mackay of Bighouse; and before delivery several of his creditors proceeded to

---

3. Composition: the acceptance of a smaller sum in payment of a larger sum, usually by the creditors of a bankrupt.

   * 2. Vernon 71. Child contra Danbridge [1688; reprinted in *The English Reports*, vol. 23, p. 655].

   4. "Intention."

   † Dict[ionary,] tit[le] (Fraud) [Kames, *Dictionary*, vol. 1, pp. 335–36: Sir John Inglis of Cramond contra Royal Bank, 8 December 1736; M 4937].

   5. "Surrender of goods." Using this procedure, "a bankrupt in prison giving up his whole estate to his creditors upon oath, may apply to the Court of Session for liberation." N. Bailey, *An Universal Etymological Dictionary*, 28th ed. (Edinburgh: Neill, 1800).

   6. In this case, Joseph Cave, the purchaser from Sir John Inglis, bought barley while insolvent, and within three days of making a *cessio bonorum:* "The Lords found, that the presumptive fraud must be confined to three days before the *cessio bonorum*" (Kames, *Dictionary*, vol. 2, p. 336).

execution[7] against him. A few days after delivery, he made over the salmon to William Forsyth, another merchant of the same town, in part payment of a debt due to Forsyth; who was in the knowledge that Barclay was in labouring circumstances, and that the price of the salmon was not paid. Execution thickened more and more upon him, and he broke in ten days or a fortnight after the salmon were delivered to Forsyth. From these circumstances the court presumed an intention in Barclay to defraud Bighouse: and considering that Forsyth's purchase was not made *bona fide,* they found him liable to pay to Bighouse the value of the salmon.*

Next of other transactions brought about by deceitful means. By a marriage- <92> settlement *A* is tenant for life of certain mills, remainder to his first son in tail.[8] The son, knowing of the settlement, encourages a person, after taking a thirty-years lease of these mills, to lay out a considerable sum in new buildings, and other improvements, intending to take the benefit after his father's death. This is a deceit which justice discountenances; and therefore it was decreed, that the lessee should enjoy for the residue of the term that was current at the father's death.†,[9] The defendant on a treaty of marriage for his daughter with the plaintiff, signed a writing comprising the terms of the agreement. Designing afterward to get loose from the agreement, he ordered his daughter to entice the plaintiff to deliver up the

---

7. "Putting into effect a court order." In Scotland, it also refers to the document which attests that the officer has carried this out.

* Mackay of Bighouse contra William Forsyth merchant in Cromarty, January 20. 1758 [M 4944, from Kames, *Select Decisions,* p. 198].

8. In order to preserve family property, eighteenth-century marriage settlements conferred only a life interest in the property on the husband (who became "tenant for life"). In contrast with estates in "fee simple" (where absolute rights were granted), such estates were granted in "fee tail," with the settlement specifying "remainders in tail," setting out who would obtain the property after the expiry of the life-estate—generally the "heirs of his body." See J. H. Baker, *An Introduction to English Legal History,* 4th ed. (London: Butterworths, 2002), pp. 293–94.

† Abridgement cases in equity, cap. 47. sect. B. par. 10 [1 Eq. Cas. Abr. 356–57, reprinted in *The English Reports,* vol. 21, p. 1099. The reference is to *Hanning* v. *Ferrers* (1712)].

9. Discussing this case, the first edition adds (p. 6): "Here was no actual damage, but only a risk; for the lessee would have enjoyed the full benefit of his lease had the lessor lived thirty years. 2*do,* The part the son acted was fraudulent, and undoubtedly subjected him to make reparation. And 3*tio,* The proper and natural reparation was to secure the lessee against the wrong-doer."

writing, and then to marry him. She obey'd; and the defendant stood at the
corner of the street to see them go along to be married. The plaintiff was relieved on the point of deceit. A man having agreed to be bound for certain
provisions in his son's contract of marriage, upon a promise from the son to
discharge the <93> same, which accordingly was done before the marriage:
and after the marriage, money having been lent to the son upon the faith
of the said provisions in his contract; the discharge was set aside at the instance of the creditors, as being a deceitful contrivance between father and
son to entrap them.* In a suit by the indorsee of a note or ticket, the debtor
pleaded compensation[10] upon a note for the equivalent sum, granted him
by the indorser, bearing the same date with that upon which the process
was founded. The court deemed this a deceitful contrivance to furnish the
indorser credit; and therefore refused to sustain the compensation.†

A having an incumbrance upon an estate, is witness to a subsequent
mortgage, but conceals his own incumbrance. For this wrong his incumbrance shall be postponed.‡ To mortgage land as free when there is
an incumbrance upon it, is a cheat in the borrower; to which cheat the
in- <94> cumbrancer is accessory by countenancing the mortgage, and
subscribing it as a witness. The hurt thus done to the lender by putting him
off with a lame security, was properly repaired by preferring him before the
incumbrancer. The following cases are of the same kind. A man lends his
mortgage-deed to the mortgager, to enable him to borrow more money.
The mortgagee being thus in combination with the mortgager to deceive
the lender, is accessory to the fraud. And the hurt thereby done was properly repaired by postponing his mortgage to the incumbrance which the
lender got for his money.§ A counsel having a statute from *A* which he

---

* Stair, January 21. 1680, Caddel contra Raith [M 4275].

10. The provision in Scots law whereby mutual debts can be extinguished by setting
one off against the other. Under the statute 1592 c. 143 (*APS* iii: 573: c. 61, Compensation
Act); this may be pleaded by way of exception or defense before a decree, but not by way
of suspension or reduction after a decree.

† Fountainhall, Forbes, June 11. 1708, Bundy contra Kennedy [M 4907, 4908].

‡ 2 Vern[on] 151. Clare contra Earl of Bedford [reprinted in *The English Reports*, vol.
23, p. 703. The case referred to is discussed in the report of the case of *Hunsden* v. *Cheyney*].

§ 2 Vern[on] 726. Peter contra Russel [1716, reprinted in *The English Reports*, vol. 23,
p. 1076].

conceals, advises *B* to lend *A* £1000 on a mortgage, and draws the mortgage with a covenant against incumbrances. The statute was postponed to the mortgage.* *A* being about to lend money to *B* on a mortgage, sends to inquire of *D,* who had a prior mortgage, whether he had any incumbrance on *B's* estate. If it be proved that *D* denied he had any incumbrance, <95> his mortgage will be postponed.[†,11] An estate being settled by marriage-articles upon the children of the marriage, which estate did not belong to the husband, but to his mother: yet she was compelled in equity to make good the settlement; because she was present when the son declared that the estate was to come to him after her death, and because she was also one of the instrumentary witnesses.[‡,12]

SECTION V

What remedy is applied by a court of equity against the wrongs above stated.

It is proper to be premised, that regulations for preventing harm cannot be other but prohibitory; and consequently cannot afford opportunity for the

---

* [M. Bacon,] New abridgment of the law, vol. 2 [1736,] p. 598. Draper contra Borlace [1699; the case referred to is reported in 2 Vernon's Chancery Cases 370, reprinted in *The English Reports,* vol. 23, p. 833].

† 2 Vern[on] 554. Ibbotson contra Rhodes [1706, reprinted in *The English Reports,* vol. 23, p. 958].

11. In the discussion of this case in the first edition (p. 8), the comment is added, "A lie being a moral wrong, is sufficient, independent of all connections, to oblige the wrong-doer to repair the prejudice done by it, even where he has no purpose to benefit himself."

‡ 2 Vern[on] 150, Hunsdens contra Cheiney [1690, reprinted in *The English Reports,* vol. 23, p. 703].

12. When this case is discussed in the first edition (p. 8), the following comment is added: "The mother's connection here with the parties-contracters, and the countenance she gave to the contract, made it her duty, without artifice or dissimulation, to speak out the truth. Her artful silence therefore was a wrong, which subjected her to repair the prejudice occasioned by it. The parties could not be restored *in integrum,* because marriage had followed. The only reparation then that could be, was to pay the prejudice upon the wrong-doer, by obliging her to make good the settlement. Such reparation falls heavy on her, because it deprives her of her property. But in all views it is more equitable that the guilty suffer than the innocent."

interposition of any court of law till the wrong be committed. To restore
the party injured to his former situation, where that method is practicable,
will be preferred <96> as the most complete remedy. Thus goods stolen are
restored to the owner; and a disposition of land procured by fear, or undue
influence, is voided, in order that the disponer may be restored to his property. But it seldom happens that there is place for a remedy so complete: it
holds commonly, as expressed in the Roman law, that *factum infectum fieri
nequit,*[1] and when that is the case, the person injured, who cannot be restored to his former situation, must be contented with reparation in money.

The first question that occurs here is, Whether in money-reparation,
consequential damage can be stated? Consequential damage is sometimes
certain, sometimes uncertain. A house of mine rented by a tenant, is un-
lawfully demolished: the direct damage is the loss of the house: the consequential damage is the loss of the rent; which in this case is certain,
because the unlawful act necessarily relieves the tenant from paying rent.
Again, a man robs me of my horse: the direct damage is the horse lost
to me: the consequential damage is the being prevented from making
profit by him; which is not <97> certain, because the opportunity of making profit might have failed me, and possibly might have been neglected
though it had offered. In the case first mentioned, the loss of the rent,
being certain, comes properly under the estimation of actual damage;
and consequently will not be excluded by a court of common law. But
consequential damage that is uncertain, is not always taken into the account. And the reason follows. It is regularly incumbent on the man who
claims reparation, to prove the extent of the damage he has sustained;
which cannot be done with respect to consequential damage, as far as uncertain. But as it is undoubtedly a prejudice to be deprived of profit that
probably might have been made; the claimant is in equity relieved from
this proof, where the direct damage is the effect of a criminal act: every
presumption is turned against the delinquent; and he is charged with
every probable article of profit, unless he can give convincing evidence
that the profit claimed could not have been made. And this is conformable to the rules of equity; for as the profits are rendered uncertain by a

---

1. "A thing which is done cannot be undone."

<98> criminal act, the consequences of this uncertainty ought to affect the delinquent, not his party who is innocent. Here is a fair opportunity for the interposition of equity. A court of common law cannot listen to any proof but what is complete; and cannot award damages except as far as rendered certain by evidence. A court of equity, with respect to criminal acts, turns the uncertainty against the delinquent; and by that means affords complete reparation to the person injured. Thus, in a spuilzie,[2] which is a claim for damages in a civil court founded on the violent abstraction of moveable goods, the profit that might have been made by the horses carried off, termed *violent profits,* makes always an article in the estimation of damage. The rule is different, where the damage is occasioned by a culpable act only; for as there is nothing here to vary the rule of law, *Quod affirmanti incumbit probatio,*[3] no article of profit will be sustained but what can be rendered certain by evidence. This, it is true, may possibly be prejudicial to the person who is hurt by the culpable act: but *humanum est errare;*[4] and it is more expedient that he <99> suffer some prejudice, than that men should be terrified from industry and activity, by a rigorous and vague claim.[a] This doctrine is espoused by Ulpian:* "Item Labeo scribit, si cum vi ventorum alio modo, nisi praecisis funibus explicare se potuit, nullam actionem dandam. Idemque Labeo, et Proculus, et circa retia piscatorum, in quae navis inciderat, aestima-

2. See glossary, "spuilzie."
3. "The burden of proof is on him who affirms."
4. "To err is human."
a. In the English courts of common law there is no accurate distinction made between damage certain and uncertain. Damages are taxed by the jury, who give such damages as in conscience they think sufficient to make up the loss, without having any precise rule.
* l. 29 §3. ad leg[em] Aquil[iam] [the *lex Aquilia,* D 9.2.29.3: Watson i: 287: "Furthermore, Labeo writes that when a ship was blown by the force of the wind into the anchor ropes of another vessel and the sailors cut the ropes, no action should be allowed if the vessel could be extricated in no other way than by severing the ropes. And both Labeo and Proculus thought the same about fishermen's nets in which a fishing boat got caught; but clearly, if this was caused through the fault of the sailors, action could be brought under the *lex Aquilia.* But where action is brought for wrongful damage to the nets no account is to be taken of the fish which were not caught because of the damage, as it is so uncertain whether they would have been caught. The same is true in the cases of the prospective catches of both hunters and bird catchers"].

runt. Plane, si culpa nautarum id factum esset, lege Aquilia agendum. Sed ubi damni injuria agitur, ob retia, non piscium, qui capti non sunt, fieri aestimationem; cum incertum fuerit, an caperentur. Idemque et in venatoribus, et in aucupibus probandum." The following instance is an apt illustration of this doctrine. The Duke of Argyle's right of admiralty reach- <100> es over the western islands; on the coast of which a wrecked ship, floating without a living creature in it, was laid hold of and sold by authority of the Duke's depute to one Robertson, who refitted the ship at a considerable charge, and provided a crew to carry her to Clyde. Sir Ludovick Grant, who had a deputation from the Admiral of Scotland, misapprehending the bounds of his jurisdiction, gave orders for seizing the ship as his property; and these orders were put in execution after the ship was refitted by Robertson. As soon as the mistake was discovered, the ship was redelivered. But Robertson, who lost considerably by the delay, brought a process against Sir Ludovick for damages, and obtained a decree* for a large sum, to which the direct damage amounted. It was considered, that the defendant's error was culpable in acting rashly without duly examining the limits of his jurisdiction, which might have been ascertained by inspecting the Duke's title on record. But as to the consequential damage, namely, the profits Robertson could have made by the ship <101> had he not been unjustly deprived of the possession, which must be uncertain, the court unanimously rejected that branch of the claim.

The next question is, Whether in estimating damage there be ground in any case for admitting the *pretium affectionis*.[5] Paulus answers, That there is not: "Si servum meum occidisti, non affectiones aestimandas esse puto, (veluti si filium tuum naturalem quis occiderit, quem tu magno emptum velles), sed quanti omnibus valeret. Sextus quoque Pedius ait, pretia rerum, non ex affectione, nec utilitate singulorum, sed communiter fungi. Itaque eum, qui filium naturalem possidet, non eo locupletiorem esse,

---

* December 21. 1756.

5. "The price of feelings"; that is, emotional damages: "the imaginary value put upon a subject by the fancy of the owner, or by the regard in which he held it," William Bell, *Dictionary and Digest of the Law of Scotland,* rev. ed. by George Ross (Edinburgh: Bell & Bradfute, 1861).

quod eum plurimo, si alius possideret, redempturus fuit: nec illum, qui filium alienum possideat, tantum habere, quanti eum patri vendere posset: in lege enim Aquilia (damnum) consequimur, et amisisse dicemur, quod aut consequi potuimus, aut erogare cogimur."* As this response is given in general terms, without distinction of cases, it must be considered as declaratory of the common <102> law. The same rule must obtain in equity where the wrong is culpable only. But in repairing mischief done intentionally, the *pretium affectionis* ought in equity to be admitted; because otherwise the person who suffers obtains no adequate reparation; and also because that otherwise there is no proper distinction made between a crime and a fault.

CHAPTER II

Powers of a Court of Equity to remedy what is imperfect
in common law, with respect to protecting the weak of
mind from harming themselves by unequal bargains and
irrational deeds.

The weakness and imbecility of some men make them a fit prey for the crafty and designing. But as every deed, covenant, or transaction, procured by undue influence, comes under the foregoing chapter, the present chapter is confined to cases where equity protects individuals <103> who are not misled by undue influence, from hurting themselves by their own weakness and imbecillity. And here, though for the sake of commerce utility will not

---

* l. 33. ad legem Aquiliam [the *lex Aquilia,* D 9.2.33.pr.: Watson i: 288: "If you kill my slave, I think that personal feelings should not be taken into account (as where someone kills your natural son whom you would be prepared to buy for a great price) but only what he would be worth to the world at large. Sextius Pedius says that the prices of things are to be taken generally and not according to personal affections nor their special utility to particular individuals; and accordingly, he says that he who has a natural son is none the richer because he would redeem him for a great price if someone else possessed him, nor does he who possesses someone else's son actually have as much as he could sell him for to his father. For under the *lex Aquilia,* we sue for the amount of the harm suffered, and we are said to have lost either whatever we could have gained or what we are obliged to pay out"].

listen to a complaint of inequality among *majores, scientes, et prudentes;*[1] yet the weak of mind ought to be excepted; because such persons ought to be removed from commerce, and their transactions be confined to what is strictly necessary for their subsistence and well-being. And this is justly confining to the weak of mind a rule against inequality in bargains, which the Romans, ignorant of commerce, made general in respect to every person.

I begin with deeds granted by persons under age, who cannot be supposed mature in judgment. A reduction upon the head of minority and lesion, unknown in the common law, is an action sustained by a court of equity for setting aside any unequal transaction done during nonage. But inequality ought not to be regarded in a deed that proceeds from a virtuous and rational motive, which would be a laudable deed in one of full age. I give the following examples. A young man under age, having no means of his own, <104> is alimented and educated by a near relation, till he happens to succeed to an opulent fortune. Full of gratitude, he grants to his benefactor a remuneratory bond for a moderate sum, and dies without arriving to full age. A court of equity will never give countenance to the heir attempting to reduce this bond; for gratitude is a moral duty, and the young man was in conscience bound to make a grateful return. A court of equity, it is true, has not many opportunities to enforce the duty of gratitude, because it can seldom be brought under a general rule; but here the court may safely interpose to support a grateful return, the extent of which is ascertained by the young man himself. I put another case. A man of an opulent fortune dies suddenly without making provisions for his younger children. His eldest son and heir supplies this omission by giving suitable provisions, and dies under age. I put a third case. A man of an opulent fortune dies suddenly, leaving a numerous family of children, all of the female sex, without making provisions for them. A collateral heir-male[2] succeeds, who supplies this <105> omission by giving suitable provisions, but dies under age. A court of equity would deviate from the spirit of its institution, if it should authorise a reduction of such provisions by the granter's heir, upon the head of minority

---

1. "People who are of age, are conscious of what they are doing, and have good sense."

2. A male heir, not in a direct line of descent from the deceased, but in a diverging line of descent.

and lesion. For a rational and laudable deed never can be lesion in any proper sense.

The same doctrine is applicable to those who have a natural imbecillity which continues for life. A transaction made by such a person is not voided by a court of equity, unless it appear irrational and the effect of imbecillity. Where this is the case, it becomes indeed necessary that the court interpose, though there can be no general rule for direction.

The protection afforded by equity to the weak in mind, is extended to save them from hurting themselves by irrational settlements. The opinions of men with respect to the management of affairs and the exercising acts of property, are no less various than their faces: and as the world is seldom agreed about what is rational and irrational in such matters, there can be no rule for restraining the settlements of those who are not remarkably weak, <106> unless such settlements be not only irrational but absurd. But as the weak and facile are protected against unequal bargains, there is the same reason for their being protected against absurd settlements. Take the following example. In a process at the instance of a brother next of kin, for voiding a testament made by his deceased sister in favour of a stranger; it came out upon proof, that, some time before making the testament, the testatrix, being seized with madness, was locked up; and that not long after making the testament her madness recurred, and continued till her death; that at the time of the testament she was in a wavering state, sometimes better, sometimes worse; in some instances rational, in others little better than delirious, never perfectly sound in mind. In particular, it appeared from the proof, that when in better health, she expressed much affection for her brother the pursuer; but that, when the disease was more upon her, she appeared to have some grudge or resentment at him without any cause. The testament was holograph;[3] and the scroll she copied was furnished by the defendant, in whose favour <107> the testament was made, who had ready access to her at all times, while her brother lived at a distance. In reasoning it was yielded, that the woman was capable of making a testament, and that the testament challenged might be effectual at common law. But then it was urged, That though a testament made in

3. Handwritten by the testator.

the condition of mind above described, preferring one relation before another, a son before a father, or a sister before a brother, might be supported in equity as well as at common law; yet that the testament in question, proceeding not from rational views, but from a diseased mind occasioning a causeless resentment against the pursuer, ought not to be supported in equity, being a deed which the testatrix herself must have been ashamed of had she recovered health. Weight also was laid upon the following circumstance, That the testament was made *remotis arbitris*,[4] and kept secret; which showed the defendant's consciousness, that the testatrix would have been easily diverted by her friends from making so irrational a settlement. In this view, it was considered as a wrong in him to take from her, in these circumstances, an irrational <108> deed; and consequently, that he ought to be restrained in equity from taking any benefit by it. The testament was voided.*

A temporary weakness ought, for the time of its endurance, to have the same effect in law with one that is perpetual: for which reason a discharge obtained from a woman during the pains of childbirth was reduced; *Fountainhall, 7th December* 1686.[5]

CHAPTER III

Powers of a court of equity to remedy what is imperfect
in common law, with respect to the natural duty of
benevolence.

In the Introduction there was occasion to observe, that the virtue of benevolence is by various connections converted <109> into a duty; and that duties of this kind, being neglected by the common law, are enforced by a court of equity. This opens a wide field of equity, boundless in appearance, and which would be so in reality as well as in appearance, were it not for one circumstance, That the duty of benevolence is much more

4. "Witnesses being absent."
* January 26. 1759, Tulloch contra Viscount of Arbuthnot [M 11672, from Kames, *Select Decisions,* p. 207].
5. [A. against B.: M 6298].

limited than the virtue. The virtue of benevolence may be exercised in a great variety of good offices: it tends often to make additions to the positive happiness of others, as well as to relieve them from distress or want. But abstracting from positive engagement, the duty of benevolence is, with respect to pecuniary interest, confined to the latter. No connection, no situation, nor circumstance, makes it my duty to enlarge the estate of any person who has already a sufficiency, or to make him *locupletior*,[1] as termed in the Roman law. For even in the strictest of all connections, that of parent and child, I feel not that I am in conscience or in duty bound, to do more than to make my children independent, so as to preserve them from want:[a] <110> all beyond is left upon parental affection. Neither doth gratitude make it my duty to enrich my benefactor, but only to aid and support him when any sort of distress or want calls for help. A favour is

---

1. "Richer"; enriched.

a. This proposition is illustrated in the following case. Mary Scot, daughter of Scot of Highchester, having, by unlucky circumstances, been reduced to indigence, was alimented by her mother Lady Mary Drummond, at the rate of £20 yearly. Lady Mary, at the approach of death, settled all her effects upon Mary Sharp, her daughter of another marriage, taking no other notice of her daughter Mary Scot, but the recommending her to the charity of Mary Sharp. After the mother's death, Mary Scot brought a process for aliment against her sister Mary Sharp, founded chiefly on the said recommendation. A proof was taken of the extent of the effects contained in the settlement to the defendant, which amounted to about £300 Sterling. No action, either in law or equity, could be founded on the recommendation, very different in its nature from an obligation or a burden. But it was stated, that the pursuer, being very young when her father died, was educated by her mother to no business by which she could gain a livelihood: and it occurred to the court, that though the *patria potestas* [paternal power] is such, that a peer may breed his son a cobler, and after settling him in business with a competent stock, is relieved from all further aliment; yet if a son be bred as a gentleman, without being instructed in any art that can gain him a farthing, he is intitled to be alimented for life; for otherwise a palpable absurdity will follow, That a man may starve his son, or leave him to want or beggary. Thus, Lady Mary Drummond, breeding her daughter to no business, was by the law of nature bound to aliment her for life, or at least till she should be otherwise provided; and the pursuer therefore being a creditor for this aliment, has a good action against her mother's representatives. The court accordingly found the pursuer intitled to an aliment of £12 Sterling yearly, and decerned [decreed] against the defendant for the same.—*8th March* 1759, *Mary Scot contra Mary Sharp* [M App. I, Parent & Child, No. 1; from Kames, *Select Decisions,* p. 209. On the Scots law imposing a duty on the parent to maintain or aliment the child, see Bankton, *Institute,* vol. 1, pp. 155–56].

indeed scarce felt to be such, but when it prevents or relieves from harm; and a favour naturally is returned in kind. <111>

Here is a clear circumscription of equity, as far as concerns the present chapter. A court of equity cannot force one man, whether by his labour or money, to add to the riches of another; because, abstracting from a promise, no connection makes this a duty. What then is left for a court of equity, is, in certain circumstances, to compel persons to save from mischief those they are connected with, or to relieve them from want or distress. Benevolence in this case is a strong impulse to afford relief; and in this case benevolence, assuming the name of *pity* or *compassion,* is by a law in <112> our nature made a positive duty. In all other cases, benevolence is a virtue only, not a duty: the exercise is left to our own choice; and the neglect is not punished, though the practice is highly rewarded by the satisfaction it affords. In this branch of our nature, a beautiful final cause is visible: the benevolence of man, by want of ability, is confined within narrow bounds; and in order to make the most of that slender power he has of doing good, it is wisely directed where it is the most useful, namely, to relieve others from distress.

It appears then, that equity, with respect to the duty of serving others, is not extended beyond pity or compassion. But it is circumscribed within still narrower bounds; for compassion, though a natural duty, is not adopted in its utmost extent by courts of equity. In many cases, this duty is too vague and undetermined to be reached by human laws; and a court of equity pretends not to interpose, but where the duty, being clear and precise, can be brought under general rules.* Some of the connections that occasion duty so pre- <113> cise I shall proceed to handle, confining myself to those that are in some measure involved in circumstances; for the more simple connections, such as that of parent and child, require little or no elucidation. Though all the duties of this kind that are enforced by a court of equity, belong to the principle of justice; they may however be divided into different classes. The present chapter is accordingly divided into two sections. In the first are handled connections that make benevolence a duty when not prejudicial to our interest. In the second are

---

* See the Introduction.

handled connections that make benevolence a duty even against our inter-est. These connections are distinguishable from each other so clearly, as to prevent any confusion of ideas; and the foregoing order is chosen, that we may pass gradually from the slighter to the more intimate connections. To prompt a man to serve those with whom he is connected, requires not any extraordinary motive, when the good office thwarts not his own interest: any slight connection is sufficient to make this a duty, and therefore such connections are first discussed. It requires a more intimate connection, to <114> make it our duty to bestow upon another any part of our sub-stance. Self-interest is not to be overcome but by connections of the most intimate kind, which therefore are placed last in order.

SECTION I

Connections that make benevolence a duty when not prejudicial to our interest.

The connection I shall first take under consideration, is that which sub-sists between a creditor and a cautioner. The nature of this engagement demands benevolence on the part of the creditor. The cautioner, when he pays the debt, suffers loss by the act of the creditor, though not by his fault; and the creditor will find himself bound in humanity, as far as consistent with his own interest, to assist the cautioner in operating his relief against the principal debtor. He ought in particular to convey to the cautioner, the bond with the execution done upon it, in order that the cautioner may the more speedily <115> obtain relief from the principal. The law, favouring this moral act, considers the money delivered to the creditor, not as payment, but as a valuable consideration for assigning his debt and execution to the cautioner. I cannot explain this better than in the words of Papinian, the most eminent of all the writers on the Roman law: "Cum possessor unus, expediendi negotii causa, tributorum jure conveniretur; adversus caeteros, quorum aeque praedia tenentur, ei, qui conventus est, actiones a fisco praestantur: scilicet ut omnes pro modo praediorum pe-cuniam tributi conferant: nec inutiliter actiones praestantur tametsi fiscus pecuniam suam reciperaverit, quia nominum venditorum pretium acceptum videtur."* From which consideration it follows, that this assignment may be demanded and granted *ex post facto,* if the precaution be omitted when the money is paid.

From this connection it also follows, that the creditor is bound to convey to the cautioner every separate security he has for the debt; and consequently, that if the cre- <116> ditor discharge or pass from his separate security, the cautioner, as far as he suffers thereby, hath an exception in equity against payment.

I must observe historically, that there are many decisions of the court of session, declaring the creditor not bound to grant the assignment first mentioned. These decisions, remote in point of time, will not be much regarded; because the rules of equity lay formerly in greater obscurity than at present. And there is an additional reason for disregarding them, that they are not consistent with others relating to the same subject. If it be laid down as a rule, That the creditor is not bound to assign his bond and execution, it ought to follow, that neither is he bound to assign any separate security: if it be not his duty to serve the cautioner in the one case, it cannot be his duty to serve him in the other. And yet it is a rule established in this court, That the cautioner, making payment of the debt, is intitled to every separate security of which the creditor is possessed. One is at no loss to discover the cause of this discrepancy: when the question is about a separate security upon <117> which the cautioner's relief may wholly depend, the principle of equity makes a strong impression: its impression is slighter when the question is only about assigning the bond, which has no other effect but to save a process.

It is of the greater consequence to settle with precision the equitable rule that governs questions between the creditor and cautioner, because upon it depends, in my apprehension, the mutual relief between co-cautioners. Of two cautioners bound for the same debt at different times and in dif-

* l. 5. De censibus [On censuses, D 50.15.5.pr.: Watson iv: 932: "If in order to expedite the affair a single owner is prosecuted under the law of taxation, the man who is prosecuted is allowed by the imperial treasury actions against the others whose estates are equally liable, of course, so that all may contribute the tax money according to the size of their estates. Nor are the actions allowed to no purpose, although the imperial treasury has recovered its money, since the sum is regarded as received from the debts of sellers"].

ferent deeds, one pays the debt upon a discharge without an assignment: where is the legal foundation that intitles this man to claim the half from his fellow-cautioner? The being bound in different deeds, affords no place for supposing an implied stipulation of mutual relief: nay, supposing them bound in the same deed, we are not from that single circumstance to imply a mutual consent for relief, but rather the contrary when the clause of mutual relief is omitted; for, in general, when an obvious clause is left out of a deed, it is natural to ascribe the omission to design rather than to forgetfulness. <118> The principal debtor is *ex mandato*[1] bound to relieve all his cautioners: but there is no medium at common law, by which one cautioner can demand relief from another. And with respect to equity, the connection of being bound for payment of the same debt, is too slight to intitle that cautioner who pays the whole debt, to be indemnified in part out of the goods of his fellow. It appears then, that the claim of mutual relief among co-cautioners can have no foundation other than the obligation upon the creditor to assign upon payment. This assignment in the case of a single cautioner must be total; in the case of several must be *pro rata;* because the creditor is equally connected with each of them. The only difficulty is, that at this rate, there is no mutual relief unless an assignment be actually given. But this difficulty is easily surmounted. We have seen above, that such assignment may be granted *ex post facto:* hence it is the duty of the creditor to grant the assignment at whatever time demanded; and if the creditor prove refractory, the law will interpose to hold an assignment as granted, because it ought to be granted. And this suppletory or im- <119> plied legal assignment, is the true foundation of the mutual relief among co-cautioners, which obtains both in Scotland and England.

Utility concurs to support this equitable claim: no situation with regard to law would be attended with more pernicious consequences, than to permit a creditor to oppress one cautioner and relieve others: judges ought to be jealous of such arbitrary powers, which will generally be directed by bad motives; often by resentment, and, which is still worse, more often by

---

1. According to the mandate; that is, by the contract of suretyship: from *mandatum,* the Roman consensual contract by which one party gratuitously undertook a commission for the other.

avarice. It is happy therefore for mankind, that two different principles co-incide in matters of this kind, to put them upon a just and salutary footing.

The creditor, as has been said, being bound to all the cautioners equally, cannot legally give an assignment to one of them in such terms as to intitle him to claim the whole from the other cautioners. In what terms then ought the assignment to be granted? or when granted without limitation, what effect ought it to have in equity? This is a question of some subtilty. To permit the assignee to demand the whole from any single cau- <120> tioner, deducting only his own part of the debt, is unequal; because it evidently gives the assignee an advantage over his co-cautioners. On the other hand, the assignee is in a worse situation than any other of them, if he must submit to take from each of them separately his proportion of the debt: upon this plan, the cautioner who pays the debt, is forc'd to run the circuit of all his co-cautioners; and if one or two prove insolvent, he must renew the suit against the rest, to make up the proportions of those who are deficient. To preserve therefore a real equality among the cautioners, every one of them against whom relief is claimed, ought to bear an equal proportion with the assignee. To explain this rule, I suppose six cautioners bound in a bond for six hundred pounds. The first paying the debt, is in-titled to claim the half from the second, who ought to be equally burdened with the first. When the first and second again attack the third, they have a claim against him each for a hundred pounds; which resolves in laying the burden of two hundred pounds upon each; —and so on till the whole cautioners be discussed.[2] This <121> method not only preserves equality, but avoids after-reckonings in cases of insolvency.

So far clear when relief can be directly obtained. But what if the assignee be put to the trouble of adjudging for his relief? In that case, the assignment is a legal title to lead an adjudication for the whole debt. Equity is satisfied, if no more be actually drawn out of the estate of the co-cautioners, than what that co-cautioner is bound to contribute as above. And in leading the adjudication, not even the adjudger's own proportion of the debt ought to be deducted: it is a benefit to the other cautioners that the security be as

2. Discussion (benefit of): the right of a surety to require the creditor to take proceed-ings to obtain payment from the principal debtor before seeking payment from the surety. Adapted in Scots law from the Roman law *beneficium ordinis* (privilege of order).

extensive as possible; for it intitles the adjudger to a greater proportion of the subject or price, in competition with extraneous creditors.

The same principles and conclusions are equally applicable to *correi debendi*,[3] where a number of debtors are bound conjunctly and severally to one creditor. Equity requires the utmost impartiality in him to his debtors: if for his own ease he take the whole from one, he is bound to grant an assignment precisely as in the case of co-cautioners. Utility joins with equity <122> to enforce this impartiality. And it makes no difference whether the *correi debendi* be bound for a civil debt, or be bound *ex delicto;*[4] for in both causes equally it is the duty of the creditor to act impartially, and in both cases equally utility requires impartiality.

Another connection, of the same nature with the former, is that between one creditor who is infeft in two different tenements for his security, and another creditor who hath an infeftment on one of the tenements, of a later date. Here the two creditors are connected, by having the same debtor, and a security upon the same subject. Hence it follows, as in the former case, that if it be the will of the preferable creditor to draw his whole payment out of that subject in which the other creditor is infeft, the latter for his relief is intitled to have the preferable security assigned to him: which can be done upon the construction above mentioned; for the sum recovered by the preferable creditor out of the subject on which the other creditor is also infeft, is justly understood to be advanced by the latter, being a sum which he was intitled to, and <123> must have drawn had not the preferable creditor intervened; and this sum is held to be the purchase-money of the conveyance. This construction, preserving the preferable debt entire in the person of the second creditor, intitles him to draw payment of that debt out of the other tenement. By this equitable construction, matters are restored to the same state as if the first creditor had drawn his payment out of the separate subject, leaving the other entire for payment of the second creditor. Utility also concurs to support this equitable claim.

It is scarce necessary here to observe, that a supposed conveyance, sufficient as above mentioned to found a claim of relief among co-cautioners,

3. "Joint debtors."
4. "Because of a delict."

will not answer in the present case. In order to found an execution against
land, there must be an infeftment; and this infeftment must be conveyed
to the person who demands execution. Any just or equitable consideration
may be sufficient to found a personal action; but even personal execution
cannot proceed without a formal warrant, and still less real execution.

But now, admitting it to be the duty of <124> the preferable creditor
to assign, the question is, To what extent. Whether ought the assignment
to have a total effect, or only to put the disappointed creditor in the same
situation as if the preferable creditor had drawn his payment proportionally out of both subjects? It will be made appear by and by, that the assignment must be confined to the latter effect in the case of two secondary
creditors. But there is no equity to limit the assignment in this manner,
where there is no interest in opposition but that of the debtor. He has no
equitable interest to oppose a total assignment; and the second creditor has
an equitable claim to all the aid the first creditor can afford him.

The rules of equity must be the same in every country where law is
cultivated. By the practice in England,* if the creditors sweep away the
personal estate, the real estate will be charged for payment of the legacies.
In this case, the legatees need no assignment to found their equitable claim
against the heir who succeeds to the real estate.

We proceed to another connection, which <125> is that between the
preferable creditor infeft in both tenements, and two secondary creditors,
one infeft in one of the tenements, and one in the other. The duty of the
preferable or catholic creditor,⁵ with relation to these secondary creditors, cannot be doubtful considering what is said above. Equity as well
as expediency bars him from arbitrary measures. He is equally connected
with his two fellow-creditors, and he must act impartially between them.
The equitable measure is, to draw his payment proportionally out of both
tenements; but if, for his own ease or conveniency, he chuse to draw the
whole out of one, the postponed creditor is intitled to an assignment; not
indeed total, which would be an arbitrary act, but proportional, so as to

---

* 2 Chancery Cases 4 [Anonymous (1679), reprinted in *The English Reports,* vol. 22,
p. 817].

5. A catholic creditor: one whose debt is secured over the whole property of the debtor,
or several different parts of it.

intitle him to draw out of the other subject, what he would have drawn out of his own, had the preferable creditor drawn proportionally out of both subjects. I need scarce mention, that the same rule which obtains in the case of secondary creditors, must equally obtain among purchasers of different parcels of land, which before the purchase were all *in cumulo*[6] burdened with an <126> infeftment of annualrent. A man grants a rent-charge out of all his lands, and afterwards sells them by parcels to diverse persons: the grantee of the rent-charge levies his whole rent from one of these purchasers: this purchaser shall be eased in equity by a contribution from the rest of the purchasers.*

A case connected with that last handled, will throw light upon the present subject. Let it be supposed, that the catholic or preferable creditor purchases one of the secondary debts: will this vary the rule of equity? This purchase in itself lawful, is not prohibited by any statute, and therefore must have its effect. The connection here between the creditors is by no means so intimate, as to oblige any one of them, at the expence of his own interest, to serve the others. There is no rule in equity to bar the catholic creditor from drawing full payment of the secondary debt out of the tenement which it burdens, reserving his catholic debt to be made effectual out of the other tenement; though of consequence the secondary creditor upon that tenement <127> is totally disappointed. This secondary creditor has no claim for an assignment, total or partial, when the interest of the catholic creditor stands in opposition. But here the connection among the parties must, in my apprehension, have the following equitable operation, that the catholic creditor, by virtue of his purchase, cannot draw more than the sum he paid for it. Equity in this case will not allow the one to profit by the other's loss. But a hint here must suffice; because the point belongs more properly to another head.†

The following case proceeds upon the principle above laid down. The husband, on the marriage, charged the lands with a rent-charge for a jointure to his wife, and afterward devised part of these lands to the wife. After

---

6. "Collectively."

* Abridg. cases in equity, cap. 18. sect. A. §1 [1 Eq. Cas. Abr. 113; reprinted in *The English Reports*, vol. 21, p. 921].

† Immediately below, sect. 2. art. 1.

the husband's death, the heir prayed that the lands devised to the wife might bear their proportion of the rent-charge: the bill was dismissed, because the grantee of the rent-charge may distrain[7] in all or any part of the lands for her rent; and there is no equity to abridge her remedy.* <128>

If the catholic creditor, after the existence of both secondary debts, renounce his infeftment with respect to one of the tenements, which makes a clear fund for the secondary creditor secured upon that tenement; such renunciation ought to have no effect in equity against the other secondary creditor, because it is an arbitrary deed, and a direct breach of that impartiality which the catholic creditor is bound to observe with relation to the secondary creditors. It is in effect the same with granting a total assignment to one of the secondary creditors against the other.

In every one of the cases mentioned, the catholic creditor is equally connected with each of the secondary creditors, and upon that account is bound to act impartially between them. But this rule of equity cannot take place where the connections are unequal. It holds here as among blood-relations: those who are nearest to me, are intitled to a preference in my favour. The following case will be a sufficient illustration. A man takes a bond of borrowed money with a cautioner; obtains afterward an infeftment from the <129> principal debtor as an additional security; and last of all, another creditor for his security obtains infeftment upon the same subject. Here the first mentioned creditor has two different means for obtaining payment: he may apply to the cautioner, or he may apply to the land in which he is infeft. He proceeds to execution against the land, by which he cuts out the second creditor. Is he bound to grant an assignment to the second creditor against the cautioner, total or partial? The second creditor is in this case not intitled to demand an assignment: on the contrary, the preferable creditor, taking payment from the cautioner, is bound to give him a total assignment; because he is more intimately connected with the cautioner than with the second creditor. A cautionary engagement is an act of pure benevolence; and when a creditor lays hold of this engagement to oblige one man to pay another's debt, this connection makes it

---

7. See glossary, "distraint/distress."

* 1 Vern[on] 347 [*Knight* v. *Calthorpe* (1685), reprinted in *The English Reports*, vol. 23, p. 513].

evidently the duty of the creditor to aid the cautioner with an assignment, in order to repair his loss; and it proceeds from the same intimacy of connection, that, as above mentioned, he is obliged to include <130> in this assignment every separate security he has for the debt. It is his duty accordingly to convey to the cautioner the real security he got from the principal debtor. Nor is the interest of the second creditor regarded in opposition; for he is no other way connected with the preferable creditor, but by being both of them creditors to the same person, and both of them infeft on the same subject for security.

A question of great importance, that has frequently been debated in the court of session, appears to depend upon the principles above set forth. The question is, Whether a tenant in tail be bound to extinguish the annual burdens arising during his possession, so as to transmit to the heirs of entail the estate in as good condition as when he received it. To treat this question accurately, we must begin with considering how the common law stands. With respect to feu-duties,[8] cess,[9] and teind,[10] these are *debita fructuum*[11] and at common law afford an action for payment against every person who levies the rents, and against a tenant in tail in particular.[12] But this is not the case of the entailer's personal debts, which burden the <131> heirs of entail personally, but not the fruits. Let us consider what that difference will produce. An heir in a fee-simple[13] is liable to the debts of his predecessor, and every heir is so liable successively. But this obligation respects the creditors only; and affords no relief to one heir against another either for principal or interest. Does an entail make a difference at common law? A tenant in tail possesses the rents: but these rents are his property, just as much if the estate were a fee-simple; and the consuming

8. Feudal duties payable in money or in kind, in respect of land held by feudal holding.

9. A land tax on the produce and rent of real property, originally imposed in 1652 (Scotland).

10. Tithes collected for the maintenance of the Scottish Kirk.

11. A debt chargeable on the fruits of the land, as opposed to *debita fundi,* debts chargeable on the land itself.

12. In the second edition (p. 92), Kames notes at this point, "With respect then to the foregoing articles, there is no occasion for equity: the common law burdens every tenant in tail with what of them become due during his possession." He adds an additional paragraph: see Appendix, p. 522, Extract [2nd: 92–93].

13. See glossary, "debita fructuum."

rents belonging to himself, cannot subject him as tenant in tail more than if his estate were a fee-simple. Hence it appears clear, that at common law a tenant in tail is not bound to relieve the heirs of entail of any growing burdens, unless what is a *debitum fructuum.*

A court of equity, less confined than a court of common law, finds this case resolvable into one above determined, namely, that of *correi debendi,* where several debtors are conjunctly bound for payment of one debt. There is no difference between *correi debendi* and heirs of entail, but that the former are all of them liable at <132> the same time, the latter only successively; which makes no difference either in equity or in expediency, the same impartiality being required of the creditor with respect to both. While the debt subsists, the creditor is bound to lay the burden of his interest upon each heir equally; consequently each heir is bound to pay the interest that arises during his time. And if the principal be demanded, the heir who pays is only entitled to an assignment of the principal sum, and of the interest that shall arise after his own death. This rule accordingly obtains in England, as where a proprietor of land, after charging it with a sum of money, devises it to one for life, remainder to another in fee. Equity will compel the tenant for life to pay the arrears due on the rent-charge, that all may not fall upon the remainder-man.*

A tenant by curtesy[14] is, like a tenant in tail, bound to extinguish the current burdens. The curtesy is established by customary law; and a court of equity is intitled to supply any defect in law, whether written or customary, in order to make the law rational. The law, autho- <133> rising the husband to possess the wife's estate, intends no more but to give him the enjoyment of it for life, without waste, confining him to act like a *bonus paterfamilias.*[15,†]

The following case seems to require the interposition of a court of equity; and yet whether its powers reach so far is doubtful. A man assigns to a relation of his £500 contained in a bond specified, without power of

---

* 1 Chancery Cases 223 [*Hayes* v. *Hayes* (1674), reprinted in *The English Reports,* vol. 22, p. 772].

14. See glossary, "curtesy."

15. "A good head of a family" (Roman law).

† Home, Jan. 3. 1717, Anna Monteith [M 3117, from Kames, *Remarkable Decisions* i: 3, No. 2].

revocation, reserving only his own liferent. Many years after, forgetting the assignment, he makes a will, naming this same relation his executor and residuary legatee,[16] bequeathing in the testament the foresaid bond of £500 to another relation. The testator's effects, abstracting from the bond, not exceeding in value £500, it becomes to the executor nominate a matter indifferent, whether he accept the testament, or betake himself to his own bond. But it is not indifferent to others; for if he undertake the office of executor, he must convey the bond to the special legatee; if he cling to the bond, rejecting the office, the testament falls to the ground, and the next of kin will take <134> the effects, leaving nothing to the special legatee. The interest of others ought not to depend on the arbitrary will of the executor nominate; and yet, as far as appears, there is no place here for the interposition of equity. The privilege of accepting or rejecting a right, no man can be deprived of; and, admitting this privilege, the consequences that follow seem to be out of the reach of equity.

Land-estates that are conterminous, form such a connection between the proprietors, as to make certain acts of benevolence their duty, which belong to the present subject. To save my ground from water flowing upon it from a neighbouring field, a court of equity will intitle me to repair a bulwark within that field, provided the reparation do not hurt the proprietor.* The following is a similar case. The course of a rivulet which serves my mill happens to be diverted, a torrent having filled with stones or mud the channel in my neighbour's ground above. I will be permitted to remove the obstruction though in my neighbour's property, in <135> order to restore the rivulet to its natural channel. My neighbour is bound to suffer this operation, because it relieves me from damage without harming his property.

But in order to procure any actual profit, or to make myself *locupletior,* equity will not interpose or intitle me to make any alteration in my neighbour's property, even where he cannot specify any prejudice by the alteration. The reason is given above, That equity never obliges any man, whether by acting or suffering, to encrease the estate of another. Thus, the Earl of Eglinton having built a mill upon the river of Irvine, and stretched

---

16. The person designated to receive the residue of the deceased's estate.

* l. 2. §5. in fine, De aqua et aquae pluviae arcen[dae (On Water and the Action to ward off Rainwater), D 39.3.2.5].

a dam-dike cross the channel, which occasioned a restagnation to the prejudice of a superior mill; Fairly, the proprietor of this mill, brought a process, complaining that his mill was hurt by the back-water, and concluding that the Earl's dam-dike be demolished, or so altered as to give a free course to the river. The restagnation being acknowledged, the Earl proposed to raise the pursuer's mill-wheel ten inches, which would make the mill go as well as formerly; offering security against all fu- <136> ture damage: and urged, that to refuse submitting to this alteration would be acting *in aemulationem vicini* which the law doth not indulge. The court judged the defendant's dam-dike to be an encroachment on the pursuer's property, and ordained the same to be removed or taken down as far as it occasioned the restagnation.*

SECTION II

Connections that make benevolence a duty even against our interest.

These connections must be very intimate; for, as observed in the beginning of the present chapter, it requires a much stronger connection to oblige me to bestow upon another any portion of my substance, than merely to do a good office which takes nothing from me. The bulk of these connections, though extremely various, may be brought under the fol- <137> lowing heads. 1st, Connections that intitle a man to have his loss made up out of my gain. 2d, Connections that intitle a man who is not, properly speaking, a loser, to partake of my gain. 3d, Connections that intitle one who is a loser to a recompence from one who is not a gainer.

ARTICLE I. *Connections that intitle a man to have his loss made up out of my gain.*

No personal connection, supposing the most intimate, that of parent and child, can make it an act of justice, that one who is a gainer, should re-

---

* Jan. 27. 1744, Fairly contra Earl of Eglinton [M 12781, from Kames, *Remarkable Decisions* ii. 79].

pair the loss sustained by another, unless there be also some connection between the loss and gain; and that connection is a capital circumstance in the present speculation. The connections hitherto mentioned relate to persons; this relates to things. If, for example, I lay out my money for meliorating a subject that I consider to be my own, but which is afterward discovered to be the property of another; my loss in this case is <138> intimately connected with his gain, because in effect my money goes into his pocket.

The connection between the loss and gain may be more or less intimate: and its different degrees of intimacy ought to be carefully noted.[1] When this connection is found in the highest degree, there is scarce requisite any other circumstance to oblige one to apply his gain for making up another's loss: in its lower degrees no duty arises, unless the persons be otherwise strongly connected. Proceeding then to trace these degrees, the lowest I have occasion to mention, is where the loss and gain are connected by their relation to the same subject. For example, a man purchases at a low rate one of the preferable debts upon a bankrupt estate; and upon a sale of the estate draws more than the transacted sum: he gains while his fellow-creditors lose considerably. The next degree going upward, is where my gain is the occasion of another's loss. For example, a merchant foreseeing a scarcity, purchases all the corn he can find in the neighbourhood, with a view to make great profit: before he opens his granaries, I import a <139> large cargo from abroad, retailing it at a moderate price, under what my brother-merchant paid for his cargo; by which means he loses considerably. The third, pretty much upon a level with the former, is where another's loss is the occasion of my gain. For example, my ship loaded with corn proceeds, in company with another, to a port where there is a scarcity: the other ship being foundered in a storm, and the cargo lost, my cargo by that means draws a better price. The fourth connection is more intimate, the loss and the gain proceeding from the same cause. In the case last mentioned, suppose the weaker vessel, dashed against the

1. In the first edition (p. 21), he adds, "because it is reasonable to presume, what will be found true by induction, That a man's duty to apply his gain for repairing another's loss, depends greatly on the strength of this connection." The second edition (p. 96) includes a similar sentence.

other in a storm, is sunk: here the same cause by which the one proprietor loses, proves beneficial to the other. The last connection I shall mention, and the completest, is where that which is lost by the one is gained by the other; or, in other words, where the money of which the one is deprived benefits the other. This is the case first mentioned, of money laid out by a *bona fide possessor,* in meliorating a subject that is afterward claimed by the proprietor. <140> The money that the former loses is gained by the latter.

A famous maxim of the Roman law, *Nemo debet locupletari aliena jactura,*[2] is applicable to this article: and in order to ascertain, if it can be done, what are the connections that make it the duty of one man to part with his gain for repairing another's loss, I shall begin with a commentary upon that maxim. I observe first, That it is expressed abstractly, as holding true in general, without distinction of persons; and therefore that the duty it establishes must be founded upon a real connection, independent altogether of personal connections: which leads us to examine what that real connection must be. *Nemo debet locupletari aliena jactura,* or, No person ought to profit *by* another's loss, implies a connection between the loss and the gain: it implies that the gain arises *by* the loss, or *by means* of the loss. Taking therefore the maxim literally, it ought to take place where-ever the gain is occasioned by the loss, or perhaps occasions the loss; which certainly is not good law. In the second and third cases above mentioned, the same cause that destroys <141> the one merchant is profitable to the other: yet no man who in such circumstances makes profit, finds himself bound in conscience to make up the other's loss. It appears then, that this maxim, like most general maxims, is apt to mislead by being too comprehensive. Upon serious reflection, we find, that what a man acquires by his own industry, or by accident, however connected with the loss sustained by another, will not be taken from him to make up that loss, if there be no personal connection. The only real connection that of itself binds him, is where another's money is converted to his use. This circumstance, though without any intention to benefit him, will bind him in conscience to make up the other's loss as far as he himself is a gainer. Here the maxim, *Nemo debet locupletari aliena jactura,* taken in its most extensive sense, is appli-

---

2. "No one should be enriched at another's expense."

cable; and the single case, as far as I understand, where it is applicable. The most noted case of this kind is, where the possessor of a subject which he *bona fide* considers to be his own, bestows his money on reparations and meliorations,[3] intending nothing but his own benefit: the <142> proprietor claims the subject in a process, and prevails: he profits by the meliorations; and the money bestow'd on these meliorations is converted to his use. Every one must be sensible of a hardship that requires a remedy; and it must be the wish of every disinterested person, that the *bona fide possessor* be relieved from the hardship. That the common law affords no relief, will be evident at first sight: the labour and money of the *bona fide possessor* is sunk in the subject, and has no separate existence upon which to found a *rei vindicatio:*[4] the proprietor, in claiming the subject, does no more but exercise his own right; which cannot subject him personally to any demand. If then there be a remedy, it can have no other foundation but equity; and that there is a remedy in equity, will appear from the following considerations. Man being a fallible creature, society would be uncomfortable were individuals disposed in every case to take advantage of the mistakes and errors of others. But the author of our nature has more harmoniously adjusted its different branches to each other. To make it a law in our nature, never to take advantage of <143> error in any case, would be giving too much indulgence to indolence and remission of mind, tending to make us neglect the improvement of our rational faculties. On the other hand, to make it lawful to take advantage of error in every case, would be too rigorous, considering how difficult it is for a man to be always upon his guard. The author of our nature has happily moulded it so as to avoid these extremes. No man is conscious of wrong when, to save himself from loss, he takes advantage of an error committed by another: if there must be a loss, the moral sense dictates, that it ought to rest upon the person who has committed an error, however innocently, rather than upon him who has been careful to avoid all error. But *in lucro captando,*[5] the moral sense teaches a different lesson: every one is conscious of wrong, when an error is laid hold of to make gain by it. The consciousness of injustice, when such advantage

3. See glossary, "meliorations."
4. An action by the owner of a thing to recover it.
5. "In seeking a profit."

is taken, is indeed inferior in degree, but the same in kind with the injustice of robbing an innocent person of his goods or of his reputation. This doctrine is supported by utility as well as by ju- <144> stice. Industry ought to be encouraged; and chance as much as possible ought to be excluded from all dealings, in order that individuals may promise to themselves the fruits of their own industry. This affords a fresh instance of that beautiful harmony which subsists between the internal and external constitution of man. A regular chain of causes and effects, leaving little or nothing to accident, is advantageous externally by promoting industry, and internally by the delight it affords the human mind. No scene is more disgustful than that of things depending on chance, without order or connection. When a court of equity therefore preserves to every man, as much as possible, the fruits of his own industry; such proceeding, by rectifying the disorders of chance, is authorised by utility as well as by justice. And hence it is a principle of morality, founded both on the nature of man and on the interests of society, That we ought not to make gain by another's error.

This principle is clearly applicable to the case above mentioned. The titles of land-property being intricate, and often uncertain, instances are frequent, where a <145> man in possession of land, the property of another, is led by unavoidable error to consider it as belonging to himself: his money is bestowed without hesitation on repairing and meliorating the subject. Equity will not permit the owner to profit by such a mistake, and in effect to pocket the money of the innocent possessor: he will be compelled by a court of equity to make up the loss, as far as he is *locupletior.* Thus the possessor of a tenement, having, on the faith and belief of its being his own, made considerable meliorations, was found intitled to claim from the proprietor the expence of such meliorations as were profitable to him by raising the rent of his tenement.* In all cases of this kind, what is lost to the one accrues to the other. The maxim then must be understood in this limited sense; for no connection between the loss and gain inferior in degree to this, will, independent of personal connections, be a sufficient foundation for a claim in equity against the per- <146> son who gains, to make up the other's loss.

* Stair, January 18. 1676, Binning contra Brotherstanes [M 13401].

But supposing the subject meliorated to have perished before bringing the action, is the proprietor notwithstanding liable? I answer, That where equity makes benevolence a duty to those who benefit us without intending it, it is not sufficient that there has been gain one time or other: it is implied in the nature of the claim, that there must be gain at the time of the demand; for if there be no gain at present, there is no subject out of which the loss can be made up.

It will not be thought an unnecessary digression to observe a peculiarity in the Roman law with respect to this matter. As that law stood originally, the *bona fide possessor* had no claim for his expences. This did not proceed from ignorance of equity, but from want of a *formula*[6] to authorise the action; for at first when brieves or forms of action were invented,* this claim was not thought of. But an exception[7] was soon thought of to intitle the *bona fide possessor* to retain the subject, till he got payment of his expence; and this ex- <147> ception the judges could have no difficulty to sustain, because exceptions were not subjected to any *formula.* The inconvenient restraint of these *formulae* was in time broken through, and *actiones in factum*[8] or *upon the case,*[9] were introduced, which are not confined to any *formula.* After this innovation, the same equity that gave an exception, produced also an *actio in factum;* and the *bona fide possessor* was made secure as to his expences in all cases, namely, by an exception while he remained in possession, and by an action if he happened to lose the possession.

Another case, differing nothing from the former in effect, though considerably in its circumstances, is where, upon a fictitious mandate, one purchases my goods, or borrows my money, for the use of another. That other is not liable *ex mandato* because he gave no mandate: but if I can

6. *Formulae:* model pleas developed in Rome by the praetor, authorizing the judge to find for the plaintiff if certain facts were proved.

* See [Kames,] Historical Law tracts [1758, vol. 2], tract 8 ["History of Brieves," pp. 2–20].

7. A form of defense to an action. In Roman law, an *exceptio* was a plea by the defendant alleging facts or legal provisions to deny the claim.

8. *Actio in factum:* "an action in regard to the fact"; that is, an action in Roman law granted by the praetor when no standard action was available.

9. See glossary, "action on the case."

prove that the money or goods were actually applied for his use, equity affords me a claim against him, as far as he is a gainer. Thus, in an action for payment of merchant-goods purchased in name of the defendant, and applied to his use, the defendant insisted, that he gave no com- <148> mission; and that if his name was used without his authority, he could not be liable. "It was decreed, That the goods being applied to the defendant's use, he was liable, unless he could prove that he paid the price to the person who bespoke the goods."* This case, like the former, rests entirely upon the real connection between the loss and gain, independent of which there was no connection between the parties. And in it, perhaps more clearly than in the former, every one must be sensible, that the man who reaps the benefit is in duty bound to make up the other's loss. Hence the action *de in rem verso*,[10] the name of which we borrowed from the Romans. In a case precisely similar, the court inclined to sustain it relevant to assoilzie the defendant, that the goods were gifted to him by the person who purchased them in his name. But as donation is not presumed, he was found liable, because he could not bring evidence of the alleged donation.† Upon the supposition of a gift, it could not well <149> be specified that the defendant was *locupletior:* a man will spend liberally what he considers as a present, though he would not lay out his money upon the purchase.

Having endeavoured to ascertain, with all possible accuracy, that degree of connection between the loss and gain, which is requisite to afford a relief in equity by obliging the person who gains to make up the other's loss, I proceed to ascertain the precise meaning of loss and gain as understood in the maxim. And the first doubt that occurs is, Whether the term *locupletior* comprehends every real benefit, prevention of loss as well as a positive increase of fortune; or whether it be confined to the latter. I explain myself by examples. When a *bona fide possessor* rears a new edifice upon another man's land, this is a positive accession to the subject, which makes the proprietor *locupletior* in the strictest sense of the word. But it may hap-

---

* Stair, February 20. 1669, Bruce contra Stanhope [M 13403].

10. An action (*actio*) for money applied to the defendant's advantage (*in rem versum:* turned to his account); to reverse an unjust enrichment.

† July 1726, Hawthorn contra Urquhart [M 13407, from Kames, *Dictionary*, vol. 2, p. 317].

pen that the money laid out by the *bona fide possessor* is directed to prevent
loss; as where he fortifies the bank of a river against its incroachments,
where he supports a tottering edifice, or where he transacts[11] a claim that
threatened to carry off <150> the property. Is the maxim applicable to cases
of this kind, where loss is only prevented, without any positive increase
of wealth or fortune? When a work is done that prevents loss, the subject
is thereby improved and made of greater value. A bulwark that prevents
the encroachments of a river, makes the land sell at a higher price; and a
real accession, such as a house built, or land enclosed, will not do more.
The only difference is, that a positive accession makes a man richer than
he formerly was; a work done to prevent loss makes him only richer than
he would have been had the work been left undone. This difference is too
slight to have any effect in equity. The proprietor gains by both equally;
and in both cases equally he will feel himself bound in justice to make up
the loss out of his gain. A *bona fide possessor* who claims money laid out
by him to support a tottering edifice, is *certans de damno evitando*[12] as well
as where he claims money laid out upon meliorations; and the proprietor
claiming the subject, is *certans de lucro captando*[13] in the one case as well
as in the other. Here equity supports the claim of him who is <151> *certans
de damno evitando;* for, as observed above, there is in human nature a perception of wrong, where a man avails himself of an error to make profit at
another's expence. Nor does the principle of utility make any distinction.
It is a great object in society, to rectify the disorders of chance, and to
preserve to every man, as much as possible, the fruits of his own industry;
which is the same whether it has been applied to prevent loss, or to make
a real accession to a man's fortune. In the cases accordingly that have occurred, I find no distinction made; and in those which follow, there was no
benefit but what arose from preventing loss. A ship being ransomed from
a privateer, every person benefited must contribute a proportion of the
ransom.* A written testament being voided for informality, the executor
nominate was allowed the expence of confirming the testament, because

11. *Transaction:* an agreement between parties to settle a disputed claim.
12. "Striving to avoid a loss."
13. "Striving to make a profit"; attempting to obtain an advantage.
* Fountainhall, June 29. 1710, Ritchie contra Lord Salton [M 13421].

to the executrix *qua* next in kin, pursuer of the reduction, it was profitable by saving her the expence of a confirmation.* <152>

From what is said, it may possibly be thought, that the foregoing rule of equity is applicable where-ever it can be subsumed, that the loss sustained by one proves beneficial to another. But this will be found a rash thought, when it is considered, that one may be benefited without being in any proper sense *locupletior* or a gainer upon the whole. I give an example. A man erecting a large tenement in a borough, becomes bankrupt by overstretching his credit. This new tenement, being the chief part of his substance, is adjudged by his creditors for sums beyond the value. In the mean time, the tradesmen and the furnishers of materials for the building, trusting to a claim in equity, forbear to adjudge. They are losers to the extent of their work and furnishings; and the adjudgers are in one sense *locupletiores,* as by means of the tenement they will draw perhaps ten shillings in the pound instead of five. Are the adjudgers then, in terms of the maxim, bound to yield this profit, in order to pay the workmen and furnishers? By no means. For here the benefit is partial only, and produceth not upon the whole <153> actual profit: on the contrary, the adjudgers, even after this benefit, are equally with their competitors *certantes de damno evitando.* The court of session accordingly refused to sustain the claim of the tradesmen and furnishers.† Hence appears a remarkable difference between property and obligation. Money laid out upon a subject by the *bona fide possessor,* whether for melioration or to preserve it from damage, makes the proprietor *locupletior,* and a *captator lucri ex aliena jactura.*[14] But though a creditor be benefited by another's loss, so as by that means to draw a greater proportion of his debt; he is not however a gainer upon the whole, but is still *certans de damno evitando.* And when the parties are thus *in pari casu*[15] a court of equity cannot interpose, but must leave them to the common law.

I add another limitation, which is not peculiar to the maxim under

---

* Fountainhall, Feb. 26. 1712, Moncrieff contra Monypenny [M 13410].

† Dec. 4. 1735, Burns contra creditors of Maclellan [M 13402, from Kames, *Dictionary,* vol. 2, p. 316].

14. "One who strives to obtain a profit from another's loss."

15. "In a similar condition."

consideration, but arises from the very constitution of a court of equity. It is not sufficient that there be gain, even in the strictest sense: it is necessary that the gain be clear and certain; <154> for otherwise a court of equity must not undertake to make up the loss out of that gain. The principle of utility, in order to prevent arbitrary proceedings, prohibits a court of equity to take under consideration a conjectural loss or a conjectural gain; because such loss or gain can never be brought under a general rule. I give the following illustrations. Two heritors having each of them a salmon-fishing in the same part of a river, are in use to exercise their rights alternately. One is interrupted for some time by a suit at the instance of a third party: the other by this means has more capture than usual, though he varies not his mode of fishing. What the one loses by the interruption, is probably gained by the other, at least in some measure. But as what is here transferred from the one to the other cannot be ascertained with any degree of certainty, a court of equity must not interpose. Again, a tenant upon the faith of a long lease, lays out considerable sums upon improving his land, and reaps the benefit a few years. But the landlord, who holds the land by a military tenure, dies suddenly in the flower of his age, <155> leaving an infant heir: the land by this means comes into the superior's hand, and the lease is superseded during the ward. Here a great part of the extraordinary meliorations which the lessee intended for his own benefit, are converted to the use of the superior. Yet equity cannot interpose, because no general rule can be laid down for ascertaining the gain made by the superior. The following case confirms this doctrine. In an action at a tercer's[16] instance for a third of the rents levied by the fiar, the court refused to sustain a deduction claimed by the defendant, namely, a third of the factor-fee[17] paid by him for levying the rents; though it was urged, that the pursuer could not have levied her third at less expence.* The loss here was not ascertained, and was scarce capable of being ascertained; for no one could say what less the factor would have accepted for levying two-thirds of the rent than for levying the whole. Neither was the profit capable to

16. The holder of a terce, a liferent given to a widow of one-third the heritage of which her husband died infeft.
17. A fee paid to a factor (agent).
* Durie, March 27. 1634, Lady Dunfermline contra her son [M 13408].

be ascertained: the lady herself might have levied her share, or have got a friend to serve her *gratis.* <156>

I shall close with one further limitation, which regards not only the present subject, but every claim that can be founded on equity. Courts of equity are introduced in every country to enforce natural justice, and by no means to encourage any wrong. Whence it follows, that no man is intitled to the aid of a court of equity, where he suffers by his own fault. For this reason the proprietor is not made liable for the expence of profitable meliorations, but where the meliorations were made *bona fide* by a person intending his own profit, and not suspecting any hazard. It is laid down however in the Roman law, That the necessary expence laid out in upholding the subject, may be claimed by the *mala fide possessor.** If such reparations be made while the proprietor is ignorant of his right, and the ruin of the edifice be thereby prevented, there possibly may be a foundation in utility for the claim: but I deny there can be any foundation in justice. And therefore, if a tenant, after being ejected by legal execution, shall obstinately persist to plough and <157> sow, he ought to have no claim for his seed nor his labour. The claim in these circumstances hath no foundation either in justice or utility: yet the claim was sustained.†

But there are many personal connections joined with a much slighter real connection than that above mentioned, which intitle a man to have his loss made up out of my gain. Of which take the following examples.

There are three creditors connected by their relation to the same debtor who is a bankrupt, and by their relation to two land-estates *A* and *B* belonging to the debtor, the first creditor being preferably secured on both estates, one of the secondary creditors being secured upon *A,* the other upon *B.* The catholic creditor purchases one of the secondary debts under its value, by which he is a gainer; for by his preferable debt he cuts out the other secondary creditor, and by that means draws the whole price of the two subjects. The question is, Whether equity will suffer him to retain his gain against the other <158> secondary creditor, who is thus cut out of his security. It cannot indeed be specified here, as in the case of the *bonae fidei possessor rei*

---

* l. 5, C. De rei vindic[atione (On real actions for the recovery of property), C 3.32.5].
† Stair, February 22. 1671, Gordon contra Macculloch [M 13400].

alienae,[18] that money given out by the one is converted to the use of the other: but then the loss and gain are necessarily connected by having a common cause, namely, the purchase made by the catholic creditor. This connection between loss and gain, joined with the personal connections above mentioned, make it the duty of the catholic creditor to communicate his profit, in order to make up the loss that the other creditor sustains. And one with confidence may deliver this opinion, when the following circumstance is added, that the loss was occasioned by the catholic creditor, in making a purchase that he was sensible would ruin his fellow-creditor.

The next case in order is of two assignees to the same bond, ignorant of each other. The cedent or assignor contrives to draw the purchase-money from both, and walks off in a state of bankruptcy. The latter assignment, being first intimated,[19] will be preferred. But to what extent? Will it be preferred for the whole <159> sum in the bond, or only for the price paid for it? The circumstances here favour the postponed assignee, though they have not the same weight with those in the former: the material difference is, that the assignee preferred made his purchase without knowing of his competitor, and consequently without any thought of distressing him. The personal connection however, joined with the necessary connection between the loss and gain, appears sufficient to deprive the last assignee of his gain, in order to make up the loss sustained by the first. The case would be more doubtful, had the first assignment been first completed; because it may appear hard, that the intervention of a second purchaser should deprive the first of a profitable bargain. I leave this point to be ripened by time and mature deliberation. The progress of equity is slow, though constant, toward the more delicate articles of natural justice. If there appear any difficulty about extending equity to this case, the difficulty probably will vanish in course of time.

One thing is certain, that in the English court of chancery there would be no <160> hesitation to apply equity to this case. That court extends its power a great way farther; farther indeed than seems just. A stranger, for

18. "The bona fide possessor of another person's things."

19. *Intimation:* formal notice given (for example, via a notarial instrument) by an assignee to the debtor of the assignment, necessary for the complete transfer of the right assigned.

example, who purchases a prior incumbrance, can draw no more from the other incumbrancers than the sum he really paid:* and to justify this extraordinary opinion, it is said, "That the taking away one man's gain to make up another's loss, is making them both equal." This argument, if it prove any thing, proves too much, being applicable to any two persons indifferently who have not the smallest connection, supposing only the one to have made a profitable, the other a losing bargain. There ought to be some connection to found such a demand: the persons ought to be connected by a common concern; and the loss and gain ought to be connected, so at least as that the one be occasioned by the other. The first connection only is found in this case: a stranger who purchases a prior incumbrance is indeed, by a common subject, connected with the other incumbrancers: but this purchase does not harm the other incumbrancers; for when the <161> purchaser claims the debt in its utmost extent, it is no more than what his author[20] could do. The rule of chancery, in this view, appears a little whimsical: it deprives me of a lucrative bargain, the fruit of my own industry, to bestow it, not upon any person who is hurt by the bargain, but upon those who are in no worse condition than before the bargain was made. Neither am I clear, that this rule can be supported upon a principle of utility: for though it is preventive of hard and unequal bargains; yet as no prudent man will purchase an incumbrance on such a condition, it is in effect a prohibition of such purchases, which would prove a great inconveniency to many whose funds are locked up by the bankruptcy of their debtors.

That an heir acquiring an incumbrance should be allowed no more but what he really paid, or, which comes to the same, that he should be bound to communicate eases,[21] is a proposition more agreeable to the principles of equity. This is the law of England,† and it is the law of Scot- <162> land with regard to heirs who take the benefit of inventory.[22] But the case of an

---

* 1. Vernon 476 [*Williams* v. *Springfeild* (1687), reprinted in *The English Reports,* vol. 23, p. 602].

20. *Author:* the person from whom the property is purchased, in contrast to *ancestor,* from whom property is inherited.

21. *Ease:* a reduction or remission of an amount of service due.

† 1 Salkeld 155 [*Anonymous* (1708), reprinted in *The English Reports,* vol. 91, p. 143].

22. See glossary, "benefit of inventory."

heir is very different from that of a stranger. He hath in his hand the fund for payment of the creditors, which he ought faithfully to account for; and therefore he is not permitted to state any article for exhausting that fund beyond what he hath actually expended: if a creditor accept less than his proportion, the fund for the other creditors is so much the larger.

A cautioner upon making payment obtaining an ease, must communicate the same to the principal debtor, upon a plain ground in common law, that being secure of his relief from the principal debtor, he has no claim but to be kept *indemnis*.[23] But supposing the principal debtor bankrupt, I discover no ground other than paction, that can bind one cautioner to communicate eases to another: and yet it is the prevailing, I may say the established, opinion, That a cautioner who obtains an ease must communicate the benefit to his co-cautioner. I am aware of the reason commonly assigned, That cautioners for the same debt are to be considered as in a society, obliged to bear the loss equally. <163> But this, I doubt, is arguing in a circle: they resemble a society, because the loss must be equal; and the loss must be equal, because they resemble a society. We must therefore go more accurately to work. In the first place, let us examine whether an obligation for mutual relief ought to be implied. This implication, at best doubtful, supposes the cautioners to have subscribed in a body. And therefore, to leave no room for an implied obligation, we need but suppose, that two persons, ignorant of each other, become cautioners at different times, and in different deeds. It appears, then, that common law affords not an obligation for mutual relief. The matter is still more clear with regard to equity: for the connection between two cautioners can never be so intimate, as to oblige the one who is not a gainer to make up the other's loss; which is the case of the cautioner who obtains an ease, supposing that ease to be less than that proportion of the debt which he stands bound to pay. Upon the whole, my notion is, that if a cautioner, upon account of objections against the debt, or upon account of any circumstance that regards the principal <164> debtor, obtain an ease, he is bound to communicate that ease to his fellow-cautioner, upon the following rational principle, That both cautioners ought equally to partake of an ease, the motive to which

23. "Free from loss or damage."

respects them equally. This appears to be the *ratio decidendi*[24] in the case reported by Stair, July 27. 1672, Brodie contra Keith.[25] But if upon prompt payment by one cautioner after the failure of others, or upon any consideration personal to the cautioner, an ease be given; equity, I think, obliges not the cautioner to communicate the benefit to his fellow-cautioners. And this was decreed, Stair, July 8. 1664, Nisbet contra Leslie.[26]

There is one circumstance that, without much connection real or personal, extends to many cases the maxim, *Nemo debet locupletari aliena jactura;* and that is fraud, deceit, or any sort of wrong. If by means of a third person's fraud one gains and another loses, a court of equity will interpose to make up the loss out of the gain. And this resolves into a general rule, "That no man, however innocent, ought to take advantage of a tortious act by which <165> another is hurt." Take the following example. A second disposition of land, though gratuitous, with the first infeftment, is preferred at common law before the first disposition without infeftment, though for a valuable consideration. But as the gratuitous disponee is thus benefited by a moral wrong done by his author, he ought not, however innocent, to take advantage of that moral wrong to hurt the first disponee. This circumstance makes the rule applicable, *Non debet locupletari aliena jactura;* and therefore a court of equity will compel him, either to give up his right to the land, or to repair the loss the first disponee has suffered by being deprived of his purchase.

The following cases rest upon the same principle. A disposition by a merchant of his whole estate to his infant-son, without a reserved life-rent or power to burden, was deemed fraudulent, in order to cheat his correspondents, foreign merchants, who had traded with him before the alienation, and continued their dealings with him upon the belief that he was still proprietor; and their claims, though posterior <166> to the disposition, were admitted to affect the estate.*

24. "The reason for deciding"; that is, the principle or rule on which the decision is grounded.

25. M 3393.

26. M 3392.

* Stair, July 2. 1673, Street contra Mason [(M 4914). For Kames's discussion of this case in the third edition, where it is placed in book 3, chap. 5, on equity's powers in relation to bankrupts, see Appendix, p. 515, Extract (1st: 236–37).]

Where a tutor acting to the best of his skill for the good of his pupil, happens, in the ordinary course of administration, to convert a moveable debt into one that is heritable, or an heritable debt into one that is moveable; such an act, after the pupil's death, will have its effect with respect to the pupil's succession, by preferring his heir or executor, as if the act had been done by a proprietor of full age. But where the tutor acts in this manner unnecessarily, with the sole intention to prefer the heir or the executor, this is a tortious act, contrary to the duty he owes his pupil, which will affect the heir or executor, though they had no accession to the wrong. In common law the succession will take place according to the tutor's act, whether done with a right or a wrong intention; but this will be corrected in equity, upon the principle, That no person ought to take advantage of a tortious act that harms another.

A donation *inter virum et uxorem*[27] is re- <167> vocable; but not a donation to the husband or wife's children, or to any other relation. A wife makes a donation of her land-estate to her husband; who afterward, in order to bar revocation, gives up the disposition granted to him, and instead of it takes a disposition to his eldest son. Will this disposition be revocable? Where a wife out of affection to her husband's eldest son makes a deed in his favour, it is not revocable, because it is not a *donatio inter virum et uxorem.* But in this case it is clear, that the donation was intended for the husband, and that the sole purpose of the disposition to the son was to bar revocation; which was an unlawful contrivance to elude the law. It would be wrong therefore in the son, however innocent, to take advantage of his father's tortious act, calculated to deprive the woman of her privilege; and therefore the disposition to him will be revocable in equity, as that to the father was at common law. <168>

ARTICLE II. *Connections that intitle a man who is not a loser, to partake of my gain.*

For the sake of perspicuity, this article shall be divided into two branches: 1st, Where the gain is the operation of the man who claims to partake of it. 2d, Where he has not contributed to the gain.

27. Gift "between man and wife."

I introduce the first branch with a case which will be a key to the several matters that come under it. Two heirs-portioners, or in general two proprietors of a land-estate *pro indiviso*,[1] get for a farm a rent of eighty pounds yearly; and an offer of ten pounds additional rent if they will drain a lake in it. John is willing; but James refuses, judging it impracticable, or at least too expensive. John proceeds at his own risk; and for the sum of £100 drains the lake. He cannot specify any loss by this undertaking; because the sum he laid out is fully compensated by the five pound additional rent accruing to him: and therefore the maxim, *Nemo debet locupletari aliena jactura,* is not applicable to <169> his case. But James is a profiter, not only by John's advancing the money, but at his risk; for if the undertaking had proved abortive, John would have lost both his labour and money. Is it just that James should be permitted to lay hold of an additional rent of £5, without defraying any part of the expence? He cannot justify this to his own conscience, nor to the world. The moral sense dictates, that where expence is laid out in improving or repairing a common subject, no one ought to take the benefit, without refunding a part of the expence in proportion to the benefit received.

This leads to a general rule, That expence laid out upon a common subject, ought to be a burden upon the benefit procured. And this rule will hold even against the dissent of any of the parties concerned; for they cannot in conscience take the benefit without the burden. A dissent cannot have any effect in equity, but only to free the person dissenting from any risk.

The following cases come clearly under the same general rule. One of three joint proprietors of a mill, having raised a decla- <170> rator of thirlage,[2] and, notwithstanding a disclamation by the others, having insisted in the process till he obtained a decree; the others who reaped the profit equally with him, were made liable for their share of the expence.* And one of many co-creditors having obtained a judgment against the debtor's relict,[3]

---

1. "Undivided."
2. A servitude enjoyed by mill owners: possessors of lands subject to the servitude were bound to grind their grain at a particular mill.
* Stair, January 6. 1676, Forbes contra Ross [M 13414].
3. Widow.

finding her liable to pay her husband's debts; the other creditors who shared
the benefit were decreed to contribute to the expence.* For the same reason, where a tenement destroyed by fire was rebuilt by a liferenter, the
proprietor, after the liferenter's death, was made liable for the expence of
rebuilding, as far as he was *lucratus*[4] thereby.[†] And if rebuilt by the proprietor, the liferenter will be liable for the interest of the sum expended as far
as he is *lucratus*.[‡] Action was sustained at the instance of a wadsetter for
declaring, that his intended reparation of a harbour in the wadset-lands,
would be profitable to the re- <171> verser; and that the reverser,[5] upon
redemption, should be bound to repay the expence thereof.[§] Upon the
same principle, if a lessee erect any buildings by which the proprietor is
evidently *lucratus* at the end of the lease, there is a claim in equity for the
expence of the meliorations. But reparations, though extensive, will scarce
be allowed where the lessee is bound to uphold the houses; because a lessee
who bestows such reparation without his landlord's consent, is understood
to lay out his money in order to fulfil his obligation, without any prospect
of retribution.[||] The present minister was not found liable for the meliora-
tions of the glebe[6] made by his predecessor.[**] But what if meliorations be
made, inclosing, draining, stoning, &c. which are clearly profitable to all
future possessors? If the expence of these, in proportion to the benefit, be
not in some way refunded, glebes will rest in their original state forever.
I do not say, <172> that the minister immediately succeeding ought to be
liable for the whole of this expence: for as the benefit is supposed to be
perpetual, the burden ought to be equally so: which suggests the following
opinion, That the sum-total of the expence ought to be converted into a

* Bruce, July 30. 1715, Creditors of Calderwood contra Borthwick [M 1197].
4. "A gainer."
† Forbes, Feb. 20. 1706, Halliday contra Garden [M 13419].
‡ Stair, Jan. 24. 1672, Haket contra Watt [M 13412].
5. The proprietor of land who has granted a wadset of the land, and who has the
right to recover the land (or the right of *reversion*), on repayment of the money advanced to him.
§ Durie, July 22. 1626, Morison contra Earl of Lothian [M 13402].
|| Gilmour, Feb. 1664, Hodge contra Brown [M 2651].
6. Lands belonging to the church.
** Nicolson, (Kirkmen), June 14. 1623, Dunbar contra Hay [M 13399, in Kames,
Dictionary, vol. 2, p. 316].

perpetual annuity, to be paid by the ministers of this parish; for the only equitable method is, to make each contribute in proportion to the benefit he receives.

The following case belongs undoubtedly to the maxim of equity under consideration; and yet was judged by common law, neglecting the equitable remedy. In a shipwreck, part of the cargo being saved, was delivered to the owners for payment of the salvage. The proprietor of the ship claiming the freight of the goods saved *pro rata itineris*,[7] the freighters admitted the claim; but insisted, that as the salvage was beneficial to him on account of his freight, as well as to them on account of their goods, he ought to contribute a share. His answer was sustained to free him from any part, That the expence was wholly laid out on recovering the freighter's goods; and therefore that they <173> only ought to be liable.* The answer here sustained resolves into the following proposition, That he only is liable whose benefit is intended: which holds not in equity; for at that rate, the *bona fide possessor*, who in meliorating the subject intends his own benefit solely, has no claim against the proprietor. Here the freighters and the proprietor of the ship were connected by a common interest: the recovering the goods from shipwreck was beneficial to both; to the freighters, because it put them again in possession of their goods; and to the proprietor of the ship, because it gave him a claim for freight. The salvage accordingly was truly *in rem versum*[8] of both; and for that reason ought to be paid by both in proportion to the benefit received. This case may be considered in a different light that will scarce admit a dispute. Suppose that the owners of the cargo, in recovering their goods to the extent of £1000, have laid out £100 upon salvage: they have in effect saved or recovered but £900; and beyond that sum they cannot be liable for the freight: which in numbers <174> will bring out a greater sum than what results from the rule above mentioned.

It will not escape the reader, that equity is further extended in this

---

7. In proportion to the amount of the journey completed; that is, a claim to be paid freight charges for the proportion of the voyage that was actually completed.

* January 18. 1735, Lutwich contra Gray [M 13422, from Kames, *Dictionary*, vol. 2, p. 320].

8. To the enrichment ("turned to his account").

branch than in the former; and he will also discover a solid reason for the difference. With respect to matters contained in the former branch, the real connection is only, that what is lost by the one is gained by the other; as in the case of a *bona fide possessor rei alienae.*[9] But the real connection in the present branch is so far more intimate, that every acquisition must benefit all equally, and every loss burden all equally.

It appears, that a benefit accruing to another by my labour, occasionally only, not necessarily, will not intitle me to a claim where I am not a loser. To make the truth of this observation evident, a few examples will be sufficient. A drain made by me in my own ground for my own behoof, happens to discharge a quantity of water that stagnated in a superior field belonging to a neighbour. Justice does not intitle me to claim from this neighbour any share of the expence laid out upon the drain. The drain has answered my intention, and overpays the sum be- <175> stowed upon it: therefore my case comes not under the maxim, *Nemo debet locupletari aliena jactura.* Neither can I have any claim upon the rule, That expence laid out upon a common subject ought to be a burden upon the benefit procured; for here there is no common subject, but only another person accidentally or occasionally benefited by an operation intended solely for my own benefit. And Providence has wisely ordered that such a claim should have no support from the moral sense; for as there can be no precise rule for estimating the benefit that each of us receives from the drain, the subjecting my neighbour to a claim would tend to create endless disputes between us. For the same reason, if my neighbour in making an inclosure take advantage of a march-fence built by me, he will not be liable to any part of the expence bestowed by me upon it; because the benefit, as in the former case, is occasional only or consequential.

From the nature of the claim handled in the present branch, it follows, that if the party against whom the claim is laid, <176> renounce the benefit, he cannot be subjected to the burden.

With respect to the branch now handled, the circumstance that the benefit accruing to another was occasioned by my means, is the connection that intitles me to a proportion of the sum I laid out in procuring that

9. "The possessor in good faith of another person's property."

benefit. But with respect to the second branch, which we are next to enter upon, it must require some personal relation extremely intimate to intitle me to partake of another man's profit when I have not contributed to it. And this will be made evident by the following examples.

When land is held ward, and the superior is under age, a gift of his ward is effectual against his vassal as well as against himself. But where the gift of ward was taken for behoof of the superior, it was the opinion of the court, that the vassal also had the benefit thereof upon paying his proportion of the composition.* Against this opinion it was urged, That a vassal must reckon upon being liable to all casualties arising from the nature of <177> his right; and that there is no reason for limiting the superior's claim, more than that of any other donatar.[10] But it was answered, That the relation between superior and vassal is such, as that the superior cannot *bona fide* take advantage against his vassal of a casualty occasioned by his own minority. The same rule was applied to a gift of marriage taken for behoof of the superior.† And it appearing that the superior had obtained this gift for alledged good services, without paying any composition, the benefit was communicated to the vassal without obliging him to pay any sum.‡

If a purchaser of land, discovering a defect in the progress,[11] secure himself by acquiring the preferable title; common law will not permit him to use this title as a ground of eviction, and to make his author, bound in absolute warrandice, liable for the value of the subject: for the purchaser is not intitled to the value unless the land be evicted from him; and therefore he cannot have any claim upon the <178> warrandice beyond the sum he paid for the title. This point is still more clear upon the principle of equity above mentioned. The connection is so intimate between a purchaser, and a vender bound in absolute warrandice, that every transaction made by either, with relation to the subject purchased, is deemed to be for behoof of both.

---

   * Dirleton, December 1. 1676, Grierson contra Ragg [M 7761, Grierson contra Laird of Lag. Composition to a superior: the payment made by a purchaser to obtain an entry into the land held of the superior.].
   10. One to whom a donation has been made, usually of escheated land.
   † Harcase (Ward and Marriage), Jan. 1686, Drummelzier contra Murray of Stanhope [M 7763].
   ‡ Ibid.
   11. *Progress of titles:* series of title deeds which constitute the holder's title to lands.

But now supposing several parcels of land to be comprehended under one title-deed. One parcel is sold with absolute warrandice; and the purchaser, discovering the title-deed to be imperfect, acquires from a third party a preferable title to the whole parcels. He is no doubt bound to communicate the benefit of this acquisition to the vender, as far as regards the parcel he purchased. But there is nothing at common law to bar him from evicting the other parcels from the vender. Whether a relief can be afforded in equity, is doubtful. The connection between the parties is pretty intimate: the purchaser is bound to communicate to the vender the benefit of his acquisition with respect to one parcel, and it is natural to extend the same benefit to the whole. One case <179> of this nature occurred in the court of session. A man having right to several subjects contained in an adjudication, sold one of them with absolute warrandice; and the purchaser having acquired a title preferable to his author's adjudication, claimed the subjects that were not disponed to him. The court restricted the claim to the sum paid for the preferable title.* It is not certain whether this decree was laid upon the principle above mentioned: for what moved some of the judges was the danger of permitting a purchaser acquainted with the title-deeds of his author, to take advantage of his knowledge by picking up preferable titles; and that this, as an unfair practice, ought to be prohibited.

ARTICLE III. *Connections that intitle one who is a loser to be indemnified by one who is not a gainer.*

Cases daily occur, where, by absence, infancy, inadvertence, or other circum- <180> stances, effects real or personal are left without proper management, and where ruin must ensue, if no person of benevolence be moved to interpose. Here friendship and good-will have a favourable opportunity to exert themselves, and to do much good, perhaps without any extraordinary labour or great expence; and when a proprietor is benefited by such acts of friendship or benevolence, justice and gratitude claim from him a retribution, to the extent at least of the benefit received. Here the

---

* February 21. 1741, James Drummond contra Brown and Miln [M 1705].

maxim, *Nemo debet locupletari aliena jactura,* is applicable in the strictest sense. Hence the *actio negotiorum gestorum* in the Roman law, which for the reason given is adopted by all civilized nations.

But what if this friendly man, after bestowing his money and labour with the utmost precaution, happen to be unsuccessful? What if, after laying out his money profitably upon repairing houses or purchasing cattle for my use, the benefit be lost to me by the casual destruction of the subject; would it be just that this friend, who had no view but for my interest, should run the risk? As there was <181> no contract between us, a claim will not be sustained at common law for the money expended. But equity pierces deeper, in order to fulfil the rules of justice. Service undertaken by a friend upon an urgent occasion, advances gratitude from a virtue to be a duty; and binds me to *recompense* my friend as far as he has laid out his own money in order to do me service. The moral sense teaches this lesson; and no person, however partial in his own concern, but must perceive this to be the duty of others. Utility also joins with justice to support this claim of recompence. Men ought to be invited to serve a friend in time of need: but instead of invitation, it would be a great discouragement, if the money advanced upon such service were upon their own risk, even when laid out with the greatest prudence.[a] This doc- <182> trine is laid down by Ulpian in clear terms: "Is autem, qui negotiorum gestorum agit, non solum si effectum habuit negotium quod gessit, actione ita utetur: sed sufficit, si

a. The Roman writers found this duty upon their *quasi*-contracts, of which *negotiorum gestio* is said to be one. And to understand this foundation, the nature of *quasi*-contracts must be explained. In human affairs certain circumstances and situations frequently happen that require a covenant, which nothing can prevent but want of opportunity. The present case affords a good illustration. A sudden call forces me abroad, without having time to regulate my affairs: disorder ensues, and a friend undertakes the management. Here nothing prevents a mandate but want of opportunity; and it is presumed that the mandate would not have been wanting, had I known the good intentions of my friend. Equity accordingly holds the mandate as granted, and gives the same actions to both that the common law gives in pursuance of a mandate. Though this serves to explain the Roman *quasi*-contracts, yet it seems a wide stretch in equity to give to a supposition the effects of a real contract; especially without any evidence that the person who undertakes the management would have been my choice. But I have endeavoured to make out in the text, that this claim for recompence has a solid foundation in justice, and in human nature, without necessity of recurring to the strained supposition of a contract.

utiliter gessit, etsi effectum non habuit negotium. Et ideo, si insulam fulsit, vel servum aegrum curavit, etiamsi insula exusta est, vel servus obiit,
aget negotiorum gestorum. Idque et Labeo probat."*,1

From what is said above it is evident, <183> that the man who undertakes my affairs, not to serve me, but to serve himself, is not intitled to
the *actio negotiorum gestorum.* Nor, even supposing me to be benefited by
his management, is he intitled to have his loss repaired out of my gain: for
wrong can never found any claim in equity. Yet Julianus, the most acute
of the Roman writers, answers the question in the affirmative. Treating
of one who *mala fide* meddles in my affairs, he gives the following opinion: "Ipse tamen, si circa res meas aliquid impenderit, non in id quod ei
abest, quia improbe ad negotia mea accessit, sed in quod ego locupletior factus sum, habet contra me actionem."† It appears at the same time,
from *l. ult, C. De negot. gest,* that this author was of a different opinion,
where the management of a man's affairs was continued against his will;
for there no action was given.2 This, in my apprehension, is establishing
a distinction without a difference: for no man can hope for my consent
to continue the management of my affairs, when he began that management, not to serve me, but with a view to his own interest. A <184> pro-

---

* l. 10. §1. [De] Negot[iis] gest[is. (Unauthorized Administration), D 3.5.9.1: Watson i: 101: "A person who brings an action for unauthorized administration will have
the use of that action not only if he was successful in the business he transacted, but it is
enough that he acted beneficially, even if what he did was unsuccessful. For this reason,
if he shored up a tenement or took care of a sick slave, even if the tenement was burned
down or the slave died, he will bring an action for unauthorized administration. Labeo
too supports this view"].

1. For Kames's significantly different approach to this subject in the first edition (pp.
34–35), where he rooted the obligation in quasi-contract, see Appendix, p. 487, [Extract 1st:
34–35].

† l. 6, §3. De negot[iis] gest[is (Unauthorized Administration), D 3.5.5.5: Watson i:
99: "However, on his side, if he has been put to some expense with regard to my affairs,
he has an action against me not for the amount of his loss, because he came to my business with dishonest intent, but for the amount I have been made richer"].

2. C 2.18.24: the text reads: "secundum iuliani sententiam nullam esse adversus eum
contrarium actionem, scilicet post denuntiationem, quam ei dominus transmiserit nec
concedens ei res eius attingere, licet res bene ab eo gestae sint" (according to the opinion of Julian, no counterclaim lies against him, that is, after notification sent by the
owner, not permitting the other to meddle with his property, even though things may
have been well managed by him).

hibition involved in the nature of the thing, is equivalent to an express prohibition.

The master of a ship, or any other, who ransoms the cargo from a privateer, is, according to the doctrine above laid down, intitled to claim from the owners of the cargo the sum laid out upon their account: they profit by the transaction, and they ought to indemnify him. But what if the cargo be afterward lost in a storm at sea, or by robbery at land? The owners are not now profiters by the ransom, and therefore they cannot be made liable upon the maxim, *Nemo debet locupletari aliena jactura.* They are however liable upon the principle here explained. The moment the transaction was finished they became debtors to the ransomer for the sum he laid out profitably upon their account. He did not undertake the risk of the cargo ransomed; and therefore the casual loss of the cargo cannot have the effect to deprive him of his claim.[3]

The *lex Rhodia de jactu,*[4] a celebrated maritime regulation, has prevailed among all civilized nations ancient and modern. Where in a storm weighty goods of little <185> value are thrown over board to disburden the ship, the owners of the remaining cargo must contribute to make up the loss. This case, as to the obligation of retribution, is of the same nature with that now mentioned, and depends on the same principle. The throwing overboard weighty goods of little value, is beneficial to the owners of the more precious goods, which by that means are preserved; and, according to the foregoing doctrine, these owners ought to contribute for making up the loss of the goods thrown into the sea, precisely as if there had been a formal covenant to that effect. But what if the whole cargo be afterward lost, by

---

3. In the first edition (p. 36), Kames put the principle in explicitly quasi-contractual terms abandoned by the second edition: "The ransomer is considered in the same light as if he had acted by commission; and the owners are in equity bound to him, not less strictly than if they had granted a commission. Where equity lays hold of one man's gain to make up another's loss, it is not sufficient that there have been gain sometime or other. It is implied in the very nature of the claim, that there must be gain at the time of the demand; for if there be no gain at present, there is no subject to be laid hold of by a court of equity for making up the loss. But when there is a ground in equity for making a man liable as if he had made an agreement, variation in circumstances can have no effect upon this claim more than upon a claim at common law founded upon an agreement actually made."

4. "The Rhodian law of jettison."

which eventually there is no benefit? If lost at sea in the same voyage, the owner of the goods thrown overboard has certainly no claim; because at any rate he would have lost his goods along with the rest of the cargo. But as soon as the cargo is laid upon land, the obligation for retribution is purified; the value of the goods abandoned to the sea, is or ought to be in the pocket of the owner; and the delay of payment will not afford a defence against him, <186> whatever becomes of the cargo after it is landed.[5]

It is a question of greater intricacy, Whether the goods saved from the sea ought to contribute according to their weight or according to their value. The latter rule is espoused in the Roman law: "Cum in eadem nave varia mercium genera complures mercatores coegissent, praetereaque multi vectores, servi, liberique in ea navigarent, tempestate gravi orta, necessario jactura facta erat. Quaesita deinde sunt haec: An omnes jacturam prestare oporteat, et si qui tales merces imposuissent, quibus navis non oneraretur, velut gemmas, margaritas? et quae portio praestanda est? Et an etiam pro liberis capitibus dari oporteat? Et qua actione ea res expediri possit? Placuit, omnes, quorum interfuisset jacturam fieri, conferre oportere, quia id tributum observatae res deberent: itaque dominum etiam navis pro portione obligatum esse. Jacturae summam pro rerum pretio distribui oportet. Corporum liberorum aestimationem nullam fieri posse."* This

---

5. In the first edition (p. 37), Kames used much more explicitly contractual language in explaining this example, writing, "And it will be remarked, that this circumstance would afford a good defence against a contribution, had there even been an actual agreement for throwing overboard the coarsest goods in place of the more valuable. But supposing the cargo to be lost at land, by robbers, for example, or fire, it appears to me that the claim stands good notwithstanding. For nothing but want of time prevented an explicit agreement for substituting coarse goods in place of the more valuable; and equity considers the case as if the agreement had been made. In this view the owners of the goods which were preserved from being thrown into the sea must contribute, whether at present they be profiters or not. The robbery or fire will afford them no defence; because it can never be made certain that the coarse goods, had they not been thrown overboard, would have suffered the same fate."

* l. 2, §2, De lege Rhodia de jactu [On the Rhodian Law of Jettison, D 14.2.2.2: Watson i: 419: "A vessel carrying diverse cargoes shipped by many merchants in addition to many passengers, both slave and free, was overtaken by a serious storm and had to be lightened. The questions put were whether the people whose goods, such as jewels and pearls, added no weight to the ship had to contribute like everyone else, in what proportion the loss should be split, whether anything was due in respect of the free pas-

rule is adopted <187> by all the commercial nations in Europe, without a single exception, as far as I can learn. And in pursuance of the rule, it is also adopted, That the owner of the ship ought to contribute, because the shipwreck being prevented by throwing overboard part of the cargo, his claim for freight is preserved to him. "Thus, if, in stress of weather, or in danger and just fear of an enemy, goods be thrown overboard, in order to save the ship and the rest of the cargo, that which is saved shall contribute to repair that which is lost, and the owners of the ship shall contribute in proportion."*

These authorities notwithstanding, to which great regard is justly due, it is not in my power to banish an impression, That the rule of contribution ought to be weight, not value. In every case where a man gives away his money or his goods for behoof of a plurality connected by a common interest, two things are evident: first, That his equitable claim for a recompence cannot exceed the loss he has sustained; <188> and next, That each individual is liable to make up the loss of that part which was given away on his account. When a ransom is paid to a privateer for the ship and cargo, a share of the money is understood to be advanced for each proprietor, in proportion to the value of his goods; and that share each must contribute, being laid out on his account, or for his service. That the same rule is applicable where a ship is saved by abandoning part of its cargo, is far from being clear. Let us proceed warily, step by step. The cargo in a violent storm is found too weighty for the ship, which must be disburdened of part, let us suppose the one half. In what manner is this to be done? The answer would be easy, were there leisure and opportunity for a regular operation: each person who has the weight of a pound aboard, ought to throw the half into the sea; for one person is not bound to abandon a greater proportion than another. This method, however, is seldom

---

sengers, and by what action the matter should be proceeded with. It was agreed that all those who had benefited by the jettison must make their contribution, including the owner of the ship for his part, because the contribution is levied on property preserved. The total amount of the loss should be apportioned in relation to the market value of the property, freemen not being valued"].

* Shower's Cases in parliament 19 [*Sheppard* v. *Wright* (1698) in Sir Bartholomew Shower, *Cases in Parliament Resolved and Adjudged, upon petitions and writs of error* (London: A. & J. Churchill, 1698), pp. 18, 19; reprinted in *The English Reports,* vol. I, p. 13].

or never practicable; because in a hurry the goods at hand must be heaved over: and were it practicable, it would not be for the common interest to abandon goods of little <189> weight and great value, along with goods of great weight and little value. Hence it comes to be the common interest, and, without asking questions, the common practice, to abandon goods the value of which bears no proportion to their weight. This, as being done for the common interest, intitles the proprietors of these goods to a recompence from those for whose service the goods were abandoned. Now the service done to each proprietor is, instead of his valuable goods, to have others thrown overboard of a meaner quality; and for such service all the recompence that can be justly claimed is the value of the goods thrown overboard. Let us suppose with respect to any owner in particular, that regularly he was bound to throw overboard twenty ounces of his goods: all that he is bound to contribute, is the value of twenty ounces of the goods that in place of his own were actually thrown overboard. In a word, this short-hand way of throwing into the sea the least valuable goods, appears to me in the same light, as if the several owners of the more valuable part of the cargo, had each of them purchased a quantity of the mean <190> goods to be thrown into the sea instead of their own.

I must observe at the same time, that the doctrine of the Roman law appears very uncouth in some of its consequences. Jewels, and I may add bank-bills, are made to contribute to make up the loss, though they contribute not in any degree to the distress; nor is a single ounce thrown overboard upon their account: nay, the ship itself is made to contribute, though the *jactura*[6] is made necessary, not by the weight of the ship, but by that of the cargo. On the other hand, passengers are exempted altogether from contributing, for a very whimsical reason, That the value of a free man cannot be estimated in money: and yet passengers frequently make a great part of the load. If they contribute to the necessity of disburdening the ship, for what good reason ought they to be exempted from contributing to make up the loss of the goods thrown into the sea upon their account?

Under this article comes a case that appears to be *in apicibus juris*.[7] A

6. "Jettison."
7. "Among the subtleties of the law."

bond extinguished by payment is assigned for a valuable consideration, and the assignee, <191> ignorant of the payment, obtains payment a second time from the debtor's heir. After several years the error is discovered, but the cedent by this time has become bankrupt. The heir is at common law entitled to demand from the assignee the sum he paid; as twice payment can have no support in law. The assignee paying this sum is barred by the insolvency of the cedent from any relief against him. What does equity rule in this intricate case, where there is a real connection between the parties by their concern in the same subject? A strong circumstance for the assignee is, that the payment he received from the heir *bona fide,* was to him invincible evidence, that he could have no claim against the cedent. He was led into that mistake by the heir's remissness or rather rashness in paying without examining his father's writings. They are equally *certantes de damno vitando;* and yet the heir's claim at common law must be sustained, if there be nothing in equity to balance it. The balance in equity is, that the loss ought to rest on the heir, by whose remissness it was occasioned, and not on the assignee, who had it not in his power <192> to prevent it. But as the assignee's loss is only the price he paid to the cedent, his equitable defence against the heir can go no further. This principle of equity is acknowledged by the court of session, and has been frequently applied. Thus an heir having ignorantly paid a debt to an assignee, and several years after having discovered that his ancestor had paid the debt to the cedent, he insisted in a *condictio indebiti.*[8] The defendant was assoilzied, because the cedent had become insolvent after the erroneous payment.* In this case it seems to have been overlooked, that the assignee was not intitled to withhold from the heir more than what he himself had paid to the cedent. So far he was *certans de damno vitando:* to demand more was *captare lucrum ex aliena jactura.*[9] A creditor, after receiving a partial payment, assigned the whole sum for security of a debt due by him to the assignee; who having got payment of the whole sum from the debtor, ignorant of the partial payment, was on discovery of the fact

8. An action to recover money paid by mistake, which was not due (*indebitus*).

* 24th July 1723, Duke of Argyle contra Representatives of Lord Halcraig [M 2929, from Kames, *Remarkable Decisions* i: 78, No. 39].

9. "To seek to make a gain by another's loss."

sued for restitution *condictione in-* <193> *debiti.* His defence was sustained, That he was not bound to restore what he received in payment of a just debt.* This judgement is founded on a mistake in fact. The debt due to the assignee by the cedent was a just debt; but the sum paid by the debtor to the assignee was not in payment of that debt, but of the debt due by him to the cedent, which was not wholly just, as part had been formerly paid. The debtor therefore was well intitled to demand the overplus from the assignee, because a second payment can have no support from law. But probably the cedent had become insolvent after the erroneous payment, which brings this case under the rule of equity handled above. <194>

CHAPTER IV

Powers of a court of equity to remedy what is imperfect
in common law with respect to deeds and covenants.

We have seen above, that, abstracting from positive engagements, the affording relief to a fellow-creature in distress, is the only case that exalts our benevolence to be an indispensable duty. A man however is singly the most helpless of all animals; and unless he could rely upon assistance from others, he would in vain attempt any work that requires more than two hands. To secure aid and assistance in time of need, the moral sense makes the performance of promises and covenants a duty; and to these accordingly may justly be attributed, the progress at least, if not the commencement, of every art.

Among the various principles that qualify men for society, that by which one man can bind <195> himself to another by an act of will, is eminent. By that act, a new relation arises between them: the person bound is termed *obligor,* the other *obligee.* But a man may exert an act of will in favour of another without binding himself, which is the case of a testament or latter-will: during the testator's life, his will expressed in his testament, differs not from a resolution, as he is bound by neither; but after death it differs widely, for death puts an end to the power of alteration.

* Stair, 23d February 1681, Earl Mar contra Earl Callender [M 2927].

A testament therefore must be effectual by the testator's death, or it never can be effectual.

Where two persons bind themselves to each other by mutual acts of will, this is termed a *contract* or *covenant*. Where one binds himself to another without any reciprocal obligation, that act of will is termed a *promise*. I promise to pay to John £100. An *offer* is a different act of will: it binds not unless it be accepted; and acceptance is an act of will of a fourth kind. Where one by an act of will conveys a subject to another, that is a fifth kind; and that act expressed in writing is termed a *deed*. <196>

Nature, independent of will, bars absolutely men from harming each other. It binds them positively to afford relief to the distressed as far as they are able. But in no case is a man bound to add to the estate of another, or to make him *locupletior,* as termed in the Roman law, otherwise than by voluntary engagement. This distinguishes the obligation of a voluntary engagement from the other duties mentioned. The latter cannot be transgressed without making others suffer in person, in goods, or in reputation: but in relieving from the obligation of a promise or covenant, the person in whose favour it is made, is indeed deprived of any benefit from it, but suffers no positive loss or damage: to him it is *lucrum cessans*[1] only, not *damnum datum.*[2] Hence it is, that the moral sense is less rigid as to voluntary engagements, than as to duties that arise without consent. To fulfil a rational promise or covenant, is a duty no less inflexible than to fulfil the duties that arise without consent. But as man is a fallible being, liable to fraud and deceit, and apt to be misled by ignorance and error, the moral sense would be ill suited to his na- <197> ture, did it compel him to fulfil every engagement, however irrational, however rashly or ignorantly made. Deplorable indeed would be our condition, were we so strictly bound by the moral sense: the innocent would be a prey to the designing, the ignorant would be over-reached by the crafty, and society be an uncomfortable state. But the author of our nature leaves none of his works imperfect: the moral sense, corresponding to the fallibility of our nature, binds us by no engagement but what is fairly entered into with every

---

1. "A gain lost."
2. "Damage done."

consequence in view, and what in particular answers the end for which it was made.[3]

Few persons pass much of their time without having purposes to fulfil, and plans to execute; for accomplishing which, means are employ'd. Among these means, deeds and covenants make a capital figure; no man binds himself or others for the sake merely of binding, but in order to bring about a desired event. Every deed and covenant may accordingly be considered to be a mean employed to bring about some end or event.

Sometimes the desired event is mention- <198> ed in the deed or covenant, and expressly agreed on to be performed; in which case performance concludes the transaction, being all that was intended. A bond for borrowed money is a proper example; what is stipulated in the bond to be performed, is repayment of the money, beyond which the parties have no view; and that end is accomplished when the money is repaid. A legacy bequeathed in a testament is another example: payment of the legacy is the only end in view; and that end is accomplished when the legatee receives the money. But in many deeds and contracts, the fact appointed to be done, is not ultimate, but intended to bring about a further end. Thus, when I buy a stone horse for propagation, the contract is performed upon delivery of the horse to me. But this performance does not fulfil my promise: I have a further end in view, which is to breed horses; and unless the horse be fit for that end, my purpose in contracting is frustrated. I purchase a hogshead of flax-seed for raising a crop of flax. It is not enough that the seed be delivered to me: if it be <199> rotten, the end I have in view is disappointed.

This suggests a division of voluntary engagements into two kinds: the first, where the performance mentioned is ultimate by fulfilling all that was intended; the other, where the performance mentioned is not ultimate, but intended as a mean to a further end, not mentioned. In this kind, a contract is a mean to bring about the immediate end, namely, the performance of what was mentioned and agreed on; and this immediate end is a mean to bring about the ultimate end.

3. In the second edition, a shorter passage, Appendix, p. 523, Extract [2nd: 119], takes the place of the three paragraphs above.

In contracts of this kind, there is place for judging how far the means are proportioned to the end: they may be insufficient to bring about the end; they may be more than sufficient; and they may have no tendency to bring about the end. Here equity may interpose, to vary these means in some cases, and to proportion them more accurately to the ultimate end: in other cases, to set aside the contract altogether, as insufficient to bring about the ultimate end. Hence it is, that such contracts are termed *contracts bonae fidei*,[4] that is, contracts in which equity may inter- <200> pose to correct inequalities, and to adjust all matters according to the plain intention of the parties. With respect to contracts where the performance stipulated is the ultimate end, there is evidently no place for the interposition of equity; for what defence can a man have, either in law or in equity, against performing his engagement, when it fulfils all that he had in view in contracting? Contracts accordingly of that kind, are termed *contracts stricti juris.*

To the distinction between contracts *bonae fidei* and *stricti juris,* great attention is given in the Roman law. We are told, that equity may interpose in the former, and that the latter are left to common law. But as to what contracts are *bonae fidei,* what *stricti juris,* we are left in the dark by Roman writers. Some of their commentators give us lists or catalogues; but they pretend not to lay down any precise rule by which the one kind may be distinguished from the other. I have endeavoured to supply that defect: whether satisfactorily or not, is the province of others to judge.

Have we in Scotland any action similar <201> to what in the Roman law is termed *Condictio ex poenitentia?*[5] Voet, upon the title *Condictio causa data,*[6] &c. says, that the *condictio ex poenitentia* is not admitted in

---

4. Roman contracts *bonae fidei* (of good faith) stood in contrast to those *stricti iuris* (by strict law). Roman law divided the kinds of contract according to whether the formula used to redress breaches was one that allowed the judge to use his discretion—considering issues such as whether the parties had acted fairly and in good faith—or was one that required only the strict observance of outward formalities.

5. An action in Roman law to recover money paid, after a party to a transaction changed his mind (*poenitentia*), before the other had performed.

6. *Condictio causa data causa non secuta:* an action in Roman law to recover property transferred for a purpose which failed to come about.

modern practice, because every paction is now obligatory.[7] I admit, that every paction is obligatory so far as to produce an action; but that does not bar an equitable defence. And it appears to me, that there are contracts where repentance may be sustained in equity as a good defence; as where the contract is of a deep concern to one of the parties, and of very little to the other. For example, I bargain with an undertaker to build me a dwelling-house for a certain sum, according to a plan concerted. Before the work is begun, the plan is discovered to be faulty in many capital articles. Am I bound notwithstanding to fulfil my covenant with the undertaker? Will not ignorance here relieve me, as error would do, where it is *lucrum cessans* only to the undertaker, and a very deep loss to me? Suppose again, that upon a more narrow inspection into my finances, the sum agreed on for building is found to be more than I ought to afford. Or what if, *rebus integris*,[8] I suc- <202> ceed to an estate with a good house upon it, or am invited by an employment to settle elsewhere? If I be relieved, the undertaker is at liberty to accept of employment from others; and perhaps of more beneficial employment than mine: if I be kept bound, a great interest on my side is sacrificed to a trifling interest on his. Covenants, intended for the support of society, ought not rashly to be converted to the ruin of an individual. It is a delicate point to determine in what cases a court of equity ought to interpose. All arbitrary questions are dangerous, and this is one of them. The court of session, however, must not decline such questions where it is to relieve from deep inequality and distress. In the cases above mentioned, they certainly would not refuse to interpose.[9]

7. Johannes Voet, *Commentarius ad Pandectas* (The Hague: Anthony van Dole, 1734), book XII, tit. 4, s. 6, p. 646.

8. "Matters being complete"; that is, no performance of the contract having taken place.

9. This topic is treated at greater length in the first edition (pp. 113–14) and second edition (pp. 165–66), which both devote a separate section to it. Before giving the example of the building contract, Kames makes the following comments: "It may indeed appear singular, that there should be a covenant of such a nature, as to afford on the one side an exception founded on *poenitentia* merely, or change of mind, and not on the other. I incline however to be of opinion, that this privilege hath an equitable foundation in every case where the covenant is made chiefly or solely for the benefit of one of the contracters, and where of consequence it is indifferent to the other whether the covenant be performed or not. For example, I promise a man a sum of money to

Great interest on the one side, and very little on the other, is not the only instance where a court of equity will admit of repentance. Of all articles of commerce, that of land is of the highest importance. For that reason, repentance is permitted in a verbal bargain of land, however fair and equal the bargain may be. It requires <203> writing to fix the bargain. Marriage is a contract still more important, as the happiness of one's whole life may depend on it. Hence it is that nothing but a contract *de praesenti*[10] can bind. Repentance is permitted of every agreement that can be made about a future marriage. Thus a bond granted by a woman to marry the obligee under a penalty, will not be effectual even for the penalty.*

This chapter, consisting of many parts, requires many divisions; and in the divisions that follow a proper arrangement is studied, which ought to be a capital object in every didactic subject.

SECTION I

Where will is imperfectly expressed in the writing.

In applying the rules of equity to deeds and covenants, what comes first under consideration is, whether the will be fully <204> or fairly taken down in the writing. A man, expressing his thoughts to others, is not always accurate in his terms; neither is the writer always accurate in expressing the will of his employer: and between the two, errors are often multiplied. Thus, clauses in writings are sometimes ambiguous or obscure, sometimes too limited, sometimes too extensive. As in common law the words are strictly adhered to, such imperfections are remedied by a court of equity. It admits words and writing to be the proper evidence of will;

---

manumit his slave. This man is not interested to demand performance of the promise, because he gains no more by the money than he loses by the manumission. Herefore, from the nature of the thing, the privilege of repentance ought to be indulged me. The common law however in this case affords me no relief, because every covenant is binding by the common law. But it is the province of a court of equity to afford relief where the common law is oppressive" (first ed., p. 113).

10. *Verba de praesenti:* words of present consent.

* 2. Vernon 102 [*Key* v. *Bradshaw* (1689), reprinted in *The English Reports,* vol. 23, p. 675].

but excludes not other evidence. Sensible that words and writing are not always accurate, it endeavours to reach will, which is the substantial part; and if, from the end and purpose of the engagement, from collateral circumstances, or from other satisfying evidence, will can be ascertained, it is justly made the rule, however it may differ from the words. The sole purpose of the writing is to bear testimony of will; and if that testimony prove erroneous, it can avail nothing against the truth. This branch of equitable jurisdiction, which comprehends both deeds and covenants, is founded on the <205> principle of justice, which declares for will against every erroneous evidence of it.

This section may be divided into three articles. First, Where the words leave us uncertain about will. Second, Where they are short of will. Third, Where they go beyond it.

ARTICLE I. *Where the words leave us uncertain about will.*

This imperfection may be occasioned by the fault of the writer, mistaking the meaning of his employer; or by the fault of the employer, exerting an act of will imperfectly, or expressing his will obscurely. But I purposely neglect these distinctions; because in most of the cases that occur, it is extremely doubtful upon whom the inaccuracy is to be charged. Nor will this breed any confusion; for from whatever cause the doubt about will arises, the method of solving it is the same, namely, to form the best conjecture we can, after considering every relative circumstance. <206>

Contracts shall furnish the first examples. In a bargain of sale, the price is referred to a third person: the referee dies suddenly without naming the price; and there is no performance on either side. There being no remedy here at common law, because the price is not ascertained, can a court of equity supply the defect in order to validate the bargain? This question depends on what the parties intended by the reference. If they intended not to be bound but by the opinion of the referee, it is in effect a conditional bargain, never purified, which no court will make effectual. But if it was intended, that the sale should in all events stand good, leaving only the price to be determined by the referee; the unexpected accident of his death cannot resolve the bargain; upon which account, it belongs to a court of equity, in place of the referee, to name a price *secundum arbitrium boni vi-ri.*[1] A man having purchased land, obliged himself in a backbond[2] to redispone, upon receiving back the price from the vender within a time specified. The vender having died within the time, it was questioned, Whether his heir was privileged to redeem the <207> land. If it was the meaning of the contract to confine the privilege of redemption to the vender personally, his heir could have no right. But if it was understood sufficient that the price should be repaid within the time specified, the heir was intitled to redeem, as the predecessor was. This construction, as the more equal and rational, was adopted by the court of session. And, accordingly, the land was found legally redeemed, upon the heir's offering the price before the term was elapsed.* A gentleman having given a bond of provision to his sister for 3000 merks, took from her a backbond, importing, "That the sum being rather too great for his circumstances, she consented that the same should be mitigated by friends to be mutually chosen, their mother being one." After the mother's decease without mitigation, the brother's creditors insisting for a mitigation *secundum arbitrium boni viri,* the defence was, That the condition of the mitigation had failed by the mother's death; and therefore that the bond must subsist <208> *in totum.*[3] The defence was sustained.† Supposing the backbond to be conditional, the judgment is right. But as it seems the more natural construction, that there should be a mitigation if the brother's circumstances required it, the unexpected death of the mother ought not to have prevented the mitigation.[4]

1. "According to the decision of a good man."

2. An instrument which qualifies another, unqualified instrument.

* Stair, 9th January 1662, Earl of Moray contra Grant [M 10322].

3. "In its entirety."

† 19th February 1734, Corsan contra Maxwell of Barncleuch [M 673, from Kames, *Dictionary,* vol. 1, p. 53].

4. In his discussion of this case in the first edition, in place of these two sentences Kames wrote (p. 50): "Supposing the backbond to be merely a gratuitous deed, in which view it seems to have been taken, the decision is just. But I cannot enter into this view. I conceive the backbond to be the counter-part of the bond, and that both of them make parts of a mutual engagement. From the very terms of this engagement, the brother was entitled to a mitigation of the sum contained in his bond; and therefore, since the method laid down for the mitigation failed, justice required other means to be substituted." His discussion in the second edition (p. 146) reflects that given in the first.

The next examples shall be of deeds. The minister of Weem settled his funds upon five trustees, and their successors, for the use of the schoolmasters of that parish, declaring the major part to be a quorum. Two only of the trustees having accepted and intermeddled with the funds, a process was brought against them by the representatives of the minister, claiming the funds upon the following ground, That the deed of mortification[5] was conditional, requiring the acceptance of a quorum at least of the trustees; and therefore void, the condition not having been purified. The defence was, That the deed of mortification was pure, vesting a right in the schoolmasters of Weem; that the nomination of trustees was only <209> intended, like the nomination of an executor, to make the funds effectual; and that it was not intended to make the deed depend on their acceptance or non-acceptance. The deed was sustained; the court being of opinion, that it would have been effectual though all the trustees had declined acceptance.[*,6] I illustrate this by an opposite case, where it was understood that no right was created by the deed. Lady Prestonfield made a settlement of considerable funds, to Sir John Cunninghame her eldest son, and Anne Cunninghame her eldest daughter, as trustees for the ends and purposes following. First, the yearly interest to be applied for the education and support of such of her descendents as should happen to be in want or stand in need thereof, and that at the discretion of the trustees. Second, failing descendents, the capital to return to her heirs. The trustees declining to accept this whimsical settlement, a process for voiding it was brought by the heir-at-law, in which were called all the existing descendents of the <210> maker. As here it appeared to be the maker's will to leave all to the discretion of the trustees, without the least hint of giving any right to her

5. Giving property for religious or charitable purposes.

* December 1752, Campbell contra Campbell of Monzie and Campbell of Achallader [M 16203].

6. In the first edition, Kames adds the following comment (pp. 53–54): "In this case it was evidently the purpose of the granter, in all events, to make a provision for the schoolmasters of Weem; and the naming trustees must be considered as a means only chosen by him to fulfil his purpose. Justice requires that when such means fail, others should be substituted; and therefore if the court of session had declined to interpose in this case, it would have been defeating the granter's will instead of fulfilling it."

descendents independent of the trustees, the deed was declared void by their non-acceptance.*

Colonel Campbell being bound in his contract of marriage to secure the sum of 40,000 merks, and the conquest during the marriage,[7] to himself and spouse in conjunct fee and liferent, and to the children to be procreated of the marriage in fee,[8] did, by a deathbed deed settle all upon his eldest son, burdened with the sum of 30,000 merks to his younger children, to take place if their mother could be prevailed on to give up her claim to the liferent of the conquest, and restrict herself to a less jointure: otherwise the provision to the younger children to be void; in which event, it was left upon the Duke of Argyle and Earl of Ilay to name such provisions to the children as they should see convenient. The referees having declined to accept, the question occurred between the heir and the younger children, What <211> was the Colonel's intention, whether to make a provision for his younger children, referring the quantum only to the Duke and Earl; or to make the provision conditional, that it should not be effectual unless the referees named a sum. The court adopted the latter construction; and refused to interpose in place of the referees to name a sum.† The judgement probably would have been different, had no provision been made for the children in the contract of marriage.[9]

---

* 22 January 1758, Sir Alexander Dick contra Mrs Fergusson and her children [M 7446].

7. See glossary, "conquest."

8. Conjunct rights are those taken jointly. Between husband and wife, where rights were taken "in conjunct fee and liferent, and the heirs of their body," the husband was taken to be the sole owner of the fee, and the wife a liferenter: see Erskine, *Institute,* vol. 2, p. 560 (book III, tit. 8, s. 36).

† 22d December 1739, Campbell contra Campbells [M 674 and M 6849, from Kames, *Dictionary,* vol. 1, pp. 53, 465].

9. In his discussion of the case in the first edition (p. 55), Kames adds the following comment: "The settlement appears to me in a very different light. The Colonel's will to provide his children in all events, is clearly expressed. As he was doubtful what the sum should be in case their mother insisted upon her jointure, he left it upon the referees to name the sum, not doubting their acceptance. This reference I consider to be the means chosen by the Colonel for accomplishing his purpose of providing his children; but not so as to exclude all other means. His younger children were entitled to a provision by his will; and failing the means chosen by him for acertaining the extent, justice required that other means should be substituted, in order to make their claim effectual. This case

A married woman gives a security on her estate to her husband's creditors; but with what intention it is not said. If a donation was intended, she has no claim for relief against her husband: but *in dubio*,[10] a cautionary engagement will be presumed; which affords her a claim.* A court of common law would hardly be brought to sustain a claim of this nature, where there is no clause in the deed on which it can be founded.[11] <212>

Where a man provides a sum to his creditor, without declaring it to be in satisfaction, it will be sustained as a separate claim at common law. But as the granter probably intended that sum to be in satisfaction, according to the maxim, *Quod debitor non praesumitur donare*,[12] a court of equity, supplying a defect in words, decrees the sum to be in satisfaction. Thus, a man being bound for £10 yearly to his daughter, gave her at her marriage a portion of £200. Decreed, That the annuity was included in the portion.† But where a man leaves a legacy to his creditor, this cannot be constructed as satisfaction; for in that case it would not be a legacy or donation.

Anthony Murray, *anno* 1738, made a settlement of his estate upon John and Thomas Belscheses [that is, Belsches], taking them bound, among

---

resembles very much that above mentioned concerning a sum settled upon trustees for the use of the schoolmasters of Weem. The settlement upon trustees was a means only for making the mortification effectual; and the failure of the trustees, could have no other effect than to make way for supplying other means." In the second edition (p. 148), Kames includes a similar passage.

10. "In case of doubt."

* Stair, 11th January 1679, Bowie contra Corbet [M 13405]; Fountainhall, 16th July 1696, Leishman contra Nicols [M 13406]; 29th November 1728, Trail of Sabae contra Moodie [M 13407, from Kames, *Dictionary*, vol. 2, p. 318].

11. In the first edition, discussing this case, Kames commented: "Whether a claim ought to be sustained in equity, depends upon the construction of the transaction. If intended a donation, there is no claim: but if intended a cautionary engagement only, which *in dubio* ought to be presumed, the husband was undoubtedly bound in conscience for an equivalent; and justice calls for the power of a court of equity to make the obligation effectual. This is doing no more than supplying as usual an article omitted; for had the matter been thought of, a clause would have been added for indemnifying the wife. And the decisions of the court of session are all of them agreeable to this doctrine."

12. "A debtor is not presumed to make a gift."

† Tothill's Reports, 78 [*Kirrington* v. *Astie* (1637) in William Tothill, *The Transactions of the High Court of Chancery both by Practice and Precedent* (London: R. Best and J. Place, 1649), p. 141, reprinted in *The English Reports*, vol. 21, p. 128].

other legacies, to pay £300 Sterling to their sister Emilia, at her marriage. Anthony altered this settlement *anno* 1740, in favour of his heir-at-law; obliging him, however, to pay the legacies contained in the former settlement. In the year 1744, Anthony executed a bond to Emilia upon <213> the narrative[13] of love and favour, binding himself to pay to her in liferent, and to her children *nati et nascituri*[14] in fee, at the first term after his decease, the sum of £1200 Sterling. The doubt was, whether both sums were due to Emilia, or only the latter. It was admitted, that both sums would be due at common law, which looks no farther than the words. But that this was not the intention of the granter, was urged from the following circumstance, That in the bond for the £1200 there is no mention of the former legacy, nor of any legacy; which clearly shews, that Anthony had forgot the first legacy, and consequently that he intended no more for Emilia but £1200 in whole. Which was accordingly decreed.*

ARTICLE 11. *Where the words are short of will.*

Between this article and a following section, intitled *Imply'd will,* there is much affinity; but as the blending together <214> things really distinct, tends to confusion of ideas, I have brought under the present article, acts of will that are indeed expressed, but so imperfectly as to leave room for doubt whether the will does not go farther than is spoken out; leaving to the section *Imply'd will* articles essential to the deed or covenant, that must have made a part of the maker's will, and yet are totally omitted to be expressed.

In England, where estates are settled by will, it is the practice to make up any defect in the words, in order to support the will of the devisor. But here it is essential, that the will be clearly ascertained, in order that the court may run no hazard of overturning the will, instead of supporting it. An executor being named with the usual power of managing the whole money and effects of the deceased, the following clause subjoined "And I hereby debar and seclude all others from any right or interest in my said

13. Recital in a deed, setting for the cause of its being granted.
14. "Born and to be born."
* 22 December 1752, Emilia Belsches and her husband contra Sir Patrick Murray [M 11361 and 11363, from Kames, *Select Decisions,* p. 34].

executry," was held by the court to import an universal legacy in favour of the executor.* A man having two nephews who were his <215> heirs at law, made a settlement in their favour, dividing his farms between them, intending probably an equal division. A farm was left out by the omission of the clerk, which the scrivener swore was intended for the plaintiff. The court refused to amend the mistake, leaving the farm to descend as *ab intestato* [by intestacy].† For here it was not clear that the maker of the deed intended an equal division.

There being an entail of the estate of Cromarty to heirs-male, the Earl, in his contract of marriage, *anno* 1724, became bound, in case of children of the marriage who should succeed to and enjoy the estate, to infeft his lady in a liferent-locality[1] of forty chalders victual;[2] and in case of no children to succeed to and enjoy the estate, he became bound to make the said locality fifty chalders. The following clause is added: "That if at the dissolution of the marriage there should be children succeeding to and enjoying the estate, but who should afterward decease during the life of his said spouse, she from that period should be entitled to fifty chalders, as if the said children <216> had not existed." The Earl being forfeited in the year 1745, having issue both male and female, a claim was entered by his lady for the jointure of fifty chalders, to take effect after her husband's death. Objected by his Majesty's Advocate, That she is intitled to forty chalders only, there being sons of the marriage, who but for the forfeiture would have succeeded to the estate. Here evidently the words fall short of intention; for as the claimant would have had a jointure of fifty chalders if the Earl's brother or nephew had succeeded to the estate, there can be no doubt that had the event of forfeiture been foreseen, the Earl would have given her at least fifty chalders. The claim accordingly was sustained.‡

Walter Riddel, in his contract of marriage 1694, became bound to settle his whole land-estate on the heir-male of the marriage. In the year 1727,

---

* 1st February 1739, John Beizly contra Gabriel Napier [M 6591, from Kilkerran, 326].

† 1. Vernon 37 [*Lee* v. *Henley* (1681) reprinted in *The English Reports,* vol. 23, p. 292].

1. The liferent created in marriage contracts in favor of a wife; "locality" is an appropriation of certain lands to the wife in liferent.

2. *Chalder:* a unit of measure of capacity; made up of 16 bolls.

‡ 26th January 1764, Countess of Cromarty contra the Crown [M 6601, from Kames, *Select Decisions,* p. 278].

purposing to fulfil that obligation, he disponed to his eldest son the lands therein specified, burdened with his debts, reserving to himself an annuity of 2000 merks only. <217> The lands of Stewarton, which came under the said obligation, were left out of the disposition 1727. But that they were omitted by oversight, without intention, was made evident from the following circumstances: first, That the title-deeds of that farm were delivered to the son along with the other title-deeds; second, That he took possession of the whole; third, That a subsequent deed by the father *anno* 1733, proceeds upon this narrative, "That the whole lands belonging to him were conveyed to his son by the disposition 1727." Many years after, the father, having discovered that Stewarton was not mentioned in the said disposition, ventured to convey that farm to his second son, who was otherwise competently provided. It was not pretended, that Stewarton was actually conveyed to the eldest son, which could not be but in a formal disposition; but as there was clear evidence of the father's obligation to convey it with the rest of the estate, which obligation he was still bound to fulfil, the court judged this a sufficient foundation for voiding <218> the gratuitous disposition to the second son.*

In the cases mentioned, writing is necessary as evidence only: it is of no consequence what words be used in the nomination of an heir or of an executor, provided the will of the maker be ascertained. But in several transactions, writing, beside the evidence it affords, is an indispensable solemnity. Land cannot be conveyed without a procuratory or a precept,[3] which must be in a set form of words. A man may lend his money upon a verbal paction, but he cannot proceed directly to execution, unless he have a formal bond containing a clause of registration, authorising execution. Neither can such a bond be conveyed to a purchaser, otherwise than by a formal assignment in writing. Here a new speculation arises, What power a court of equity hath over a writing of this kind? In this writing, no less than in others, the words may happen erroneously to be more extensive than the will of the granter; or they may happen to be more limited. Must the words in all cases <219> be the sovereign rule? Far from it. Though in certain transactions

---

* January 4. 1766, Riddel contra Riddel of Glenriddel [M 13019, Kames, *Select Decisions,* p. 311].

3. A warrant, or authority granted.

writ[4] is an essential solemnity, it follows not that the words solely must be regarded, without relation to will; for to bind a man by words where he hath not interposed his will, is contrary to the most obvious principles of justice. Hence it necessarily follows, that a deed of this kind may, by a court of equity, be limited to a narrower effect than the words naturally import; and that this ought to be done, where from the context, from the intendment of the granter, or from other convincing circumstances, it can be certainly gathered, that the words by mistake go beyond the will. But though in ordinary cases, such as those above mentioned, the defect of words may be supplied, and force given to will, supposing it clearly ascertained; yet this cannot be done in a deed to which writ is essential. The reason is, that to make writ an essential solemnity, is in other words to declare, that action must not be sustained except as far as authorised by writ. However clear therefore will may be, a court of equity hath not authority to sustain action upon it, independent of <220> the words where these are made essential; for this, in effect, would be to overturn law, which is beyond the power of equity. A case that really happened, is a notable illustration of this doctrine. A bond of corroboration granted by the debtor with a cautioner, was of the following tenor: "And seeing the foresaid principal sum of 1000 merks, and interest since Martinmas 1742, are resting unpaid; and that *A* the creditor is willing to supersede payment till the term after mentioned, upon *B* the debtor's granting the present corroborative security with *C* his cautioner; therefore *B* and *C* bind and oblige them, conjunctly and severally, &c. to content and pay to *A* in liferent, and to her children in fee, equally among them, and failing any of them by decease, to the survivors, their heirs or assignees, in fee, and that at Whitsunday 1744, with 200 merks of penalty, together with the due and ordinary annualrent[5] of the said principal sum from the said term of Martinmas 1742," &c. Here the obligatory clause is imperfect, as it omits the principal sum corroborated, name- <221> ly, the 1000 merks, a pure oversight of the writer. In a suit upon this bond of corroboration against the heir of the cautioner, it was objected, That upon this bond no action could lie against him for payment of the principal sum. It was obvious to the court, that the

4. That is, writing.
5. Interest.

bond, though defective in the most essential part, afforded clear evidence of C's consent to be bound as cautioner. But then it occurred, that a cautionary engagement is one of those deeds that require writing in point of solemnity. A defective bond, like the present, whatever evidence it may afford, is still less formal than if it wanted the requisites of the act 1681.[6] Action accordingly was denied; for action cannot be sustained upon consent alone where a formal deed is essential.* The following case concerning a registrable bond, or, as termed in England, *a bond in judgment,* is another instance of refusing to supply a defect in words.[7] A bond for a sum of money bore the following clause, *with interest and penalty,* without specifying any sum in name of penalty. The creditor moved <222> the court to supply the omission, by naming the fifth part of the principal sum, being the constant rule as to consensual penalties. There could be no doubt of the granter's intention; and yet the court justly thought that they had not power to supply the defect.†

But though a defect in a writ that is essential in point of solemnity, cannot be supplied so as to give it the full effect that law gives to such a deed, it will however be regarded by a court of equity in point of evidence. A bond of borrowed money, for example, null by the act 1681 because the writer's name was neglected, may, in conjunction with other evidence, be produced in an action for payment; in order to prove delivery of the money as a loan, and consequently to found a decree for repayment.

ARTICLE III. *Where the words go beyond will.*

It is a rule in daily practice, That <223> however express the words may be, a court of equity gives no force to a deed beyond the will of the granter.[1]

6. Act 5, parl. 1681; *APS* viii: 242: 1681, c. 5, Act concerning probative witnesses in writs & Executions [Subscription of Deeds Act 1681].

* 2d June 1749, Colt contra Angus [M 17040, from Kames, *Remarkable Decisions* ii: 206].

7. See glossary: "registrable bond"; "bond in judgment."

† Fountainhall, 6th January 1705, Leslie contra Ogilvie [M 7429].

1. In the first edition, in which this material is put in a separate chapter dealing with the common law's working of injustice in respect of rights founded on will, Kames prefaces this sentence with the following statement (p. 78): "The power of a court of equity to limit a deed within narrower bounds than the words naturally import, is already explained. It is made evident, that this ought to be done, when from the context, from

This rule is finely illustrated in the following case. John Campbell, provost of Edinburgh, did in July 1734 make a settlement of the whole effects that should belong to him at the time of his death, to William his eldest son, with the burden of provisions to his other children, Matthew, Daniel, and Margaret. Daniel being at sea in a voyage from the East Indies, made his will, May 1739, in which he "gives and bequeaths all his goods, money, and effects, to John Campbell his father; and in case of John's decease, to his beloved sister Margaret." The testator died at sea in the same month of May; and in June following John the father also died, without hearing of Daniel's death, or of the will made by him. William brought an action against his sister Margaret and her husband, concluding, That Daniel's effects, being vested in the father, were conveyed to him the pursuer by the father's settlement; and that the substitution in favour of Margaret, contained in Daniel's will, was thereby altered. It was answered, <224> That nothing could be intended by the Provost, but to settle his proper estate upon his eldest son, without any intention to alter the substitution in his son Daniel's testament, of which he was ignorant: That words are not alone, without intention, sufficient to found a claim; and therefore, that the present action ought not to be sustained. "The court judged, That the general disposition 1734, granted by John Campbell to his son, the pursuer, several years before Daniel's will had a being, does not evacuate the substitution in the said will."* Charles Farquharson writer, being in a sickly condition and apprehensive of death, did, *anno* 1721, settle all the effects real and personal that should belong to him at his death, upon his eldest brother Patrick Farquharson of Inverey, and his heirs; reserving a power to alter, and dispensing with the delivery. Charles was at that time a bachelor, and died so. Being restored to health, he not only survived his brother Patrick, but also Patrick's two sons, who successively inherited the estate <225> of Inverey. Patrick left daughters; but as the

---

the end and purpose of the deed, or from other circumstances, it can with certainty be gathered, that the words by mistake go beyond the will. It is also made evident, that this power comprehends grants as well as covenants, not even excepting deeds where writ is an essential solemnity."

* 13th June 1740, Campbell contra his Sister [M 14856 and 14857, from Kames, *Remarkable Decisions* ii: 25–26].

investitures[2] were to heirs-male, Charles was infeft as heir-male, died in possession, and left the estate open to the next heir-male. Against him a process is raised by the daughters of Patrick, claiming the estate of Inverey upon the settlement 1721 as belonging to Charles at the time of his death, and consequently now to them as heirs of line to Patrick. The defence was, That here the words of the settlement are more extensive than the will of the granter, which was only to augment the family-estate by settling his own funds on Patrick the heir of the family; that this purpose was fulfilled by the coalition of both estates in the defendant, the present head of the family; whereas the claim made by the pursuers, the purpose of which is to take from the representative of the family the family-estate itself, is not only destitute of any foundation in the maker's will, but is in direct opposition to it. The court judged, That the pursuers had no action on the deed 1721 to oblige the defendant to denude of the e- <226> state of Inverey.* A contract of marriage providing the estate to the heirs-male of the marriage, whom failing, to the husband's other heirs-male, contained the following clause, "And seeing the earldom of Perth is tailzied[3] to heirs-male, so that if there be daughters of the marriage they will be excluded from the succession; therefore the said James Lord Drummond and his heirs become bound to pay to the said daughters, at their age of eighteen or marriage, the sums following; to an only daughter 40,000 merks," &c. The estate being forfeited for treason committed by the eldest son of the marriage, the only daughter of the marriage claimed the 40,000 merks as being excluded from the succession by the existence of an heir-male. Objected by the King's Advocate, That the provision not being to younger children in general, but to daughters only, upon consideration that the estate was entailed to heirs-male, was obviously intended to be conditional, and only to take effect failing sons of the mar- <227> riage; and that here inadvertently the words are more extensive than the will. It carried however, by a narrow plurality, to sustain the claim.† But the judgement was reversed in the House of Lords.

2. *Investiture:* the act by which a transfer of the right to land is effected, by means of a charter and instrument of sasine, duly registered.

* 10th February 1756, Heirs of line of Patrick Farquharson contra his Heir-male [M 6596, from Kames, *Select Decisions,* p. 142].

3. Entailed.

† 10th July 1752, Lady Mary Drummond contra the King's Advocate [M 6402, from Kames, *Select Decisions,* p. 18].

The same rule obtains with respect to general clauses in discharges, submissions,[4] assignments, and such like, which are limited by equity where the words are more extensive than the will. Thus, a general submission of all matters debateable, is not understood to comprehend land or other heritable right.* Nor was a general clause in a submission extended to matters of greater importance than those expressed.† *A* had a judgement of £6000 against *B*. *B* gave *A* a legacy of £5, and died. *A*, on receipt of this £5, gave the executor of *B* a release in the following words. "I acknowledge to have received of *C* £5, left me as a legacy by *B*, and do release to him all demands which I <228> against him, as executor to *B*, can have for any matter whatever." It was adjudged, That the generality of the words *all demands* should be restrained by the particular occasion mentioned in the former part, namely, the receipt of the £5, and should not be a discharge of the judgement.‡

A variety of irritancies contrived to secure an entail against acts and deeds of the proprietor, furnish proper examples of this doctrine. Where such irritancies are so expressed as to declare the proprietor's right voidable only, not *ipso facto* void, an act of contravention may be purged before challenge, and even at any time before sentence in a process of declarator. But what shall be said upon clauses declaring the proprietor to fall from his right *ipso facto* upon the first act of contravention? Supposing the entailer by this clause to have only intended to keep his heirs of entail to their duty, which *in dubio* will always be presumed, his purpose is fulfilled if the estate be relieved from the debts and deeds of the tenant in tail. <229> The words indeed are clear; but words unsupported by will have no effect in law. The act 1685 concerning tailzies declares, "That if the provisions and irritant clauses are not repeated in the rights and conveyances by which the heirs of tailzie bruik[5] or enjoy the estate, the omission shall import a contravention of the irritant and resolutive clauses against the person and his

---

4. That is, to arbitration.

* Hope, (Arbiter), 4th March 1612, Paterson contra Forret [M 5064, from Kames, *Dictionary,* vol. 1, p. 345].

† Haddington, 4th March 1607, Inchaffray contra Oliphant [M 5063, from Kames, *Dictionary,* vol. 1, p. 345].

‡ Abridgement Cases in equity, chap. 25, sect. C. note at the end [*Knight* v. *Cole* (1689) in 1 Eq. Cas. Abr. 170; reprinted in *The English Reports,* vol. 21, p. 965].

5. *Bruik:* brook, to enjoy the use of, profit by.

heirs who shall omit to insert the same, whereby the estate shall *ipso facto* fall, accresce,[6] and be devolved upon the next heir of tailzie; but shall not militate against creditors,"[7] &c. Here the words go inadvertently beyond will. It cannot be the will of any entailer, to forfeit his heir for an omission that the heir supplies *rebus integris*. Nor could it be the intendment of the legislature to be more severe than entailers themselves commonly are. This irritancy, according to order, ought to come in afterward in treating of equity with respect to statutes; but by the intimacy of its connection with the irritancies mentioned, it appears in a better light here.

The foregoing irritancies relate to grants and single deeds. The following is an ex- <230> ample of a conventional irritancy,[8] an irritancy *ob non solutum canonem*[9] in a lease or feu-right. Such a clause expressed so as to make the right voidable only upon failure of payment, is just and equal; because, by a declarator of irritancy, it secures to the superior or landlord payment of what is due to him, and at the same time affords to the vassal or tenant an opportunity to purge the irritancy by payment. And even supposing the clause so expressed as to make failure of payment an *ipso facto* forfeiture, it will be held by a court of equity, that the words go inadvertently beyond the will; and a declarator of irritancy will still be necessary, in order to afford an opportunity for purging the irritancy.

Conditional bonds and grants afford proper examples of the same kind. These are of two sorts. One is where the condition is ultimate; as for example, a bond for money granted to a young woman upon condition of her being married to a man named, or a bond for money to a young man upon condition of his entering into holy orders. The other is where the condition is a means to a certain end; <231> as for example, a bond for a sum of money to a young woman upon condition of her marrying with

6. *Accretion:* the perfection of a defective title by some of the party who conveyed an imperfect title to the current holder: that is, when A, who has conveyed to B, has an imperfect title, which is later perfected, this "accresces to" and perfects B's title.

7. Act 22, parl. 1685; *APS* viii: 477: 1685, c. 26, Act concerning Tailzies [Entail Act 1685].

8. See glossary, "irritancy."

9. "On the ground of unpaid feuduty."

consent of certain friends named, the intendment of which is to prevent an unsuitable match. Conditions of the first sort are taken strictly, and the sum is not due unless the condition be purified [that is, fulfilled]. This is requisite at common law; and no less so in equity, because justice requires that a man's will be obey'd. To judge aright of the other sort, we ought to lay the chief weight upon the ultimate purpose of the granter; which, in the case last mentioned, is to confine the young woman to a suitable match. If she therefore marry suitably, though without consulting the friends named, I pronounce that the bond ought to be effectual in equity, though not at common law. The reason is given above, that the ultimate will or purpose ought to prevail in opposition to the words.[10] I am aware, that in Scotland we are taught a different lesson. In bonds of the sort under consideration, a distinction is made between a suspensive condition, and one that is resolutive.[11] If the bond to the young woman contain a resolutive condition only, namely, *if she <232> marry without consent she shall forfeit the bond,* it is admitted, that the forfeiture will not take effect unless she marry unsuitably. But it is held by every one, that if the condition be suspensive, as where a bond for money is granted to a young woman, *on condition that if she marry it be with consent of certain friends named,* it must be performed in the precise terms of the clause; because, say they, the will of the granter must be the rule; and no court has power to vary a conditional grant, or to transform it into one that is pure

---

10. In the first edition, in place of this sentence, Kames writes (p. 56): "If the condition was adjected as a means only to prevent an unsuitable match, the granter's ultimate purpose is fulfilled by her marrying suitably; and the bond for that reason ought to be due in equity. Means are employed in order to an end; and if the end be accomplished, the means have had all the effect that was intended, and it would be unjust to give them further effect. To think otherwise involves an evident absurdity, that of preferring the means to the end." In the second edition (p. 154), he writes, "If the condition was adjected as a means only to prevent an unsuitable match, the granter's ultimate purpose is fulfilled by her marrying suitably; and the bond for that reason ought to be due in equity. Means are employed in order to an end; and if the end be accomplished, the means have had all the effect that was intended, and it would be unjust to give them any further effect. To think otherwise involves an evident absurdity, that of preferring the means to the end."

11. See glossary: "condition suspensive" and "condition resolutive."

and simple. This argument is conclusive where a condition is ultimate, whether suspensive or resolutive; but not where the condition is a means to an end. The granter's will, it is true, ought to be obey'd; but whether his will with regard to the means, or his will with regard to the end? The means are of no significancy but as productive of the end; and if the end be accomplished without them, they can have no weight in equity or in common sense. Let us try the force of this reasoning by bringing it down to common apprehension. Why is a resolutive condition disregarded, where the ob- <233> ligee marries suitably? For what reason but that it is considered as a mean to an end; and that if the end be accomplished, the granter's purpose is fulfilled? Is not this reasoning applicable equally to a suspensive condition? No man of plain understanding, unacquainted with law, will discover any difference. And accordingly, in the later practice of the English court of chancery, this difference seems to be disregarded. A portion of £8000 is given to a woman, provided she marry with consent of *A;* and if she marry without his consent, she shall have but £100 yearly. She was relieved, though she married without consent; for the proviso is *in terrorem* only.*

One having three daughters, devises lands to his eldest, upon condition that within six months after his death she pay certain sums to her two sisters; and if she fail, he devises the land to his second daughter on the like condition. The court may enlarge the time for payment, though the premises are devised over.[12] And in all cases where compensation can be made for <234> the delay, the court may dispense with the time, though even in the case of a condition precedent.† This practical rule is evidently derived from the reasoning above stated.

Take another example that comes under the same rule of equity. A claim is transacted,[13] and a less sum accepted, upon condition that the

---

* Abridg. Cases in equity, chap. 17. sect. C, §1 [*Bellasis* v. *Ermin* (1663) in 1 Eq. Cas. Abr. 110, reprinted in *The English Reports,* vol. 21, p. 918].

12. That is, although the will makes provision for the property to pass to another person, in case of failure.

† Abridg. Cases in equity, chap. 17, sect. B, §5 [*Woodman* v. *Blake* (1691) in 1 Eq. Cas. Abr. 109, reprinted in *The English Reports,* vol. 21, p. 917].

13. *Transaction:* an agreement between parties to settle a disputed claim.

same be paid at a day certain, otherwise the transaction to be void. It is the general opinion, that where the clause is resolutive, equity will relieve against it after the stipulated term is elapsed, provided the transacted sum be paid before process be raised; but that this will not hold where the clause is suspensive. In my apprehension, there is an equitable ground for relief in both equally. The form may be different, but the intention is the same in both, namely, to compel payment of the transacted sum; and therefore if payment be offered at any time before a declarator of irritancy, with damages for the delay, the conditional irritancy has had the full effect that was intended. Equity therefore requires a decla- <235> rator of irritancy, whether the clause be suspensive or resolutive; and the defendant ought to be admitted to purge the failure by offering payment of the transacted sum. The case, I acknowledge, is different where the transacted sum is to be paid in parcels, and at different periods; as for example, where an annuity is transacted for a less yearly sum. A court of equity will scarce interpose in this case, but leave the irritancy to take place *ipso facto,* by the rules of common law; for if the irritant clause be not in this case permitted to operate *ipso facto,* it will be altogether ineffectual, and be no compulsion to make payment. If a declarator be necessary, the defendant must be admitted to purge before sentence; and if it be at all necessary, it must be renewed every term where there is a failure of payment. This would be unjust, because it reduces the creditor to the same difficulty of recovering the transacted sum, that he had with respect to his original sum; which, in effect, is to forfeit the creditor for his moderation, instead of forfeiting the debtor for his ingratitude.

The examples above given coincide in the following particular, that the acts of <236> contravention can be purged, so as to restore matters to the same state as if there had been no contravention. But there are acts incapable of being purged, such as the cutting down trees by a tenant. Now, suppose a lease be granted with a clause of forfeiture in case of felling trees, will equity relieve against this forfeiture in any case? If the act of contravention was done knowingly, and consequently criminally, there can be no equity in giving relief; but if it was done ignorantly and innocently, a court of equity ought to interpose against the forfeiture, upon making up full damages to the landlord. Take the following instance. The plaintiff, tenant for life of a copyhold-estate, felled trees, which, at a court-baron, was found a waste,[14] and consequently a forfeiture. The bill was to be relieved against the forfeiture, offering satisfaction if it appeared to be a waste. The court decreed an issue,[15] to try whether the primary intention in felling the trees was to do waste; declaring, That in case of a wilful forfeiture it would not relieve.* <237>

A power granted to distribute a sum or a subject among children, or others, is limited in equity to be exercised *secundum arbitrium boni viri,* unless an absolute power be clearly expressed. A man devised to his wife his personal estate, upon trust and confidence,[16] "That she should not dispose thereof but for the benefit of her children." She by will gave to one but five shillings, and all the rest to another. The court set aside so unequal a distribution.† A man by will directed that his land should descend to his daughters, "in such shares as his wife by a deed in writing should appoint." The wife makes an unequal distribution. The court at first declared, the circumstances must be very strong, as bribery, for instance, or corruption, that could take from the wife a power given her by the will: but afterward declared the case was proper for equity, and that the plaintiff might be relieved. Here the plaintiff was allowed but a small proportion; and for any causeless displeasure she might have been put off with a single barren acre; that the court in the latter case, would have a jurisdiction; and <238> therefore in the case that really happened.‡

---

14. Permanent harm to real property caused by the tenant, for which legal liability was incurred.

15. That is, the Court of Chancery referred a disputed question of fact to a common law court for determination by a jury.

* 1. Chancery cases 95 [*Thomas* v. *Porter* (1668) reprinted in *The English Reports,* vol. 22, p. 711].

16. That is, in trust.

† 1. Vernon 66 [*Gibson* v. *Kinven* (1682) reprinted in *The English Reports,* vol. 23, p. 315].

‡ 1. Vernon 355. 414 [*Wall* v. *Thurborne* (1685–86) reprinted in *The English Reports,* vol. 23, pp. 519, 555].

SECTION II

Implied will.

In framing a deed it belongs to the granter to declare his will and purpose: the proper clauses for expressing these are left to the writer. But seldom it happens that every particular is expressed: nor is it necessary; for where a man declares his will with respect to a certain event, he undoubtedly wills every necessary mean; which is only saying, that he is not a changeling. I grant, for example, to a neighbour, liberty of my coal-pit for the use of his family. It follows necessarily, that he have a coal-road through my land, if he have not otherwise access to the pit. The same holds in covenants. A clause in a lease entitling the lessee to take possession at a time specified, implies ne- <239> cessarily authority from the landlord to remove the tenant in possession.

Tacit will, where made clear from circumstances, ought to have the same authority with expressed will: the only use of words is to signify will or intention; and from the very nature of the thing, will or intention cannot have greater authority when expressed in words, than when ascertained with equal clearness by any other signs or means. A court of common law rarely ventures to dive into tacit will. But it is one of the valuable powers of a court of equity, to imply will where it is not expressed; without which deeds and covenants would often fall short of their purposed end. But a judge ought to be extremely cautious in the exercise of this power, to avoid counteracting will, instead of supporting it; an error that seems to have been committed in the following case.[1] The sum of £120 was given with an apprentice; and as the master was sick when the articles were drawn, it was provided, that if he died within a year £60 should be returned. He having died within three weeks, a bill was brought in chancery to have a greater sum returned. And <240> notwithstanding the express provision, it was decreed that a hundred guineas should be returned.*

1. For the introduction to the corresponding section in the second edition, see Appendix, Extract [2nd: 130–31].

* [1] Vernon 460 [*Newton* v. *Rowse* (1687), reprinted in *The English Reports*, vol. 23, p. 586].

As tacit will is to be gathered from various circumstances, particularly from the nature and intendment of the deed or covenant, general rules are not to be expected. All I can venture on, is to give examples of various kinds, which may enure the student of law to judge, in what cases will ought to be imply'd, in what not. For the sake of perspicuity, these examples shall be put in different classes. And first, of *accessories*.[2] Where a subject is conveyed, every one of its accessories are understood to be conveyed with it, unless the contrary be expressed. An assignment, for example, of a bond of borrowed money, implies a conveyance of what executions have passed upon it: these may be of use to the assignee; but can avail nothing to the cedent after he is denuded. Thus, an assignment to a bond was understood to comprehend an inhibition[3] that followed upon it; though there was no general clause that could compre- <241> hend the inhibition.* In an infeftment of annualrent a personal obligation for payment is now common. In the conveyance of an infeftment containing that obligation, no mention was made of it. It was however imply'd by the court of session; as there appeared no intention to relieve the debtor.[†] Tenants, taken bound by lease to carry their corn-rent to the place of sale, were decerned to perform that service to the proprietor's widow, infeft in a liferent-locality.[‡] Such implication is not made with respect to penal accessories: these will not go to the assignee, unless expressly convey'd. The superior of a feu-right dispones the same for a valuable consideration; but antecedently the feuer[4] had incurred an irritancy upon failing to pay his feu-duty. Is the purchaser entitled to reduce the feu upon that head? The irritancy is indeed an accessory to the superiority; but loosely con- <242> nected and easily separated. The punishment is what few superiors are so

2. *Accessory obligations:* obligations which "cannot subsist by themselves, but are accessions to, or make part of, other obligations to which they are interposed": Erskine, *Institute,* vol. 2, p. 469 (book III, tit. 3, sect. 60).

3. A form of execution against a debtor prohibiting him from burdening or disposing of heritable property to the prejudice of a creditor.

* Harcase, (Assignation), January 1682, Williamson contra Threapland [M 6306].

† Dury [Durie], 23d November 1627, Dunbar contra Williamson [M 570].

‡ Fountainhall, 29th July 1680, Countess-dowager of Errol contra the Earl [M 6550, from Kames, *Dictionary,* vol. 1, p. 440].

4. "Vassal."

hardhearted as to inflict; and a superior who declines the taking advantage of it for himself, will not readily bestow the power on another. If intended therefore to be convey'd, it must be expressed; for it will not be imply'd by a court of equity.

A discharge of the principal debt includes accessories by imply'd will. An agent, for example, employ'd to carry on a process, states an account without any article for pains. He receives payment of the sum in the account, and gives a discharge. The article for pains is understood to be also discharged. Imply'd will is extended still farther. The extract of a decree[5] implies the passing from any claim for costs of suit; because no rational person who purposes to claim such costs will reserve them for a new process, when by delaying extract it is so much more easy to claim them in the same process.

So much for accessories. Next, of *consequents.* A commission being given to execute any work, every power necessary to carry it on is implied. Example: A man commissioned to navigate a ship, <243> termed the *master,* can bind his owners to pay what money he has borrowed in a foreign country for repairing the ship.

I shall add but one class more, which is, where in a settlement upon one person a benefit is understood to be conferred on another. Thus, where a man devises land to his heir after the death of his wife, this by necessary implication is a good device to the wife for life: by the words of the will, the heir is not to have it during her life; and none else can have it, as the executors cannot intermeddle.* But if a man devises land to a stranger after the death of his wife, this does not necessarily infer, that the wife should have the estate for her life: it is but declaring at what time the stranger's estate shall commence; and in the meantime the heir shall have the land.[†,a]

I close this head with the following reflection, That the power of implying will <244> can only be of use where tacit will is authoritative: it can avail

---

5. Procuring a written instrument signed by a court official containing a statement of a decree.

* [M. Bacon,] New abridgment of the law, vol. 2. [1736,] p. 66.

† Ibid.

a. This is a proper example of a maxim in the Roman law, *Positus in conditione non censetur positus in institutione* [The disposition in the contract is not supposed to be the disposition in practice].

nothing where writing, and consequently words, are essential. To make a valid entail, for example, words are essential: tacit will avails nothing.

SECTION III

Whether an omission in a deed or covenant can be supplied.[1]

With regard to the former section, a court has no occasion to extend its equitable power farther than to dive into tacit will and to bring it into daylight. With respect to the present section, the court is called on to extend its power a great way farther, in order to do justice. In framing a deed or covenant, every necessary circumstance is not always in view: articles are sometimes omitted essential to the deed or covenant; which therefore ought to be supplied, in order to do justice to the parties concerned. It is a bold step in a court to supply will in any particu- <245> lar, which so far is making a will for a man who omitted to make one for himself; but where will is declared with respect to capital articles, so as to create a right to one or to both of the parties, it is the duty of a court of equity to supply omissions, in order to make the rights created effectual: a right is created by what is actually agreed on; the court is bound to give force to that right, according to the maxim, That right ought never to be left without remedy.

This extraordinary power ought never to be exercised but where it clearly follows, from the nature of the writing, from the intendment of parties, or from other pregnant circumstances, that there really is an omission of some clause that would have been expressed had it occurred to the parties. If a court should venture to interpose without being certain that the clause was not purposely left out, they would be in hazard of making a will for a man, and overturning that which he himself made. But where they are satisfied that there is really an omission, their supplying the omission is not making a will for a man, <246> but, on the contrary, is completing his will.

1. In the second edition (p. 132), Kames begins this section thus: "Before entering into particulars, it must be premised in general, that a court of common law cannot supply any imperfection in a deed or covenant. Such extraordinary power is reserved for a court of equity, authorised by the principle 'That where a right is created it ought

This doctrine will be illustrated by the following examples. In a wadset the naming a consignator[2] is omitted; which could not be done purposely, a consignator being an essential person in following out an order of redemption. From the nature of the contract, the granter is intitled to redeem; and to make his right effectual, the court will name a consignator. Upon a wadset granted to be held of the superior, an infeftment passed; but it was omitted to provide, that the wadsetter, on redemption, should surrender the subject to the superior for new infeftment to the reverser. The court of session, considering that this is a proper clause, and that the wadsetter could not have objected to it had it occurred in framing the wadset, decreed him to grant a procuratory[3] of resignation.*

A man lent a sum on bond, payable to himself and to his children *nominatim*[4] in fee, with the following provision, <247> "That in case of the decease of any of the said children, the share of that child shall be equally divided among the survivors." One of the children, a son, having predeceased his father, leaving issue, it was questioned, whether his share of the bond descended to his issue, or accresced to the survivors. Here was evidently an omission; as the granter could not intend to exheredate[5] the issue of any of his children. And accordingly the issue of the son were preferred.† Papinian, the greatest of the Roman lawyers, delivers the same

---

to be made effectual.' Hence a practical rule to guide us through all the mazes of this intricate subject: Where ever it appears to be the will of the granter of a deed, or of parties engaged in a covenant, to create a right, it is the duty of a court of equity to supply every defect in order to make the right effectual. If there be no right created, a court of equity has not power, more than a court of common law, to supply any defect. For this in effect would be to create a right; or, in other words, to make a will for a man who has made none for himself: a court of equity cannot make a deed for an individual, more than it can make a statute for the whole people."

2. A person authorized to accept the delivery of money from a debtor, where the creditor refuses to accept it.

3. A mandate or commission granted by one person to act for another.

* Dury [Durie], 9th February 1628, Simson contra Boswell [M 6540]; Gosford, 25th June 1625, Duke Lauderdale contra Lord and Lady Yester [M 6545, from Kames, *Dictionary*, vol. 1, p. 440].

4. "By name."

5. "Disinherit."

† 21st November 1738, Magistrates of Montrose contra Robertson [M 6398, from Kilkerran 455].

opinion in a similar case: "Cum avus filium ac nepotem ex altero filio heredes instituisset, a nepote petiit, ut *si intra annum trigesimum moriretur, hereditatem patruo suo restitueret:* nepos, liberis relictis, intra aetatem suprascriptam vita decessit: fideicommissi conditionem, conjectura pietatis, respondi defecisse, quod minus scriptum quam dictum fuerat inveniretur."* Our author supposes, that the testator had provided for the issue of his grandchildren, but <248> that the provision had been casually omitted by the writer. This is cutting the Gordian knot, instead of untying it; for what if the writer had not received any such instruction? There is no occasion for Papinian's conjecture: it was obviously an omission, which a court of equity ought to supply, in order to do justice, and to fulfil the intendment of the creditor.[6]

A man believing his wife to be pregnant, left a legacy to a friend in the following terms, "That if a male child was brought forth, the sum should be 4000 merks; if a female, 5000 merks." The wife produced no child. As a legacy was intended even in case of a child, it cannot be thought that the friend should have no legacy if no children were born. The clause therefore is evidently imperfect, a member being wanting, that of the testator's dying without children. The want of that member was a pure omission, which the testator would have supplied had the event occurred to him; and which a court of equity may supply, in order fully to accomplish the intendment of those who are <249> no longer in being to speak for them-

---

* l. 102. De cond[icionibus et] demonst[rationibus] et causis [et modis eorum, quae in testamento scribuntur (On conditions, particularizations, explanations for and modalities of provisions in wills), D 35.1.102: Watson iii: 199: "A grandfather instituted as heirs his son and a grandson by another son; he then requested the grandson, should he die before the age of thirty, to make over the [whole] inheritance to his uncle. The grandson died leaving issue but before attaining thirty. My ruling was that considerations of duty meant that the condition of the *fideicommissum* failed, because less was expressed than was intended"].

6. In the first edition (p. 94), Kames commented that the reason given by Papinian was "slight and precarious," and added: "For what if this event was really overlooked? Supposing this to be the fact, we are left without a reason. The solid foundation of the opinion is, that a deed ought not to be made effectual in equity, when by oversight it extends to an event that was not in the view of the granter. So much easier is it to judge or perceive what is right, than to give a solid reason for our judgment." He then proceeds to the exposition in Appendix, pp. 499–500, Extracts [1st: 94–95] and [1st: 96]. A similar comment is included in the second edition (p. 137).

selves. The court of session accordingly found the highest sum due *ex prae-sumpta voluntate testatoris.*[7],* They could go no further without exerting an act of power altogether arbitrary; as they had no *data* for determining what greater length the testator himself would have gone. Here it is proper to be observed, that in the former cases mentioned, a right was created, to make which effectual a court of equity ought to lend their aid. In the present case, there was no right created; and a court of equity had no call to interpose, but in order to give the most liberal effect to deeds made by persons deceased. The present case then is much more delicate than any formerly mentioned.

But now, what if the wife had brought forth twins? Though the testator gave a legacy in the event of a single child, it follows not necessarily, that he would have given a legacy had he foreseen the birth of two children. Therefore, as it is not certain that in the case here figured there is <250> any omission, a court cannot interpose, without hazarding the making a will for a man that he himself would not have made.[8] I venture this opinion even against the authority of Julianus, the most acute of all the writers on the Roman law. "Si ita scriptum sit, 'Si filius mihi natus fuerit, ex besse heres esto, ex reliqua parte uxor mea heres esto; si vero filia mihi nata fuerit, ex triente heres esto, ex reliqua parte uxor heres esto:' et filius et filia nati essent: dicendum est, assem distribuendum esse in septem partes, ut ex his filius quatuor, uxor duas, filia unam partem habeat: ita enim secundum voluntatem testantis, filius altero tanto amplius habebit quam uxor, item uxor altero tanto amplius quam filia. Licet enim subtili juris regulae conveniebat, ruptum fieri testamentum, attamen, quum ex utroque nato testator voluerit uxorem aliquid habere, ideo ad hujusmodi sententiam

7. "From the presumed will of the testator."

* Dirleton, 18th July 1666, Wedderburn contra Scrimzeor [M 6587].

8. When discussing this problem in the first edition, Kames was more critical in his tone (pp. 51–52): "Here was a *casus incogitatus* about which the testator had interposed no will. The legatee therefore had no claim, and the court cannot make a will for any man. It is not a good reason for depriving a man's natural heirs of a sum, that the testator himself would probably have done the same, had he foreseen the event. At this rate, had the testator's wife brought forth twins, some part of the lagacy must have been due, and this part must have been determined by the arbitrary will of the judges. There would be no bounds to the powers of a court of equity were this admitted; and equity would deviate into iniquity."

humanitate suggerente decursum est; quod etiam Juventio Celso appertis-
sime placuit."* <251>

In a contract of marriage there was the following clause: "And in case
there shall happen to be only one daughter, he obliges him to pay the
sum of 18,000 merks; if there be two daughters, the sum of 20,000 merks,
11,000 to the eldest, and 9000 to the other; and if there be three daughters, the sum of 30,000 merks, 12,000 to the eldest, 10,000 to the second,
and 8000 to the youngest." There the contract stops, because probably
a greater number was not expected. The existence of a fourth daughter
brought on the question, Whether she could have any share of the 30,000
merks, or be left to insist for her legal provision *ab intestato* [from an
intestacy]. As it appeared to be the father's intention to provide for all
the children of the marriage, and as he certainly would have provided for
the fourth daughter, it belonged to a court of equity to supply the omission, by naming to her such a sum as he himself would have done. The
court decreed 4500 merks to the fourth daughter, as her proportion of the
30,000 merks; and restricted the eldest daughter to 10,500, the second
to 8500, and the <252> third to 6500.†,9 The following case stands on the

---

* l. 13. pr. De liberis et posthumis heredibus instituendis [The Institution of Children and *Posthumi* as Heirs, D 28.2.13.pr.: Watson ii: 821: "If a will was drawn as follows, 'if a son is born to me let him be my heir in respect of two thirds, let my wife be
heir in respect of the remaining part; but if a daughter is born to me, let her be heir to
the extent of a third; let my wife be heir in respect of the remaining part,' and both a
son and daughter were born the decision must be that the whole inheritance should
be divided into seven parts, so that the son gets four of them, the wife two, and the
daughter one; for in this way, in accordance with the wishes of the testator, the son will
have as much more again as the wife and the wife as much more again as the daughter;
for although it was agreed that by a nice rule of law the will was broken, yet, as the
testator wished his wife to have something against both children, humanity suggested
that a decision of this kind should be reached, which very clearly had the approval also
of Juventius Celsus"].

† 18th July 1729, Anderson contra Anderson [M 6590, from Kames, *Dictionary*, vol.
I, p. 441].

9. When discussing this problem in the first edition, Kames took a critical approach
(p. 52): "It was undoubtedly the father's purpose to provide all the children he expected from that marriage; but the existence of a fourth daughter was a *casus incogitatus* for which no provision was made. A judge must have a strong impulse to make
a settlement upon a child neglected by oversight and not of design. But if a court of
equity undertake in any case to make a provision for a child, who is omitted by the

same foundation. "Clemens Patronus testamento caverat, 'Ut si sibi filius natus fuisset, heres esset: si duo filii, ex aequis partibus heredes essent: si duae filiae, similiter: si filius et filia, filio duas partes, filiae tertiam dederat.' Duobus filiis et filia natis, quaerebatur quemadmodem in proposita specie partes faciemus: cum filii debeant pares, vel etiam singuli duplo plus quam soror accipere. Quinque igitur partes fieri oportet, ut ex his binas masculi, unam foemina accipiat."*

No article concerning law ought to be more relished, than the authority a court of equity is endued with to make effectual deeds and covenants, not only according to the actual will of the parties, but according to their honest wishes. With respect to family-settlements in particular, a man in his last moments has entire satisfaction in reflecting, that his settlement will be made effectual after his death, candidly and fairly, as if he himself were at hand to explain his views. So great stress is laid up- <253> on will as the fundamental part of every engagement, that where it is clear, defects in form are little regarded by a court of equity. Take the following instances. A man settles his estate on his eldest son in tail, with a power, by deed or will under seal, to charge the land with any sum not exceeding £500. A deed is prepared and engrossed, by which he appoints the £500 to his younger children; but dies without its being signed and sealed. Yet this in

---

father, it is but one step farther to make a provision to children in every case where it was intended, though left undone; as, for example, where a bond is writ out but not signed, or signed by the granter but not by the witnesses. I imagine that our judges have been misled here, as in many other instances, by a blind attachment to the Roman law, from which the decision now mentioned is copied." By the time of the second edition (p. 134), he modified his view: "Though the existence of a fourth daughter was a *casus incogitatus,* for which no provision was made; yet as it appeared to be the father's intention to provide for all the children of that marriage, there was a right created in the fourth daughter by this intention, which intitled her to a share of the 30,000 merks."

* l. 81. pr. De heredibus instituendis [The Institution of Heirs, D 28.5.82.pr: Watson ii: 848: "Clemens Patronus had provided in his will that if a son had been born to him, he should be heir and, if two sons, they should be heirs in equal shares; if two daughters, similarly; if a son and a daughter, he had given the son two shares and the daughter a third share. Two sons and a daughter having been born, the question was asked how we should make up the shares in the case proposed, as the sons ought to be equal, even also each receive twice as much as their sister. Therefore, five shares ought to be created so that the males may have two of them each and the female one"].

equity shall amount to a good execution of his power, the substance being performed.* Here there could be no doubt about the man's will creating a right to his younger children. The power he reserved of charging the estate by deed or will under seal, was not intended to make their right conditional, but to give them the highest security that is known in law. This security was indeed disappointed by the man's sudden death; but he had sufficiently declared his purpose to give them £500, which afforded them a good claim in equity for that sum. Provost Aberdeen wishing to have a country-seat <254> near the town of Aberdeen, purchased the lands of Crabstone from Farquharson of Invercauld, for £3900 Sterling; and missive letters were exchanged, agreeing that the lands should be disponed to the Provost in liferent, and in fee to any of his children he should name. The title-deeds were delivered to a writer, who, by the Provost's order, made out a scroll of the disposition, to the Provost in liferent, and to Alexander the only son of his second marriage in fee. A disposition was extended 12th June 1756, and dispatched to Invercauld, inclosed in the following letter, subscribed by the Provost: "This will come along with the amended disposition; and upon its being delivered to me duly signed, I am to put the bond for the price in the hands of your doer." Invercauld not being at home, the packet was delivered to his lady. As soon as he came home, which was on the 21st of the said month, he subscribed the disposition, and sent it with a trusty hand to be delivered to the Provost at Aberdeen. But he, having been taken suddenly ill, died on the 24th of June, a few hours before the express arrived; whereby it happened, that <255> the disposition was not delivered to him, nor the bond for the price subscribed by him. This unforeseen accident gave rise to a question between Robert, the Provost's eldest son and heir, and the said Alexander, son of the second marriage. For Robert it was pleaded, That the disposition remained an undelivered evident under the power of the granter; nor could it bind the Provost, since it was not accepted by him; and laying aside that incompleted deed, nothing remained binding but the mutual missives; the benefit of which must descend to the Provost's heir at law, seeing none of his

---

* Abridg. Cases in equity, ch. 44. sect. B. §14 [*Smith* v. *Ashton* (1675) 1 Eq. Cas. Abr. 345, reprinted in *The English Reports,* vol. 21, p. 1091].

children is named in these missives. It was answered for Alexander, That his father's will being clearly for him, it is the duty of the court of session to make it effectual. And he accordingly was preferred.* A settlement being made on a young woman, proviso that she marry with consent of certain persons named, the consent to be declared in writing; a consent by parole was deemed sufficient.† For it was not understood to be the will of <256> the maker to forfeit the young woman merely for the want of form, when the substance was preserved. Land cannot be charged but by a formal deed; for such is the common law. But a court of equity may supply a defective deed, considered as a satisfactory evidence of will, by subjecting the heir personally.[10] In one case, the court of session made a wide step. In a disposition the granter reserved power to burden the land with a sum to particular persons named. The disponee was made liable for the sum, though the disponer had made no step toward exercising the power.‡ This indeed was a favourable case, the power reserved being to provide younger children. And yet, were this extension of equity to be justified, I cannot discover any bounds to equitable powers. What better evidence can be required of the disponer's resolution not to exert his reserved power, than his forbearing to exert it?

I must observe upon this section in general, that to ascertain what was a man's will, to make it effectual, and to supply omissions, afford a spacious field in equity <257> for supporting deeds and covenants, upon which the prosperity of society and many of its comforts greatly depend. But as far as I discover, equity, which has a free course in supporting will, never is exerted against it. It ventures not to alter a man's will, far less to void it: it cannot even supply will where totally wanting. Where a deed or covenant

---

* 13th December 1757, Alexander Aberdeen contra Robert Aberdeen [M 6598, from Kames, *Select Decisions*, p. 189].

† 1. Modern Reports [300,] 310 [*Fry* v. *Porter* (1670) in (Anthony Colquitt), *Modern Cases, or Select Cases Adjudged in the Courts of Kings Bench, Chancery, Common-pleas, and Exchequer since the Restauration of His Majesty King Charles II* (London: T. Basset, J. Wright, R. Chiswell, and S. Heyrick, 1682), reprinted in *The English Reports*, vol. 86, p. 898].

10. Kames here alludes to the notion that whereas common law courts settled questions of right, courts of equity operated by directing the conscience of the parties.

‡ Gosford, 15th February 1673, Graham contra Morphey [M 4100].

is fairly made without any reserved power to alter, what before was voluntary, becomes now obligatory; and it must have its course, whatever be the consequence. However clear it may be, that it would not have been made had the event been foreseen, yet no court of law is impowered to void the writing or to alter it; for this would be to make a settlement for a man who himself made none. Power so extensive would be dangerous in the hands of even the most upright judges. I dare not except a British parliament.

Were a court of law endued with a power to alter will, or to supply its total absence, the following cases would be a strong temptation to exercise the power. A gratuitous bond by a minor being voided at the instance of his heir, because a <258> minor cannot bind himself without a valuable consideration; the obligee insisted for an equivalent out of the moveables left by the minor, on the following ground, That he could have left the same sum to his friend by way of legacy. It was admitted, that if the heir's challenge had been foreseen, the minor probably would have given a legacy instead of a bond: but that in fact the minor gave no legacy; and no court can make a testament for a man, who himself made none: which accordingly was found.*,[11] The bond here was complete in all its parts, and no article omitted that a court of equity could supply. There was indeed a defect of foresight with respect to what might happen; but a court of equity does not assume a power to supply defects of that kind. The like was found with respect to a gratuitous disposition of an heritable subject, which was voided as being granted on deathbed. The disponee claimed the value from the executor, presuming that the deceased, had

---

* Fountainhall, 15th December 1698, Straiton contra Wight [M 10326].

11. Commenting on this case in the second edition (p. 149), Kames notes: "In this case, as it appears to me, the *ratio decidendi* is taken from the common law, not from equity. One thing seems clear, that the minor intended in all events to bestow the sum named upon his friend the obligee; for if he was willing to bind himself personally to pay the sum, he could not have the least hesitation to bind his representatives by bequeathing it as a legacy. And if this be admitted, the consequence is fair, that the friend thereby acquired a right, which it was the duty of the court of session to make effectual, by sustaining a claim against the executor in the same manner as if the sum had been a legacy."

the event been foreseen, would have given an equivalent out of his movables. But as in fact the deceased signified no will nor <259> intention to burden his executor, the judges refused to make him liable.*,12 The Roman law concerning a *legatum rei alienae*13 adheres to the same principle. Where a testator legates a subject as his property, which after his death is discovered to be the property of another, the heir is not bound to give an equivalent, because *deficit voluntas testatoris.*14 But if the testator knew that the subject was not his, it must have been his will, if he did not mean to be jocular, that it should be purchased by his heir for the legatee; and this implied will was accordingly made effectual by the Pretor as a judge of equity.

---

* Dirleton, 12th November, Stair, 26th November, 1674, Paton contra Stirling [M 12588]; Fountainhall, 22d November 1698, Cumming contra Cumming [M 5399].

12. The case is discussed at greater length in the first edition (pp. 50–51): "A gratuitous disposition of an heritable subject being voided, because granted on death-bed, the disponee insisted against the executor for value, founding his claim upon the will of the deceased, presumed from the deed, of which the natural construction is, 'That if the disposition by any means prove ineffectual, the disponee shall be entitled to an equivalent.' Answered, 1mo, The voidance of the disposition, as granted on death-bed, was a *casus incogitatus,* about which no person can say what would have been the will of the disponer had he foreseen the event. 2do, supposing it probable in the highest degree, that the disponer would have provided an equivalent had he foreseen the event, yet in fact as he has not interposed any will in this matter, judges have no power to supply the defect. The court was of opinion, that the disposition could not affect the executry either as a debt or as a legacy. This is a just decree; for a gratuitous deed, which has no foundation other than will merely, cannot be supported in any particular, except so far as will is actually interposed." In the second edition, a different commentary is included (pp. 149–50): "This judgement must be approved; for it is far from being clear that the value of the heritable subject was intended in all events to be made effectual to the disponee. It may be a man's will to alien from his heir an heritable subject, though he would not burden his executors with the value, supposing them to be a number of younger children. This argument goes on the supposition that the disponer knew the subject to be heritable. But what if by mistake he took it to be moveable? This is more doubtful. And yet even upon that supposition it would be bold to give an equivalent; because a man may have motives for bestowing upon his friend a certain subject, who would not be disposed to burden either his heir or executor with an equivalent sum."

13. "A legacy of a thing which does not belong to the testator."

14. "The will of the testator is lacking."

SECTION IV

A deed or covenant that tends not to bring about the end for which it was made.

Where a man exerts an external act, however inconsiderately, he cannot be relieved, *quia factum infectum fieri ne-* <260> *quit.*[1] But a man making a deed or covenant may be relieved by a sentence of the judge; and will be relieved if a good cause be shown. With respect particularly to the subject of the present section, a deed or covenant, as laid down in the beginning of this chapter, is a mean employed to bring about a certain end or event: whence it follows, that it ought to be voided where it fails to be a mean, or, in other words, where it tends not to bring about the end or event desired. To think otherwise, is to convert a mean into an end, or to adhere to the mean without regard to the end.[2] Common law, regarding the words only, may give force to such a deed or covenant; but equity pierces deeper into the nature of things. Adverting to the fallibility of our nature, it will not suffer one to be bound by such an engagement; and considers, that when he is freed from it, it is only *lucrum cessans*[3] to the party who insists on its performance, not *damnum datum.*[4]

To prevent mistakes in the application of the foregoing doctrine, it is necessary to be observed, that the end here understood is not that which may be secretly <261> in view of the one or the other party, but that which is spoken out, or understood by both; for a thought retained within the mind, cannot have the effect to qualify an obligation more than to create it. The overlooking this distinction has led Puffendorff into a gross error: who puts the case,* That a man, upon a false report of all his horses being destroy'd, makes a contract for a new set; and his opinion is, that in equity the purchaser is not bound. This opinion is of a man unacquainted with

---

1. "A thing which is done cannot be undone."
2. For the fuller formulation of the means/ends distinction in the first and second editions, see Appendix, Extracts [1st: 85–87] and [2nd: 139–40].
3. "A gain lost."
4. "Damage done."
* lib. 3. cap. 6. §7 [Samuel von Pufendorf, *Of the Law of Nature and Nations,* trans. B. Kennet (Oxford, 1703), p. 215].

the world and its commerce. Were mistakes of that kind indulged with a remedy, there would be no end of law-suits. At this rate, if I purchase a quantity of body or table linen, ignorant at the time of a legacy left me of a large quantity, I ought to be relieved in equity, having now no occasion for the goods purchased. And for the same reason, if I purchase a horse by commission for a friend, who happens to be dead at the time of the purchase, there must be a relief in equity, though I made the purchase in my own name. But there is no foundation for this opinion in equity, <262> more than at common law. If a subject answer the purpose for which it is purchased, the vender has no farther concern: he is entitled upon delivery to demand the price, without regarding any private or extrinsic motive that might have led his party to make the purchase. In general, a man who exposes his goods to sale must answer for their sufficiency; because there is no obligation in equity to pay a price for goods that answer not the purpose for which they are sold by the one, and bought by the other: but if a purchaser be led into an error or mistake that regards not the subject nor the vender, the consequences must rest upon himself.

I shall only add upon this general head, that the end purposed to be brought about by a deed or covenant ought to be lawful; for to make effectual an unlawful act is inconsistent with the very nature of a court of law. Thus a bond granted by a woman, binding her to pay a sum if she should marry, is unlawful, as tending to bar population; and therefore will be rejected even by a court of common law. And the same fate will attend every obligation granted *ob turpem causam;*[5] a bond, <263> for example, granted to a woman as a bribe to commit adultery or fornication. So far there is no occasion for a court of equity.

The first example shall be from deeds. Upon a young man living abroad under sentence of forfeiture, his father settled an annuity for life, ignorant that it would fall to the crown. This deed will not bind the granter; for it does not produce the end or effect intended. To sustain it, would be to give force to the mean without regarding the end.

Here a subtile question casts up, What in the view of law is to be held

5. "On account of an immoral consideration" (from C 4.7: *de condictione ob turpem causam*).

the end upon which the fate of the deed or covenant depends: is a court of equity confined to the immediate end, or may it look forward to consequences. An example will explain the question. In a contract of marriage, the estate is settled on heirs-male of the marriage. The eldest son, being forfeited for high treason, is forced to abandon his native country. The father makes a settlement, excluding him from the succession, in order to prevent his estate from falling to the crown. Can this <264> settlement be supported by a court of equity? I doubt. The contract of marriage was a proper mean for the end in view, namely, that the estate should descend to the heirs-male of the marriage. The contractors had no farther view; and if a court were to be sway'd by unforeseen consequences, deeds and covenants could not be much relied on. Suppose that after the father's death a pardon is procured for the son, must not this have the effect to void the last settlement, and to restore the son to his right as heir of the marriage? Yet in a case still more delicate, the court of session gave judgment for the father, influenced probably by an overflow of compassion and humanity. James Thomson, in his marriage-contract, provided his estate and conquest to the heirs of the marriage. The heir, a son idle and profligate, became a notour bankrupt;[6] which induced the old man to settle his estate on his grandchildren by that son, burdened with the liferent of the whole to him. A reduction being brought of this settlement as in defraud of the marriage-contract, the court of session repelled the reason of <265> reduction, and sustained the settlement.* Beside setting the father free from a rational and solemn contract, there was a very material point in equity against sustaining the settlement, which seems to have been overlooked. What if the whole debts, or the bulk of them, were contracted by the son for necessaries before his bankruptcy? On that supposition, the creditors were *certantes de damno vitando:* the children, on the other hand, were *certantes de lucro acquirendo.* Take a different view of the case: What if the bankrupt, by some fortunate adventure, a lottery-ticket for example, had been enabled to pay all his debts: would he not have been entitled as a free

---

6. A "notorious bankrupt," defined by legislation of 1696 (*APS* x:33: c.5, An Act for declaring notour bankrupts).

* 11th February 1762, Thomson and his Creditors contra his Children [M 13018, from Kames, *Select Decisions,* p. 251].

man to claim the benefit of the contract of marriage, seeing the only cause for disinheriting him was now removed? If so, a contract of marriage is but an unstable security, as it may depend on future contingencies whether it will be effectual or no.

In questions between husband and wife, a contract of marriage is a contract in the <266> strictest sense; but in questions with the heirs, it is rather to be considered as a deed; in which light it is viewed above. I proceed now to give examples relative to what are properly contracts. In a contract of sale, the circumstance regarded at common law, is the agreement of the parties, the one to sell the other to purchase the same subject. What are its qualities, whether the price be adequate, and whether it will answer the end for which it is purchased, are left to the regulation of equity. The last belongs to the present section; one instance of which makes a figure in practice, to wit, where goods sold are by some latent insufficiency unfit for the purchaser's use. A horse is bought for a stallion that happens to be gelt, or a hogshead of wine for drinking that happens to be sour. If the purchaser be notwithstanding bound, he is compelled to accept goods that are of no use to him, and over and above to pay a full price for what is of little or no value. It would, on the other hand, be to act against conscience, for the vender to take a full price in such a case. Supposing the goods to be sufficient at the time of the bargain, but in- <267> sufficient at the time of delivery, the loss naturally falls on the vender, who continues proprietor till the subject be delivered. If insufficient at the time of the bargain, there is an additional reason for setting it aside, namely error; for error relieves the person who is *certans de damno vitando* against the person who is *certans de damno captando*, which will be more fully explained afterward.[a]

A large cargo of strong ale was purchased from a brewer in Glasgow,

---

a. The laws of Hindostan go a great way farther against the vender of insufficient goods, farther indeed than either equity or utility will justify. "If a man have sold rice or wheat for sowing, and they do not spring up, the vender shall make good the crop." [Cf: (Nathaniel Brassey Halhed,) *A Code of Gentoo Laws, or Ordinations of the Pundits, from a Persian Translation* (London, 1776), p. 11. This reference is new to the third edition. Boswell recorded seeing Kames in January 1778: "He was keeping his bed with a cold, but was in good humour, his spirits clear and lively. He had the Gentoo Laws, just published, lying on a little table," *Private Papers of James Boswell from Malahide Castle,* ed. G. Scott and F. A. Pottle, 18 vols. (New York, 1928–34), vol. 15, p. 267.]

in order to be exported to New York. In a suit for the price, the following defence was sustained, That having been not properly prepared for the heat of that climate, it had bursted the bottles, and was lost. It was not supposed, that the brewer had been guilty of any wilful wrong; but the defence was sustained upon the following rule of equity, That a man who purchases <268> goods for a certain purpose, is not bound to receive them unless they answer that purpose; which holds *a fortiori* where the vender is himself the manufacturer. And where the insufficiency cannot be known to the purchaser but upon trial, the rule holds even where the goods are delivered to him. It was also in view, that if the brewer be not answerable for the sufficiency of ale sold by him for the American market, that branch of commerce cannot be carried on.*

An insolvent debtor makes a trust-right[7] in favour of his creditors; and, among his other subjects, dispones to the trustees his interest in a company-stock. A creditor of the company, who was clearly preferable upon the company-stock before the bankrupt's private creditors, being ignorant of his preference, accedes to the trust-right, and consents to an equal distribution of the bankrupt's effects. Being afterward informed of his preference, he retracts while matters are yet entire. *Quaer.*[8] Is he bound by his agreement? He undoubtedly draws by it all the benefit he <269> had a prospect of; and considering the agreement singly, without relation to the end, he is bound; and so says common law. But equity considers the end and purpose of the agreement; which is, that this man shall draw such proportion of the bankrupt's effects as he is intitled to by law. The means concerted, that he shall draw an equal proportion, contribute not to this end, but to one very different, namely, that he shall draw less than what is just, and the other creditors more. Equity relieves from an engagement where such is the unexpected result; there being no authority from the intendment of parties to make it obligatory where it answers not the purposed end.

---

* 13th December 1765, Baird contra Pagan [M 14241, from Kames, *Select Decisions,* p. 309].

7. That is, a trust deed, transferring the debtor's assets to a trustee to hold for the benefit of his creditors.

8. "Question."

Having laid open the foundation in equity for giving relief against a covenant where performance answers not the end purposed by it, I proceed to examine whether there be any relief in equity after the covenant is fulfilled. I buy, for example, a lame horse unfit for work; but this defect is not discovered till the horse is delivered, and the price paid. If the vender hath engaged to warrant the horse as sufficient, he is liable at common law to ful- <270> fil his covenant. But supposing this paction not to have been interposed, it appears to me not at all clear, that there is any foundation in equity for voiding the sale thus completed. The horse is now my property by the purchase, and the price is equally the vender's property. If he knew that the horse was lame, he is guilty of a wrong that ought to subject him to the highest damages:* but supposing him *in bona fide,* I see no ground for any claim against him. The ground of equity that relieves me from paying for a horse that can be of no use, turns now against me in favour of the vender; for why should he be bound to take my horse, of no use to him? The Roman law indeed gave an *actio redhibitoria*[9] in this case, obliging the vender to take back the horse, and to return the price. But I discover a reason for this practice in a principle of the Roman law, that squares not with our practice, nor with that of any other commercial nation. The principle is, That such contracts as are intended to be equal, ought to answer the intention: and therefore in such contracts the Roman Pretor never permitted any <271> considerable inequality. Hence the *actio quanti minoris,*[10] which was given to a purchaser who by ignorance or error paid more for a subject than it is intrinsically worth: and it follows upon the same plan of equity, that if a subject be purchased which is good for nothing, the *actio quanti minoris* must resolve into an *actio redhibitoria.* But equity may be carried

---

* l. 13. pr. [De] Actionibus empt[i et venditi (The Actions for Sale and Purchase), D 19.1.13.pr.: Watson ii: 548: "Julian . . . says that if (the seller) acted unknowingly in selling a diseased herd or an unsound timber, then in an action on purchase he will be held responsible for the difference from the smaller amount I would have paid had I known of this. But if he knew but kept silent and so deceived the buyer, he will be held responsible to the buyer for all losses he sustained due to this sale"].

9. A redhibitory action: An action to cancel a sale because of defects in the goods sold, and to return them to the vendor.

10. An action for the shortfall in value, whereby the purchaser could recover a sum overpaid for a defective item.

so far as to be prejudicial to commerce by encouraging law-suits; and for that reason we admit not the *actio quanti minoris:* the principle of utility rejects it, experience having demonstrated that it is a great interruption to the free course of commerce. The same principle of utility rejects the *actio redhibitoria* as far as founded on inequality; and after a sale is completed by delivery, I have endeavoured to show, that if inequality be laid aside, there is no foundation for the *actio redhibitoria.* In Scotland, however, though the *actio quanti minoris* is rejected, the *actio redhibitoria* is admitted where a latent insufficiency unqualifies the subject for the end with a view to which it was purchased. This practice, as appears to me, is out of all rule. If we adhere strictly to equity without regarding utili- <272> ty, we ought to sustain the *actio quanti minoris,* as well as the *actio redhibitoria.* But if we adhere to utility, the great law in commercial dealings, we ought to sustain neither. To indulge debate about the true value of every commercial subject, would destroy commerce: and for that reason, equity, which has nothing in view but the interest of a single person, must yield to utility, which regards the whole society.

SECTION V

Equity with respect to a deed providing for an event that now can never happen.

This section chiefly concerns settlements *intra familiam*[1] and such like, which on the part of the maker are gratuitous. I cannot easily figure a case relative to a covenant where it can obtain.

A bachelor in a deadly disease, daily expecting death, settles his estate on a near relation, without reserving a power to alter, which he had no prospect of needing. He recovers as by a miracle, and lives <273> many years. The deed, being in its tenor pure, is effectual at common law. But as death was the event provided for, which did not happen, and as he had no intention to give away his estate from himself, it will not be sustained in equity. And indeed it would be hard to forfeit the poor man for a mis-

1. "Within a family."

take in thinking himself past recovery. In this example, the failure of the event is accidental, independent of the granter's will. But equity affords relief, even where the failure is owing to the granter himself. An old man, on a preamble that he was resolved to die a bachelor, settles his estate on a near relation, reserving his liferent and power to alter. In dotage, he takes a conceit for a young woman, marries her, but dies suddenly without altering his settlement. Seven or eight months after, a male child is born, who claims the estate. The deed cannot stand in equity, being made for an event that has not fallen out, to wit, the granter's dying without children.[2] Take another example which depends on the same principle. In the year 1688, the Duchess of Buccleugh obtained from the crown a gift of her husband the Duke of Mon- <274> mouth's personal estate, which fell under his forfeiture. As by this means their younger son the Earl of Deloraine was left unprovided, she gave him a bond for £20,000. The Duke's forfeiture being afterward rescinded, the Earl of Deloraine, executor decerned to him,[3] claimed from his mother the Duke's personal estate. The Duchess was willing to account; but insisted that payment of the bond should be held as part-payment of the personal estate. Which was accordingly found.* Here the event provided for, which was the Earl's being deprived

2. Discussing this example in the first edition, Kames adds the following comment (p. 93): "I endeavour to confirm this reasoning by the following reflections. A man's will occasioned by error or oversight, ought not to be regarded in opposition to what evidently would have been his will had all the circumstances been in view. It is no doubt one of the most useful branches of judicial power, to give the utmost effect to the settlements of those who are no longer in this world to act for themselves. A man dies in peace, when he trusts that his deeds will be made effectual, fairly and candidly, according to his intention. But it is neither humanity with respect to the deceased, nor justice with respect to the living, to enforce a settlement in an event which the maker would avoid with horror were he alive. Equity therefore will never interpose in favour of such a deed. And it contributes in the highest degree to peace of mind, that a man in his last moments can with assurance rely upon the justice of the laws of his country; entertaining a full conviction, that, after his death, his concerns will be regulated in the same manner as if he himself had direction of them." For the treatment in the second edition, see Appendix, p. 525, Extract [2nd: 136], where he takes a different view of conditions from that stated at the end of this section.

3. That is, decreed to be the executor (executor-dative).

* 7th December 1723, Earl Deloraine contra Duchess of Buccleugh [M 6396, from Kames, *Dictionary*, vol. 1, p. 428].

of his legal right by his father's forfeiture, had failed; and consequently the bond could not be effectual in equity. There was beside a still stronger objection against it, namely, that the pursuer had now right to the very subject out of which the bond was intended to be paid.

Cases of this nature are resolved by lawyers into a conditional grant, imply'd, they say, though not expressed. A condition may be imply'd in the case last mentioned; but the circumstances of the two <275> former will not admit such implication. In the first, the granter is described as having lost all hope of recovery; in which he would not readily think of making his death a condition of the grant. Neither in the other is there any foundation for implying a condition *si sine liberis,*[4] as the granter declared his firm intention to die a bachelor. In cases of this nature, there is no necessity of cutting the Gordian knot by a supposed condition. It is loosed with great facility, by applying to it a maxim, That a deed providing for an event that has failed, cannot in equity be effectual.

SECTION VI

Errors in deeds and covenants.[1]

In the beginning of this chapter it is laid down, that the moral sense, respecting the fallibility of our nature, binds us by no engagement but what is fairly done with every circumstance in view; and consequently, that equity will afford relief <276> against rashness, ignorance, and error. In handling the circumstance last mentioned, it will contribute to perspicuity, that we distinguish errors that move a person to enter into a deed or covenant, from errors that are found in the deed or covenant itself. Errors of the former kind happen more frequently with respect to deeds: of the latter kind, seldom but in contracts. I begin with the first kind, of which the following is an example. My brother having died in the East Indies, leaving children, a boy is presented to me as my nephew, with credentials in appearance sufficient. After executing a bond in his favour for a moder-

---

4. "If [he dies] without children."

1. For the treatment of this topic in the first (and second) editions, see Appendix, Extract [1st: 109–13].

ate sum, the cheat is discovered. The moral sense would be little concordant with the fallibility of our nature, did it leave me bound in this case. And supposing the cheat not to be discovered till after my death, a court of equity, directed by the moral sense, will relieve my heir. Here the relief is founded on error solely; for the boy is not said to have been privy to the cheat, or to have understood what was transacting for his behoof. To the same purpose Papinian, "Falsam causam legato non obesse, verius <277> est; quia ratio legandi legato non cohaeret. Sed plerumque doli exceptio locum habebit, si probetur alias legaturus non fuisse."* The circumstances of the following case make it evident, that the error was the sole motive, bringing it under the exception mentioned by Papinian. "Pactumeius Androsthenes Pactumeiam Magnam filiam Pactumeii Magni ex asse heredem instituerat; eique patrem ejus substituerat. Pactumeio Magno occiso, et rumore perlato quasi filia quoque ejus mortua, mutavit testamentum, Noviumque Rufum heredem instituit, hac praefatione: 'Quia heredes quos volui habere mihi, continere non potui, Novius Rufus heres esto.' Pactumeia Magna supplicavit Imperatores nostros; et, cognitione suscepta, licet modus institutione contineretur, quia falsus non solet obesse, tamen ex voluntate testantis putavit Imperator ei subveniendum: igitur pronunciavit, 'Hereditatem ad Magnam pertinere, sed legata ex posteriore testamento eam praestare debere, proinde atque si in posterioribus tabulis ipsa <278> fuisset heres scripta.'"† The testament could not stand in equity,

---

* l. 72. §6. De condition[ibus] et demonstr[ationibus et causis et modis eorum, quae in testamento scribuntur (On conditions, particularizations, explanations for, and modalities of provisions in wills), D 35.1.72.6: Watson iii: 194: "The truer view is that an incorrect motivation is no impediment to a legacy because the reason for a bequest is no part of the bequest; still the defense of bad faith will generally be applicable if it be established that the testator would not otherwise have made the legacy"].

† l. ult. De hered[ibus] instit[uendis (On the institution of heirs), D 28.5.93: Watson ii: 850: "Pactumeius Androsthenes had instituted Pactumeia Magna, the daughter of Pactumeius Magnus, as heir in respect of his whole inheritance and had substituted her father to her. When Pactumeius Magnus had been killed and a rumour had reached him that Pactumeius Magnus's daughter also was dead, he changed his will and instituted Novius Rufus as heir, prefacing the institution as follows: 'Because the heirs whom I wished that I might have I could not have, let Novius Rufus be heir.' Pactumeia Magna petitioned our emperors and, having held a *cognitio* (that is, a judicial inquiry or cognizance), although a limitation was placed on the institution, because an erroneous (limitation) does not usually form an obstacle (to an institution), the emperor took

proceeding from an erroneous motive. To sustain such a testament, would
be to disinherit the favourite heir, contrary to the will of the maker. As to
the legacies contained in the latter testament, they were justly sustained, as
there appeared no evidence nor presumption that the testator was moved
by an error to grant them.

In many cases it may be doubted, whether error was the sole motive,
or one of them only. To solve that doubt, the nature of the deed will have
great influence. A rich man executes a bond for a small sum in favour of
an indigent relation, upon the narrative, that he had behaved gallantly
in a battle, where he was not even present. Equity will not relieve the
granter against this bond, because charity of itself was a good cause for
granting. The following texts of the *Corpus Juris* belong to the same head.
"Longe magis legato falsa causa adjecta, non nocet: veluti cum quis ita
dixerit, 'Titio, quia me absente negotia mea curavit, stichum do, lego.'
Vel ita: 'Titio, quia patro- <279> cinio ejus capitali crimine liberatus sum,
stichum do, lego.' Licet enim neque negotia testatoris unquam gesserit
Titius, neque patrocinio ejus liberatus sit, legatum tamen valet. Sed si conditionaliter enunciata fuerit causa, aliud juris est: veluti hoc modo, 'Titio,
si negotia mea curaverit, fundum meum do, lego.'"* Again: "Quod autem
juris est in falsa demonstratione, hoc vel magis est in falsa causa: veluti ita,
'Titio fundum do, quia negotia mea curavit.' Item, 'Fundum Titius filius
meus praecipito, quia frater ejus ex arca tot aureos sumpsit': licet enim
frater hujus pecuniam ex arca non sumpsit, utile legatum est."†

---

the view that, nevertheless, having regard to the testator's wishes, she should be helped.
Therefore, he gave judgment that the inheritance belonged to Magna but that she must
pay the legacies given in the later will, just as if she herself had been appointed heir in
the later will"].

* §31. Instit. de legatis [On Legacies, Inst 2.20.31: Birks & McLeod 85: "Still less does
it matter if the testator discloses a false belief in the background. Take 'I give and bequeath Stichus to Titius because he managed my affairs in my absence' or 'I give and
bequeath Stichus to Titius because by his advocacy I was acquitted of a capital charge.'
Here the legacy is valid even if Titius never managed his affairs or secured his acquittal.
It is different if it is put conditionally: 'I give and bequeath land to Titius, if it was he
who managed my affairs in my absence'"].

† l. 17. §2. De condit[ionibus] et demonst[rationibus et causis et modis eorum, quae
in testamento scribuntur (On conditions, particularizations, explanations for, and modalities of provisions in wills), D 35.1.17.2: Watson iii: 184: "The law in respect of false
particularization applies the more to a false explanation, for example, 'I give the estate

With respect to a deed entirely gratuitous to a person unconnected with the granter, and above taking charity, an error like what is mentioned above, will be held more readily the sole motive; and consequently a ground in equity for voiding the deed.

Where there is any foundation of controversy, a transaction putting an end to it must be effectual; for where there is a <280> rational motive for making a deed, the making of it will never be held to proceed from error. But where a man is moved to make a transaction on supposition of a claim that has no foundation, as in the case of a forged deed, he will be relieved from the transaction in equity, the motive being erroneous.* An unequal transaction may be occasioned by error; but here utility forbids relief; for to extinguish law-suits, the great source of idleness and discord, is beneficial to every member of society.

We proceed now to errors found in a deed or covenant after it is made. These are of two kinds: one prevents consent altogether; as where the purchaser has one subject in view, the vender another. And as no obligation can arise where there is no agreement, such a covenant, if it can bear that name, is void at common law, and there is no occasion for equity. The other kind is where the error is in the qualities of a subject, not in the subject itself; a purchase, for example, of a horse understood to be an Arabian of true blood, but discovered after to be a mere Ple- <281> beian. The bargain is effectual at common law; and the question is, Whether or how far there ought to be a relief in equity.

We begin with errors that regard the subject itself. If in the sale of a horse, the vender intended to sell the horse *A,* the purchaser to buy the horse *B,* there is no agreement: the one did not agree to sell the horse *B,* nor the other to buy the horse *A.* The same must hold in every bargain of sale, whatever the subject be.

Next, where an error respects not the subject, but its qualities. I purchase, for example, a telescope, believing it to be mounted with silver, though the mounting is only a mixed metal. Or, I purchase a watch, the

---

to Titius because he looked after my affairs' or 'let my son Titius take the estate as a preferred gift because his brother abstracted so many gold pieces from the chest'; the legacy is valid, even though the brother did not take the money from the chest"].

* l. 42. Cod. De transact[ionibus (On negotiated settlements), C 2.4.42].

case of which I take to be gold, though only silver gilt. Equity will not relieve me from the bargain, as the instrument equally answers its end, whether more or less ornamented. The most that can result from such an error, is to abate the price, in order to make the bargain equal; and this was done in the Roman law. But a claim of that nature, impeding the free course of commerce, is rejected by commercial nations. <282>

It is a very different case, where the error is such as would have prevented the purchase had it been discovered in time, termed in the Roman law, *Error in substantialibus.*[2] Example: A horse is purchased as a stallion for breed; but unknown to both, he happened to be gelt before the bargain. It may be doubted, whether such a bargain be not effectual at common law, as the error is only in the quality of the horse; but undoubtedly it may be set aside in equity, upon a principle mentioned more than once above, That the vender *certans de lucro captando,* ought not to take advantage of the purchaser's error, who is *certans de damno vitando.* Another principle concurs, handled sect. 4 of the present chapter, that one is not bound to fulfil a contract which answers not the purposed end.

We proceed to errors that respect the property of the subject sold. As here the Roman law affords not much light, we have the greater need to proceed warily. I sell to John a horse understood by both of us to be my property. After all is agreed on, it is discovered to be his property. The bargain is void even at common <283> law, as it is incapable of being fulfilled on either side. I cannot convey the property to him, nor can he receive the property from me. It was not my intention to sell a horse that did not belong to me; nor was it his intention to pay for his own horse. The case where the horse belongs to a third person, is in effect the same. I did not intend to sell a horse that belongs not to me; nor did John intend to purchase a horse from me that belongs to a third person. If the mistake be discovered before delivery to John, I am bound in justice to deliver the horse to the proprietor, not to John; and John is under no obligation to pay the price. If the discovery be not made till after John has received the horse and paid the price, there is no obligation on either side, but that I restore the price, as the bargain was void from the beginning.

2. Error as to the fundamental nature, or going to the root of the contract.

That the same doctrine ought to obtain in the sale of land, is extremely evident. And as in a sale of land writing is essential, the warrandice contained in the disposition,[3] or in the minute of sale, ought not to go further than to oblige the vender to repeat[4] the price in case of eviction; un- <284> less the circumstances of the bargain be such as to justify a more extensive warrandice. Hence it follows, that the clause of warrandice in a disposition or minute of sale of land, even what is termed absolute warrandice, ought to be confined to a repetition of the price upon eviction, unless the vender be further bound in express terms. Yet absolute warrandice here is by the generality of lawyers understood as binding the vender to make up to the purchaser all the loss he sustains by eviction, which in effect is the value of the subject at that time. Whether this be a just conception, deserves the most serious consideration, being of capital importance in the commerce of land.

That the eviction of land ought not to subject the vender to harder terms than the eviction of a moveable, is a doctrine that at least has a plausible appearance. A plausible appearance however is not sufficient: let us enter into particulars, in order to try whether some lurking objection may not be detected that will overturn it. If none can be detected, we may rest secure that the doctrine is solidly founded in principles. In communing about a sale <285> of land, the title-deeds are produced for the inspection of the purchaser: there is a search of the records; and the bargain is not concluded till the purchaser have full satisfaction that the vender is proprietor. If there happen, after the strictest examination, to be a latent defect in the progress, it is not to be charged on the vender more than on the purchaser. For what good reason then ought he to be made liable for the value of the land as at the time of eviction? The land was understood by both parties to belong to the vender: he wanted to have money for his land; the purchaser to have the land for his money; neither of which purposes can be fulfilled. The purchaser is not bound, because he cannot have the land he bargained for: the vender is not bound, because he agreed to sell his own land, not that of another. Suppose the eviction has taken place while

---

3. A unilateral deed by which property is transferred.
4. That is, "repay": from *repetition,* the repayment of money which was not owed.

the subject remains with the vender, the minute of sale is void, no less than in the case first mentioned, where the one has it in view to purchase the horse *A*, the other to sell the horse *B*. Nor can it make any difference that the purchaser is infeft before eviction. The infeft- <286> ment is void, as taken without consent of the proprietor: and after restoring the price, both parties are free as before they entered into the contract. Upon the whole, the vender must restore the price, because he cannot perform the mutual cause. And as for the purchaser, he can have no claim for the value of the subject evicted; because there can be no claim, either for a subject or its value, at the instance of a person who has no right to the subject. Add another argument no less conclusive. From a contract binding on no person, no claim can arise to any person; not even the claim against the vender for restoring the price, which arises not from the contract, but from being in his hand *sine causa*.[5] Hitherto every particular is the same as in the sale of a moveable. The only difference that can found an argument of favour, is on the side of a vender of land. As in the sale of a moveable all rests on the information of the vender; it might be thought, that more is incumbent on him than on a vender of land, whose affirmation is not relied on, but the progress.

So much for common law. Let us now <287> examine, whether there be any ground in equity for subjecting the vender of land to all the loss that the purchaser may suffer by eviction. A bargain of sale is intended to be fair and equal. The purchaser gets the land, the vender the price, and both are equally accommodated. By eviction, the vender is the only sufferer. Land is seldom alienated but to pay debt. The vender is deprived of the price: his debts remain unpaid; and he is reduced to poverty. But what does the purchaser suffer? He is indeed deprived of what he probably reckons a good bargain; but the price, which is restored to him, will give him the choice of as good a bargain in any corner of Scotland. This is a just state of the case; upon which I put the following question, Is there any equity for subjecting the vender, after restoring the price, to pay what more the land may be worth at the time of eviction? Before answering this question, let the following case be considered. Soon after the purchaser's

---

5. Without legal cause or reason.

entry to the land, a valuable lead or coal mine is accidentally discovered, for which the purchaser paid nothing, the parties having had no view to it. This mine <288> belongs to the evicter, and to neither of the contractors. Suppose now the purchase to have been only of a few acres, the mine may intrinsically be worth a hundred times the price. Not satisfied with saying, that I see no equity for obliging the vender to pay this immense sum; I have no hesitation to affirm positively, that it would be highly unjust. This example deserves attention. Would it not require the most express terms in a clause of warrandice to oblige the vender to pay such a sum? One thing will certainly be granted me, that such a contract entered into by a facile person, or by a minor even with consent of curators, would be voided without hesitation. There may indeed be good ground to demand caution from the vender to restore the price in case of eviction; considering that venders of land are seldom in opulent circumstances. More cannot justly be demanded.

The hardship is here intolerable, which no man with his eyes open will submit to. But now, supposing, for argument's sake, the purchaser's claim, however much above the price, to be well founded; is there nothing to be said for the vender, <289> where the land happens to fall in value below the price? If the purchaser, upon a rise of the market, be intitled to draw from the vender more than the price, ought not the vender to have the benefit of a falling market to pay less than the price? I cannot invent a case where the maxim, *Cujus commodum, ejus debet esse incommodum,*[6] is more directly applicable. It is evident, however, that the vender must restore the price wholly, as the bargain was from the beginning void; and for the same reason, the purchaser can have no claim for more than the price.

Viewing this case with regard to expediency, it is of importance to the public, that the commerce of land, the most useful of all, be free, easy, and equal. If a vender must be so deeply burdened as above, and laid open to such consequences, no man will sell land but in the most pinching necessity. Men at any rate are abundantly averse to sell land, which reduces many to low circumstances; and if this law should obtain, there would be few sales but by public authority. Nor is this all. This law, as to

6. "The person who has the advantage should also have the disadvantage."

meliorations, would be of no use to the purchaser, who <290> is secured absolutely without need of oppressing the vender: he is intitled to retain possession, till the evicter make good to him all the expence profitably laid out upon the subject.

Hitherto of a complete progress. Very different is the case where the progress is acknowledged to be incomplete. If in this case the vender be unwilling to sell under the market-price, he must submit to the hazard of eviction, and give warrandice to make up to the purchaser what he loses by eviction, being the value of the subject at the time of eviction. It is a chance-bargain, importing, that if the land sink in value below the price, the purchaser is intitled to that value only; and is intitled to double or triple the price, if the land rise so high in value.

What then is the true import of a clause of absolute warrandice in a sale of land? In the sale of a moveable, there is no warrandice. The vender is held to be proprietor, of which the purchaser is satisfied without requiring warrandice. Neither is there use for warrandice against incumbrances; because a moveable passes from hand to hand, without being subjected to <291> any incumbrance. But in a sale of land warrandice is necessary; for though there may be no doubt of the vender's right, yet it is proper that the purchaser be secured against incumbrances, to many of which that appear not on record land is subjected. Clauses of warrandice are different, according to the nature of the bargain. In some contracts of sale, the vender gives warrandice against his own facts and deeds only; in some, against the facts and deeds of his predecessors and authors; in some, against all incumbrances whatever; and this last is termed *absolute warrandice.* But of whatever tenor the warrandice be, it will not be understood to guard against a preferable title of property, unless expressed in the clearest terms. The reason is given above, that to extend warrandice so far, where the progress is good and the price adequate, is repugnant to common law, to equity, and to expedience.

The authors of our styles[7] have had a just conception of this matter. Every clause of warrandice I have seen ingrossed[8] in a disposition of land

7. Model forms of deeds.
8. That is, drawn in a deed.

for a just price, and where the progress was held sufficient, is <292> confined to incumbrances, without any mention of eviction on a preferable right of property. The style follows: "warranting the land from all wards, reliefs, nonentries, marriages of heirs, liferent escheats, recognitions, liferent infeftments, annualrents, and from all and sundry other burdens and incumbrances whatever, whereby the land may be evicted, or possession impeded, at all hands, and against all deadly, as law will." Nor a syllable of eviction upon a preferable title of property; which, as it cuts deeper than any incumbrance, would be placed in the front were it intended. Nor let the concluding words, *at all hands and against all deadly,* create any doubt; it being an infallible rule in the construction of writs, Never to extend a general clause beyond the particulars to which it is added. This rule holds, even where the general clause is expressed absolutely, without reference to any of the antecedent articles in particular. In the present case, we have scarce occasion for that rule, as the general clause has an immediate reference to incumbrances, and to nothing else. <293>

It is admitted by all lawyers, that in the conveyance of claims or debts, absolute warrandice does not secure the purchaser against eviction upon a preferable title; and I am utterly at a loss to see, that the same precise words should have a different meaning in a conveyance of land. Lord Stair indeed endeavours to account for this difference; but without success, as far as I can comprehend. His words are, "Warrandice has no further effect than what the party warranted truly paid for the right whereby he was or might be distressed, though less than the value of the right warranted. This will not hold in warrandice of land; as to which land of equal value, or the whole worth of what is evicted as it is at the time of the eviction, is inferred; because the buyer had the land with the hazard of becoming better or worse, or the rising or falling of rates, and therefore is not obliged to take the price he gave."* I cannot avoid observing, that two very different subjects are jumbled together in this passage; namely, the purchasing a competing right in order to pre- <294> vent eviction, and the effect of warrandice where land is actually evicted. These are different propositions depending on different principles, and entirely unconnected;

---

* Institut. book 2. title 3. sect. 46 [Stair, *Institutions,* pp. 375–76].

yet are opposed to each other as if they were parts of the same proposition. Can any accuracy be expected in such a manner of handling a question? His Lordship beside stops short in the middle. In the case of rising of rates, the purchaser, says he, is not obliged to take the price he gave. Not a word upon the case of falling of rates. His Lordship upon maturer thinking would have seen, that as the subject never belonged to the purchaser, he could have no claim for it or its value against the vender; and he also would have seen, that from a contract binding neither party, no claim can arise to either party. But this is not all. I am at a loss to conceive that the hazard of becoming better or worse, can be of any weight in this case. One thing I clearly conceive, that if this circumstance have any weight, it will make absolute warrandice to have the same effect in the conveyance of debts, that it is said to have in the conveyance of land. Real debts[9] produced in a rank- <295> ing[10] are commonly at first of uncertain value. An adjudication is purchased for a trifle, which, by objections sustained against competing creditors, draws at the conclusion a large sum. There is here perhaps more hazard of becoming better or worse, than in the purchase of land: yet, after the purchaser of the adjudication has laid out a considerable sum in obtaining a high place in the ranking, he has upon eviction no claim against the vender but for the price he paid: he must rely on the evictor for recovering the expence of process. Sensible I am from my own experience, how difficult it is to guard against errors in the hurry of composition. Lord Stair was an able lawyer; and, not to mention the case of a mine discovered after the purchase, had he but thought on useful improvements laid out by the purchaser, he certainly would not have thought it reasonable that the vender should be liable for the value of these, considering that the evicter is bound for it. The following scene might have occurred to his Lordship. After adjusting the progress and the price, "Nothing remains," says the intended purchaser, "but that you <296> warrant the expence I intend to lay out upon inclosing, plant-

9. Real debts or real burdens (*debita fundi*): obligations laid on lands to pay money, declared in a deed naming the creditor, the lands affected, and the amount of the burden.

10. *Ranking and sale:* a process whereby the heritable property of an insolvent was sold, and the proceeds distributed among his creditors.

ing, and other improvements.[" "]Are you not secured by law?" answers the vender: "you are intitled to retain possession till you obtain full satisfaction from the evicter. You have thus real warrandice, and need not the addition of personal." "I insist however for your warrandice," replies the other: "one cannot be made too secure." "After being absolutely secure," rejoins the vender, "beyond the possibility of a disappointment, your demand for my warrandice has no meaning but to have it in your power to oppress me. A demand so irrational proves you either to be a fool or a knave: I reject all dealing with you." As no man of sense would advise the vender to submit to that demand, I hold it as demonstration, that the expence of profitable improvements cannot be understood to be comprehended in a clause of absolute warrandice. As to voluptuary expences,[11] termed so by Roman writers, the law, it is true, gives no security in case of eviction; nor is there reason for it. A man embellishes his person, his house, his fields, in order to make <297> a figure. In case of a voluntary sale, he reckons not upon any additional price for a fine garden, and as little in case of eviction. And were the vender to be made liable, it would oblige venders to be extremely cautious about the person they sell to; no man could sell an acre or two without the hazard of absolute ruin. Upon these acres the purchaser erects a palace, adorns his gardens with temples, triumphal arches, cascades, &c. &c. sufficient to exhaust the riches of a nabob. The poor vender all this while sits trembling at every joint for fear of eviction.

I put a case the most favourable that can be for the purchaser, to which the argument urged by Lord Stair is directly applicable. By a gradual rise of the market without a farthing laid out on it, the land purchased thirty years ago has risen in value a third or fourth part above the price paid for it. There lies no claim against the evicter for this additional value; and it is so much lost to the purchaser if the vender be not liable. This probably is the case his Lordship had in view. If the vender, *major, sciens, et prudens,*[12] bound himself to make up that loss, he must sub- <298> mit. But I state a plain question, Is there any thing in justice, or in the nature of a contract of sale, to lay this risk on the vender? In making the bargain, both parties are equally *in bona*

---

11. "Such repairs as are only for pleasure but yield no profit": Bankton, *Institute,* vol. I, p. 236.

12. "A person who is of age, conscious of what he is doing, and of good sense."

fide, the progress is held to be good by both; and both are losers; not equally indeed, for the vender, who must restore the whole price, is the greatest loser. Say, what is it that intitles the purchaser to draw from the vender the present value of the land? Not the contract, for a contract that does not bind can produce no action: not the property of the land, which did not pass to the purchaser. The only remaining foundation I can think of, is to claim that loss on the footing of damage. Neither can this hold, as there can be no claim for damage, except from express paction or from a delict; and the case supposed admits of neither. Nor could Lord Stair have a view to either, when the opinion he gives is founded solely on the rising or falling of rates.

This interesting point of law was judicially handled in a late process, Lord Napier *contra* the Representatives of Mr William Drummond, who sold the estate of <299> Edinbelly to his Lordship. The progress had been held sufficient by the purchaser; and the warrandice was in the ordinary style, the same that is above mentioned. It was found however by decree of the court of session, "That the representatives of Mr William Drummond are liable to Lord Napier for the value of the estate of Edinbelly, evicted from him, as the same was at the time of eviction."* This judgement has a formidable appearance against the doctrine above inculcated. Yet as far as could be gathered from the reasoning of the judges, what moved them was not the terms of the absolute warrandice, but the two following arguments: First, That possessors of land ought not to be discouraged from making ornamental improvements; and, next, That though many evictions must have happened, there is not on record a single instance of a process for eviction: whence it was presumed, that the present value must have been submitted to by the vender, otherwise that it would have been demanded from him in a process. And the inference was, that <300> it is now too late to alter a practice so long established. To the first answered, That the possessor has absolute security for profitable improvements, which, as beneficial to the public, deserve every encouragement; but that ornamental improvements, being a species of luxury, are entitled to no favour; and were they intitled, that the evicter only ought to be subjected, as they were occasioned by his delay or negligence; especially as he now has the plea-

* 6th August 1776.

sure of them. Answered to the second, The presumption lies clearly on the other side. No man who has produced a progress to the satisfaction of the purchaser, will upon eviction find himself bound in conscience to pay the present value of the land, including all the improvements, voluptuary as well as profitable. And as there is no instance of a decree against the vender for that value, there is the highest probability that the demand has never exceeded the price, which will always be admitted without a process. As for embellishments in particular, the taste for them is but creeping in; and they are so rare in Scotland, as to afford no probabi- <301> lity that they ever were claimed upon eviction.

The arguments I have endeavoured to obviate, were spoken out; but what I conjecture chiefly influenced the judges, was the authority of Lord Stair; which could not fail to have great weight, considering that for a course of years it had been inculcated into every student as a rule of law, and adopted by every member of the court. Men, who in early youth have sucked in a maxim whether of law or of religion, are impregnable by argument. Much superior to that of reason must the authority be, which can operate a conversion. In matters arbitrary and doubtful, I chearfully submit to the authority of eminent writers, to that especially of Lord Stair, who is our capital writer on law. But neither reason nor common sense will justify such deference, with regard to points that are resolvable into principles.

But now, waving that subject, I have another attack to make on his Lordship, and on its offspring the late judgement of the court, which will open the eyes of our men of law, if any thing can. Though his Lordship's opinion respects voluntary <302> sales only, yet it must equally hold in judicial sales, as the fluctuating value of land is the same whether sold publicly or privately. Yet this opinion is not made the rule in judicial sales. The practice is, that each creditor gives warrandice against eviction to the extent of what he draws of the price; justly, because the creditors cannot retain the price, if the purchaser be deprived of the land. But warrandice is never exacted from them for the value of the land in case of eviction. This has not only been the uniform practice from the commencement of judicial sales, but is a practice authorised by an express act of sederunt,* declar-

* Last of March 1685 [AS 167].

ing, "That the creditors preferred to the price, shall, upon payment, dispone to the purchaser their rights and diligences, with warrandice *quoad*[13] the sums received by them; so that in case of eviction of the lands disponed, they shall be liable to refund these sums in whole or in part effeiring[14] to the eviction. And this is declared to be the import of any former obligements of warrandice given by creditors in the case foresaid." Here we have <303> constant and uniform practice for a long course of time, authorised by the supreme court of the nation; which equals in authority an act of parliament. Now as, with respect to the present point, no difference can be figured between a public and a private sale, the rule laid down for the former must equally obtain with regard to the latter, were the case of the latter otherwise doubtful. Had the practice in public sales been suggested to the court, or had it occurred to any of the judges, we may rest with assurance, that a different judgment would have been given in the case of Lord Napier.

I have insensibly been led, from the close and concise manner of a didactic work, into a sort of dissertation. But the importance of the subject will I hope plead for me.

Hitherto of errors discovered in the contract itself. We proceed to errors arising in the performance of a contract. Under this head comes erroneous payment, or *solutio indebiti,*[15] as termed in the Roman law. Of this there are two kinds; one where payment is erroneously made of an extinguished debt, supposed to be subsisting; and <304> one where a debt really subsisting is paid by a man who mistakes himself to be the debtor. To judge rightly of the former, the following preliminaries will pave the way. The sale of a subject as existing which does not exist, is void: the vender cannot deliver a *non ens;*[16] and the purchaser is not bound to pay the price unless he get what he bargained for. In like manner, where an extinguished debt is assigned, understood to be subsisting, the assignment is void; and if the price have been paid, it must be restored on discovery of the error. This doctrine is applicable to the case in hand. As it is unjust in a creditor

13. "To the extent of."
14. *Effeir:* to fall by right; to appertain.
15. "The payment of what is not owing."
16. A nonentity; thing not existing.

to take twice payment, he can have no pretext for detaining the second payment made erroneously by the debtor. The same must follow, where the second payment has been made to the creditor's heir, who, though *in bona fide,* can have no better right than his predecessor had. The same will also follow in the case of an executor-creditor.[17,*] An assignee to a debt extinguished by payment obtains payment from <305> the debtor's heir; both of them being ignorant of the former payment. The error is discovered *rebus integris.*[18] The heir must have back the money he paid, being in the hands of the assignee *sine causa;* and the assignee is intitled to draw from the cedent the price he paid for a *non ens.* So far clear. But what if the error be discovered several years after, when the cedent happens to be insolvent? This intricate case is handled above, where it comes in more properly. There it is laid down, that the assignee having been deprived of his recourse against the cedent by the debtor's rashly paying the debt a second time, neglecting to look into his affairs, the loss ought to rest on him. The argument is still stronger for the assignee, where a debt is purchased on condition that the debtor's heir grant a bond of corroboration. This bond indeed corroborating a *non ens* cannot be effectual; but as the purchase was made on the faith of it, the loss occasioned by the cedent's bankruptcy, ought to fall on the heir, who was at least rash or incautious, not on the purchaser, who acted prudently. And when <306> the price he paid to the cedent is made up to him by the heir, matters are restored to their original state, as if the bargain had not been made. There may be bargains against which there can be no restitution; as where a bond is assigned to a husband in name of tocher[19] with his wife, which happens to be corroborated by the debtor's heir before it was assigned to the husband. As the marriage was made on the faith of the bond of corroboration, the granter of the bond can have no relief, but must pay the whole to the husband. And so says Paulus: "Si quis indebitam pecuniam, per errorem, jussu

17. A person who, in order to recover a debt in legal proceedings has himself confirmed as executor in respect of some items only of the deceased's assets.

* Stair, Gosford, 10th January 1673, Ramsay contra Robertson [M 2924 and 2926; the Gosford report is in Kames, *Dictionary,* vol. 1, p. 186].

18. "Matters being complete"; that is, no performance of the contract having taken place.

19. "Dowry."

mulieris, sponso ejus promisisset, et nuptiae secutae fuissent, exceptione doli mali uti non potest. Maritus enim suum negotium gerit; et nihil dolo facit, nec decipiendus est: quod fit, si cogatur indotatam uxorem habere. Itaque adversus mulierem condictio ei competit; ut aut repetat ab ea quod marito dedit, aut ut liberetur, si nondum solverit."*

We proceed to the case where a debt really subsisting is paid by a man who er- <307> roneously understands himself to be the debtor. This case has divided the Roman writers. To the person who thus pays erroneously, Pomponius gives a *condictio indebiti.*[20,†] Paulus is of the same opinion.[‡] Yet this same Paulus, in another treatise, refuses action.[§] The solution of this question seems not to be difficult.[21] Were it the effect of the erroneous payment to extinguish the debt, a *condictio* could not be sustained against the creditor: a man who does no more but receive payment of a just debt, cannot be bound to repeat. But the following reasons evince, that a debt

---

* l. 9. §1, De condict[ione] causa data [causa non secuta (On the *condictio* for non-reciprication), D 12.4.9.1: Watson i: 376: "Suppose that, on the authority of a woman, someone promises her fiancé money mistakenly supposed to be owed, and the marriage does follow. He cannot use the defense of fraud; for the husband is only looking to his own interest and is not perpetrating any fraud. Nor ought he to be let down, which he would be if forced to take an undowered wife. So the *condictio* must go against the woman either to get back from her the payment to the husband or, if nothing has yet been paid, to effect a discharge"].

20. An action to recover money paid by mistake, which was not due (*indebitus*).

† l. 19. §3. [De condict[ione] indeb[iti] (On the *condictio* for money not owed), D 12.6.19.3: Watson i: 381].

‡ l. 65. §ult. eod. [De condictione indebiti (On the *condictio* for money not owed), D 12.6.65.9: Watson i: 388].

§ l. 44. eod. [De condictione indebiti (On the *condictio* for money not owed), D 12.6.44: Watson i: 386].

21. In the first edition, Kames wrote, on this point (p. 92), "The solution of this question seems not to be difficult. A man pays a debt due by another, thinking by mistake that he himself is debtor. The sum here delivered to the creditor, operates necessarily as extinction of the debt. It is delivered with that intention, and is accepted with the same intention. Every circumstance is here found that is necessary to extinguish the debt. If the debt then be extinguished, no claim can lie against the *quondam* creditor, either in law or equity, for restoring the money; and all that remains to the person who has thus paid erroneously, is an action against the true debtor for the sum paid to the creditor; which hath a good foundation in equity upon the following principle, *Quod nemo debet locupletari aliena jactura.*" By the second edition (pp. 144–45), he had changed his mind on this, taking the view given in the text above.

is not extinguished by erroneous payment. First, There is nothing that can hinder the creditor, upon discovery of the mistake, to restore the money, and to hold by the true debtor. Second, The true debtor, notwithstanding the erroneous payment, is intitled to force a discharge from the creditor, upon offering him payment; which he could not do were the debt already extinguished. Hence it follows, that the creditor holds the putative debt- <308> or's money *sine justa causa*[22] and consequently, that a *condictio indebiti* against him is well founded. But the circumstance that operates in the case first mentioned, where there exists no debt, operates equally here. Upon receiving payment *bona fide* from the putative debtor, the creditor thinks no more of a debt he considers to be extinguished; and therefore, if the real debtor become insolvent after the payment, the inconsiderateness of the putative debtor will subject him to the loss; which may instruct him to be more circumspect in time coming.

With respect to payment erroneously made by the debtor to one who is not the creditor, see book 2. chap. 5.

The legal consequences of the payment of a debt by a man who knows himself not to be the debtor, are handled book 1. part 2. at the end. <309>

SECTION VII

A deed or covenant being void at common law as ultra vires, *can a court of equity afford any relief?*

A Principle in logics, That will without power cannot produce any effect, is applicable to matters of law; and is thus expressed, That a deed *ultra vires*[23] is null and void. Common law adheres rigidly to this principle, without distinguishing whether the deed be wholly beyond the power of the maker, or in part only. If it be one deed, it admits of no division at common law, but must be totally effectual or totally void. The distinction is reserved to a court of equity, which gives force to every rational deed as far as the maker's power extends. Take the following illustrations.

22. "Without just cause."
23. Beyond the power of the grantor.

If one having power to grant a lease for ten years grants it for twenty, the lease is in equity good for ten years.* For here <310> there can be no doubt about will; and justice requires, that the lease stand good as far as will is supported by power. A tack set by a parson for more than three years without consent of the patron, is at common law void totally, but in equity is sustained for the three years.† But a college having set a perpetual lease of their teinds for 50 merks yearly, which teinds were yearly worth 200 merks; and the lease being challenged for want of power in the makers, who could not give such a lease without an adequate consideration, it was found totally null, and not sustained for any limited time or higher duty.‡ For a court of equity, as well as a court of common law, must act by general rules; and here there was no rule for ascertaining either the endurance of the lease, or the extent of the duty. Further, a court of equity may separate a deed into its constituent parts, and support the maker's will as far as he had power: but here the li- <311> miting the endurance and augmenting the duty so as to correspond to the power of the makers, would be to frame a new lease, varying in every article from the lease challenged.

By the act 80, parl 1579,[24] "All deeds of great importance must be subscribed and sealed by the parties, if they can write; otherwise by two notaries before four witnesses, present at the time, and designed by their dwelling-places; and the deeds wanting these formalities shall make no faith." With respect to this statute, a deed is held by the court of session to be of great importance when what is claimed upon it exceeds in value £100. And upon the statute thus constructed, it has often been debated, Whether a bond for a greater sum than £100 subscribed by one notary only and four witnesses, or two notaries and three witnesses, be void; or whether it ought to be sustained to the extent of £100. A court of common law, adhering to the words of the statute, will refuse action upon it.

---

* 1. Chancery cases 23 [*Pawcy* v. *Bowen* (1663), reprinted in *The English Reports*, vol. 22, p. 674].

† Stair, 18th July 1668, Johnston contra Parishioners of Hoddam [M 6848].

‡ Stair, 13th July 1669, Old College of Aberdeen contra the Town [M 2533].

24. *APS* iii: 145: 1579, c. 18, Anent the inserting of witnessis in obligationis and writtis of importance [Subscription of Deeds Act 1579].

And such was the practice originally of the court of ses- <312> sion.* But a court of equity, regarding the purpose of the legislature, which is to make additional checks against falsehood in matters of importance, will support such deeds to the extent of £100: for a deed becomes of small importance when reduced to that sum, and ought to be supported upon the ordinary checks. And accordingly the court of session, acting in later times as a court of equity, supports such bonds to the extent of £100.[†] But in applying the rules of equity to this case, the bond ought to be for a valuable consideration, or at least be rational: if irrational, it is not intitled to any support from equity.

Oral evidence is not sustained in Scotland to prove a verbal legacy exceeding £100, but if it be restricted to that sum, witnesses are admitted.[‡,25]

When arbiters take upon them to determine articles not submitted, the award or <313> decreet-arbitral[26] is at common law void even as to the articles submitted. A decreet-arbitral is considered as one entire act, which must stand or fall *in totum.* Equity, prone to support things as far as rational, separates the articles submitted from those not submitted, and sustains the proceedings of the arbiters as far as they had power. Thus, if two submit all actions subsisting at the date of the submission, and the arbitrators release all actions to the time of the award, the award shall be good for what is in the submission, and void for the residue only.[§] A decreet-arbitral being challenged, as *ultra vires compromissi*[27] with respect

* Hope, (Obligation), November 29. 1616, Gibson contra Executors of Edgar [M 6839, in Kames, *Dictionary,* vol. 1, p. 463]; Durie, 13th November 1623, Marshall contra Marshall [M 6839].

† Dictionary of Decisions, (Indivisible) [Kames, *Dictionary,* vol. 1, p. 464, citing Durie, 7th Auchinleck, *(Legacy)* 11th July 1629, Wallace contra Muir: M 6847. Durie 1st December 1629, executrix of Scot contra Rae's legatars: M 6847].

‡ Durie, 7th July 1629, Wallace contra Muir [M 1350]; Durie, 1st December 1629, Executrix of Scot contra Raes [M 6847].

25. The second edition (p. 170) proceeds at this point to discuss the case of Charles M'Kinnon of M'Kinnon contra Sir James M'Donald, 14 Feb. 1765 (reported by Kames in *Select Decisions of the Court of Session, from the Year 1752 to the Year 1768,* p. 298 [M 5279]), which is discussed in vol. 2 of the third edition, p. 112). See Appendix, p. 527, Extract [2nd: 170].

26. The decision of an arbiter.

§ [M. Bacon, A] New abridgment of the law, vol. 1. [1736], p. 139, 140.

27. Beyond the powers given by the submission to arbitration.

to mutual general discharges which were ordered to be granted, though some particular claims only were submitted; the decreet-arbitral was sustained as far as relative to the articles submitted, and found void as to the general discharges only.* Arbiters having decreed a sum to themselves and their clerk, for which the submission gave no <314> authority; yet the decreet-arbitral, as far as supported by the submission, was found good even at common law, so as to have the privilege of the regulations 1695,[28] not to be liable to any objection but falsehood, bribery, and corruption. Upon this ground, an objection of iniquity was repelled as incompetent.† Here the objection of iniquity had but an indifferent look: an objection carrying a strong appearance of justice, would probably have been better received.

Family-settlements are commonly more complex than any of the cases mentioned above, consisting of many parts interwoven so intimately, that if one be withdrawn as *ultra vires,* the rest must tumble. There is no remedy but to adjust the will to the present circumstances, in such a manner as the maker himself would have done had he foreseen the event. Take the following examples. A man having two sons, John and James, makes a deed, settling upon them his estate, consisting of two baronies, to John one of the baronies, the other to James. John's part is evicted by one having a preferable right. The deed, as far <315> as in favour of James, will be supported at common law, which regards the words only without piercing deeper. But a court of equity considers, that to give to one of the brothers the whole that remains of the estate, and nothing to the other, is inconsistent with the will of the maker, who proportioned his estate between them in the same deed by a single act of will. Therefore to support that will as far as the present circumstances can admit, the court will divide the remaining estate between the brothers, in the same proportion that the whole was divided by the maker. And this may be done boldly; as being what the granter himself would have done, had he foreseen the event. The following example is of the same kind. A man settles his estate of £1000 yearly rent on his eldest son, burdened with £8000 to his eight

---

* Fountainhall, 25th December 1702. Crawford contra Hamilton [M 6835].

28. See Articles of Regulation concerning the Session, section 25: Act of Sederunt, 2 November 1695, in *AS* 209, 215.

† March 1777, Jack contra Cramond [M App. 1, Arbitration, No. 5].

other children. A farm making half of the estate is evicted. The children notwithstanding claim their whole provision; which perhaps would be sustained at common law, as there is no condition expressed. But assuredly, the provision was not intended to be made effectual, even though there should not remain a shilling <316> to the heir. In order to fulfil the maker's will as far as the present circumstances admit, a court of equity will restrict the provision to £4000, which is giving to the younger children the same proportion of their father's effects that was originally intended. But let it be remarked, that the result will be different where there is a bond of provision for £8000, and the estate settled on the heir by a different deed, or left to be taken up *ab intestato* [by intestacy]. He will be subjected to all the debts, and to the bond of provision among the rest. Take a third example. A man having three daughters, settles his land-estate on the eldest, with competent provisions to the other two. As this settlement happened to be made on deathbed, it was reduced by the younger sisters, who by that means came to be heirs-portioners[29] with the eldest. Can they claim their provisions over and above? Here the whole was done in the same deed, and by a single act of will. It was not the intention of the father, that the eldest should have the estate independent of her sister's provisions; and as little that they should have their provisions independent of their eldest sister's right to <317> the estate. A court of equity, therefore, to support the father's deed as far as possible, will reject the claim for the provisions. The younger sisters disobeying their father's will, are not permitted to take any benefit from it. Equity suffers no person to approbate and reprobate the same deed. The younger sisters, therefore, if they adhere to their reduction, must give up their provisions.[30] The following is a similar example. John Earl of Dundonald, by a deed of entail, settled his land-estate on his heirs-male; with the same breath settled his moveables by a testament; and executed bonds of provision to his daughters. These several writings, done *unico contextu*[31] in pursuance of one act of will, and making a complete settlement of his estate real and personal, remained with him undelivered.

29. Co-heirs; females succeeding jointly to a heritage for which there is no male heir.
30. This case is identified in the first edition (p. 95) and second edition (p. 138) as Stair, Feb. 1, 1671, Pringle contra Pringle [M 6374]. See Appendix, p. 500, Extract [1st: 94–95].
31. In one connection; as part of one single continuous process.

After the Earl's death, certain lands contained in the entail being found to be still remaining *in hereditate jacente*[32] of a remote predecessor, they were claimed by the daughters as heirs of line. It was objected, That the whole settlement was one act of will, and one deed, though in different writings; that the pursuers could not approbate and reprobate; <318> and that therefore, if they claimed the lands contrary to their father's will, they could take no benefit by that will. It was accordingly found, That the pursuers might chuse either, but could not have both.*

The settlement of an estate by marriage-articles upon the heirs of the marriage, is not intended to bar the husband from a second marriage, or from making rational provisions to the issue of that marriage. A man thus bound makes exorbitant provisions to the issue of a second marriage, such as his whole estate, or the greater part. This settlement, as a breach of engagement, is wholly void at common law; and it is a matter of delicacy for a court of equity to interpose where there is no rule for direction. It would, however, be inconsistent with common sense, that children should suffer as much by excess of affection in their father, as by his utter neglect. As it would be a reproach on law, that the children should be left without remedy, the court of session ventures <319> to interpose, by sustaining the provisions to such an extent as to be consistent with the engagement the father came under in his first contract of marriage. The court, however, never interposes without necessity; and if common law afford any means for providing the children, the matter is left to common law. The following case will illustrate this observation. Colonel Campbell, being bound by marriage-articles to provide to the issue the sum of 40,000 merks, with the conquest, did, by a deathbed-settlement, appoint his eldest son to be heir and executor; leaving it upon the Duke of Argyle and the Earl of Ilay to name rational provisions to his younger children. The referees having declined to act, the younger children insisted to have the settlement voided, as contradictory to the marriage-articles. It was urged for the heir, That the Colonel had power to divide the special sum and conquest, by

32. "In the estate of a deceased person."
* 20th February 1729, Countess of Strathmore and Lady Catharine Cochrane contra Marquis of Clydesdale and Earl of Dundonald [M 6377, from Kames, *Dictionary*, vol. 1, p. 427].

giving more to one child and less to another; and that though the whole happens to be settled on the eldest son, by accident not by intention, it belongs to the court of session to remedy the inequality, by doing what was expected from the referees, <320> namely, to appoint rational provisions to the younger children. The court voided the settlement totally; which intitled the children *per capita* to an equal division of the subjects provided to them in the marriage contract.*

SECTION VIII

Where there is a failure in performance.

In order to distinguish equity from common law upon this subject, we begin with examining what power a court of common law has to compel persons to fulfil their engagements. That this court has not power to decree specific performance, is an established maxim in England, founded upon the following reason, That in every engagement there is a term for performance; before which term there can be no demand; and after the term is past, performance at the term is imprestable.[1,†] <321> A court of common law, confined to the words of a writing, hath not power to substitute equivalents; and therefore all that can be done by such a court, is to award damages against the party who has failed. Even a bond of borrowed money is not an exception; for after the term of payment, the sum is ordered to be paid by a court of common law, not as performance of the obligation, but as damage for not performance. This, it must be acknowledged, is a great defect; for the obvious intention of the parties in making a covenant, is not to have damages, but performance. The defect ought to be supplied; and it is supplied by a court of equity upon a principle often mentioned, That where there is a right it ought to be made effectual. By every covenant that

---

* 22d December 1739, Campbell contra Campbells [M 674 and 6849, from Kames, *Dictionary,* vol. 1, pp. 53, 465].

1. "Unperformable."

† See Vinnius's commentary upon §2. De verborum obligationibus. Institutes [Commentary on Inst. 3.15.2 (On the Verbal Obligation), in A. Vinnius, *In quatuor libros Institutionum imperialum commentarius,* ed. J. G. Heineccius (Leiden: Joannes van der Linden, 1726), lib. III, tit. xvi, pp. 614–17].

is not conditional, there is a right acquired to each party: a term specified
for performance is a mean to ascertain performance, not a condition; and
when that mean fails, it is the duty of a court of equity to supply another
mean, that is, to name another day.

To illustrate this doctrine, several cases shall be stated. In a minute
of sale of land, <322> a term is specified for entering the purchaser into
possession, and for paying the price. The matter lies over till the term is
past, without a demand on either side. At common law, the minute of sale
is rendered ineffectual; because possession cannot be delivered, nor the
price be paid, at a term that is now past: neither can damage be awarded
for non-performance, as neither of the contractors has been *in mora*.[2]
But the remedy is easy in a court of equity; namely, to assign a new term
for specific performance; which fulfils the purpose of the covenant, and
makes the rights therefrom arising effectual.[3] But the naming a new term
for performance, must vary the original agreement. The price cannot bear
interest from the term named in the minute, because the purchaser got not
possession at that term: nor is the vender liable from that term to account
for the rents, because he was not bound to yield possession till the price
should be offered. These several prestations must take place from the new
term named by the court of equity.

Supposing now a *mora* on one side. The <323> purchaser, for example,
demands performance at the term stipulated; and years pass in discussing
the vender's defences. These being over-ruled, the purchaser insists for
specific performance. What doth equity suggest in this case? for now, the
term of performance being past, performance cannot be made in terms of
the original articles. One thing is evident, that the purchaser must not suffer by the vender's failure; and therefore, a court of equity, though it must
name a new term for performance, may, at the instance of the purchaser,

2. *Mora:* delay; normally a claimant's delay in asserting a right or claim, to the prejudice of the defender.

3. When this case is discussed in the first edition, Kames adds the following explanation (p. 48): "A term specified for performance is not readily supposed to imply a
condition: it is considered only as a means to bring about the end proposed; and when
it proves ineffectual, it is the province of a court of equity to supply other means; that
is, in the present case to name another day for performance. This is what the parties
themselves would have done, had they foreseen the event."

appoint an account to be made on the footing of the original articles. If the rent exceed the interest of the price, the balance may be justly claimed by the purchaser. But what if the interest of the price, as usual, exceed the rent? The vender will not be intitled to the difference; because no man is intitled to gain by his failure. In a word, the purchaser can claim damage in the former case, so far as he loses by the vender's failure. But in the latter case, he gains by the failure, and has no damage to claim. This, at first view, may seem to clash with the maxim, *Cujus commodum, ejus* <324> *debet esse incommodum.*[4] There is no clashing in reality: the vender suffers justly for his failure; but the purchaser cannot suffer, who was always ready to perform. This gives the true sense of the maxim, That it holds only between persons who are upon an equal footing; not between persons where the one is guilty, the other innocent. I need scarce add, that the option given to the purchaser upon the vender's *mora,* is given to the vender upon the purchaser's *mora.*

It frequently happens, that specific performance is imprestable; as where I sell the same horse first to John, and then to James. The performance to John becomes imprestable after the horse is delivered to James; and therefore, instead of specific performance, a court of equity must be satisfied, like a court of common law, to decree damages to John; according to the maxim, *Loco facti impraestabilis succedit damnum et interesse.*[5]

This suggests an inquiry, whether in awarding damages there be any difference between common law and equity. An obligor, bound to perform what he undertakes, ought to make up the loss occa- <325> sioned by his failure; and such failure accordingly affords a good claim for damages at common law as well as in equity. Thus, the purchaser of an estate from an apparent heir,[6] having, along with the disposition, received a procuratory to serve and infeft the apparent heir, employs his own doer to perform that work. By the doer's remissness, the heir-apparent dies without being infeft, which renders the disposition ineffectual. The doer is bound at common law to make up

4. "The person who has the advantage should also have the disadvantage."
5. "Damages and interest follow in place of something which cannot be performed."
6. The heir to an estate, who has the right to enter into the succession, but who has not yet completed his title to his ancestor's estate, and who must decide within a year and a day whether to take up or renounce the succession.

the purchaser's loss, though it be *lucrum cessans*[7] only; and a court of equity can go no further. In cases of that nature, if skill be professed, unskilfulness will not afford a defence. "Proculus ait, si medicus servum imperite secuerit, vel locato vel ex lege Aquilia competere actionem."* "Celsus etiam imperitiam culpae adnumerandum scripsit. Si quis vitulos pascendos vel sarciendum quid poliendumve conduxit, culpum eum praestare debere; et quod imperitia peccavit, culpam esse; quippe ut artifex conduxit."† Upon this rule the fol- <326> lowing case was determined. An advocate being debtor to his client, wrote and delivered him a bill of exchange for the sum. Being sued for payment, he objected, That the bill was null, containing a penalty. The advocate probably was ignorant that this was a nullity; but he undertook the trust of drawing the bill, and therefore was bound for its sufficiency.‡,[8] Where a prisoner for debt makes his escape, it must be admitted, that the creditor is hurt in his interest; but he cannot prove any damage; for it is not certain that he would have recovered payment by detaining the debtor in prison, and it is possible he may yet recover it. But to be deprived of the security he has by his debtor's imprisonment, is undoubtedly a hurt or prejudice; and the common law gives reparation by making the negligent jailor liable for the debt, as equity doth in similar cases. A messenger who neglects to put a caption[9] in execution, affords another instance of the same kind. By his negligence he is subjected to the debt, which is said to be *litem suam facere*.[10] <327> The

---

7. "A gain lost."

* l. 7 §8. Ad legem Aquil[iam (the *Lex Aquilia*), D 9.2.7.8: Watson i: 279: "Proculus says that if a doctor operates negligently on a slave, an action will lie either on the contract for his services or under the *lex Aquilia*"].

† l. 9. §5. Locati conducti [Lease and Hire, D 19.2.9.5, Watson ii: 560: "Celsus wrote that inexperience should also be counted as fault; if someone contracts to pasture calves or to repair or adorn something, he should be held responsible for fault, and it is fault when he errs due to inexperience, since, as Celsus says, it was obviously as a craftsman that he took the job"].

‡ 26th November 1743, Garden contra Thomas Rigg Advocate [M 10450 and 11274].

8. In the first edition, this case is discussed in the section where Kames talks of personal objections. He describes it thus (p. 139): "A bill of exchange granted by an advocate to his client, was objected to by the former because it bore a penalty. The defendant was barred *personali objectione* from insisting upon this nullity."

9. See glossary, "caption."

10. "To make a suit of one's own"; that is, to be liable for an action because of one's own misconduct.

undertaking an office implies an agreement to fulfil the duty of the office: negligence accordingly is a breach of agreement, which subjects the officer to all consequences, whether actual damage or other prejudice. At the same time, it ought not to escape observation, that as neglect singly without intention of mischief is no ground for punishment, damages are the only means within the compass of law for compelling a man to be diligent in his duty. So far the remedy afforded by a court of common law is complete, without necessity of recurring to a court of equity.

Certain covenants unknown to common law, belong to a court of equity. This was the case of a bill of exchange, before it was brought under common law by act of parliament;[11] and while it continued in its original state, damages from failure of performance could not be claimed but in a court of equity. A policy of insurance is to this day unknown at common law; and consequently every wrong relative to it must be redressed in a court of equity.[12]

And now as to the rules for estimating actual damage upon failure to perform a <328> covenant. A failure of duty, whether the duty arise from a covenant, or from any other cause, is a fault only, not a crime; and upon such failure no consequential damage that is uncertain ought to be claimed.* There is the greatest reason for this moderation with respect to

11. In Scotland, the Bills of Exchange Act 1681 (act 20, parl. 1681; *APS* viii: 352: 1681, c. 86: Act concerning bills of exchange) introduced a summary proceeding on foreign bills of exchange; a procedure extended to inland bills by the Inland Bills Act 1696 (act 36, parl. 1696; *APS* x: 77: 1696, c. 38: Act anent inland bills and precepts). In England, cases involving bills of exchange were dealt with by the common law courts, following the custom of merchants.

12. English common law courts heard cases relating to insurance throughout the eighteenth century. Its principles were particularly developed in the King's Bench during the time of Lord Mansfield (on which, see James Oldham, *The Mansfield Manuscripts and the Growth of English Law in the Eighteenth Century,* 2 vols., Chapel Hill and London: University of North Carolina Press, 1992, vol. 1, chap. 7). The first Scottish treatise writer on insurance was John Millar Jr., whose *Elements of the Law of Insurances* (Edinburgh: J. Bell, 1787) noted (at pp. 17–18) that "the first decisions [in Scotland] which, strictly speaking, relate to *insurance,* are all, except one, within the course of the last ten years. During this period, however, the trade of insuring has risen to a very great height; and the decisions of the Court of Session, upon that subject, have become proportionably comprehensive and systematic."

* See above, p. 69.

covenants, where the failure is often occasioned by a very slight fault, and sometimes by inability without any fault. This rule is adopted by writers on the Roman law: "Cum per venditorem steterit quo minus rem tradat, omnis utilitas emptoris in aestimationem venit: quae modo circa ipsam rem consistit. Neque enim, si potuit ex vino puta negotiari, et lucrum facere, id aestimandum est, non magis quam si triticum emerit, et ob eam rem quod non sit traditum, familia ejus fame laboraverit: nam pretium tritici, non servorum fame necatorum, consequitur."* "Venditori si emptor in pretio solvendo moram fecerit, usuras duntaxat praestabit, non omne omnino quod venditor, mora non facta, consequi potuit; veluti si negotiator fuit, et, <329> pretio soluto, ex mercibus plus quam ex usuris quaerere potuit."†

At a slight view it might be thought, that to reject uncertain damage here is inconsistent with what is laid down above concerning a jailor or a messenger. But upon a more accurate view it will appear, that uncertain damage is not admitted in either case. The creditor's risk upon escape of his prisoner is certain, however uncertain the consequences may be. It is this risk only that is estimated; and it is estimated in the most accurate manner, by relieving the creditor, and laying it on the jailor or messenger. Upon the whole, with respect to estimating actual damage from breach of covenant, there appears no defect in common law more than in estimating risk, to make the interposition of equity necessary.

Hitherto of a total failure. Next where the failure is partial only. Many obligations are of such a nature as to admit no medium between complete performance and total failure. Other obligations admit a partial perfor-

---

* l. 21. §3. [De actionibus] Empti et venditi [On the actions for Sale and purchase, D 19.1.21.3: Watson ii: 552: "When the seller is responsible for non-delivery of an object, every benefit to the buyer is taken into account provided that it stands in close connection with this matter. If he could have completed a deal and made a profit from wine, this should not be reckoned in, no more than if he buys wheat and his household suffers from starvation because it was not delivered; he receives the price of the grain, not the price of slaves killed by starvation"].

† l. 19. De peric[ulo] et commod[o] rei vend[itae (On the risk and benefit of the thing sold), D 18.6.20: Watson ii: 541: "If the purchaser is late in paying the price, he will have only to pay interest, not everything that the vendor might have gained if he had not been in delay; for instance, if the vendor was a trader and could have gained more than the amount of interest by his dealings"].

mance, and conse- <330> quently a failure that is but partial. A bargain and sale of a horse furnishes examples of both. The vender's performance is indivisible: if he deliver not the horse, his failure is total. The obligation on the purchaser to pay the price, admits a performance by parts: if he have paid any part of the price, his performance is partial, and his failure partial.

Many obligations *ad facta praestanda*[13] are of the last kind. A waggoner who engages to carry goods from London to Edinburgh, and yet stops short at Newcastle, has performed his bargain in part, and consequently has failed only in part. The like, where a ship freighted for a voyage, is forced, by stress of weather, to land the cargo before arriving at the des-tined port. In cases of that kind the question is, What is the legal effect of a partial failure? The answer is easy at common law, which takes the bar-gain strictly according to the strict meaning of the words. I am not bound to pay the price or wages till the whole goods be delivered as agreed on. But in order to answer the question in equity, a culpable failure must be distinguished from a failure occasioned by acci- <331> dent or misfortune: a culpable failure can expect no relief from equity; the rule being general, That equity never interposes in favour of a wrong-doer: but where the failure is occasioned by accident or misfortune, the price or wages will be due in proportion to what part of the work has been done; and the claim rests on the following maxim, *Nemo debet locupletari aliena jactura.*[14] Thus, where a man undertakes to build me a house for a certain sum, and dies before finishing, his representatives will be entitled to a part of the sum, proportioned to the work done; for in that proportion I am *locupletior ali-ena jactura.* And in the case above mentioned, if the waggoner die at New-castle, or be prevented by other accident from completing his journey, he or his executors will have a good claim *pro rata itineris.* By the same rule, the freight is due *pro rata itineris,* as was decreed Lutwidge *contra* Gray.*

A process was lately brought before the court of session upon the fol-lowing fact. Mariners were hired at Glasgow to per- <332> form a trading voyage, first to Newfoundland, next to Lisbon, and last to the Clyde. A

---

13. "For the performance of certain acts."
14. "No one should be enriched at another's expense."
  * See the Dictionary, title (*Periculum*) [Kames, *Dictionary,* vol. 2, p. 59: Lutwidge contra Gray, 12 February 1732; also M 10111].

certain sum per month was agreed on for wages, to be paid where the voyage should be completed. The Glasgow cargo was safely landed in Newfoundland; and a cargo of fish, received there, was delivered at Lisbon. In the homeward passage, the ship with the Lisbon cargo being taken by a French privateer, the mariners, when liberated from prison, claimed their wages *pro rata itineris.* This cause was compromised. It can scarce however admit of a doubt, but that the rule, *Pro rata itineris,* must hold with respect to mariners, as well as with respect to the freighter of a ship. And accordingly it is a common saying, That the freight is the mother of the seamen's wages; meaning, that where the former is due, the latter must also be due.

What is said above is applicable to a lease. A lease, in its very nature supposes a subject possessed by one, for the use of which he pays a yearly sum to another: the possession and rent are mutual causes of each other, and cannot subsist separately. Land set in lease happens to be swal- <333> lowed up by the sea: this puts an end to the lease. Here the failure is total. A total sterility is in effect the same. Let us now suppose the sterility to be partial only. What says common law? It says, that such sterility will not intitle the lessee to any deduction of rent; that he must abandon the farm altogether, or pay the whole rent. In the following case, several rules of equity concerning sterility are opened. In January 1755, Foster and Duncan set to Adamson and Williamson a salmon-fishing in the river Tay, opposite to Errol, on the north side of a shallow, named the *Guinea-bank,* to endure for five years. The river there is broad; but the current, being narrow, passed at that time along the north side of the said bank, the rest of the river being dead water. As one cannot fish with profit but in the current, the lessees made large profits the first two years, and were not losers the third; but the fourth year the current changed, which frequently happens in that river, and instead of passing as formerly along the north side of the bank, passed along the south side, which was a part of the river let to others; by which means the fishing let to Adam- <334> son and Williamson became entirely unprofitable during the remainder of their lease. The granters of the lease having brought a process against the lessees for £36 Sterling, being the rent for the two last years, the defence was, a total sterility by the change of the current as aforesaid; and a proof being taken, the facts appeared to be what are above stated. It was pleaded for the pursuers, That whatever may be thought with respect to a total sterility during the whole years of the lease, or during the remaining years after the lease is offered to be given up, the sterility here was temporary only: for as the stream of the river Tay is extremely changeable, it might have returned to its former place in a month, or in a week; and as the lessees adhered to the lease, and did not offer to surrender the possession, they certainly were in daily expectation that the current would take its former course. A tenant cannot pick out one or other steril year to get free of that year's rent: if equity afford him any deduction, it must be upon computing the whole years of the lease; for if he be a gainer upon the whole, which is the present case, he has no claim <335> in equity for any deduction.[15] It was carried, however, by a plurality, to sustain the defence of sterility, and to assoilzie the defenders from the rent due for the last two years.[16] This judgement seems no better founded in equity than at common law. And it is easy to discover what moved the plurality: In a question between a rich landlord and a poor tenant, the natural bias is for the latter: the subject in controversy may be a trifle to the landlord, and yet be the tenant's all. Let us put an opposite case. A widow with a numerous family of children has nothing to subsist on but her liferent of a dwelling-house, and of an extensive orchard. These she leases to a gentleman in opulent circumstances, for a rent of £15 for the house, and £25 for the orchard. He possesses for several years with profit. The orchard happens to be barren the two last years of the lease, and he claims a deduction upon that account. No one would give this cause against the poor widow. Such influence have extraneous circumstances, even where the judges are not conscious of them.[17]

Partial failure has hitherto been consi- <336> dered in its consequences with respect to the person who has failed to execute a commission. I proceed to the effect of a failure with respect to those who give the commis-

---

15. In the second edition, in place of this sentence, Kames inserted the comments to be found in Appendix, p. 528, Extract [2nd: 172].

16. Foster and Duncan contra Adamson and Williamson, 16 July 1762: M 10131 from Kames, *Select Decisions*, p. 264.

17. In the second edition (p. 173), Kames added the comment, "I am not certain but some of the judges considered this as a *rei interitus* to afford a defence at common law; a very great mistake, as a thing cannot be understood to be totally destroy'd while we have daily expectation of its being restored to its former condition."

sion. A submission is a proper example. It being the professed intention of a submission to put an end to all the differences that are submitted, the arbiters, chosen to fulfil that intention, are bound by acceptance to perform. An award or decreet-arbitral is accordingly void at common law, if any article submitted be left undecided; for in that case the commission is not executed. Nor will such a decreet-arbitral be sustained in a court of equity, where claims made by the one party are sustained, and the other left to a process; which is partial and unfair. But where the claims are all on one side, and some of them only decided, equity will support the decreet-arbitral; it being always better to have some of the claims decided than none. But in this case, the decreet-arbitral, so far as it goes, must be unexceptionable; for a court of equity will never support a deed or act void at common law, except as far as it is just. <337>

SECTION IX

Indirect means employed to evade performance.

Among persons who are sway'd by interest more than by conscience, the employing indirect means to evade their engagements, is far from being rare. Such conduct, inconsistent with the candour and *bona fides* requisite in contracting and in performing contracts, is morally wrong; and a court of equity will be watchful to disappoint every attempt of that kind. Thus, if a man, subjected to a thirlage of all the oats growing on his farm that he shall have occasion to grind, sell his own product of oats, and buy meal for the use of his family, with no other view but to disappoint the thirlage; this is a wrong *contra bonam fidem contractus,*[1] which will subject him to the multure[2] that would have been due for grinding the oats of his own farm. The following case is an example of the same kind. A gentleman be- <338> ing abroad, and having no prospect of children, two of his nearest relations agreed privately, that if the estate should be disponed to either, the other was to have a certain share. The gentleman, ignorant of this

1. "A contract against good faith."
2. A toll paid to the proprietor of a mill in return for grinding corn; paid from a proportion of the grain ground.

agreement, settled his estate upon one of them, reserving a power to alter. The disponee sent his son privately to Denmark, where the gentleman resided: upon which the former deed was recalled, and a new one made upon the son. In a process, after the gentleman's death, for performance of the agreement, the defence was, That the agreement had not taken place, as the disposition was not in favour of the defendant, but of his son. The court judged, That the defendant had acted fraudulently in obtaining an alteration of the settlement, in order to evade performance of the agreement; and that no man can take benefit by his fraud. For which reason he was decreed to fulfil the engagement, as if the alteration had not been made.*,3 <339>

CHAPTER V

Powers of a court of equity to remedy what is imperfect in common law with respect to statutes.

Considering the nature of a court of common law, there is no reason that it should have more power over statutes than over private deeds. With respect to both it is confined to the words; and must not pretend to pronounce any judgement upon the spirit and meaning in opposition to the

* Stair, 15th July 1681, Campbell contra Moir [M 4889].

3. The discussion of this case in the first edition adds the following comment (p. 9): "This case deserves peculiar attention. And, in the first place, I must cursorily observe, That the wrong here was, properly speaking, not fraud, because no artifice was used to deceive or circumvent. It was obviously however a transgression of that fair and candid dealing, which the connection of the parties and the nature of the agreement required. But what deserves chiefly to be observed is, That no action could lie on this agreement at common law, nor even in equity, because the event in which it was to be made effectual did not exist. The disposition was not to either of the parties, but to the son of one of them. Neither could there lie upon the wrong an action at common law for reparation, because the party injured could only qualify *lucrum cessans,* not *damnum datum.* But there behoved to be reparation in a court of equity; and as the wrong-doer had no power over the estate which was settled on his son, the only reparation that could be afforded was an equivalent in money. And this is one of the rare cases where a court of equity must give a sum of money as reparation. And there appears not any reason to debar a court of equity from giving a reparation, where the circumstances admit not a reparation more compleat."

words. And yet the words of a statute correspond not always to the will of the legislature; nor are always the things enacted proper means to answer the end in view; falling sometimes short of the end, and sometimes going beyond it. Hence to make statutes effectual, there is the same necessity for the interposition of a court of equity, that there is with respect to deeds and covenants. But in order to <340> form a just notion of the powers of a court of equity with respect to statutes, it is necessary, as a preliminary point, to ascertain how far they come under the powers of a court of common law; and with that point I shall commence the enquiry.

Submission to government is universally acknowledged to be a duty: but the true foundation of that duty seems to lie in obscurity, though scarce any other topic has filled more volumes. Many writers derive this duty from an original compact between the sovereign and his people. Be it so. But what is it that binds future generations? for a compact binds those only who are parties to it; not to mention that governments were established long before contracts were of any considerable authority.* Others, dissatisfied with this narrow foundation, endeavour to assign one more extensive, deriving the foregoing duty from what is termed in the Roman law a *quasi-contract.* "It is a rule," they say, "in law, and in common sense, That a man who lays hold of a benefit, must take it with its conditions, and submit to its necessary consequences. Thus one <341> who accepts a succession, must pay the ancestor's debts: he is presumed to agree to this condition, and is not less firmly bound than by an explicit engagement. In point of government, protection and submission are reciprocal; and the taking protection from a lawful government, infers a consent to submit to its laws." This ground of submission is not much more extensive than the former; for both proceed upon the supposition, that without consent expressed or imply'd no person owes obedience to government. At this rate, the greater part of those who live under government are left in a state of independency; for seldom is there occasion to afford such peculiar protection to private persons, as necessarily to infer their consent. Consider farther, that the far greater part of those who live in society, are not capable to understand the foregoing reasoning: many of them have not even the

* See [Kames,] Historical law-tracts [vol. 1, 1758], tract 2 [pp. 91–121].

slightest notion of what is meant by the terms *protection* and *submission*. I am inclined therefore to think, that this important duty has a more solid foundation; and, comparing it with other moral duties, I find no reason to doubt, <342> that like them it is rooted in human nature.* If a man be a social being and government be essential to society, it is not conformable to the analogy of nature, that we should be left to an argument for investigating the duty we owe our rulers. If justice, veracity, gratitude, and other private duties, be supported and enforc'd by the moral sense, it would be strange if nature were deficient with respect to the public duty only. But nature is not deficient in any branch of the human constitution: government is no less necessary to society, than society to man; and by the very frame of our nature we are fitted for government as well as for society. To form originally a state of society under government, there can be no means, it is true, other than compact; but the continuance of a state, and of government over multitudes who never have occasion to promise submission, must depend on a different principle. The moral sense, which binds individuals to be just to each other, binds them equally to submit to the laws of their society; and we have a clear con- <343> viction that this is our duty. The strength of this conviction is no where more visible than in a disciplined army. There, the duty of submission is exerted every moment at the hazard of life; and frequently where the hazard is imminent, and death almost certain. In a word, what reason shows to be necessary in society, is, by the moral sense, made an indispensable duty. We have a sense of fitness and rectitude in submitting to the laws of our society; and we have a sense of wrong, of guilt, and of meriting punishment, when we transgress them.ª <344>

* See [Kames,] Essays on the principles of morality and natural religion, part 1. ess. 2. chap. 7 [2nd ed., 1758, pp. 76–90; cf. Liberty Fund ed., pp. 46–54].

a. In examining this matter, it would not be fair to take under consideration statutes relating to justice, because justice is binding independent of municipal law. Consider only things left indifferent by the law of nature, which are regulated by statute for the good of society; the laws, for example, against usury, against exporting corn in time of dearth, and many that will occur upon the first reflection. Every man of virtue will find himself bound in conscience to submit to such laws. Nay, even with respect to those who by interest are moved to transgress them, I venture to affirm, that the first acts, at least, of transgression, are seldom perpetrated with a quiet mind. I will not even except what is called *smuggling;* though private interest authorised by example, and the trifle

Hence it clearly follows, that every voluntary transgression of what is by statute ordered to be done or prohibited, is a moral wrong, and a transgression of the law of nature. This doctrine will be found of great importance in the present enquiry.

Many differences among statutes must be kept in view, in order to ascertain the powers of a court of common law con- <345> cerning them. Some statutes are compulsory, others prohibitory; some respect individuals, others the public; of some the transgression occasions damage, of others not; to some a penalty is annexed, others rest upon authority.

I begin with those which rest upon authority, without annexing any penalty to the transgression. The neglect of a compulsory statute of this kind will found an action at common law to those who have interest, ordaining the defendant either to do what the statute requires, or to pay damages. If, again, the transgression of a prohibitory statute of the same kind harm any person, the duty of the court is obvious: The harm must be repaired, by voiding the act where it can be voided, such as an alienation after inhibition; and where the harm is incapable of this remedy, damages must be awarded. This is fulfilling the will of the legislature, being all that is intended by such statutes.

But from disobeying a statute, prejudice often ensues, which, not being pecuniary, cannot be repaired by awarding a sum in name of damages.

---

that is lost to the public by any single transgression, obscure commonly the consciousness of wrong; and perhaps, after repeated acts, which harden individuals in iniquity, make it vanish altogether. It must however be acknowledged, that the moral sense, uniform as to private virtue, operates with very different degrees of force with relation to municipal law. The laws of a free government, directed for the good of the society, and peculiarly tender of the liberty of the subject, have great and universal influence: they are obeyed chearfully as a matter of strict duty. The laws of a despotic government, on the contrary, contrived chiefly to advance the power or secure the person of a tyrant, require military force to make them effectual; for conscience scarce interposes in their behalf. And hence the great superiority of a free state, with respect to the power of the governors as well as the happiness of the subjects, over every kingdom that in any degree is despotic or tyrannical. [In the first edition (p. 60), this note commences with the following observation: "The sense of duty in submitting to the authority of a government, is in some instances so weak, as that I shall not be surprised to find its existence called in question. We have examples without end, of every art put in practice to evade payment of taxes. It is almost become a maxim, that cheating the government is no fault."]

Statutes relating to the public are for the most part of this nature; <346> and many also in which individuals are immediately concerned.[a] To clear this point, we must distinguish as formerly between compulsory and prohibitory statutes. The transgression of a prohibitory statute is a direct contempt of legal authority, and consequently a moral wrong, which ought to be redressed; and where no sanction is added, it must necessarily be the purpose of the legislature to leave the remedy to a court of law. This is a clear inference, unless we suppose the legislature guilty of prohibiting a thing to be done, and yet leaving individuals at liberty to disobey with impunity. To make the will of the legislature effectual in this case, different means must be employ'd according to the nature of the subject. If an act done *prohibente lege*[1] can be undone, the most effectual method of redressing the wrong is to void the act. If the act cannot be undone, the only means left is punishment. And accordingly, it is a rule <347> in the law of England,[*] that an offender for contempt of the law, may be fined and imprisoned at the King's suit.[b]

On the other hand, the transgression of a compulsory statute ordering a thing to be done, infers not necessarily a contempt of legal authority. It may be an act of omission only, which is not criminal; and it will be construed to be such, unless from collateral circumstances it be <348> made evident, that there was an intention to contemn the law. Supposing then the transgression to be an act of omission only, and consequently not an

a. This branch, by the general distribution, ought regularly to be handled afterward, part 2. of this first book; but by joining it here to other matters with which it is intimately connected, I thought it would appear in a clearer light.

1. "Law forbidding," that is, forbidden by law.

* 2. Instit. 163 [Coke, 2 *Institutes*, p. 163].

b. If this doctrine to any one appear singular, let it be considered, that the power insisted on is only that of authorizing a proper punishment for a crime after it is committed, which is no novelty in law. Every crime committed against the law of nature, may be punished at the discretion of the judge, where the legislature has not appointed a particular punishment; and it is made evident above, that a contempt of legal authority is a crime against the law of nature. But to support this in the present case, an argument from analogy is very little necessary; for, as observed above, it is obviously derived from the will of the legislature. I shall only add, that the power of naming a punishment for a crime after it is committed, is greatly inferior to that of making a table of punishments for crimes that may be committed hereafter, which is a capital branch of the legislative authority.

object of punishment, the question is, What can be done, in order to fulfil the will of the legislature. The court has two methods: one is, to order the statute to be fulfilled; and if this order be also disobey'd, a criminal contempt must be the construction of the person's behaviour, to be followed, as in the former case, with a proper punishment. The other is, to order the thing to be done under a penalty. I give an example. The freeholders are by statute bound to convene at Michaelmas, in order to receive upon the roll persons qualified; but no penalty is added to compel obedience. In *odium*[2] of a freeholder who desires to be put upon the roll, they forbear to meet. What is the remedy here where there is no pecuniary damage? The court of session may appoint them to meet under a penalty. For, in general, if it be the duty of judges to order the end, they must use such means as are in their power. And if this can be done with respect to a private person, it follows, that where a <349> thing is ordered to be done for the good of the public, it belongs to the court of session, upon application of the King's Advocate, to order the thing to be done under a penalty. In a process at the instance of an heritor intitled to a salmon-fishing in a river, against an inferior heritor, for regulating his cruive and cruive-dike, concluding, That he should observe the Saturday's slap;[3] that the hecks of his cruives should be three inches wide, &c. it was decreed, That the defendant should be obliged to observe these regulations under the penalty of £50 Sterling. It was urged for the defendant, That the pursuer ought to be satisfied with damages upon contravention, because the law has imposed no penalty, and the court can impose none. Answered, That it is beyond the reach of art to ascertain damage in this case; and therefore that to enforce these regulations a penalty is necessary. And if this remedy be neglected by the legislature, it must be supplied by a court of equity upon the principle, That if there be a right it ought to be made effectual.

What next come under consideration are statutes forbidding things to be done un- <350> der a penalty; for to the omission of a thing ordered to be done, a penalty is seldom annexed. These are distinguishable into two kinds. The first regard the more noxious evils, which the legislature

---

2. "Hatred."

3. *Saturday's slap:* a gap in a weir to allow fish to swim upstream to spawn.

prohibits absolutely; leaving the courts of law to employ all the means in their power for repressing them; but adding a penalty beforehand, because that check is not in the power of courts of law. The second regard slighter evils, to repress which no other means are intended to be applied but a pecuniary penalty only. Both kinds are equally binding in conscience; for in every case it is a moral wrong to disobey the law. Disobedience however to a statute of the second class, is attended with no other consequence but payment of the penalty; whereas the penalty in the first class is due, as we say, *by and attour*[4] *performance;* and for that reason, a court of law, beside inflicting the penalty, is bound to use all the means in its power to make the will of the legislature effectual, in the same manner as if there were no penalty. And even supposing that the act prohibited is capable of being voided by the sentence of a court, the penalty ought still to <351> be inflicted; for otherwise it will lose its influence as a prohibitory means.

Prohibitory statutes are often so inaccurately expressed, as to leave it doubtful whether the penalty be intended as one of the means for repressing the evil, or the only means. This defect occasions in courts of law much conjectural reasoning, and many arbitrary judgements. The capital circumstance for clearing the doubt, is the nature of the evil prohibited. With respect to every evil of a general bad tendency, it ought to be held the will of the legislature, to give no quarter: and consequently, beside inflicting the penalty, it is the duty of courts of law to use every other mean to make this will effectual. With respect to evils less pernicious, it ought to be held the intention of the legislature, to leave no power with judges beyond inflicting the penalty. This doctrine will be illustrated by the following examples. By the act 52, parl. 1587, "He who bargains for greater profit than 10 *per cent.* shall be punished as an usurer."[5] Here is a penalty without declaring such bargains null: and yet it has ever been held the intendment of this act to dis- <352> charge usury totally; and the penalty is deemed as one mean only of making the prohibition effectual. There was accordingly never any hesitation to sustain action for voiding usurious bargains, nor even to make the lender liable for the sums received by him

---

4. Over and above, in addition to.
5. *APS* iii: 451: 1587, c. 35, Act concerning the punishment of usury.

above the legal interest. This then is held to be a statute of the first class. The following statutes belong to the second class. An exclusive privilege of printing books, is given to authors and their assigns for the term of fourteen years. Any person who within the time limited prints or imports any such book, shall forfeit the same to the proprietor, and one penny for every sheet found in his custody; the half to the King, and the other half to whoever shall sue for the same.* With respect to the monopoly granted by this statute, it has been justly established, that a court of law is confined to the penalty, and cannot apply other means for making it effectual, not even an action of damages against an interloper.† "Members of the college of justice are <353> discharged to buy any lands, teinds, &c. the property of which is controverted in a process, under the certification of losing their office."‡ It has been always held the sense of this statute, to be satisfied with the penalty, without giving authority to reduce or void such bargains.⁶

But though contracts or deeds contrary to statutory prohibitions of the kind last mentioned are not subject to reduction, it is a very different point, Whether it be the duty of courts of law to sustain action upon such a contract or deed. And yet this distinction seems to have been overlooked in the court of session:⁷ for it is the practice of that court, while they inflict the penalty, to support with their authority that very thing which is prohibited under a penalty. Thus, a member of the college of justice, buying land while the property is controverted in a process, is deprived of his office; and yet, with the same breath, action is given him to make the minute of sale <354>

---

* 8 Ann. 18 [8 Anne, c. 19 (1709): An Act for the encouragement of learning, by vesting the copies of printed books in the authors or purchasers of such copies, during the times therein mentioned].

† June 7. 1748, Booksellers of London contra Booksellers of Edinburgh and Glasgow [M 8295, from Kames, *Remarkable Decisions* ii: 154; also M 8302, M 8305].

‡ Act 216. parl. 1594 [*APS* iv: 68: 1594, c. 26, Anent the bying of landis and possessionis dependand in pley be Jugeis or memberis of courtis (Land Purchase Act 1594)].

6. In the first edition, Kames adds (p. 64), "The *lex furia* among the Romans, prohibiting legacies above a certain sum, is held to be a law of this kind. Legacies above that sum were not voided, the penalty only was exacted."

7. In the first edition, Kames notes more strongly (p. 64), "With respect to the statutes last mentioned, I observe with regret, that their intendment has generally been misapprehended."

effectual.* This, in effect, is considering the statute, not as prohibitory of such purchases, but merely as laying a tax upon them, similar to what at present is laid upon plate, coaches, &c. I take liberty to say, that this is a gross misapprehension of the spirit and intendment of the statute. Comparing together the statutes contained in both classes, both equally are prohibited: the difference concerns only the means employ'd for making the prohibition effectual. To repress the less noxious evils, the statutory penalty is thought sufficient: to repress the more noxious evils, beside inflicting the statutory penalty, a court may employ every lawful mean in its power. But evidently both are intended to be repressed; and justly, because both in different degrees are hurtful to the society in general, or to part of it. This article is of no slight importance. If I have set in a just light the spirit and intendment of the foregoing statutes, it follows of conse- <355> quence, that an act prohibited in a statute of the second class ought not to be countenanced with an action, more than an act prohibited in a statute of the first class. Courts of law were instituted to enforce the will of the national legislator, as well as of the Great Legislator of the universe, and to put in execution municipal laws as well as those of nature. What shall we say then of a court that supports an act prohibited by a statute, or authorises any thing contradictory to the will of the legislature? It is a transgression of the same nature, though not the same in degree, with that of sustaining action for a bribe promised to commit murder or robbery. With regard then to statutes of this kind, though a court is confined to the penalty, and cannot inflict any other punishment, it doth by no means follow, that action ought to be sustained for making the act prohibited effectual: on the contrary, to sustain action would be flying in the face of the legislature. The statute, for example, concerning members of the college of justice, is satisfied with the penalty of deprivation, without declaring the bargain <356> null; and therefore to sustain a reduction of the bargain would be to punish beyond the words, and perhaps beyond the intention, of the statute. But whether action should be sustained to make the bargain effectual, is a

* Haddington, June 5. 1611, Cunninghame contra Maxwell [M 9495, from Haddington report in Kames, *Dictionary*, vol. 2, p. 24]; Durie, July 30. 1635, Richardson contra Sinclair [M 3210]; Fountainhall, December 20. 1683, Purves contra Keith [M 9500].

consideration of a very different nature: the refusing action is made necessary by the very constitution of a court of law; it being inconsistent with
the design of its institution, to enforce any contract or any deed prohibited
by statute. It follows indeed from these premises, that it is left optional to
the vender to fulfil the contract or no at his pleasure; for if a court of law
cannot interpose, he is under no legal compulsion. Nor is this a novelty. In
many cases beside the present, the rule is applicable, *Quod potior est conditio possidentis*,[8] where an action will not be given to compel performance,
and yet if performance be made, an action will as little be given to recall it.

Pondering this subject sedately, I can never cease wondering to find the
practice I have been condemning extended to a much stronger case, where
the purpose of the legislature to make an absolute prohibition is clearly expressed. The case I have <357> in view relates to the revenue-laws, prohibiting certain goods to be imported into this island, or prohibiting them to be
imported from certain places named. To import such goods, or to bargain
about their importation, is clearly a contempt of legal authority; and consequently a moral wrong, which the smuggler's conscience ought to check
him for, and which it will check him for, if he be not already hardened
sinner. And yet, by mistaking the nature of prohibitory laws, actions in the
court of session have been sustained for making such smuggling-contracts
effectual. They are not sustained at present; nor I hope will be. "Non du-
bium est, in legem committere eum, qui verba legis amplexus, contra legis
nititur voluntatem. Nec poenas insertas legibus evitabit, qui se contra juris sententiam saeva praerogativa verborum fraudulenter excusat. Nullum
enim pactum, nullam conventionem, nullum contractum inter eos videri
volumus subsecutum, qui contrahunt lege contrahere prohibente. Quod ad
omnes etiam legum interpretationes, tam veteres quam novellas, trahi gen-
eraliter imperamus; ut legislatori quod fieri non vult, tantum pro- <358>
hibuisse sufficiat: caeteraque, quasi expressa, ex legis liceat voluntate col-
ligere: hoc est, ut ea, quae lege fieri prohibentur, si fuerint facta, non solum
inutilia, sed pro infectis etiam habeantur: licet legislator fieri prohibuerit
tantum, nec specialiter dixerit *inutile esse debere quod factum est.*"*

8. The condition of the person in possession is stronger.
* l. 5. C. De legibus [C 1.14.5: Concerning statutes: "There is no doubt that a person
who follows the letter of the law, but violates its intention, breaks the law. Nor will a

So much upon the powers of a court of common law with respect to statutes. Upon the whole it appears, that this court is confined to the will of the legislature as expressed in the statutory words. It has no power to rectify the words, nor to apply any means for making the purpose of the legislature effectual, other than those directed by the legislature, however defective they may be. This imperfection is remedied by a court of equity, which enjoys, and ought to enjoy, the same powers with respect to statutes that are explained above with respect to deeds and covenants. To give a just notion of these powers concerning the present subject, the following distinction will contribute. Statutes, as far as they regard matter of law and come under the cognisance of a court of equity, <359> may be divided into two classes. First, Those which have justice for their object, by supplying the defects, or correcting the injustice, of common law. Second, Those which have utility for their sole object. Statutes of the first class are intended for no other purpose but to enlarge the jurisdiction of courts of common law, by empowering them to distribute justice where their ordinary powers reach not: such statutes are not necessary to a court of equity, which, by its original constitution, can supply the defects and correct the injustice of law: but they have the effect to limit the jurisdiction of a court of equity; for the remedies afforded by them must be put in execution by courts of common law, and no longer by a court of equity. All that is left to a court of equity concerning a statute of this kind, is to supply the defects and correct the injustice of common law, as far as the statute is incomplete or imperfect; which, in effect, is supplying the defects of the statute. But it is not a new power bestowed upon a court of equity as to statutes that are imperfect: the court only goes on to exercise its wonted

---

person who fraudulently justifies himself by fiercely privileging the words, against the meaning of the law, escape the punishment provided for by law. For we wish that no pact, agreement or contract shall come into effect between those who make contracts which the law prohibits. And we order that this shall apply generally to the interpretation of all laws, both old and new; so that it will be sufficient for the legislator to have forbidden what he wishes not to be done; and the rest may be inferred from the intention of the law, as if it had been expressed; that is to say, that which the law prohibits to be done, if it is done, shall be regarded not only as invalid, but as never having been done: although the legislator has only prohibited doing it, and has not specifically said that *what has been done shall be invalid*"].

powers with respect to matters of justice <360> that are left with it by the statute, and not bestowed upon courts of common law. I explain myself by an example. When goods were wrongously taken away, the common law of England gave an action for restitution to none but the proprietor; and therefore when the goods of a monastery were pillaged during a vacancy, the succeeding abbot had no action. This defect in law with respect to material justice, would probably have been left to the court of chancery, had its powers been unfolded when the statute of Marlebirge supplying the defect was made;* but no other remedy occurring, that statute empowers the judges of common law to sustain action. Had the statute never existed, action would undoubtedly have been sustained in the court of chancery: all the power that now remains with that court, is to sustain action where the statute is defective. The statute enacts, "That the successor shall have an action against such transgressor, for restoring the goods of the monastery." Attending to the words singly, which a court of common law must do, the remedy is incomplete; <361> for trees cut down and carried off are not mentioned. This defect in the statute, is supplied by the court of chancery. And Coke observes, that a statute which gives remedy for a wrong done, shall be taken by equity.[9] After all, it makes no material difference, whether such interposition of a court of equity, be considered as supplying defects in common law, or as supplying defects in statutes. It is still enforcing justice in matters which come not under the powers of a court of common law.

Statutes that have utility for their object, are of two kinds. First, Those which are made for promoting the positive good and happiness of the society in general, or of some of its members in particular. Second, Those which are made to prevent mischief. Defective statutes of the latter kind may be supplied by a court of equity; because, even independent of a statute, that court hath power to make regulations for preventing mischief. But that court hath not, more than a court of common law, any power to supply defective statutes of the former kind; because it is not impowered originally to interpose in any matter that hath no other tendency but

---

* 52. Henry III. cap. 29 [Statute of Marlbridge 1267].

9. The proposition can be seen stated most directly in the index to Coke, 2 *Institutes.*

merely to promote the posi- <362> tive good of the society. But this is only mentioned here to give a general view of the subject: for the powers of a court of equity as directed by utility are the subject of the next book.

Having said so much in general, we are prepared for particulars; which may commodiously be distributed into three sections. First, Where the will of the legislature is not justly expressed in the statute. Second, Where the means enacted fall short of the end purposed by the legislature. Third, Where the means enacted reach unwarily beyond the end purposed by the legislature.

SECTION I

Where the will of the legislature is not justly expressed in the statute.

This section, for the sake of perspicuity, shall be divided into three articles. First, Where the words are ambiguous. Second, Where they fall short of will. Third, Where they go beyond will. <363>

ARTICLE I. *Where the words are ambiguous.*

The following is a proper instance. By the act 250. parliament 1597,[1] "Vassals failing to pay their feu-duties for the space of two years, shall forfeit their feu-rights, in the same manner as if a clause irritant were engrossed in the infeftment." The forfeiting clause here is ambiguous: it may mean an *ipso facto* forfeiture upon elapsing of the two years; or it may mean a forfeiture if the feu-duty be not paid after a regular demand in a process. Every ambiguous clause ought to be so interpreted as to support the rules of justice, because such must be constructed the intendment of the legislature: and that by this rule the latter sense must be chosen, will appear upon the slightest reflection. The remedy here provided against the obstinacy or negligence of an undutiful vassal, could never be intended a trap for the innocent, by forfeiting those who have failed in payment through

---

1. *APS* iv: 133: 1597, c. 17, All fewis may be decernit null ffor nocht payment of the dewtie albeit na provisioun be maid thairanent in the infeftment [Feu-duty Act 1597].

ignorance or inability. The construction chosen making the right voidable only, not void *ipso* <364> *facto,* obliges the superior to insist in a declarator of irritancy or forfeiture, in order to void the right; which gives the vassal an opportunity to prevent the forfeiture, by paying up all arrears. By this method, it is true, the guilty may escape: but this is far more eligible in common justice, than that the innocent be punished with the guilty.

ARTICLE II. *Where the words fall short of will.*

In the act of Charles II. laying a tax on malt-liquors,[1] there are no words directing the tax to be paid, but only a penalty in case of not payment. The exchequer, which, like the session, is a court both of common law and of equity, supplies the defect; and, in order to fulfil the intendment of the statute, sustains an action for payment of the tax.

ARTICLE III. *Where the words go beyond will.*

By the act 5. parl. 1695,[1] it is enacted, "That hereafter no man binding for and <365> with another conjunctly and severally, in any bond or contract for sums of money, shall be bound longer than seven years after the date of the bond." It appearing to the court, from the nature of the thing, and from other clauses in the statute, that the words are too extensive, and that the privilege was intended for none but for cautioners upon whose faith money is lent, they have for that reason been always in use to restrict the words, and to deny the privilege to other cautioners.

The act 24. parl. 1695,[2] for making effectual the debts of heirs who after three years possession die in apparency,[3] is plainly contrived for debts only that are contracted for a valuable consideration. The act however is expressed in such extensive terms, as to comprehend debts and deeds, gratuitous as well as for a valuable consideration. The court therefore, re-

---

1. 12 Charles II c. 24, ss. 16–18 (1660) (An Act for takeing away the Court of Wards and Liveries and Tenures in Capite and by Knights Service and Purveyance, and for Setling a Revenue upon his Majesty in lieu thereof).

1. *APS* ix: 366: 1695, c. 7, Act anent principals and cautioners [Cautioners Act 1695].

2. *APS* ix: 427: 1695, c. 39, Act for obviating the frauds of appearand heirs.

3. The period of time before an heir-apparent has decided to take up or renounce his succession.

stricting the words to the sense of the statute, never sustains action upon this statute to gratuitous creditors.

The regulations 1695,[4] admitting no objection against a decreet-arbitral but bribery and corruption only, reach unwarily <366> beyond the meaning of the legislature. A decreet-arbitral derives its force from the submission; and for that reason every good objection against a submission must operate against the decreet-arbitral.[5]

By the statute 9° Annae, cap. 14,[6] "The person who at one time loses the sum or value of £10 Sterling at game, and pays the same, shall be at liberty within three months to sue for and recover the money or goods so lost, with costs of suit. And in case the loser shall not within the time foresaid really and *bona fide* bring his action, it shall be lawful for any one to sue for the same, and triple value thereof, with costs of suit." Here there is no limitation mentioned with respect to the popular action: nor, as far as concerns England, is it necessary; because, by the English statute 31st Eliz. cap. 5.[7] "No action shall be sustained upon any penal statute made or to be made, unless within one year of the offence." A limiting clause was necessary with regard to Scotland only, to which the said statute of Elizabeth reacheth not; and therefore, as there is no limitation expressed in the act, a court of common law in <367> Scotland must sustain the popular action for forty years, contrary evidently to the will of the legislature, which never intended a penal statute to be perpetual in Scotland, that in England is temporary. As here, therefore, the words go beyond will, it belongs to the court of session to limit this statute, by denying action if not brought within one year after the offence. Hence, in the decision January 19. 1737, Murray contra Cowan,[8] where an action was sustained even after the year, for recovering money lost at play with the triple value, the court of session acted as a court of common law, and not as a court of equity.

4. See Articles of Regulation concerning the Session, section 25 (*AS* 209, 215).

5. The second edition (p. 188) adds the following sentence: "But a submission is in its nature a mutual contract; and therefore every objection that in its nature is effectual to cut down the submission as a mutual contract, must be equally effectual to cut down the decreet-arbitral founded upon it."

6. An Act for the better preventing excessive and deceitful gaming, 1710.

7. 31 Eliz. c. 5, s. 5 (An Act concerning informers, 1589).

8. M 4508, from Kames, *Dictionary,* vol. 1, p. 322.

The following is an instance from the Roman law with respect to the *hereditatis petitio,*[9] of words reaching inadvertently beyond the will of the legislator. "Illud quoque quod in oratione Divi Hadriani est, *Ut post acceptum judicium id actori praestetur, quod habiturus esset, si eo tempore, quo petit, restituta esset hereditas,* interdum durum est: quid enim, si post litem contestatam mancipia, aut jumenta, aut pecora deperierint? Damnari debebit secundum verba orationes: quia po- <368> tuit petitor, restituta hereditate, distraxisse ea. Et hoc justum esse in specialibus petitionibus Proculo placet: Cassius contra sensit. In praedonis persona Proculus recte existimat: in bonae fidei possessoribus Cassius. Nec enim debet possessor aut mortalitatem praestare, aut propter metum hujus periculi temere indefensum jus suum relinquere."*

SECTION II

Where the means enacted fall short of the end purposed by the legislature.

The first instance shall be given of means that afford a complete remedy in some cases, and fall short in others *ubi par est ratio.*[1] In order to fulfil justice, the will of the legislature may be made effectual by a court of equity, whatever defect there may be in the words. Take the following examples. In the Roman law, Ulpian mentions the following edict. "Si quis id quod, jurisdictionis perpetuae <369> causa, in albo, vel in charta, vel in alia ma-

---

9. A Roman law action by which an heir claimed an inheritance by virtue of his right of succession.

* l. 40. De hereditatis petitione [On the claim for an inheritance, D 5.3.40.pr.: Watson i: 194: "The following principle too, which occurs in a speech of the deified Hadrian, is sometimes harsh, that after acceptance of suit, the plaintiff is given what he would have had if the inheritance had been made over to him at the time of making his claim. For what if after joinder of issue slaves or working or herd animals have died? According to the wording of the speech, payment for them will have to be imposed because the claimant could have disposed of them if the inheritance had been made over. Proculus held that this was just in particular cases, whereas Cassius took the opposite view. As regards the grabber, Proculus is right; as regards possessors in good faith, Cassius. For the possessor ought not to have to guarantee against death or, through fear of this, to have to let his case go undefended without good cause"].

1. "Where the reason is the same."

teria propositum erit, dolo malo corruperit; datur in eum quingentorum aureorum judicium, quod populare est."[2] Upon this edict Ulpian gives the following opinion. "Quod si, dum proponitur, vel ante propositionem, quis corruperit; edicti quidem verba cessabunt; Pomponius autem ait sententiam edicti porrigendam esse ad haec."*

"Oratio Imperatorum Antonini et Commodi, quae quasdam nuptias in personam senatorum inhibuit, de sponsalibus nihil locuta est: recte tamen dicitur, etiam sponsalia in his casibus ipso jure nullius esse momenti; ut suppleatur, quod orationi deest."[†]

"Lex Julia, quae de dotali praedio prospexit, Ne id marito liceat obligare, aut alienare, plenius interpretanda est: ut etiam de sponso idem juris sit, quod de marito."[‡]

By the statute of Glocester, "A man shall have a writ of waste against him <370> who holdeth for term of life or of years."[§] This statute, which supplies a defect in the common law, is extended against one who possesses for half a year or a quarter. For (says Coke) a tenant for half a year being within the same mischief shall be within the same remedy, though it be out of the letter of the law.[||]

An heir, whether apparent only, or entered *cum beneficio*,[3] cannot act more justly with respect to his predecessor's creditors, than to bring his

2. D 2.1.7.pr.: Watson i: 40: "If anyone should maliciously obliterate from a tablet, paper, or other material what has been stated with respect to jurisdiction to be exercised permanently, not that to be held only for a single occasion, an action, which anyone may bring, is given against him for five hundred aurei."

* l. 7. §2. De jurisdic[tione (On the administration of justice), D 2.1.7.2: Watson i: 40: "But should anyone obliterate the notice while it is being put up or before it has been put up, the words of the edict will not strictly apply. However, Pomponius says that the principle of the edict should be extended to these cases"].

† l. 16. De sponsalibus [On betrothals, D 23.1.16: Watson ii: 656: "An oration of the Emperors Antoninus and Commodus, which prohibited senators from marrying certain people, did not say anything about betrothals. Still betrothals in these circumstances are quite rightly held to be void at common law, so as to supply the omission in the oration"].

‡ l. 4. De fundo dotali [On dotal land: D 23.5.4: Watson ii: 693: "The *lex Julia* which applies to dotal land and provides that a husband cannot encumber or alienate it, ought to be widely interpreted so as to cover a betrothed man as well as a husband"].

§ 6. Edward I. cap. 5 [1278].

|| 1. Instit. 54. b [Coke, 1 *Institutes*, p. 54b].

3. That is, *cum beneficio inventarii:* "with the benefit of an inventory"; for which see glossary.

predecessor's estate to a judicial sale. The price goes to the creditors, which is all they are intitled to in justice; and the surplus, if any be, goes to the heir, without subjecting him to trouble or risk. The act 24, parl. 1695,[4] was accordingly made, empowering the heir-apparent to bring to a roup or public auction his predecessor's estate, whether bankrupt or not. But as there is a solid foundation in justice for extending this privilege to the heir entered *cum beneficio,* he is understood as omitted *per incuriam;*[5] and the court of session supplied the defect, by sustaining a process at the instance of the heir <371> *cum beneficio,* for selling his predecessor's estate.*

By the common law of Scotland, a man's creditors after his death had no preference upon his estate: the property was transferred to his heir, and the heir's creditors came in for their share. This was gross injustice; for the ancestor's creditors, who lent their money upon the faith of the estate, ought in all views to have been preferred. The act 24, parl. 1661,[6] declares, "That the creditors of the predecessor doing diligence[7] against the apparent heir, and against the real estate which belonged to the defunct, within the space of three years after his death, shall be preferred to the creditors of the apparent heir." The remedy here reaching the real estate only, the court of session completed the remedy, by extending it to the personal estate,† and also to a personal bond limited to a substitute named.‡ And, as being a court of equity, it was well authorised to make this extension; for to <372> withdraw from the predecessor's creditors part of his personal estate, is no less unjust than to withdraw from them part of his real estate.

One statute there is, or rather clause in a statute, which affords a plentiful harvest of instances. By the principles of common law an heir is intitled to continue the possession of his ancestor; and formerly, if he could colour his possession with any sort of title, however obsolete or defective, he not only enjoy'd the rents, but was enabled by that means to defend his posses-

4. *APS* ix: 427: 1695, c. 39, Act for obviating the frauds of appearand heirs.

5. "By mistake."

* Feb. 27. 1751, Patrick Blair [M 5353].

6. *APS* vii: 63: 1661, c. 88, Act concerning appearand airs their payment of their oun & their predecessours debts.

7. That is, execution against debtors.

† Stair, Dec. 16. 1674, Kilhead contra Irvine [M 3124].

‡ Forbes, Feb. 9. 1711, Graham contra Macqueen [M 3128].

sion against the creditors.* Among many remedies for this flagrant injustice, there is a clause in the act 62. parl. 1661,[8] enacting, "That in case the apparent heir of any debtor shall acquire right to an expired apprising,[9] the same shall be redeemable from him, his heirs and successors, within ten years after acquiring of the same, by the posterior apprisers, upon payment of the purchase-money." This remedy has been extended in many particulars, in order to fulfil the end intended by the legislature. For, 1mo, Tho' <373> the remedy is afforded to apprisers only, it is extended to personal creditors. 2do, It has been extended even to an heir of entail, impowering him to redeem an apprising of the entailed lands, after it was purchased by the heir of line. 3tio, Though no purchase is mentioned in this clause but what is made by the heir-apparent, the remedy however is extended against a presumptive heir, who cannot be heir-apparent while his ancestor is alive. 4to, It was judged, That an apprising led both against principal and cautioner, and purchased by the heir-apparent of the principal, might be redeemed by the creditors of the cautioner. This was a stretch, but not beyond the bounds of equity: the cautioner himself, as creditor for relief, could have redeemed this apprising in terms of the statute; and it was thought, that every privilege competent to a debtor ought to be extended to his creditors, in order to make their claims effectual. 5to, The privilege is extended to redeem an apprising during the legal, though the statute mentions only an expired apprising. And, lastly, Though the privilege of redemption is limited to ten years after the purchase <374> made by the heir-apparent, it was judged, that the ten years begin not to run but from the time that the purchase is known to the creditors. These decisions all of them are to be found in the Dictionary, vol. 1, p. 359.[10]

It is chiefly to statutes of this kind that the following doctrine is applicable. "Non possunt omnes articuli singillatim aut legibus aut senatuscon-

---

* See [Kames,] Historical law-tracts, tract 12. toward the close [1758 ed., vol. 2, pp. 157–58].

8. *APS* vii: 317: 1661, c. 344, Act for ordering the payment of debts betwixt creditor and debtor [Diligence Act 1661].

9. The diligence (execution against a debtor) used for transferring land to a creditor in satisfaction of the owner's debt. See glossary, "apprising."

10. "Redemption of apprisings from apparent heirs," Kames, *Dictionary*, vol. 1, pp. 359–60.

sultis comprehendi: sed cum in aliqua causa sententia eorum manifesta est, is, qui jurisdictioni praeest, ad similia procedere, atque ita jus dicere debet. Nam, ut ait Pedius, quoties lege aliquid, unum vel alterum introductum est, bona occasio est, caetera, quae tendunt ad eandem utilitatem, vel interpretatione vel certe *jurisdictione,* suppleri."*

The next branch is of means that are incomplete in every respect, where the very thing in view of the legislature is but imperfectly remedied. Of this take the following illustrious example, which at the same time furnishes an opportunity to explain the nature and effect of an adjudication after its legal is expired.[11] <375>

An adjudication during the legal is a *pignus praetorium:*[12] and expiry of the legal is held to transfer the property from the debtor to the creditor; precisely as in a wadset or mortgage, where the redemption is limited within a day certain. Yet the rule which, with relation to a wadset, affords an equity of redemption after the stipulated term of redemption is past,[†] has never been extended, directly at least, to relieve against an expired legal. This subject therefore is curious, and merits attention.

In a poinding[13] of moveables, the debtor has not an equity of redemption, because the moveables are transferred to the creditor at a just value. The same being originally the case of an apprising of land, the legal reversion of seven years introduced by the act 36, parl. 1469,[14] was in reality a privilege bestowed upon the debtor, without any foundation in equity;

* l. 12 & 13. De legibus [On statutes: D 1.3.12–13: Watson i: 12: "It is not possible for every point to be specifically dealt with either in statutes or in *senatus consulta;* but whenever in any case their sense is clear, the president of the tribunal ought to proceed by analogical reasoning and declare the law accordingly. For, as Pedius says, whenever some particular thing or another has been brought within statute law, there is good ground for other things which further the same interest to be added in supplementation, whether this be done by [juristic] interpretation or *a fortiori* by judicial decision].

11. *Legal:* the period of time allowed to the person whose land is in the process of adjudication, within which the money owed may be paid and the land freed of the adjudication.

12. "A magisterial pledge": that is, a pledge given to a creditor by the order of a magistrate.

† Pag. 54.

13. Taking the debtor's moveables by way of execution.

14. *APS* ii: 96: 1469, c. 12, Anent the distrenying of tenandis for the lordis dettis [Diligence Act 1469].

and therefore equity could not support an extension of the reversion one hour beyond the time granted by the statute. But the nature of an apprising was totally reversed, by an oppressive and dishonest practice of <376> attaching[15] land for payment of debt, without preserving any equality between the debt and the land; great portions of land being frequently carried off for payment of inconsiderable sums. An apprising, as originally constituted, was a judicial sale for a just price: but an execution, by which land at random is attached for payment of debt without any estimation of value, ought to have been reprobated as flying in the face of law. By what means it happened that creditors were indulged to act so unjustly, I cannot say; but so it is, that such apprisings were supported even against the clearest principles of common law. An apprising so irregular cannot indeed be held as a judicial sale for a just price: the utmost indulgence that could be given it, was to hold it to be a security for payment of debt. Accordingly the act 6, parl. 1621,[16] considers it in that light, enacting, "That apprisers shall be accountable for their intromissions[17] within the legal, first in extinction of the interest, and thereafter of the capital"; which, in effect, is declaring the property to remain with the debtor, as no man is bound to account for rents that are his <377> own. And it is considered in the same light by the act 62. parl. 1661,[18] "ranking *pari passu*[19] with the first effectual apprising, all other apprisings led within year and day of it": creditors real or personal may be ranked upon a common subject *pari passu,* or in what order the legislature thinks proper; but such ranking evidently implies that the property belongs to the debtor.[a]

An apprising, then, or, instead of it, an adjudication, has, during the

15. To seize under legal authority.

16. *APS* iv: 609: 1621, c. 6, Act anent Comprysingis [Diligence Act 1621].

17. The act of dealing with another person's property.

18. *APS* vii: 317: 1661, c. 344, Act for ordering the payment of debts betwixt creditor and debtor [Diligence Act 1661].

19. "By equal step"; that is, proportionally, without preference.

a. Stair declares positively for this doctrine. "An apprising is truly a *pignus praetorium:* the debtor is not denuded, but his infeftment stands. And if the apprising be satisfied within the legal, it is extinguished, and the debtor need not be re-invested. Therefore he may receive vassals during the legal; and if he die during the legal, his apparent heir, intromitting with the mails and duties, doth behave himself as heir." *Book* 2. *tit.* 10. §1 [Stair, *Institutions,* p. 513; Kames's transcription of Stair is not exact].

legal, sunk down to be a *pignus praetorium,* or a judicial security for debt; and the remaining question is, Whether it be converted into a title of property upon expiry of the legal? The act 1621 above mentioned makes apprisers accountable for their in- <378> tromission within the legal; and if they be not accountable after, ought it not to be inferred, that they must be held to be proprietors? It may indeed be clearly inferred from the act, that they are not accountable after the legal is expired; but it follows not that the property must be held to be in them: I instance a proper wadsetter, who is not proprietor of the subject, and yet is not liable to account. I say further, that a court of equity, though it has no power to overturn express law, is not bound by any inference drawn from a statute, however clear, except as far as that inference is supported by the rules of justice. And in that view we proceed to inquire, what are the rules of justice with respect to an apprising or an adjudication after expiration of the legal.

According to the original form of an apprising, requiring a strict equality between the debt and the value of the land, it was rational and just, that the property of the land should instantly be transferred to the creditor in satisfaction of the debt; but it could no longer be rational or just to transfer the property, after it became cu- <379> stomary to attach land at random without regarding its extent. The debtor's whole land-estate was apprised, and is now adjudged by every single creditor, however small his debt may be; and therefore to transfer to an appriser or adjudger the property of the land *ipso facto,* upon the debtor's failure to make payment within the legal, would be a penal irritancy of the severest kind. On the other hand, this supposed *ipso facto* transference of the property is penal upon the creditor where the land adjudged by him happens to be less in value than his debt: in that case, it would be glaring injustice to force the land upon him in payment of his debt. Nay more, it is repugnant to first principles, that a man should be compelled to take land for his debt, however valuable the land may be: it may be his choice to continue possession as creditor, after the legal as well as before; and this must be understood his choice, if he do not signify the contrary. To relieve the creditor as well as the debtor from the foregoing hardships, equity steers a middle course. It admits not an *ipso facto* transference of the property, upon expiry of the legal; but <380>

only gives the creditor an option, either to continue in his former situation, or to take the land for his debt; which last must be declared in a process, intitled *a declarator of expiry of the legal.* This removes all hardship: land is not imposed upon the creditor against his will: the debtor, on the other hand, has an opportunity to purge his failure, by making payment: and if he suffer a decree to pass without offering payment, it is just that the property be transferred to the creditor in satisfaction of the debt; for judicial proceedings ought not for ever to be kept in suspense. Thus, the law is so constructed as to make the property transferable only, and not to be transferred but by the intervention of a declarator. The declarator here, serves the same double purpose that it serves in the *lex commissoria in pignoribus:*[20] it is a declaration of the creditor's will to accept the land for his money; and it relieves the debtor from a penal irritancy, by admitting him to purge at any time before the declaratory decree pass.

We proceed to examine how far the practice of the court of session concerning apprisings and adjudications, is conform- <381> able to the principles above laid down. And I must prepare my reader beforehand to expect here the same wavering and fluctuation between common law and equity, that in the course of this work is discovered in many other instances. I observe, in the first place, That though the court, adhering to common law, has not hitherto sustained to the debtor an equity of redemption after expiry of the legal, yet that the same thing in effect is done indirectly, through the influence of equity. Some pretext or other of informality is always embraced to open an expired legal, in order to afford the debtor an opportunity to redeem his land by payment of the debt. And this has been carried so far, as to open the legal to the effect solely of intitling the debtor to make payment, holding the legal as expired with respect to other effects, such as that of relieving the creditor from accounting for the rents levied by him, unless during the ten years that the legal is current by statute.*,[21]

---

20. Agreements for strict foreclosure of pledges.
  * Forbes, February 2. 1711, Guthrie contra Gordon [M 1020].
  21. The first edition (p. 132) and second edition (p. 195) add the following comment: "Here is a strange jumble betwixt common law and equity. The freeing the

In another particular, our practice appears to deviate far from just principles. <382> With respect to the adjudger, it is justly held, that the debt due to him cannot be extinguished without his consent; whence it necessarily follows, that, even after the legal is expired, he must have an option, to adhere to his debt, or to take the land instead of it. This is established in our present practice: and what man is so blind as not to perceive what necessarily follows? An adjudger, upon whose will it depends to continue creditor, or to take himself to the land, cannot be proprietor of that land: before the property can be transferred to him, he must interpose his will, which is done by a declarator; and so far our practice proceeds upon just principles. But whether what is held with respect to the debtor be consistent with that practice, we next enquire. It is held, that the debtor's power of redemption is confined within the legal; that, by expiry of the legal, he is forfeited *ipso facto* of his property; and consequently that he has no power to redeem, nor to purge his failure of payment. Here we find a direct inconsistency in our practice: with respect to the creditor, the property is not his, till he obtain a declarator of expiry of the legal: with respect <383> to the debtor, the property without a declarator is lost to him *ipso facto,* by expiry of the legal. Can any man say who is proprietor in the interim? These notions cannot be reconciled; but the cause of them may be accounted for. In our practice, there is a strong bias to creditors in opposition to their debtors. This bias hath bestow'd on an appriser the equitable privilege of an option between the debt and the land upon which he is secured: the rigor, on the other hand, with which debtors are treated, has denied them the equitable privilege of purging an irritant clause at any time before the door be shut against them by a declaratory decree.

----

creditor from accounting for the rents after the lapse of the ten years, supposes the property to have been transferred to him *ipso facto* by the lapse of these years, which indeed is the case by the common law. The admitting again payment, to be made after the ten years, is supposing, upon principles of equity, that the property is not transferred before a declarator of expiry of the legal [see glossary, "legal"]; for upon no other supposition can payment be forced upon the adjudger after the statutory reversion is expired."

SECTION III

Where the means enacted reach unwarily beyond the end purposed by the legislature.

By the common law of England, ecclesiastics were at liberty to grant leases without limitation of time. As this liberty might be exercised greatly to the hurt <384> of their successors in office, the statute 13° Eliz. cap. 10.[1] was made, prohibiting ecclesiastics from granting a lease for a longer time than twenty-one years, or three lives. In the construction of this statute, it is held, that a lease during the life of the granter is good were he to live a century; for not being within the mischief, it is not within the remedy.

The act 6. parl. 1672,[2] requires, "That all executions of summons shall bear expressly the names and designations of the pursuers and defenders." This regulation was necessary in order to connect the execution with the summons. For as at that period it was common to write an execution upon a paper apart, bearing a reference in general to the summons, in the following manner, "That the parties within expressed were lawfully cited," &c. the execution of one summons might be applied to any other, so as to become legal evidence of a citation[3] that was never given. But as there can be no opportunity for this abuse where an execution is written upon the back of the summons, it belongs to a court of equity, with respect to a case where the statutory remedy is un- <385> necessary, to relieve so far from the enacting clause; which is done by declaring, that it is not necessary to name the pursuers and defenders where the execution is written on the back of the summons.*

---

1. 13 Eliz. c. 10 (1570): Fraudulent deeds made by spiritual persons to defeat their successors of remedy for dilapidations, shall be void etc.

2. *APS* viii: 64: 1672, c. 6, Act discharging second summonds etc. [Summons Execution Act 1672].

3. *Citation:* the procedure by an officer of the court that calls on a party to appear in court, to answer an action or to testify.

* Feb. 20. 1755, Sir William Dunbar contra John Macleod younger of Macleod [M 3746, from Kames, *Select Decisions,* p. 111].

By the 34 and 35 Henry VIII. cap. 5. §14.[4] it is declared, That a will or testament made of any manors, lands, &c by a feme covert,[5] shall not be effectual in law. This could not be intended to render ineffectual a will made by a woman whose husband is banished for life by act of parliament. And accordingly such will was sustained.*

The statutes introducing the positive and negative prescriptions, have for their object public utility; and the supplying defects in these statutes rests upon the same principle; a subject that belongs to the next book, which contains the proceedings of a court of equity acting upon the principle of utility. But to mitigate these statutes with respect to articles that happen to be oppressive and unjust, is a branch of <386> the present subject; and to examples of that kind I proceed. Common law, which limits not actions within any time, affords great opportunity for unjust claims, which, however ill founded originally, are brought so late as to be secure against all detection. It is not wrong in common law to sustain an old claim, for a claim may be very old and yet very just: but to sustain claims without any limitation of time, gives great scope to fraud and forgery; and for that reason public utility required a limitation. Upon that principle the statutes 1469[6] and 1474[7] were made, denying action upon debts and other claims beyond forty years. A court of common law proceeding upon these statutes, cannot sustain action after forty years, even where a claim is evidently well founded, as where it is proved to be so by referring it to the oath of the defendant. In this case, the means enacted go evidently beyond the end purposed by the legislature; which intended only to secure against suspicious and ill-founded claims, not to cut off any just debt; and in this view nothing further could be intended than to introduce a presumption against every claim brought after forty <387> years; reserving to the pursuer to bring positive evidence of its being a subsisting claim, and justly

4. 1542: Statute of Wills.

5. A married woman.

* 2 Vernon 104 [*Countess of Portland* v. *Prodgers* (1689), reprinted in *The English Reports*, vol. 23, p. 677].

6. Act 28, parl. 1469; *APS* ii: 95: 1469, c. 4, Anent the prescriptioun of obligationis nocht followit within the space of fourty yeris [Prescription Act 1469].

7. Act 54, parl. 1474; *APS* ii: 107: 1474, c. 9, Anent the act of prescripcione of obligacionis [Prescription Act 1474].

due. Yet the court of session, acting as a court of common law, did in one instance refuse to sustain action after the forty years, though the debt was offered to be proved by the oath of the defendant.* In another point they act properly as a court of equity. Persons under age are relieved from the effect of these statutes, for an extreme good reason, That no presumption can lie against a creditor while under age, for delaying to bring his action.

The same construction in equity is given to the English act of limitation concerning personal actions:[8] it is held, That a bare acknowledgment of the debt is sufficient to bar the limitation;† importing, that the legislature intended not to extinguish a just debt, but only to introduce a presumption of payment. But with this doctrine I cannot reconcile what seems to be established in the English courts of e- <388> quity, "That if a man by will or deed subject his land to the payment of his debts, debts barred by the statute of limitations shall be paid; for they are debts in equity, and the statute hath not extinguished the obligation, though it hath taken away the remedy."‡ This differs widely from the equitable construction of the statute; for if its intendment be to presume such debts paid, they cannot even in equity be considered as debts, unless the statutory presumption be removed by contrary evidence. The following case proceeds upon the same misapprehension of the statute: "It hath also been ruled in equity, that if a man has a debt due to him by note, or a book-debt, and has made no demand of it for six years, so that he is barred by the statute of limitations; yet if the debtor or his executor, after the six years, puts out an advertisement in the Gazette,[9] or any other news-paper, that all persons who have any debts owing to them may apply to such a place, and that they shall be paid; this, though general, (and <389> therefore might be intended of legal subsisting debts only), yet amounts to such an acknowledgement of that debt which was barred, as will revive the right, and bring it out of the statute again."§

* Fountainhall, Dec. 7. 1703, Napier contra Campbell [M 10656].
8. 21 Jac. I, cap. 16 (An Act for limitation of actions, and for avoiding of suits in law, 1623).
† [M. Bacon,] Abridg. of the law, vol. 3. [1740,] p. 517.
‡ [M. Bacon,] Abridg. of the law, vol. 3. [1740,] p. 518.
9. The *London Gazette,* used to give notice in England of bankruptcy proceedings.
§ [M. Bacon,] Abridg. of the law, vol. 3. [1740,] p. 518.

To the case first mentioned of referring a debt to the defendant's oath, a maxim in the law of England is obviously applicable, "That a case out of the mischief, is out of the meaning of the law, though it be within the letter." A claim, of whatever age, referred to the defendant's oath, is plainly out of the mischief intended to be remedied by the foregoing statutes; and therefore ought not to be regulated by the words, which in this case go beyond the end purposed. Coke* illustrates this maxim by the following example. The common law of England suffered goods taken by distress[10] to be driven where the creditor pleased; which was mischievous, because the tenant, who must give his cattle sustenance, could have no knowledge where they were. This mischief was remedied by statute 3. Edward I. cap. 16.[11] <390> enacting, "That goods taken by distress shall not be carried out of the shire where they are taken." Yet, says our author, if the tenancy be in one county and the manor in another, the lord may drive the distress to his manor, contrary to the words of the statute; for the tenant, by doing of suit and service to the manor,[12] is presumed to know what is done there.

The act 83. parl. 1579,[13] introducing a triennial prescription of shop-accounts, &c. is directed to the judges, enacting, "That they shall not sustain action after three years," without making any distinction between natives and foreigners. Nor is there reason for making a distinction; because every claimant, native or foreigner, must bring his action for payment in the country where the debtor resides; and for that reason both equally ought to guard against the prescription of that country. When such is the law of prescription in general, and of the act 1579 in particular, I cannot avoid condemning the following decision. "In a pursuit for an account of drugs, furnished from time to time by a London druggist to an E- <391> dinburgh apothecary, the court repelled the defence of the triennial prescription, and decreed, That the act of limitation in England, being the

---

* [Coke,] 2 Instit[utes,] 106.
10. See glossary, "distraint."
11. 1275: First Statute of Westminster.
12. See glossary, "suit and service to the manor."
13. *APS* iii: 145: 1579, c. 21, Anent prescriptioun in certane causis of debt [Prescription Act 1579].

locus contractus,[14] must be the rule."* There is here another error beside that above mentioned. The English statute of limitation has no authority with us, otherwise than as inferring a presumption of payment from the delay of bringing an action within six years; and this presumption cannot arise where the debtor is abroad, either in Scotland or beyond seas.

If the prescription of the country where the debtor dwells be the rule which every creditor foreign or domestic ought to have in view, it follows necessarily, that a defendant, to take advantage of that prescription, must be able to specify his residence there, during the whole course of the prescription. While the debtor resides in England, for example, or in Holland, the creditor has no reason to be upon his guard against the Scotch triennial prescription: and supposing the action to be brought the next day after the debtor settles <392> in Scotland, it would be absurd that the creditor should be cut out by the triennial prescription. I illustrate this doctrine by a plain case. A shop-keeper in London furnishes goods to a man who has his residence there. The creditor, trusting to the English statute of limitation, reckons himself secure if he bring his action within six years; but is forc'd to bring his action in Scotland, to which the debtor retires after three years. It would in this case be unjust, to sustain the Scotch triennial prescription as a bar to the action; in which view, the means enacted in the statute 1579 are unwarily too extensive, forbidding action after three years, without limiting the defence to the case where the defendant has been all that time in Scotland.

Equity is also applied to mitigate the rigor of statute-law with respect to evidence. By the English statute of frauds and perjuries, it is enacted, "That all leases, estates, interests of freehold or terms of years, made or created by parole and not put in writing, shall have the force and effect of leases or estates at will[15] only."† In the construction of this statute the following point was resolved, That if there <393> be a parole-agreement for

14. "The place where the contract was made."

* November 1731, Fulks contra Aikenhead [M 4507, from Kames, *Dictionary*, vol. 1, p. 322].

15. *Estate at will:* a tenancy which is terminable at will, and has no fixed period of duration.

† 29. Charles II. cap. 3 [29 Car. II, c. 3, s. 1: An act for prevention of frauds and perjuries, 1677].

the purchase of land, and that in a bill brought for a specific performance, the substance of the agreement be set forth in the bill, and confessed in the answer, the court will decree a specific performance; because in this case there is no danger of perjury, which was the only thing the statute intended to prevent.* Again, whatever evidence may be required by law, yet it would be unjust to suffer any man to take advantage of the defect of evidence, when the defect is occasioned by his own fraud. There are accordingly many instances in the English law-books, where a parole-agreement intended to be put into writing, but prevented by fraud, has been decreed in equity, notwithstanding the statute of frauds and perjuries. Thus upon a marriage-treaty, instructions given by the husband to draw a settlement, are by him privately countermanded: after which he draws in the woman, upon the faith of the settlement, to marry him. The parole-agreement will be decreed in equity.† <394>

Statutory irritancies in an entail are handled book 1. part 1. chap. 4. sect. 1. art. 3.

Whether can a statutory penalty be mitigated by a court of equity? See below, chap. 8.

CHAPTER VI

Powers of a court of equity to remedy what is imperfect in common law with respect to matters between debtor and creditor.

With respect to this subject, we find daily instances of oppression, sometimes by the creditor, sometimes by the debtor, authorised by one or other general rule of common law, which happens to be unjust when applied to some singular case out of the reason of the rule. In such cases, it is the duty of a court of equity, to interpose and to relieve from the oppression. To trust this power with some <395> court, is evidently a matter of neces-

---

* Abridg. cases in equity, ch. 4, sect. B, §3 [*Croyston* v. *Banes* (1702), 1 Eq. Cas. Abr. 19, reprinted in *The English Reports,* vol. 21, p. 841].

† Ibid. §4 [*Sir George Maxwell* v. *Lady Mountacute* (1719), 1 Eq. Cas. Abr. 20, reprinted in *The English Reports,* vol. 21, p. 842].

sity; for otherwise wrong would be authorised without remedy. Such oppression appears in different shapes and in different circumstances, which I shall endeavour to arrange properly; beginning with the oppression a creditor may commit under protection of common law, and then proceeding to what may be committed by a debtor.

SECTION I

Injustice of common law with respect to compensation.

By the common law of this land, when a debtor is sued for payment, it will afford no defence that the plaintiff owes him an equivalent sum. This sum he may demand in a separate action; but in the mean time, if he make not payment of the sum demanded, a decree issues against him, to be followed with execution. Now this is rigorous, or rather unjust. For, with respect to the plaintiff, unless he mean to oppress, he cannot wish better payment <396> than to be discharged of the debt he owes the defendant. And, with respect to the defendant, it is gross injustice to subject him to execution for failing to pay a debt, when possibly the only means he has for payment is that very sum the plaintiff detains from him. To that act of injustice, however, the common law lends its authority, by a general rule, impowering every creditor to proceed to execution when his debtor fails to make payment. But that rule, however just in the main, was never intended to take place in the present case; and therefore a court of equity remedies an act of injustice occasioned by a too extensive application of the rule beyond the reason and intention of the law. The remedy is, to order an account in place of payment, and the one debt to be hit off against the other. This is termed the *privilege of compensation,* which furnishes a good defence against payment. Compensation accordingly was in old Rome sustained before the Praetor; and in England has long been received in courts of equity. In Scotland indeed it has the authority of a statute;* which it seems was <397> thought necessary, because at that period the court of session

---

* Act 143. parl. 1592 [*APS* iii: 573: 1592, c. 61, That compensatioun de liquido ad liquidum be admittit in all jugementis (Compensation Act 1592)].

was probably not understood to be a court of equity.* But perhaps there was a further view, namely, to introduce compensation as a defence into courts of common law; and with that precise view did compensation lately obtain the authority of a statute in England:† the defence of compensation was always admitted in the court of chancery; but by authority of the statute, it is now also admitted in courts of common law.

In applying, however, the foregoing statute, the powers of a court of equity are more extensive, than of a court of common law. A court of common law is tied to the letter of the statute, and has no privilege to inquire into its motive. But the court of session, as a court of equity, may supply its defects and correct its excesses. Yet I know not by what misapprehension, the court of session, with regard to this statute, hath always been considered as a court of common law, and not as a court of equity; a misapprehension the less excusable, considering the subject of <398> the statute, a matter of equity, which the court itself could have introduced had the statute never been made. I shall make this reflection plain, by entering into particulars. The statute authorises compensation to be pleaded in the original process only, by way of exception, and gives no authority to plead it whether in the reduction or suspension¹ of a decree. The words are, "That a liquid debt be admitted by way of exception before decreet by all judges, but not in a suspension nor reduction of the decreet." This limitation is proper in two views. The first is, that the omitting or forbearing to plead compensation in the original process is not a good objection against the decree. The other view is, that it would afford too great scope for litigiosity, were defendants indulged to reserve their articles of compensation as a ground for suspension or reduction. Attending to these views, a decree purely in absence ought not to bar compensation; because it is often pronounced when the party hath not an opportunity to appear. For that reason, a party who is restored to his defences in a suspension, upon showing that his absence <399> was not contumacious, ought to be at

---

* See the Introduction.

† 2. Geo. II. cap. 22. §11 [An act for the relief of debtors with respect to the imprisonment of their persons, 1729, s. 13].

1. *Suspension:* the process in Scots law by which execution on a sentence or decree is stayed until a final decision has been made by the supreme court.

liberty to plead every defence, whether in equity or at common law. And yet our judges constantly reject compensation when pleaded in a suspension of a decree in absence, though that case comes not under the reason and motive of the statute. The statute, in my apprehension, admits of still greater latitude; which is, that after a decree *in foro*[2] is suspended for any good reason, compensation may be received in discussing the suspension;[3] for the statute goes no farther but to prohibit a decree to be suspended merely upon compensation. Nor can it have any bad effect to admit compensation when a cause is brought under review by suspension because of error committed in the original process: on the contrary, it is beneficial to both by preventing a new law-suit.

If the decisions of the court of session upon the different articles of this statute show a slavish dependence on the common law; the decisions which regulate cases of compensation not provided for by the statute breathe a freer spirit, being governed by true principles of equity. The first case that presents itself, is, where one only <400> of the two concurring debts bears interest. What shall be the effect of compensation in that case? Shall the principal and interest be brought down to the time of pleading compensation, and be set off at that period against the other debt which bears not interest? Or shall the account be instituted as at the time of the concourse,[4] as if from that period interest were no longer due? Equity evidently concludes for the latter; for it considers, that each had the use of the other's money; and that it is not just the one should have a claim for interest while the other has none: interest is a premium for the use of money, and my creditor in effect gets that premium by having from me the use of an equivalent sum. And accordingly, it is the constant practice of the court, to stay the course of interest from the time the two debts concurred. But as it would be unjust to make a debtor pay interest for money he must retain in his hand ready to answer a demand, therefore in such a case compensation is excluded.[5] Example. A

---

2. "In court."

3. See glossary, "suspension."

4. That is, at the moment of the set off, or *concursus debiti et crediti*.

5. In place of this sentence, the equivalent passages in the first edition (pp. 142–43) and second edition (p. 204) read: "But this obviously can only hold where the compen-

tacksman[6] lends a considerable sum to his landlord, agreeing in the bond to suspend the payment during the currency of the tack, but <401> stipulating to himself a power to retain the interest annually out of the tack-duty. The tacksman makes punctual payment of the surplus tack-duties, as often as demanded: but, by some disorder in the landlord's affairs, a considerable arrear is allowed to remain in the hands of the tacksman. The landlord pleading to make the tack-duties in arrear operate *retro* against the bonded debt, so as to extinguish some part of the principal annually, the *retro* operation was not admitted: because, in terms of the contract, the tacksman was bound to keep in his hand the surplus tack-duties ready to be paid on demand; and for that reason it would be unjust to make him pay interest for this sum; or, which comes to the same, it would be unjust to make it operate *retro,* by applying it annually in extinction of the bonded debt bearing interest.*

In applying compensation, both claims must be pure; for it is not equitable to delay paying a debt of which the term is past, upon pretext of a counter-claim that cannot at present be demanded, or that <402> is uncertain as to its extent. But what if the pursuer be bankrupt, or be *vergens ad inopiam?*[7] The common law authorises a bankrupt to insist for payment equally with a person solvent: but it is not just to oblige me to pay what I owe to a bankrupt, and to leave me without remedy as to what he owes me. This therefore is a proper case for the interposition of equity. It cannot authorise compensation in circumstances that afford not place for it; but it can prevent the mischief in the most natural manner, by obliging the bankrupt to find security to make good the counter-claim when it shall become due; and this is the constant practice of the court of session.

---

sation is mutual. A debtor who cannot retain by compensation is supposed to have the money always ready to meet a demand. In this situation, it would be unjust to oblige him to pay 5 *per cent.* premium, or any premium, for money which must lie dead in his hand without being put to any use; and it would be equally unjust to make the claim for that money operate *retro,* in order to cut down a debt due to him bearing interest, which, in effect, is making the dead sum bear interest against him."

6. Leaseholder.

* July 21. 1756, Campbell contra Carruthers [M 2551, from Kames, *Select Decisions,* p. 158].

7. "On the brink of insolvency."

Compensation would be but an imperfect remedy against the oppression of the common law, if it could not be applied otherwise than by exception. The statute, it is true, extends the remedy no farther; but the court of session, upon a principle of equity, affords a remedy where the statute is silent. Supposing two mutual debts, of which the one only bears interest, the creditor in the barren debt demands his money; which the debtor pays without <403> pleading compensation, and then demands the debt due to himself with the interest. Or let it be supposed, that payment of the barren debt is offered, which the creditor must accept, however sensible of the hardship. In these cases there is no opportunity to apply the equitable rule, That both sums should bear interest, or neither. Therefore, to give opportunity for applying that rule, a process of mutual extinction of the two debts ought to be sustained to the creditor whose sum is barren; to have effect *retro* from the time of concourse: and this process accordingly is always sustained in the court of session.

We next take under consideration the case of an assignee. And the first question is, Whether the process of mutual extinction now mentioned be competent against an assignee. To prevent mistakes, let it be understood, that an assignment intimated is, in our present practice, a proper *cessio in jure*,[8] transferring the claim *funditus* from the assignor or cedent to the assignee. This being taken for granted, it follows, that compensation cannot be pleaded against an assignee: for though one of the claims is now transferred to him, that cir- <404> cumstance subjects him not to the counterclaim; and therefore there is no mutual concourse of debts between the parties, upon which to found a compensation.

Let us suppose, that the claim bearing interest is that which is assigned. This claim, principal and interest, must be paid to the assignee, because he is not subjected to the counter-claim. Must then the assignee's debtor, after paying the principal and interest, be satisfied to demand from the cedent the sum due to himself which bears not interest? At that rate, the creditor whose claim bears interest, will always take care by an assignment to prevent compensation. This hardship is a sufficient ground for the in-

---

8. *Cessio in jure:* transfer in law. In Roman law, *in jure cessio* was a means of transferring ownership by means of a fictitious suit in the form of a *rei vindicatio.*

terposition of equity. If the cedent hath procured an undue advantage to himself, by making a sum bear interest in the name of an assignee, which would not bear interest in his own name, the debtor ought not to suffer; and the proper reparation is to oblige him to pay interest *ex aequitate*,[9] though the claim at common law bears none.

But if the debt assigned be that which bears not interest, a total separation is <405> thereby made between the two debts. And what after this can prevent the counter-claim with its interest from being made effectual against the cedent? No objection in equity can arise to him, seeing, with his eyes open, he deprived himself of the opportunity of compensation, the only mean he had to avoid paying interest upon the counter-claim.

In handling compensation as directed by equity, I have hitherto considered what the law ought to be, and have carefully avoided the intricacies of our practice, which in several particulars appears erroneous. To complete the subject, I must take a survey of that practice. By our old law, derived from that of the Romans, and from England, a creditor could not assign his claim; all he could do was to grant a procuratory *in rem suam;*[10] which did not transfer the *jus crediti*[11] to the assignee, but only intitled him *procuratoria nomine*[12] to demand payment. From the nature of this title it was thought, that compensation might be pleaded against the assignee as well as against the cedent: and indeed, considering the title singly, the opinion is right; because the pleading compensation against <406> a procurator, is in effect pleading it against the cedent or creditor himself. The opinion however is erroneous; and the error arises from overlooking the capital circumstance, which is the equitable right that the assignee, though considered as a procurator only, hath to the claim assigned, by having paid a price for it. Equity will never subject such a procurator or assignee to the cedent's debts, whether in the way of payment or compensation. And as for the statute, it affords not any pretext for sustaining compensation against such an assignee; being made to support compensation against

---

9. "In accordance with equity."

10. Procuratory *in rem suam:* an authority given to another to act "in his own affairs"; by which the assignee was authorized by the creditor to sue the debtor in his own name.

11. "The right of a creditor"; that is, the personal right vested in a creditor to the debt.

12. "In the name of a procurator"; that is, in his capacity as procurator.

the rigour of common law; but to support it only as far as just. It could not therefore be the intention of the legislature, in defiance of justice, to make compensation effectual against an assignee who pays value. Nor must it pass unobserved, that, as our law stands at present, this iniquitous effect given to compensation is still more absurd, if possible, than it was formerly. In our later practice an assignment has changed its nature, and is converted into a proper *cessio in jure,* divesting the cedent *funditus,* and vesting the assignee. Whence it follows, that, af- <407> ter an assignment is intimated, compensation is barred from the very nature of the assignee's right, even laying aside the objection upon the head of equity. But we began with sustaining compensation against an assignee for a valuable consideration, in quality of a procurator; not adverting, that though his title did not protect him from compensation, his right as purchaser ought to have had that effect: and by the force of custom we have adhered to the same erroneous practice, though now the title of an assignee protects him from compensation, as well as the nature of his right when he pays value for it.

SECTION II

Injustice of common law with respect to indefinite payment.

Next of oppression or wrong that may be committed by a debtor, under protection of common law.

Every man who has the administration of his own affairs, may pay his debts in <408> what order he pleases, where his creditors interpose not by legal execution. Nor will it make a difference, that several debts are due by him to the same creditor; for the rule of law is, That if full payment be offered of any particular debt, the creditor is bound to accept, and to give a discharge.

But now supposing a sum to be delivered by the debtor to the creditor as payment, but without applying it to any one debt in particular, termed *indefinite payment,* the question is, By what rule shall the application be made when the parties afterward come to state an account? If the debts be all of the same kind, it is of no importance to which of them the sum

be applied: otherwise, if the debts be of different kinds, one for example
bearing interest, one barren. The rule in the Roman law is, *Quod electio est
debitoris;*[1] a rule founded on the principles of common law. The sum delivered to the creditor is in his hand for behoof of the debtor, and therefore it
belongs to the debtor to make the application. But though this is the rule
of common law, it is not the rule of justice: if the debtor make an undue
<409> application, equity will interpose to relieve the creditor from the
hardship. A debtor, it is true, delivering a sum to his creditor, may direct
the application of it as he thinks proper: he may deliver it as payment of a
debt bearing interest, when he is due to the same creditor a debt bearing
none; yet a remedy in this case is beyond the reach of equity. But where
the money is already in the hand of the creditor indefinitely, the debtor
has no longer the same arbitrary power of making the application: equity
interposing, will direct the application. Thus, indefinite payment comes
under the power of a court of equity.

In order to ascertain the equitable rules for applying an indefinite payment, a few preliminary considerations may be of use. A loan of money is
a mutual contract equally for the benefit of the lender and borrower: the
debtor has the use of the money he borrows, and for it pays to the creditor
a yearly premium. With respect therefore to a sum bearing interest, the
debtor is not bound, either in strict law or in equity, to pay the capital
until the creditor make a demand. A debt <410> not bearing interest is
in a very different condition: the debtor has the whole benefit, and the
creditor is deprived of the use of his money without a valuable consideration; which binds the debtor, in good conscience, either to pay the sum,
or to pay interest. Though this be a matter of duty, it cannot however be
enforced by a court of equity in all cases; for it may be the creditor's intention to assist the debtor with the use of money without interest: but upon
the first legal expression of the creditor's will to have his money, a court of
equity ought to decree interest.

Another preliminary is, that where a cautioner accedes to a bond of
borrowed money, the debtor is in conscience bound to pay the sum at the
term covenanted, in order to relieve his cautioner, who has no benefit by

---

1. "That the debtor has the choice."

the transaction. The case is different where the cautioner shows a willingness to continue his credit.

Entering now into particulars, the first case I shall mention is, where two debts are due by the same debtor to the same creditor, one of which only bears interest. An indefinite payment ought undoubtedly <411> to be applied to the debt not bearing interest; because this debt ought in common justice to be first paid, and there is nothing to oblige the debtor to pay the other till it be demanded. A man of candour will make the application in this manner; and were there occasion for a presumption, it will be presumed of every debtor that he intended such application. But the judge has no occasion for a presumption: his authority for making the application is derived from a principle of justice. The same principle directs, that where both debts bear interest, the indefinite payment ought first to be applied for extinguishing what is due of interest; and next for extinguishing one or other capital indifferently, or for extinguishing both in proportion.[a]

The second case shall be of two debts bearing interest; one of which is secured by infeftment or inhibition. It is equal to the debtor which of the debts be first paid: <412> and therefore, the indefinite payment ought to be applied to the debt for which there is the slenderest security; because such application is for the interest of the creditor. Take another case of the same kind. A tenant in tail owes two debts to the same creditor; one of his own contracting, and one as representing the entailer. Every indefinite payment he makes ought to be ascribed to his proper debt, for payment of which there is no fund but the rents during his life. This, it is true, is against the interest of the substitutes:[2] but their interest cannot be regarded in the application of rents which belong not to them but to the tenant in tail: and next, as they are *certantes de lucro captando,* their interest cannot weigh against that of a creditor, who is *certans de damno evitando.*

---

a. The rule here laid down seems to be unknown in England. Sometimes it is found that *electio est debitoris,* and sometimes that it is *creditoris. Abridg. cases in equity, cap.* 22. *sect. D.* §1. & 2 [*Heyward* v. *Lomax* (1681) and *Manning* v. *Westerne* (1707), 1 Eq. Cas. Abr. 147, reprinted in *The English Reports,* vol. 21, p. 948].

2. *Substitutes in an entail:* those heirs who succeed in case of failure of the person granted the settlement.

Third case. A debtor obtains an ease, upon condition of paying at a day certain the transacted sum bearing interest: he is also bound to the same creditor in a separate debt not bearing interest. The question is, To which of these debts ought an indefinite payment to be applied? It is the interest of the debtor that it be ap- <413> plied to the transacted sum: it is the interest of the creditor that it be applied to the separate debt not bearing interest. The judge will not prefer the interest of either, but make the application in the most equitable manner, regarding the interest of both: he will therefore, in the first place, consider which of the two has the greatest interest in the application; and he will so apply the sum as to produce the greatest effect. This consideration will lead him to make the application to the transacted sum: for if the transaction be in any degree lucrative, the debtor will lose more by its becoming ineffectual, than the creditor will by wanting the interim use of the money due to him without interest. But then, the benefit ought not to lie all on one side; and therefore equity rules, that the debtor, who gets the whole benefit of the application, ought to pay interest for the separate sum; which brings matters to a perfect equality between them. For the same reason, if the application be made to the debt not bearing interest, the transaction ought to be made effectual, notwithstanding the term appointed for paying the transacted sum be elapsed. <414>

Fourth case. Suppose the one debt is secured by adjudication the legal of which is near expiring, and the other is a debt not bearing interest. And, to adjust the case to the present subject, we shall also suppose, that the legal of an adjudication expires *ipso facto* without necessity of a declarator. An indefinite payment here ought to be applied for extinguishing the adjudication. And, for the reason given in the preceding case, the separate debt ought to bear interest from the time of the indefinite payment.

Fifth case. An heir of entail owes two debts to the same creditor; the one a debt contracted by the entailer not bearing interest, the other a debt bearing interest contracted by the heir, which may found a declarator of forfeiture against him. An indefinite payment ought to be applied to the first-mentioned debt, because it bears not interest: for with regard to the heir's hazard of forfeiture, the forfeiture, which cannot be made effectual but by a process of declarator, may be prevented by paying the debt. And the difficulty of procuring money for that purpose, is an event <415> too distant and too uncertain to be regarded in forming a rule of equity.

Sixth case. Neither of the debts bear interest; and one of them is guarded by a penal irritancy, feu-duties for example, due more than two years. In this case, the feu-duties ought to be extinguished by the indefinite payment; because such application relieves the debtor from a declarator of irritancy, and is indifferent to the creditor as both debts are barren. Nor will it be regarded, that the creditor is cut out of the hope he had of acquiring the subject by the declarator of irritancy; because in equity the rule holds without exception, *Quod potior debet esse conditio ejus qui certat de damno evitando, quam ejus qui certat de lucro captando.*[3]

Seventh case. If there be a cautioner in one of the debts, and neither debt bear interest, the indefinite payment ought undoubtedly to be applied for relieving the cautioner. Gratitude demands this from the principal debtor, for whose service solely the cautioner gave his credit. It may be more the interest of the creditor to have the application made to the other debt, which is not so well secured: but the <416> debtor's connection with his cautioner is more intimate than with his creditor; and equity respects the more intimate connection as the foundation of a stronger duty.

Eighth case. Of the two debts, the one is barren, the other bears interest, and is secured by a cautioner. The indefinite payment ought to be applied to the debt that bears not interest. The delaying payment of such a debt, where the creditor gets nothing for the use of his money, is a positive act of injustice. On the other hand, there is no positive damage to the cautioner, by delaying payment of the debt for which he stands engaged. There is, it is true, a risk; but seeing the cautioner makes no legal demand to be relieved, it may be presumed that he willingly submits to the risk.

Ninth case. One of the debts is a transacted sum that must be paid at a day certain, otherwise the transaction to be void: or it is a sum which must be paid without delay, to prevent an irritancy from taking place. The other is a bonded debt with a cautioner, bearing interest. The indefinite payment must be applied to <417> make the transaction effectual, or to

---

3. That the condition of him who is striving to avoid a loss should be stronger than that of him who is striving to make a gain.

prevent the irritancy. For, as in the former case, the interest of the creditor, being the more substantial, is preferred before that of the cautioner; so, in the present case, the interest of the debtor is for the same reason preferred before that of the cautioner.

Tenth case. An indefinite payment made after insolvency to a creditor in two debts, the one with, the other without a cautioner, ought to be applied proportionally to both debts, whatever the nature or circumstances of the debts may be: for here the creditor and cautioner being equally *certantes de damno evitando,* ought to bear the loss equally. It is true, the debtor is more bound to the cautioner who lent his credit for the debtor's benefit, than to the creditor who lent his money for his own benefit; but circumstances of this nature cannot weigh against the more substantial interest of preventing loss and damage. <418>

SECTION III

Injustice of common law with respect to rent levied indefinitely.

By the common law of this land, a creditor introduced into possession upon a wadset, or upon an assignment to rents, must apply the rent he levies toward payment of the debt which is the title of his possession; because for that very purpose is the right granted. Rent levied by execution, upon an adjudication for example, must for the same reason be applied to the debt upon which the execution proceeds. Rent thus levied, whether by consent or by execution, cannot be applied by the creditor to any other debt however unexceptionable.

But this rule of common law may in some cases be rigorous and materially unjust; to the debtor sometimes, and sometimes to the creditor. If a creditor in possession by virtue of a mortgage or improper wadset, purchase or succeed to an adjudication of the same land, it is undoubt- <419> edly the debtor's interest that the rents be applied to the adjudication, in order to prevent expiry of the legal, not to the wadset which contains no irritancy nor forfeiture upon failure of payment. But if the creditor purchase or succeed to an infeftment of annualrent, upon which a great sum of interest happens to be due, it is beneficial to him that the rents be ascribed for extinction of that interest, rather than for extinction of the wadset-sum which bears interest. These applications cannot be made, either of them, upon the principles of common law; and yet material justice requires such application, which is fair and equitable weighing all circumstances. No man of candour in possession of his debtor's land by a mortgage or improper wadset, but must be ashamed to apply the rents he levies to the wadset, when he has an adjudication, the legal of which is ready to expire. And no debtor of candour but must be ashamed to extinguish a debt bearing interest, rather than a debt equally unexceptionable that is barren.

Equity therefore steps in to correct the oppression of common law in such cases; <420> and it is lucky that this can be done by rules, without hazard of making judges arbitrary. These rules are delineated in the section immediately foregoing; and they all resolve into a general principle, which is, "That the judge ought to apply the rents so as to be most equal with respect to both parties, and so as to prevent rigorous and hard consequences on either side."

But this remedy against the rigour of common law, ought not to be confined to real debts that intitle the creditor to possess. In particular cases, it may be more beneficial to the debtor or to the creditor, without hurting either, to apply the rents for payment even of a personal debt, than for payment of the debt that is the title of possession. What if the personal debt be a bulky sum, restricted to a lesser sum upon condition of payment being made at a day certain? It is the debtor's interest that the rents be applied to this debt in the first place; as, on the other hand, it is the creditor's interest that they be applied to a personal debt which is barren. A court of equity, disregarding the rigid principles of common law, and consider- <421> ing matters in the view of material justice, reasons after the following manner. A personal creditor has not access to the rents of his debtor's land till he lead an adjudication. But if the creditor be already in possession, an adjudication is unnecessary: such a title, it is true, is requisite to complete the forms of the common law; but equity dispenses with these forms, when they serve no end but to load the parties with expence. And thus where the question is with the debtor only, equity relieves the creditor in possession from the ceremony of leading an adjudication upon his separate debt: and no person can hesitate about the equity of a rule, that is no less beneficial to the debtor by relieving him from the expence of legal execution, than to the creditor by relieving him from trouble and advance of money. Thus an executor in possession, is by equity relieved from the useless ceremony of taking a decree against himself for payment of debt due to him by the deceased: and for that reason, an executor may pay himself at short-hand. In the same manner, a wadsetter in possession of his debtor's land, has no occasion to <422> attach the rents by legal execution for payment of any separate debt due to him by the proprietor: his possession, by construction of equity, is held a good title; and by that construction the rents are held to be levied indefinitely; which makes way for the question, To which of the debts they ought to be imputed? The same question may occur where possession is attained by legal execution, without consent of the debtor. A creditor, for example, who enters into possession by virtue of an adjudication, acquires or succeeds to personal debts due by the same debtor: these, in every question with the debtor himself, are justly held to be titles of possession, to give occasion for the question, To what particular debt the rent should be imputed.

Having said so much in general, the interposition of equity to regulate the various cases that belong to the present subject, cannot be attended with any degree of intricacy. The road is in a good measure paved in the preceding section; for the rules there laid down with regard to debts of all different kinds, may, with very little variation, be readily accommoda- <423> ted to the subject we are now handling. For the sake, however, of illustrating a subject that is almost totally overlooked by our authors, I shall mention a few rules in general, the application of which to particular cases will be extremely easy. Let me only premise what is hinted above, that the creditor in possession can state no debts for exhausting the rents, but such as are unexceptionably due by the proprietor: for it would be against equity as well as against common law, that any man should be protected in the possession of another's property, during the very time the question is depending, whether he be or be not a creditor. Let such debts then be the only subject of our speculation. And the first rule of equity is, That the imputation be so made, as to prevent on both hands irritancies and forfeitures. A second rule is, That, *in pari casu,*[4] personal debts ought to be paid before those which are secured by infeftment. And thirdly, with respect to both kinds, That sums not bearing interest be extinguished before sums bearing interest.

It is laid down above, that where the legal of an adjudication is in hazard of ex- <424> piring, equity demands, that the rents be wholly ascribed to the adjudication. But it may happen in some instances to be more equitable, that the creditor be privileged to apply the rents to the bygone interest due upon his separate debts: and this privilege will be indulged him, provided he renounce the benefit of an expired legal.

The foregoing rules take place between creditor and debtor. A fourth rule takes place among creditors. The creditor who attains possession by virtue of a preference decreed to him in a competition with co-creditors, cannot apply the rents to any debt but what is preferable before those debts which by the other creditors were produced in the process of competition: for after using his preferable right to exclude others it would be unjust to apply the rents to any debt that is not effectual against the creditors who are excluded. This would be taking an undue preference upon debts that have no title to a preference.[5]

Hitherto I have had nothing in view but the possession of a single fund, and the rules for applying the rent of that fund <425> where the possessor hath claims of different kinds. But, with very little variation, the foregoing rules may be applied to the more involved case of different funds. A creditor, for example, upon an entailed estate, has two debts in his person; one contracted by the entailer, upon which an adjudication is led against the entailed estate; another contracted by the tenant in tail, which can only affect the rents during his life. It is the interest of the substitutes, that the rents be imputed toward extinction of the entailer's debt, because they are not liable for the other. The interest of the creditor in possession upon his adjudication is directly opposite: it is his interest that the personal debt be first paid, for which he has no security but the rents during his debtor's life. Here equity is clearly on the side of the creditor: he is *certans de damno*

---

4. "In a similar condition."
5. Priority of payment given to one creditor over another.

evitando, and the substitutes *de lucro captando.* And this coincides with the second case stated in the foregoing section of indefinite payment. <426>

CHAPTER VII

Powers of a court of equity to remedy what is imperfect in common law with respect to a process.

Under the shelter of common law, many act imprudently, many indecently, and not a few act against conscience and moral honesty. The two first are repressed by censure, public and private: the last, a more serious matter, is repressed by a court of equity; which will not sustain either a claim or a defence against conscience, however well founded it may be at common law. The party will be repelled *personali objectione*[1] from insisting on his claim or defence. This personal objection is with respect to the pursuer the same with what is termed *exceptio doli*[2] in the Roman law. I proceed to examples; and first of the personal objection against a claimant. An informal relaxation[3] of a <427> debtor denounced rebel on a horning,[4] is no relaxation; and therefore will not prevent single escheat.[5] But the creditor on whose horning the escheat had fallen, craving preference on the escheated goods; it was objected, That he had consented to the relaxation, which removed the informality as to him; and that equity will not suffer him to act against his own deed. The court accordingly excluded him *personali objectione* from quarrelling the

1. "By a personal exception," that is, an exception pertaining to the individual.

2. "A defense or plea of fraud."

3. Letters whereby a debtor was "relaxed" from personal diligence (that is, execution of judgment), either by consent of the creditor or because of an error in the proceedings. Formal relaxation required the use of the signet, the seal used to authenticate summonses before the Court of Session.

4. The denunciation of a person as an outlaw. Here, Kames refers to a debtor against whom letters of horning have issued, and who has failed to comply and has hence been proclaimed a rebel.

5. The forfeiture to the crown of movable estate. Until 1748, such forfeiture was suffered by those who had been denounced for nonpayment or nonperformance of a civil obligation (as well as those who had committed criminal offenses). This civil forfeiture was abolished by 20 Geo. II c. 50.

relaxation.* In a competition between two annualrenters, the first of whom was bound to the other as cautioner; it was objected to the first claiming preference, That it was against conscience for him to use his preferable infeftment against a creditor whose debt he was bound to pay. The court refused to sustain this personal objection; leaving the second annualrenter to insist personally against the first as cautioner.† This was acting as a court of common law, not as a court of equity. The preferable <428> annualrenter ought to have been barred *personali objectione* from obstructing execution for payment of a debt, which he himself was bound to pay as cautioner. In the Roman law, he would have been barred by the *exceptio doli*.

Next as to personal objections of this kind against defendants. A cautioner for a curator being sued for a sum levied by the curator, the cautioner objected, That the person for whom he stands bound as cautioner could not be curator, as there is a prior act of curatory standing unreduced. An endeavour to break loose from a fair engagement being against conscience, the cautioner was repelled *personali objectione* from insisting in his objection.‡,6 A verbal promise to dispone lands is not made effectual in equity; because a court of equity has no power to overturn common law, which indulges repentance till writ be interposed. But a disponee to land insisting upon performance, the disponer objected a nullity in the disposition. He was barred *personali objectione* from <429> pleading the objection, because he had verbally agreed to ratify the disposition.§,7

* Forbes, 10th February 1710, Wallace contra Creditors of Spot [M 10444].
† Forbes, 28th June 1711, Baird contra Mortimer [M 10445].
‡ Durie, 5th December 1627, Rollock contra Corsbies [M 2075].
6. When discussing these cases, and personal objections, in the first edition (p. 139), Kames adds the following example: "A person interdicted insisting in an action against his interdictor for loosing the interdiction, it was objected, That the pursuer being denunced rebel upon a horning, was barred thereby from appearing in court either as a pursuer or defendant. The court would not allow this objection, though good in itself, to be moved on the part of the defendant, whose duty it was as interdictor, to take care of the pursuer, and even to free him from the interdiction, unless he could alledge a just reason for denying the pursuer that privilege." The case is cited as "Haddington, March 3, 1607 Earl Athole *contra* Edzel" [M 10429, Haddington's report in Kames, *Dictionary,* vol. 2, p. 83].
§ 22d February 1745, Christies contra Christie [M 8437, from Falconer i: 81].
7. In the first edition, Kames adds the comment (p. 139), "A court of equity declining to sustain an action upon a verbal promise to dispone land, acts not unjustly; but only

There is one case in which the personal objection cannot be listened to, and that is, where an objection is made to the pursuer's title. The reason is, that it is *pars judicis*[8] to advert to the pursuer's title, and never to sustain process upon an insufficient title, whether objected to or not. Thus, against a poinding of the ground, which requires an infeftment, it being objected, That the pursuer was not infeft, it was answered, That the defendant, who is superior, has been charged by the pursuer to infeft him; and that the defendant ought to be barred *personali objectione* from pleading an objection arising from his own fault. The court judged, That it is their duty to refuse action, unless upon a good title; and that no personal objection against a defendant can supply the want of a title.*

END of the FIRST VOLUME

---

refuses to lend its authority to a just claim that is rejected by the common law. But it is repugnant to the very nature of a court to authorize either an unjust claim, or an unjust defence, which would be a positive act of injustice."

8. "The part of the judge": the judge's duty.

* Durie, 20th June 1627, Laird Touch contra Laird Hardiesmill [M 10430]; Stair, Gosford, 25th June 1668, Heriot contra Town of Edinburgh [M 6901].

PRINCIPLES

OF

EQUITY.

THE THIRD EDITION.

IN TWO VOLUMES.

VOL. II.

EDINBURGH:

Printed for J. Bell, and W. Creech, *Edinburgh*;

and T. Cadell, *London*.

MDCCLXXVIII.

PRINCIPLES OF EQUITY

Powers of a Court of Equity derived from the Principles of Justice.

Part I

Powers of a court of equity to remedy the imperfections
of common law with respect to pecuniary interest.

CHAPTER VIII

Powers of a court of equity to remedy what is imperfect
in common law with respect to legal execution.

This chapter splits naturally into two sections. First, Where the common
law is defective. Second, Where it is oppressive or unjust. <2>

SECTION I

Where the common law is defective.

It is natural to believe, and it holds in fact, that the different executions
for payment of debt founded on common law, relate to those cases only

which most frequently occur in practice. Upon a debtor's failing to make payment, his land is attached by an apprising, his moveables by poinding, and the debts due him by arrestment and forthcoming.[1] But experience discovered many profitable subjects that cannot be brought under any of the foregoing executions. And even with respect to common subjects, several peculiar circumstances were discovered to which the executions mentioned are not applicable. A court of common law, which cannot in any article exceed the bounds of common law, has not power to supply any of these defects. This power is reserved to a court of equity acting upon a principle of justice often above mentioned, namely, That where- <3> ever there is a right it ought to be made effectual.

This section comprehends many articles. 1st, Subjects that cannot be attached by the executions of common law. 2d, Circumstances where even common subjects are withdrawn from these executions. 3d, These executions are in some cases imperfect. 4th, They serve only to make debts effectual, and give no aid to other claims.

ARTICLE I. *Subjects that cannot be attached by the executions of common law.*

The common law is defective with respect to a variety of subjects that cannot be attached by any of its executions; a reversion, for example, a bond secluding executors,[2] a sum of money with which a disposition of land is burdened, &c. These are all carried by an adjudication invented by the sovereign court. They could not be carried by an apprising in the form of common law: nor can they be carried by an adjudication put in place

---

1. "Arrestment and forthcoming": *Arrestment* is the attaching of a debtor's property in the hands of a third person; *forthcoming* is the action used to make the property attached available to the arrester. The action of forthcoming is brought against the arrestee (the person holding the goods) and the "common debtor," that is, the party owing a debt to both the arrester and arrestee. See Kames's discussion below, pp. 334–35.

2. Under the 1661 Act concerning heritable and moveable bonds (*APS* vii: 230), obligations bearing interest descended to executors; but the act excepted bonds which excluded (or secluded) executors, where the bond passed to the heirs. See further Erskine, *Institute,* vol. 1, p. 172 (book II, tit. 2, sect. 12).

of an apprising by the act 1672,[3] which by the act <4> itself is confined to land, and to what rights are properly accessory to land, real servitudes, for example, and such like. But this is not all. There are many other rights and privileges, to attach which no execution is provided. A debtor has, for example, a well-founded claim for voiding a deed granted by him in his minority greatly to his hurt and lesion: but he is bankrupt, and perversely declines a process, because the benefit must accrue to his creditors: he will neither convey his privilege to them, nor insist on it himself. A reduction on the head of deathbed[4] is an example of the same kind. There are many others. If a man fail to purge an irritancy, the common law admits not his creditors to purge in his name; and they cannot in their own, unless the privilege be conveyed to them. A court of equity supplies these defects of common law; and, without necessity either of a voluntary or judicial conveyance, intitles creditors at short-hand to avail themselves of such privileges. They are impowered to prosecute the same for their own advantage; in the same manner as if the debtor had <5> done them justice, by making a conveyance in their favour.

ARTICLE II. *Circumstances where even common subjects are withdrawn from these executions.*

I give the following instances. First, The apprisings of common law reach no land but where the debtor is infeft. The apprising a minute of sale of land and a disposition without infeftment, was introduced by the sovereign court.

Second, John is creditor to James, and James to William. To convey the last-mentioned debt to John, common law requires an arrestment and process of forthcoming. But what if before John proceed to execution, William die, and no person is found to represent him? In this case there is no place for an arrestment; and yet John ought not to be disappointed of

---

3. Act 19, parl. 1672; *APS* viii: 93: 1672, c. 45, Act concerning adjudications [Adjudications Act 1672].

4. In Scots law, the "law of deathbed" provided that an heir in heritage could reduce all voluntary deeds granted to his prejudice by his predecessor within sixty days of his death, provided he was then suffering from the illness of which he later died. It was based on a presumption that the granter would not have been of sound mind.

his payment. The court of session must supply the defect, by adjudging to John the debt due by William to James.

Third, Execution for payment of debt supposes a *mora*[5] on the debtor's part; and <6> a judge cannot warrantably authorise such execution where there is no *mora*. This holds even in a process for payment. Nor is there any foundation in equity, more than at common law, for a process before the term of payment. Where the debtor is ready to fulfil his engagement at the term covenanted, and is guilty of no failure, justice will not suffer him to be vexed with a process. But with respect to an annuity, or any sum payable at different terms, if the debtor be once *in mora* to make a process necessary for payment of a part actually due, a decree may not only be pronounced for payment of that part, but also for what will afterward become due, superseding execution till the debtor be *in mora*. Equity supports this extension of the common law, which is beneficial to the creditor by easing him of trouble, and no less to the debtor by preventing the costs that he would otherwise be subjected to in case of future *mora*.

From these principles it appears, that a process for poinding the ground before the term of payment, ought not to be sustained, more than a process against the debtor personally for payment. I observe in- <7> deed, that a process of mails and duties[6] has been sustained after the legal term of Martinmas, though Candlemas be the customary term of payment.* But the reason of this singularity is, that originally Martinmas was the conventional term of corn-rent, and for that reason was established to be the legal term. It crept in by practice to delay payment till Candlemas, in order to give the tenant time to thrash out his corns. And for some centuries, this delay was esteemed an indulgence only, not a matter of right. But, now that long custom has become law, and that a tenant is understood not to be bound to pay his corn-rent before Candlemas, a court, whether

---

5. "Delay" or default; normally a claimant's delay in asserting a right or claim, to the prejudice of the defender.

6. An action for the rents of an estate (from *mails and duties,* the rents of an estate, whether in cash or grain). It could be used by a proprietor, or by one claiming the right to the property, or as a form of execution against a debtor by which a heritable creditor procured the rents of the property to be paid directly to him.

* Durie, February 5. 1624, Wood contra Waddel [M 8126].

of common law or of equity, will not readily sustain the process before Candlemas.

A process of forthcoming is in a different condition; for being held necessary to complete the right of the arrester, it may in that view proceed before the term of payment of the debt arrested.* The same <8> holds in a process for poinding the ground,[7] if it be necessary to complete a base infeftment[8] by making it public.†

There is one general exception to the foregoing rule, That if a debtor be *vergens ad inopiam*,[9] execution may in equity proceed against him for security. Thus arrestment in security was sustained where the debtor was in declining circumstances.‡ The defendant's testator gave the plaintiff £1000, to be paid at the age of twenty-one years. The bill suggested, that the defendant wasted the estate; and pray'd he might give security to pay this legacy when due; which was decreed accordingly.§

Fourth, In the common law of England there is one defect that gives access to the most glaring injustice. When a man dies, his real estate is withdrawn from his personal creditors, and his personal estate from his real creditors. The common law <9> affords not to a personal creditor execution against the land of his deceased debtor, nor to a real creditor execution against the moveables; and by this means a man may die in opulent circumstances, and yet many of his creditors be forfeited. Whether the court of chancery interposes in this case, I am uncertain. In the following case it cannot, I am certain, fail to interpose; and that is, where a debtor, having a near prospect of death, bestows all his money on land, in order to disappoint his personal creditors. The common law affords not a remedy, because the pur-

---

* Durie, Feb. 21. 1624, Brown contra Johnston [M 8127]. Durie, July 3. 1628, Scot contra Laird of Drumlanrig [M 846].

7. To take goods on land in virtue of a real burden imposed on the land.

8. Infeftment of land to be held under the grantor, rather than directly under his superior; subinfeudation.

† Gilmour, February 1662, Douglas contra Tenants of Kinglassie [M 1282].

9. "On the brink of insolvency."

‡ Stair, July 17. 1678, Laird Pitmedden contra Patersons [M 813]. Home, Feb. 27. 1758, Meres contra York-building company [M 800, from Kames, *Remarkable Decisions* i: 205, No. 106].

§ 1. Chancery Cases 121 [*Duncumban* v. *Stint* (1669), reprinted in *The English Reports*, vol. 22, p. 723].

chasing land is a lawful act; and the common law looks not beyond the act itself. But the court of chancery is not so circumscribed. If the guilt appear from circumstances, the court will relieve against the wrong, by decreeing satisfaction to the personal creditors out of the real estate.

Fifth, A process at common law reacheth no man but within the jurisdiction. If a debtor therefore be in foreign parts, a judgement cannot pass against him, because he cannot be cited to appear in court; and execution cannot be issued against his effects without a judgment. This defect, <10> which interrupts the course of justice, is in Scotland remedied by a citation at the market-cross of Edinburgh, pier and shore of Leith, introduced by the sovereign court, acting upon the foregoing principle, That where there is a right, it ought to be made effectual. In England, a person abroad cannot be cited to appear even in the court of chancery. This court however affords a remedy. It will not warrant a citation against any person who is not within the jurisdiction of the court: but it will appoint notice to be given to the debtor; and if he appear not in his own defence, the court will out of his effects decree satisfaction to the creditor. Thus, upon an affidavit that the defendant was gone into Holland to avoid the plaintiff's demand against him, and he having been arrested on an attachment, and a *cepi corpus*[10] returned by the sheriff, the court of chancery granted a sequestration of the real and personal estate.* By virtue of the same power supplying the defects of common law, the court of session gives authority to attach moveables in this country belonging to a foreigner, <11> in order to convert them into money for payment to the creditor who applies for the attachment. And as the foreigner cannot be cited to appear in the court of session, notice will be appointed to be given him, that he may appear if he think proper. Where a debtor, lurking somewhere in Scotland, cannot be discovered, the court of session makes no difficulty to order him to be cited at that head borough with which he appears to have the greatest connection.

---

10. "I have taken the body": the return made by an English sheriff who had arrested a defendant against whom the process of *capias ad respondendum* (to secure his appearance in court) had issued.

* 1. Vernon 344 [*Frederick* v. *David* (1685), reprinted in *The English Reports*, vol. 23, p. 510].

ARTICLE III. *These executions are in some cases imperfect.*

The executions of common law, even where there is sufficiency of effects, fall sometimes short of the end proposed by them, that of operating payment. I give for example the English writ *Elegit,*[1] that which corresponds the nearest to our adjudication. The chief difference is, that an *Elegit* is a legal security only, and transfers not the property to the creditor. Hence it follows, that though the interest of the debt exceed the rent of the land, the cre- <12> ditor must be satisfied with the possession; and hath no means at common law to obtain payment of his capital, or in place of it to obtain the property of the land. But as in this case, the execution is obviously imperfect, hurting the creditor without benefiting the debtor, the court of chancery will supply the defect, by ordering the land to be sold for payment of the debt.

ARTICLE IV. *They serve only to make debts effectual, and give no aid to other claims.*

Beside for payment of debt, execution sometimes is necessary for making other claims effectual; and here also the common law is imperfect. To remedy this imperfection, adjudications in implement,[1] declaratory adjudications,[2] &c. were in Scotland invented by the sovereign court. The following case shows the necessity of a declaratory adjudication.

Sir Robert Munro, debtor to Andrew Drummond banker, assigned to John Gordon, "in trust, and for the use of the said <13> Andrew Drum-

---

1. A writ of execution used in England on a judgment for debt or damages. Under this writ, a plaintiff obtained the defendant's chattels to satisfy the debt. If they were insufficient, he was entitled to take half of the profits from the defendant's land until the debt was satisfied.

1. The procedure used when a party selling heritable property (the grantor) fails to fulfill his obligation to convey a complete title to the grantee. In this process, the grantee asks that, in "implement" of the grantor's obligation, the property in question should be "adjudged" from the grantor and declared to belong to the grantee.

2. A procedure, developed in the mid-eighteenth century, to make effective the rights of beneficiaries of landed property held in trust in Scotland. By this procedure, the court could decree the trust at an end and order the feudal superior to grant charters to infeft the beneficiary.

mond," certain subjects, and in particular an adjudication led by him against Mackenzie of Redcastle's estate. After Gordon's death, Andrew Drummond, upon this adjudication, as his title, brought a process of mails and duties against the tenants of Redcastle. The objection was, That the pursuer, having no conveyance from Gordon, has no title to carry on this process. The judges agreed upon the following propositions: 1st, That the trust being given to John Gordon only, and not to his heirs, was at an end by his death; for there cannot be a trust without a trustee. 2d, That Sir Robert Munro being divested by the trust-deed, the adjudication returns not to him by the death of the trustee. 3d, That though the person for whom the trust is created may in his own name insist in every personal action flowing from the trust, yet none but the trustee can insist in any real action founded on the adjudication; because the trustee only is vested in it. These points being settled, the difficulty was, to find out a legal method for establishing the adjudication in the person of Andrew Drummond; and the judges came <14> all into the following opinion, That Andrew Drummond's only method was, to raise a declaratory adjudication, calling all parties that may appear to have interest, namely, the representatives of John Gordon and of Sir Robert, and concluding, that the adjudication thus left *in medio*³ should be adjudged to him, in order to make effectual the purposes of the trust. This can be done by the court of session supplying defects in common law. An action was competent to Andrew Drummond against John Gordon himself, to denude of the adjudication; and the declaratory adjudication comes in place of that action.*

The common law is defective with respect to those who are *in meditatione fugae*⁴ in order to avoid payment of their debts; but a court of equity lends a helping hand, by granting warrant for seizing the debtor, and incarcerating him, unless he find bail for his appearance. But this is not done rashly, upon the naked complaint of the creditor. He is bound first to give e- <15> vidence of his debt: he is bound next to explain the reasons of his suspicion; and if these be found groundless, or no sufficient

---

3. "In the middle," referring to a fund in dispute (Scots law).

* Andrew Drummond contra Mackenzie of Redcastle, June 30. 1758 [M 16206, from Kames, *Select Decisions*, p. 203].

4. "Thinking about fleeing."

cause of suspicion, the warrant will be refused: he is bound to give his oath of credulity, that he verily believes his debtor to be *in meditatione fugae.* And in the last place, he is bound to give security for damages in case of wrongous detention.* Damages will be awarded accordingly, if upon trial it be found, either that his claim of debt was groundless, or that he fail to prove the facts alleged by him to justify his suspicion of a *meditatio fugae.*

SECTION II

Where the common law with respect to execution is oppressive or unjust.

Execution for payment of debt is the operation of the judge or magistrate, interposing in behalf of a creditor to whom the debtor refuses or neglects to do justice. <16> It is the duty of a debtor to convert his effects into money in order to pay his debts; and if he prove refractory or be negligent, it is the duty of the judge to interpose, and in his stead to do what he himself ought to have done.† Hence it appears, that the judge ought not to authorise execution against any subject which the debtor himself is not bound to surrender to his creditors. But a court of common law, confined by general rules, regards no circumstance but one singly, Whether the subject belong to the debtor: if it be his property, execution issues; and it is not considered whether it would be just in the debtor to apply this subject for payment of his debts. A man who by fraud or other illegal means has acquired the property of a subject, is not bound to convey that subject to his creditors: on the contrary, he is in conscience bound to restore it to the person injured, in order to repair the wrong he has done. And in such a case a court of law ought not to interpose in behalf of the creditors, but in behalf of the person injured. A court of <17> equity accordingly, correcting the injustice of common law, will refuse its aid to the creditors; who ought not to demand from their debtor what in conscience he ought to restore to another; and will give its aid to that other for recovering a subject of which he was unjustly deprived.

* See act of sederunt, December 18. 1613.
† [Kames,] Historical law-tracts, tract. 12. at the beginning ["History of Execution for Obtaining Payment after the Death of the Debtor," 1758 ed., vol. 2, p. 102].

Having thus given a general view of the subject, I proceed to particulars; and shall first state a case, where a merchant, in immediate prospect of bankruptcy, purchases goods and takes delivery without any view of paying the price. This is a gross cheat in the merchant, which binds him in common justice to restore the goods. A court of common law, however, regardless of that circumstance, will authorise the bankrupt's creditors to attach these goods for their payment, as being his property. This act of injustice ought to be redressed by a court of equity: if the goods be claimed by the vender, the court of equity, barring execution by the creditors, will decree the goods to be restored to him. Thus, a reduction upon the head of the cheat mentioned, was sustained against the bankrupt's creditors arresting the subject purchased in the hands of the person to whom <18> it was delivered for behoof of the purchaser.* Mrs Rolland obtained a *cessio bonorum* anno 1748, and began again to trade as formerly. In the year 1749, she purchased a cargo of wine from Main and Company in Lisbon. She commissioned another cargo from them May 1750, which was arrested at Leith by one of her creditors against whom she had obtained the *cessio bonorum*. The venders appeared in the forthcoming, and were preferred to the cargo for payment of the price, upon the following medium, That it was fraudulent in Mrs Rolland to commission goods from her foreign correspondents, when she must have been conscious that they would not have trusted her had they been informed of the *cessio*.†

The same must hold with respect to land, when purchased fraudulently: when the purchaser's creditor commences his adjudication, the vender will be admitted for his <19> interest, and the following objection will be sustained in equity, "That the land ought not to be adjudged to the creditor, but restored to him the vender, to repair the wrong done him." I put

---

* Stair, Fountainhall, December 22. 1680, Prince contra Pallat [M 4932 and 4933]; Dalrymple, Bruce, January 18. 1715, Main contra Maxwell [M 945]; December 8. 1736, Sir John Inglis contra Royal Bank [M 4937, from Kames, *Dictionary,* vol. 1, p. 336].

† Andrew Forbes contra Main and Company, February 25. 1752 [M 4937, from Kames, *Select Decisions,* p. 4; also M 4938 and 4940. The report of this case in Kames, *Select Decisions,* p. 4, says: "the Mains appearing in the furthcoming before the Judge-Admiral, were preferred for the price of the cargo, which was not paid; upon this ground, that Mrs Rolland acted fraudulently in concealing her circumstances from her Lisbon correspondents" (for an explanation of 'forthcoming', see glossary, arrestment and forthcoming.)].

another case. In a process of adjudication, a man who had purchased the land by a minute of sale before the adjudication was commenced, appears for his interest: ought he not to be preferred? His objection against the adjudger appears good in two respects: it would, in the first place, be unjust in the proprietor to grant to his creditor a security upon that subject; and it is therefore unjust in the creditor to demand the security by legal execution: in the next place, it would be unjust in the court to authorise execution against a subject which the debtor is not bound to surrender to his creditors; but, on the contrary, is strictly bound to convey it in terms of the minute of sale.

I illustrate this doctrine by applying it to a subject of some importance that has been frequently canvassed in the court of session. A factor[1] having sold his constituent's[2] goods, took the obligation for the price in his own name, without mention- <20> ing his constituent. The factor having died bankrupt, the question arose, Whether the sum in this obligation was to be deemed part of his moveable estate affectable by his creditors; or whether he was to be deemed a nominal creditor only, and a trustee for his constituent. The common law, regarding the words only, considers the obligation as belonging to the deceased factor: but equity takes under consideration the circumstances of the case, which prove that the obligation was intended to be taken *factorio nomine,*[3] or ought to have been so intended; and that the factor's creditors are in equity barred from attaching a subject which he was bound to convey to his constituent. The constituent was accordingly preferred.* A employs B as his factor to sell cloth. B sells on credit, and before the money is paid dies bankrupt. This money shall be paid to A, and not to the administrator of B: for a factor is in effect a trustee only for his principal.† Hugh Murray, na- <21> med executor in Sir James Rochead's testament, appointed a factor to act for him. At clearing accounts there was a balance of £268 Sterling in the hands of the

---

1. An agent.

2. *Constituent:* the principal who appoints an agent.

3. "In the name of the factor."

* Stair, June 9. 1669, Street contra Home [M 15122]. The like, Forbes, March 15. 1707, Hay contra Hay [M 15128].

† 2 Vernon 638 [*Burdett* v. *Willett* (1708), reprinted in *The English Reports,* vol. 23, p. 1017].

factor, for which he granted bill to Murray his constituent, and of the same date obtained from him a discharge of the factory. Murray the executor having died insolvent, the said bill as belonging to him was confirmed by his creditors. Sir James's next of kin claimed the sum in the bill as part of his executry, or as the produce of it. They urged, That though the bill was taken payable to Murray singly, yet the circumstances of the case evince, that it was taken payable to him in quality of executor, and that he was bound to account for it to Sir James's next of kin. They accordingly were preferred.* For the same reason, if an executor, instead of receiving payment, take a new bond from a debtor of the deceased with a cautioner, and discharge the original bond, this new bond, being a *surrogatum*[4] in place of the former, will be considered in equity as part of the effects of the deceased: and will not be af- <22> fectable by the creditors of the executor.[†] And if the debt be lost by the bankruptcy of the debtor and his cautioner, equity will not charge the executor with it, but will only decree him to assign the security.[‡] Boylstoun having given money to one Makelwood to buy a parcel of linen-cloth for him, she bought the goods, but without mentioning her employer. Her creditors having arrested these goods, Boylstoun appeared for his interest. The vender deposed, that he understood Makelwood to be the purchaser for her own behoof. She deposed upon the commission from Boylstoun, and that with his money she bought the cloth for his behoof. The court, in respect that the goods being sold to Makelwood for her own behoof became her property, therefore preferred her creditors the arresters.[§] This was acting as a court of common law. The property no doubt vested in Makelwood, because the goods were sold and delivered to her for her own behoof: but that circumstance is far <23> from being decisive in point of equity. It ought to have been considered, that though the transference of property be ruled by the will of the vender, yet that it depends on the will of the purchaser whether to accept delivery for

* January 4. 1744, Sir John Baird contra Creditors of Murray [M 7737 and 7738, from Kames, *Remarkable Decisions,* ii: 77-8].

4. "Substitute."

† Stair, book 3. tit. 8. §71 [Stair, *Institutions,* p. 768].

‡ 1. Chancery cases 74 [*Armitage* v. *Metcalf* (1666), reprinted in *The English Reports,* vol. 22, p. 701].

§ Stair, January 24. 1672, Boylstoun contra Robertson [M 15125].

his own behoof or for behoof of another. Here it clearly appeared, that Makelwood bought the goods for behoof of Boylstoun; and that in effect she was trustee only in the subject: the legal right was indeed in her, but the equitable right clearly in Boylstoun. It ought to have been considered further, that Makelwood having laid out Boylstoun's money in purchasing the cloth, was bound in justice to deliver the cloth to Boylstoun; and therefore, that he in equity ought to have been preferred to her creditors, even though she had been guilty of making the purchase for her own behoof.

Such is the relief that by a court of equity is afforded to the person who has the equitable claim, while matters are entire and the subject *in medio*. But now, supposing the execution to be completed and the property to be transferred to the creditor ignorant of any claim against his <24> debtor, as for example by a poinding or by an adjudication with a decree declaring the legal to be expired; what shall be the operation of equity in that case? In answer to this question, it holds in general without a single exception, That a *bona fide* purchaser lies not open to a challenge in equity more than at common law; because no man can be deprived of his property except by his consent or his crime.

I proceed to another branch of the subject. Execution both personal and real for payment of debt is afforded by the law of all countries: but execution intended against the refractory only, is sometimes extended beyond the bounds of humanity; and equity is interposed against rigorous creditors, where it can be done by some rule that is applicable to all cases of the kind. Two rules have been discovered, which judges may safely apply without hazard of becoming arbitrary. The first governs those cases where there is such a peculiar connection between the debtor and creditor, as to make kindness or benevolence their reciprocal duty. In such cases, if the creditor carry his execution to extremity, and deprive the debtor of bread, he <25> acts in contradiction to his positive duty, and a court of equity will interpose to prevent the wrong. The rule is, That a competency must be left to the debtor to preserve him from indigence. Thus, in the Roman law, parents have *beneficium competentiae*[5] against their children, and a

---

5. "The privilege of competency"; the right of the debtor, who assigns his property to his creditors, to be ordered to pay only as much as he reasonably can, leaving him enough to live on (Scots and Roman law).

patron against his client;* a man against his wife;† and the same obtains in an *actio pro socio.*[6,‡] The rule was applied by the court of session to protect a father against his children, February 21. 1745, Bontein of Mildovan, where two former decisions on the other side were over-ruled. The common law, in affording execution against a debtor, intends not to indulge the rigour of creditors acting in direct contradiction to their duty. But as in making laws it is impracticable to foresee every limitation, the rule must be made general, leaving to a court of equity to make exceptions in singular cases.

The other rule is more general, and still more safe in the application. Personal exe- <26> cution was contrived to force the debtor, by the terror and hardship of personal restraint, to discover his effects, and to do justice to his creditors. But if the *squalor carceris,*[7] a species of torture, cannot draw a confession of concealed effects, the unhappy prisoner must be held innocent; and upon that supposition, personal restraint is no less inconsistent with justice than with humanity. Hence the foundation of the *Cessio bonorum,* by which the debtor, after his innocence is proved by the torture of personal restraint, recovers his liberty, upon conveying to his creditors all his effects. And in Scotland this action was known as far back as we have any written law.

APPENDIX TO CHAPTER VIII

When a creditor leads an adjudication for a greater sum than is due, it is held that at common law the adjudication is totally void. The reason given is, That an adjudication, being an indivisible right, cannot subsist in part and fall in part. At <27> the same time it is admitted, that where the *pluris*

* l. 17. De re judicata [On Judgment: D 42.1.17: Watson iv: 538: "Those who can be sued for what they can afford include a parent, a patron, a patroness, or their children and parents. Equally, a husband is sued in respect of dowry for what he can afford"].

† §37. Instit. de actionibus [On Actions, Inst 4.6.37].

6. "Action on a partnership."

‡ l. 16. De re judicata [On judgment, D 42.1.16: Watson iv: 538: "There are people who are sued for what they can afford, that is, not taking account of what others owe them. These are mainly those sued in the action of partnership (which means a partnership of all assets)"].

7. "The strictness of imprisonment": that imprisonment which a creditor can enforce on the debtor to induce him to pay his debt (Scots law).

petitio[1] is occasioned by an innocent error, without any *mala fides* in the creditor, the adjudication ought to be supported as a security for what is justly due, not only in accounting with the debtor, but even in a competition with co-creditors; and that in fact it receives this support from the court of session acting as a court of equity. If this be the true foundation of the practice, it belongs to the present chapter; being an example of equity correcting the rigor of common law with respect to execution.

But that this practice cannot be founded on equity, appears to me clear from the following considerations. In the first place, it is made evident above, that one *certans de damno evitando* may take advantage of an error committed by another; and that equity prohibits not such advantage to be taken, except where positive gain is made by it.* This rule is applicable to the present case. A creditor demanding his payment in a competition, is *certans de damno evitando:* and that, in order to ob- <28> tain preference, he may lawfully avail himself of an error committed by a co-creditor; and consequently, that to support a void adjudication against him, is not agreeable to any rule of equity. In the next place, an adjudication *ex facie*[2] null as proceeding without citing the debtor, is not supported to any effect whatever either against a competing creditor, or even against the debtor himself. Nor is there any support given to an adjudication against an apparent heir, when it proceeds without a special charge,[3] or where the lands are not specified in the special charge. This leads me to reflect upon the difference between intrinsic objections, which render the adjudication void and null, and extrinsic objections, which only tend to restrict it. If the *pluris petitio* be an objection of the former sort, the adjudication, being void totally at common law, cannot be supported in equity, more than an adjudication that proceeds without calling the debtor: if it be an objection of the latter sort, there may possibly be a foundation at common law for supporting the adjudication in part, even against a competing creditor, though there be no founda- <29> tion in equity. The question then is, To which class this objection belongs?

1. An excessive claim, claiming more than is due.
* Vol. I. p. 150 [p. 95 above].
2. "On the face of it."
3. See glossary, "special charge."

Intrinsic objections, generally speaking, resolve into an objection of want of power. A judge, unless the debtor be called into court, cannot adjudge his land to his creditor; and if he proceed without that solemnity, he acts *ultra vires,* and the adjudication is void. The case is the same, where an adjudication is led against an apparent heir, without charging him to enter to the estate of his ancestor. To determine what must be the effect of a *pluris petitio,* an adjudication shall be considered in two lights; first as a judicial sale, and next as a *pignus praetorium.*[4] If a man voluntarily give off land to his creditor for satisfaction of £1000, understood at the time to be due, though the debt be really but £900, the sale is not void; nor is it even voidable. The property is fairly transferred to the creditor, of which he cannot be forfeited when he is guilty of no fault; and all that remains is, that the *quondam*[5] creditor, now proprietor, be bound to make good the difference. A judicial sale of land for payment of debt, stands precisely on the same footing: it cannot <30> be voided upon account of a *pluris petitio* more than a voluntary sale. I illustrate this doctrine, by comparing an adjudication considered as a judicial sale, with a poinding, which is really a judicial sale. A man poinds his debtor's moveables for payment of £100, and the poinding is completed by a transference of these moveables to the creditor, for satisfaction of the debt. It is afterward discovered, that £90 only was due. Will this void the execution, and restore the goods to the debtor? No person ever dreamed that an innocent *pluris petitio* can have such effect with respect to a poinding. By the original form of this execution, the debtor's goods were exposed to public auction, and the price was delivered to the creditor in payment *pro tanto:*[6] the purchaser surely could not be affected by any dispute about the extent of the debt; and the result must be the same where the goods are adjudged to the creditor for want of another purchaser. With regard to all legal effects, he is held the purchaser, and is in reality so; and if it shall be found that the execution has proceeded for a greater sum than was really due, this circumstance will found a <31> personal action to the *quondam* debtor, but by no means a *rei vindicatio.*[7]

4. "A magisterial pledge": that is, a pledge given to a creditor by the order of a magistrate.
5. "Former."
6. "For so much," as far as it goes.
7. A real action by the owner of a thing to recover it.

But too much is said upon an adjudication considered as a judicial sale; for during the legal at least, it is not a judicial sale, but a *pignus praetorium* only; and this I have had occasion to demonstrate above.* If a man shall grant to his creditor real security for £1000, when in reality £900 is only due, will this *pluris petitio* void the infeftment? There is not the least pretext for such a consequence: the sum secured will indeed be restricted, but the security stands firm and unshaken. It will be evident at first glance, that the same must be the case of an adjudication led innocently for a greater sum than is due: a *pignus praetorium* must, with respect to the present point, be precisely of the same nature with a voluntary pledge.

Hence it clearly appears, that the sustaining an adjudication for what is truly due, notwithstanding a *pluris petitio,* is not an operation of equity, to have place regularly in the present treatise; but truly an operation of common law, which sustains not a *pluris petitio* to any other ef- <32> fect than to restrict the sum secured to what is truly due, without impinging upon the security. And this was the opinion of the court given in the case of the creditors of Easterfearn, 6 November 1747, engrossed in Lord Kilkerran's collection.[8] An adjudication was objected to upon a most dishonest *pluris petitio.* The adjudication however was sustained as a security for the sum truly due. Equity could afford no aid to such an adjudication. What the court went upon was, That at common law a *pluris petitio* is not sufficient to annul a right in security, but only to restrict it. This is not a vain dispute; for beside resting the point upon its true foundation which always tends to instruction, it will be found to have considerable influence in practice. At present, an adjudication, where there is a *pluris petitio,* is never supported against competing creditors farther than to be a security for the sums due in equity, striking off all penalties: and this practice is right, supposing such adjudication to be null at common law, and to be supported by equity only. But if a *pluris petitio* have not the effect at common

---

* Vol. I. p. 380 [p. 217 above].

8. Ross of Calrossie, and other postponed creditors of Ross of Easterfearn contra Balnagowan and Davidson, in Sir James Fergusson of Kilkerran, *Decisions of the Court of Session from the Year 1738 to the Year 1752* (Edinburgh: J. Bell and W. Creech, 1775), p. 17; M 112. This example was not included in the equivalent passages in the first edition (p. 162) and second edition (p. 228).

law to void the adjudication, but only to re- <33> strict the sum secured, there is no place for striking off the penalties, more than where there is no *pluris petitio*. Equity indeed interposes to restrict penalties to the damage that the creditor can justly claim by delay of payment; but this holds in all adjudications equally, not excepting those that are free of all objections.

That it is lawful for one *certans de damno evitando* to take advantage of another's error, is an universal law of nature; that it has place in covenants, is shown in a former chapter; and that it should have place among creditors, is evidently agreeable to justice, which dictates, that if there must be a loss, it ought to rest upon the creditor who hath been guilty of some error, rather than upon the creditor who hath avoided all error. When matters of law are taken in a train, and every case is reduced to some principle, judges seldom err. What occasions so many erroneous judgments, is the being sway'd by particular circumstances in every new case, without thinking of recurring to principles or general rules. By this means we are extremely apt to go astray, carrying equity sometimes too far, and sometimes <34> not far enough. Take the following remarkable instance. Among the creditors of the York-buildings company, a number of annuitants for life, infeft for their security, occupied the first place; and next in order came the Duke of Norfolk, infeft for a very large sum. These annuities were frequently bought and sold; and the purchasers, in some instances, instead of demanding a conveyance of the original bonds secured by infeftment, returned these to the company, and took new personal bonds in their stead, not imagining that by this method the real security was unhinged. These new bonds being objected to by the Duke of Norfolk, as merely personal and incapable to compete with his infeftment, the court pronounced the following interlocutor:[9] "In respect that the English purchasers, ignorant of the laws of Scotland, had no intention to pass from their real security; and that the Duke of Norfolk, who had suffered no prejudice by the error, ought not to take advantage of it; therefore find the said annuitants preferable as if they had taken assignments to the original bonds, instead of delivering them up to the <35> company." This was stretching equity beyond all bounds; and in effect judging that a creditor is barred by equity

9. Judgment.

from taking advantage of any error committed by a co-creditor. Upon a reclaiming petition[10] the interlocutor was altered, and the Duke of Norfolk preferred.* And this judgment was affirmed in the House of Lords.

CHAPTER IX

Power of a court of equity to inflict punishment, and to mitigate it.

It is an inviolable rule of justice as well as of expediency, That no man be allowed to reap the fruits of his fraud, nor to take benefit by any wrong he has done. If, by the tortious act, another be hurt in his rights or privileges, there is ground for reparation at common law; which <36> subject is handled in the beginning of this work. But wrong may be done without impinging upon any right or privilege of another; and such wrongs can only be redressed in a court of equity, by inflicting punishment in proportion to the offence. In slight offences it is satisfied with forfeiting the wrong-doer of his gain: in grosser offences, it not only forfeits the gain, but sometimes inflicts a penalty over and above. I begin with cases of the first kind.

A man having two estates, settles them upon John and James, his two sons. John discovering accidentally a defect in his father's titles to the estate settled on James, acquires a preferable title, and claims that estate from his brother. This palpable transgression, not only of gratitude, but of filial affection, was never committed by any person with a quiet mind; and yet, upon the principles of common law, this odious man must prevail. But a court of equity will interpose,[1] and bar him from taking any benefit from this immoral act, by limiting his claim to the sum laid out upon the purchase.

10. A process to submit the decisions of the Lords Ordinary of the Court of Session to review by the Inner House of the court (or to submit decisions of the Inner House itself to review).

* Feb. 14. 1752, Duke of Norfolk contra Annuitants of the York-building company [M 7062, from Kames, *Select Decisions*, p. 1].

1. When this example was used in the first edition (p. 117), Kames added: "It will not permit *A* [that is, John] to accuse himself, by maintaining that he made the purchase for his own behoof. It will hold the purchase as made for behoof of his brother, and

If a gratuitous disposition be granted <37> with a proviso that the disponee shall perform a certain fact, his acceptance of the disposition subjects him at common law to performance. But let us suppose that a man makes a settlement of his estate, burdening his heir with a legacy to a certain person named; and that afterward, in a separate deed, he appoints that person to be tutor to his children. Here the legacy being given without any condition, is due at common law whether the legatee undertake the tutory or not. But every one must be sensible, that it is an act of ingratitude in the legatee to decline the trust reposed in him, and that he is in conscience bound either to undertake the tutory or to surrender the legacy. If, therefore, he be so unjust as to claim the legacy without undertaking the trust, a court of equity will punish him with the loss of his legacy.* Many examples of the same kind are found in the Roman law. A *libertus* claiming a legacy left him by his patron,[2] will be removed *personali objectione*,[3] or *exceptione doli*[4] in the language of the Roman law, if he have been guilty of in- <38> gratitude to his patron; even where the act of ingratitude is otherwise laudable, as where after the death of the patron the *libertus* informed against him as a smuggler.† But the connection between a master and his manumitted slave was so intimate, as to make a step of this kind be reckoned highly ungrateful. Again, a legatee who conceals a testament in order to disappoint it, is for his ingratitude to the testator removed *personali objectione* from claiming his legacy.‡ I shall add but one other example: "Meminisse autem oportebit, eum, qui testamentum inofficiosum improbe dixit, et non obtinuit, id quod in testamento accepit perdere, et id fisco vindicari quasi indigno oblatum. Sed ei demum aufertur quod testamento datum est, qui usque ad sententiam, lite improba, persevera-

---

afford him no claim beyond the sum expended in making the purchase. The maxim, *Quod nemo debet locupletari aliena jactura,* obtains here as well as in many other cases."

    * See Dirleton, 16th June 1675, Thomson contra Ogilvie [M 6362].

    2. The former slave owner, known as "patron" in relation to his manumitted slave (*libertus*).

    3. "By a personal exception," that is, an exception pertaining to the individual.

    4. "By the defense of fraud."

    † l. 1. De his quae ut indign[is auferuntur (On legacies taken away on the grounds of unfitness, D 34.9.1): Watson iii: 177].

    ‡ l. 25. C. De legatis [On legacies, C 6.37.25].

verit: caeterum, si ante sententiam destitit vel decessit, non ei aufertur quod datum est."*

When a man is thus forfeited of a good claim, the question is, What becomes of <39> the subject claimed; whether doth it accrue to the fisk[5] as *bona vacantia,*[6] or is it left with the person against whom the claim is laid? Ulpian, in the text last cited, gives his opinion for the fisk; thinking probably that the legacy becomes a subject without a proprietor; and that if no person can claim, it must go to the fisk. Paulus takes the other side: "Amittere id quod testamento meruit, et eum, placuit, qui tutor datus excusavit se a tutela. Sed hoc legatum, quod tutori denegatur, non ad fiscum transfertur, sed filio relinquitur cujus utilitates desertae sunt."† And this seems to be the more solid opinion. The legatee is not guilty of any wrong with respect to the crown, but only with respect to the testator and his heir. Nor can the legacy be ranked *inter bona vacantia;* for the legatee continues proprietor, and is only barred from the use of his property by an exception competent to the heir, not against the legatee's right, but only to defend himself against payment. There is an additional reason for this defence against payment, which is, that the heir <40> should have some compensation as a *solatium*[7] for that distress of mind he must feel, when

* l. 8. §14. De inoff[icioso] test[amento (On the undutiful will), D 5.2.8.14: Watson i: 177: "One should bear in mind that a person who has without justification brought a complaint of undutiful will and been unsuccessful loses what he received under the will, and this is claimed for the imperial treasury on the ground that he did not deserve it. But only the person who has continued with an unjustified suit right up to the judges' verdict has what he was given under the will taken from him. But if he has left off or died before the verdict, what he was given is not taken from him"].

5. *Fisc:* the public treasury.

6. "Vacant goods," that is, goods without an owner. Often used when property has not been disposed of by will and there is no heir entitled to it.

† l. 5. §2. De his quae ut indign[is auferuntur (On legacies taken away on the grounds of unfitness, D 34.9.5.2): Watson iii: 178: "It is agreed that anyone who is appointed a tutor but excuses himself from administering the tutelage should lose that to which he is entitled under the will. If, however, he has already received it he should not be permitted to excuse himself from administering the tutelage. The position is, I think, different in the case of someone who is only entitled to a legacy under the will, and who is asked by the mother of the *pupillus* to become his tutor but chooses not to do so, since such a person has done nothing contrary to the wishes of the deceased. A legacy thus denied to a tutor does not pass to the imperial treasury but is left to the son whose interests have been ignored"].

7. "Solace"; compensation for grief (Scots law).

treated ill by those who owed gratitude to his father or ancestor. In our law accordingly, the heir is relieved from the legacy.[8]

But supposing both parties equally criminal, Ulpian's opinion upon that supposition seems to be well founded. I give for an example an obligation granted *ob turpem causam,*[9] paid and discharged. Here both parties are equally guilty; and hence the maxim in the Roman law, *Quod in turpi causa potior est conditio possidentis;*[10] meaning that the obligee is barred *personali objectione* from demanding payment; and that if payment be made, the *quondam* obligor is equally barred from claiming restitution. This maxim may hold between the parties; but not against the fisk.

Stellionate,[11] which consists in aliening to different persons the same subject, is a crime punishable by statute.*,[12] I sell my land to John by a minute of sale. I sell it a second time to James, who is first infeft. If James was ignorant of my bargain with John, his purchase will stand <41> good in equity as well as at common law; because he made a lawful purchase, and had no intention to hurt John. But what shall be the consequence, supposing James when he made his purchase to have been in the knowledge of my bargain with John? It will make no difference at common law, which only considers that James is preferable by his first infeftment, and that John is not more hurt than if his bargain had been unknown to James. But it was a tortious act in James to receive from me what I could not lawfully give; and he is punished for the tortious act by voiding his purchase. Thus, if A, having notice that lands were contracted to be sold to B, purchase these lands, such purchase will be voided in equity.† Again, in a case of

---

8. In the second edition (p. 231), this sentence reads, "In our law accordingly the legacy is allowed to remain with the heir: equity forfeits the wrong-doer, and bestows the legacy on the family that is burdened with it."

9. On account of an immoral consideration (from C.4.7: *de condictione ob turpam causam*).

10. "In cases of an immoral consideration, the person in possession is a stronger position."

11. *Stellionatus:* underhand dealing.

* Act 105. parl. 1540 [*APS* ii: 375: 1540, c. 23, Provisioun and panis of thame committand fraud in alienatioun or utherwyis].

12. The material which follows is placed in the first edition in a section devoted to "Personal Circumstances that unhinge in Equity legal Rights founded on Will." For the introductory passage, see Appendix, p. 509, Extract [1st: 114–15].

† Abridg. cases in equity, chap. 42. sect. A. §1 [*Abney* v. *Kendal* (1663) 1 Eq. Cas. Abr. 330, reprinted in *The English Reports,* vol. 21, p. 1081].

two purchasers of the same land in Yorkshire, where the second purchaser, having notice of the first purchase and that it was not registered, went on and purchased and got his purchase registered,[13] it was decreed, that the first purchaser was preferable.* A, <42> who purchased land though he knew that the vender was but tenant for life and that the property was in his son, sold the land afterward to B, who had no notice of the settlement. Upon a bill brought by the son after the death of his father against A and B, it was decreed, That as to B, who was purchaser without notice, the bill should be dismissed; but that A should account for the purchase-money he received, with interest from the death of the tenant for† life.[a] <43>

Next of conveying a subject attached by inchoated[14] execution. The conveying a subject thus legally attached is not stellionate, because it comes not under the definition of granting double rights. But the disponer is guilty of a moral wrong, in attempting to disappoint his creditor by withdrawing the subject from his execution, to which wrong the purchaser is accessory if he had notice of the execution; and for that reason, though the purchaser's title be first completed, he will be postponed to the creditor in a court of equity, as a punishment. Thus the porteur[15] of a bill of ex-

---

13. In England, legislation was passed in the eighteenth century to provide for the registration of title deeds in Middlesex and the West Riding of Yorkshire. For Yorkshire, see the statutes of 1707 (6 Anne c. 35) and 1735 (8 Geo. 2 c. 6).

* Ibid. chap. 47. sect. B. §12 [*Blades* v. *Blades* 1 Eq. Cas. Abr. 358, reprinted in *The English Reports*, vol. 21, p. 1100].

† Abridg. cases in equity, chap. 42. sect. A, §5 [*Ferrars* v. *Cherry* (1700), reprinted in *The English Reports*, vol. 21, pp. 1081–82].

a. From this and other similar cases contained in the chancery-reports, one would imagine it to be a rule established in England, that a *bona fide* purchaser, even from a person who has no right, is secure in equity. But if such purchaser be secure, it cannot be upon any principle in equity: for equity forfeits no man of his property unless he be guilty of some wrong; and though a *bona fide* purchase be an equitable title, the title of the true proprietor claiming his subject is no less so. If a *bona fide* purchaser from a person who has no right be preferred before the former proprietor, this preference can have no foundation but the common law. That such was once the common law is certain, [Kames,] *Historical law-tracts, tract* 3. [1758 ed., vol. 1, pp. 140–42]; and, from the decrees above mentioned, it would appear, that the law of England continues the same to this day.

14. Partially completed.

15. The payee: "A bill of exchange, in its proper sense, is a security invented by merchants, in different countries, for the more easy remittance of money from the one to the other; which has since spread itself into almost all pecuniary transactions. It is a deed or obligation, which, on account of commerce, is peculiarly favoured by law, and

change, having indorsed the same for ready money after it was attached by
an arrestment laid in the hands of the acceptor, the arrestor was preferred
before the indorsee, for the reason above mentioned, that the latter, when
he took the indorsation was in the knowledge of the arrestment.* This
lays open the foundation of a proposition established in practice, That
inchoated execution renders the subject litigious.[16] After an adjudication,
for example, is commenced, it is <44> wrong in the debtor to sell the land;
and it is wrong for any one to purchase.

We proceed to the case of a creditor, who, for his security, takes a conveyance to a subject which he knows was formerly disponed to another for
a valuable consideration. What pleads for this creditor's preference, is the
necessity of providing for his security when he cannot otherwise obtain
payment. But the debtor is undoubtedly criminal in granting the security:
he is guilty of stellionate, and the creditor is accessory to the crime. This
circumstance ought to bar him in equity from taking the benefit of his real
security against the first disponee; for I hold it to be clear in principles,
that the motive of preventing loss, is in no case a sufficient excuse for doing an unjust act, or for being accessory to it.

Such is the relief that is afforded to the equitable claim against a purchase made *mala fide.* Let us now suppose, that a purchase is fairly made
without notice, and that the property is transferred to the purchaser. I put
a strong case, that a man is guilty of stellionate, by selling his land a second
time, and that the second purcha- <45> ser, ignorant of the other, obtains

---

may be defined, A mandate or request from one person to another, desiring him to pay
a sum therein named to a third person on his account, either upon presenting of the
bill, or within a time specified within the bill. . . . The person who writes this letter,
or bill, is stiled the *drawer;* and he to whom it is written, the *drawee* [or *acceptor*]; and
the third person, to whom it is made payable, the *payee* or *porteur.* Thus, it is evident
that the porteur or creditor in the bill has a double security for his money; he has the
drawee, and failing his accepting or paying, he goes back upon the drawer. . . . But the
porteur not only has a right to receive payment, but a right to assign his property in
the bill, which is termed *indorsation.*" *Ars Notariatus: or, the art and office of a notary-
public, as the same is practised in Scotland,* 3rd ed. (Edinburgh: W. Gordon and C. Elliot,
1777), pp. 261–63.

* June 1728, Competition between Logan and M'Caul [M 1694, from Kames, *Dictionary,* vol. 1, p. 105].

16. *To render property litigious:* to prohibit its alienation, in order to defeat an action
or execution which has commenced but has not been completed.

the first infeftment. To make the question of importance, let it also be supposed, that the price is paid by the first purchaser, and that the common
author is now bankrupt. Some circumstances at first view seem to weigh
against the second purchaser: The common author is guilty of stellionate;
and though the second purchaser is not accessory to the crime, he takes
however the benefit of an iniquitous deed; which may be reckoned not
altogether fair. But upon mature reflection it will be found, that justice
militates not against him. By obtaining the first infeftment he becomes
proprietor: and it only remains to be considered, whether there be any
ground in equity or justice to forfeit him of his property. Such forfeiture
cannot otherwise be just than as a punishment for a crime, and therefore
it cannot be applied against the innocent. Hence an inviolable rule of
justice, That the innocent cannot be deprived of their property unless by
their own consent. By this rule, the second purchaser first infeft is secure:
he is secure by the common law, because he has the first infeftment; and
he is secure by equity, be- <46> cause, having purchased *bona fide,* he is
innocent.

A is tenant in tail, remainder to his brother B in tail. A not knowing
of the entail, makes a settlement on his wife for life as a jointure, without
levying a fine,[17] or suffering a recovery.[18] B, who knew of the entail, in-
grosses this settlement, but does not mention any thing of the entail; because, as he confessed in his answer, if he had spoken of it, his brother, by
a recovery, might have cut off the remainder, and barred him. B, after the
brother's death, recovered an ejectment[19] against the widow by force of the

17. Fine: A method of conveying land in England, abolished in 1833, taking the form
of a fictitious personal action between the parties—in which the grantee of the land
claimed to have been deforced of the land by the grantor—ending in a legal compromise, or final concord. Since the grantor admitted that the lands are already those of
the grantee, there was no need for a livery of seisin.

18. A method of conveying land in England (abolished in 1833), taking the form of a
feigned or collusive real action between the parties, in which the grantee successfully
"recovered" the land.

19. A method to try title to land in England, developed in the sixteenth and seventeenth centuries. The action of ejectment (*ejectio firmae*) was a tort action (which was
simpler than the older real actions) in which a person claiming to have been wrongfully
ejected from his land sought to recover possession. The nominal parties in the suit were
fictitious ("John Doe" and "Richard Roe"), so that no physical ejectment took place.

entail. She was relieved in chancery; and a perpetual injunction granted for this wrong done by B in concealing the entail; for if the entail had been disclosed, the settlement would have been made good by a recovery.* The connection which B had with the parties, partly by blood, and partly by being employed to ingross the settlement, made it his duty to inform them of the entail. And his wilful transgression of this duty was a moral wrong, which justly de- <47> prived him of the benefit he projected to himself by concealing the entail.

In a case that has some analogy to the foregoing, the court of session, as a court of equity, stretched their powers a great way further; further, I am persuaded, than can be justified. An heiress's infeftment upon a service to her predecessor, being, after her death, challenged in a reduction as null and void, with the view to disappoint her husband of his curtesy; the court decreed, That the heiress's infeftment not having been challenged till after her death, it was sufficient to support the curtesy, upon the following ground of equity, That had it been challenged during her life, the nullity might and would have been supplied.† One is prone to approve this judgement; and yet there appear unsurmountable difficulties. For, first, it is not said that the pursuer of the reduction was in the knowledge of these nullities during the life of his predecessor the heiress. 2dly, What if they had been known to him? Can silence alone be considered as criminal, where there is no other <48> connection but that of predecessor and successor?

In the foregoing instances, the ill-doer is deprived of the gain he made: in what follow, a punishment is inflicted upon him. A defendant, sued for his rent, deposed that he had no lease: being afterward sued to remove, he produced a current lease. He was barred *personali objectione* from founding any defence upon it.‡ Which in effect was forfeiting him of his lease as a punishment for his perjury. A man, by adding a seal to a note, which is

---

* Preced. chan. 35. Raw contra Potts [Thomas Finch (ed.), *Precedents in Chancery: Being a Collection of Cases Argued and Adjudged in the High Court of Chancery from the Year 1689 to 1722*, 2nd ed. (London: H. Lintot, 1747), reprinted in *The English Reports*, vol. 24, p. 19].

† June 1716, Hamilton contra Boswell [M 3117, from Kames, *Dictionary*, vol. 1, p. 205].

‡ Maitland, 7th December 1563, Laird Innerquharitie contra Ogilvies [M 10429, from Maitland report in Kames, *Dictionary*, vol. 2, p. 81].

sufficient without a seal, was punished with the loss of his security.* And accordingly it is a rule, "That a wrongful manner of executing a thing shall void a matter that might have been executed lawfully."† A bond being vitiated in the sum by superinduction of pounds for merks, was not sustained for the original sum, but was found null *in totum*.‡ It is not clear what <49> was the *ratio decidendi;*[20] whether a penalty was intended for falsifying the bond, or whether the court meant only to refuse action upon a bond that was vitiated; which they might well do, because the word *pounds* was an evident vitiation, by being superinduced over another word that could not be known to be *merks* but by conjecture. The trying case would have been a reference to the defender's oath, that he really borrowed the sum originally contained in the bond. Would the Court of Session have refused to sustain this claim, yea or no? They could not have refused upon any footing but *per modum poenae*.[21] The court of session denied action upon a bond that was purposely antedated in order to save it from an§ inhibition.ᵃ <50>

* 2 Vern[on] 162 [*Sir William Beversham's sister's case,* discussed in *Hitchcock* v. *Sedgwick* (1690), reprinted in *The English Reports,* vol. 23, p. 707].

† [M. Bacon,] New abridg. of the law, vol. 2. [1736,] p. 594.

‡ November 26. 1723, Macdowal of Garthland contra Kennedy of Glenour [M 17063, from Kames, *Dictionary,* vol. 2, p. 554].

20. "The reason for deciding"; that is, the principle or rule on which the decision is grounded.

21. "By way of punishment."

§ Durie, February 10. 1636, Edmondston contra Syme [M 17062. The headnote of this case reads, "A bond was antidated in order to save it from inhibition. Found null *in toto*"].

a. This judgement has not a foot to stand upon but that of punishment: and yet the *ratio decidendi* was very different, if we can trust the compiler [that is, Durie, in M 17063], namely, "Quia quod non est verum de data quam prae se fert, presumitur non esse omnino verum, nec ullo tempore fuisse gestum" [Because it is untrue regarding the date it displays, it cannot be presumed in any way to be true, nor to have happened at any time]. It is amusing to observe how well an argument passes in Latin, that would make but a shabby figure in English. But to judge well, and to give a solid reason for one's judgement, are very different talents. There is in the mind of man a disposition to let nothing pass without a reason; but that disposition is easily gratified, for with the plurality any thing in the form of a reason is sufficient. Mascardus, *De probationibus,* lays down the following rule: "That a thousand witnesses, without being put upon oath, afford not evidence in a court of justice" [Josephus Mascardus, *De probationibus,* 3 vols. (Frankfurt am Main: E. Kempffer, 1619), vol. 3, p. 451: Conclusio 1369. 9: "Ampliatur

What is the legal effect of bribery in the election of a member to serve in parliament, or of magistrates to serve in boroughs? Common law, with respect to electors, considers only whether the man was intitled to vote, disregarding the motive that induced him to prefer one candidate before another; and therefore this matter comes under a court of equity. And as good government requires a freedom and independency in voting, a court of equity will set aside every vote obtained by bribery; for the candidate who is guilty of bribery will not be permitted to be- <51> nefit himself by his crime: and even the candidate's own vote is set aside though not obtained by bribery, as a punishment justly inflicted upon him for corrupting others.

By the common law of England, the wife's adultery did not deprive her of her dower,[22] even though a divorce had followed.* Upon this account the act 13° Edward I. cap. 34.[23] was made, enacting, "That if a wife willingly leave her husband, and continue with her adulterer, she shall be barred for ever of her dower, unless her husband willingly, and without coercion of the church, be reconciled to her." Elisabeth Clement, after living with her husband for three months, deserted him, and lived in open adultery with another man, by whom she had a child. Being cited before the kirk-session[24] of Crieff, she confessed her guilt, and suffered public penance in presence of the congregation. After her husband's decease, she claimed from his representatives the third part of his moveables, and the terce of his land. Her claim was sustained, <52> notwithstanding her adultery, which was not denied. What moved the plurality of the judges was, that since there was no divorce, the pursuer's adultery did not deprive her of her quality of relict, nor consequently of her legal provisions. This may be right at common law; but it ought to have been considered, that a woman

---

secundo conclusio, vt procedat, etiamsi essent mille testes, qui non iurati deponerent; quia defectus iuramenti non suppletur, per numerum"]. What is the reason given? It is, that numbers do not supply the want of an oath; which is no more but the same assertion in different words.

22. A widow's right to a life-interest in one-third of the land held in fee by the husband [English law].

* Coke, 2 Instit[utes] 435.

23. Statute of Westminster II (1285).

24. That is, prosecuted in the church court.

who hath behaved so undutifully as a wife, is justly deprived of the privileges of a wife; and that she ought not to have the aid of a court of equity to make these privileges effectual. The English statute rests obviously upon this equitable foundation; and now that the principles of equity are ripened, the same ought to obtain with us without a statute.*

A statutory penalty cannot be extended beyond the words; but it may be limited within the words, upon circumstances that infer innocence. Captain Forbes, who had no land in the shire of Cromarty, was however by act of parliament appointed commissioner of supply for that shire, under the name and designation of "Captain John Forbes of New, factor upon the an- <53> nexed estate of Cromarty." A complaint being exhibited against him for acting as commissioner of supply without having the qualification of £100 valued rent, the court judged, That he had no title to act. But in respect he had acted many years without challenge *qua* factor upon the said estate, as former factors had done, and in respect the objection against him was not clear and in a similar case had been found by the court to be no objection, his *bona fides* was sustained to free him from the penalty. And yet upon a reclaiming petition this interlocutor was altered, and he was found liable for the penalty. The judges continued in their former opinion, that he acted *bona fide;* but the plurality thought that they had no power to mitigate the statutory penalty; which was in effect maintaining a very absurd proposition, That a punishment may be inflicted on an innocent person for an error in judgement merely. The doctrine of *bona fides* will only hold in statutory penalties; for in a crime against the law of nature, *bona fides* will never be supposed. And with respect to statutory penalties, many of them are enacted in terms so ambiguous, as to make <54> it extremely doubtful in what cases the penalty is incurred. A man happens to mistake the statute; or rather, happens to judge differently from what is afterward found to be its meaning in a court of law: is it consistent with the rules of morality, or of common justice, to subject this innocent person to the penalty?

Upon the same ground, a conventional penalty is equally subject to

---

* Elisabeth Clement contra Sinclair, 4th March 1762 [M 337, from Kames, *Select Decisions*, p. 261].

mitigation. But in that case, it is sometimes difficult to say, what is to be held a penalty, what not. Take the following instance. A proprietor lets a farm, two thirds to be in grass; but with liberty to the tenant to add to the corn part upon paying five shillings for each acre taken from grass. This paction has nothing penal in it. But what if, instead of five shillings, £50 be stipulated? This cannot be called properly an oppressive bargain, because the tenant may keep free of it. Nor can it be oppressive in the landlord to afford his tenant an option, however unequal. But now suppose an express prohibition against adding to the corn part, and stipulating a penalty of £50 each acre in case of contravention. <55> This penalty would undoubtedly be mitigated by the court of session; and yet the two cases mentioned are fundamentally the same, differing in the form of words only.

Part II

Powers of a court of equity to remedy the imperfection of common law with respect to matters of justice that are not pecuniary.

The goods of fortune, such as admit an estimation in money, are the great source of controversy and debate among private persons. And, for that reason, when civil courts were instituted, it was not thought necessary to extend their jurisdiction beyond pecuniary matters: the improvement was indeed so great as to be held complete. But time unfolded many interesting articles that are not pecuniary. <56> Some of them, making a figure, are distributed among different courts: a claim of peerage, for example, is determined in the House of Lords; of bearing arms, in the Lyon Court; and of being put upon the roll of freeholders, in the court of Barons. Even after this distribution, there remain many rights established by law, and wrongs committed against law, that are not pecuniary; which being left unappropriated, must be determined in a court of equity: for the great principles so often above mentioned, That where there is a right it ought to be made effectual, and where there is a wrong it ought to be repressed, are equally applicable, whether the interest be pecuniary or not pecuniary.

To collect all the rights established and wrongs committed that are not pecuniary, would be an endless labour: it would be useless as well as endless; for the remedy is not at all intricate. The only question of difficulty is, In what courts such matters are to be tried and to this question no general answer can be given, other than that the chancery in England and session in Scotland, are the proper courts, where there is no peculiar court established for <57> determining the point in controversy. Take the following example. The qualifications of a man claiming to be a freeholder, must be judged by the freeholders of the county, convened at their Michaelmas head-court: but the law has provided no remedy for a wrong that may be committed by the freeholders, namely, their forbearing to meet at the Michaelmas head-court in order to prevent a man from applying to be put upon the roll; and therefore it is incumbent upon the court of session to redress this wrong, by ordering the freeholders to meet under a penalty.

Two branches of law come under this part of the work, so extensive as to require different chapters. In the first is treated, how far a covenant or promise in favour of an absent person, is effectual. In the other, immoral acts that are not pecuniary. <58>

CHAPTER I

How far a covenant or promise in favour of an absent person, is effectual.

I am aware that the interest which arises to the absent from a promise or covenant, being commonly pecuniary, ought in strict form to have been handled above. But the interest of the person who obtains the obligation for behoof of the absent, is not pecuniary; and the connection of these different interests, arising from the same promise or covenant, makes it necessary that they should be handled together.

Promises and covenants are provided by nature for obliging us to be useful to others, beyond the bounds of natural duty. They are perfected by an act of the will,[1] expressed externally by words or by signs. And they are

1. In the second edition (p. 238), this sentence reads: "They are perfected by a peculiar act of the will, termed *consent*, expressed externally by words or by apt signs." In the earlier edition, this paragraph begins with the following remark: "In treating of

binding by the very constitution of our nature, the moral sense dic- <59>
tating that every rational promise ought to be performed.

No circumstance shows more conspicuously our destination for society,
than the obligation we are laid under by our very nature to perform our
promises and covenants. And to make our engagements the more extensively useful in the social state, we find ourselves bound in conscience, not
only to those with whom we contract, but also to those for whose benefit
the contract is made, however ignorant of the favour intended them. If
John exact from me a promise to pay £100 to James, I stand bound in
conscience to perform my promise. It is true, that the promise being made
to John, it is in his power to discharge the same; and therefore, if he be
silent without requiring me to perform, my obligation is in the mean time
suspended, waiting the result of his will. But as John's death puts an end
to his power of relieving me from my obligation, the suspension is thereby
removed, and from that moment it becomes my indispensable duty to pay
the £100 to James. <60>

The binding quality of a promise goes still farther. If I promise John to
educate his children after his death, or to build a monument for him, conscience binds me also in this case: which is wisely ordered by the author of
our nature; for a man would leave this world discontented, if he could not
rely upon the promises made to him of fulfilling his will after his death.
And though my friend dies without an heir to represent him, I find myself,
however, bound in conscience to execute his will. Here then comes out a
singular case, an obligor without an obligee. And if it be demanded what
compulsion I am under to perform, when a court of law cannot interpose
unless there be an obligee to bring an action the answer is, that I stand
bound in conscience, as men were by a covenant before courts of law were
instituted. Nor is this case altogether neglected by law. It is extremely
probable, that a court of equity would compel me to execute the will of my
deceased friend, upon a complaint brought by any of his relations, though
they could not state themselves as obligees. <61>

Such are the binding qualities of a promise, and of a covenant, by the

---

this nice subject, I cannot hope to give satisfaction to the reader, without first explaining, more minutely than has hitherto been necessary, the nature of a promise and of a
covenant; particularly how far they are binding in conscience, and how far in law."

law of our nature. We proceed to show how far these qualities are supported by municipal law.

For a long period after courts of law were instituted, covenants and promises were left upon conscience, and were not inforc'd by any action. This in particular was the case among our Saxon ancestors: they did not give an action even upon buying and selling, though the most necessary of all covenants. The Romans were more liberal; and yet they confined their actions to a few covenants that are necessary in commerce. At the same time, the action given to inforce these covenants was confined within the narrowest bounds. In the first place, as only pecuniary interest was regarded, no action was given upon a covenant, unless the plaintiff could show that it tended to his pecuniary interest.* And accordingly, an action was denied upon a contract to pay a sum of money to a third person. In the next place, though that person had a pecuniary interest to <62> have the contract performed, yet action was not given him: because, in the Roman law, no action was given upon a contract but to those who were parties to it.† And hence the noted Roman law maxim, *Quod alii per alium non acquiritur obligatio.*[2]

But by confining the actions upon a covenant within so narrow bounds, many moral rights and obligations are left unsupported by law. The Roman law, in particular, is signally defective in denying support to any right but what terminates upon pecuniary interest. If I exact a promise in favour of a stranger, action for performance is deny'd me, it being held that I am not interested to have it performed. Is the case the same where the promise is in favour of a friend, or of a distant relation? Perhaps it may. Let us then suppose the promise to be made in favour of my benefactor, or of my child, perhaps my heir. Have not I to whom the promise was made, an interest to exact performance? No person of feeling can answer with confidence in the nega- <63> tive. Intricate questions of this kind lead to

---

* l. 38. §17. De verborum oblig[ationibus (On verbal contracts), D 45.1.38.17: Watson iv: 655–56].

† l. 11, De obligationibus et actionibus [(On obligations and actions), D 44.7.11: Watson iv: 642].

2. One man cannot incur a liability through another. For the treatment of this maxim in the first edition, see Appendix, p. 510, Extract [1st: 165].

a general doctrine founded on human nature, That the accomplishment of every honest purpose is a man's interest. And accordingly, in the affairs of this world, it is far from being uncommon to prefer the interest of ambition, of glory, of learning, of friendship, to that of money. This doctrine, by refinement of manners, prevails now universally. In the case stated, that I have an equitable interest to exact the promise in favour of my friend, is acknowledged; and a court of equity will accordingly afford me an action to compel performance.

But has my friend an action if I forbear to interpose? He has no action at common law, because the promise was not made to him. And as little has he an action in equity during my life; for the following reason, that it depends on me, to whom the promise was made, whether it shall be performed or not. It is in my power to pass from or discharge the promise made to me; and as this power continues for life, the obligor cannot be bound to pay to my friend, while it remains un- <64> certain whether it may not be my will to discharge the obligation.*,3

I illustrate this doctrine by the following examples. I give to my servant money to be delivered to my friend as a gift, or to my creditor as payment. The money continues mine till delivery; and I have it in my choice to take it back, or to compel delivery. The friend or creditor has no action. He has not a real action, because the property of the money is not transferred to him: he has not a personal action, while it continues in my power to recal the money. If delivery be delay'd, he will not naturally think of any remedy other than of making his complaint to me. Yet the court of session taught a very different doctrine in the following case. In a minute of sale of land, the purchaser was taken bound to pay the price to a creditor of the vender's: action was sustained to this creditor for payment to him of the price; though it was pleaded for the vender, That the pursuer not being a party to the minute of sale, no right could arise <65> to him from it, and that the vender's mandate or order might be recalled by him at his

---

* l. 3, De servis exportandis [On slaves to be exported, D 18.7.3: Watson ii: 542]. l. 1. C. Si mancipium ita fuerit alienat[um, ut manumittatur vel contra (If a slave has been alienated under the condition that he be manumitted, or the reverse), C 4.57.1].

3. In the first edition, Kames added a paragraph at this point, suggesting that the third party had no claim after the death of the promisee. See Appendix, p. 511, Extract [1st: 166].

pleasure.* But the court afterward determined more justly in the following cases, founded on the same principle. A proprietor having resigned his estate in favour of his second son and his heirs-male, with power to his eldest son and the heirs-male of his body to redeem; did afterward limit the power of redemption, that it should not be exercised unless with the consent of certain persons named; and impowering those persons to discharge the reversion altogether if they thought proper, which accordingly they did after the father's death. In a declarator at the instance of the second son to ascertain his right to the estate, it was objected by the eldest, That, by the settlement, he had a *jus quaesitum*,[4] which could not be taken from him. The discharge was sustained.[†,5] Sir Donald Baine of Tulloch dis- <66> poned his estate to his eldest son John; and took from him bonds of provision in name of his younger children. It was found, that as these bonds were never delivered, it was in Sir Donald's power to discharge or cancel them at pleasure.[‡] The like was found 2d July 1755, Hill *contra* Hill.[6]

To return to the case figured of a promise exacted by me in favour of an absent person. My death makes a total change, by giving him an action which he had not during my life: for if the obligor, who formerly was bound at my instance, remain still bound in conscience, as is made evident above, it follows, that the person in whose favour the promise was made, must be intitled to demand performance. This will readily be yielded where the paction is for a valuable consideration: if John give a sum to James, for which James promises to John that he will build a house to William, James cannot both retain the money and refuse performance. The same must follow though the paction be gratuitous; for James is in <67>

* Stair, July 7. 1664, Ogilvie contra Ker [M 7740]; Durie, January 9. 1627, Supplicants contra Nimmo [M 7740].

4. "An acquired right"; or right to recover from someone under an obligation.

† Fountainhall, January 2. 1706, Dundas contra Dundas [M 4089].

5. In the first edition, Kames inserted an argument at this point to show that the third party cannot recover after the promisee's death: see Appendix, p. 511, Extract [1st: 167–68]. This argument was abandoned by the second edition and the argument which follows in the text above was presented (pp. 241ff.).

‡ July 6. 1717, Rose contra Baine of Tulloch [M 11505, from Kames, *Remarkable Decisions,* i: 10, No. 6].

6. M 11580, from Kames, *Select Decisions,* 121.

conscience bound to perform his promise; and William of course must be intitled to demand performance.

From these premises it follows, that the man who thus makes a contract for the benefit of an absent person, may renounce his power of discharging the contract; which renunciation delivered, will instantly intitle that person to demand performance. Such renunciation may also be inferred *rebus et factis*.[7] As for example, where a man dispones his estate to his eldest son, and takes from him a bond of provision to his younger children by name: while the bond is in the father's custody, it continues under his power; but if he deliver the bond to his children, he is understood to renounce his power, which will intitle them to demand payment.*

In the Roman law, a stipulation in favour of the heir was early made effectual, by sustaining an action to the heir.[†] By that law, a son might stipulate in favour <68> of his father, and a slave in favour of his master. In the progress of equity this privilege was further extended. Where a man stipulated in favour of his daughter, an *utilis actio*[8] was given to the daughter, which is an action in equity.[‡] Yet a daughter's paction in favour of her mother did not avail the mother.[§] A man's stipulation in favour of his grandchildren profited them.[||] Where there was a *rei interventus*,[9] an *utilis actio* was given to the absent person whoever he was.** But among the Romans a gratuitous stipulation in favour of a stranger never produced an action to the stranger.[††]

---

7. "By the facts and circumstances."

* Dirleton, November 20. 1667, Trotters contra Lundy [M 11498].

† l. 38, §12 & 14, De verborum oblig[ationibus (On verbal contracts), D 45.1.38.12 and D 45.1.38.14: Watson iv: 655].

8. In Roman law, an action which arose through the modification of an existing action, extending the law to cover situations not covered by the original action.

‡ l. 45, §2, De verborum oblig[ationibus (Verbal contracts), D 45.1.45.2; Watson iv: 657].

§ l. 26. §4. De pactis dotal[ibus (On dotal pacts), D 23.4.26.4: Watson ii: 687].

|| l. 7. C. De pactis conven[tis (On agreements): C 5.14.7].

9. "Things intervening": In Roman law, a party under an imperfect obligation lost the right not to perform the obligation if he permitted the other party to act on the assumption that the obligation was complete: these "intervening" circumstances removed his right to rescind the obligation.

** l. 3. C. De donat[ionibus] quae sub modo [On gifts subject to a qualification, C 8.54.3].

†† §4. Instit. de inutil[ibus] stipul[ationibus (On ineffective stipulations), Inst 3.19.4].

The foregoing doctrine unfolds the nature of *fideicommissary* settlements[10] among the Romans. Of these settlements Justinian* gives the following history, That they were a contrivance to elude a regulation that rendered certain persons incapable of taking benefit by a testament; that <69> it being in vain to settle upon such a person an estate by testament, another person was named heir, to whom it was recommended to settle the estate as intended; and that Augustus Caesar gave here a civil action to make the settlement effectual. But did Augustus make effectual a settlement executed in defraud of the law? I can hardly be of that opinion. If the law was inexpedient, why not openly rescind it? Augustus was too wise a prince to set thus a public example of eluding law. Justinian, I suspect, did not understand the nature of these settlements. It was a maxim in the Roman law, derived from the nature of property, That a man cannot name an heir to succeed to his heir.† Because this could not be done directly, it was attempted indirectly by a *fideicommissary* settlement: I name my heir regularly in my testament, and I order him to make a testament in favour of the person I incline should succeed him. Such settlements did at first depend entirely on the faith of the heir in possession, who upon that account was termed *Heres fiducia-* <70> *rius:* the person appointed to succeed him, termed *Heres fideicommissarius,* had not an action at common law to compel performance; for the fiduciary heir was not bound to him, but to the testator solely. But here was a *rei interventus,* a subject in the hands of the fiduciary heir, which, by accepting the testament, he bound himself to settle upon the *fideicommissary* heir; and he is therefore bound in conscience to settle it accordingly. The *fideicommissary* heir has beside an equitable claim to the subject founded on the will of the testator. These things considered, it appears to me plain, that Augustus Caesar, with respect to such settlements, did no more but supply a defect in common law, by appointing an action to be sustained to the *fideicommissary* heir.

What is just now said serves to explain the nature of trusts, where a sub-

---

10. A form of trust in Roman law, whereby the testator left his property to an heir with instructions to pass it on subsequently to another party. This is discussed by Kames in detail below.

* §1. Inst. de fideicommiss[ariis] hered[itatibus] (On trusts of estates), Inst 2.23.1].

† See [Kames,] Historical law-tracts, tract 3 [1758 ed., vol. 1, p. 190].

ject is vested in a trustee for behoof of a third party, the children *nascituri* of a marriage, for example. A trust of this nature, analogous to a *fideicom-missary* settlement among the Romans, comes not under the cognizance of a court of common law; because the person in whose favour the trust is e- <71> stablished, not being a party to the agreement, has not at common law an action to oblige the trustee to fulfil his engagement: but he hath an action in equity as above mentioned. And hence it is, that in England such trusts must be made effectual in the court of chancery.

Reviewing what is said above, I am in some pain about an objection that will readily occur against it. A legatee, by the common law of the Romans, had an action against the heir for performance; and yet a lega-tee is not made a party in the testament; nor is the heir, by accepting the testament, bound to him, but to the testator solely. To remove this objection, it will be necessary to give an account of the different kinds of legacies well known in the Roman law; and upon setting this subject in its true light, the objection will vanish. In the first place, where a legacy is left of a *corpus*,[11] the property is transferred to the legatee *ipso facto* upon the testator's death, conformable to a general rule in law, That subjects are transferred from the dead to the living without necessity of delivery: for after the proprietor's death, there is no person who can make <72> deliv-ery; and if will alone, in this case, have not the effect to transfer property, it never can be transferred from the dead to the living. Upon that account, a legatee of a *corpus* has no occasion to sue the heir for delivery: he hath a *rei vindicatio*[12] at common law. The next kind of legacy I shall mention, is where a bond for a sum of money is bequeathed directly to Titius. The subject here, as in the former case, vests in the legatee *ipso facto* upon the testator's death. The legatee has no occasion for an action against the heir; for in quality of creditor he has at common law an action against the debtor for payment. A third sort of legacy is, where the testator burdens his heir to pay a certain sum to Titius. This is the only sort, resembling a *fideicommissary* settlement, to which the maxim can be applied *Quod alii per alium non acquiritur obligatio*. But as an action at common law for

---

11. That is, *corpus patrimonii:* the whole estate.
12. A real action by the owner of a thing to recover it.

making other legacies effectual was familiar, the influence of connection, without making nice distinctions, produced an action at common law for this sort also. Therefore all that can be made of this instance, is to prove what will appear in many instances, that <73> common law and equity are not separated by any accurate boundary.

Our entails upon the common law are in several respects similar to the Roman *fideicommissary* settlements; and so far are governed by the principles above established. I give the following instances. A man makes an entail in favour of his son or other relation, disponing the estate to him, substituting a certain series of heirs, and reserving his own liferent. The institute,[13] though fettered with irritant and resolutive clauses, is however vested in the full property of the estate;* and the substitutes, for the reason above given, have not an action at common law to oblige the institute to make the entail effectual in their favour. But the institute resembles precisely a Roman *heres fiduciarius,* and is bound in equity to fulfil the will of the entailer, by permitting the substitutes to succeed in their order.

I give a second instance, in order to clear up a celebrated question often debated in the court of session, namely, Whether an entail, such as that above men- <74> tioned, after being completed with infeftment, can be altered or discharged even by the joint deed of the entailer and institute. Our lawyers have generally leaned to the negative. The institute, they urge, fettered by the entail, has not power to alter or discharge; and the will of the entailer, who is not now proprietor, cannot avail. This reasoning is a mere sophism. The full property is vested in every tenant in tail, no less than in him who inherits a fee-simple. A tenant in tail is indeed limited as to the exercise of his powers of property: he must not alien, and he must not alter the order of succession. But these, and such like limitations, proceed not from defect of power *qua proprietor,* but from being bound personally, by acceptance of the entail, not to exercise these powers.† This distinction with respect to the present question is of moment. A man cannot exercise any power beyond the nature of his right: such an act is void;

---

13. The person to whom an estate is first given in a settlement.

* See Historical law tracts, tract 3. toward the close ["History of Property," 1758 ed., vol. i, pp. 201–16].

† This doctrine is more fully explained in tract 3. above cited.

and every person is intitled to object to it. But no person, other than the obligee, is intitled to object to the trans- <75> gression of a covenant or personal obligation. The entailer, in the case stated, is the obligee: it is he who took the institute bound to limit as above the exercise of his property; and he therefore has it in his choice, to keep the heir bound, or to release him from his obligation. To be in a condition to grant such release, it is necessary indeed that he be obligee, but it is not necessary that he be proprietor.

Hence it appears, that the substitutes have no title while the entailer is alive, to restrain the institute from the free use of his property. They have no claim personally against the institute; who stands bound to the entailer, not to them: nor have they any other ground for an action, seeing the full property of the estate is vested in the institute, and no part in them. In a word, it depends entirely upon the entailer, during his life, whether the entail shall be effectual or no; and while that continues to be his privilege, the substitutes evidently can have no claim. Nay more, I affirm, that the entailer cannot deprive himself of this privilege, even though he should expressly renounce it in the deed of entail. The substitutes are <76> not made parties to the entail, and the renunciation, though in their favour, is not made to them. The renunciation is at best but a gratuitous promise, which none are intitled to lay hold of but that very person to whom it is made.

A great change indeed is produced by the entailer's death. There now exists no longer a person who can loose the fetters of the entail. The institute must for ever be bound by his own deed, restraining him from the free exercise of his property; and as the substitutes, by the entailer's will, have in their order an equitable claim to the estate, a court of equity will make this claim effectual.

But here a question naturally arises, Why ought not the entailer's privilege to discharge the fetters of the entail, descend to his heirs. The solid and satisfactory answer is what follows. No right or privilege descends to an heir, but what is pecuniary and tends to make him *locupletior:* but the privilege of discharging the fetters of an entail makes not the heir *locupletior,* and therefore descends not to him.

Similar to the rule above explained, *Alii per alium non acquiritur obli-*

gatio, is the fol- <77> lowing rule, *Alii per alium non acquiritur exceptio.*[14] These rules, governed by the same principle, throw light upon each other; and ought therefore to be handled together. I obtain from a man a promise to discharge his debtor, the question is, What shall be the effect of that promise. The Roman lawyers answer, that I cannot have an action to compel performance, because I have no interest that performance should be made; and that the debtor cannot have an action to compel performance, because he was not a party to the agreement.*

But the Roman writers were certainly guilty of an oversight in not distinguishing here a *pactum liberatorium*[15] from a *pactum obligatorium.*[16] Admitting the latter to be limited as above by the common law of the Romans; it can be made evident from the principles of that very law, that the former cannot be so limited, but must be effectual to him for whose behoof it is made, whether the person who obtained it be connected with him or no. The difference indeed with respect to the present <78> point between these pactions, arises not from any difference in their nature, but from the nature of a court of law. Courts of law, as above mentioned, were originally circumscribed within narrow bounds; and with respect to the Roman courts in particular, many *pacta obligatoria* were left upon conscience unsupported by these courts. Such a constitution indeed confines courts within too narrow limits with respect to their power of doing good; but then it does not lead them to do any wrong. The case is very different with respect to *pacta liberatoria:* it is unjust in the creditor to demand payment, after he has promised, even gratuitously, to discharge the debt; and a court of law would be accessory to that act of injustice, if it sustained action after such a promise. The court therefore must refuse to sustain action; or rather must sustain the *pactum liberatorium* as a good exception to the action.† And it makes no difference, whether the person who obtained the promise be dead or alive. For while the prom-

---

14. "One man cannot acquire a defense through another."

* l. 17. §4. De pactis [On pacts, D 2.14.17.4: Watson i: 67].

15. A "liberating agreement"; an agreement freeing parties from an obligation (from a real right in Roman law).

16. "An agreement imposing an obligation."

† See Historical law-tracts, tract 2 ["History of Promises and Covenants," 1758 ed., vol. 1, p. 96].

ise subsists, it must bar the creditor from <79> claiming payment; and must bar every court from supporting such a claim. It is true indeed, that while the person who obtained the promise is alive, it is in his power to discharge the promise; and consequently to intitle the creditor to an action: but till that discharge be obtained, it would be unjust in any court to sustain action.

Some of the Roman writers, sensible that an action for payment ought not to be sustained to a creditor who has passed from his debt, endeavour to make this opinion consistent with the rule *Alii per alium non acquiritur exceptio,* by a subtilty that goes out of sight. They insist, that the debtor cannot found a defence upon a paction to which he was not a party: but they yield, that the paction, though not effectual to the debtor, is effectual against the creditor; and they make it effectual against him, by sustaining to the debtor an *exceptio doli.**

Upon the same principle, if a third person pay a debt knowingly and take a discharge in name of the debtor, the <80> debtor, though the discharge be not delivered to him, can defend himself by an *exceptio doli* against the creditor demanding payment from him: for the creditor who has received payment from the third person, cannot in conscience demand a second payment from the debtor. But tho' he be barred from demanding a second payment, it does not follow that the debt is extinguished. That it remains a subsisting debt will appear from considering, 1mo, That the transaction between the creditor and the third person may be dissolved as it was established, namely, by mutual consent, and by cancelling the discharge. 2do, The debtor, notwithstanding the erroneous payment, has it in his power to force a discharge from the creditor upon offering him payment: neither of which could happen, were the debt extinguished. It only remains to be observed, that, when a debt is thus paid by a third person, it is in the debtor's choice to refund the money to the third person, or to pay it to the creditor. But if he defend himself against the creditor by an *exceptio doli,* which imports his ratification of the payment, the sustaining this exception hath <81> two effects: 1st, It operates to him a legal extinc-

---

* l. 25. §2. l. 26. De pactis [On pacts, D 2.14.25.2, D 2.14.26: Watson i: 68]; l. 26. §4. De pactis dotalibus [On dotal pacts, D 23.4.26.4: Watson ii: 691].

tion of the debt; and, next, It intitles the third person to demand the sum
from him.

CHAPTER II

Powers of a court of equity to repress immoral acts that are not pecuniary.

I have had occasion to mention above, that an attempt to correct all the
wrongs that are not pecuniary, would be endless; and in a measure useless,
as the method of repressing them all is the same, which is to declare them
void. One species of immoral acts deserves peculiar notice, not only as a
transgression of duty, but as tending to corrupt our morals.

Individuals in society are linked together by various relations that require a suitable conduct.[1] The relations in particular that imply subordination, make the corner-stone of government, and ripen men <82> gradually
for behaving in it with propriety. The reciprocal duties that arise from
the relation of parent and child, of preceptor and scholar, of master and
servant, of the high and low, of the rich and poor, and such like, accustom
men both to rule and to be ruled. It is for that reason extremely material,
that the duties arising from subordination be preserved from encroaching
on each other: to reverse them, would reverse the order of nature, and tend
to unhinge government. To suffer, for example, a young man to assume
rule over his father, is to countenance an immoral act and breach of duty;
having at the same time a tendency to destroy subordination.

A young man, in his contract of marriage, consented to be put under
interdiction[2] to his father and father-in-law; and in case of their failure, to
the eldest son of the marriage. They having failed, the court refused to sustain an interdiction where the father is interdicted and the son interdictor.*

---

1. The equivalent passages in the first edition (pp. 173–74) and second edition (p.
250) add: "and that we should act according to the relations in which we are engaged,
appears not only proper, but, by the moral sense, is made a matter of strict duty" [2nd
ed.: "our duty"].

2. *Voluntary interdiction:* a system of voluntary restraint provided for those who are
liable to imposition. See glossary, "interdiction."

* Durie, 18th January 1622, Silvertonhill contra his Father [M 9451].

A bond was granted by a man to his wife, bearing, "That by his facility he might be misled to dispose of <83> a liferent he had by her, and therefore binding himself not to dispone without her consent." Upon this bond followed an inhibition; which was in effect putting the husband under interdiction to his wife. The court refused to sustain this act; because a married woman, being *sub potestate viri*,[3] cannot be a curator to any person; and to make her a curator to her husband would be to overturn the order of nature.*

Other acts tending to or arising from depravation of manners, are also rejected by a court of equity. Thus, a man who had fallen out with his mother, settled his mansion-house on his brother; and took from him a bond in his sister's name, that he should not permit his mother to set foot in the house. The bond was set aside.[†,4] <84>

---

3. "Under the power of her husband."

* Stair, 27th February 1663, Lady Milton contra Milton [M 9452].

† 1 Vernon 413 [*Traiton* v. *Traiton* (1686), reprinted in *The English Reports,* vol. 23, p. 554].

4. The first edition (pp. 174–75) and second edition (p. 251) include additional examples: see Appendix, p. 512, Extract [1st: 174–75].

Powers of a Court of Equity founded on the principle of Utility

Justice is applied to two particulars, equally capital; one to make right effectual, and one to repress wrong. With respect to the former, utility coincides with justice: with respect to the latter, utility[1] goes farther than justice. Wrong must be done before justice can interpose; but utility lays down measures to prevent wrong. With respect to measures for the positive good of society, and for making men still more happy in a social state, these are reserved to the legislature.[a] It is not <85> necessary that such extensive powers be trusted with courts of law: the power of making right effectual, of redressing wrong, and of preventing mischief, are sufficient.

As the matters contained in this book come within a narrow compass, I shall not have occasion for the multiplied subdivisions necessary in the former. A few chapters will exhaust the whole; beginning with those mischiefs or evils that are the most destructive, and descending gradually to those of less consequence. I reserve the last place for the power of a court

1. The equivalent passages in the first edition (p. 173) and the second edition (p. 249) add the phrase "having a more extensive view."

a. And to interpose for advancing the positive good of but one or a few individuals, is still farther beyond the powers of a court of equity; though the court of chancery has sometimes ventured to exert itself for this narrow purpose, actuated by a laudable zeal to do good, carried indeed beyond proper bounds. I give the following instance. Eighteen tenants of a manor have right to a common, and fifteen of them agree to inclose. The inclosing will be decreed tho' opposed by three: for it shall not be in the power of a few wilful persons to oppose a public good; *Abridg. cases in equity, cap.* 4. *sect. D.* §2 [*Anon* (1663), 1 Eq. Cas. Abr. 24, reprinted in *The English Reports*, vol. 21, p. 846].

of equity to supply defects in statutes preventive of harm, whether that harm be of more or less importance: it is proper that matters so much connected should be handled together. <86>

CHAPTER I

Acts in themselves lawful reprobated in equity as having a tendency to corrupt morals.

Society cannot flourish by pecuniary commerce merely: without benevolence the social state would neither be commodious nor agreeable. Many connections there are altogether disinterested; witness the connection between a guardian and his infant, and in general between a trustee and the person for whose behoof the trust is gratuitously undertaken. In such a case, to take a premium for executing any article of the trust, being a breach of duty, will be discountenanced even at common law. Thus a bond for 500 merks granted to an interdictor by one who purchased land from the person interdicted was voided.* If the sale was a rational measure, <87> it was the interdictor's duty to consent to it without a bribe: if a wrong measure, the interdictor's taking a sum for his consent, was taking a bribe to betray his trust.

Equity goes farther: it prohibits a trustee from making any profit by his management directly or indirectly. An act of this nature may in itself be innocent; but is poisonous with respect to consequences; for if a trustee be permitted, even in the most plausible circumstances, to make profit, he will soon lose sight of his duty, and direct his management chiefly for making profit to himself. It is solely on this foundation that a tutor is barred from purchasing a debt due by his pupil, or a right affecting his estate. The same temptation to fraudulent practice, concludes also against a trustee who has a salary, or is paid for his labour. A *pactum de quota litis*[1]

---

* Haddington, penult July 1622, Carnousie contra Achanachie [M 9455, from Haddington's report in Kames, *Dictionary*, vol. 2, p. 20].

1. "An agreement about a portion of the amount in issue"; that is, a contract by which a client agrees to pay his advocate a part of the sum he wishes to recover in litigation, in exchange for services in recovering it.

between an advocate and his client, which tends to corrupt the morals of the former, and to make him swerve from his duty, is discountenanced by all civilized nations. A bargain betwixt such persons may be fair, and may even be advantageous to the client: but utility re- <88> quires that it be prohibited; for if indulged in any circumstances, it must be indulged without reserve. It is for the same reason, that a member of the college of justice is prohibited by statute* from purchasing land that is the subject of a law-suit; and that a factor on a bankrupt-estate is prohibited by an act of sederunt† from purchasing the bankrupt's debts. The same rule is extended against private factors and agents without an act of sederunt. Debts due by a constituent purchased by his factor or agent will be held as purchased for behoof of the constituent; and no claim be sustained but for the transacted sum.[2] It was decreed in chancery, That a bond for £500 for procuring a marriage between two persons equal in rank and fortune, is good. But on an appeal to the House of Lords, the decree was reversed.‡ Such a bond to a match-maker, tending to ruin persons of fortune and quality, ought not to be sus- <89> tained; and the countenancing such bonds would be of evil example to guardians, trustees, servants, who have the care of persons under age.[3]

---

* Act 216. parl. 1594 [*APS* iv: 68: 1594, c. 26, Anent the bying of landis and possessionis dependand in pley be Jugeis or memberis of courtis (Land Purchase Act, 1594)]; the same, 13. Edward I. cap. 49 [Second Statute of Westminster, 1285].

† 25th December 1708 [Act of Sederunt anent factors upon, and tacksmen of sequestrated estates: *AS* 228].

2. The equivalent passages in the first edition (p. 176) and the second edition (p. 256) add the following example: "A bond given to the defendant to procure in marriage to the plaintiff a young gentlewoman of £. 2000 fortune, was decreed to be given up, because the match was unequal the plaintiff being sixty years of age and having seven children." The example is *Drury* v. *Hook* (1686), 1 Eq. Cas. Abr. 89, reprinted in *The English Reports*, vol. 21, p. 900 (cited as Abridg. Cases in Equity, chap. 13, sect. F, §2).

‡ Abridg. cases in equity, chap. 13. sect. F. §3 [*Hall* v. *Potter* (1695), 1 Eq. Cas. Abr. 89, reprinted in *The English Reports*, vol. 21. pp. 900–901].

3. The equivalent passages in the first edition (p. 177) and the second edition (p. 256) add the following text: "But if the sum be paid to the broker, neither law nor equity furnishes an action against him for restitution. For even supposing this to be a *turpis causa*, the rule applies, *quod potior est conditio possidentis*. And yet action was furnished in the court of chancery for restoring the money." Reference is made to *Goldsmith* v. *Bruning* (1700), 1 Eq. Cas. Abr. 89, reprinted in *The English Reports*, vol. 21, p. 901.

CHAPTER II

Acts and covenants in themselves innocent, prohibited in
equity, because of their tendency to disturb society, and
to distress its members.

The spirit of mutiny showed itself some time ago among the workmen in
the city of London, and rose to such a height as to require the interposition of the legislature.[1] The same spirit broke out afterward among the
journeymen-tailors of Edinburgh, who erected themselves into a club or
society, keeping in particular a list of the journeymen out of service, under
pretext of accommodating the masters more easily with workmen, but in
reality to enable themselves to get new masters if they differed with those
they served. Any <90> of them that deserted their service, entered their
names in that list, and were immediately again employed by other masters who wanted hands. The master-tailors suffered many inconveniences
from this combination, which among other hardships produced increase
of wages from time to time. The journeymen, for saving time, had always
breakfasted in the houses of their masters; but upon a concert among
them, they all of them deserted their work about nine in the morning,
declaring their resolution to have the hour between nine and ten to themselves in all time coming; a desertion that was the more distressing, as it
was made when the preparing cloathing for the army required the utmost
dispatch. This occasioned a complaint to the bailies[2] of Edinburgh; who
found, "That the defenders, and other journeymen-tailors of Edinburgh,
are not intitled to an hour of recess for breakfast; that the wages of a
journeyman-tailor in the said city ought not to exceed one shilling per
day; and that if any journeyman-tailor, not retained or employed, shall
refuse to work when required by a master on the foresaid terms, <91>
unless for some sufficient cause to be allowed by the magistrates, the offender shall upon conviction be punished in terms of law." This cause
being brought to the court of session by advocation, it was thought of suf-

---

1. 1721 Tailors' Combination Act, 7 Geo. I s. 1, c. 13: An act for regulating the journeymen taylors within the weekily bills of mortality.
2. A municipal office or magistrate in Scotland, equivalent to an English alderman.

ficient importance for a hearing in presence; and the result was, to approve of the regulations of the magistrates.

The only difficulty was, whether the foresaid regulations did not incroach upon the liberty of the subject. It was admitted that they did in some measure; but the court was satisfied of their necessity from the following considerations. Arts and manufactures are of two kinds. Those for luxury and for amusement are subjected to no rules, because a society may subsist comfortably without them. But those which are necessary to the well-being of society must be subjected to rules; otherwise it may be in the power of a few individuals to do much mischief. If the bakers should refuse to make bread, or the brewers to make ale, or the colliers to dig coal, without being subjected to any control, they would be masters of the lives of the inhabitants. To remedy such an evil, <92> which is of the first magnitude, there must be a power placed somewhere; and this power has been long exercised by magistrates of boroughs and justices of peace, under review of the sovereign court. The tailors, by forbearing to work, cannot do mischief so suddenly: but people must be clad; and if there be no remedy against the obstinacy of tailors, they may compel people to submit to the most exorbitant terms.

Another point debated was the propriety of the foregoing regulations. Upon which it was observed, that the regulation of the wages is even admitted by the defenders themselves to be proper, because they have acquiesced in it without complaint. And yet if this article be admitted, the other regulations follow of necessary consequence; for it is to no purpose to fix wages without also fixing the number of working hours; and it is to no purpose to fix either, if the defenders have the privilege to work or not at their pleasure. Their demand of a recess between nine and ten, which they chiefly insist for, is extremely inconvenient, because of the time it consumes, especially in a wet day, when <93> they must shift and dry themselves to avoid sullying the new work they have on hand. And as for health, they will never be denied, either by their masters or by the judge, a whole day at times for exercise.*

---

* Tailors of Edinburgh contra Their Journeymen, December 10. 1762 [M 7682, from Kames, *Select Decisions,* p. 268].

When the malt-tax was ordered to be levied in Scotland, the Edinburgh brewers, dissatisfied with the same, entered into a combination to forbear brewing. The court of session, upon the principle above mentioned, ordered them to continue their brewing as formerly under a severe penalty.[3]

The journeymen-woolcombers in Aberdeen did in the year 1755 form themselves into a society, exacting entry-money, inflicting penalties, &c. to be under the management of stewards, chosen every month: and though their seeming pretext was to provide for their poor, yet under that pretext several regulations were made, cramping trade, and tending to make them independent of their employers. A complaint against the society, by the procurator-fiscal[4] of the bailie-court of Aberdeen, <94> being removed to the court of session by advocation,[5] the following interlocutor was pronounced: "The Lords, having considered the plan upon which the society of woolcombers is erected, the regulations at first enacted, though afterward abrogated, and the rules still subsisting, find, That such combinations of artificers, whereby they collect money for a common box, inflict penalties, impose oaths, and make other by-laws, are of dangerous tendency, subversive of peace and order, and against law: therefore they prohibit and discharge the defenders, the woolcombers, to continue to act under such combination or society for the future, or to enter into any such-like new society or combination, as they shall be answerable: but allow them, at the sight of the magistrates of Aberdeen, to apply the money already collected, for discharging the debts of the society; the remainder to be distributed among the contributors, in proportion to their respective contributions."

Upon a reclaiming petition, answers, replies, and duplies,[6] the court adhered to the foregoing interlocutor, as far as it finds the society complained of to be of danger- <95> ous tendency, and consequently *contra bonos*

---

3. This episode was widely discussed in the eighteenth-century literature as an example of the Court of Session exercising its *nobile officium*. See Bankton, *Institute*, vol. 2, pp. 517–18. For the act of sederunt, see *AS*, 280.

4. The prosecutor in Scottish inferior courts, representing the Lord Advocate.

5. Advocation: a form of process in Scotland by which cases are removed from inferior to superior courts, either to review the decision of the inferior court or to continue the process in the Court of Session.

6. Duplie: a defender's rejoinder to the pursuer's reply (Scots law).

mores;[7] but they remitted to the Ordinary to hear the parties, Whether the woolcombers may not be permitted, under proper regulations, to contribute sums for maintaining their poor.*

The journeymen-weavers in the town of Paisley, emboldened by numbers, began with mobs and riotous proceedings, in order to obtain higher wages. But these overt acts having been suppressed by authority of the court of session, they went more cunningly to work, by contriving a kind of society termed the *defence-box;* and a written contract was subscribed by more than six hundred of them, containing many innocent and plausible articles, in order to cover their views, but chiefly contrived to bind them not to work under a certain rate, and to support out of their periodical contributions those who by insisting on high wages, might not find employment. Seven of the subscribers being charged upon the contract for payment of their stipulated contributions, brought a suspension, in which it was decreed, That <96> this society was an unlawful combination, under the false colour of carrying on trade; and that the contract was void, as *contra utilitatem publicam.*[8,†]

CHAPTER III

Regulations of commerce, and of other public concerns, rectified where wrong.

It belongs to a court of police to regulate commerce and other public matters. The court of session is not a court of police; but it is a court of review, to take under consideration the proceedings of courts of police, and to rectify such as are against the public interest. This jurisdiction is inherent in the court of session as the supreme court in civil matters, founded on the great principle, That every wrong must have a remedy.

In the year 1703 the magistrates and <97> town-council of Stirling made an act confirming a former act of council in favour of the town weavers,

---

7. "Against good morals."

* Procurator-fiscal contra Woolcombers in Aberdeen, December 15. 1762 [M 1961].

8. "Against public utility."

† January 21. 1766, Barr contra Curr, &c. [M 9564, from Kames, *Select Decisions,* p. 312; also M 9565].

and prohibiting all country weavers from buying woollen or linen yarn brought to the town for sale, except in public market after eleven fore-noon, under the pain of confiscation. This act of council was not a little partial: the weavers in the neighbourhood were confined to the market, while the town weavers were left at liberty to make their purchases at large. The former brought a process before the court of session, insisting to have the market at an earlier hour, in order that they might not be prevented by the latter from purchasing; and also, that the prohibition of purchasing yarn privately should be made general to comprehend the town weavers as well as those of the country. The court not only appointed an earlier hour for the market; but put both parties upon an equal footing, by prohibiting yarn to be purchased before the opening of the market.*

Regulations that encroach on freedom <98> of commerce, by favouring some to the prejudice of others, is what renders a monopoly odious in the sight of law. However beneficial a monopoly may be to the privileged, it is a wrong done to the rest of the people, by prohibiting them arbitrarily from the exercise of a lawful employment. Monopolies therefore ought to be discountenanced by courts of justice, not excepting those granted by the crown. And I am persuaded, that the monopolies granted by the crown last century, which were not few in number, would have been re-jected by our judges, had their salaries been for life, as they now happily are. I venture a bolder step, which is to maintain, that even the parliament itself cannot legally make such a partial distinction among the subjects. My reason is, that admitting the House of Commons to have the powers of a Roman dictator *ne quid respublica detrimenti capiat,*[1] it follows not that such a trust will include a power to do injustice, or to oppress the many for the benefit of a few. How crude must have been our notions of government in the last century, when monopolies granted by the King's sole authority, were ge- <99> nerally thought effectual to bind the whole nation! I am acquainted with no monopolies that may be lawfully granted

---

* 14th November 1777, Paterson and others contra Rattray and others.

1. Literally, "that no harm comes to the republic." In Rome, when the Republic was judged to be in danger, the Senate could revive the ancient absolute power of the consuls (and give them a power of martial law), through a decree (or *senatus consultum*) with the formula "*videant consules* [let the consuls see] *ne quid respublica detrimenti capiat.*"

but what are for the public good, such as, to the authors of new books and new machines, limited to a time certain. The profit made in that period is a spur to invention: people are not hurt by such a monopoly, being deprived of no privilege enjoyed by them before the monopoly took place; and after expiry of the time limited, all are benefited without distinction.

In the year 1722 certain regulations were made in the bailie-court of Leith, concerning the forms of procedure in the administration of justice, and the qualification of practitioners before that court; among other articles providing, "That when the procurators[2] are not under three in number, none shall be allowed to enter, except such as have served the clerk or a procurator for the space of three years as an apprentice, and one year at least after; beside undergoing a trial by the procurators of court, named by the magistrates for that effect." John Young, craving to be entered procurator, as having served an apprenticeship to an <100> agent of character before the court of session, this regulation of the bailie-court of Leith was objected. The bailies having found the petitioner not qualified in terms of the regulations, the cause was advocated;[3] and the court found the said article void, as *contra utilitatem publicam,* by establishing a monopoly.*

CHAPTER IV

Forms of the common law dispensed with in order to abridge law-suits.

Retention which is an equitable exception resembling compensation, was introduced by the Court of Session without authority of a statute. The statute 1592, authorising compensation,[1] speaks not of an obligation *ad factum praestandum,*[2] nor of any obligation but for payment of money; and yet it would be hard, that a man should have the authority of a <101>

---

2. Legal representatives or attorneys.

3. That is, removed by the process of advocation.

* 21st December 1765, John Young contra Procurators of the bailie-court of Leith [M 9564, in Kames, *Select Decisions,* p. 309].

1. Act 143, parl. 1592; *APS* iii: 573: 1592, c. 61, That compensatioun de liquido ad liquidum be admittit in all jugementis [Compensation Act 1592].

2. "For specific performance": an obligation (imposed by the court) to perform the act.

court to make his claim effectual against me, while he refuses or delays to satisfy the claim I have against him. So stands, however, the common law, which is corrected by a court of equity for the public good. Supposing parties once in court upon any controversy, the adjusting, without a new process, all matters between them that can at present be adjusted, is undoubtedly beneficial, because it tends to abridge law-suits. This good end is attained, by bestowing on the defendant a privilege to with-hold performance from the pursuer, till the pursuer *simul et semel*[3] perform to him. This privilege is exercised by pleading it as an exception to the pursuer's demand; and the exception, from its nature, is termed *Retention*.

Compensation, as we have seen, is founded on the principle of equity. And it is also supported by that of utility; because the finishing two counter-claims in the same process tends to lessen the number of law-suits. Retention is founded solely on utility, being calculated for no other end but to prevent the multiplication of law-suits. The utility of retention has gained it admittance in all civilized nations. In <102> the English court of chancery particularly, it is a well-known exception, of which I give the following instance. "If the plaintiff mortgage his estate to the defendant, and afterward borrow money from the defendant upon bond, the redemption ought not to take place unless the bonded debt be paid as well as the mortgage-money."*

From what is said, every sort of obligation affords, as it would appear, a ground for retention, provided the term of performance be come, and no just cause for withholding performance. It shall only be added, that for the reasons given with respect to compensation,† retention cannot be pleaded against an assignee for a valuable consideration.

A directed B to pay C what sums C should want. C accordingly received two sums (among others) from B, for which he gave receipts as by the order of A. A and C came to account, which being stated, they gave mutual releases. But the two sums not being entered in the books of A, were not accounted for by C. B not ha- <103> ving received any allowance from A for the two sums, prefers his bill against C to have the money re-

---

3. "Together at one time."

* 1. Vernon 244 [*Baxter* v. *Manning* (1684), reprinted in *The English Reports*, vol. 23, p. 441: this case concerns the English doctrine of the equity of redemption].

† Vol. 1. p. 395 [p. 224 above].

turned to him. C confessed the receipts, but insisted, that the money was delivered to him by the order of A, and that B being a hand only had no claim. But the court decreed, That the plaintiff had a fair claim against the defendant to avoid circuity of suits: for otherwise it would turn the plaintiff on A, and A again on the defendant in equity to set aside the release, and to have an allowance of these sums. And the decree was affirmed in the House of Lords.*

By the common law of this land, a creditor introduced into possession upon a wadset, upon an assignment to rents, or upon an adjudication, is bound to surrender the possession as soon as the debt is paid by the rents levied. He obtained possession in order to levy the rents for his payment; and when payment is obtained, he is no longer intitled to possess. He perhaps is creditor in other debts that may intitle him to apprehend possession *de novo:* but these will not, at common law, im- <104> power him to detain possession one moment after the debt that was the title of his possession is paid. He must first surrender possession; and he may afterward apply for legal authority to be repossessed for payment of these separate debts. A court of equity views matters in a different light. The debtor's claim to have his land restored to him is certainly not founded on utility, when such claim can serve no other end but to multiply expence, by forcing the creditor to take out execution upon the separate debt, in order to be repossessed. A maxim in the Roman law concludes in this case with force, *Frustra petis quod mox es restituturus;*[4] and this maxim accordingly furnisheth to the creditor in possession a defence that is a species of retention. There is, indeed, the same reason for sustaining the exception of retention in this case, that there is in personal debts, namely, utility, which is interposed to prevent the multiplying of lawsuits, prejudicial to one of the parties at least, and beneficial to neither.

But this relief against the strictness of common law, ought not to be confined to real debts which intitle the creditor to pos- <105> sess. It may sometimes happen, as demonstrated above,† to be more beneficial to the

---

* Shower's cases in parliament, 17 [*Dolphin* v. *Haynes* (1697), reprinted in *The English Reports,* vol. 1, p. 12].

4. "Vainly you seek what you are soon to restore."

† Vol. 1. p. 420 [p. 237 above].

debtor or to the creditor, without hurting either, that the rents be applied for payment even of a personal debt, than for payment of the debt which is the title of possession. And where-ever the rents may be applied for payment of a personal debt, the creditor must be privileged to hold possession till that debt be paid.

CHAPTER V

Bona fides as far as regulated by utility.

My first head shall be *bona fide* payment. It may happen by mistake that payment is made, not to the person who is really the creditor, but to one understood to be the creditor. However invincible the error may be, payment made to any but to the creditor avails not at common law; because none but the cre- <106> ditor can discharge the debt. What remedy can be afforded by a court of equity where a debt is *bona fide* paid to another than the true creditor, I proceed to explain.

It is an observation verified by long experience, That no circumstance tends more to the advancement of commerce, than a free circulation of the goods of fortune from hand to hand. In this island, commercial law is so much improved, as that land, moveables, debts, have all of them a free and expedite currency. A bond for borrowed money, in particular, descends to heirs, and is readily transferable to assignees voluntary or judicial. But that circumstance, beneficial to commerce, proves in many instances hurtful to debtors. Payment made to any but the creditor, frees not the debtor at common law: and yet circumstances may be often such, as to make it impracticable for the debtor to discover that the person who produceth a title, fair in appearance, is not the creditor. Here is a case extremely nice in point of equity. On the one hand, if *bona fide* payment be not sustained, the hardship will be great upon the debtor, who must <107> pay a second time to the true creditor. On the other hand, if the exception of *bona fide* payment be sustained to protect the debtor from a second payment, the creditor will be often forfeited of his debt without his fault. Here the scales hang even, and equity preponderates not on either side. But the principle of utility affords relief to the debtor, and exerts all its weight in his scale: for if a debtor were not secure by voluntary payment, no man would venture to pay a shilling by any authority less than that of the sovereign court; and how ruinous to credit this would prove, must be obvious without taking a moment for reflection.

To bring this matter nearer the eye, we shall first suppose that the putative creditor proceeds to legal execution, and in that manner recovers payment. Payment thus made by authority of law, must undoubtedly protect the debtor from a second payment. And this leads to another case, That the debtor, to prevent legal execution which threatens him, makes payment voluntarily. The payment here is made indeed without compulsion, because there is no actual execution: but then it is not made without authority; for, by the sup- <108> position, execution is awarded, and nothing prevents it but payment. The third case is of a clear bond, upon which execution must be obtained as soon as demanded; and the debtor pays, knowing of no defence. Why ought not he also to be secure in this case? That he be secure, is beneficial to creditors as well as to debtors, because otherwise there can be no free commerce of debts. This exception then of *bona fide* payment, is supported by the principle of utility in two different respects: it is beneficial to creditors, by encouraging debtors to make prompt payment; and by removing from them the pretext of insisting upon anxious and scrupulous defences, which, under the colour of paying securely, would often be laid hold of to delay payment: it is beneficial to debtors, who can pay with safety without being obliged to suffer execution.

But here the true creditor is not left without a remedy. The sum received by the putative creditor is in his hand *sine justa causa,*[1] and he is answerable for it to the true creditor. In this view, the operation of *bona fide* payment is only to substitute one debtor for another, which may as <109> often be beneficial to the true creditor, as detrimental.

An executor under a revoked will, being ignorant of the revocation, pays legacies; and the revocation is afterward proved: he shall be allowed these legacies.*

If, in making payment to the putative creditor, the debtor obtain an ease, the exception of *bona fide* payment will be sustained for that sum

1. "Without just cause."

* 1. Chancery cases 126 [*Hele* v. *Stowel* (1669), reprinted in *The English Reports,* vol. 22, p. 725].

only which was really paid.* This rule is founded on equity; for here the true creditor is *certans de damno evitando,* and the debtor *de lucro captando.*

My next head shall be a *bona fide* transaction with a putative proprietor. Such transactions are void at common law as *ultra vires;* and were there no remedy in equity, the paying debt to a putative creditor would not be more hazardous, than transactions with a putative proprietor. The remedy with respect to the former is stated above; and the remedy with respect to the latter, far from oppression on either side, must give satisfaction to every rational enquirer. Where a person in posses- <110> sion of land performs acts of property in the ordinary way of management, levying rents, granting leases, selling corns, cattle, or what else the land produces, no person thinks of enquiring about his title. It would be an insufferable hardship on those who deal with him, and a great obstruction to commerce, were such acts void as *ultra vires.* But with respect to acts of extraordinary administration, such as selling land, or borrowing money upon real security, it is expected that the possessor should make good his title; without which no prudent person will deal with him. If the title be found infirm, a court of equity can afford no remedy: it cannot interpose on the footing of justice between the proprietor on the one hand and the purchaser on the other, who are equally *certantes de damno vitando,* nor on the footing of utility, which pleads not for the one more than for the other. The parties must be left to common law, which intitles the proprietor to vindicate his subject, or to be relieved from debt he did not contract. This latter branch is so clearly founded on principles, that probably it has never been drawn into controversy. With respect to <111> the former, less clear, take the following examples. Count Antonius Lesly, an alien, was served and infeft in the estate of Balquhain as heir of entail; it being at that time understood, that alienage deprives not a man of his birthright in Scotland. But his title being afterward called in question by Peter Lesly-Grant, the next substitute, insisting that an alien cannot acquire land in Scotland either by purchase or succession, the reason of reduction was sustained, first in the court of session, and next in the House of Lords; which rendered the Count's right void from the beginning. Before his right was challenged, he had sold many trees come to maturity, and received the

---

* Stair, July 19. 1665, Johnston contra Macgregor [M 1790].

price. The court, in respect of his *bona fides,* relieved him from accounting for the price. This at first seemed to be a question of some intricacy; but it was soon found to resolve into an established maxim, *Quod bona fide possessor rei alienae facit fructus consumptos suos.*[2] Trees are the product of land as well as corn or cattle; and it would be no less severe to oblige a putative proprietor to account for the price of full-grown trees than to account for the price of ripe corn. <112> The following case is far more delicate. The brother of the deceased Missinish, being the nearest heir in existence, was admitted to serve heir to the estate. The right of the brother thus served was but conditional, as there was a possibility of a nearer heir; and the widow of the deceased brought forth a son, which voided the service from the beginning. But the brother served and infeft having sold land for payment of the family-debts, while there was yet little prospect of a nearer heir, the sale was supported by the court of session, upon evidence brought that it was *in rem versum*[3] of the infant-heir.[4] The favourableness of this case had, I conjecture, no slight influence in procuring the judgement. It lies open to objections that seem not easily solved. First, What room was there for *bona fides* while it remained uncertain whether the widow might not be pregnant? and surely the debts could not be so pressing as not to bear the delay of a few months. Next, Had the interest of the debts exceeded the rents of the estate, to make it necessary to dispose of the whole, a sale upon that supposition might be held to be *in rem versum* of the in- <113> fant-heir: but it does not appear so clearly that the sale of a part could be *in rem versum;* because, by exact and frugal management during the minority of the heir, the debts might have been so much reduced as to make it proper to preserve the estate entire.

I close this chapter with the acts and deeds of a putative judge; of which the case of Barbarius Philippus is an illustrious instance.* Having been elected a Roman Praetor, he determined many causes, and transacted ev-

---

2. The possessor in good faith of another person's property is entitled to the fruits which he consumes.

3. To the enrichment ("turned to his account").

4. The case was Charles M'Kinnon of M'Kinnon contra Sir James M'Donald, 14 Feb. 1765, reported by Kames in *Select Decisions of the Court of Session, from the Year 1752 to the Year 1768,* p. 298 [M 5279]. For Kames's comments on the case in the second edition, see Appendix, p. 527, Extract [2nd: 170].

* l. 3. De officio Praet[orum (Duties of Praetors): D 1.14.3: Watson i: 30].

ery sort of business that belonged to the office. He was discovered to be a slave, which rendered all his acts and deeds void at common law; because none but a freeman was capable to be a Roman Praetor. With respect to third parties, however, their *bona fides* supported all his acts and deeds as if he really had been a Praetor. <114>

CHAPTER VI

Interposition of a court of equity in favour even of
a single person to prevent mischief.

This subject is so fully explained in the introduction as to require very little addition. It exhibits a court of equity in a new light; showing that this court, acting upon the principle of utility, is not confined to what is properly termed *jurisdiction;* but, in order to prevent mischief even to a single person, may assume magisterial powers. It is by such power that the court of session names factors to manage the estates of those who are in foreign parts, and of infants who are destitute of tutors. The authority interposed for selling the land-estate of a person under age, is properly of the same nature; for the inquiry made about the debts, and about the rationality of a sale, though in the <115> form of a process, is an expiscation merely.

By the Roman law, a sale made by a tutor of his pupil's land-estate without authority of a judge, was void *ipso jure*,[1] as *ultra vires*. This seems not to have been followed in Scotland. Maitland reports a case,* where it was decreed, that such a sale *sine decreto*[2] is not void, but that it is good if profitable to the infant. And I must approve this decision as agreeable to principles and to the nature of the thing. The interposition of a court beforehand, is not to bestow new powers upon a tutor, but to certify the necessity of a sale, in order to encourage purchasers by rendering them secure. But if, without authority of a court, a purchaser be found who pays a full price, and if the sale be necessary, where can the objection lie? So far indeed a court may justly go, as to presume lesion from a sale *sine decreto*, until the tutor justify the sale as rational, and profitable to the infant. <116>

1. "By the law itself": that is, at law.
* Dec. 1. 1565, Douglas contra Foreman [M 16230, in Kames, *Dictionary*, vol. 2, p. 489].
2. "Without a decree."

CHAPTER VII

Statutes preventive of wrong or mischief extended by a court of equity.

Statutes as hinted above,* that have utility for their object, are of two kinds: First, Statutes directed for promoting the positive good of the whole society, or of some part: Second, Statutes directed to prevent mischief only. Defective statutes of the latter kind may be supplied by a court of equity; because, independent of a statute, it is impowered to prevent mischief. But that court has not, more than a court of common law, any power to supply defective statutes of the former kind; because it belongs to the legislature only to make laws or regulations for promoting good positively.

Usury is in itself innocent, but to prevent oppression it is prohibited by statute. Gaming is prohibited by statute; as also <117> the purchasing law-suits by members of the college of justice. These in themselves are not unjust; but they tend to corrupt the morals, and prove often ruinous to individuals. Such statutes, preventive of wrong and mischief, may be extended by a court of equity, in order to complete the remedy intended by the legislature. It is chiefly with relation to statutes of this kind that Bacon delivers an opinion with great elegance: "Bonum publicum insigne rapit ad se casus omissos. Quamobrem, quando lex aliqua reipublicae commoda notabiliter et majorem in modum intuetur et procurat, interpretatio ejus extensiva esto et amplians."†

In this class, as appears to me, our statute 1617 introducing the positive prescription[1] ought to be placed. For it has not, like the Roman *usucapio*,[2] the penal effect of forfeiting a proprietor for his negligence, and of transferring his property to another: it is contrived, on the contrary, to se-

---

* Vol. 1. p. 339, 340 [pp. 195–96 above].

† De augmentis scientiarum, l. 8. cap. 3, aphor. 12 [Bacon, *Works*, vol. 1, p. 250: "Great public good attracts to itself cases which have not been provided for. For which reason, when any law contemplates and procures advantages to the state in a noteworthy way and to an extraordinary degree, let its interpretation be extensive and broad"].

1. Act 12, parl. 1617; *APS* iv: 543: 1617, c. 12, Anent prescriptioun of heretable rights [Prescription Act 1617].

2. The acquisition of ownership by prescription; that is, long possession commenced in good faith.

cure every man in his land-property, by denying action upon old obsolete claims, which by common law are perpetual. A <118> claim may be very old and yet very just; and it is not therefore wrong in the common law to sustain such a claim. But the consequences ought to be considered: if a claim be sustained beyond forty or fifty years because it may be just, every claim must be sustained however old; and experience discovered, that this opens a wide door to falsehood. To prevent wrong and mischief, it was necessary that land-property should by lapse of time be secured against all claims; and as with respect to antiquated claims there is no infallible criterion to distinguish good from bad, it was necessary to bar them altogether by the lump. The passage quoted from Bacon is applicable in the strictest manner to this statute, considered in the light now mentioned; and it hath accordingly been extended in order to complete the remedy afforded by the legislature. To secure land-property against obsolete claims, it must be qualified, that the proprietor has possessed peaceably forty years by virtue of a charter and seisin. So says the statute; and if the statute be taken strictly, no property is protected from obsolete claims, but where infeftment is the title <119> of possession. But the court of session, preferring the end to the means, and consulting its own powers as a court of equity to prevent mischief, secures by prescription every subject possessed upon a good title, a right to tithes for example, a long lease of land, or of tithes, which are titles that admit not infeftment.

As the foregoing statute was made to secure land from obsolete and unjust claims, the statute 1469[3] introducing the negative prescription of obligations, was made to secure individuals personally from claims of the same kind. As this statute is preventive of mischief, it may be extended by a court of equity to complete the remedy. It has accordingly been extended to mutual contracts, to decrees *in foro contradictorio,*[4] and to reductions of deeds granted on deathbed.[a] <120>

---

3. Act 28, parl. 1469; *APS* ii: 95: 1469, c. 4, Anent the prescriptioun of obligationis nocht followit within the space of fourty yeris [Prescription Act 1469].

4. "In a court of counterarguments"; that is, in a court where both parties have put forward arguments.

a. I am aware, that the statutes introducing the negative prescription have, by the court of session, been considered in a different light. They have been held as a forfeiture even of a just debt: for it was once judged, that after the forty years the defendant

Considering the instances above mentioned, it must, I imagine, occasion some surprise, to find a proposition cherished by our lawyers, That correctory statutes, as they are termed, ought never to be extended. We have already seen this proposition contradicted, not only by solid principles, but even by the court of session in many instances. With relation to statutes in particular correctory of injustice or of wrong, no man can seriously doubt that a court of equity is empowered to extend such statutes, in order to complete the remedy prescribed by the legislature: and the same is equally clear with relation to statutes supplying defects in common law. As to the statutes under consideration, intended to prevent mischief, it might, I own, have once been more doubtful, whether these could be extended; for of all the powers assumed by a court of equity, it is probable that the power of preventing mischief <121> was the latest. But in England this power has been long established in the court of chancery; and experience has proved it to be a salutary power. Why then should we stop short in the middle of our progress? No other excuse can be given for such hesitation, but that our law, considered as a regular system, is of a much later date than that of England.

The foregoing are instances where the court of session, without hesitation, have supplied defects in statutes made to prevent mischief. But to show how desultory and fluctuating the practice of the court is in that particular, I shall confine myself to a single case on the other side, which makes a figure in our law. In the transmission of land-property, by succession as well as by sale, we require infeftment. An heir however, without completing his right by infeftment, is intitled to continue the possession of his ancestor.* In this situation, behaving as proprietor, he contracts debts, and unless he be reduced to the necessity of borrowing large sums,

---

was not bound to give his oath upon the verity of the debt; and that though he should acknowledge the debt to be just, yet he was not liable *in foro humano* [in the human court], however he might be liable *in foro poli et conscientiae* [in the court of heaven and the conscience]; *Fountainhall, December 7. 1703, Napier contra Campbell* [M 10656]. That this is a wrong construction of these statutes I have endeavoured to show above, pp. 385, 386 [p. 220 above].

* See [Kames,] Historical Law-tracts, tract 5 ["History of the Privilege which an Heir-Apparent in feudal holdings has, to continue the possession of his ancestor," 1758 ed., vol. 1, pp. 263–84].

those he deals with are seldom so scrupu- <122> lous as to enquire into his title. By the common law however, the debtor's death before infeftment is, as to the real estate, a forfeiture of all his personal creditors. This is a mischief which well deserved the interposition of the legislature; and a remedy was provided by act 24, parl. 1695, enacting, "That if an apparent heir have been in possession for three years, the next heir, who by service or adjudication connects with the predecessor last infeft, shall be liable to the apparent heir's debts *in valorem*[5] of the heritage."[6] There can be no doubt, that this statute was intended to procure payment to those who deal *bona fide* with an heir-apparent. And yet, if we regard the words only, the remedy is imperfect; for what if the next heir-apparent, purposely to evade the statute, shall content himself with the possession and enjoyment of the heritage, without making up titles by service or adjudication? Taking the statute strictly according to the words, the creditors will reap little benefit: if the debts be considerable, no heir will subject himself by completing his titles, when he has full enjoyment of the rents, without that solemnity. For- <123> merly, the heir-apparent in possession had no interest to forbear the completing his titles: his forbearing must have proceeded from indolence or inattention. But if the remedy intended by the statute reach not an heir-apparent though in possession, a strong motive of interest will make him forbear to complete his titles. In this view, the statute, if confined to the words, is perfectly absurd; for what can be more absurd than to leave it in the power of the heir-apparent to disappoint the creditors of the remedy intended them? It is always in his power, by satisfying himself with a possessory title, to disappoint them: and as by a possessory title he has the full enjoyment of the estate, he will always disappoint them, if he regard his own interest. The legislature in this case undoubtedly intended a complete remedy; and the consideration now mentioned, peculiar to this case, is a strong additional motive for the interposition of a court of equity to fulfil the intendment of the legislature. And yet, misled by the notion that correctory laws ought not

---

5. "According to the value."
6. *APS* ix: 427: 1695, c. 39, Act for obviating the frauds of appearand heirs.

to be extended, the court of session hath constantly denied action to the creditors of an <124> heir who dies in apparency, against the next heir in possession, unless he has completed his title to the estate by service or adjudication.

There is another palpable defect in this statute which ought also to be supplied. A predecessor may have a good title to his estate without being infeft; and yet, regarding the words only, the heir-apparent is not liable upon this statute, unless where he connects with a predecessor infeft. I put the following case. John purchases an estate, takes a disposition with procuratory[7] and precept,[8] but dies without being seised. James, his heir-apparent, enters into possession without making up titles, and contracts debt after being in possession three years. After his death, William, the next heir-apparent, makes up his titles by a general service. This case comes not under the words of the statute; but as it undoubtedly comes under the mischief which the legislature intended to remedy, it is the duty of a court of equity to complete the remedy.

In one case the court, from a due sense of their equitable powers, ventured upon a remedy where this statute was defective. <125> Some acres and houses having been disponed for a valuable consideration by an heir-apparent three years in possession, the next heir-apparent foreseeing that he would be barred by the act 1695 from objecting to this alienation if he should enter heir, bethought himself of a different method. He sold the subject for twenty guineas, and granted bond to the purchaser, who led an adjudication against the estate, and upon that title brought a reduction of the disposition in his own name. But the court decreed, that this case fell under the meaning of the statute, though not under the words; and therefore that the pursuer was barred from challenging the disposition.*

---

7. *Procuratory of resignation:* a written mandate given by a vassal, authorizing his feu to be returned to his superior, to be granted out to a new vassal.

8. *Precept of sasine:* An order from a feudal superior to give infeftment of certain lands to his vassal.

* Burns of Dorater contra Pickens, July 11. 1758 [M 5275, from Kames, *Select Decisions,* p. 205].

What if the heir forbearing to enter in order to evade the act 1695, shall contract debt to the value of the subject, upon which adjudications are led *contra hereditatem jacentem?*[9] Here the estate is applied for payment of the heir's debts, and consequently converted to his use as much as if he were entered. Would the court of session give no relief in this case to the cre- <126> ditors of the interjected heir-apparent? Would they suffer the purpose of the statute to be so grossly eluded?

A word or two upon statutes contrived to advance the positive good of the society in general, or of individuals in particular, making them *locupletiores,* as termed in the Roman law. To supply defects in such a statute is beyond the power even of a court of equity. The statute 1661, act 41, obliging me to concur with my neighbour in erecting a march-dike,[10] is of that nature. There is no provision in the act for upholding the march-dike after it is made; and the defect cannot be supplied by any court. Upon my neighbour's requisition I must join with him to build a march-dike; but I am bound no further; and therefore the burden of upholding must rest upon himself. Monopolies or personal privileges cannot be extended by a court of equity;* because that court may prevent mischief, but has no power to advance the positive good of any person. As to penal statutes, it is clear, in the first place, that to augment a penalty beyond <127> that directed by a statute is acting in contradiction to the statute, which enacts that precise penalty, and not a greater. In the next place, to extend the penalty in a statute to a case not mentioned, is a power not trusted with any court, because the trust is not necessary. A penalty is commonly added to a statutory prohibition, for preventing wrong or mischief. A court of equity may extend the prohibition to similar cases, and even punish the transgression of their own prohibition.† But with respect to a prohibition that regards utility only not

9. "Against a neglected inheritance"; that is, against a succession which an heir has not taken up. The phrase is used in reference to a creditor's ability to pursue a debtor's estate, when the heir has not taken up the succession.

10. *APS* vii: 263: 1661, c. 284, Act for planting & incloseing of land [March Dykes Act 1661].

* l. 1. §2. De constitut[ionibus] princ[ipum (On Enactments by Emperors), D 1.4.1.2: Watson i: 14].

† Book 1. part 1. chap. 5.

justice, it is a prerogative peculiar to the legislature to annex beforehand a penal sanction.

CONCLUSION OF BOOK II
Justice and Utility compared.

The principle of justice, though more extensive in its influence than that of utility, is in its nature more simple: it never looks beyond the litigants. The principle of utility, on the contrary, not <128> only regards these, but also the society in general; and comprehends many circumstances concerning both. Being thus in its nature and application more intricate than justice, I thought it not amiss to close this book with a few thoughts upon it. In the introduction there was occasion to hint, that utility cooperates sometimes with justice, and sometimes is in opposition to it. There are several instances of both in the first book, which I propose to bring under one view, in order to give a distinct notion of the co-operation and opposition of these principles.

It is scarce necessary to be premised, that in opposing private utility to justice, the latter ought always to prevail. A man is not bound to prosecute what is beneficial to him: he is not even bound to demand reparation for wrong done him. But he is strictly bound to do his duty; and for that reason he himself must be conscious, that in opposition to duty interest ought to have no weight. It is beside of great importance to society that justice have a free course; and accordingly public utility unites with justice to enforce right against interest. Private interest therefore, <129> or private utility, may, in the present speculation, be laid entirely aside; and it is barely mentioned to prevent mistakes.

Another limitation is necessary. It is not every sort of public utility that can outweigh justice: it is that sort only which is preventive of mischief affecting the whole or bulk of the society: public utility, as far as it concerns positive additional good to the society, is a subject that comes not within the sphere of a court of equity.

Confining our view then to public utility, that which is preventive of mischief to the whole or great part of the society, I venture to lay down the following proposition, That where-ever it is at variance with justice, a court of equity ought not to enforce the latter, nor suffer it to be enforced by a court of common law. In order to evince this proposition, which I shall endeavour to do by induction, the proper method will be, to give a table of cases, beginning with those where the two principles are in strict union, and proceeding orderly to those where they are in declared opposition.

These principles for the most part are good friends. The great end of establish- <130> ing a court of equity is, to have justice accurately distributed, even in the most delicate circumstances; than which nothing contributes more to peace and union in society. As this branch therefore of utility is inseparable from justice, it will not be necessary hereafter to make any express mention of it. It must be always understood when we talk of justice.

We proceed to other branches of utility, which are not so strictly attached to justice, but sometimes coincide with it, and sometimes rise in opposition. One of these is the benefit accruing to the society by abridging law-suits. In the case of compensation, utility unites with justice to make compensation a strong plea in every court of equity. Retention depends entirely upon the utility of abridging law-suits. But if it have no support from justice, it meets on the other hand with no opposition from it.

In the case of *bona fide* payment the utility is different. It is the benefit that arises from a free course to money-transactions, which would be obstructed if debtors, by running any risk in making payment, were encouraged to state anxious or <131> frivolous defences. The exception of *bona fide* payment is sustained upon no ground but that of preventing the mischief here described. Justice weighs equally on both sides: for if the exception be not sustained, the honest debtor bears the hazard of losing his money; if it be sustained, the hazard is transferred upon the creditor.

But there are cases where justice and utility take opposite sides: which, in particular, is the case where a transaction[1] extremely unequal is occasioned by error. Here the justice of affording relief is obvious: but then a transaction by putting an end to strife is a favourite of law; and it is against the interest of the public to weigh a transaction in the nice balance of grains and scruples. A man, by care and attention in making a transaction, may avoid

---

1. An agreement between parties to settle a disputed claim.

error; but the bad consequences of opening transactions upon every ground of equity cannot be avoided. Justice therefore must in this case yield to utility; and a transaction will be supported against errors sufficient to overturn other agreements. I give another example. In the Roman law, *laesio ultra duplum*[2] was sustained to avoid a bargain: but in Britain we re- <132> fuse to listen to equity in this case; for if complaints of inequality were indulged, law-suits would be multiplied, to the great detriment of commerce.

If the discouraging law-suits be sufficient to with-hold relief in equity, the hazard of making judges arbitrary is a much stronger motive for with-holding that relief. However clear a just claim or defence may be, a court of equity ought not to interpose, unless the case can be brought under a general rule. No sort of oppression is more intolerable than what is done under the colour of law: and for that reason, judges ought to be confined to general rules, the only method invented to prevent legal oppression. Here the refusing to do justice to a single person makes no figure, when set in opposition to an important interest that concerns deeply the whole society. And it seems to follow, from the very nature of a court of equity, that it ought to adhere to general rules, even at the expence of forbearing to do justice. It is indeed the declared purpose of a court of equity, to promote the good of society by an accurate distribution of justice: but the means ought to be subor- <133> dinate to the end; and therefore, if in any case justice cannot be done but by using means that tend to the hurt of society, a court of equity ought not to interpose. To be active in such a case, involves the absurdity of preferring the means to the end.

Thus we may gather by induction, that in every case where it is the interest of the public to with-hold justice from an individual, it becomes the duty of a court of equity in that circumstance, not only to abstain from enforcing the just claim or defence, but also to prevent its being enforced at common law. But the influence of public utility stops here, and never authorises a court of equity to enforce any positive act of injustice.* For, first, I cannot discover that it ever can be the interest of the public to

2. "Loss of more than half." In Roman law, the seller of a thing for which the buyer paid less than half its value could rescind the sale for *laesio enormis* (excessive loss).

* See this doctrine illustrated, [Kames,] Historical Law-tracts, tract 2 [1758 ed., vol. 1, p. 97].

require the doing an unjust action. And, next, if even self-preservation will not justify any wrong done by a private person,* much less will public utility justify any wrong done or enforced <134> by a court of equity. It is inconsistent with the very constitution of this court, to do injustice, or to enforce it.ᵃ

---

* [H. Home, Lord Kames,] Sketches of the History of Man, [2nd ed., 1778,] vol. 4. p. 31 (Liberty Fund ed., p. 716).

a. The following case is an illustrious instance of this doctrine. A ship-cargo of negroes, young and old, being imported into Jamaica for sale, Mr Wedderburn purchased a boy not above twelve years of age, educated him for a house-servant, and employ'd him as his slave while he continued in Jamaica. The negro being now fully grown, was brought to Scotland by his master, where he got a wife and had children. Never having received any wages, he became uneasy for want of means to maintain his family. He absented, and endeavoured to procure money by a lawful employment. Mr Wedderburn applied to the sheriff of Perth to oblige his slave to return to him. The sheriff found, "That slavery is not recognised by the law of this kingdom, and is inconsistent with the principles thereof; that the regulations in Jamaica concerning slaves extend not to this kingdom; and therefore repelled Mr Wedderburn's claim to perpetual service from the negro." The cause being advocated to the court of session, was held to be of such importance as to demand a hearing in presence [of the whole court]. The sum of the argument for the negro was what follows. It was premised, that not one of the causes assigned by writers for justifying slavery is applicable to the negro in question. It is not alledged that he was taken captive in war; and he was too young for committing any crime that deserved so severe a punishment. As to consent, it is not said that he ever <135> consented or showed any willingness to be a slave. He could expect no redress in Jamaica; but when he came to a land of liberty, where he could hope for protection, he left his master, and asserted his claim to be free. Now as all men are born free, and in a state of independence, except upon their parents, and as the negro in question has done no act to deprive him of that valuable right, he is protected by the law of nature, and by every principle of justice, from being made a slave. Slavery, it is true, is supported by the practice of Jamaica. But even supposing it to be authorised by the municipal law of that country, yet the judges in Scotland do not give blind obedience to any foreign law. If a foreign decree or a foreign statute be brought here for execution, our judges listen cordially to any objection in equity that may lie against it; and never interpose their authority for execution unless where it is founded on material justice. Mr Wedderburn can have no pretext other than the law of Jamaica for claiming this man as a slave. And as this claim is repugnant to the law of nature and to every just principle, the court of session would be accessory to a gross wrong if they should enforce that claim. Courts were instituted to make justice effectual, and never to transgress it. The court accordingly remitted the cause to the sheriff; which in effect was refusing to interpose their authority in behalf of Mr Wedderburn's claim. But they avoided the giving any opinion with respect to the law or practice of Jamaica, how far effectual by long custom for the sake of commerce (15 January 1778, John Wedderburn contra Joseph Knight a negro) [M 14545]. <136>

BOOK III

Hitherto our plan has been, to set forth the different powers of a court of equity; and to illustrate these powers by apt examples selected from various subjects where they could be best found. Our plan in the present book is, to show the application of these powers to various subjects, handled each as an entire whole: and the subjects chosen are such as cannot easily be split into parts to be distributed under the different heads formerly explained. Beside, as the various powers of a court of equity have been sufficiently illustrated, as well as the principles on which they are founded, I thought it would be pleasant as well as instructive to vary the method, by showing the operation of these powers upon particular subjects. The first and second books may be considered as theoretical, explaining the powers of a court of equity: the present book is practical, showing the application of these powers to several important subjects. <137>

CHAPTER I

What equity rules with respect to rents levied upon an erroneous title of property.

With respect to land possessed upon an erroneous title of property, it is a rule established in the Roman law and among modern nations, That the true proprietor asserting his right to the land, has not a claim for the rents levied by the *bona fide* possessor, and consumed. But though this subject is handled at large both by the Roman lawyers and by their commentators, we are left in the dark as to the reason of the rule, and of the principle upon which it is founded. Perhaps it was thought, that the proprietor has not an action at common law for the value of the product consumed by the *bona fide* possessor; or perhaps, that the action, as rigorous, is rendered ineffectual by equity. So far indeed it is evident, that as no title of <138> property can absolutely be relied on, sad would be the condition of land-holders, were they liable forty years back, for rents which they had reason to believe their own, and which without scruple they bestow'd on procuring the necessaries and conveniences of life.

Though in all views the *bona fide* possessor is secure against restitution, it is however of importance to ascertain the precise principle that affords him security; for upon that preliminary point several questions depend. We shall therefore without further preface enter into the enquiry.

The possessor, as observed, must be protected either by common law or by equity. If common law afford to the proprietor a claim for the value of his rents consumed, it must be equity correcting the rigor of common law that protects the possessor from this claim: but if the proprietor have not a claim at common law, the possessor has no occasion for equity. The matter then is resolvable into the following question, Whether there be or be not a claim at common law. And to this que- <139> stion, which is subtile, we must lend attention.

Searching for materials to reason upon, what first occurs is the difference between natural and industrial fruits. The former, owing their existence not to man but to the land, will readily be thought an accessory that must follow the land. The latter will be viewed in a different light; for industrial fruits owe their existence to labour and industry, more than to land. Upon this very circumstance does Justinian found the right of the *bona fide* possessor: "Si quis a non domino quem dominum esse crediderit, bona fide fundum emerit, vel ex donatione, aliave qualibet justa causa, aeque bona fide acceperit; naturali rationi placuit, fructus, quos percepit, ejus esse pro cultura et cura. Et ideo, si postea dominus supervenerit, et fundum vindicet, de fructibus ab eo consumptis agere non potest."* And

---

* §35. Instit. De rer[um] divisione [On the classification of things: Inst. 2.1.35: Birks & McLeod 59: "Suppose you believe that someone is owner of a piece of land when in fact he is not, and you buy it from him in good faith or, still on the assumption of good faith, receive it as a gift or on some other legally sufficient ground. The law decided, true to first principles, that fruits which you harvest become yours because of your work in growing and looking after them. So if the owner appears and vindicates the land, he cannot claim in respect of fruits you have consumed"].

upon this foundation Pomponius pronounces, that the *bona fide* possessor acquires right to the industrial fruits only: "Fru- <140> ctus percipiendo, uxor vel vir, ex re donata, suos facit: illos tamen quos suis operis adquisierit, veluti serendo. Nam si pomum decerpserit, vel ex sylva cedit, non fit ejus: sicuti nec cujuslibet bonae fidei possessoris; quia non ex facto ejus is fructus nascitur."* Paulus goes further. He admits not any distinction between natural and industrial fruits; but is positive, that both kinds equally, as soon as separated from the ground, belong to the *bona fide* possessor: "Bonae fidei emptor non dubie percipiendo fructus, etiam ex aliena re, suos interim facit, non tantum eos qui diligentia et opera ejus pervenerunt, sed omnes; quia quod ad fructus attinet, loco domini pene est. Denique etiam, priusquam percipiat, statim ubi a solo separati sunt, bonae fidei emptoris fiunt."†

But now, after drawing so nigh in appearance to a conclusion, we stumble upon an unexpected obstruction. Is the foregoing doctrine consistent with the principle, <141> *Quod satum solo cedit solo?*[1] If corns while growing make part of the land, and consequently belong to the proprietor of the land, the act of separation cannot have the effect to transfer the property from him to another. And if this hold as to fruits that are industrial, the argument concludes with greater force if possible as to natural fruits. What then shall be thought of the opinions delivered above by the Roman writers? Their authority is great I confess, and yet no authority will justify us in deviating from clear principles. The fruits, both industrial and natural, after separation as well as before, belong to the proprietor of the land. He

---

* l. 45. De usuris [et fructibus et causis et omnibus accessionibus et mora (On interest, fruits, incidentals, accessions and delay), D 22.1.45: Watson ii: 642: "Husband or wife who gather fruits from a gift acquire them provided they get them by their own efforts, as by sowing. If, however, they pick an apple or cut wood, they do not, nor does any possessor in good faith, since these are not fruits of their efforts"].

† l. 48. pr. De adquir[endo] rer[um] dom[inio (On acquisition of ownership of things), D 41.1.48.pr: Watson iv: 498: "A purchaser in good faith undoubtedly acquires ownership for the time being by gathering fruits, even those of someone else's property, not only the fruits which are produced by his care and toil but all fruits, because, in the matter of fruits, he is virtually in the position of an owner. Indeed, even before he gathers them, the fruits belong to the purchaser in good faith as soon as they are severed from the soil"].

1. "Whatever is planted in the soil goes with the soil."

has undoubtedly an action at common law to vindicate the fruits while extant: and if so, has he not also a claim for the value after consumption?

However prone to answer the foregoing question in the affirmative, let us however suspend our judgement till the question be fairly canvassed. It is indeed clear, that the fruits while extant, the *percepti*[2] as well as *pendentes*,[3] belong to the proprietor of the land, and can be claimed by a *rei vin-* <142> *dicatio*.[4,a] But is it equally clear, that the *bona fide* possessor who consumes the fruits is liable for their value? Upon what medium is this claim founded? The fruits are indeed consumed by the possessor, and the proprietor is thereby deprived of his property: but it cannot be subsumed, that he is deprived of it by the fault of the possessor; for, by the supposition, the possessor was *in bona fide* to consume, and was not guilty of the slightest fault. Let us endeavour to gather light from a similar case. A man buys a horse *bona fide* from one who is not proprietor: upon urgent business he makes a very severe journey; and the horse, unable to support the fatigue, dies. Is the purchaser answerable for the value of the horse? There is no principle upon which that claim can be founded. In general, a proprietor deprived of his goods by the fact of another, cannot claim the value upon any principle but that of reparation: but it is a rule established both in the law of nature <143> and in municipal law, That a man free from fault or blame, is not liable to repair any hurt done by him: one in all respects innocent, is not subjected to reparation more than to punishment.* And thus it comes out clear, that there is no action at common law against the *bona fide* possessor for the value of the fruits he consumes: such an action must resolve into a claim of damages, to which the innocent cannot be subjected.

And if *bona fides* protect the possessor when he himself consumes the fruits, it will equally protect his tenants. A man who takes a lease from

2. *Fructus percepti:* fruits which have been gathered in.

3. *Fructus pendentes:* hanging fruits; that is, those still in the soil or on the trees which produced them.

4. A real action by the owner of thing to recover it.

a. Whether he may not in equity be liable for some recompence to the person by whose labour the industrial fruits were raised, is a different question.

* See *Sketches of the History of Man* [2nd ed., 1778], vol 4. p. 71 (Liberty Fund ed., pp. 734–35).

one who is held to be proprietor of the land, is *in bona fide* as well as his landlord. The fruits, therefore, that the tenant consumes or disposes of, will not subject him to a claim of damages; and if the proprietor have no claim for their value, he can as little claim the rent paid for them.

As common law affords not an action in this case, equity is still more averse. The proprietor no doubt is a loser; and, which is a more material circumstance, <144> what he loses is converted to the use of the *bona fide* possessor. But then, though the proprietor be a loser, the *bona fide* possessor is not a gainer: the fruits or rents are consumed upon living, and not a vestige of them remains.[a] Thus, equity rules even where the claim is brought recently. But where it is brought at a distance of time, for the rents of many years, against a possessor who regularly consumed his annual income, and had no reason to dread or suspect a claim, the hardship is so great, that were it founded in common law, the *bona fide* possessor would undoubtedly be relieved by equity.

What is now said suggests another case. Suppose the *bona fide* possessor to be *locupletior* by the rents he has levied. It is in most circumstances difficult to ascertain this point: but circumstances may be supposed that make it clear. The rents, for example, are assigned by the *bona fide* possessor for payment of his debts: the creditors continue in possession till their claims <145> are extinguished; and then the true proprietor discovering his right, enters upon the stage. Here it can be qualified, that the *bona fide* possessor is *locupletior,* and that he has gained precisely the amount of the debts now satisfied and paid. Admitting then the fact, that the *bona fide* possessor is enriched by his possession, the question is, Whether this circumstance will support any action against him. None at common law, for the reason above given, that there is nothing to found an action of reparation or damages in this case, more than where the rents are consumed upon living. But that equity affords an action is clear; for the maxim, *Nemo debet locupletari aliena jactura*[5] is applicable to this case in the strictest sense: the effects of the proprietor are converted to the use of the *bona fide* possessor:

a. The *bona fide* possessor cannot be reached by an *actio in rem versum;* for this action takes place only where the goods applied to my use are known by me to belong to another.

5. "No one should be enriched at another's expense."

what is lost by the one, is gained by the other; and therefore equity lays hold of that gain to make up the loss. This point is so evidently founded on equity, that even after repeated instances of wandering from justice in other points, I cannot help testifying some surprise, that the learned Vinnius, not to mention Voet and other commentators, should reject the <146> proprietor's claim in this case.[6] And I am the more surprised, that in this opinion they make a step no less bold than uncommon, which is, to desert their guides who pass for being infallible, I mean the Roman lawyers, who justly maintain, that the *bona fide* possessor is liable *quatenus locupletior.*[7] "Consuluit senatus bonae fidei possessoribus, ne in totum damno adficiantur, sed in id duntaxat teneantur in quo locupletiores facti sunt. Quemcunque igitur sumptum fecerint ex hereditate, si quid dilapidaverunt, perdiderunt, dum re sua se abuti putant, non praestabunt: nec si donaverint, locupletiores facti videbuntur, quamvis ad remunerandum sibi aliquem naturaliter obligaverunt."*

Where the *bona fide* possessor becomes *locupletior* by extreme frugality and parsimony, it may be more doubtful whether a claim can lie against him. It must appear hard, that his starving himself and his family, or his extraordinary anxiety to lay up a stock for his children, should subject him to a claim which his prodigality <147> would free him from; and yet I can-

6. The equivalent passage in the first edition (p. 193) reads, "I cannot help testifying some surprise at the stupidity of Vinnius, Voet, and other commentators, who reject the proprietor's claim even in this case." Kames's references are to A. Vinnius, *In quatuor libros institutionum imperialum commentarius* (ed. J. G. Heineccius, Leiden: Joannes van der Linden, 1726), lib. II, tit. i, sect. 35, p. 185, and Johannes Voet, *Commentarius ad Pandectas* (The Hague: Anthony van Dole, 1734), vol. 2, p. 736 (book XLI, tit. i, sect. 29). Both of these jurists noted that where the *bona fide* possessor was sued in a claim for an inheritance, he would have to hand back fruits used up to the extent to which he had been enriched, for which they cited the passage drawn on by Kames here (D 5.3.25.11).

7. "To the extent to which he is enriched."

* l. 25. §11. De hered[itatis] pet[itione (On the claim for an inheritance), D 5.3.25.11: Watson i: 190–91: "The senate took thought for the interests of possessors in good faith; they are not to suffer an overall loss but are to be liable only to the extent they have become richer. Therefore, while they are under the impression it is their own property they are misusing, they will not be liable for any loss they have put the inheritance to if they have caused the deterioration or loss of anything; and if they have made a gift, they will not be deemed to have become richer in spite of the fact that they have put someone under a moral obligation to make a return-gift"].

not see that this consideration will prevent the operation of the maxim, *Nemo debet locupletari aliena jactura.*

The foregoing disquisition is not only curious but useful. Among other things, it serves to determine an important question, Whether *bona fides,* which relieves the possessor from accounting for the rents, will at the same time prevent the imputation of these rents towards extinction of a real debt he has upon the land. A man, for example, who has claims upon an estate by infeftments of annualrent, adjudications, or such like, enters into possession upon a title of property, which he believes unexceptionable. When the lameness of his title is discovered, his *bona fides* will secure him from paying the rents to the true proprietor: but will it also preserve his debts alive, and save them from being extinguished by his possession of the rents? The answer to this question depends upon the point discussed above. If the proprietor have, at common law tho' not in equity, a claim for the value of the rents consumed by the *bona fide* possessor, this value, as appears to me, must go in <148> extinction of the debts affecting the subject. For where the proprietor, instead of demanding the money to be paid to himself, insists only, that it shall be apply'd to extinguish the real incumbrances; equity interposeth not against this demand, which is neither rigorous nor unjust: and if equity interpose not, the extinction must take place. If, on the other hand, there be no claim at common law for the value of the rents consumed, I cannot perceive any foundation for extinguishing the real debts belonging to the possessor; unless the following proposition can be maintained, That the very act of levying the rents extinguishes *ipso facto* these debts, without necessity of applying to a judge for his interposition.[8] This proposition holds true where a real debt is the title for levying the rents; as, for example, where they are levied upon a poinding of the ground, or upon an adjudication completed by a decree of mails and duties. But it cannot hold in the case under consideration; because, by the very supposition, the rents are levied upon a title of property, and not by virtue of the real debts.

I illustrate this point by stating the fol- <149> lowing case. An adjudger

8. In place of the two preceding sentences, the first edition contains the text in Appendix, p. 513, Extract [1st: 194].

infeft enters into possession of the land adjudged after the legal is expired, considering his adjudication to be a right of property. After many years possession, the person against whom the adjudication was led, or his heir, claims the property; urging a defect in the adjudication which prevented expiration of the legal. It is decreed accordingly, that the adjudication never became a right of property, but that the legal is still current. Here it comes out in fact, that the land has all along been possessed upon the title of a real debt, extinguishable by levying the rents, though by the possessor understood to be a title of property. Even in this case, the levying the rents will not extinguish the debt. I give my reason. To extinguish a debt by voluntary payment two acts must concur; first, delivery by the debtor in order to extinguish the debt; and, next, acceptance by the creditor as payment. In legal payment by execution there must also be two acts; first, the rent levied by the creditor in order to be apply'd for payment of the debt; and, next, his holding the same as payment: neither of which acts <150> are found in the case under consideration. The rent is levied, not by virtue of execution in order to extinguish a debt, but upon a title of property: neither is the rent received by a creditor as payment, but by a man who conceives himself to be proprietor.

The foregoing reasoning, which because of its intricacy is drawn out to a considerable length, may be brought within a narrow compass. A *bona fide* possessor who levies and consumes the rents, is not liable to account to the proprietor whose rents they were; nor is subjected to any action whether in law or in equity; and for that reason his possession of the rents will not extinguish any debt in his person affecting the subject. But if it can be specified that he is *locupletior* by his possession, that circumstance affords to the proprietor a claim against him in equity; of which the proprietor may either demand payment, or insist that the sum be applied for extinguishing the debts upon the subject.

In these conclusions I have been forc'd to differ from the established practice of the court of session, which indeed protects the *bona fide* possessor from payment; but <151> always holds the possession as sufficient to extinguish the real debts belonging to the possessor. But I have had the less reluctance in differing from the established practice, being sensible that this matter has not been examined with all the accuracy of which it is susceptible. In particular, we are not told upon what ground the practice is founded: and if it be founded on the supposition that the proprietor has a legal claim for his rents levied by the *bona fide* possessor, I have clearly proved this a supposition to have no foundation.

Another important question has a near analogy to that now discussed. If the *bona fide* possessor have made considerable improvements upon the subject, by which its value is increased, will his claim be sustained as far as the proprietor is benefited by these improvements, or will it be compensated by the rents he has levied? Keeping in view what is said upon the foregoing question, one will readily answer, that the proprietor, having no claim for the rents levied and consumed by the *bona fide* possessor, has no ground upon which to plead compensation: But upon a more <152> narrow inspection, we perceive, that this question depends upon a different principle. It is a maxim suggested by nature, That reparations and meliorations bestowed upon a house or upon land ought to be defray'd out of the rents. Governed by this maxim, we sustain no claim against the proprietor for meliorations, if the expence exceed not the rents levied by the *bona fide* possessor. It is not properly compensation; for the proprietor has no claim to found a compensation upon. The claim is rejected upon a different medium: the rents while extant belong to the proprietor of the land: these rents are not consumed, but are bestowed upon meliorations; and the *bona fide* possessor who thus employs the proprietor's money, and not a farthing of his own, has no claim either in law or in equity. Such accordingly is the determination of Papinian, the most solid of all the Roman writers: "Sumptus in praedium, quod alienum esse apparuit, a bona fide possessore facti, neque ab eo qui praedium donavit, neque a domino peti possunt: verum exceptione doli posita, per officium judicis aequitatis ratione servantur; scilicet si <153> fructuum ante litem contestatam perceptorum summam excedant. Etenim, admissa compensatione, superfluum sumptum, meliore praedio facto, dominus restituere cogitur."*

---

* l. 48. De rei vindicatione [On *vindicatio* of property, D 6.1.48: Watson i: 208: "Where a possessor in good faith has incurred expense on land which is shown to belong to someone else, he can recover it neither from one who gave him the land as a gift nor from the owner. However, he can be indemnified by raising the defense of fraud, at the judge's discretion based on principles of fairness, so long as his expenses exceed

CHAPTER II

Powers of a court of equity with respect to a conventional
penalty.

A penal sum is inserted in a bond or obligation as a spur on the debtor to
perform.[1] With respect to an obligation *ad factum praestandum*,[2] no law can
compel the obligor to perform, otherwise than indirectly by stipulating a
penal sum in case of failure. This is explained by Justinian in the following
words. "Non solum res in stipulatum deduci possunt, sed etiam facta; ut si
stipulemur aliquid fieri vel non fieri. Et in hujusmodi stipulationi- <154>
bus optimum erit poenam subjicere, ne quantitas stipulationis in incerto
sit, ac necesse sit actori probare quod ejus intersit. Itaque si quis, ut fiat
aliquid, stipuletur; ita adjici poena debet, *si ita factum non erit, tunc poenae
nomine decem aureos dare spondes.*"*,[3] This sum comes in place of the fact
promised to be done; and when paid relieves from performing the fact.
The only thing that a court of equity has to mind with respect to a stipulation of this kind, is, that advantage be not taken of the obligant to engage
him for a much greater sum than the damage on failure of performance
can amount to. If exorbitant, it is so far penal, and will be mitigated by

---

the amount of profits which he received before joinder of issue. Thus, since set-off is
allowed, the owner is made to pay the amount spent in excess of profits, where the land
has been improved"].

1. In the first edition (p. 197) and second edition (p. 277), the equivalent chapter
begins with the following distinction: "Conventional penalties are of two kinds. A sum
of money substituted in place of an obligation to perform a fact, is an example of the
one kind; and a penal sum added to enforce the performance of any obligation, is an
example of the other kind."

2. "For the performance of a certain act."

* §7. Inst. De verb[orum] oblig[atione (On obligations by words, Inst 3.15.7): Birks
& McLeod 107: "Not only things but also services can be made the subject of stipulations, as where we stipulate for something to be done or not to be done. The best plan
here is to insert a penalty to avoid leaving the value of the stipulation uncertain, which
would put the onus on the plaintiff to prove the quantum of his interest. If someone
stipulates for something to be done, he ought to attach a penalty in this way: '*If it is not
done, do you promise to pay me a penalty of 10?*'"].

3. A different argument is set forth from this point to the end of the equivalent chapters in the first and second editions: see Appendix, p. 528, Extract [2nd: 277–83].

the court. But unless the excess be considerable, the court will not readily interpose. Thus, a farm being let to a tenant under the condition, that if he entered not, he should pay a year's rent; the whole was decreed against him on his failure: for the landlord's damage might have amounted to a year's rent.*

As payment of a bond for money can be compelled by legal execution, the penal <155> clause in such a bond differs from the former. In our bonds for borrowed money, the debtor is taken bound to pay the principal and interest, and "to pay over and above a fifth part more of liquidate expences in case of failzie."[4] This lump sum is a modification or liquidation of the damage the creditor may happen to suffer by delay of payment, advantageous to both parties by saving the trouble and expence of proving the quantum of the damages. Here, as in the former case, if the penal sum correspond in any moderate degree to the damage that may ensue from the delay, equity will not interpose. But as money-lenders in Scotland were not long ago in condition to give law to the borrowers, their practice was to stipulate exorbitant sums as liquidate expences, which, as rigorous and oppressive, are always mitigated in equity. "The court of session (says Lord Stair) modifies exorbitant penalties in bonds and contracts, even though they bear the name of liquidate expences with consent of the parties, which necessitous debtors yield to. These the Lords retrench to the <156> real expence and damage of the parties."† This penal sum is now constantly made the fifth part of the principal sum; from which our scribes never swerve, though nothing can be more absurd. It is commonly no less expensive to recover £5 than to recover £5000; yet in the former the penalty is no more but twenty shillings, in the latter no less than £1000. How disproportioned are these sums to their destined purpose? and yet for preventing such inequality the court of session has not hitherto ventured to interpose. Why not an act of sederunt, confining the penalty in a bond to £100, or some such moderate sum, however great the principal may be?

An English double bond has the effect of a conventional penalty. It was originally intended to evade the common law, which prohibits the taking

* Durie, 15th July 1637, Skene [*contra* Anon. M 8401].
4. Failure or nonperformance.
† [Stair,] Book 4. tit. 3. §1 [that is, sect. 2; Stair, *Institutions,* p. 813].

interest for money. That prohibition is no longer in force:[5] the double bond however is continued, as it supplies the want of a conventional penalty. The penal sum is upon failure due at common law; but in equity it is restricted to damages. "After the <157> day of payment, the double sum becomes the legal debt; and there is no remedy against such penalty, but by application to a court of equity, which relieves on payment of principal, interest, and costs."*

A debtor who by failure of payment draws a process upon him, and has no defence that he can urge *bona fide,* must submit to the penalty restricted to the pursuer's expense. No other excuse will avail him. Failure is often occasioned by want of money: but were such an excuse admitted, it would never be wanting; and the conventional penalty would lose its effect. Imprisonment on suspicion of treason would not be sustained as an excuse, were the debtor even refused the use of pen, ink, and paper, to request aid from his friends. The creditor goes on with all the artillery of the law; and must have his expenses out of the penalty, because the misfortune of his debtor cannot affect him.

The only doubt is, where the debtor or his heir, trusting to a defence in appear- <158> ance good, ventures to stand a process, and at last is over-ruled; whether the creditor be intitled to the modified penalty. This question merits a deliberate discussion; in order to which, it will be necessary to examine what ground there is for costs of suit, abstracting from a conventional penalty. Any voluntary wrong is a foundation for damages, even at common law; but a man free from fault or blame, is not liable for damages, or liable to repair any hurt he may have occasioned;[†] whence it follows, that there is no foundation even at common law, for subjecting to costs of suit a defendant who is *in bona fide.* Equity is still more averse from subjecting an innocent person to damages; and considering the fallibility of man, his case would be deplorable, were he bound to repair all

5. The canon law regarded it as sinful to take interest on a loan, and usurers were punished in medieval church courts. The English common law did not invalidate such agreements, though statutes (dating from the Tudors) set a limit to the amount of interest which could lawfully be charged. An Act of Anne in 1713 (12 Anne s. 2 c. 16) set the legal rate of interest at 5 percent.

* [M. Bacon, A] *New abridgment of the law,* vol. 3. [1740,] p. 691.

† See the chapter immediately foregoing.

the hurt he may occasion by an error or mistake. What then shall be said of the act 144. parl. 1592,[6] appointing, "That damage, interest, and expences of plea, be admitted by all judges, and liquidated in the decree, whether condemnator[7] or absolvitor"?[8] <159> If this regulation could ever be just, it must have been among a plain people, governed by a few simple rules of law, supposed to be universally known. Law, in its present state, is too intricate for presuming that every person who errs is *in mala fide;* and yet, unless *mala fides* be presumed in every case, the regulation cannot be justified.

These things being premised, we proceed to examine, whether a defender who is *in bona fide* can be subjected to costs by virtue of a conventional penalty. Suppose a defence urged against payment, so doubtful in law as to divide the judges, who at last gave it against the defendant by the narrowest plurality: Or suppose the cause to depend on an obscure fact requiring a laborious investigation; as where I owe £1000 by bond to my brother, who dies without children, so far as known to his relations. A woman appears with an infant, alledging a private marriage. I stand a process: the proof, drawn out to a great length, appears still dark and doubtful: judgement is at last pronounced against me by a plurality. Will justice permit me to be loaded with an immense sum of costs <160> for not submitting to the claim without trial? To extend a conventional penalty to such cases, would be in effect to punish men, for adhering, after the best advice, to what appears their rights and privileges: the grievance would be intolerable. Many a man, through the dread of costs, would be deterred from insisting on a just defence, and tamely submit to be wronged.

It appears therefore clear, that to extend against a *bona fide* defendant the penal clause in a bond, would be rigorous and unjust. And to make it still more clear, I put the following question. Let us suppose, that in a bond of borrowed money the debtor is taken expressly bound to pay the costs of suit, however plausible his defence may be, however strong his *bona fides:* would not such a clause be rejected by the court of session as exacted from a necessitous debtor by a rigorous and oppressive creditor?

6. *APS* iii: 573: 1592, c. 62, Anent damnage and expenssis of pley [Expenses Act 1592].
7. A decision against the defendant; condemnatory.
8. A decree or decision in favor of the defendant.

If the question be answered in the affirmative, which cannot be doubted, the necessary consequence is, that the penal clause, in its ordinary style, cannot be understood to have that meaning. <161>

But at that rate, it will be urged, a conventional penalty is of no use to the creditor where it is most needed, namely, in a process for recovering payment; that if the debtor be *in bona fide,* the penalty will not reach him; and if he be litigious, that there is no use for the penalty, as he is subjected to costs at common law. I answer, That the penal clause is of use even in a process. Litigiosity must be evident to infer costs at common law; but the slightest fault, or even doubt, on the defendant's part, though far from amounting to litigiosity, will subject him to the modified penalty. And Lord Stair accordingly, in the passage partly quoted above, says, "That in liquidating the pursuer's expence, the Lords take slender probation of the true expence, and do not consider whether it be necessary or not, provided it exceed not the sum agreed on; whereas in other cases they allow no expence but what is necessary or profitable."[9] <162>

CHAPTER III

What obligations and legacies transmit to heirs.

If the obligee's heirs be named in the obligation, they will succeed whether he die before or after the term of payment, because such is the will of parties. The present question relates to obligations where the obligee's heirs are not named. Such obligations by the common law transmit not to heirs; because the common law regards what is said to be the only proof of will:[1] but equity is not so peremptory nor superficial. It considers, that in human affairs errors and omissions are frequent, and that words are not always to be absolutely relied on: it holds indeed words to be the best evidence of will, but not to be the only evidence. If therefore any suspicion lie, that the will is not precisely what is expressed, every rational circumstance is laid hold of to ascertain, with all the ac-

---

9. Stair, *Institutions,* 4.3.2, p. 813.

1. The first edition has the additional words (p. 204) "and if heirs be not expressly called to the succession, they are, by construction of common law, purposely omitted."

curacy <163> possible, what really was the will of the granter, or of the contractors.*

With respect to this point, the motive that produced the obligation is one capital circumstance. Where there is no motive but good-will merely, the words are strictly adhered to; as there is nothing to infer that more was intended than is expressed. Therefore my gratuitous promise of a sum to John, is void at common law, if he die without receiving payment; for as heirs are not named, they have no claim. Nor in equity have they any claim, if the obligee die before the term of payment. But where the obligee survives the term without receiving payment, his heirs have a good claim upon the following rule in equity, That what ought to have been done is held as done.† If payment had been made, as ought to have been done, at the term specified in the deed, the sum would have been an addition to the stock of the obligee, which would have accrued to his representatives; and it would be a reproach to justice, were they left to suffer by the <164> obstinacy or neglect of the obligor. It would be a reproach still greater, that the obligor's fault in postponing payment should liberate him from his obligation. The sum is, In a deed flowing from a motive of pure benevolence, the granter's will must govern, which is understood to be in favour of the grantee only, if heirs be not mentioned. In commercial obligations, on the contrary, where there is *quid pro quo,* the obligee's will governs; and he is understood to purchase for his heirs as well as for himself, if the contrary be not expressed. The not mentioning heirs is an omission, which will be supplied by a court of equity; as justice will not permit the obligor to enjoy the valuable consideration without performing the equivalent pactioned.² Thus, a bond for borrowed money, though the creditor only be mentioned, and not heirs, descends to his heirs, where he dies before the term of payment, as well as after.

Men are bound to educate their children till they be able to provide for themselves; and any further provision is understood to be gratuitous.

* See vol. 1. pp. 201, 202 [p. 121 above].

† See [Henry Home, Lord Kames,] Elucidations respecting the Common and Statute law [of Scotland (Edinburgh: William Creech, 1777)], p. 62.

2. See Appendix, p. 514, Extract [1st: 205], for a different formulation (in the first and second editions) of the point made in the previous two sentences.

Hence, a bond of provision to children is deemed a gratuitous <165> deed; and for that reason, if the children die before the term of payment, equity gives no aid to their heirs. If heirs be named in the bond, they have right at common law: if not named, neither equity nor common law gives them right. Thus, in a contract of marriage certain provisions being allotted to the children, the portions of the males payable at their age of twenty-one years, and of the females at eighteen, without mentioning heirs or assignees; the assignees and creditors of some of the children who died before the term of payment, were judged to have no right.* I cannot so readily acquiesce in the following decision, where a bond of provision payable to a daughter at her age of fourteen, and to her heirs, executors, and assignees, was voided by her death before the term of payment.† The addition of *heirs, executors, and assignees,* was thought to regard the child's death after the term of payment; and not to be an indication of the granter's will that the bond should be effectual though the child died before the term of <166> payment. The clause, I admit, is capable of that restricted meaning: but I can find no reason for this restriction; and in all cases it is safest to give words their natural import, unless it be made clear that the granter's meaning was different. And accordingly Chalmers having settled his estate upon his nephew, with the burden of a sum certain to Isabel Inglis, wife of David Millar, and to her heirs, executors, or assignees, payable year and day after his death, with interest after the term of payment; and Isabel having died before Chalmers, leaving a son who survived him; the sum was decreed to that son as a conditional institute.[3,‡]

Even a bond of provision, or any gratuitous deed, will descend to heirs, as above said, if such was the granter's intention. Nor is it necessary in equity that such intention be expressed in words: it is sufficient that it be made evident from circumstances.

What is said above seems a more clear and satisfactory reason for ex-

---

* Stair, January 17. 1665, Edgar contra Edgar [M 6325].

† Stair, February 22. 1677, Belsches contra Belsches [M 6327].

3. *Conditional institute:* an *institute* is the person entitled to take up possession of heritable property as the immediate disponee of the granter; where the institution of that person was made conditional on certain events, it was a *conditional institute.*

‡ Millar contra Inglis, July 16. 1760 [M 8084].

cluding heirs where the creditor in a bond of provision dies before the term of payment, than <167> what is commonly assigned, that the sum in the bond, being destined as a stock for the child, ceases to be due, since it cannot answer the purpose for which it was intended. Were this reason good, it would hold equally whether the child die before or after the term of payment; and therefore in proving too much it proves nothing.

In what cases a legacy descends to heirs, is a question that takes in a great variety of matter. To have a distinct notion of this question, legacies must be divided into their different kinds. I begin with the legacy of a *corpus*.[4] The property here is transferred to the legatee *ipso facto* upon the testator's death. The reason is, that will solely must in this case have the effect to transfer property, otherwise it could never be transferred from the dead to the living: a proprietor after his death cannot make delivery; and no other person but the proprietor can make a legal delivery. Now if the legatee be vested in the property of the subject legated, it must upon his death descend to his heirs even by common law.

But what if the legatee die before the testator? In this case the legacy is void. <168> The testator remains proprietor till his death, and the subject legated cannot by his death be transferred to a person who is no longer in existence. Nor can it be transferred to that person's heirs, because the testator did not exert any act of will in their favour.

The next case I put is of a sum of money legated to Titius. A legacy of this sort, giving the legatee an interest in the testator's personal estate, and intitling him to a proportion, vests in the legatee *ipso facto* upon the testator's death. And for the same reason that is given above, the legacy even at common law will transmit to heirs, if the legatee survive the testator; if not, it will be void. But what if the legacy be ordered to be paid at a certain term? It is to be considered, whether the term be added for the benefit of the testator's heir, in order to give him time for preparing the money; or whether it be added to limit the legacy. A term for payment given to the testator's heir, will not alter the nature of the legacy, nor prevent its vesting in the legatee upon the testator's death; and consequently such a legacy will transmit to heirs, even where the legatee dies before the term of pay-

---

4. *Corpus patrimonii:* the whole estate.

ment, provided <169> he survive the testator. *Dies cedit etsi non venerit.*[5] But where the purpose of naming a term for payment is to limit the legacy, the legatee's death before that term will bar his heirs, because he himself had never any right. Here *dies nec cedit nec venit.*[6] In order to determine what was the intention of the testator in naming a day for payment, the rule laid down by Papinian is judicious: *Dies incertus conditionem in testamento facit.** A day certain for performance is commonly added in favour of the testator's heir, in order to give him time for providing the money. An uncertain day respects commonly the condition of the legatee; as where a legacy is in favour of a boy to be claimed when he arrives at eighteen years of age, or of a girl to be claimed at her marriage. In such instances, it appears to be the will of the testator, that the legacy shall not vest before the term of payment. The *dies incertus*[7] is said to make the legacy conditional; not properly, for the naming a day of payment, certain or uncertain, is not a condition. But as the uncertain term for pay- <170> ment has the effect to limit the legacy in the same manner as if it were conditional; for that reason, the uncertain term is said to imply a condition, or to make the legacy conditional.

A third sort of legacy is where the testator burdens his heir to pay a certain sum to Titius singly, without the addition of heirs. The heirs at common law have no right even where Titius survives the testator, because there is not here, as in the former cases, any subject vested in Titius to descend to his heirs; nor can heirs, at common law, claim upon an obligation which is not in their favour. But equity sustains an action to them: for no day being named, the death of the testator is the term of payment; and equity will not suffer the testator's heir to profit

---

5. The right has vested in the person, even if it has not become enforceable. [*Dies cedit:* the time for enjoyment of the right has begun (literally, "the day begins to run"); *dies venit:* the right is vested and actionable (literally, "the day has come").]

6. The right has neither vested nor become enforceable.

* l. 75, De condicion[ibus] et demon[strationibus et causis et modis eorum, quae in testamento scribuntur (On conditions, particularizations, explanations for, and modalities of provisions in wills), D 35.1.75: Watson iii: 194, "A date uncertain of realization constitutes in a will a condition"].

7. "Uncertain day."

by delaying payment. Where a term of payment is added by the testator, the case becomes the same with that of a gratuitous obligation *inter vivos.*[8] <171>

CHAPTER IV

Arrestment and process of forthcoming.

Current coin is the only legal subject for payment of debt, which accordingly the creditor is bound to accept of. Sometimes however, for want of current coin, the creditor submits to take satisfaction in goods; and sometimes he is put off with a security, an assignment to rents, for example, or to debts, which empowers him to operate his payment out of these subjects. Legal execution, copying voluntary acts between debtor and creditor, is of three kinds. The first, compelling payment of the debt, resembles voluntary payment. This was the case of poinding in its original form;* and it is the case of a decree for making *corpora*[1] forthcoming, as will be seen afterwards. The second re- <172> sembles voluntary acceptance of goods for satisfying the debt; which is the case of poinding according to our present practice. The goods are not sold as originally; but after being valued, are delivered *ipsa corpora*[2] to the creditor. The third resembles a voluntary security: it gives the creditor a security upon his debtor's funds, and enables him to operate his payment accordingly. This is the case of an adjudication during the legal; which empowers the creditor to draw payment out of the debtor's rents by a decree of mails and duties against the tenants. A decree for making forthcoming sums of money due to the debtor, is of the same nature: it is a security only, not payment; and consequently, if my debtor, against whom the decree of forthcoming is obtained, prove insolvent, the

8. "Between living people."

* [Kames,] Historical Law-tracts, tract 10 ["History of Execution against Moveables and Land for payment of debt," 1758 ed., vol. 2, pp. 49–72].

1. *Corpora* of moveable property: that is, tangible moveable goods, in contrast to intangible ones, such as obligations to pay debt. The first edition (p. 208) and second edition (p. 288) use the word *moveables* in place of *corpora*.

2. Physically (that is, the very goods).

sum is lost to me, not to my creditor who obtained the decree: his security indeed is gone; but the debt which was secured remains entire.[3]

So much for preliminaries. And as to the subject of the present chapter, I begin with the several kinds of arrestment. The first I shall mention is that which proceeds on a judicial order to secure the per- <173> son of one accused of a crime. The next is for securing moveable effects in the hands of the possessor, till the property be determined. This arrestment, termed *rei servandae causa,*[4] is a species of sequestration: it is a sequestration in the hands of the possessor. The goods are thus secured till the property be determined; and the person declared proprietor, takes possession *via facti.*[5] A third arrestment is that which is preparatory to a process of forthcoming raised by a creditor for recovering payment out of his debtor's moveables, whether *corpora* or *debita.*[6]

A debtor's corporeal moveables in his own possession are attached by poinding, corresponding to the *Levari facias* in England.[7] But where such moveables are in the possession of any other, and the particulars unknown, there can be no place for poinding. The creditor obtains a warrant or order from a proper court to arrest them in the hands of the possessor, to hinder him from delivering them up to the proprietor. The service of this order is termed *an arrestment;* and the person upon whom it is served is termed the *arrestee.* The first step of the process of forthcoming consequent <174> upon the arrestment is an order to sell the goods secured by the arrestment. The price is delivered to the creditor for his payment; and the debt is thereby extinguished in whole or in part, which completes the process. A process of forthcoming upon sums arrested is in the same form; with this only difference, that instead of selling *corpora,* a decree of forthcoming goes out against the arrestee, and payment is recovered from him accordingly.

3. This material is more fully explained in the first and second editions: see Appendix, p. 514, Extract [1st: 209].

4. "To preserve the assets."

5. "By way of deed."

6. That is, "tangible or intangible property."

7. *Levari facias:* a writ of execution in England issued to a sheriff ("that you cause to be levied") ordering the seizure of a judgment debtor's chattels and income to satisfy the debt.

An arrestment of this kind is not to be considered as necessary to found a process of forthcoming. This process is founded on common law, and may proceed without an arrestment; which will appear from the following consideration. If I have not money to pay my debt, I ought to convey to my creditor what other things I am master of, that he may convert them into money for his payment. If I refuse to do him that act of justice, a court of law will interpose, and do what I ought to have done. The court will adjudge my land to belong to him; or they will ordain my effects to be made forthcoming to him. An arrestment indeed commonly precedes; but <175> its only purpose is, to secure the subject in the hands of the arrestee till a process of forthcoming be raised. In that respect, an arrestment resembles an inhibition, which is not a step of execution, but only an injunction to the debtor, prohibiting him to alien his land or to contract debt, in order to preserve the fund entire for the creditor's adjudication. A forthcoming is of the same nature with an adjudication: an heritable subject is attached by the latter; a moveable, by the former. A process of adjudication is carried on every day without a preparatory inhibition; and a process of forthcoming may be carried on equally without a preparatory arrestment.

Though what is above laid down belongs to common law, it is however proper here, as an introduction to the matters of equity that follow. The subject to be handled is the operations of common law and of equity with respect to a competition between an arrestment and other rights, voluntary or legal. With respect to the arrestment of a *corpus,* all are agreed, that it is a sequestration merely in the hands of the possessor, and transfers no right to the creditor. The goods secured <176> by the arrestment, are in the process of forthcoming sold as the property of the debtor; and the price is applied for payment of the debt due by him to the arrester. For that reason, an arrestment cannot bar a poinding carried on by another creditor. If the subject belong to the debtor, poinding goes on of course by the authority of common law.

It is natural to assimilate the arrestment of a debt to that of a moveable, in being prohibitory only, and in transferring no right to the creditor. Yet many hold that the former has a stronger effect than the latter, by transferring to the creditor some sort of right, signified by the term *nexus realis.*[8] To ascertain the nature and effect of such an arrestment, the best way is to give an accurate analysis of it. The letter or warrant for arrestment, to which the arrestment itself is entirely conformable, is in the following words: "To fence and arrest all and sundry the said A. B. his readiest goods, gear, debts, &c. in whosoever hands the same can be apprehended, to remain under sure fence and arrestment, at the instance of the said complainer, ay and while payment be <177> made to him." Upon this warrant and arrestment following upon it, it will be observed, first, That no person is named but the arrester and his debtor. It is not a limited warrant to arrest in the hands of any particular person; but an authority to arrest in the hands of any person that the creditor suspects may owe money to his debtor. Secondly, The arrestee is not ordered or authorised to make payment to the arrester: the order he receives, is to keep the money in his hand till the arrester be satisfied. These particulars make it plain, that an arrestment, like an inhibition, is merely prohibitory; and that it transfers not any right to the arrester. And this point is put out of doubt by the summons of forthcoming, concluding, "That the defender should be decerned and ordained to make forthcoming to the complainer the sum of resting and owing by him to A. B. (the complainer's debtor against whom the execution passes), and arrested in the defender's hands at the complainer's instance." It is the decree of forthcoming, therefore, that intitles the creditor to demand the sum arrested, to be applied <178> for payment of the debt upon which the arrestment and forthcoming proceeded; and the preparatory arrestment has no other effect, but to prevent alienation before the process of forthcoming is raised.

If it hold true, that arrestment is prohibitory only, and that my creditor arresting in the hands of my debtor, hath no right to the sum arrested till he obtain a decree of forthcoming, it follows upon the principles of common law, that this sum, belonging to me after arrestment as well as before, lies open to be attached by my other creditors; and that, in a competition among these creditors, all of them arresters, the first decree of forthcoming must give preference. For the first order served upon my debtor binds him to the creditor who obtained the order; after which he cannot legally

8. "A real fetter"; an encumbrance to property (Scots law).

pay to any other. Thus stands the common law, which is followed out in a course of decisions, mostly of an old date, giving preference, not to the first arrestment, but to the first decree of forthcoming.

Whether equity make any variation, shall be our next inquiry. It is the privilege of a debtor, with respect to his own funds, <179> to apply which of them he pleases for payment of his debts. Upon the debtor's failure, this choice is transferred to the creditor, who may attach any particular subject for his payment. In that case, the debtor is bound to convey to his creditor the subject attached, for his security: it is undoubtedly the duty of the debtor to relieve his creditor from the trouble and expence of execution; and, consequently, to relieve him from execution against any particular subject, by surrendering it voluntarily, unless he find other means of making payment. The creditor's privilege to attach any particular subject for his payment, and the debtor's relative obligation to save execution by surrendering that subject to his creditor, are indeed the foundation of all execution. A judge authorising execution, supplies only the place of the debtor; and consequently cannot authorise execution against any particular subject, unless the debtor be antecedently bound to surrender the same to his creditor.* This branch of the debtor's duty explains a rule in law, "That inchoated <180> execution makes the subject litigious, and ties up the debtor's hands from aliening." If it be his duty to prevent execution by surrendering this subject to his creditor, it is inconsistent with his duty to dispose of it to any other person.

In applying the rules of equity to an arrestment, the duty now unfolded is of importance. If the debtor ought to convey to his creditor the subject arrested, no other creditor who knows the debtor to be so bound, can justly attach that subject by legal execution: for it is unjust to demand from a debtor a subject he is bound to convey to another.† And if a creditor shall act thus unjustly, by arresting a subject which he knows to be already arrested by another creditor, a court of equity will disappoint the effect of the second arrestment, by giving preference to the first.

Our writers, though they have not clearly unfolded the debtor's ob-

---

* See above, p. 16 [p. 253 above].
† See above, p. 17 [p. 253 above].

ligation to the first arrester, have, however, been sensible of it; for it is obviously with reference to this obligation, that an arrestment is said to make a *nexus realis* upon the subject. I know but of two ways by which a man <181> can be connected with a debt: one is where he has the *jus exigendi*,[9] and one where the creditor is bound to make it over to him. It will be admitted, that an arrestment has not the effect of transferring to the arrester the debt arrested: the arrester has not even the *jus exigendi* till he obtain a decree of forthcoming. And if so, a *nexus realis*, applied to the present subject, cannot import other than the obligation which the creditor is under to make over the debt to the arrester. Thus, by the principles of equity, the first arrestment is preferable while the subject is *in medio;*[10] but if a posterior arrester, without notice of a former, obtain payment upon a decree of forthcoming, he is secure in equity, as well as at common law; and his discovery afterward of a prior arrestment will not oblige him to repay the money.* This equitable rule of preferring the first arrestment while the subject is *in medio,* is accordingly established at present, and all the late decisions of the court of session proceed upon it.

An arrestment, as observed above, hath not the effect at common law to bar poind- <182> ing; but in equity, for the reason now given, an arrestment made known to the poinder, ought to bar him from proceeding in his execution, as well as it bars a posterior arrestment. A creditor ought not, by any sort of execution, to force from his debtor what the debtor cannot honestly convey to him. And yet, though in ranking arrestments the court of session follows the rules of equity, it acts as a court of common law in permitting a subject to be poinded after it is arrested by another creditor. I shall close this branch of my subject with a general observation, That the equitable rules established above, hold only where the debtor is solvent: it will be seen afterward, that in the case of bankruptcy, all personal creditors ought to draw equally.

So much about arresters competing for the same debt. Next about an arrester competing with an assignee. Touching this competition, one pre-

---

9. "The right to enforce payment"; that is, the right of a creditor to enforce immediate payment of a debt.
10. "In the middle," referring to a fund in dispute (Scots law).
  * See above, pp. 23, 24 [p. 257 above].

liminary point must be adjusted, namely, How far an arrestment makes the subject arrested litigious; or, in other words, How far it bars voluntary deeds. It is obvious, in the first place, that an arrestment makes the sub- <183> ject litigious with respect to the arrestee, because it is served upon him: the very purpose of the arrestment is, to prohibit him from paying the debt arrested, or from giving up the goods. In the next place, as a creditor may proceed to arrestment without intimating his purpose to his debtor, an arrestment cannot bar the debtor's voluntary deeds, till it be notified to him: the arrestment deprives him not of his *jus crediti*,[11] nor of his property; and while he continues ignorant of the arrestment, nothing bars him, either in law or in equity, from conveying his right to a third party. Upon that account, intimation to him is an established practice in the country from whence we borrowed an arrestment: "Quamvis debitor debitoris mei a me arrestari nequeat, cum mihi nulla ex causa obligatus sit, tamen, quod Titius debitori meo debet, per judicem inhibere possum, ne debitori meo solvatur, sine mea vel judicis voluntate. De quo arresto debitorem meum certiorem facere debeo, eique diem dicere; quo si compareat, nec justam causam alleget ob quam arrestum relaxari debeat, vel si non compareat, judex ex pecunia arre- <184> stata mihi solvendum decernet."* The same doctrine is laid down by Balfour,† "That an arrestment of corns, goods, or gear, ought to be intimated to the owner thereof; and that if no intimation be made, it is lawful for the owner to dispose of the same at his pleasure." Thirdly, With respect to others, an arrestment, though notified to the arrester's debtor, makes not the subject litigious; for any person

11. "The right of a creditor"; that is, the personal right vested in a creditor to the debt.

* Sande Decis. Fris. l. 1. tit. 17. def. 1 [Johan van den Sande, *Decisiones Frisicae; sive rerum in suprema frisiorum curia judicatarum libri quinque* (Amsterdam: T. Myls, 1698; 1st ed. 1633), p. 34: "Even though my debtor's debtor cannot be arrested by me, since he is under no legal obligation to me, through a judge I can nevertheless prevent what Titius owes to my debtor from being paid to my debtor without my consent or that of a judge. I must inform my debtor of this arrestment, and fix a day for his appearance in court; and if he appears and shows no just cause why this arrestment should be released, or does not appear, the judge will decree payment to me from the money arrested"].

† Title, Arrestment, cap. 3 [Sir James Balfour of Pittendreich, *Practicks, or a System of the More Ancient Law of Scotland,* 2 vols. (Edinburgh: A. Kincaid and A. Donaldson, 1754); facsimile reprint, ed. P. G. B. McNeill (Edinburgh: Stair Society, 1962), vol. 2, p. 538].

ignorant of the arrestment, is at liberty to take from the arrester's debtor a conveyance to the subject arrested. The cedent aliens indeed *mala fide* after the arrestment is notified to him; but the purchaser is secure if he be *in bona fide:* the property is legally transferred to him; and there is nothing in law nor in equity to deprive a man of a subject honestly acquired. That an arrestment makes not the subject litigious with regard to third parties, will be clear from considering, that an effect so strong is never given to any act, unless there be a public notification: a process in the court of session <185> is supposed to be known to all; and, as it is a rule, *Quod nihil innovandum pendente lite,*[12] any person who transacts either with the plaintiff or defendant, so as to hurt the other, does knowingly an unlawful act, which for that reason will be voided: an inhibition and interdiction are published to all the lieges,[13] who are thereby put *in mala fide* to purchase from the person inhibited or interdicted: an apprising renders the subject litigious as to all, because the letters are publicly proclaimed or denounced, not only upon the land, but also at the market-cross of the head-borough of the jurisdiction where the land lies;* and an adjudication has the same effect, because it is a process in the court of session: a charge of horning bars not the debtor from aliening, till he be publicly proclaimed or denounced rebel; and it must be evident, that an arrestment served upon my debtor, cannot hurt third parties dealing with me, more than a horning against myself. In a word, litigiosity, so as to affect third parties, never takes place without public notification. <186>

Were we to draw an argument from an inhibition, it might be inferred, that even the actual knowledge of an arrestment should not bar one from purchasing the subject arrested. But the argument from an inhibition concludes not with respect to an arrestment; and in order to show the difference, it will be necessary to state the nature of an inhibition in a historical view.

This writ prohibits the alienation of moveable subjects as well as of immoveable; and to secure against alienation, the writ is published to the lieges, to put every man upon his guard against dealing with the person

---

12. "No alteration should take place while a lawsuit is pending."
13. That is, subjects of the monarch.
 * Stair, lib. 3. tit. 2. §14. [Stair, *Institutions,* p. 597].

inhibited. This writ must have been the invention of a frugal age, before the commerce of money was far extended. While inhibitions were rare, their publication could be kept in remembrance; a debtor inhibited would be a remarkable person, to make every one avoid dealing with him. But when the commerce of money was farther extended, and debts were multiplied, an inhibition was no longer a mark of distinction. And as inhibitions could no longer be kept in memory, they became a load upon the commerce of move- <187> ables past enduring; for no man was in safety to purchase from his neighbour a horse, or a bushel of corn, till first the records of inhibitions were consulted. A Lycurgus intending to bar commerce, in order to preserve his nation in poverty, could not have invented a more effectual scheme. This execution, inconsistent with commerce as far as it affects moveables, is also inconsistent in itself, tending directly to disappoint its own end. The purpose of an inhibition is to force payment; and the effect of it is to prevent payment, by locking up the debtor's moveables, which commonly are the only ready fund for procuring money.

These reasons have prevailed upon the court of session to refuse any effect to an inhibition as far as it regards moveables. An inhibition indeed, with respect to its form and tenor, continues the same as originally; and accordingly every debtor inhibited is to this hour discharged to alien his moveables, no less peremptorily than to alien his land. This inconsistence cannot be remedied but by the legislature; for the court of session cannot alter a writ of the common law, more than it can al- <188> ter any other branch of the common law. But the court of session, as a court of equity, can redress the rigor, injustice, or oppression, of the common law: and tho' it hath no power to alter the style of an inhibition, it acts justly in refusing to give force to it as far as it affects moveables; because so far it is an oppressive and inconsistent execution. This argument, as above hinted, may seem to apply to an arrestment, that even the knowledge of this execution ought not to bar any person from purchasing the subject arrested, whether it be a debt, or a *corpus*. But this holds not in practice: and there is good reason for distinguishing, in this particular, an arrestment from an inhibition: the latter prohibits, in general, the debtor to alien any of his moveables, and for that reason is rigorous and oppressive: the former is of particular subjects only; nor doth it affect any moveables in the debtor's own possession, for which reason, the execution so limited is neither rigorous nor oppressive. An arrestment, therefore, as to the subjects affected by it, is allowed in practice to have the full effect that is given it at common law. But with respect to a <189> third party, it has a more ample effect in equity than at common law: for though a man who *bona fide* purchases a subject arrested, is secure in equity as well as at common law; yet a *mala fide* purchase, though effectual at common law, will undoubtedly be voided in a court of equity.

Having discussed preliminary points, we proceed to the subject proposed, competition between an arrester and an assignee. I begin with arrestment of a moveable bond,[14] assign'd before the arrestment, but intimated after. The intimation by our law makes a complete conveyance of the bond into the person of the assignee; after which the sum cannot be made forthcoming to the arrester for his payment: the very foundation of his claim is gone; for neither law nor equity will permit any subject to be taken in execution that belongs not to the debtor. Many decisions, it is true, prefer the arrester; upon what medium, I cannot comprehend. Our decisions, however, are far from being uniform upon this point. I give the following example. John assigns the rent of his land for security and payment of a debt due by him. He hath another creditor <190> who afterward raises a process of adjudication affecting the same land. The assignee intimating his right after the citation, but before the decree of adjudication, is preferred before the adjudger.* An arrestment surely makes not a stronger *nexus* upon the subject than is made by a citation upon a summons of adjudication; and if an assignment be preferred before the latter, it ought also to be preferred before the former. But I say more. Let it be supposed, that after the citation upon the summons of adjudication, but before intimation of the assignment, the rent is arrested by a third creditor. The decree of adjudication is preferred before the arrestment.† If so, here is a circle absolutely inextricable, an adjudication preferred before

---

14. A simple bond for the repayment of borrowed money; in contrast to a heritable bond, a bond for a sum of money to which is joined a conveyance of land or heritable property to be held as security for the debt.

* Durie, March 2. 1637, Smith contra Hepburn [M 2804].

† Dalrymple, June 26. 1705, Stewart contra Stewart [M 2767].

an arrestment, the arrestment before an assignment, and the assignment before the adjudication. This proves demonstrably that the assignee ought to be preferred before the arrester, as well as before the adjudger. The court went still further, in preferring an assignee before <191> an arrester. An English assignment to this day is a procuratory *in rem suam* only, carrying the equitable right indeed, but not the legal right. And yet with respect to a bond due to Wilson residing in England, by the Earl of Rothes in Scotland, an English assignment by Wilson of the said bond was of itself, without intimation, preferred before an arrestment served afterward upon the Earl.[15] The preference thus given was clearly founded on equity; because the court of session, as a court of equity, could not justly make forthcoming to a creditor of Wilson for his payment, a subject that Wilson had aliened for a valuable consideration, and to which the purchaser had the equitable, though not the legal right. But if this be a just decision, which it undoubtedly is, nothing can be more unjust, than to prefer an arrestment before a Scotch assignment of a prior date, even after it is completed by intimation; for here the assignee has both the equitable and legal right.

The next case I put, is where, in a process of forthcoming upon an arrestment, an assignee appears with an assignment prior to the arrestment, but not intimated. <192> I have already given my reason for preferring the assignee, as the court did with respect to an English assignment: and yet the ordinary practice is to prefer the arrestment; which one will have no hesitation to believe, when an arrestment is preferred even where the assignment is intimated.

The preference due to the assignee is in this case so clear, that I am encouraged to carry the doctrine farther, by preferring an assignee even before a poinder; provided the assignee appear for his interest before the poinding be completed. The poinder no doubt is preferable at common law, because till an assignment be completed by intimation, the debtor continues proprietor. The assignee however has the equitable right; and justice will not permit goods that the debtor has aliened for a valuable consideration to be attached by any of his creditors. The result will be different, where the poinding is completed, and the property of the goods

15. See Wilson's Assignees contra Earl of Rothes, 27 February 1759 [M 1802].

is transferred to the creditor, before the assignee appears. In this case, the poinder is secure; because no man can be forfeited of his property who has committed no fault. <193>

I proceed to an assignment dated after arrestment, but intimated before competition. Supposing the assignee to be *in bona fide,* he is clearly preferable; for the intimation vests in him the legal as well as equitable right; which bars absolutely the cedent and his creditors: and this reason is good at common law to prefer the assignee, even supposing he had notice of the arrestment before he took the assignment. But in equity the arrester is preferable where the assignee is *in mala fide,* for the following reason. The debtor, after his subject is affected by an arrestment, is bound in duty to make over the subject to his creditor the arrester: if he transgress by conveying the subject to one who knows of the arrestment, both are guilty of a moral wrong, which equity will redress by preferring the arrester.

Let us drop now the intimation, by putting the case, that in a process of forthcoming upon an arrestment, an assignee appears for his interest, craving preference upon an assignment bearing date after the arrestment, but before the citation in the process of forthcoming. Supposing the as- <194> signee *in mala fide,* he will in equity be postponed to the arrester for the reason immediately above given. But what shall be the rule of preference where the assignee purchases *bona fide?* The arrester and he have each of them an equitable right to the subject; neither of them has the legal right. This case resembles that of stellionate, where a proprietor of land sells to two different purchasers ignorant of each other: neither of whom has the legal right, because there is no infeftment; but each of them has an equitable right. In these cases, I cannot discover a rule for preference; nor can I extricate the matter otherwise than by dividing the subject between the competitors. And after all, whether this may not be cutting the Gordian knot instead of untying it, I pretend not to be certain.

Upon the whole, an arrestment appears a very precarious security till a process of forthcoming be commenced. This process indeed is a notification to the debtor not to alien in prejudice of the arrestor, and at the same time a public notification to the lieges not to purchase the subject arrested. <195> And by this process the subject is rendered litigious; though the same privilege is not indulged to an inhibition as far as moveables are concerned.

CHAPTER V

Powers of a court of equity with relation to bankrupts.

In the two foregoing books are contained many instances of equity remedying imperfections in common law as to payment of debt. But that subject is not exhausted: on the contrary, it enlarges upon us, when we take under consideration the law concerning bankruptcy. And this branch was purposely reserved, to be presented to the reader in one view; for the parts are too intimately connected to bear a separation without suffering by it.

This branch of law is of great importance in every commercial country; and in order to set it in a clear light, I cannot think of a better arrangement than what <196> follows. First, To state the rules of common law. Second, To examine what equity dictates. Third, To state the regulations of different countries. And to conclude with the proceedings of the court of session.

The rules of common law are very short, but very imperfect. Any deed done by a bankrupt is effectual at common law, no less than if he were solvent: nor is legal execution obstructed by bankruptcy; a creditor, after his debtor's bankruptcy, having the same remedy for recovering payment, that he had before. The common law considers only whether the subject convey'd by the bankrupt or attached by his creditors, was his property: if it was, a court of common law supports both. Let him alien his moveables, or his land, intentionally to defraud his creditors, common law, however, regardless of intention, considers such acts as legal exertions of property, and consequently effectual.

In order to determine what justice dictates in this case, it becomes necessary in the first place to ascertain, what circumstances make bankruptcy in the common <197> sense of mankind. A man, while he carries on trade, or hath any business that affords him a prospect of gain, is not bankrupt though his effects may not be sufficient to pay his debts; for he has it in view to pay all: but if his business fail him, and leave him no prospect of paying his debts, he is in the common sense of mankind insolvent or bankrupt; his creditors must lose by him.

This situation, though not uncommon, is yet singular in the eye of justice. *Property* and *interest*, for the most part strictly united, are here disjoined: the bankrupt continues proprietor of his estate, but his creditors are the only persons interested in it: they have the equitable right, and nothing remains with him but the legal right. In this view, a bankrupt may not improperly be held as a trustee, bound to manage his effects for behoof of his creditors: the duty of a bankrupt is in effect the same with that of a trustee, as both of them ought to make a faithful account of the subjects under their management. While a debtor continues solvent, he may pay his creditors in what order he pleases; because no creditor suffers by the prefer- <198> ence given to another. But upon his bankruptcy or insolvency, that privilege vanishes: he is bound to all his creditors equally; and justice dictates, that he ought to distribute his effects among them equally. A creditor demanding payment from his debtors, or from their cautioners bound conjunctly and severally, ought to behave with impartiality:* much more is this incumbent upon a bankrupt in making payment to his creditors. No distinction ought to be made but between real and personal creditors: a real security fairly obtained from a debtor in good circumstances, is not prejudicial to the other creditors; and if unexceptionable originally, it cannot be voided by what may afterward happen to the debtor. There is no injustice therefore in the preference given to real creditors before personal.[a] <199>

To confirm this doctrine, I appeal to the general sense of the nation, vouched by act 5. parl. 1696,[1] which, taking for granted that a bankrupt ought to behave with impartiality to his creditors, prohibits him to prefer any of his creditors before the rest, and annuls every one of his deeds giving

---

* Vol. 1. p. 172 et seqq. [p. 105ff above].

a. The following rule is contained in a code of Hindostan laws. "When several men are creditors to the same debtor, they shall make a sort of common stock of their debts, and receive their respective shares of each payment. If any creditor refuse to accede to this agreement, he shall lose his share" [Quotation from (Nathaniel Brassey Halhed), *A Code of Gentoo Laws, or Ordinations of the Pundits, from a Persian Translation* (London, 1776), p. 11].

1. *APS* x: 33: 1696, c. 5, Act for declaring nottour bankrupt [Bankruptcy Act 1696].

such undue preference. And I appeal also to the English bankrupt-statutes, which evidently rest upon the same foundation.

Thus stands the duty of a bankrupt with respect to his creditors, founded on the rules of justice. The duty of the creditors with respect to each other may seem not so evident. It is the privilege of a creditor who obtains not satisfaction, to draw his payment out of the debtor's effects; and it will not readily occur, that the debtor's insolvency, the very circumstance which enhances the value of the privilege, should be a bar to it. This way of thinking is natural; and hence the following maxims that have obtained an universal currency: *Prior tempore potior jure:*[2] *Vigilantibus non dormientibus jura subveniunt.*[3] In rude times, before the connections of society have taken deep root, selfish prin- <200> ciples prevail over those that are social. Thus in the present case, a creditor, partial to his own interest, is apt to confine his thoughts to the power he hath over his debtor; overlooking, or seeing but obscurely, that where the debtor is bankrupt, his creditors, connected now with each other by a common fund, ought to divide that fund equally among them. But by refinement of manners, man becomes more a social than a selfish being; and, by the improvement of his faculties, he discovers the lawful authority of social duties, as what he is bound to fulfil even in opposition to his own interest. By such refinement it is at last perceived, that by the debtor's insolvency, his personal creditors have all of them an equal claim upon his effects; that a creditor, taking measures to operate his payment, ought to consider the connection he has with his fellow creditors, engaged equally with him upon the same fund; and therefore that justice requires an equal distribution. In every view we take of the subject, we become more and more satisfied that this rule is agreeable to justice. To make the distribution of the common fund depend on <201> priority of execution, exhibits the appearance of a race, where the swiftest obtains the prize: a race is a more manly competition, because there is merit in swiftness; none in priority of execution, which depends upon accident more frequently than upon expedition. It is natural for savage animals to fall out about their prey, and to rob each other; but social

2. "The earlier in time, the stronger in right." The third edition misspells *potior* as *potio.*

3. "The law helps the vigilant, not those who sleep."

beings ought to be governed by the principle of benevolence: creditors in particular, connected by a common fund and equally interested, should not like enemies strive to prevent each other; but like near relations should join in common measures for the common benefit.

This proposition is put past doubt by the following argument. A debtor, after his insolvency, is bound to distribute his effects equally among his creditors; and it would be an act of injustice in him to prefer any of them before the rest. It necessarily follows, that a creditor cannot be innocent, who, knowing the bankruptcy, takes more than his proportion of the effects: if he take more by voluntary payment, he is accessory to an unjust act done by the bankrupt; and it will not be <202> thought that he can justly take more by execution than by voluntary payment. If he should attempt such wrong, it is the duty of the judge to refuse execution.*

That creditors having notice of their debtor's bankruptcy are barred from taking advantage of each other, shall now be taken for granted. It is not so obvious what effect bankruptcy ought to have against creditors who are ignorant of it. I begin with payment made by a bankrupt in money or effects, which transfers the property to his creditor. It is demonstrated above,† that even in the case of stellionate, the second purchaser, supposing him *in bona fide,* and not partaker of his author's fraud, is secure by getting the first infeftment; and that his purchase cannot be cut down in equity more than at common law. The reasoning there concludes with equal if not superior force in the case of bankruptcy: it is unjust in a bankrupt to prefer one creditor before another; but if he offer payment, the creditor who accepts, supposing him ignorant <203> of the bankruptcy, is innocent, and therefore secure: the property of the money or effects being transferred to him in lieu of his debt, there is no rule in equity more than at common law to forfeit him of his property. The same reasoning concludes in favour of a creditor, who, ignorant of the bankruptcy, recovers payment by a poinding, or by a forthcoming upon an arrestment.

Next comes the case of a real security, which transfers not the property of the subject. It is observed above, that a real security, obtained before

* See book I. part I. chap. 8. sect. 2.

† pp. 41, 42 [pp. 266–67 above].

bankruptcy, is in all events a preferable debt. But what if it be obtained after bankruptcy? The creditor, who, ignorant of his debtor's bankruptcy, obtains from him such security, whether by legal execution or by voluntary deed, is indeed not culpable in any degree. But before this security existed, each of the creditors had an equitable right to a proportion of the bankrupt's effects; which right cannot be hurt by legal diligence, and still less by a partial deed of the bankrupt, who acts against conscience in preferring one of his creditors before the rest. Where payment is <204> actually made, a court of equity can give no relief, for two reasons: first, the innocent creditor, to whom the money was paid, cannot be deprived of his property; and next, a debt extinguished by payment cannot be reared up in order to compel the *quondam* creditor to enter the lists again with the remaining creditors. But where the creditor is still *in petitorio*,[4] demanding preference by virtue of his real security, the court cannot listen to his claim; because to prefer him would be to forfeit the other creditors of what they are justly intitled to.

If in a bankrupt it be unjust to divide his effects unequally among his creditors, it is still more unjust to hurt his whole creditors by gratuitous alienations or gratuitous bonds. A gratuitous alienation transferring the property, cannot, it is true, be voided, if the donee be not in the knowledge of the bankruptcy: but he is liable for the value to the bankrupt's creditors, upon the rule of equity, *Nemo debet locupletari aliena jactura;*[5] which is not applicable to an alienation before bankruptcy, because by such an alienation the creditors are not hurt. But against a gratuitous bond <205> claimed after bankruptcy, though executed and delivered while the granter was solvent, the rule *Nemo debet locupletari aliena jactura* is applicable; because the taking payment is a direct prejudice to the creditors by lessening their fund; and for that reason, a court of equity will not interpose to make such a bond effectual. It deserves attention, that this principle operates in favour of a creditor who lent his money even after the date of the gratuitous bond.*

The equitable right to the debtor's effects, which upon his insolvency

---

4. "In a petitory action."
5. "No one should be enriched at another's expense."
* Dirleton, January 21. 1677, Ardblair contra Wilson [M 4928].

accrues to his creditors, makes it a wrong in him to sell any of his effects privately without their consent. The sale indeed is effectual at common law; but the purchaser, supposing his knowledge of the bankruptcy, is accessory to the wrong, and the sale is voidable upon that ground. The principle of utility also declares against a sale of that nature: for to permit a bankrupt to alien his effects privately, even for a just price, is throwing a temptation in his way to defraud his creditors, by the oppor- <206> tunity it affords him to walk off with the money.

Thus we see, that in applying the rules of equity to the case of bankruptcy, two preliminary facts are of importance; first, the commencement of the bankruptcy; and, next, what knowledge creditors or others have of it: the former is necessary to be ascertained in every case; the latter frequently. The necessity of such proof tends to darken and perplex law-suits concerning bankruptcy. To ascertain the commencement of bankruptcy must always be difficult, considering that it depends on an internal act of the debtor's mind deeming his affairs irretrievable: and the difficulty is greatly increased, when the knowledge of the bankruptcy comes also to be a point at issue; for such knowledge must be gathered commonly from a variety of circumstances that are scarce ever the same in any two cases. To avoid such intricate expiscation, which tends to make law-suits endless and judges arbitrary, it has been a great aim of the legislature in every commercial country, to specify some ouvert act that shall be held not only the commence- <207> ment of bankruptcy, but also a public notification of it.

But if the specifying a legal mark of bankruptcy be of great importance, the choice of a proper mark is no less nice than important. Whether in any country a choice altogether unexceptionable has been made, seems doubtful. It ought, in the first place, to be some act that cannot readily happen except in bankruptcy: for to fix a mark of bankruptcy on one who is not a bankrupt, would be a great punishment without a fault. Secondly, It must be an act that will readily happen in bankruptcy, and which a bankrupt cannot prevent: for if it be in his power to suppress it altogether, or for any time, he may in the interim do much wrong that will not admit a remedy.

Having thus gone through the rules of common law and the rules of equity concerning bankruptcy, we are, I presume, sufficiently prepared for the third article proposed, namely, to state the regulations of different countries upon that subject. And to bring the present article within reasonable compass, I shall confine myself to the Roman law, the English law, and to that <208> of Scotland, which may be thought sufficient for a specimen. I begin with the Roman law. A debtor's absconding intitled his creditors to apply to the court for a *curator bonis;*[6] and after the creditors were put in possession by their *curator,* no creditor could take payment from the bankrupt.* This *missio in possessionem,*[7] however, seems not to have been deemed a public notification of bankruptcy; for even after that period, a purchaser from the bankrupt was secure, if it could not be proved that he was *particeps fraudis.*[8,†] But every gratuitous deed was rescinded, whether the acquirer was accessory to the wrong or no;‡ and in particular a gratuitous discharge of a debt.§

Before the *missio in possessionem* the debtor continued to have the management as while he was solvent; and particularly was intitled to pay his creditors in what order he thought proper. It is accordingly laid down, That a creditor, who before the *missio in possessionem* receives payment, is se- <209> cure, though he be in the knowledge of his debtor's insolvency. *Sibi enim vigilavit,*[9] says the author:‖ a doctrine very just with respect to a court of common law, but very averse to Praetorian law or that of equity.

The defects of the foregoing system are many, but so obvious as to make a list unnecessary. I shall mention two particulars only, being of great importance. The first is, that the necessity of establishing a public mark of bankruptcy which every one is presumed to know, seems to have been altogether overlooked by the Romans. Even the *missio in possessionem,* as

6. The administrator of the estate of an insolvent debtor.

* l. 6. §7. Quae in fraud[em] cred[itorum (In fraud of creditors), D 42.8.6.7: Watson iv: 559] l. 10. §16. eod. [D 42.8.10.16: Watson iv: 562].

7. "Admission into possession"; a coercive measure in Roman law, by which the Praetor authorized a claimant to enter into possession of his adversary's property.

8. "An accomplice in fraud."

† l. 9. eod. [D 42.8.9: Watson iv: 561].

‡ l. 6. §11. eod. [D 42.8.6.11: Watson iv: 560–61].

§ l. 1. §2. eod. [D 42.8.1.2: Watson iv: 559–60].

9. "For he is looking after his own interests."

‖ l. 6. §7. Quae in fraud[em] cred[itorum (In fraud of creditors), D 42.8.6.7: Watson iv: 559].

mentioned above, was not held such a mark. It is true, that after such possession no creditor could take payment from the bankrupt. But why? Not because of the creditor's *mala fides,* but because of the creditors in general, being put in possession of the bankrupt's funds, acquired thereby a *jus pignoris;*[10] and in the division of the price were accordingly intitled each to a rateable proportion. I observe next, that it is a great oversight in the Roman law, to neg- <210> lect that remarkable period which runs between the first act of bankruptcy and the *missio in possessionem.* In that period generally all contrivances are set on foot to cover the effects of the bankrupt, or to prefer favourite creditors.

In England, the regulations concerning bankrupts are extended farther than in the Roman law, and are brought much nearer the rules of equity above laid down. The nomination of commissioners by the chancellor upon application of the creditors, is, in effect, the same with the nomina-tion of a *curator bonis* in the Roman law. But the foregoing defects of the Roman law are supplied, by declaring a debtor's absconding or keeping out of the way, termed *the first act of bankruptcy,* to be a public mark or notification of bankruptcy, of which no person is suffered to plead ig-norance. From that moment the hands both of the bankrupt and of his creditors are fettered: he can do no deed that is prejudicial to his creditors in general, or to any one in particular: they, on the other hand, are not permitted to receive a voluntary payment, nor to operate their payment by legal execution. <211>

It is perhaps not easy to invent a regulation better calculated for ful-filling the rules of equity, than that now mentioned. It may be thought indeed, that the absconding or keeping out of the way, supposing it mo-mentary only, is a circumstance too slight and too private to be imposed upon all the world as notorious. But the English bankrupt-statutes are confined to mercantile people, who live by buying and selling: and with respect to a merchant, his absconding or keeping out of the way is a mark of bankruptcy neither slight nor obscure. Merchants convene regularly in the exchange; a retailer ought to be found in his shop or warehouse; and their absconding or absence without a just cause is conspicuous. A creditor

10. "A right of pledge": the creditor's right in property pledged to secure a debt.

may happen, for some time, to be ignorant of the first act of bankruptcy; but a singular case must not be made an exception: justice must be distributed by general rules, tho' at the expence of a few individuals; in order to prevent judges from becoming arbitrary, and law-suits endless. There is indeed a hardship in this regulation with respect to commerce, which is softened by <212> a late statute,* enacting, That money received from a bankrupt in the course of trade and dealing before the commission of bankruptcy sued forth, whether in payment of goods sold to the bankrupt, or of a bill of exchange accepted by him, shall not be claimed by the assignees to the bankruptcy, unless it be made appear, that the person so receiving payment was in the knowledge of the debtor's bankruptcy. This is in effect declaring with respect to payment received in the course of trade, that the issuing the commission of bankruptcy is to be deemed the first public mark or notification of bankruptcy, and not what is called the first act of bankruptcy.

The first bankrupt-act we have in Scotland is an act of sederunt ratified by statute 1621, cap. 18,[11] intitled, "A ratification of the act of the Lords of Council and Session against unlawful dispositions and alienations made by dyvours[12] and bankrupts." In this act of sederunt, two articles only are brought under consideration. First, Fraudulent contrivances to withdraw a bankrupt's effects from his <213> creditors, by making simulate and feigned conveyances. Second, The partiality of bankrupts, by making payment to favourite creditors, neglecting others. With respect to the first, it is set forth in the preamble, "That the fraud, malice, and falsehood of dyvours and bankrupts was become so frequent as to be in hazard of dissolving all trust and commerce among the subjects of this kingdom; that many, by their apparent wealth in land and goods, and by their show of conscience and honesty, having obtained credit, intend not to pay their debts, but either live riotously, or withdraw themselves or their goods

* 19. Geo. II. cap. 32 [An Act for amending the law relating to bankrupts, 1746].

11. Act of sederunt 12 July 1620, ratified in 1621, c. 18: *APS* iv: 615, An ratificatioun of the act of the lordis of counsell and sessioun made in Julij 1620 aganis unlauchfull dispositiones and alienationes made by dyvoures and banckruptis [Bankruptcy Act 1621].

12. *Dyvour:* a bankrupt, who made cession of all his goods in favor of his creditors and who was required to wear "the dyvour's habit"—a yellow hat or bonnet—and to sit on a pillory near the market cross of Edinburgh.

forth of this realm to elude all execution of justice: and to that effect, and in manifest defraud of their creditors, make simulate and fraudful alienations, dispositions, and other securities of their lands, reversions, teinds, goods, actions, debts, and other subjects belonging to them, to their wives, children, kinsmen, allies, and other confident and interposed persons, without any true, lawful, or necessary cause, and without any just or true price; whereby the creditors and cau- <214> tioners are falsely and godlessly defrauded of their just debts, and many honest families are ruined." For remedying this evil, it is ordained and declared, "First, That all alienations, dispositions, assignations, made by the debtor, of any of his lands, teinds, reversions, actions, debts, or goods, to any conjunct or confident person, without true, just, and necessary causes, and without a just price really paid, shall be of no force or effect against prior creditors. Second, Whoever purchases from the said interposed persons any of the bankrupt's lands or goods, at a just price, or in satisfaction of debt, *bona fide,* without being partaker of the fraud, shall be secure. Third, The receiver of the price shall make the same forthcoming to the bankrupt's creditors. Fourth, It shall be sufficient evidence of the fraud intended against the creditors, if they verify by writ, or by oath of the party-receiver of any right from the dyvour or bankrupt, that the same was made without any true, just, and necessary cause, or without any true price; or that the lands or goods of the bankrupt being sold by the <215> interposed person, the price is to be converted to the bankrupt's profit and use. Fifth, All such bankrupts, and interposed persons for covering or executing their frauds, and all others who shall give counsel and assistance to the said bankrupts in devising and practising their frauds and godless deceits to the prejudice of their true creditors, shall be reputed and holden dishonest, false, and infamous persons, incapable of all honours, dignities, benefices, and offices, or to pass upon an inquest or assize, or to bear witness in judgement or outwith, in any time coming."

The clause restraining a bankrupt's partiality in making payment to favourite creditors and neglecting others, is expressed in the following terms: "If any bankrupt, or interposed person partaker of his fraud, shall make any voluntary payment or right to any person, in defraud of the more timely diligence of another creditor, having served inhibition, or used horning, arrestment, comprising, or other lawful mean to affect the bankrupt's lands, goods, or price thereof: in that case the bankrupt, or interposed <216> person, shall be bound to make the same forthcoming to the creditor having used the more timely diligence. And this creditor shall likewise have good action to recover from the co-creditor posterior in diligence what was voluntarily paid to him in defraud of the pursuer."

With respect to the article concerning fraud, this act is an additional instance of what I have had more than one opportunity to observe, that the court of session, for many years after its institution, acted as a court of common law only. No wrong calls louder for a remedy than frauds committed by bankrupts in withdrawing their effects from their creditors; and yet from the preamble of the act it appears, that the court of session had not, before that period, assumed the power to redress any of these frauds. Nor is it clear that the power was assumed by the session as a court of equity: it is more presumeable that the court considered itself as a court of common law acting by legislative authority; first by authority of its own act, and afterward by authority of the act of parliament:—I say by authority of its own act; for the court of session <217> being empowered by parliament to make regulations for the better administration of justice, an act of sederunt originally was held equivalent to an act of parliament.[a]

This act, framed as we ought to suppose by the wisest heads of the nation, is however not only shamefully imperfect, but in several particulars grossly unjust. No general regulations are established concerning the conduct of the bankrupt, of his creditors, or of the judges: no overt act is fixed as a public notification of bankruptcy: nor is there any regulation barring the creditors from taking advantage of each other by precipitancy of execution. Such blindness is the less excusable in judges to whom the Roman law was no stranger; and who, in an English bankrupt-statute passed a few

a. Acts by a bankrupt defrauding his creditors, as mentioned at the beginning of this chapter, are left without remedy by common law. As bankruptcy does not divest a man of his property, he is understood at common law to have the same power over his estate that he had before, however prejudicial to his creditors his acts and deeds may be, and however ill intended.

years before, had a good model to copy after, and to <218> improve. But
this act, which has occasioned many irregular and even unjust decisions,
must be examined more particularly.

In the first place, There cannot be a more pregnant instance of unskilfulness in making laws, than the clause confining the evidence of fraud to
the writ or oath of the person who benefits by it. A very little insight into
human nature would have taught our judges, that it is in vain to think
of detecting fraud by such evidence. Covered crimes must be detected by
circumstances, or not at all; and such matters, being beyond the reach of
a general rule, ought to be left with judges, without any rule other than
to determine every case according to its peculiar circumstances. We shall
accordingly have occasion to see, that the court of session were forc'd to
abandon the evidence established by themselves; and in every instance
to indulge such proof as the nature of the case will admit. In the second
place, With respect to deeds done against creditors, it must appear strange,
that the act of sederunt should be confined to actual fraud; a crime that
merits punish- <219> ment, and to which accordingly a punishment is
annexed in the act itself. It bars not a gratuitous deed in favour of children
or others, however prejudicial to creditors; provided it be not granted purposely to hurt them, but to benefit the donees. This palpable defect in the
act will be accounted for by an observation one has occasion to make daily,
that in reforming abuses, there is commonly a degree of diffidence, which
prevents the innovation from being carried its due length. The repressing
actual fraud was a great improvement, which filled the mind, and scarce
left room for a thought of further improvement. And, in all probability,
it appeared a bolder step to supply the defect of common law by voiding
frauds committed by bankrupts, than to supply the defect of the statute
by voiding also gratuitous deeds.

So much upon the first article. With respect to the second, contrived
to restrain the bankrupt from acting partially among his creditors, it is
not in my power to give it any colour either of justice or expediency. I
have been much disposed to think, that an inchoated act of execution was
in- <220> tended by the legislature to be the public notification of bankruptcy, so often mentioned. But I am obliged to relinquish that thought,
when I consider, that our statute 1621 is not confined to merchants, but

comprehends the whole body of the people; and that an inchoated act of horning or arrestment is scarce a mark of bankruptcy at present, far less when the act was made, with respect especially to landed men. And that in fact it was not intended a mark or notification of bankruptcy, is clear from the following considerations, that creditors are not barred by it from forcing payment by legal execution; nor even the bankrupt from acting partially among his creditors, except with regard to those only who have commenced execution: all the other creditors are left at his mercy as much as before the act was made. This however is an omission only; and I could wish, for the honour of my country, that nothing but an omission could be objected to this clause: but it is fruitless to disguise that it is grossly unjust. There ought, no doubt, to be a remedy against the creditor who obtains payment by the bankrupt's partiality: but to <221> make him surrender the whole to the creditor who has got the start in execution, is an unjust remedy; for justice only requires that he should surrender a part, that both may be upon a level. To make him surrender the whole, is indeed an effectual cure to the bankrupt's partiality, but a cure that is worse than the disease; worse, I say, because the partiality of an individual is a spectacle much less disgusting than is the partiality of law. This regulation is unjust, even supposing the bankruptcy to be known to the creditor who receives payment. But how much more glaring the injustice, where he happens to be ignorant of that fact? the money he receives becomes undoubtedly his property; and justice forfeits no man of his property without a fault. Nor is this all. The regulation, in itself unjust, is no less so with respect to consequences. Voluntary payment effectually binds up the creditor from legal execution: in the mean time the funds of the bankrupt are swept away by other creditors: and the creditor is forfeited for condescending to take payment, being left without a remedy. Viewing now this regulation with respect to u- <222> tility, it appears no less inexpedient than unjust: to excite creditors to take the start in execution, it holds out a premium, to which they are not intitled by the rules of justice; a premium that tends to a very unhappy consequence, namely, to overwhelm with precipitant execution honest dealers, who, treated with humanity, might have emerged out of their difficulties, and have become bold and prosperous traders.

The next bankrupt-statute, in order of time is the act 62, parl. 1661,[13] ranking *pari passu* with the first effectual apprising, all apprisings of a prior date, and all led within year and day of it; for I shall have occasion to show afterward, that this statute ought to be classed with those concerning bankruptcy, though not commonly considered in that light. But the connection of matter, more intimate than that of time, leads me first to the act 5. parl. 1696,[14] intended evidently to supply the defects of the act 1621. Experience discovered in the act 1621 one defect mentioned above, that no ouvert act is ascertained, to be held the first act of bankruptcy as well as a public notification of it. This <223> defect is supplied by the act 1696, in the following manner. An insolvent debtor under execution by horning and caption, is declared a notour bankrupt, provided he be imprisoned, or retire to a sanctuary, or fly, or abscond, or defend his person by force. This is one term, and counting sixty days back, another term is fixed; after which all partial deeds by a bankrupt among his creditors are prohibited. The words are, "All dispositions, assignations, or other deeds, granted by the bankrupt at any time within sixty days before his notour bankruptcy, in favour of a creditor, directly or indirectly, for his satisfaction or further security, preferring him to other creditors, shall be null and void."

It will be observed, that this statute, with respect to the legal commencement of bankruptcy, differs widely from those made in England. And indeed, to have copied these statutes, by making absconding, or keeping out of the way, the first act of bankruptcy, would in this country have been improper. In England, arrestment of the debtor's person till he find bail being commonly the first act of exe- <224> cution, a debtor, to avoid imprisonment, must abscond or keep out of the way the moment his credit is suspected; and therefore in England, absconding or keeping out of the way is a mark of bankruptcy not at all ambiguous. But in Scotland, this mark of bankruptcy would always be too late; for with us there must be several steps of execution before a bankrupt be forc'd to abscond, letters of horning, a charge, a denunciation, a caption. In this country therefore it was necessary to specify some mark of bankruptcy antecedent to ab-

---

13. *APS* vii: 317: 1661, c. 344, Act for ordering the payment of debts betwixt creditor and debtor [Diligence Act 1661].

14. *APS* x: 33: 1696, c. 5, Act for declaring nottour bankrupt [Bankruptcy Act 1696].

sconding. The mark that would correspond the nearest to absconding in England, is denunciation upon a horning; for after receiving a charge, the debtor, if he have any credit, will be upon his guard against denunciation, supposing it to be established as a public notification of bankruptcy. But our legislature perhaps showed greater penetration, in commencing bankruptcy from a term of which even the bankrupt must be ignorant. Sudden bankruptcy is so rare, as scarce to deserve the attention of the legislature. A man commonly becomes bankrupt long before he is publicly known to be so by <225> ultimate execution; and considering that the suspicious period, during which a debtor is tempted to act fraudulently, commences the moment he foresees the ruin of his credit, which is generally more than two months before his notour bankruptcy, it appears the safest course to tie up a bankrupt's hands during that period. Such retrospect from notour bankruptcy cannot be productive of any wrong, if it have no other effect but to void securities, which creditors obtain by force of execution, or by the voluntary deed of their debtor. And therefore the statute 1696, as far as concerns the commencement of bankruptcy, seems wise and political; and perhaps the best that is to be found in any country.

The statute adheres strictly to the principles of equity above laid down, as far as it voids every security granted to one creditor in prejudice of the rest, within sixty days before notour bankruptcy. But I must add, with regret, that it goes unwarily too far when it voids also without distinction conveyances made in satisfaction or payment of debt. To deprive a man of a subject, the property of which <226> he has obtained *bona fide* in lieu of a debt, is, as observed above, inconsistent with an inviolable rule of justice, That an innocent man ought never to be forfeited of his property: and therefore a conveyance of this nature ought not to be voided, unless the creditor receiving satisfaction be in the knowledge of his debtor's bankruptcy.

But this is an error of small importance compared with what follows. After the commencement of bankruptcy, ascertained as above, a bankrupt is prohibited to act partially among his creditors; and yet creditors are permitted, as in the act 1621, to act partially among themselves, and to prevent[15] each other by legal execution. To permit a creditor to take by

15. That is, pre-empt.

legal execution what he is prohibited to receive voluntarily, is a glaring absurdity. Payment or satisfaction obtained *bona fide,* whether from the bankrupt himself, or by force of execution, ought to be sustained: but after the commencement of bankruptcy, there is the same justice for voiding a security obtained by execution, that there is for voiding a security obtained <227> voluntarily from the bankrupt. And yet our legislature has deviated so widely from justice, as to give full scope to execution even after notour bankruptcy. Nothing can be conceived more gross. It had been a wise regulation, that upon notour bankruptcy a factor should be appointed, to convert the bankrupt's effects into money, and to distribute the same among the creditors at the sight of the court of session. This regulation, established in Rome and in England, ought not to have been overlooked. But if it was not palatable, our legislature ought at least to have prohibited more to be taken by any execution, than a rateable proportion; for after notour bankruptcy no creditor can be *in bona fide* to take payment of his whole debt.

The injustice and absurdity of permitting a creditor to take by execution what he is discharged to receive from his debtor voluntarily, though left without remedy by our two capital bankrupt-statutes, have not however been altogether overlooked. And I now proceed to the regulations made to correct that evil, which, for the sake of connection, I have reserved to the last place, though one of these regulations comes in <228> point of time before the act 1696. The great load of debt contracted during our civil wars in the reign of Charles I. and the decay of credit occasioned thereby, produced the act 62. parl. 1661,[16] laying down regulations suited to the times, for easing debtors and restoring credit. Among other articles, "All apprisings deduced since the 1st of January 1652, before the first effectual apprising, or after, but within year and day of the same, are appointed to come in *pari passu,* as if one apprising had been deduced for the whole." This regulation is general without respect to bankruptcy. But whatever stretches may be necessary for a particular exigency, it is evident, that the regulation cannot be justified as a perpetual law, except

16. *APS* vii: 317: 1661, c. 344, Act for ordering the payment of debts betwixt creditor and debtor [Diligence Act 1661].

upon supposition that all the apprisings are deduced after the debtor is insolvent. A debtor while he is in good circumstances, may pay his debts or grant real securities in what order he pleases. By using this privilege he harms none of his creditors: they have no ground for challenging such a deed at the time when it is granted; and his supervening bankruptcy cannot afford them a ground <229> of challenge which they had not at first. A security obtained by an apprising or adjudication is precisely similar. If the debtor be solvent when an adjudication is obtained by a creditor, the other creditors suffer not by it; and the adjudger who has thus fairly obtained a security, must be intitled to make the best of his right, whether the debtor afterward become insolvent or no. I have reason therefore to place the foregoing statute, considered as perpetual, among those which have been enacted in the case of bankruptcy: and in order to fulfil the rules of justice, the court of session, as a court of equity, will consider it in that light. The involved circumstances of debtors and creditors at the time of the statute, made it a salutary regulation to bring in apprisers *pari passu,* even where the debtor was solvent, though evidently a stretch against justice: but to adhere strictly to the regulation at present, when there is not the same necessity, is to adhere rigidly to the words against the mind and intendment of the legislature; for surely it could not be intended, that a creditor should for ever be deprived of the preference he obtains by being the first <230> adjudger, even where the other creditors are not hurt by that preference. That after the debtor's bankruptcy a creditor should not have more than his proportion of the common fund, is extremely just; and so far the statute ought to be held perpetual. What farther is enacted to answer a particular purpose, ought to be considered as temporary; because the legislature could not mean it to be perpetual.

If then the foregoing statute be held to be perpetual, it must be confined to the case of bankruptcy; and in that view it deserves to be immortal. The first adjudication may be justly held a public mark or notification of the debtor's bankruptcy, warning the other creditors to bestir themselves; and a year commonly is sufficient for them to lead adjudications, which, by authority of the statute, will intitle each creditor to a proportion of the debtor's real estate. This was a happy commencement of a much wanted reformation. The court of session, taking example, ventured to declare by an act of sederunt,* That the priority of a creditor's confirmation shall <231> afford no preference in competition with other creditors confirming within six months of the death of their debtor.[17] By another act of sederunt,[†] All arrestments within sixty days preceding the notour bankruptcy, or within four months thereafter, are ranked *pari assu;* and every creditor who poinds within sixty days preceding the notour bankruptcy, or within four months thereafter, is obliged to communicate a proportion to the other creditors suing him within a limited time.[‡] In the heat of reformation, the last-mentioned regulation is carried too far. Poinding operates at once a transference of the property and a discharge of the debt; and supposing a poinder to be ignorant of his debtor's insolvency, which is frequently the case where the execution precedes the notour bankruptcy, there is no rule in equity more than at common law to oblige the poinder to communicate any proportion to the other creditors. Nay, it is possible that a debtor may be solvent within sixty days of his notour bankruptcy: a poinding against him in that case, which wounds <232> not the other creditors, ought not to afford them the shadow of a claim.[a]

The principles of equity ripening gradually, our zeal for the act 1661 has increased; and there is a visible tendency in our judges to make the remedy still more complete. In order to that end, the court of session, as a court of equity, might have enlarged the time given by the statute for leading adjudications. The principles of justice authorise a still bolder step, which is, to put upon an equal footing all adjudications led upon debts existing before the first adjudication. But the court of session, wavering always as

---

    * Feb. 28. 1662 [Act anent executors-creditors, in *AS* 82].

    17. *Confirming:* this refers to the confirmation of the creditor of the deceased debtor as executor-creditor.

    † August 9. 1754 [Act of sederunt anent poindings and arrestments [10 August 1754], in *AS* 478].

    ‡ Act of sederunt, ibid.

    a. Experience soon suggested, that the two last-mentioned acts of sederunt required several emendations; for which reason, being temporary only, they were allowed to run out. And thus again we were laid open to the rapacity of creditors endeavouring to prevent one another by legal execution; till a remedy was provided by a British statute, that shall be mentioned at the end of this chapter *cum elogio* [with praise], being the most perfect bankrupt-statute that ever was contrived by the wit of man, as far as moveables are concerned.

to their equitable powers, have not hitherto ventured so far. Not adverting to an obvious doctrine, That in order to fulfil justice it is <233> lawful to improve means laid down in a statute, the court of session hath not attempted directly to enlarge the time for bringing in adjudgers *pari passu:* but they do the same thing every day indirectly; for upon the application of any creditor, setting forth, "That if the common *induciae*[18] required in the processes of constitution[19] and adjudication be not abridged in his favour, he cannot hope to complete his adjudication within year and day of the adjudication first effectual," the court, without requiring any cause to be assigned for the delay, give authority for adjudging summarily; which in effect is declaring, that all adjudgers shall have the benefit of the statute, provided the summons of adjudication be within year and day of the first effectual adjudication. It may be questioned whether this be not too indulgent: the extraordinary privilege of shortening the forms, ought not to be permitted, unless the creditor can assign some good cause for his delay; because law ought not to be stretched in favour of those who suffer by their own fault or neglect. It is curious at the same time to observe, that a court, like an individual, <234> afraid of a bold step, will, to shun it, venture upon one no less bold in reality, though perhaps less so in appearance: for to abridge or dispense with forms, salutary in themselves and sanctified by inveterate practice, is an act of authority no less extraordinary, than to enlarge the time afforded in a statute for ranking adjudgers *pari passu.*

But after all, the foregoing regulations for putting creditors upon a level in the case of bankruptcy, are mere palliatives: they soften the disease, but strike not at the root. The court of session tried once a bolder and more effectual remedy, borrowed from the law of Rome and of England, that of naming a factor for managing and disposing of the bankrupt's moveable funds, in order that the price may be equally distributed among the creditors. It was made for a trial, and in that view was made temporary. Why it was not renewed and made perpetual, I cannot guess, if it was not that the court doubting of its powers, thought a statute necessary. One thing

---

18. The period allowed for the appearance of a person served with legal process (from *indutiae,* "a pause").

19. *Constitute:* to determine or establish a debt in court.

is certain, that the late bankrupt-statute, mentioned below, was <235> framed by the judges of that court, and procured upon their application.

According to the method proposed in the beginning, nothing now remains but the operations of the court of session, to which I proceed, beginning with decisions relative to the statutes, and concluding with decisions founded on equity independent of the statutes. And first, the statute 1621 has been extended to a lease of land set to a trustee at an undervalue, in order that the bankrupt himself might enjoy the profits. A lease of this nature, though not comprehended under the words of the act, comes plainly under its spirit and intention; and therefore it was the duty of the court to extend the act to that case. A fraudulent bond granted by a bankrupt in order to withdraw from the true creditors a part of the fund for the bankrupt's own behoof, is another example of the same kind. For, as Sir George Mackenzie observes in his explication of this act, "Though neither tacks nor bonds be comprehended under the letter of the law, yet the reason of the law extends to them; and in laws founded on the principles of reason, extensions from the <236> same principles are natural. And in laws introduced for obviating of cheats, extensions are most necessary, because the same subtle and fraudulent inclination that tempted the debtor to cheat his creditors, will tempt him likewise to cheat the law, if the wisdom and prudence of the judge do not interpose."[20] A discharge granted by the bankrupt in order to cover a debt from his creditors for his own behoof, will also come under the act by an equitable interpretation.[21]

With respect to the evidence required in the first article of the statute 1621, for detecting fraudulent deeds, the court of session hath assumed a power proper and peculiar to a court of equity. It has been forc'd to abandon the oath or writ of the partaker of the fraud, being a means altogether insufficient to answer the purpose of the statute, and in place of it to lay hold of such evidence as can be had. It is accordingly the prac-

20. Sir George Mackenzie, *Observations upon the 18th Act of the 23d Parliament of King James the Sixth against Dispositions Made in Defraud of Creditors &c,* in *The Works of That Eminent and Learned Lawyer Sir George Mackenzie of Rosehaugh,* 2 vols. (Edinburgh: James Watson, 1716–22), vol. 2, p. 8.

21. In the first edition, Kames here includes a paragraph discussing *Street v. Mason.* See Appendix, p. 515, Extract [1st: 236–37]. In the third edition, the case is discussed above, p. 102.

tice of the court, after weighing circumstances, to presume sometimes in favour of the deed till fraud be proved, and sometimes against the deed till a proof be brought of its being fair and honest. Thus a bond bearing bor- <237> rowed money, granted by a bankrupt to a conjunct and confident person,[22] was presumed to be fairly granted for the cause expressed; and the burden of proving it to have been granted without any just cause, was, in terms of the act, laid upon the pursuer of the reduction.* A disposition by a bankrupt of his whole heritage to his son-in-law, upon the narrative of a price paid, was found probative, unless redargued[23] by the disponee's oath.† A disposition by a bankrupt to his brother, bearing to be for security of a sum instantly borrowed, was sustained; but admitting the cause expressed to be redargued by the disponee's oath. And the judges distinguished this case from that of a disposition bearing a valuable consideration in general, which must be otherwise verified than by the disposition.‡

On the other hand, in a reduction upon the act 1621 of a bond bearing borrowed money granted by a bankrupt to his brother, the judges thought, that though <238> bonds *inter conjunctos*[24] may prove where commercial dealings appear; yet as no such dealings were alleged, and as the creditor's circumstances made the advancement of so large a sum improbable, the bond was not sustained as probative of its cause.§ A disposition of land by a bankrupt to his brother, bearing a valuable consideration in general, was not sustained as probative of its narrative in prejudice of prior creditors; and it was laid on the disponee to astruct[25] the same.‖ And he having specified, that it was for a sum of money advanced in specie to his brother,

22. Someone related by blood and connected by interest; or (under the Act 1621, c. 18) someone to whom an alienation of property is made by an insolvent person, without cause.

* Durie, Jan. 22. 1630, Hope Pringle contra Carre [M 12553: Hoppringle contra Ker].

23. *Redargue:* disprove or refute.

† Durie, Jan. 17. 1632, Skene contra Beatson [M 896].

‡ Gosford, Nov. 28. 1673, Campbell contra Campbell [M 9396].

24. "Between family members."

§ Fountainhall, Forbes, Dec. 5. 1707, Maclearie contra Glen [M 12565, M 12563: M'Lierie contra Glen].

25. Establish.

‖ Stair, Nov. 29. 1671, Whitehead contra Lidderdale [M 12557].

which he offered to depone upon, the court found this not relevant.* In a similar case, the disponee having produced two bonds due to him by the disponer, and offering to give his oath that these were the cause of the disposition, the court thought this sufficient.† <239>

A disposition by a bankrupt to a conjunct or confident person, referring to a prior engagement as its cause, is not sustained unless the prior engagement be instructed.[26] Thus an assignment made by a bankrupt to a conjunct and confident person, bearing to be a security for sums due to the assignee, was presumed to be *in fraudem creditorum,*[27] unless the assignee would bring evidence of the debts referred to in the deed.‡ And the assignee specifying, that he took the assignment for behoof of a third party, one of the bankrupt's creditors, the assignment was sustained.§ An assignment by a bankrupt to his brother, bearing to be a security for debts owing to him, was presumed gratuitous, unless the assignee would instruct otherwise than by his own oath, that he was creditor.‖ To support the narrative of a disposition by a bankrupt to his son, bearing for its cause cer- <240> tain debts undertaken by the son, it was judged sufficient that the son offered to prove by the creditors mentioned in the disposition, that he had made payment to them in terms of the disposition.** A disposition by a bankrupt to his brother, bearing to be a security for certain sums due by bond, was thought sufficiently supported by production of the bonds, unless the pursuer would offer to prove, that the bonds were granted after insolvency. Here no suspicious circumstances occurred, other than the conjunction itself; and if such a proof of a valuable consideration be not held sufficient, all commerce among relations will be at an end. It might upon the same footing be doubted, whether even a proof by witnesses

* Stair, Dec. 14. 1671, inter eosdem [Whitehead contra Lidderdale, M 12557].

† Stair, Dec. 15. 1671, Duff contra Forbes of Culloden [M 12430].

26. *Instruct:* to confirm by evidence (Scots law).

27. "In fraud of the creditors."

‡ Durie, Haddington, Feb. 12. 1622, Dennison contra Young [M 12549, in Kames, *Dictionary,* vol. 2, p. 252].

§ Hope, (De creditoribus), Feb. 27. 1622, inter eosdem [that is, Dennison contra Young: M 12549; in Kames, *Dictionary,* vol. 2, p. 252].

‖ Durie, Jan. 29. 1629, Auld contra Smith [M 12552]; Stair, July 15. 1670, Hamilton contra Boyd [M 12555].

** Stair, Jan. 9. 1672, Robertson contra Robertson [M 12559].

of the actual delivery of the money would be sufficient, which might be done simulately, in order to support a bond, as well as a bond be granted simulately in order to support a disposition.* It will be observed, that some of the foregoing cases are of bonds granted after bankruptcy, as for <241> borrowed money, which ought not to be sustained in equity. But the court of session, as will be seen afterward, is in the practice of sustaining such bonds, for no better reason than that they are not prohibited by the bankrupt-statutes.

With respect to the second article of the act 1621, prohibiting payment to be made in prejudice of a creditor who is *in cursu diligentiae*,[28] the court of session ventured to correct the injustice of this article, by refusing to oblige a creditor who had obtained payment, to deliver the money to the creditor first in execution; unless it could be verified, that at the time of the payment the debtor was commonly reputed a bankrupt.† A debtor commonly reputed a bankrupt will always be held such by his creditors; and a creditor knowing of his debtor's bankruptcy cannot justly take more than his proportion. Where payment is made before inchoated execution, and yet within threescore days of notour bankruptcy, the court of session hath no occasion to extend its equitable powers to <242> support such payment, which stands free of both statutes; for the statute 1621 challenges no payments but what are made after inchoated execution, and payments are not at all mentioned in the statute 1696. Payments after notour bankruptcy are in a different case: they are barred in equity, though not by this statute.

The second branch of the act 1621, securing a creditor who has commenced execution against the partiality of his debtor, is so strictly interpreted by the court of session, that where a security is voided by a creditor prior in execution, the whole benefit is given to him. And the act 1696 is so strictly interpreted, that moveables being delivered to a creditor in satisfaction of his debt, the transaction was voided because delivery was made within sixty days before notour bankruptcy;‡ though, abstracting

---

* Fountainhall, Feb. 22. 1711, Rule contra Purdie [M 12566].

28. "In the course of doing diligence"; that is, in the course of executing a judgment.

† Dalrymple, Bruce, June 7. 1715, Tweedie contra Din [M 1039].

‡ Dalrymple, Jan. 27. 1715, Forbes of Ballogie [M 1124]; July 19. 1728, Smith contra Taylor [M 1128 and 1189].

from the injustice of depriving an innocent man of his property, the court, in interpreting a rigorous statute, ought to have limited the words within their narrowest meaning, by finding, that <243> moveables, the commerce of which ought to be free, are not comprehended in the statute.

By the act 1696, as above observed, "All dispositions, &c. granted by a debtor within sixty days before his notour bankruptcy, in favour of a creditor, for his satisfaction or security, preferring him before other creditors, are declared null and void." This clause admits a double meaning: it may import a total nullity; or it may import a nullity as far only as that creditor is preferred before others. The former meaning would be rational, supposing the creditors to be barred from execution as the bankrupt is from alienation: but as they are left free, the latter meaning ought to be adopted, as what answers the purpose of the legislature, and fulfils the rules of justice. And yet, I know not by what misapprehension, the former is adopted by the court of session. A disposition accordingly of this kind was voided totally; without even giving the disponee the benefit of a *pari passu* preference with the other creditors, who had attached the subject by legal execu- <244> tion.* This is laying hold of the words of a statute, without regarding its spirit and intendment. It is worse: it is giving a wrong sense to an ambiguous clause, in opposition to the spirit and intendment. The obvious purpose of the act 1696 is not to deprive a bankrupt altogether of the management of his affairs, for in that case a *curator bonis* must have been appointed, but only to bar him from acting partially. It clearly follows, that a court of equity, supporting the spirit of the law, ought not to have carried the reduction farther than to redress the inequality intended by the disposition. Yet the court of session, in this case, was no less partial to the pursuers of the reduction, than the disposition was to the defendant; and their decree exceeded the bounds of justice on the one side, as much as the bankrupt's disposition did on the other. The solidity of this reasoning will be clearly apprehended, in applying it to a security granted by a debtor in good credit, but who, within sixty days after, becomes a notour bankrupt. The <245> creditor, being *in optima fide*[29] to take a security

---

* Fountainhall, Dalrymple, Dec. 4. 1704, Man contra Reid [M 1008]; July 19. 1728, Smith contra Taylor [M 1128 and 1189, in Kames, *Dictionary,* vol. 1, pp. 83–84].
29. "In the best faith."

in these circumstances, merits no punishment. Another creditor, however, anxious about his debt, attaches the subject by legal execution; and thus gets the start of the disponee, whose hands by the disposition are tied up from execution. Could one listen with patience to a decision that voided the disposition altogether, and preferred the other creditor?

With respect to particulars that come not under either of the bankrupt-statutes, but are left to be regulated by equity, it is distressing to observe the never-ceasing fluctuation of the court of session between common law and equity. In many instances, the court hath given way to the injustice of common law without affording a remedy; for a very odd reason indeed, That no remedy is provided by statute. In other instances, the court, exerting its equitable powers, has boldly applied the remedy. I proceed to examples of both.

A sale by a notour bankrupt after the act 1696, was supported for the following reason, That it is not prohibited by the act.* <246> Very true. But, as above demonstrated, it is prohibited by justice and by utility; and upon these *media* it ought to have been voided. And a bond for money was sustained, though lent to a known bankrupt.† In those days, it seems to have been assumed as a maxim, That every exercise of property even by a notour bankrupt, however destructive to his creditors, is lawful, except what are prohibited in express terms by the bankrupt-statutes. Upon the statute 1696 it has been disputed, whether an act be challengeable where no subject is aliened, and yet a partial preference is given. The case was as follows. An heir-apparent having given infeftments of annualrent, did thereafter grant a procuratory to serve himself heir, that his infeftment might accresce to the annualrent-rights. In a competition between these annualrenters and posterior adjudgers, it was objected against the procuratory, That it was granted by a notour bankrupt, and therefore null by the statute 1696; the purpose of which is to annul every partial preference by a bankrupt, *direct or indirect*. It <247> was answered, That the statute mentions only alienations made by the bankrupt, and reaches not every act that may be attended with a consequential damage or benefit to some

---

* Bruce, January 1. 1717, Burgh contra Gray [M 1125].
† Stair, June 28. 1665, Monteith contra Anderson [M 1044].

of the creditors. The court preferred the annualrenters.* Had the service been before the bankruptcy, there could be no reason in equity against it: but a man, who, conscious of his own bankruptcy, performs any act in order to prefer one creditor before another, is unjust; and the creditor who takes advantage of that act, knowing his debtor to be bankrupt, is partaker of the wrong. The court therefore denying a remedy in this case, acted as a court of common law, overlooking its equitable powers.

Opposite to the foregoing instances, I shall mention first a donation, the motive of which is love and favour to the donee, without any formed intention to wrong the creditors, though in effect they are wronged by it. That this case is not provided for in the statute 1621, is evident from every clause in it. Fraud only is repressed: not fraud in a lax sense, signify- <248> ing every moral wrong by which a creditor is disappointed of his payment; but fraud in its proper sense, signifying a deliberate purpose to cheat creditors; that sort of fraud which is criminal and merits punishment: which is put beyond doubt by the final clause, inflicting a punishment fully adequate to fraud in its proper sense. But a gratuitous bond or alienation, of which the intention is precisely what is spoken out, without any purpose to cover the effects from the creditors, is not a fraud in any proper sense, at least not in a sense to merit punishment. This then is left upon equity: and the court of session, directed by the great principle of equity, *Nemo debet locupletari aliena jactura,*[30] makes no difficulty to cut down a gratuitous bond or alienation granted by a bankrupt. With respect to a gratuitous bond, the court I believe has gone farther: it has preferred the creditors upon an eventual bankruptcy, even where the granter was solvent when he made the donation. And indeed the court cannot do otherwise, without deviating from the principle now mentioned. <249>

Next comes a security given by a bankrupt in such circumstances as not to be challengeable upon either of the statutes, being given, for example, before execution is commenced against the bankrupt, and more than sixty days before his bankruptcy becomes notorious. It is made out above, that a court of equity ought to void such a security, even though the creditor,

---

* February 1728, Creditors of Graitney competing [M 1127, in Kames, *Dictionary,* vol. 1, p. 83].

30. "No one should be enriched at another's expense."

ignorant of his debtor's bankruptcy, obtained the same *bona fide.* The court of session, it is true, hath not hitherto ventured to adopt this equitable regulation in its full extent; but it hath made vigorous approaches to it, by voiding such security where-ever any collateral circumstance could be found that appeared to weigh in any degree against the creditor. Thus, a security given by a bankrupt to one of his creditors, who was his near relation, was voided, though the disposition came not under either of the bankrupt-statutes.* In the same manner, a disposition *omnium bonorum,*[31] as a security to a single creditor, is always voided. And here it merits ob-<250> servation, that the court of session acting upon principles of equity, is more correct in its decrees, than where it acts by authority of the statutes; witness the following case. "A debtor against whom no execution was commenced, having granted a disposition *omnium bonorum* as a security to one of his creditors, another creditor arrested in the disponee's hands, and in the forthcoming insisted, that the disposition was null, and that the subject ought to be made forthcoming to him upon his arrestment. The court reduced to the effect of bringing in the arrester *pari passu.*"† The following case, though varying in circumstances, is built upon the same foundation. Robert Grant, conscious of his insolvency, and resolving to prefer his favourite creditors, executed privately in their favour a security upon his land-estate, which in the same private manner he completed by infeftment. This security being kept latent, even from those for whom it was intended, gave no alarm, and Robert Grant did not become a notour bankrupt for many months after. But the <251> peculiar circumstances of this case, a real security bestow'd on creditors who were not making any demand, seisin given clandestinely, &c. were clear evidence of the granter's consciousness of his bankruptcy, as well as of his intention to act partially and unjustly among his creditors; and the court accordingly voided the security as far as it gave preference to the creditors therein named; *November* 10. 1748, *Sir Archibald Grant contra Grant of Lurg.*[32]

---

* Fountainhall, January 28. 1696, Scrymzeour contra Lyon [M 903].

31. "Of all goods."

† February 25. 1737, Cramond contra Bruce [M 893, in Kames, *Dictionary,* vol. 1, p. 67].

32. M 949, from Kames, *Remarkable Decisions,* ii: 167; also M 952.

The principle upon which this decision is founded was admitted in the following case;* though the judgement was laid on a speciality. Fenwick Stow merchant in Berwick, having been employed by the Thistle Bank of Glasgow as an agent for circulating their notes, was indebted to them, February 1768, the sum of £2000. Finding himself insolvent, without hope of retrieving his circumstances, he set on foot a most unjust plan, that of securing his favourite creditors, at the expence of the rest. In that view, he executed privately three heritable bonds, on his land-estate <252> in Scotland, two to his near relations, and the third to the Thistle Bank for the said £2000. These bonds were kept latent,[33] even from the persons concerned, till late in June 1768; at which time, being *in actu proximo*[34] of absconding, the bond to the Thistle Bank was sent to them by post 29th of that month. Upon the 3d July 1768, he left Berwick abruptly, and fled to London; and infeftment was taken upon the bond to the Thistle Bank 13th July. By the debtor's sudden elopement, his other Scotch creditors were deprived of an opportunity to render him notour bankrupt: but upon notice of his absconding, border-warrants were taken out for apprehending his person; and sundry inhibitions were raised and executed 12th and 13th July. In a competition among the bankrupt's creditors, the case between the Thistle Bank and the adjudging creditors was debated in presence; and the following argument was urged for the latter.

A merchant in the course of business purchases goods, draws bills, grants securities. He may even pay one creditor before another, as long as he has a prospect to pay all. But where he is so far dipt as <253> to despair of retrieving his circumstances, and yet delays to declare himself insolvent till he has distributed his effects among his favourite creditors; such management is grossly unjust: it is a fraud which no court of equity will countenance; and it is the very fraud which is the inductive cause of the bankrupt-act 1696. For what other reason are partial preferences cut down by that act, but because they are unjust or fraudulent? And what

* 4th August 1774, Creditors of Fenwick Stow contra Thistle Bank of Glasgow.
33. Concealed. "Rights which remain unknown and concealed are ineffectual against creditors, when in the person of relatives and confidants" (William Bell, *Dictionary and Digest of the Law of Scotland*, rev. ed. George Ross, Edinburgh: Bell & Bradfute, 1861).
34. "On the verge of."

is remarkable in that act, even the *bona fides* of a creditor who obtains a preference, does not secure him, if the preference be granted by the debtor within threescore days of his notour bankruptcy. Nor ought *bona fides* to be regarded in this case: it is fraudulent to prefer a favourite creditor: the *bona fides* of that creditor vanisheth when he is made acquainted with the condition of his debtor; and he is *particeps fraudis* if he pretend to hold the security.

It is a gross mistake that the act 1696 is the only law we have for repressing the partial deeds of a bankrupt. It required indeed a statute to make bankruptcy operate *retro;* and it required a statute to cut down a partial preference *funditus,* so as not even <254> to rank it *pari passu* with other debts. Such effects are far above the power of any court. But though the characteristics of notour bankruptcy are necessary each of them to produce these extraordinary effects, yet the act says not nor insinuates, that any bankrupt who falls not precisely under the description of the statute may without control commit the grossest injustice by preferring one creditor before another. It would be strange indeed to annul *in totum* all partial deeds by one who is a bankrupt in terms of the act 1696, if granted within sixty days antecedent to the notour bankruptcy; and yet to leave a bankrupt at freedom to distribute his effects as he pleases, if but a single circumstance be wanting of those specified in the statute. Our law is not so imperfect. For every wrong there ought to be a remedy; and the court of session, directed by the great principle of justice, will correct every wrong a bankrupt can do to his creditors. So far as the bankrupt-statutes extend, they act as a court of common law: beyond these bounds, they act as a court of equity. Take the following instances of the latter. A debtor advertises his insolvency in the <255> news-papers, and appoints a day for the meeting of his creditors; who meet and name trustees. The bankrupt surely will not after this be suffered to give a real security to one of his creditors in prejudice of the rest; and yet all these steps may have been taken without a single execution against him. A person insolvent having been charged with horning retires to the sanctuary,[35] or steps over the

---

35. The abbey of Holyrood House had the privilege of giving sanctuary to debtors. The 1696 Act for declaring nottour bankrupt (c. 5) made retirement to the abbey by an insolvent a legal bankruptcy.

border. Tho' this case falls not under the act 1696, yet no one can doubt but that every partial preference granted by him will be cut down by the court of session. A peer cannot be brought under the description of the statute, nor a member of the House of Commons during the sitting of parliament. Are such persons under no control with respect to their creditors? Our law would be miserably defective if they were not. Nor is it a novelty for the court of session to undertake the redressing of such wrongs. To cut down *funditus* a security granted by a bankrupt any of the sixty days that precede his bankruptcy, requires that he be a bankrupt in terms of the statute; but as it is repugnant to common justice that a person insolvent should take upon him <256> to parcel out his effects among his creditors unequally, the court of session will rectify this act of injustice by bringing them all in *pari passu*. Thus, a disposition *omnium bonorum* to one creditor has always been cut down as being a partial preference by a debtor who virtually acknowledges himself to be insolvent. A disposition to a near relation suffers the same fate, where the disponer appears to be insolvent. Now of all the cases that have happened, there is not one that bears more evident marks of partiality and injustice in preferring some creditors to the ruin of others. The fact here is the same that occurred in the case, Sir Archibald Grant *contra* Grant of Lurg, namely, a person insolvent granting of his own motive a security for a large sum to creditors who were not pressing him for payment; with the addition, in the present case, of being granted the moment before absconding. There cannot be a more bare-faced act of injustice, and none that requires more to be redressed by the court: the remedy is easy, which is to rank all the creditors *pari passu*.

It was the opinion of the court, that an insolvent person cannot prefer one creditor <257> before another; and that every such partial preference ought to be cut down. But the plurality of the judges voted for supporting the infeftment of the Thistle Bank, on the following ground, "That the Thistle Bank trusted their notes with Fenwick Stow to be put into currency for their behoof, and not with an intention to lend him money; and that Fenwick Stow became their debtor by a breach of trust, in using these notes as his own, which bound him for reparation." This argument occurred in the course of reasoning, and made a sudden impression, which

I am convinced would have been found insufficient had the cause been brought under review. For at that rate, if a man should burn my house, spuilzie my goods, run away with my money, or commit any other delict intitling me to reparation, I ought to be preferred before all his other creditors. He is indeed bound in conscience to repair the hurt he has done me; but is he not equally bound in conscience to pay the sums he has borrowed? Let it be supposed, that Fenwick Stow, instead of taking upon him arbitrarily to prefer one creditor before an- <258> other, had made a fair surrender of his effects, would the Thistle Bank in a competition have been preferred *primo loco?*[36] This would be a new ground of preference, hitherto unknown. If so, it is a clear consequence, that the bankrupt, by his voluntary deed, could not give a preference to the Thistle Bank, which they would not have been intitled to in a competition before the court of session.

After finishing the instances promised, another point demands our attention. With respect to an alienation bearing to be granted for love and favour, or made to a near relation bearing a valuable consideration, a doctrine established in the court of session by a train of decisions, appears singular. It is held, that the purchaser from such disponee, though he pay a full price, is in no better condition than his author; and that a reduction at the instance of the bankrupt's creditors will reach both equally. This doctrine ought not to pass current without examination; for its consequences are terrible. At that rate, every subject acquired upon a lucrative title is withdrawn from commerce for the space at least of forty years. What shall become <259> of those who purchase from heirs, if this doctrine hold? And if a purchaser from an heir of provision,[37] for example, be secure, why not a purchaser from a gratuitous disponee?[38] The only reason urged in support of this doctrine is, That a purchaser cannot

---

36. "In the first place."

37. One who succeeds by virtue of a provision in a settlement.

38. In the equivalent passage in the first edition (p. 243) and second edition (p. 322), the following sentence is added: "What objection should lie against the purchaser is not obvious, considering that a purchaser even from a notour bankrupt is, in the practice of the court of session, held to be secure. This is at least a good *argumentum ad hominem.*" In the following sentence, both editions have the word *appears* where the third uses *bears*.

pretend to be *in bona fide* when his author's right bears to be gratuitous, or is presumed to be so. I do not feel the weight of this reason. The act 1621 gives no foundation for such reduction: for if, even in the case of a fraudulent conveyance to an interposed person, a purchaser *bona fide* from that person be secure, what doubt can there be that a purchaser from a gratuitous disponee is also secure, especially where the gratuitous disponee is innocent of any fraud? And considering this matter with relation to equity, a gratuitous deed is not subject to reduction, unless granted by a bankrupt; and to put a man who purchases from a gratuitous disponee *in mala fide,* the bankruptcy ought also to be known to him. And yet I find not that the purchaser's knowledge of the bankruptcy has ever been held a necessary circumstance; one case excepted, re- <260> ported by Fountainhall:* "It is not sufficient to reduce the purchaser's right that he knew his author's relation to the bankrupt, unless he was also in the knowledge of the bankruptcy; because there is no law to bar a man in good circumstances from making a donation to a near relation. And knowledge, an internal act, must be gathered from circumstances, the most pregnant of which is, that the granter of the gratuitous deed was at the time held and reputed a bankrupt." But now, supposing the bankruptcy known to the purchaser, I deny that this circumstance can support the reduction either at common law or in equity: it is made evident above, that a gratuitous disponee ignorant of his author's bankruptcy, is not bound to yield the subject to the bankrupt's creditors, but only to account to them for the value; and when he disposes of the subject for a full price, this sale, far from disappointing the obligation he is under to the bankrupt's creditors, enables him to perform it. In one case only will the purchaser's right <261> be voided in equity; and that is, where the gratuitous disponee and the purchaser from him are both of them *in mala fide:* a man who takes a gratuitous disposition knowing his author to be bankrupt, is guilty of a wrong, which binds him in conscience to restore the subject itself to the bankrupt's creditors; and the person who purchases from him knowing that he is so bound, being also guilty, is for that reason bound equally to restore.

---

* November 28. 1693, Spence contra Creditors of Dick [M 1015].

The statute 1696, voiding all dispositions, assignments, or other deeds, granted by a bankrupt to a favourite creditor, appears to have no subjects in view but what are locally in Scotland, within the jurisdiction of the court of session. And indeed it would be fruitless to void a disposition of foreign effects granted by a Scotch bankrupt; because such effects will be regulated by the law of the place, and not by a decree pronounced in Scotland. Supposing then such a disposition to be granted, is there no remedy? It is certainly a moral wrong for a bankrupt to convey to one of his creditors what ought to be distributed among all; and the creditor who accepts such security knowing his debtor's <262> insolvency, is accessory to the wrong. Upon that ground, the court of session, tho' they cannot void the security, may ordain the favourite creditor to repair the loss that the other creditors have sustained by it; which will oblige the favourite creditor either to surrender the effects, or to be accountable for the value. And this was decreed in the court of session, July 18. 1758, Robert Syme clerk to the signet contra George Thomson tenant in Dalhousie.[39]

Of late it has been much controverted, whether a disposition *omnium bonorum* by a notour bankrupt to trustees for behoof of his whole creditors, be voidable upon the bankrupt-statutes. Formerly such dispositions were sustained, as not being prohibited by any clause in either of the statutes. But the court at last settled in the following opinion, "That no disposition by a bankrupt can disable his creditors from doing diligence."* This opinion, founded on justice and expediency, though not upon the bankrupt-statutes, ought to <263> govern the court of session as a court of equity. It belongs not to the bankrupt, though proprietor, to direct the management of his funds; but to his creditors, who are more interested in that management than he is. It belongs therefore to the creditors to direct the method by which the funds shall be converted into money for their payment; and if they chuse to have the effects managed by trustees,

---

39. M 1137.

* July 12. 1734, Snee contra Trustees of Anderson [M 1206, from Kames, *Dictionary*, vol. 1, p. 85]. Feb. 3. 1736, Earl of Aberdeen contra Trustees of Blair [M 1208, from Kames, *Dictionary*, vol. 1, p. 85: Earl of Aberdeen contra Creditors of Lewis of Merchiston and Scot of Blair].

it is their privilege, not the bankrupt's, to name the trustees. It follows, however, from this consideration, that those trust-rights only which are imposed by bankrupts upon their creditors, ought to be voided. There lies evidently no objection, either at common law or in equity, against a disposition *omnium bonorum* solicited by the creditors, and granted by the bankrupt to trustees of their naming. On the contrary, a trust-right of that nature, which saves the nomination of a *curator bonis,* as in Rome, or of commissioners, as in England, merits the greatest favour, being an expeditious and frugal method of managing the bankrupt's funds for behoof of his creditors. And supposing such a measure to be concerted among the bulk of <264> the creditors, a court of equity ought not to regard a few dissenting creditors who incline to follow separate measures. The trust-right is good at common law, being an alienation by a proprietor; and it is good in equity as being a just act. It must accordingly afford a preference to the creditors who lay hold of it. A dissenting creditor may, if he please, proceed to execution against his debtor, and he may attach the imaginary reversion implied in the trust-disposition: but such peevish measures cannot hurt the other creditors who are secured by the trust-right; for if that right be not voidable, it must be preferred before an adjudication, or any other execution by a dissenting creditor.

I close this chapter with observing, that since the former edition of this work,[40] all the defects above mentioned of our bankrupt-statutes are remedied by a British statute, 12th Geo. III. cap. 72;[41] of which the summary follows. Upon application of any of the bankrupt's creditors, or upon his own application, his moveable estate is sequestrated, and provision made for a fair and equal distribution of the same among the creditors. In the next place, to bar <265> the preference that a creditor formerly had access to obtain against others by legal execution, the act has a retrospect of thirty

40. The first and second editions end the equivalent chapter at the end of the previous paragraph.

41. An Act for rendering the payment of the creditors of insolvent debtors more equal and expeditious, and for regulating the diligence of the law by arrestment and poinding, and for extending the privilege of bills to promissory notes, and for limiting actions upon bills and promissory notes, in that part of Great Britain called Scotland (1772).

days; within which time an arrestment or poinding gives no preference. And now it may with confidence be pronounced, that no other country can vie with Scotland in the perfection of its bankrupt-laws.

CHAPTER VI

Powers and faculties.

Every right, real or personal, is a legal power. In that extensive sense, there are numberless powers. Every individual hath power over his own property, and over his own person; some over another's property or person. To trace all these powers would be the same with writing an institute of law. The powers under consideration are of a singular kind. They are not rights, properly speaking, but they are means by which rights can <266> be created, a power, for example, to make a man debtor for a sum, a power to charge his land with debt, a power to redeem land from the purchaser.

These powers are of two kinds; powers founded on consent, and powers founded on property. A disposition by a proprietor of land to his heir, containing a clause impowering a third person to charge the heir or the land with a sum, is an example of the first kind: a power thus created is founded on the consent of the heir, signified by his acceptance of the disposition. A power reserved in a settlement of a land-estate, to alter the settlement, or to burden the land with debt, is an example of the other kind: by such settlement the property is so far understood to be reserved to the maker, as to impower him to alter or to burden. These powers may be termed *personal* and *real.*

To explain a power of the first kind, which is commonly termed *a faculty* in contradistinction to a power founded on property, it must be considered, first, That with regard to pecuniary interest, a man may subject himself to the power of another: he may gratuitously bind himself to <267> pay a sum of money; or he may impower any person to burden him with a sum. 2d, He may also subject his property to the power of another: a proprietor can impower any person to charge his land with an infeftment of annualrent; and a real right thus established is good even at common law. Thus, it is laid down by our writers, that the proprietor's consent

will validate a resignation made by one who hath no right,* and will validate also an annualrent-right granted by one who is not proprietor.† 3d,
Though an annualrent-right thus granted by a person having a faculty to
burden the land, is a real right, no less complete than if granted by the
proprietor; yet the faculty itself is not a real right. It may indeed be exerted
while the granter continues proprietor; his consent makes it effectual: but
his consent cannot operate after he is divested of his property, more than
if he never had been proprietor: it is a consent by one to burden the
property of another; an act that can have no effect in law. Thus <268> a
power granted by a proprietor to charge his land with a certain sum, ceases
by his selling the land before the faculty is exerted. Nor in strict law can
such faculty be exerted after the granter's death. Whether equity may not
interpose, is more doubtful. Let us suppose, that a man makes a deed,
impowering certain persons to name provisions to his younger children
after his death, and to burden his heir and land-estate with the payment;
leaving at the same time his estate to descend to his heir at law by succession. This deed cannot be effectual at common law; because it is inconsistent with the nature of property that a burden can be imposed upon the
estate of any man without his consent. It seems however just, that a court
of equity should interpose to make so rational a faculty effectual against
the heir, though not to charge the estate. The faculty, it is true, cannot be
considered as a debt due by the ancestor to subject the heir by representation: but it is the will of the ancestor to burden the heir with provisions
to his younger children; and in equity the will of the ancestor ought to be
a law to the heir who succeeds <269> by that very will, implied though
not expressed. In the law of England accordingly, where lands are devised
to be sold for younger children's portions, and the executor dies without
selling, the heir is compelled to sell. And where lands were ordered to be
sold for payment of debts, without impowering any person to sell, it was
decreed that the heir should sell.‡ But a settlement of an estate made by
the proprietor upon any of his blood-relations that his wife should think

    * Stair, tit[le] Extinction of Infeftments, §7 [Stair, *Institutions*, 2.11.7, p. 529].
    † Durie, Dec. 15, 1630, Stirling contra Tenants [M 6521].
    ‡ 1. Chancery cases 176 [*Pitt* v. *Pelham* (1670), reprinted in *The English Reports*, vol.
22, p. 750].

proper to nominate after his death, is effectual at common law: for there is nothing in reason or in law to bar a proprietor from making a settlement upon any person he has a mind, whether named by himself, or by another having his authority. The settlement excludes the heir at law, and the person named has a good title by his deed.*

That sort of power which is a branch of property, is in a very different condition. It is in its nature effectual against all singular successors,[1] even *bona fide* purchasers; for a disponee to whom the pro- <270> perty is conveyed to a limited effect only, cannot bestow upon another a more extensive right than he himself has.

It may be laid down as a general rule, That powers reserved in a disposition of land, the most limited as well as the most extensive, are all of them branches of the property. To justify this rule, it must be premised, that all the powers a man hath over his own subject are included in his right of property; and that the meaning of a reservation, is not to create a new right, but only to limit the right that is convey'd. The reservation accordingly of any power over the land implies so far a reservation of the property: and this must hold, however limited the reserved power be, or however extensive, unless it be expressed in clear terms, that a faculty only is intended. A separate argument concurs for this rule. Human nature, which in matters of interest makes a man commonly prefer himself before others, founds a natural and therefore a legal presumption, that when a disponer reserves to himself any power over the subject disponed, his intention is to reserve it in the amplest and most effectual manner. And hence, <271> *in dubio,*[2] a power properly so called will be presumed, in opposition to a faculty. Thus, a reserved power to charge the estate disponed with a sum, though the most limited power that can be reserved, is held to be a reservation of the property, so as to make the reserved power good even against a purchaser from the disponee. A man disponed his estate to his eldest son, reserving a power "to affect or burden the same with a sum

---

* Nov. 28. 1729, Murray contra Fleming [M 4075, from Kames, *Dictionary,* vol. 1, p. 289].

1. Those who acquire property otherwise than by succession on the death of the owner; for example, purchasers.

2. "In case of doubt."

named for provisions to his children." The son's creditors apprised the
estate, and were infeft. Thereafter the disponer exerted his reserved power,
by granting to his children heritable bonds, upon which they also were
infeft; and in a competition they were preferred:* the reserved power was
justly deemed a branch of property, which made every deed done in pursuance of it a preferable right upon the land. James Henderson, in his eldest
son's contract of marriage, disponed to him the lands of Grange, "reserving
to himself power and faculty, even *in articulo mortis,*[3] to bur- <272> den
the land with 8000 merks to any person he should think fit." In his testament he legated the said 8000 merks to his three younger sons; who, in
a ranking of the eldest son's creditors, were preferred before all of them.[†]

But though a faculty regularly exerted while the granter continues proprietor, will lay a burden on the land effectual against purchasers, and
though a power will have the same effect at whatever time exerted, it
follows not that every exertion of a power or faculty will be so effectual:
which leads us to examine in what manner they must be exerted in order
to be effectual against purchasers. That land may be charged with debt
without infeftment, or without giving a title in the feudal form, is evident
from a rent-charge, and from a clause in a conveyance of land burdening
the land with a certain sum.[‡] That without infeftment such a burden may
be laid on land by means of a power or faculty to burden, seems equally
con- <273> sistent; and were there a record of bonds granted in pursuance
of such powers, there would be nothing repugnant to utility more than
to law in sustaining them as real rights. But as no record is appointed for
bonds of this kind, it is a wise and salutary regulation to sustain none of
them as real rights, unless where created in the feudal form to produce
infeftment; which brings them under the statute 1617,[4] requiring all sei-

---

* Stair, Dirleton, Jan. 6. 1677, Creditors of Mouswell contra Children [M 963 and
965]. Stair, Dec. 16. 1679, inter eosdem [that is, Creditors of Mouswell contra Children:
M 4104].

3. "At the point of death."

† Hendersons contra Creditors of Francis Henderson, July 8. 1760 [M 4141, from
Kames, *Select Decisions,* p. 227].

‡ See [Kames,] Historical Law-tracts, tract 4. [1758 ed., vol. 1,] p. 244.

4. Act 16, parl. 1617; *APS* iv: 545: 1617, c. 16, Anent the registratione of reversiones
seasingis and utheris writis [Registration Act 1617].

sins to be recorded. Where land stands charged with a sum by virtue of a
clause contained in the disposition, no inconvenience arises from supporting this right, according to its nature, against all singular successors; for a
purchaser from the disponee is put upon his guard by the disposition containing the burden, which disposition makes part of his title-deeds. But a
power or faculty, could it be exerted without infeftment, might occasion
great imbarrassment: the power or faculty, it is true, appears on the face of
the disposition, which is a title-deed that must be delivered to a purchaser;
but then a purchaser has no means to discover whether the power or faculty be exerted, or to what extent. Nay further, if a bond <274> be held
an exertion, there can be no limitation: for bonds referring to the faculty
may be granted for £10,000, though the faculty be limited to the tenth
part of that sum. Such uncertainty would put the land *extra commercium*[5]
during the space of the long prescription, commencing at the death of the
disponer who reserved to himself the power of burdening the land. The
foregoing regulation is accordingly in strict observance. By the decision
mentioned above, Creditors of Mouswell *contra* Children, it appears, that
when a reserved power to burden land is regularly exerted, by granting an
infeftment of annualrent, such annualrent-right is preferred even before a
prior infeftment derived from the disponee: but a bond simply is never so
preferred. Thus, a man who disponed his estate to his eldest son, reserving
to himself a power to burden the same with 5000 merks, granted thereafter
bonds for that sum to his wife and children, proceeding upon the narrative of the reserved power. After the date of these bonds, the disponee
contracted debts, which were established upon the estate by infeftments.[6]
A competition arising be- <275> tween these two sets of creditors after
the disponer's decease, the disponee's creditors were preferred upon their
infeftments.* In a disposition to the eldest son, the father having reserved
power to charge the estate with wadsets or infeftments of annualrent to the
extent of a sum specified, a bond referring to the faculty was not deemed a
real burden; and for that reason it was not held to be effectual against the

---

5. "Outside of commerce."
6. That is, becoming real debts.
* June 26. 1735, Ogilvies contra Turnbull [M 4125].

donatar of the son's forfeiture.* But where the disponer reserves a power to burden the land with a sum to a person named, the heir-male of a second marriage for example; and thereafter grants a bond to that person referring to the reserved power; it seems not unreasonable that this bond should be deemed a real burden effectual against purchasers. For here there is no uncertainty to put the land *extra commercium:* the burden can never exceed the sum specified in the disposition; and after the disponer's death, a purchaser, by inquiring at the person <276> named, has access to know whether and to what extent the power has been exerted.

If the foregoing regulation hold in reserved powers, there can be no doubt of it with respect to the faculties properly so called. The following decisions I think belong to this class. A purchaser of land took the disposition to himself in liferent, and to his son *nominatim*[7] in fee, with power to himself to dispone, wadset, &c. He afterward granted a bond, upon which the creditor adjudged the estate after the son was divested, and a purchaser infeft. The adjudication was evidently void, and the bond was decreed not to be a proper exertion of the faculty to be effectual against singular successors.† This is properly an instance of a faculty, because the power which the father provided to himself, could not be a branch of the property which was never in him. Again, a purchaser of land having taken the disposition to himself in liferent, and to his son *nominatim* in fee, with a faculty "to burden, contract debt, and to sell or otherwise dispose at his plea- <277> sure," did first grant a bond, declaring it a burden on the land, and afterward sold the land. The purchaser was preferred, the bond not being a real burden on the land.‡

The cases above mentioned are governed by the rules of common law.[8] Let us next see what equity dictates. Where a man in a gratuitous disposition of a land-estate reserves a power to burden the subject with certain

---

* Stair, July 12. 1671, Lermont contra Earl of Lauderdale [M 4100].
7. "By name."
† Home, February 1719, Rome contra Creditors of Graham [M 4113, from Kames, *Remarkable Decisions* i: 31, No. 16]. November 1725, Sinclair contra Sinclair of Barrack [M 4123: dated 23 December 1724].
‡ Forbes, December 16. 1708, Davidson contra Town of Aberdeen [M 4109].
8. The first and second editions have a fuller comment at this point: see Appendix, p. 516, Extract [1st: 251].

sums, every question relative to such reservation must be governed by his will; for an obvious reason, that the deed and every clause in it were created by him. Common law indeed, adhering to the precise words, will not intitle the granter to burden the disponee personally. But it will be considered, that in burdening the land for his own behoof, he could have no intention to exempt the disponee; and therefore that this was a pure omission, which ought to be supplied by a court of equity, in order to fulfil the will of the granter. In the decisions accordingly, Rome contra Creditors of Graham, Sinclair contra Sinclair of Barrack, and <278> Ogilvies contra Turnbull, now mentioned,* though a bond granted in pursuance of a power to burden the land was held not to be a real right; it was held however to be a burden upon the disponee personally. And in like manner, a bond granted in pursuance of a reserved power to burden the land disponed, was found effectual against the disponee personally, so as to support an adjudication of the land against the disponee after the disponer's death.† In the cases mentioned, nothing is considered in equity but the will of the granter. But where a price is paid, the will of the purchaser ought to have equal weight; and if he have not agreed to be bound personally, equity will not bind him more than common law.

With respect to faculties, there is not the same latitude of interpretation. A faculty granted to a third person gratuitously cannot be extended against the granter beyond the precise words. And it will be the same though the faculty has been granted for a valuable consideration.

A disponer, who had reserved a power <279> to burden the disponee with a sum, grants a bond for that sum, without referring to the reserved faculty. Will this bond be in equity deemed an exertion of the faculty, yea or not? If the granter have no other fund of payment, it will be presumed in equity, that he intended an exertion of the faculty: if he have a separate fund, the presumption ceases, and that fund only is attachable for payment. But what if the separate fund be not altogether sufficient? A court of equity may interpose to make what is deficient effectual by means of the reserved faculty, in order to fulfil the will of the person who granted

---

* See supra p. 275 [p. 383 above].

† January 17. 1723, Creditors of Rusco contra Blair of Senwick [M 4117, in Kames, *Dictionary*, vol. 1, p. 291].

the bond. Thus, a man, upon the narrative of love and favour, having disponed his estate to his eldest son, reserving a power to burden the estate to the extent of a sum named, granted afterward a personal bond of provision to his children without any relation to the reserved power. In a suit for payment against the disponee's representatives it was objected, That the disponer at the date of the bond had an opulent fund of moveables; and that there is no presumption he intended to charge with this debt either his son or the estate disponed. The <280> disponer's will was presumed to be, that the bond should burden his executors in the first place, and the disponee in the second place.* By marriage-articles the estate was provided to heirs-male, with power to burden it with a sum named for the heirs of a second marriage. The proprietor made a provision for the children of a second marriage, burdening his heir with the same, but not charging his estate in terms of the reserved power. At common law the estate was not subjected, because the provision was not made a burden upon it; nor was the heir subjected, because the reserved power intitled the granter to burden the estate only. The court steered a middle course in equity: the heir was made liable *ultimo loco,*[9] after his father's other estate should be discussed.†

It has been questioned, whether a reserved power to charge with a sum the land disponed, can benefit a creditor whose debt was contracted before the reserved power was created. The court thought it rea- <281> sonable that this power should be subjected to the disponer's debts, whether prior or posterior.‡ A power to charge an estate with debt, being strictly personal, is incommunicable to a creditor or to any other, even during the life of the person privileged; not to talk of his or her death. Equity however rules, that a power or faculty should be available to creditors, prior as well as posterior: for it is the duty of a debtor to use all lawful means for paying his debts, whether by selling his goods or exerting his faculties; and if he

---

* Stair, Dirleton, June 21. 1677, Hope-Pringle contra Hope-Pringle [M 4102 and 4103].

9. "In the last place."

† Fountainhall, Dalrymple, June 23. 1698, Carnegie contra Laird Kilfauns [M 4106 and 4107].

‡ Fountainhall, Dalrymple, Dec. 16. 1698, Eliot of Swinside contra Eliot of Meikledean [M 4132].

unjustly refuse, equity will hold the faculty as exerted for the benefit of the creditors. In the present case, the creditors will have access to the land for their payment, as if the debtor had exercised his faculty, and burdened the land with the sum mentioned, payable to them. But if the creditors lie dormant during their debtor's life, and make no step to avail themselves of his reserved faculty, the faculty dies with him, and they can take nothing by it. A man disponed to his sons of the second <282> marriage several parcels of land, "reserving to himself full power and faculty to alter and innovate, and to contract debt, as fully and freely as if the entire fee were in him." The question occurred, Whether these disponees were liable to their father's personal debts contracted before the existence of the said power; and the affirmative was decreed.* But in cases of this nature, the disponee, even where he is heir-apparent, is liable *in valorem*[10] only:† for the disponee is not liable at common law; and equity subjects no man farther than *in valorem* of the subject he receives.

Whether and in what cases a reserved power or faculty can effectually be exercised on deathbed, has frequently been agitated in the court of session. One point appears clear, that a reserved power to alter or burden on deathbed, contained in a disposition to a stranger, may be exercised on deathbed, supposing always the granter to be *sanae mentis.*[11] And the reason is, that the stranger laying hold of the disposition, must submit to its qua- <283> lities, and cannot object to the conditions upon which it is granted. The matter is far from being clear, where the settlement is upon the heir, who is *alioqui successurus;*[12] as to which our decisions seem not to be uniform; nor is any good rule laid down by our writers. If the heir have not by acceptance of the disposition consented to the burdening clause, his privilege of challenging a burden laid upon him on deathbed, remains entire. But if he have taken infeftment upon the disposition, and be in possession, which implies his consent to every clause in the deed,

---

* July 21. 1724, Creditors of Rusco contra Blair of Senwick [M 4117, from Kames, *Dictionary,* vol. 1, p. 292].

10. "According to value."

† Dalrymple, January 18. 1717, Abercromby contra Graham [M 4112].

11. "Of sound mind."

12. "Otherwise entitled to succeed."

will not this consent bar him from objecting to the faculty, though exerted on deathbed? This requires deliberation. What distinguishes an heir from a stranger is his dependence upon the predecessor for the estate, leaving him no freedom of choice: he must submit to the will of his predecessor under the peril of exheredation. But does this dependence presume co-action in every transaction between a man and his heir? This can hardly be maintained; for what if the reserved faculty be to burden the estate with a moderate provision to younger children, or to do any other pious or ra- <284> tional act? In such a case, no good man will with-hold his consent; and therefore in such a case there is no ground for presuming the heir's consent to have been extorted from him. This hint leads us to a distinction in answering the foregoing question. If the heir's consent be voluntary, such as he would have given in a state of independence, it must be effectual both in law and equity to support the deathbed-deed. If it be extorted by fear of exheredation, it may be good at common law, but it will be voided by a court of equity.

But this distinction, however clear in theory, seems to be not a little dark in practice; for what criterion have we for judging in what cases this consent is voluntary, in what cases extorted? The expiscation may be in-tricate, but it is necessary. Where a man settles his estate upon his eldest son, with a reserved power to alter even on deathbed, no rational man will willingly submit to be in so precarious a state; and therefore the heir's con-sent will be presumed the effect of extortion. On the other hand, where a man, settling his estate upon his eldest son, reserves only power to burden it with a moderate sum <285> to his younger children; this is a fair settle-ment, by which the heir gets more than he gives; and therefore his consent may safely be presumed voluntary. Hence in general, the heir's consent to a reserved power that bears hard upon him, will always be presumed to have been extorted: his consent, on the contrary, to a reserved power that is proper and rational, will always be presumed voluntary.

This distinction gives me the greater satisfaction, when I find that it has had an influence upon the decisions of the court of session. A reserved power to alter upon deathbed a disposition granted to an eldest son, has in no instance been supported against the heir's reduction, even where he accepted the disposition. But the exercise upon deathbed of a reserved power that is proper and rational has generally been supported. Take the following examples. The exercise of a reserved faculty to burden with a moderate sum an estate disponed to an heir, was sustained, though the faculty was exerted upon deathbed.* <286> A man having disponed his estate to his eldest son, with the burden of all provisions to his younger children granted or to be granted, a bond granted to one of his daughters *in lecto*,[13] was sustained against the heir who had accepted the disposition.†

I shall close this chapter with a separate point, concerning powers given to a plurality, whether in exercising such powers the whole must concur, or what number less than the whole may be sufficient. If the persons be named jointly, the will of the granter is clear, that the whole must concur, because such is the import of the word *jointly*. To say that any number less than the whole may be sufficient, is in other words to say, that a nomination to act jointly is the same with a nomination to act separately.

But though all must concur, it follows not that they must all agree. If they be all present, the will of the maker naming them jointly is fulfilled; and what remains is, that the opinion of the majority <287> must govern the whole body. "Celsus, lib. 2. Digestorum, scribit, Si in tres fuerit compromissum, sufficere duorum consensum, si praesens fuerit et tertius: alioquin, absente eo, licet duo consentiant, arbitrium non valere; quia in plures fuit compromissum, et potuit praesentia ejus trahere eos in ejus sententiam. Sicuti tribus judicibus datis, quod duo ex consensu, absente tertio, judicaverunt, nihil valet: quia id demum, quod major pars omnium judicavit, ratum est, cum et omnes judicasse palam est."‡

---

* Stair, June 28. 1662, Hay contra Seton [M 3246]; Stair, June 22. 1670, Douglas contra Douglas [Stair, *Decisions*, vol. 1, p. 684].

13. *In lecto mortali:* on the deathbed.

† Fountainhall, Forbes, Feb. 8. 1706, Bertram contra Weir [M 3258 and 3260].

‡ l. 17. §7. l. 18. De receptis: qui arbitr[ium receperint ut sententiam dicant (On matters referred to arbitration and those who have undertaken to arbitrate in order to make an award), D 4.8.17.7–D 4.8.18: Watson i: 152: "Celsus, the second book of his *Digest*, writes that if an arbitration is referred to three persons, it is certainly sufficient that two agree, provided the third had also been present. However, if he was absent, although two agree, the decision is not valid, because the arbitration was referred to several persons and, if present, he could have brought them over to his opinion; just as where three judges have been appointed, the judgment of two who have agreed, in the

The next question is, When a plurality are named without adding the term *jointly,* what is the legal import of such nomination? Whether is it understood the will of the maker that they must act jointly, or that they may act separately? Stair* resolves this question by an argument no less plain than persuasive: "A mandate (says he) given to ten cannot be understood as given to a lesser number. To give a mandate to Titius, Seius, and Maevius, <288> cannot be the same with giving it to any two of them." Hence it may be assumed as a rule at common law, That a number of persons named in one deed to act in the same affair, are understood to be named jointly where the contrary is not expressed.

How far in this matter common law is subjected to the correction of equity, we next proceed to inquire.[14] When a number of persons are named *jointly* to perform any work, the whole must concur in equity as well as at common law. For here the will is clearly expressed, and a court of equity hath no power to vary from will. Thus, two tutors being named *jointly* by a man to his heir, it was decreed, That the office was vacated by the death of one of them.[†]

A plurality named for carrying on any particular affair without the addition of *jointly,* affords a large field for equitable considerations. We have seen that at common law the term *jointly* is always implied or presumed. But in particular cases there are many circumstances which a court of <289> equity will lay hold of to overbalance this presumption; to reduce which under any general rule is scarce practicable: circumstances are seldom precisely the same in any two cases, and for that reason each case must be ruled by its own circumstances. All that can be said in general is, that the common law ought to take place, unless it can be clearly shown that the maker did not intend to confine his nominees to act jointly.

Since general rules cannot be expected, what remains is to state cases the most opposed to each other, and which therefore admit of different

---

absence of the third, is not valid because the majority opinion is valid only where it is apparent that all have pronounced judgment"].

    * Book I. tit. 12. §13 [Stair, *Institutions,* p. 223].

    14. The first edition (p. 255) inserts a paragraph at this point omitted in the later editions. See Appendix, p. 516, Extract [1st: 255].

    † Stair, Jan. 17. 1671, Drummond contra Feuars of Bothkennar [M 14694].

considerations. And first, If I name a plurality to perform any act that is to bind or affect me, equity as well as common law requires that the nominees act jointly. In cases of that nature, there cannot readily occur any circumstance to infer it to be my will that they may act separately: for if any one of the nominees refuse to accept, or die after acceptance, it is my privilege to make a second nomination, or to forbear altogether; and it is not presumable, that any man will give away his privilege, unless it be so declared. Thus, an award pro- <290> nounced by two arbiters and an oversman named by them, was declared void; because it proceeded upon a submission to four arbiters who were empowered to name an oversman.* And when a plurality are constituted sheriffs in that part by the court of session, no sentence can be pronounced by any of them without the rest; because (as the author expresses it) he being but one colleague joined to others, hath no power to pronounce sentence without their consent.† This holds in curators, because they are elected by the minor himself: if any of them refuse to accept, or die after acceptance, it is no hardship that the nomination should be void, because it is in the minor's power to renew the commission. But where the curators named are many in number, it will scarce be held the minor's intention to adhere to the common law by confining them to act jointly. It appears a more natural presumption, that the purpose of naming so great a number was to provide against death or non-acceptance. And accordingly <291> an act of curatory was sustained, though seven only accepted of the eight that were named.‡ Where in an act of curatory a *quorum* is named, there can be no doubt that the act is void if a sufficient number do not accept to make the *quorum*.§ For here the will of the minor is expressed in clear terms.

There is much greater latitude for interpretation of will with respect to powers intended to be exercised after the granter's death. Stair explains this matter extremely well in the following words: "A mandate *inter vivos*[15]

---

* Fountainhall, Nov. 18. 1696, Watson contra Myln [M 648].

† Balfour, (Of Judges), cap. 26. [Balfour, *Practicks,* vol. 1, p. 286].

‡ Hope, (Minor), March 11. 1612, Airth [M 8938: Laird of Airth contra Laird of ———].

§ Stair, Jan. 25. 1672, Ramsay contra Maxwell [M 9042].

15. "Between living people."

giving power is strictly to be interpreted, because the nominees failing, the power returns to the mandant. But power given by a man in contemplation of death cannot return, and therefore he is presumed to prefer all the persons nominated to any other that may fall by course of law."* This doctrine is finely illustrated in a nomination of tutors. Where a number of tutors are named simply, without confining them to act <292> jointly, the preference given to them, exclusive of the tutor-in-law,[16] manifests the will of the deceased, that the management should be carried on by any one of the nominees, rather than by the tutor-in-law. "For were it otherwise, the more guardians are appointed for the security of the infant, the less secure he would be, because upon the death of any one of them the guardianship would be at an end."† Thus three tutors being named without specifying *conjunctly* or *severally,* and one only having accepted, it was decreed, That the whole office was devolved on him.‡ And five tutors being named as above, without specifying *conjunctly* or *severally,* the nomination was sustained though two only accepted.§

Where a number of tutors are named *jointly,* it is more doubtful what is intended by such a nomination. It may have been the intention of the deceased, that no act of administration should be valid unless every person named by him did con- <293> cur; and consequently, that the death or non-acceptance of any one nominee should void the nomination, leaving place to the tutor-in-law. Or it may have been his intention, that all the nominees accepting and alive must concur in every act. The argument above mentioned urged by Lord Stair, concludes strongly for the latter interpretation; unless the former be so clearly expressed as to avoid all ambiguity. *In dubio,* it will always be presumed, that the deceased would put greater trust in his own nominees than in any person not chosen by himself.

---

* Book 1. tit. 12. §13 [Stair, *Institutions,* pp. 223–24].

16. If there is no tutor nominated by the father (tutor-nominate), a tutor-at-law takes his place. The tutor-at-law acquires his position by law, and is the nearest male over the age of twenty-five, on the father's side.

† [M. Bacon, *A*] *New Abridg[ment] of the law,* vol. 2. [1736,] p. 677.

‡ Haddington, Dec. 12. 1609, Fawside contra Adamson [M 14692, from Kames, *Dictionary,* vol. 2, p. 384].

§ Stair, Feb. 14. 1672, Elies contra Scot [M 14695].

With respect to a *quorum,* will the nomination fall altogether, where, by death or *non-acceptance,* there are not left a number of tutors sufficient to make a *quorum?* In this case, as in the former, the will of the deceased may be interpreted differently. It may have been his will to void the nomination if there remain not a number of tutors to make a *quorum.* Or it may have been his will only, that supposing a sufficient number of acting tutors to make a *quorum,* a *quorum* should be necessary to every act. The latter interpretation, for the reason above given, ought to be adopt- <294> ed, unless the former be clearly expressed. But now, admitting this interpretation, the falling of the number below a *quorum,* is a *casus incogitatus*[17] about which the deceased has interposed no act of will. To supply that defect, the court will do what they conjecture the deceased would have done had the event occurred to him. About this there can be no hesitation; as it is always to be presumed, that a man will have more confidence in a trustee named by himself, than in one that is not of his nomination. Suppose, for example, ten tutors are named, the tutor-in-law one of them, five to be a *quorum.* By death or non-acceptance the number is reduced to four, of which number the tutor-in-law is one. Can so whimsical a thing have been intended as to trust the tutor-in-law by himself, instead of confining him to act with the other three. And the argument concludes *a fortiori,* where the tutor-in-law is left out of the nomination. The same reasoning is applicable where a *sine qua non*[18] is named. This doctrine is finely illustrated in the following case. A gentleman having named his spouse, his bro- <295> ther, and several others, to be tutors and curators to his only child, "appointed, that of those who should accept and survive, the major part should be a *quorum;* that his spouse should be *sine qua non;* and in case of her death or incapacity, his brother; but that by the death or incapacity of either, the tutory and curatory should not be dissolved, but be continued with the other persons named, as long as any one of them remained alive." The only event omitted to be provided for was that which happened, namely, the widow's refusal to undertake the office; which brought on the question, Whether the nomination did

17. "A circumstance which was not thought of."
18. Tutor *sine quo non:* a tutor whose consent is indispensable.

notwithstanding subsist; or, Whether it was void to make way for the tutor-in-law? The court was of opinion, That it appeared the intention of the father to continue his nomination as long as any of the persons named should exist; which is expressed in clear terms with respect to the death or incapacity of the *sine quibus non;* and which must hold equally in the case of their non-acceptance, as no distinction can be made. The nomination accordingly was decreed to sub- <296> sist.* In several other instances, neither the failure of a *quorum* nor of a *sine quo non* was deemed sufficient to void the nomination. The court conjectured it to be the will of the deceased, to trust any of the persons named rather than the tutor-in-law.[†] But the court adopted the opposite opinion in the following instances. A man, in a nomination of tutors to his children, declared his wife to be *sine qua non.* She by a second marriage, having rendered herself incapable of the office, the court declared the nomination void.[‡]

I proceed to examples of a different kind. A man having left 2500 merks to his children, empowered four friends named to divide the same among the children. After the death of one of the four, a division made by the three survivors was not sustained, and the children accordingly were <297> decreed to have each of them an equal share.[§] Here the four being named in the same deed, and to concur in the same act, were understood to be named jointly; and as there was no circumstance to infer that the granter intended to empower any number less than the whole to make the division, there could be no reason for varying from the rule of common law.

Helen Cunningham left 4000 merks to her grandchildren, to be employed for their behoof at the sight of five persons named, of which number their father and mother were two. This sum was lent out with the approbation of all, including the father and mother, one of the nominees excepted, who was abroad at the time. The ultimate purpose of this settle-

* June 16. 1742, Dalrymple of Drummore contra Mrs Isabel Somervell [Patrick Grant of Elchies, *Decisions of the Court of Session from the Year 1733 to the Year 1754,* ed. W. M. Morison, 2 vols. (Edinburgh, 1813), vol. 2, p. 494].

† Fountainhall, 22d December 1692, Watt contra Scrymgeour [M 14701]; Fountainhall, 22d February 1693, Countess of Callender contra Earl of Linlithgow [M 14701].

‡ Fountainhall, 24th June 1703, Aikenhead contra Durham [M 14701]; 14th February 1735, Blair contra Ramsay [M 14702, from Kames, *Dictionary,* vol. 2, p. 385].

§ Fountainhall, Feb. 10. 1693, Moir contra Grier [M 14720].

ment was evidently to secure the grandchildren in the sum settled upon them; and if this was done by lending the money to a person of unexceptionable credit at the time, the granter's will and purpose was fulfilled. By naming so many persons, he made it easy for the executor to get the approbation of a sufficient number; and it could not <298> be his intention to require rigidly the concurrence of every person named. And yet the court, adhering to the words as a court of common law, found that the money was not employ'd as it ought to have been, and therefore decreed the executor to be liable.*

A reference being made by a man and his son to three friends, empowering them to name a sum to the father when he should be in want, which the son should be obliged to pay; and two having concurred in absence of the third to name the sum, it was objected by the son, That the clause, importing a joint nomination, required the concurrence of the whole. The objection was over-ruled, and the determination of the two referees sustained.†
The reference to the three friends was the means chosen for ascertaining the father's claim, but it was certainly not intended to make that claim depend on their life or acceptance. The father had a just claim whenever he came to be in want; and sup- <299> posing none of the referees had interposed, it was the duty of the court of session to make the claim effectual.

CHAPTER VII

Of the power which officers of the law have
to act *extra territorium*.[1]

A Court of equity not only varies from common law in order to fulfil the great principles of justice and utility, but countenances such variations in the conduct of individuals.[2] The present chapter is intended as an illustra-

---

* Spottiswoode, (Legacy), Feb. 13. 1624, Hunters contra Executors of Macmichael [M 8047; see also M 14719].

† Fountainhall, July 27. 1694, Riddle contra Riddle [M 14720].

1. "Beyond the territory [of their jurisdiction]."

2. The first edition (p. 260) begins this chapter thus: "Hitherto of the powers of a court of equity, varying from common law in order to fulfil the great principles of justice and utility. But the influence of a court of equity extends beyond its own peculiar

tion of this observation; for several examples shall be given, of supporting positive infringements of common law, done even by its own officers.

The legal authority of magistrates and officers of the law being territorial, is confined within precise limits. In strict reasoning, nothing can be pronounced with greater certainty, than that an officer of the law acting beyond the bounds of his <300> commission, acts illegally: and yet in practice we admit several exceptions from this rule. If goods once apprehended in order to be poinded, be driven out of the sheriffdom purposely to disappoint the poinding, it is lawful for the officer to follow and complete his poinding, in the same manner as if the goods had not been driven away.* By the statute 52 Henry III, cap. 15, "No man for any manner of cause can take a distress out of his fee, or in the king's highway."[3] But if the lord coming to distrain[4] have the view of the beasts within his fee, and before distraining the tenant chases them into the highway; it hath been found, that the lord, notwithstanding the statute, may distrain them there.[†] With regard to the power of apprehending delinquents, one instruction is, That if a delinquent fly without the bounds of a constable's charge, the constable, being in hot pursuit, may follow and apprehend him.[‡] And, by the same rule, a stranger committing a <301> riot within a barony, may, by the officers of the barony, be pursued and apprehended out of the barony.[§]

Sir Matthew Hale, in his history of the pleas of the crown,[||] handles this matter with care, and traces it through various cases. "If a warrant

---

promise. Acts promoting the same great ends, done by individuals against the strict rules of common law, are countenanced and made effectual."

* Balfour, (Poinding), March 22. 1560, Home contra Sheill [Balfour, *Practicks,* vol. 2, p. 399].

3. Statute of Marlborough 1267 (England).

4. See glossary, "distraint/distress."

† [M. Bacon,] Abridg[ment] of the law, vol. 2 [1736,] p. 111.

‡ Act 8. parl. 1617 [*APS* iv: 535: 1617, c. 8, Anent the Justices for keiping of the Kingis Majesties peace and thair constables]. Act 38 parl. 1661 [*APS* vii: 306: 1661, c. 338: Commission and Instructions to the Justices of Peace & Constables (Justices of the Peace Act 1661)].

§ Nicolson, (Forum competens), Jan. 8. 1661, Baillie contra Lord Torphichen [M 4797, from Kames, *Dictionary,* vol. 1, p. 326].

|| [Hale, *History of the Pleas of the Crown* (1736),] Vol. 2, p. 115.

or precept to arrest a felon come to an officer or other, if the felon be arrested, and after arrest escape into another county, yet he may be pursued and taken upon fresh pursuit, and brought before the justice of the county where the warrant issued; for the law adjudged him always in the officer's custody by virtue of the first arrest. But if he escape before arrest into another county, if it be a warrant barely for a misdemeanour, it seems the officer cannot pursue him into another county; because out of the jurisdiction of the justice who granted the warrant. But in case of felony, affray, or dangerous wounding, the officer may pursue him, and use hue and cry upon him into any county. But if he take him <302> in a foreign county, he is to bring him to the gaol or justice of that county where he is taken. For he doth not take him purely by the warrant of the justice, but by the authority that the law gives him; and the justice's warrant is a sufficient cause of suspicion and pursuit." Here several cases are distinguished, and different degrees of power indulged to the officer, all of them flatly contradictory to the strict rules of common law: and yet we chearfully acquiesce in the doctrine, having an impression that it is just and salutary.

Let us try what will the most readily occur, in reflecting on this subject. If a felon be once arrested and in the hands of the officer, a notion of property arises, and suggests a right similar to that of the first occupant of land. Though the felon escape, the officer, in fresh pursuit, is understood to retain a sort of possession *animo*,[5] intitling him to pursue the felon till he compass his aim, to wit, a second arrest. We naturally conclude, that the felon, being in some sense the property of the officer, may be seized where-ever he can be found; and, by virtue of that *qua-* <303> *si* property, may be carried before the judge who granted the warrant. This reasoning will appear still more satisfactory when it is applied to the case cited above from Balfour, where a poinding is inchoated by apprehension of the goods; a circumstance which undoubtedly produces some faint notion of right to the goods, intitling the poinder to seize them where-ever found.

Again, "where a felon escapes without being arrested, if the warrant be barely for a misdemeanour, it seems the officer cannot pursue him into another county. But in case of felony, affray, or dangerous wounding, the

---

5. "In his mind."

officer may pursue him into another county." Here is a distinction made, which appears to have a foundation in human nature. As this distinction cannot arise from the nature of the warrant, which is no more extensive in the one case than in the other, it must arise from the nature of the delinquence. Felony, or any capital crime, inflames the mind, and creates a strong desire of punishment: the heated imagination is hurried along, and cannot be restrained by the slight fetters of strict form. And ac- <304> cordingly, in weighing an abstract principle against the impulse of an honest passion, the mind, giving way to the latter, embraces the following sentiment, That the officer ought not to be confined within the limits of his commission. In the case of a slight misdemeanour, the result is different. Strict principles have a stronger effect upon the mind than any impulse that can arise from a venial transgression; and therefore, in judging of this case, the mind naturally rests on the limitation of the warrant.

And what is further mentioned in the foregoing quotation, will support these reflections. "A delinquent once arrested, may, upon a second arrest, be brought from another county to the judge who gave the warrant. But if arrested for the first time in a foreign county, the criminal must be carried before the judge of the county where he is taken." The distinction here made, arises from the principles above explained. It has already been observed, that the notion of a *quasi* property supplies the want of a second warrant. But an arrest for the first time in a foreign county must be governed by <305> a different rule: the mind figuring a hot pursuit of the criminal, easily surmounts any obstruction that may arise from mere form; but when the end is gained by having the felon in safe custody, the impulse of passion being over, the mind subsides; and in this condition, perceiving the defect of power, it takes the first opportunity of supplying the defect, by an application to the judge of the place.[a]

With respect to the two cases now mentioned, a remarkable difference is observable in the operations of the mind. However strong the impulse of a passion may be when it agitates the mind, yet as soon as it subsides

a. This form is now rendered unnecessary by act 24° Geo. II. cap. 55. [1751] "If a person, upon a warrant indorsed, be apprehended in another county for an offence not bailable, or if he shall not find bail, he shall be carried back into the first county, and be committed by the justices in that county, or be bailed there if the crime be bailable."

by gratification, the mind is left free to the government of reason. Thus, where a felon who was never arrested is pursued into a foreign county, the defect of power is scarce perceived during the heat of pursuit: but immediately <306> upon the arrest, the defect of power makes an impression; and reason demands that the defect be forthwith supplied. The mind is differently influenced in the case of an escape after arrest. If once a resemblance be discovered between two objects, there is a natural propensity to make the resemblance as complete as possible; which in reasoning produces an error extremely common, that of drawing the same inferences as if the resemblance were altogether complete. Thus, by getting possession of the body of a felon a faint notion of property being suggested, the mind proceeds to form all its conclusions as if the felon were truly the property of the officer.

It is extremely curious to observe, how men sometimes are influenced by principles and emotions that they themselves at the time scarce attend to; which is remarkable in writers upon law, who, little apt to regard the silent operations of the mind, are not satisfied but with reasonings drawn from principles of law. This proceeds from studying law too much as an abstract science, without considering, that all its regulations ought to be founded upon hu- <307> man nature, and be adapted to the various operations of the mind. If one of the greatest lawyers in modern times furnish this censure, few can hope to escape. And that the censure is just, will appear from considering the reasoning of our author, which is by no means satisfactory. With regard to the felon who has been once arrested, he assigns the following reason for the regulation, "That the law adjudgeth him always in the officer's custody by virtue of the first arrest." But why does the law give this judgment, when it is contrary to the fact? This question ought to have been prevented in accurate reasoning: instead of which we are left in the dark, precisely where light is the most wanted. The true answer to this question is given above, that the right of possession once fairly acquired, cannot be lost by stealth or force, and therefore is retained *animo.*[6]

Upon the other branch, the reasoning appears still more lame. The case

6. "In the mind or intention."

is of a felon apprehended for the first time out of the jurisdiction; upon which our author's reasoning is, "That the officer doth not act purely by the warrant of the justice, <308> but by the authority which the law gives him; and that the justice's warrant is a sufficient cause of suspicion and pursuit." This is extremely obscure, and unsatisfactory as far as intelligible. In the first place, it is obvious, that the reasoning, if just, is equally applicable whatever be the nature of the crime: the justice's warrant is not a sufficient cause of suspicion and pursuit where the crime is atrocious, more than where it is of the slightest kind. In the next place, supposing the justice's warrant to be a sufficient cause of suspicion, and consequently of pursuit, the person upon whose information the warrant was issued has a better cause of suspicion, and yet the law empowers not that person to apprehend or to pursue. Neither doth a sufficient cause of suspicion give authority to an officer of the law out of the jurisdiction, more than to a private person. But let a man having authority to apprehend be figured in hot pursuit of a noted criminal, the mind hurries him on till he reach his quarry where-ever found: no such impression is made by the slighter transgressions. And this difference of feel- <309> ing is the foundation of our author's doctrine; a difference that undoubtedly made an impression on him, though overlooked in his reasoning.[7]

Thus, we have endeavoured to trace out the foundation of several nice conclusions in law, that depend not on abstract reasoning, but on sentiment. In one of the cases, an imagined right over the person of a felon arrested, suggested by a slight resemblance it hath to property, is in reality the only foundation of our conclusion. In the other, what in reality determines us, is the anxiety we have to prevent the felon's escape. And whoever examines laws and decisions with due attention, will find many of them founded on impressions or emotions, still more slight than those above mentioned.

To complete the subject, nothing further seems necessary but to observe, that the foregoing principles and operations of the mind, are countenanced by courts of justice, so as even to dispense with the clearest rules

7. In the first edition (p. 264) and second edition (p. 344), the sentence reads: "a difference that undoubtedly he was sensible of, though he has not been so lucky as to put it in a clear light."

of law. These principles and operations merit regard as virtuous and laudable; but their merit chiefly depends on <310> their utility. By overcoming that scrupulous nicety of law, which often is an impediment to the administration of justice, they tend in an eminent degree to the good of society.

CHAPTER VIII

Jurisdiction of the court of session with respect to foreign matters.

The subjects hitherto treated, falling within the bounds of common law, come of course under the equitable jurisdiction of the court of session, supplying defects or correcting injustice in common law. Foreign matters, as will by and by be explained, fall not within the bounds of common law; and for that reason come not under the jurisdiction of the session, either as a court of common law or as a court of equity. Why then should the present subject be brought into a treatise of equity? Not necessarily, I acknow- <311> ledge. It is however so intimately connected with matters of equity, that the session, acting whether as a court for foreign affairs or as a court of equity, is governed by the same principles, namely, those above laid down. Of these accordingly we shall see many beautiful illustrations in handling the present subject; which, in that view, will make a proper appendix to a treatise on equity, if not a necessary part.

Such tribes as relinquished the wandering state for a settled habitation, came under new rules of law. The laws of a tribe or clan governed originally each individual belonging to it, without relation to place.* But after nations became stationary, place became the capital circumstance. Laws were made to regulate all matters at home, that is, within the territory of the state; and legislators extended not their view to what was done or suffered in a foreign country, whether by their own people or by others. Thus, laws, originally *personal,* became strictly *territorial;* and hence the established maxim, That law hath no au- <312> thority *extra territorium.* This confined notion of jurisdiction corresponded to the manners of early

---

* See [Kames,] Historical Law-tracts, tract 6 [1758 ed., vol. 1, pp. 297–98].

times: mutual fear and diffidence in days of barbarity, prevented all intercourse among nations; and individuals seldom ventured beyond their own territory. But regular government introduced more social manners: the appetite for riches unfolded itself; and individuals were put in motion to seek gain where the prospect was the fairest. In most countries accordingly, there are found many foreigners, who have an occasional residence there for the sake of commerce. This change of manners discovered the imperfection of territorial jurisdiction: a man, by retiring abroad, is secure against a prosecution, civil or criminal, for what he has done at home; and by returning home, he is secure against a prosecution for what he has done abroad: common law reacheth no person but who is actually within the territory of the state; and reacheth no cause of action but what happens within the same territory.*

The common law of England is strictly <313> territorial in the sense above described:† nor have we reason to believe that the common law of Scotland was more extensive. When therefore the foregoing defect was discovered, it became necessary to provide a remedy: and the remedy was, to bring foreign matters under jurisdiction of the King and council; to which originally, as a paramount court, all extraordinary matters were appropriated. In Scotland particularly, the act 105. parl. 1487, declares the King and council to be the only court for *the actions of strangers of other realms.*[1]

With respect to foreign matters, the jurisdiction of the King and council in both kingdoms, was distinguished from that of the ordinary courts of law in two particulars. First, The jurisdiction of the latter was territorial with respect to causes as well as with respect to persons: the jurisdiction of the former was indeed territorial with respect to persons, no person in foreign parts being subjected to the jurisdiction; but with respect to causes, it was the opposite to territorial, no cause but <314> what happened in foreign parts being competent. Next, The ordinary courts are confined to common law: but with respect to foreign matters this law can be no rule,

---

* [Kames,] Historical Law-tracts, tract 7 [1758 ed., vol. 1, pp. 358–61].

† See [Henry Home, Lord Kames, The] Statute law of Scotland abridged [Edinburgh: A. Kincaid and A. Donaldson, 1757, p. 416], note 7.

1. *APS* ii: 177: 1487, c. 10: Of jurisdictioun and process in civile accionis questionis and pleyis.

for the reason above given, that it regulates nothing *extra territorium.* The King and council accordingly judging of foreign matters, could not be governed by the common law of any country: the common law of *Britain* regulates not foreign matters; and the law of a foreign country hath no authority here. Whence it follows, that foreign matters must be governed by the rules of common justice, to which all men are subjected, or *jure gentium,*[2] as commonly expressed.

This extraordinary jurisdiction, confined originally in both kingdoms to the same court, is now exercised very differently in the two kingdoms. In Scotland, it was derived by intermediate steps from the King and council to the court of session: and accordingly, by the regulations laid down soon after the institution of that court, a jurisdiction is bestowed upon it as to foreign matters; and the actions of foreigners are privileged.* In England, <315> this extraordinary jurisdiction made a different progress. The extensive territories in France possessed by the English Kings, and the great resort of Englishmen there, occasioned numberless law-suits before the King and council. To relieve that court from an oppressive load of business, the constable and marshal court was instituted; and to this new court were appropriated foreign matters, to be tried *jure gentium.*[†] After the English conquests in France were wrested from them, this court had very little business. We find scattered instances of its acting as a criminal court, down to the reign of Charles II.; but none for centuries before of its acting as a civil court. The court of chancery, with respect to its power of supplying the defects and mitigating the rigor of common law, had succeeded to the King and council; and it would have been a natural measure to transfer to the same court the extraordinary jurisdiction under consideration, the rule of judging being the same in both. But the court of chancery being <316> at that time in its infancy, and its privileges as to extraordinary

---

2. "By the law of nations."

* Act 45. parl. 1537 [This act is not collected in *APS*. See Sir Thomas Murray of Glendook, *The Laws and Acts of Parliament Made by King James the First and His Royal Successors, Kings and Queens of Scotland,* 2 vols. (Edinburgh: D. Lindsay, 1682), vol. 1, p. 220].

† See Duck de authoritate juris Civilis, lib. 2. cap. 8. part 3. §15. &c. [Arthur Duck, *De usu et authoritate juris civili Romanorum in dominiis principum Christianorum* (London: Richard Hodgkinson, 1653), p. 151].

matters not clearly unfolded, the courts of common law, by an artifice or fiction, assumed foreign matters to themselves. The cause of action is feigned to have existed in England,* and the defendant is not suffered to traverse that allegation. This may be justly considered as an usurpation of the courts of common law upon the court of chancery; which, like most usurpations, has occasioned very irregular consequences. I shall not insist upon the strange irregularity of assuming a jurisdiction upon no better foundation than an absolute falsehood. It is more material to observe, that foreign matters ought to be tried *jure gentium,* and yet that the judges who usurp this jurisdiction have no power to try any cause otherwise than by the common law of England. What can be expected from such inconsistency but injustice in every instance? Lucky it is for Scotland, that chance, perhaps more than good policy, hath appropriated foreign matters to the <317> court of session, where they can be decided on rational principles, without being absurdly fettered as in England by common law.

To form a distinct notion of the jurisdiction of the court of session with respect to foreign matters, it may be proper to state succinctly its different jurisdictions, and to ascertain the limits of each. Considered as a court of common law, those actions only belong to it where the cause of action did arise in Scotland. With regard to persons, this court was originally limited like the courts of common law in England: it had no authority over any man but during the time he was locally in Scotland. But in this respect the court hath in latter times acquired, by prescription, an enlargement of jurisdiction: every Scotchman, at home or abroad, is subjected to the jurisdiction of the court; and, when abroad, may, by a citation at the market-cross of Edinburgh, pier and shore of Leith, be called to defend in any action before the court.† In the next place, considering this court as a court of equity, <318> empowered to supply the defects and mitigate the rigor of common law, its jurisdiction is and must be the same with what it enjoys as a court of common law. To give it a more extensive jurisdiction would be useless; and to confine it within narrower bounds would not fully answer the end of its institution, which is to redress common law

---

* See Duck de authoritate juris Civilis, lib. 2. cap. 8. part 3. §18 [Duck, *De usu et authoritate juris civili Romanorum,* p. 152].

† See [Kames,] Statute-law of Scotland abridged [1757, pp. 413–18], note 7.

when justice demands redress. In the last place, this court, with relation to foreign matters, has the same jurisdiction over persons that it has as a court of common law or of equity.[3] And accordingly the court had no difficulty to sustain a process for payment of an account contracted at Campvere in Zealand, tho' the defendant, a Scotch merchant residing there, was not in this country any time during the suit.*

The rules that govern the session as a court for foreign matters, are the same that govern it as a court of equity; for these rules are derived from the principles of justice. But it must not be held that these rules are applied precisely in the same manner: as a court of equity, the session will not venture to interpose against com- <319> mon law, unless authorised by some general rule of equity that is applicable to all cases of the kind; but as to foreign matters, which belong not to common law, every case must be judged upon its own merits. And therefore the court here is less under restraint, than in supplying the defects of common law, or in correcting its rigor.

Though with respect to foreign matters, there is, strictly speaking, but one rule for judging, namely, natural justice; yet this rule, in its application to different matters, brings out very different conclusions. And should one undertake to unfold all the various cases to which the rule may be applied, the work would be endless. Avoiding therefore this endless task, I confine my speculations to some few leading cases that have been debated in the court of session; and these, for the sake of perspicuity, shall be divided into different sections. <320>

SECTION I

Personal actions founded on foreign covenants, deeds, or facts.

According to the principles above laid down, a foreigner's covenant will produce an action against him here, provided he be found in Scotland.

---

3. In the first edition (p. 268), Kames put forward a contrary position: see Appendix, p. 517, Extract [1st: 268].

* June 27. 1760, Hog contra Tennent [M 4780 and 4783, from Kames, *Select Decisions*, p. 226].

It would be a great defect in law, were there no redress against a foreigner who retires with his effects to this country, in order to screen himself from debts contracted at home. But a momentary residence here will not presume against him: he cannot be called into court till a domicil be fixed upon him by a residence of forty days. The court of session accordingly refused to sustain an action brought by one foreigner against another for payment of debt contracted abroad; for the parties were here occasionally only, and the debtor had no domicil in Scotland.* A foreigner is sub- <321> jected to our courts for a crime committed here, or a contract made here; but to subject him instantly to answer for a debt contracted abroad, would put it in the power of malice to confine a man at home. Our law, for the facility of travelling, requires a residence of forty days to subject a foreigner to our courts.[1]

When a foreign bond stipulating the interest of the country where granted, is made the foundation of a process here, it has been doubted, whether that interest or the legal interest of this country ought to be decreed. This doubt is easily solved. An agreement to pay the interest of the country where the money is borrowed, is undoubtedly binding in conscience, and therefore ought to be made effectual in every country. Nor do we meet with any obstruction in the Scotch statutes regulating the interest of money, which are not intended to reach foreign interest. And this accordingly is the rule in the law of England.[†] Hence it appears, that the court of session erred in refusing the interest of 10 per cent. upon a double bond <322> executed in Ireland, and in restricting the penal part of the bond to 6 per cent. the legal interest here.[‡] This error will be no less evident from another consideration. The penalty of a double bond put in

---

* Haddington, Nov. 23. 1610, Vernor contra Elvies [M 4788, from Kames, *Dictionary*, vol. 1, p. 326].

1. In the first edition (p. 269) and second edition (p. 350), Kames failed to note the rule of forty days' residence, and commented on the decision of *Vernor* v. *Elvies*, "This was in effect declaring, that the court of session is a court of common law only, having no privilege to cognosce of foreign transactions; a strange mistake, considering the regulation above mentioned, expressly acknowledging a jurisdiction in this court as to foreign matters."

† Abridg. cases in equity, ch. 36. sect. E. §1 [*Earl of Dungannon* v. *Hackett* (1702), 1 Eq. Cas. Abr. 289, reprinted in *The English Reports*, vol. 21, p. 1051].

‡ Fountainhall, Jan. 27. 1710, Savage contra Craig [M 4530].

suit here, ought to be sustained to the extent of damage and costs of suit: but the damage is plainly the interest of the country where the money is lent; because had payment been duly made, the money again lent out would have produced that interest. For the same reason, supposing the rate of interest to be lower in England than here, our judges, in relieving from the penalty of a double bond, will make the English interest the rule; for the lender could not have a view to greater interest than that of his own country.

The case is different where interest is stipulated greater than is permitted in the *locus contractus*.[2] Such stipulation is usury in that country, and a moral wrong every where: I say a moral wrong, because, as every man is bound to give obedience to the laws of his own country, it is a moral <323> wrong to transgress these laws.* When action therefore is brought in a foreign country for payment of the stipulated interest, it would be unjust to make a claim founded on an immoral paction; and the judge who should sustain the claim would be accessory to the wrong. But now, admitting that the interest stipulated ought not to be sustained, it comes next to be considered, whether the interest of the *locus contractus* should be the rule, or that of the country where the action is brought, or lastly, whether interest should be rejected altogether. This is a puzzling question. One at first view will naturally reject interest altogether, as a just punishment for the wrong done. But it is not clear, that a judge can punish for a wrong committed in a foreign country. One thing indeed is clear, that action cannot be sustained upon the immoral stipulation; and therefore, if there be any claim for interest, it must be upon the maxim, *Nemo debet locupletari aliena jactura.*[3] This leads the mind to the interest of the *locus contractus*; <324> and I incline to be of opinion that that interest is due.

Under the head of covenants marriage comes celebrated abroad.[4] The municipal law of Scotland regulating the solemnities of marriage, respects

---

2. "The place where the contract was made."

* See vol. 1. p. 344 [p. 198 above].

3. "No one should be enriched at another's expense."

4. The text should read "Under the head of covenants comes marriage celebrated abroad": In the 1st (1760) ed. (p. 271) and the 2nd (1767) ed. (p. 351) the sentence reads: "Under the head of covenants comes properly marriage celebrated abroad."

no marriage but what is made in Scotland: and as foreign laws have no coercive authority here, such a marriage must be regulated by the law of nature. According to that law, the matrimonial connection is founded upon consent solely; the various solemnities required by the laws of different nations having no view but to testify consent in the most complete manner. In that view, the solemnities of the country where a marriage is celebrated, ought with us to have great weight; because they show the deliberate will and purpose of the parties. Justice however requires that a marriage be held good here, though not formal according to the law of the country where it was made, provided the will and purpose of the parties to unite in marriage clearly appear.

According to the doctrine here laid down, a child ought with us to be held legitimate by a subsequent marriage, pro- <325> vided the marriage-ceremony was performed in a country where such is the law; because marriage in such a country must import the will of the father to legitimate his bastard children. But we cannot justly give the same effect to a marriage celebrated in a country where the marriage, as in England, hath not the effect of legitimation. The reason is, that marriage in that country is not a proof of the father's will to legitimate.

A minor, in the choice he makes of curators, is not confined to his own countrymen; and therefore a foreigner chosen curator has the same authority here with a native. Neither is it of importance in what place curators be chosen; and accordingly a choice made in England of curators, whether English or Scotch, will be effectual here. The powers of a guardian to a lunatic in England are more limited. The custody of the person of an English lunatic, and the management of his land-estate, in England, belong to the court of chancery; and the chancellor names one guardian to the person, another to the estate. But the Chancellor having no power <326> over a lunatic's land in Scotland, cannot appoint a guardian to manage such land.

Having discussed civil matters, I proceed to criminal. A crime committed at sea may be tried by the court of admiralty: but, this case excepted, no crime committed in a foreign country can be tried in Scotland. The jurisdiction of the justiciary-court is strictly territorial, being confined within the limits of Scotland; and the extraordinary jurisdiction of the court of session with respect to foreign matters, reaches civil causes only. Nor is it necessary that it should be extended to crimes. It is of great importance to every nation that justice have a free course every where; and to this end it is necessary that in every country there be an extraordinary jurisdiction for foreign matters, as far as justice is concerned. But there is not the same necessity for an extraordinary jurisdiction to punish foreign delinquencies: the proper place for punishment is where the crime is committed; and no society takes concern in any crime but what is hurtful to itself. A claim for reparation arising from a foreign delinquency, is different: being founded on the rules of <327> common justice, it is a claim that undoubtedly belongs to the jurisdiction under consideration. No man who injures another, ought to reckon himself secure any where till he make reparation; and if he be obstinate or refractory, justice requires that he be compelled, where-ever found, to make reparation.

To secure the effects of the deceased from embezzlement, every person who intermeddles irregularly, is, in Scotland, subjected to the whole debts of the deceased, without limitation. This penal passive title, termed *vitious intromission,* is confined to irregular intermeddling within Scotland. The intermeddling in England with the moveable effects of a Scotchman who dies there, must be judged by the rules of natural justice; and therefore in this country cannot infer any conclusion beyond restitution or damages. <328>

SECTION II

Foreign covenants and deeds respecting land.

In order to have a distinct conception of this branch, the extent of our own municipal law with respect to land in Scotland must be ascertained; for we are not at liberty to apply the *jus gentium*,[1] or the principles of natural justice, to any case that comes under our own law. As to this preliminary point, things it is certain as well as persons are governed by municipal law. Land in particular, next to persons, is the greatest object of law; and in

1. "The law of nations."

every country the acquisition and transmission of land are regulated by
municipal law. Our law, for example, with respect to the transmission of
land-property, requires writing in a certain form. Such a writing is held a
good title of property, whether executed at home or abroad. A writing, on
the other hand, in a form different from that prescribed by our law, will be
disregarded where-ever executed: for our law regards <329> the solemnities only, not the place. Thus a testament made in England, bequeathing
land in Scotland, is not sustained by the court of session; because, by our
law, no man can dispose of his land by testament: nor will it be regarded
that land is testable in England; because every thing concerning land in
Scotland is regulated by our law. In general, the connection of a land-
estate with the territory where situated, is of the most intimate kind: it
bears the relation of a part to the whole. Thus every legal act concerning
land, the conveying it *inter vivos,* the transmitting it from the dead to the
living, the security granted on it for debt, are ascertained by the municipal
law of every country; and with respect to every particular of that kind, our
courts are tied down to their own law.

Are we then to hold, that a conveyance of land in a form different from
what is required by us, can have no effect? Suppose a man sells in England
his land-estate in Scotland, executes a deed of conveyance in the English
form, and perhaps receives payment of the price: such conveyance, not
being in the form required by the <330> law of Scotland, will not have the
effect to transfer the property. But has the purchaser any claim in Scotland
against the vender? None at common law; because a court of common law
hath not authority to transform an actual disposition into an obligation
to dispone. But such claim is supported in equity; because where a man,
in order to transfer his land to a purchaser, executes a disposition which
is afterward discovered to be imperfect, it is his duty to execute a perfect
one; and if he be refractory, it is the duty of a court of equity to compel
him, or to supply his place. If the action be laid within the territory where
the land is situated, the judge, in default of the disponer, may adjudge the
land to the plaintiff: if in any other territory, all that can ensue is damage
for not performance. I illustrate this doctrine by a similar case. A disposition of land within Scotland without procuratory or precept, will not be
regarded at common law: but a court of equity, attentive to justice, will

interpose in behalf of the purchaser, by adjudging the land to him. Thus, with respect to an informal conveyance of land within Scotland, the session <331> acts as a court of equity; and it acts as an extraordinary court for foreign matters, where a conveyance is executed abroad according to the law of the place.

A covenant was executed in England between two brothers, agreeing, that failing children the estate of the deceased should go to the survivor. The brother who first deceased had a land-estate in Scotland, a part of which he had gratuitously aliened in defraud of the covenant. A reduction was brought of this gratuitous deed by the surviving brother, and the covenant was sustained as a good title in the reduction. The covenant, though it had not the formalities of the law of Scotland, was however good evidence of the agreement; and as the deceased brother had done a moral wrong in transgressing the agreement, justice required that the wrong should be redressed, which was done by voiding the gratuitous deed.* But in a later case, the court deviated from the foregoing principle of justice. A disposition of an heritable jurisdiction in Scotland, executed in England according to <332> the English form, was not sustained even against the granter, to compel him to execute a more formal disposition.† This was acting as a court of common law. And it must not pass unobserved, that the accumulating different jurisdictions in the same court, occasions frequently mistakes of this nature; which are avoided in countries where different jurisdictions are preserved distinct in different courts.

SECTION III

Moveables domestic and foreign, and their legal effects.[1]

Local situation is essential to a moveable no less than to land: we cannot even conceive a horse or a ship but as existing in a certain place. In a legal

---

* Forbes, July 5. 1706, Cuningham contra Lady Sempill [M 4462].

† February 1729, Earl [of] Dalkeith contra Book [M 4464, from Kames, *Dictionary,* vol. 1, p. 320].

1. For the treatment of this topic in the first two editions, see Appendix, p. 517, Extract [1st: 274–77].

view, a moveable situated within a certain territory, is subjected to the judge of that territory; and every action claiming the property or possession of it, must be brought before that judge. Warrant for execution <333> must be granted by the same judge, as no other judge has authority over it.

It is a different question, by what law the judge ought to regulate his proceedings, whether by the law of his own country, or by what other law. About this question writers have differed widely. Some are of opinion, that moveables *non habent sequelam*,[2] meaning, that without regard to their local situation, they are to be held as belonging to the country of the proprietor, and to be subjected to the law of that country. Others, averse to fiction, are of opinion, that moveables like land ought to be governed by the law of the country where actually situated. Opinions so different are an incitement to trace this subject to its fountain-head, if it can be traced. That each of these opinions may be right in particular cases, is probable; for otherwise they would not be adopted: but I suspect, that neither of them will hold in general and in every case. I take first under consideration moveables accessory to an immoveable subject, the furniture of a dwelling-house, the stocking of a farm, goods in a shop for sale, the implements of a manufacture, which may be termed <334> *permanent moveables*. These are naturally considered, as belonging to the same country with the principal subject, and to be governed by the same law. This view may be enlarged, by comprehending under permanent moveables, every moveable that like those above mentioned, have beside local situation some connection with a country. So far the latter opinion appears the best founded. And that this way of thinking has long prevailed in Scotland, is made evident by the act 88. parl. 1426 enacting, "That when a Scotchman dies abroad *non animo remanendi*,[3] his Scotch effects must be confirmed in Scotland."[4] Nor will it alter the rule that the proprietor happens to be a foreigner. The succession to an immoveable subject is not

---

2. *Mobilia non habent sequelam:* moveables cannot be followed. This maxim was often used in civilian systems to hold that owners of moveable goods cannot recover them from third party bona fide purchasers; Kames's use of the maxim is, however, to point to a rule that the laws of one country cannot "follow" the property into another.

3. "Not having the intention to remain"; that is, remain abroad.

4. *APS* ii: 14: 1427, c. 8, De causis mercatorum extra regnum decedencium tractandis.

affected by that circumstance; and it is natural that an accessory should go along with its principal: the thinking mind cannot readily yield to a separation of things intimately connected, to regulate the succession of the immoveable part by the law of the country to which it belongs, and of the moveable part by the law of the proprietor's country. This argument must appear in a strong light where both parts <335> belong to a foreigner; and it can make no solid difference that the moveable part only belongs to him. We adhere to this doctrine in practice. Letters of administration from the prerogative court of Canterbury[5] will not be sustained as a title to effects in Scotland that belonged to the deceased, even though granted to those who are next in kin by the Scotch law. The powers of that court are confined within its own territory; and Scotch effects must be confirmed in Scotland. In England, a bastard enjoys the privilege of making a testament, which obtains not here. And accordingly, notwithstanding a testament made by an English bastard, his moveables here were escheated to the crown.* A nuncupative will[6] is sustained in England; but it will not carry Scotch moveables, writ with us being necessary to convey moveables from the dead to the living.† But the nomination of an executor by the proprietor in his testament, be- <336> ing effectual all the world over *jure gentium,* will be sustained here.

Moveables that are not connected with an immoveable subject, nor in any way connected with a country or territory, but merely by local situation, may be termed *transient moveables;* moveables, for example, that a proprietor carries about with him, his watch, his jewels, his garments, the money in his pocket, his horses, his coach and such like. These so far coincide with permanent moveables, as that every question concerning them must be determined by the judge of the territory where they actually are. But it follows not that the law of that territory ought to be the rule. By their intimate connection with the proprietor, the law of his country

---

5. This was the highest ecclesiastical court in the province of Canterbury in England, which heard testamentary and matrimonial suits.

* Haddington, 1st February 1611, Purves contra Chisholm [M 4494, from Kames, *Dictionary,* vol. 1, p. 320].

6. An unwritten will.

† Stair, 19th January 1665, Shaw contra Lewins [M 4494].

ought to prevail. A gentleman in the course of travelling traverses many foreign territories; and happens to die suddenly within one of them. What a strange law would it be that his succession should depend on such an accident? The nature of man is averse to chance: we love to rest on general principles and permanent facts, rejecting circumstances daily and hourly varying. A Scotchman crosses <337> the border, purposing to return home in a week; but dies suddenly in the English side by a fall from his horse. His transient effects by this accident remain in England; but it would derogate from the dignity of law to lay any weight on that circumstance; and laying it aside, what other rule is there to follow but to regulate the succession by the law of Scotland? These effects were carried by the proprietor from Scotland: he purposed to carry them back to the same country; and it is no wide stretch of thought to consider them as still continuing there. The English judges accordingly, considering them to be Scotch effects, will prefer those who are by the Scotch law next in kin to the deceased.[a] Here the opinion making the law of the proprietor's country the rule of succession, appears the best founded. This case demands peculiar attention: here <338> judges are led to found their decisions, not on their own law nor on the *jus gentium,* but on the municipal law of another country. A ship is another example of transient moveables. While it is abroad on a trading voyage, the proprietor dies at home. The ship is under a foreign jurisdiction; but when claimed there, the judge, rejecting the casual circumstance of local situation, will consider it as belonging to the country of the proprietor, and will adjudge it to those who have right by the law of that country. A Frenchman consigns goods in Edinburgh to be disposed of for his behoof; but dies before the commission is executed. The succession to these goods ought to be governed by the law of France; and the court of session, as having jurisdiction in foreign matters, will decree accordingly. In general, such moveables are held to be foreign moveables, conveyable

---

a. It may create at first some backwardness of opinion to find a rule of succession founded upon an obscure mental operation; but the argument will acquire weight on consulting the Essays on British Antiquities, essay 4, where will be found many rules of succession built upon foundations still more slender than that mentioned above [Henry Home, Lord Kames, *Essays upon Several Subjects Concerning British Antiquities* (Edinburgh: A. Kincaid, 1747), pp. 123–91].

inter vivos, and from the dead to the living, according to the law of the proprietor's country. An assignment by the foreign proprietor, formal according to the *lex loci,*[7] will be sustained here to carry such moveables. And if they belonged to an Englishman, letters <339> of administration[8] after his death will be here a valid title, without necessity of confirmation.

Upon the whole, comparing permanent and transient moveables, the local situation of the former points out the judge, without regarding the proprietor's country. But as to the latter, the proprietor's country points out the judge, without regarding the local situation.

Where a Scotchman, occasionally in England, dies there intestate, the court of session, acting as a court of common law, will adjudge his moveables situated in Scotland, of whatever kind, to those who are next in kin according to our law. But his transient moveables, locally in England, must be claimed from the English judges; who, acting as a court for foreign matters, ought to govern themselves by the law of Scotland; which brings in the relict for her share. But what if he have made a will, dividing his moveables among his blood-relations, leaving nothing to his wife? Her contract of marriage affords an effectual claim against him, which he cannot evade by any voluntary deed. And even without a contract, as the *jus relictae*[9] is e- <340> stablished by the law of Scotland beyond the power of the husband to alter, she ought to have her proportion of these transient moveables, as the English judges are in this case bound by the law of Scotland, not by their own. To fortify this doctrine, I urge the following argument. Where two persons joining in marriage are satisfied with the legal provisions, there is no occasion for a contract; and the parties may be held as agreeing that the law of the land shall be the rule. It is in effect the same, as if the parties had subscribed a short minute, bearing, that the *jus relictae* and every other particular between them should be regulated by the law of their country; and such an agreement expressed or implied, must be binding all the world over, to support the relict's claim against the testament of a deceased husband.

It may however happen, that two persons carelessly join in marriage,

---

7. "The law of the place."

8. Documents issued by English ecclesiastical courts (which had testamentary jurisdiction) appointing a person to administer the estate.

9. "The right of the widow," to a share of her husband's moveable estate [Scots law].

having an object in view very distant from a legal provision. Law does not admit of a presumption against rational conduct. But though it should be admitted, it will not avail. As every man is bound in con- <341> science to obey the laws of his country, the husband, when disposed to think, will find his wife intitled by that law to the *jus relictae;* and will see that an attempt to disappoint her would be against conscience. This must be evident to him when at home; and it must be equally evident, that change of place cannot relieve him. At any rate the *jus relictae* must have its effect as to his moveables in Scotland; and it would be not a little heteroclete that his transient effects should be withdrawn, for no better reason than that they happen accidentally to be in a foreign country where the *jus relictae* does not obtain.

SECTION IV

Debts whether regulated by the law of the creditor's country or that of the debtor.

Debts due by people of this country to foreigners, make another branch of the extraordinary jurisdiction of the court of session concerning foreign matters. The form of conveying such debts *inter vivos,* <342> of transmitting them from the dead to the living, of attaching them by execution, &c. have not hitherto been brought under general rules; and our judges are ever at a loss by what law these particulars ought to be governed, whether by our law, by that of the country where the creditor resides, or by the *jus gentium.* In order to remove this doubt, authors and lawyers are strongly disposed to assimilate debts to land, by bestowing upon them a local situation: and yet this fiction, bold as it is, removes not the doubt; for still the question recurs, Where is the debt supposed to exist, whether in the territory of the creditor or in that of the debtor. Considering a debt as a *subject* belonging to the creditor, it seems the more natural fiction to place it with the creditor as in his possession; and hence the maxim, *Mobilia non habent sequelam.* Others are more disposed to place it with the debtor; a thought suggested from considering, that the money must be demanded from the debtor, and that upon his failure the suit for payment must be in his *forum.*

It is unnecessary to bestow words upon proving, that a debt is not a *corpus* to be ca- <343> pable of loco-position, but purely a *jus incorporale.*[1] Rejecting then fictions, which never tend to sound knowledge, let us take things as they are, and endeavour to draw light from the nature of the subject. As here there are two persons connected, a debtor and a creditor, living in different countries, and subjected to different laws, it at first sight may appear a puzzling question, What law ought to govern, whether that of the debtor or of the creditor. One thing is evident, that every question concerning a subject, moveable or immoveable, must be determined by the judge whose legal powers extend over that subject; and that execution must be awarded by him only. The same rule applies to debts, according to the maxim, *Actor sequitur forum rei;*[2] whence it necessarily follows, that the form of the action, the method of procedure, and the manner of execution, must all be regulated by the law of the country where the action is brought. But though there can be no doubt about the judge, it may be a doubt what ought to be his rule in determining questions concerning the subject. With respect to that question, I submit the following hints. <344> When the creditor makes a voluntary conveyance, it is to be expected that he should speak in the style and form of his own country; and consequently, that the law of his own country should be the rule here. It would indeed be strangely heteroclete to subject him to the forms of the debtor's country, of which he is ignorant, especially if the debtor have a wandering disposition. In a word, the will of a proprietor or of a creditor, is a good title *jure gentium* that ought to be effectual every where. Thus, an assignment made by a creditor in Scotland, according to our form, of a debt due to him by a person in a foreign country, ought to be sustained in that country as a good title for demanding payment: and a foreign assignment of a debt due here, regular according to the law of the country, ought to be sustained by our judges. A foreign assignment cannot at any rate be subjected to the regulations of our act 1681[3] for preventing forgery, nor to

---

1. "An incorporeal right."
2. The plaintiff follows the forum of the defendant.
3. Act 5, parl. 1681; *APS* viii: 242: 1681, c. 5, Act concerning probative witnesses in writs and executions [Subscription of Deeds Act 1681].

any other of our regulations; because these regard no deeds but what are executed in Scotland.[4]

A judicial conveyance or legal execution will fall more naturally to be ex- <345> plained in the last section. The only remaining point is to examine by what law the creditor's succession is to be governed. Debts are part of the creditor's funds, and at his disposal. His alienations for a valuable consideration must be every where effectual, and even his donations. It is in his power alone to regulate his succession; and if he make a will, it must be effectual. But what if he die intestate; whether must the law of his country be the rule, or that of the debtor? The former undoubtedly. A man who dies intestate, is understood to adhere to the legal succession; for otherwise he would make a will. Therefore those who are heirs by the law of his own country ought to be preferred, according to his implied will. The express will of the deceased creditor must have that effect; and his implied will ought to have the same effect. The debtor has no concern but to pay safely: the law of his domicil will secure him as to that point: with regard to the creditor's succession, it can have no authority. Thus, in a competition between the brother and the nephew of Captain William Brown, who died in Scotland his native country intestate and without <346> children, concerning moveable debts due to the Captain in Ireland, the brother was preferred as next in kin by the law of Scotland; though by the laws of England and Ireland, which admit the *jus repraesentationis*[5] in the succession of moveables, a nephew and niece have the same right with a brother and sister.*

From what is said it will appear, that debts differ widely from land and from moveables. It is in vain to claim the property of any subject, unless

---

4. In the equivalent passages in first edition (p. 278) and second edition (pp. 358–59), Kames notes "that as payment must be demanded in the *forum* of the debtor, the form of the action that is brought against him, the method of procedure, the execution that passes upon the decree, and what person is liable as heir in place of the debtor dying before payment, must all be regulated by the law of the debtor's country. On the other hand, with respect to titles derived from the creditor, whether *inter vivos* or by succession, these naturally are regulated by the law of the creditor's country."

5. "The right to be represented" by another; that is, the right of the children of a deceased heir to inherit in his place.

* Nov. 28. 1744, Brown of Braid contra John Brown merchant in Edinburgh [M 4604 and 4608, from Kilkerran 199, and Falconer i: 11].

the title of property be complete and strictly formal. An equitable title in opposition to one that is legal, can never found a real action: it cannot have a stronger effect than to found an action against the proprietor to grant a more formal right; or in his default, that the court shall grant it. But in the case of a debt, where the question is not about property but about payment, an equitable title coincides in a good measure with a legal title. An assignment made by a foreign creditor according to the formalities of his country, will be sustained here as <347> a good title for demanding payment from the debtor: and it will be sustained even though informal, provided it be good *jure gentium;* that is, provided it appear that the creditor really granted the assignment. Such effect hath an equitable title; and a legal title can have no stronger effect.

It must however be admitted, that an equitable title hath not so complete an effect in a competition. Suppose an English creditor grants an assignment in the English form, of a debt due to him in Scotland: this assignment, though it transfer not the *jus crediti*[6] to the assignee, is however an order upon the debtor to pay to the assignee. But such assignment, even though the first in order of time, will not avail against a more formal assignment taken *bona fide,* and regularly intimated to the debtor. An equitable title may be good against the granter; but can never be sustained in a competition with a legal title, where both parties are *in pari casu.*[7]

I conclude this section with applying to debts, what is observed with respect to moveables in the section immediately foregoing. The nomination of an executor in a testament, is an universal title which <348> ought to be sustained every where; and is always sustained in the court of session to oblige debtors in this country to make payment.* But an executor-dative[8] with letters of administration, hath not a title to sue for payment *extra territorium.* And the same is the case of a guardian to a lunatic's estate named

6. "The right of a creditor"; that is, the personal right vested in a creditor to the debt.

7. In the first two editions, an additional paragraph is inserted here, some of whose material is placed at the very end of the third edition. (p. 434 below): see Appendix, p. 521, Extract [1st: 279–80].

* Durie, Feb. 16. 1627, Lawson contra Kello [M 4497].

8. An executor named by the court (Scots law).

in England by the chancellor: he has no title to sue for payment of the lunatic's debts in Scotland.*

SECTION V

Foreign Evidence.

Under this head come properly foreign writs; because no writ where there is wanting any solemnity of the law of Scotland, can be effectual here to any purpose but as evidence merely. And as among civilized nations, the solemnities required to make a writ effectual, are such as give <349> sufficient evidence of will; it is established as a rule with us, That contracts, bonds, dispositions, and other writs, executed according to the law of the place, are probative in this country. Thus, action is always sustained upon a foreign bond having the formalities of the place where it was granted:† and an extract of a bond from Bourdeaux subscribed by the tabellion[1] only, and bearing that the bond itself subscribed by the granter was inserted in his register, was sustained, being *secundum consuetudinem loci.*[2,‡] Depositions of witnesses taken abroad upon a commission from the court of session, were sustained here, though subscribed by the commissioners and clerk only, not by the witnesses, such being the form in the country where the depositions were taken.§

The same rule obtains even though the foreign bond bear a clause for registring in Scotland. This circumstance shows in- <350> deed, that the creditor had it in view to make his claim effectual in Scotland; but it weakens not the evidence of the bond, which therefore will be a good instruction of the claim.‖

* June 21. 1749, Morison, &c. contra Earl of Sutherland [M 4595 and 4598, from Kilkerran 209, and Falconer ii: 76 and *errata*].
† Haddington, Jan. 19. 1610, Fortune contra Shewan [M 4429, from Kames, *Dictionary*, vol. 1, p. 316].
1. A notary (France).
2. "According to local custom."
‡ Home, February 1682, Davidson contra Town of Edinburgh [M 4444, from Kames, *Dictionary*, vol. 1, p. 317].
§ Fountainhall, March 19. 1707, Cummin contra Kennedy [M 4433].
‖ Home, Feb. 14. 1721, Junquet la Pine contra Creditors of Lord Sempill [M 4451, from Kames, *Remarkable Decisions* i: 51, No. 23].

By the law of England, payment of money may be proved by witnesses; and therefore the same proof will be admitted here with respect to payment said to be made in England. For our act of sederunt confining the evidence to writ,* regards no payment but what is made in Scotland; and it would be unjust to deprive a man of that evidence which the law of his own country made him rely on. Accordingly, in every suit here upon an English bond, the defence of payment alledged made in England, is admitted to be proved by witnesses.† Yet where a bond granted in England contained a clause for registring in Scotland, the defence of payment made in England was not permitted to be pro- <351> ved by witnesses.‡ This appears to me a wrong judgement; for, as observed above, the clause of registration imported only, that the creditor had it in view to make his debt effectual in Scotland. It certainly did not bar the debtor from making payment in England; nor, consequently, from proving by witnesses that payment had been so made.

In Scotland, the cedent's oath is not good evidence against the assignee; because it is the oath, not of a party, but of a single witness. In England, an assignment being only a procuratory *in rem suam,* the cedent's oath is an oath of party, and therefore good evidence against the assignee. For that reason, an English bond being assigned in England, and a suit for payment being raised here by the assignee, a relevant defence against payment was admitted to be proved by the oath of the cedent.§ <352>

SECTION VI

Effect of a statute, of a decree, of a judicial conveyance, or legal execution, extra territorium.

Though a statute, as observed above, hath no authority as such *extra territorium;* it becomes however necessary upon many occasions to lay weight

---

* [Kames,] Historical Law-tracts, tract 2 [1758 ed., vol. i, p. 102n, referring to the Act of Sederunt, 8 June 1597, for which, see *AS* 28].

† Durie, November 16. 1626, Galbraith contra Cuningham [M 4430].

‡ Stair, Dec. 8. 1664, Scot contra Henderson [M 4450].

§ Stair, June 28. 1666, Macmorland contra Melvine [M 4447: M'Morland contra Melville].

upon foreign statutes, in order to fulfil the rules of justice. Many examples occur of indirect effects given thus to foreign statutes. One of these effects I shall mention at present for the sake of illustration; reserving others to be handled where particular statutes are taken under consideration. Obedience is due to the laws of our country, and disobedience is a moral wrong.* This moral wrong ought to weigh with judges in every country; because it is an act of injustice to support any moral wrong, by making it the foundation either of an ac- <353> tion or of an exception. I give for an example the statute prohibiting any member of a court of law to buy land about which there is a process depending.† Such a purchase being made notwithstanding, the purchaser follows the vender into a foreign country, in order to compel him by a process to make the bargain effectual. A bargain unlawful where made, becomes not lawful by change of place; and therefore the foreign judge ought not to support such unlawful bargain by sustaining action upon it. Courts were instituted to repress not to enforce wrong; and the judge who enforces any unlawful paction, becomes accessory to the wrong.

Several questions arise from the different prescriptions established in different countries. In our decisions upon that head, the case is commonly stated as if the question were, Whether a foreign prescription or that of our own country ought to be the rule? This never ought to be made a question; for our own prescription must be the rule in every case that falls under it, and not the prescription of any other coun- <354> try. The question handled in these decisions is, What effect ought to be given to a foreign prescription in cases that fall not under any of our own prescriptions? Questions of that sort may sometimes be nice and doubtful. By the English act of limitations,‡ "All actions of account and upon the case,[1] all actions of debt grounded upon any lending or contract without speciality, all actions of debt for arrearages of rent, &c. shall be sued within six years

---

* See vol. I. pp. 344, 345 [p. 198 above].

† 13. Edward I. cap. 49. [1285]; Act 216, parl. 1594 [*APS* iv: 68: 1594, c. 26, Anent the bying of landis and possessionis dependand in pley be jugeis or memberis of courtis (Land Purchase Act 1594)].

‡ 21. James I. cap. 16. §3 [Statute of Limitations, 1623].

1. Action on the case: a general form of action to remedy civil wrongs (English law).

after the cause of action." The purpose of this statute is to guard against a second demand for payment of temporary debts, such as generally are paid regularly: and to make that purpose effectual, action is denied upon such debts after six years. As statutes have no coercive authority *extra territorium,* this statute can have no effect with us, but to infer a presumption of payment from the six years delay of bringing an action. And accordingly, when a process is brought in Scotland for payment of an English debt after the English prescription has taken place, it cannot be pleaded here, that <355> the action is cut off by the statute of limitations: but it can be pleaded here, and will be sustained, that the debt is presumed to have been paid. Considering that the statute can have no authority here except to infer a presumption of payment, it follows, that the plaintiff must be permitted to defeat the presumption by positive evidence, or to overbalance it by contrary presumptions, or to show from the circumstances of his case that payment cannot be presumed. As to positive evidence, the pursuer has access to the oath of the defendant; and an acknowledgement that the debt is still existing defeats the presumption of payment.* The presumptive payment may also be counterbalanced by contrary presumptions. A case of this nature is reported by Gilmour:† "A bond prescribed by the law of England while the parties resided there, was afterwards made the foundation of a process in Scotland. The court refused to sustain the English prescription, because the <356> bond was drawn in the Scotch form betwixt Scotchmen, and bore a clause of registration for execution in Scotland." The circumstances of this case show, that the creditor's view was to receive payment in Scotland, or to raise his action there; and as a bond bearing a clause of registration prescribes not in Scotland till forty years elapse, the court justly thought, that to preserve the claim alive the creditor had no occasion to guard against any prescription but that of Scotland. To proceed, there are circumstances where the statute of limitations cannot infer any presumption of payment. What if the debtor within the six years did retire beyond sea? The forbearance in that case to bring an action against a man who cannot easily be reached, and whose residence perhaps is not

---

* February 9. 1738, Rutherford contra Sir James Campbell [M 4508, from Kames, *Dictionary,* i: 23; and Elchies, *Prescription,* No. 17].

† November 1664, Garden contra Ramsay.

known, cannot infer the slightest presumption against the creditor. The statute however, which makes no exception, must in England have been obeyed, till the defect was supplied by another statute. But the court of session is not so fettered: a presumption of payment will not be sustained when the circumstances of the case admit it not. <357>

The foregoing defect of the statute of limitations is supplied by the English statute 4to Annae, cap. 16,[2] declaring, "That where the person against whom a claim lies is beyond seas, the statute of limitation shall not run against the creditor." This statute is also defective, because it includes not Scotland; for a presumption of payment cannot justly be urged against an English creditor, who forbears to sue while his debtor is out of England though not beyond sea. Action however must be denied in England by force of the statute, though the debtor has been all along in Scotland. But this is no rule to us: we are at liberty to judge of the weight of the presumption from circumstances; and accordingly the court of session sustained action after the six years against a man who resided most of the time in Scotland.*

Though the act of limitations of James I. makes no provision for the case where the debtor happens to be in a different country, it is more circumspect as to the creditor's residence. For in the 7th section <358> it is provided, "That the prescription shall not run against the creditor while he is beyond seas":[3] and justly, because in that situation his delaying to bring an action infers not against him any presumption of payment. The case is parallel where the creditor happens to reside in Scotland, and therefore his residence there must also bar a presumption of payment. Hence it appears, that the decision, July 1717, Rae contra Wright,[4] is erroneous. James Rae a Scotch pedlar having died in England, his brother Richard intermeddled with his effects there at short-hand without any warrant. Richard, during the running of the six years, returned to Dumfries, and

---

2. An Act for the amendment of the law and the better administration of justice, 1705.

* March 4. 1755, Trustees for the creditors of Renton contra Baillie [M 11124, from Kames, *Select Decisions*, p. 113].

3. 21 James I, cap. 16 (An Act for limitation of actions and for avoiding of suits in law, 1623).

4. Rae contra Wright [M 4506], from Kames, *Remarkable Decisions* i: 16, No. 8.

died there. After the six years were elapsed, a process was brought against his executor by William Rae, a third brother, to account to him for the half of the effects thus irregularly intermeddled with. The court sustained the defence, That the action was cut off by the English statute of limitations. This was unjust. While Richard remained in England, the circumstance that William, living in Scotland, forbore to raise a suit in England, afforded not the slightest suspicion that he had <359> received payment from Richard. And suppose he had lived in England, payment could not be presumed against him, when his debtor left England before the lapse of the six years.

By established practice in England, action is not sustained upon a double bond after twenty years. The interest at the rate of 5 per cent. equals the principal in twenty years, which therefore exhausts the whole penal part of the bond, and makes the double sum due in equity as well as at common law. After this period the sum must remain barren, because interest is not stipulated in the bond: and in that view, it is justly inferred from the delay of demanding payment after the twenty years, that payment must already have been made. This in effect is an English prescription, inferring from long delay a presumption of payment. It follows therefore, if the parties have lived all along in England, that the presumptive payment from prescription ought to be sustained here.

In the English bankrupt-statute, 13th Elisabeth, cap. 7. §2. it is enacted, "That the commissioners shall have power to <360> sell all the goods of the bankrupt, real and personal, which he had before his bankruptcy, and to divide the produce among the creditors in proportion to the extent of their debts"; and §12. it is declared, "That this act shall not extend to land aliened *bona fide* before the bankruptcy."[5] Hence it appears to be the intention and effect of the statute, to bar all deeds by the bankrupt, and all execution by the creditors, after the first act of bankruptcy. And the English writers accordingly invent a cause to support these statutory effects. They hold, that the effects are vested in the commissioners *retro* from the first act of bankruptcy. "Creditors upon whatsoever security they be, come in all equal, unless such as have obtained actual execution before the

5. An Act touching orders for bankrupts, 1571.

bankruptcy, or had taken pledges for their just debts; and the reason is, because, from the act of bankruptcy, all the bankrupt's estate is vested in the
commissioners":* which is to suppose the effects of the bankrupt vested
in commissioners before they have an existence; <361> a strange bias in
some writers, that they will have recourse to absurd fictions for explaining
what is obviously reducible to rational principles! The statute has a more
solid foundation than a fiction: it is founded on equity, as is demonstrated
above.† But to confine our observations upon the statute to what more
peculiarly concerns this country, I must observe, that the great circulation
of trade through the two kingdoms since the union, makes it frequently
necessary for the court of session to take the English bankrupt-statutes
under consideration; and it has puzzled the Court mightily, what effect
should be given to them here. That a foreign statute cannot have any coercive authority *extra territorium,* is clear: but at first view it is not so clear,
that the statutory transference of property above mentioned, from the
bankrupt to the commissioners, may not comprehend effects real or personal in Scotland, or in any other foreign country; for why may not a legal
conveyance be equivalent to a voluntary conveyance by the proprietor? I
have had occasion to <362> observe above,‡ that law cannot force the will,
nor compel any man to make a conveyance. In place of a voluntary conveyance, when justice requires it to be granted, all that a court can do, or
the legislature can do, is to be themselves the disponers; and it is evident
that their deed of conveyance cannot reach any subject real or personal
but what is within their territory. This makes a solid difference between a
voluntary and a legal conveyance. The former has no relation to a place:
a deed of alienation, whether of land or of moveables, is good where-ever
granted: an Englishman, for example, has in China the same power to
alien his land in England, that he had before he left his native country; and
the power he has to dispose of his moveables will reach them in the most
distant corner of the earth. The latter, on the contrary, has the strictest
relation to place: the power of a court, and even of the legislature, being
merely territorial, reacheth not lands nor moveables *extra territorium.* We

* [M. Bacon,] New abridgement of the law, vol. 1. [1736,] p. 258.
† See above, p. 199 [p. 347 above].
‡ Sect. 4. of the present chapter.

may then with certainty conclude, that the statutory trans- <363> ference of property from the bankrupt to the commissioners, cannot carry any effects in Scotland: these are subjected to our own laws and our own judges; and cannot be convey'd from one person to another by the authority of any foreign court, or of any foreign statute. The English bankrupt-statutes however are not disregarded by us. One effect may and ought to be given them according to the rules of justice: it is the duty of the debtor to sell his effects for satisfying his creditors if he cannot otherwise procure money; and it is in particular the duty of an English bankrupt, to convey all his effects to the commissioners named by the chancellor, or to the assignees named by the creditors, in order to be sold for payment of his debts. The English statute, by conveying to the commissioners all the English funds, does for the bankrupt what he himself ought to do: but as the English statute has no authority over funds belonging to the bankrupt in Scotland, it becomes necessary for the commissioners or assignees to apply to the court of session, "specifying the debtor's bankruptcy, and his failure to make a conveyance; and there- <364> fore praying that the court will adjudge to the plaintiffs the debtor's effects in Scotland; or rather that they will order the same to be sold, and the price to be paid to the plaintiffs." For that purpose, the proper action, in my apprehension, is a process of sale of the debtor's moveables as well as of his land. Debts due here to the bankrupt may also be sold; but as against solvent debtors a process for payment is better management, it appears that, in the case of bankruptcy, this process is competent to the assignees without necessity of an arrestment.* The assignees being trustees for behoof of the whole creditors, have a just claim to the bankrupt's whole effects, to be converted into money for payment of the creditors; and in the forms of the law of Scotland there appears nothing to bar the assignees from bringing a direct action for payment against the bankrupt's debtors here, as he himself could have done before his bankruptcy. In thus appointing the bankrupt's debtors to make payment to the assignees, the court of session exerts no power but what <365> is the foundation of all legal execution, namely, the making that conveyance for the bankrupt which he himself ought to

* See above p. 174 [p. 334 above].

have made. By this expeditious method, justice is satisfied, and no person is hurt.

Whether the price of the bankrupt's moveable funds, and the sum arising from the debts due to him, ought to be distributed here among his creditors, or be remitted to England for that purpose, is a matter purely of expediency. The rule of distribution seems to be the same in both countries; and the creditors therefore have no interest in the question, but what arises from receiving payment in one place rather than in another. But if the bankrupt's lands in Scotland have been attached by execution, which is almost always the case, the price of it upon a sale must be distributed here; for the purchaser is not bound to pay the price till the real debts be convey'd to him, and the real creditors are not bound to convey till they get payment.

In the last place come foreign decrees; which are of two kinds, one sustaining the claim, and one dismissing it. A foreign decree sustaining the claim, is not <366> one of those universal titles which ought to be made effectual every where. It is a title that depends on the authority of the court whence it issued, and therefore has no coercive authority *extra territorium*. And yet as it would be hard to oblige the person who claims on a decree, to bring a new action against his party in every country to which he may retire; therefore common utility, as well as regard to a sister-court, have established a rule among all civilized nations, That a foreign decree shall be put in execution, unless some good exception be opposed to it in law or in equity: which is making no wider step in favour of the decree, than to presume it just till the contrary be proved. But this includes not a decree decerning for a penalty; because no court reckons itself bound to punish, or to concur in punishing, any delict committed *extra territorium*.

A foreign decree which, by dismissing the claim affords an *exceptio rei judicatae*[6] against it, enjoys a more extensive privilege. We not only presume it to be just, but will not admit any evidence of its being unjust. The reasons follow. A decreet- <367> arbitral is final by mutual consent. A judgement-condemnator[7] ought not to be final against the defendant,

6. A plea or defense which states that the subject matter of the action has been determined by an earlier action.

7. That is, a finding for the plaintiff.

because he gave no consent. But a decreet-absolvitor[8] ought to be final against the plaintiff, because the judge was chosen by himself; with respect to him at least, it is equivalent to a decreet-arbitral. Public utility affords another argument extremely cogent. There is nothing more hurtful to society than that law-suits be perpetual. In every law-suit there ought to be a *ne plus ultra,*[9] some step that ought to be ultimate; and a decree dismissing a claim is in its nature ultimate. Add a consideration that regards the nature and constitution of a court of justice. A decree dismissing a claim, may, it is true, be unjust, as well as a decree sustaining it. But they differ widely in one capital point: in declining to give redress against a decree dismissing a claim, the court is not guilty of authorising injustice, even supposing the decree to be unjust: the utmost that can be said is, that the court forbears to interpose in behalf of justice; but such forbearance, instead of being faulty, is highly meritorious in every case <368> where private justice clashes with public utility.* The case is very different with respect to a decree of the other kind; for to award execution upon a foreign decree without admitting any objection against it, would be, for aught the court can know, to support and promote injustice. A court, as well as an individual, may in certain circumstances have reason to forbear acting, or executing their office: but the doing injustice, or the supporting it, cannot be justified in any circumstances.†

To illustrate the practice of Scotland with respect to a foreign decree sustaining a claim, I give a remarkable case. By statute 12*mo Annae, cap.* 18, made perpetual 4*to Geo. I. cap.* 12, it is enacted, "That the collector of the customs, or any other person who shall be employed in preserving any vessel in distress, shall, within thirty days after the service performed, be paid a reasonable reward for the same; and in default thereof, that the ship or goods so saved shall remain in the custody of the collector, till such time as he and those employ'd by him <369> shall be reasonably gratified for their assistance and trouble, or good security given for that purpose."[10]

---

8. That is, a finding for the defendant.
9. "Highest point."
* See Conclusion of book 2.
† Ibid.
10. 12 Anne, c. 18, s. 22 (1713); 4 Geo. I, c. 12 (1717).

This is where the merchant claims his ship or cargo. But in case no person appear to claim, there is the following proviso: "That goods which are in their nature perishable, shall be forthwith sold by the collector; and that, after deducting all charges, the residue of the price with a fair and just account of the whole, shall be transmitted to the exchequer, there to remain for the benefit of the rightful owner; and that the same shall be delivered to him so soon as he appears, and makes a claim." Brunton and Chalmers, owners of a vessel called *The Serpent's prize,* loaded the same with 100 quarters of wheat for Zealand. In her voyage she was stranded at a place called *Redscar,* near the town of Stocktown. Chalmers having got notice of the accident, repaired immediately to Redscar; and found his wheat in the hands of John Wilson collector of the customs at Stocktown; part of it laid up in lofts, and part in the open field; the whole greatly damaged by sea-water. Finding it necessary to dispose of the wheat instantly, he <370> applied to the collector for liberty to sell; offering to put the price in his hand as security for the salvage. This being obstinately refused, he took a protest against the collector, and brought against him an action of trespass upon the case before the King's bench. And the defendant having put himself upon his country,[11] the cause came to a trial at Newcastle; where a special verdict was returned, in substance finding, "That all reasonable care was taken of the wheat by the collector and others by his order; That on the 3d of October then next following, James Chalmers applied to the collector, desiring that the wheat, being much damaged, might be forthwith sold; and that the money produced by such sale might be left in the hand of the collector to answer all charges; but did not then offer to pay to the collector any money for salvage; neither did the collector then make any demand on that account, he not knowing at that time what the salvage amounted to; but then refused to deliver the said wheat, or permit the same to be sold, he having an order from the commissioners of his Majesty's <371> customs for that purpose." And the verdict concludes thus: "But whether, upon the whole matter aforesaid by the said jurors in form aforesaid found, the within-named John Wilson be guilty of the premisses within written or not, the said jurors are altogether ignorant, and pray

11. That is, having submitted the question for determination by a jury.

advice from the court thereupon." The judge at that circuit having referred the cause to the court of King's-bench at Westminster, judgement was at last there given on the 18th July 1751, after several continuations,[12] "Finding, That the said John Wilson is not guilty of the premisses; that the said Brunton and Chalmers shall take nothing by their said bill; but that they be in mercy, &c. for their false claim; and that the said John Wilson go thereof without day, &c. And it is further considered, That the said John recover against the said Brunton and Chalmers sixty pounds, for his costs and charges laid out by him about his defence on this behalf; and that the said John have execution thereof," &c.

For this sum of £60 awarded to the collector for costs, he brought an action <372> against Brunton and Chalmers, before the court of session; and in support of his claim set forth, That it is founded on the presumption, *Quod res judicata pro veritate habetur.*[13] The defendants insisted, That this presumption must yield to direct evidence of injustice, which would clearly appear upon comparing the decree with the statute. And the following circumstances were urged. First, That though the wheat was in a perishing condition, the collector refused to permit the same to be sold, even contrary to his own interest, as the price to him was a better security for the salvage than the damaged wheat. Secondly, When the application for sale was made, the collector was not ready to make his claim for salvage, not knowing at that time the amount thereof; in which circumstances to forbid the sale, was not only rigorous, but unjust: it was, to abandon the wheat to destruction, without permitting the defendants to interpose. Even the offer of ready money to pay the salvage would not have availed them, seeing the collector was not in a condition to make any demand. This case being reported by the Lord Ordinary, it occurred at advising, that the <373> statute provides nothing about selling perishable goods, except in the case that the merchant does not appear to claim the wrecked goods. Therefore the present case is not provided for by the statute. It is a *casus omissus,*[14] which in equity must be supplied agreeably to the intendment and purpose of the statute. Viewing the matter in this light, it appeared,

12. That is, postponements, or adjournments.
13. "That a matter which has been adjudged is taken for truth."
14. An omitted case; that is, something not provided for in a statute.

in the first place, that the defendants, being proprietors of the wheat, were intitled to dispose of it, provided the collector suffered no prejudice as to his claim of salvage, which he certainly did not if the price were put in his hand. Nay his security would be improved by the sale, which would afford him current coin instead of perishing wheat. It was considered, in the second place, that this is agreeable to the intendment of the statute; for if the custom-house-officer must dispose of perishable goods where there is none to claim, much more where the owner appears, and insists for a sale. Thirdly, The statute, intitling the officer to retain the goods for security of the salvage, undoubtedly supposes that the officer can instruct his claim, in order <374> that the merchant may have instant possession of the goods, upon paying the salvage. In this view the conduct of the collector was altogether unjustifiable: the statute gives no authority for retaining the goods as a security for the salvage, unless as a *succedaneum*[15] when satisfaction is not offered in money; and as the collector here was not ready to receive satisfaction, it was a trespass[16] to retain the goods in a perishing condition. With regard to this matter in general, one observation had great weight, That it never could be the intention of the legislature, to force merchants first to pay salvage, and thereafter to undergo the risk of perishable and damnified goods, the price of which possibly might not amount to the salvage. The collector therefore could not in common justice demand more than the value of the goods for his salvage; and *a fortiori* could not demand any security beyond that value. The court accordingly unanimously refused to interpose their authority for execution upon this judgement.* <375>

The judgement of the King's-bench may possibly be justified as pronounced by a court of common law, which, in interpreting statutes, must adhere to the letter, without regarding the intention of the legislature. If so, the proprietors of the wheat ought to have applied to the chancery, or have removed their cause there by a *Certiorari*.[17] If courts of common law

---

15. Substitute.

16. That is, a wrong, tort.

* January 6. 1756, John Wilson collector of the customs at Stocktown contra Robert Brunton and James Chalmers merchants in Edinburgh [M 4551, from Kames, *Select Decisions*, p. 129].

17. A prerogative writ used in England to remove cases into the Court of King's Bench.

in England be so confined, their constitution is extremely imperfect. But supposing the court of King's-bench to have acted properly according to its constitution, it was notwithstanding right in the court of session to refuse execution upon a foreign decree that is materially unjust, or contrary to equity.

An appeal entered by Collector Wilson was heard *ex parte*,[18] and the decree of the court of session reversed; by which the £60 of costs decerned in the court of King's-bench was made effectual against Chalmers and Brunton. The decree, if I have been rightly informed, was reversed for the following reason; that in England the decree of a foreign supreme court has such credence, that judgement is immediately given, without entering into the <376> merits, provided the matter have been litigated; that in all countries the decrees of the court of admiralty are, for the sake of commerce, intitled to immediate execution; and that the same credence ought to have been given by the court of session to the judgement of the King's-bench. It would seem then, that in England greater authority is given to foreign decrees than in any other civilized country; and indeed greater than can be justified from the nature and constitution of any court. A foreign decree has no legal authority in England; and for the courts of Westminster blindly to authorise execution upon a foreign decree without admitting any objection against it, is a practice that cannot be approved, because it must frequently lead them to authorise injustice. But admitting the practice of England, it ought to have been considered, that the practice of England is no authority in Scotland. In reviewing the decrees of the court of session, the law of Scotland is the rule. And if the decree in question was agreeable to the law of *Scotland,* it ought to have been affirmed; especially as the law of Scotland with respect to foreign decrees, <377> is not only in itself rational, but agreeable to the laws of all other civilized nations, England excepted. The House of Lords, we may rest assured, could not intend to try the merits of a Scotch decree by the law or practice of England. But as the appeal was heard *ex parte,* the reversal has certainly been founded upon the erroneous supposition, That, with respect to foreign decrees, the practice of Scotland is the same with that of England.

18. Proceedings in which only one side is heard.

With respect to a judicial conveyance, or legal execution, the nature of it is sufficiently explained in a former part of this chapter, that it can carry no effects but what are subjected to the authority of the court from which execution issues. In our poinding, for example, the goods of the debtor are conveyed to his creditor, not by the will of the debtor, but by the will of the sheriff; and his will can operate no farther than to convey effects within his territory. In England, debts, like other moveables, are attached by the legal execution of *Fieri facias*,[19] similar to our poinding. But a *Fieri facias* can carry no debts but what are due by persons within the territory of the court <378> from which the execution issues. It is not a title to force payment from a debtor in Scotland: the court must be applied to within whose territory he resides; and that court will authorise the execution that is customary in Scotland, namely, an arrestment and decree of forthcoming. The same holds as to other moveables. And the titles necessary to a foreigner for attaching moveables or debts in Scotland, are set forth in the third and fourth sections of the present chapter.

19. "That you cause to be done": a writ directed to sheriffs in England to seize and sell a defendant's property in execution of the judgment of a court.

ORIGINAL INDEX

[The volumes are denoted "1st" and "2d" by Kames, and the pages by number. They relate in this volume to the page numbers bracketed <> in the text.]

208. Disposition *omnium bonorum* by a bankrupt to trustees for his creditors, 2d, 262. Statutes of bankruptcy in England, what effect they have here, 2d, 359. A reduction upon the head of bankruptcy, whether good against purchasers, 2d, 258. Bankrupt-statute 1772, 2d, 264.

Barbarius Philippus, 2d, 113.

Bargain, of hazard with a young heir, 1st, 82. Inequality not regarded *inter majores, scientes, et prudentes,* 1st, 103. But redressed where made with one weak or facile, 1st, 103.

Bastard, has not the privilege of making a testament, 2d, 335.

Beneficium competentiae, 2d, 25.

Benevolence as a virtue distinguished from benevolence as a duty, 1st, 109. In the progress of society benevolence becomes a duty in many cases formerly disregarded, 1st, 9. Duty of benevolence, how limited, 1st, 109. Duty of benevolence to children, 1st, 109. Connections that make benevolence a duty when not prejudicial to our interest, 1st, 114. Connections that make benevolence a duty even against our interest, 1st, 136.

Bona fide purchaser, 2d, 41.

Bona fide possessor *rei alienae,* has a claim for meliorations, 1st, 145. 2d, 152. Is not accountable for the rents levied and consumed by him, 2d, 111. 137; unless he be *locupletior,* 2d, 144. Will rents levied by the *bona fide* possessor impute in payment of a debt due to him, 2d, 147.

Bona fides. How far *bona fide* transactions with a putative proprietor are supported in equity, 2d, 109. How far the acts of a putative judge or

magistrate are supported in equity, 2d, 113.

Bona fides contractus, 1st, 337.

Bona fide payment, 2d, 105.

Bond secluding executors, by what legal execution it is attachable, 2d, 3. Bond of provision, cannot be claimed if the child die before the term of payment, 2d, 164. Rigorous and oppressive conditions in a bond of borrowed money, 1st, 70.

Bonos mores. Acts *contra bonos mores* repressed by equity, 1st, 17. 2d, 81.

Book. Exclusive privilege of printing books given to their authors and their assigns, 1st, 352.

Bribery in elections, 2d, 50.

Brieve, 1st, 146.

Burden. A sum with which a disposition of land is burdened, by what legal execution it is attachable, 2d, 3.

C

Catholic creditor, his duty with respect to the secondary creditors, 1st, 122. Catholic creditor purchasing one of the secondary debts, 1st, 126.

Cautioner, making payment, is intitled to have an assignment from the creditor, 1st, 114. In what terms ought this assignment to be granted, 1st, 119. Mutual relief between co-cautioners, 1st, 117. How far is a cautioner bound to communicate eases, 1st, 162.

Cess, is *debitum fructuum,* 1st, 130.

Cessio bonorum, 2d, 26.

Chance disgustful, 1st, 144.

Charity, why it is not supported by law, 1st, 23.

Children. Duty of parents to children, how far extended, 1st, 109.

PRINCIPLES Founded on in This Work

A man who is innocent is not liable to repair any hurt done by him.

Where there is a right, some court must be empowered to make it effectual.

For every wrong there ought to be a remedy.

No interest of mine, not even the preservation of life itself, authorises me to do any mischief to an innocent person.

Every man may prosecute his own right, without regarding any indirect or consequential damage that another may suffer.

Justice will not permit a man to exercise his right where his intention is solely to hurt another.

An action at law will not be sustained if the plaintiff cannot show that it will benefit him.

It is an immoral act, to strip people of their property by throwing a strong temptation in their way.

He that demands equity must give equity.

Equity holds a deed to be granted where it ought to be granted.

One is permitted to take advantage of another's error *in damno evitando*, not *in lucro captando*.

No man is intitled to the aid of a court of equity when that aid becomes necessary by his own fault.

No person, however innocent, ought to take advantage of a tortious act by which another is hurt.

A man ought not to take advantage of an improvement or reparation made upon a common subject, without refunding part of the expence, in proportion to the benefit he has received.

A thought retained within the mind cannot have the effect to qualify an obligation more than to create it.

To bind a man by words beyond consent, is repugnant to justice.

He who wills the end is understood to will the means proper for accomplishing the end.

A person honoured in a deed can take no benefit by it if he counteract the declared will of the granter.

A man who has committed no fault cannot be deprived of his property.

No person is bound to fulfil an obligation that answers not the end purposed by it.

Cujus commodum ejus debet esse incommodum [The person who has the advantage should also have the disadvantage].

Every crime against the law of nature may be punished at the discretion of the judge, where the legislature has not appointed a particular punishment.

A case out of the mischief, is out of the meaning of the law, though it be within the letter.

No man is permitted to take advantage of a defect in evidence when that defect is occasioned by his fraud.

Potior debet esse conditio ejus qui certat de damno evitando quam ejus qui certat de lucro captando [Better is the condition of him who is striving to avoid loss than the one who is striving to make a gain].

It is unjust to demand from the debtor privately, or even by legal execution, any subject that he is bound to convey to another.

No man is suffered to take benefit by his own fraud or wrong.

No person is suffered to make a defence contrary to conscience, more than to make a claim.

Frustra petis quod mox es restituturus [Vainly you seek what you are soon to restore].

The motive of preventing loss will not justify an unjust act or the being accessory to it.

MAJOR VARIANT READINGS BETWEEN THE

FIRST, SECOND, AND THIRD EDITIONS

As he was finishing the third edition of his *Principles of Equity* in March, 1778, Lord Kames told James Boswell that he was making the work "much better, and it would be a good improvement to a Lawyer to compare the last edition with this."[1] It is the third edition which is printed here, along with the Preliminary Discourse, which was included in the second edition, but dropped from the third, since Kames had in the intervening period published this material in the *Sketches of the History of Man*. Significant variations between the editions will be noted here, and extracts from the first two editions are given in the appendix.

A comparison of the three editions[2] reveals significant changes in the presentation of the material. There were substantial changes in organization between the first and second editions. Further refinements of presentation and argument were made in the third, as Kames teased out more sophisticated distinctions or as he responded to new developments.[3] The division of the work into three books, devoted to the powers of equity as derived from justice, its powers as founded on utility, and

1. Geoffrey Scott and Frederick A. Pottle, *Private Papers of James Boswell from Malahide Castle* (privately printed, 1932), vol. 15, p. 274.

2. There were to be two further editions of the text after Kames's death, one in 1800 and another in 1825. There were no changes between the third and fifth editions.

3. For instance, the first edition has no equivalent to chapter 2 of book 2 in the third edition, which deals with acts and covenants in themselves innocent, but which tend to disturb society and to distress its members. This chapter, which largely discusses case law concerning combinations of workmen, made its first appearance in the second edition, since it concerned cases which had come to court since the first edition's publication. Further case law led Kames to create an additional chapter in the third edition on "Regulations of Commerce, and of other public concerns, rectified where wrong."

the application of equity's powers to several subjects, remained constant across the editions. However, much of the material within these books was rearranged, and the arguments were refined. To allow the reader to trace how Kames rearranged the content across the editions, the table of contents of the first two editions is placed before the Appendix, with references to show where the material included in those editions was placed in the third.

The most significant structural change across the editions was Kames's reorganization of the first book between the editions of 1760 and 1767. Where the later editions divide the first book into two parts (dealing with pecuniary and nonpecuniary matters), the first edition divides it into three, separating the material on equity's intervention in pecuniary matters into two distinct parts, dealing first with equity's power to "supply what is defective" in the common law, and second with its power "to correct the injustice of the common law." In the first edition, Kames explains the underlying principles behind this distinction. The common law is defective, he argues, since it "regards no injury but what occasions actual loss or damage with respect to fortune, or actual hurt with respect to person or reputation," whereas the law of nature "prohibits every moral wrong by which one is in any way hurt in point of interest, though the hurt may not amount to actual loss or damage." Accordingly, in such cases, "it becomes the province of a court of equity to enforce the law of nature" [1st: 3]. Turning to injustices, Kames notes that since for every wrong there should be a remedy, equity must interpose where "the common law exceeds just bounds and unwarily authorises oppression and wrong." It therefore acts to restrain the common law "where a rule extends beyond its professed aim and purpose" (1st: 76: see Appendix, p. 493, Extract [1st: 76–77]). In the later editions, this categorization of material around the concepts of defects and injustices in the common law is largely[4] abandoned,

---

4. Some traces of the distinction remained. In the first edition, *defects* with respect to execution were placed in a short chapter at the end of the first book, while *injustices* with respect to execution were placed in one section of a larger chapter devoted to injustices in making debts effectual. In the third edition, these matters were gathered together in the chapter on legal execution, which was itself then divided into sections concerned with defects and injustice—thereby containing an echo of the earlier division.

with material pertaining to both aspects being consolidated into single chapters.[5]

Kames opens his substantive discussion in each edition with the subject of harms remedied by equity. The treatment of this topic in the first edition is much narrower than that taken in the second and third. In the first edition, the chapter on harms is divided into two sections, dealing with wrongs done by a man either "for his own behoof" or for the "behoof of another." In it, Kames focuses his attention primarily on fraud, dealing with cases (involving claims on estates) where a person has suffered pecuniary loss as a result of another's fraudulent conduct.[6] Much of the material which makes up these sections is reused in the subsequent editions in later chapters dealing with fraud and equity's power to punish; and a more sophisticated argument is presented in the chapter on harms. The argument now presented is that equity has a role in enforcing the moral principle of abstaining from injuring others in a number of situations where no remedy is provided at common law.[7] It intervenes in cases when harm is done by a person exercising a right or privilege, when harm is done when no right or privilege is exercised, and when undue influence or fraud are used.[8] The first two sections of the revised chapter (which address the first two of these issues) develop a distinction Kames first set out in the second edition of the *Principles of Equity*, which he subsequently included in the *Sketches of the History of Man*. He notes that while justice teaches that no man is authorised to do any mischief to another, expedience teaches that

5. Most notably, the material relating to defective deeds, which in the first edition is found in the third chapter of part 1 and the first chapter of part 2, is united into a single chapter. Similarly, Kames consolidated the two chapters dealing with defects and injustices relating to statutes. In the first edition, Kames considered a statute "defective" when the words or means enacted by it fell short of the legislative will and regarded it as an "injustice" where the words or the means went beyond the legislative will. In this case, the content was not altered by the changes in the ordering of the material.

6. As Kames explains in the second section, although the law distinguishes between accessories and principals when it comes to punishment, in matters of pecuniary loss, "every person who concurred in the wrong is subjected to reparation" [1st: 7].

7. In the third edition (3rd: 1: 44; p. 40, above), Kames made the point (omitted in the second edition) that "with respect to harm done intentionally, there is no imperfection in common law, and consequently no necessity for a court of equity."

8. In addition, the second and third editions had a final section in this chapter on remedies applied by equity.

one should not be restrained in exercising one's rights by the mere possibility that one might harm others. This distinction, found in human nature, is reflected in law. Accordingly (as Kames explains in the first section of chapter 1), while a man might lawfully exercise his rights for his own benefit, even if this were done in a way which might "consequentially" harm another, it is unlawful for him to exercise his rights with the intention of harming another [2nd: 60; 3rd: 1: 55 (p. 46 above)]. The main illustration given for the latter point is the doctrine of abuse of rights (or acting *in aemulationem vicini*),[9] something not discussed in the first edition.[10] He then turns to harms done by one not exercising a right or privilege, focusing on liability for fault in the Roman *Lex Aquilia;* and concludes that since these faults come under the common law, they leave "no gleanings to a court of equity" [2nd: 64; 3rd: 1: 65 (p. 51 above)].

The second and third editions follow with a short chapter dealing with equity's protection of the weak-minded. This chapter has no equivalent in the first edition, where the topic is covered in a long first chapter of the second part (sect. 5), on injustices with respect to rights founded on will.[11] The argument—on a new and developing area of law—became more nuanced as the editions progressed. In the first edition, Kames saw the concepts of relief on the ground of undue influence and relief of the weak-minded as linked; and he gave an example which indicated that both elements needed to be present for relief to be given (Appendix, p. 501, Extracts [1st: 97] and [1st: 98]). He also commented (1st: 99): "Where a facile

9. "In envy of the neighbor"; on which doctrine, see the glossary, "*in aemulationem vicini.*"

10. In the third edition, Kames included in this section material which in the first edition was placed in a section on "Injustice of Common Law with respect to voluntary Payment" [in chapter 4 of part 2]. The section discusses the right of a debtor to pay his original creditor before he is formally notified of the assignment of a debt. In the third edition, Kames argues that if a creditor who is aware of the assignment pays the original creditor, this is something done "intentionally to distress the assignee, without benefiting himself" [3rd: 1: 58 (p. 47 above)], and so is done *in aemulationem vicini*. In the first edition, he simply describes it as "the oppression or wrong that may be committed by a debtor under protection of the common law" [1: 150].

11. This section also includes some material (on deeds obtained by fraud or extortion) which in the later editions is placed in the expanded first chapter on harms, discussed above; as well as material on the effect of fraud by third parties (see Appendix, p. 501, Extract [1st: 100–101]), which is dealt with elsewhere in the third edition (3rd: 1: 164, p. 102 above).

man of his own accord executes a deed, however foolish, in favour of a person who has used no undue influence by fraud, by imposition, or by throwing temptations in the way, such a deed is not set aside, however great the lesion may be." However, by the time of the second edition, he treated undue influence and contracts entered into by the weak-minded in separate sections, and abandoned the contention that they were linked, dropping the example he had used to illustrate the link. This was to argue that equity could protect the weak-minded, without needing any element of undue influence or fraud.

All three editions include a chapter on defects in the common law with respect to enforcing the duty of benevolence. Each is divided into two sections, one dealing with connections which make benevolence a duty when not prejudicial to our interest, and one on connections making benevolence a duty even when against our interest. The first section is largely the same across the three editions,[12] but there are some significant changes to the second.[13] To begin with, where the first edition is only concerned with protecting those who have been losers, the later editions add a new article, discussing connections which entitle a man who is not a loser to partake of my gain.[14] Moreover, there is an important change in the argument of the

12. There are some minor additions in the later editions: for example, 3rd: 1: 130–33 (pp. 85–86 above).

13. The argument of the first article (on gains made by one applied to repair another's loss) does not change across the three editions, though the ordering of the argument does alter. In the first edition, Kames presents the argument that one man can be forced to pay for another's loss out of his gain only where there is either a strong personal or proprietorial connection. His discussion begins with the personal connections and then moves on to situations where the personal connection is weak but the link between loss and gain is strong, where the Roman maxim *nemo debet locupletari aliena jactura* is discussed. In the second and third editions, the general order is reversed: he now begins with the connection of loss and gain and proceeds to the personal connections, where the link between loss and gain is slighter.

14. This section in the later edition reuses some material placed elsewhere in the first edition. First, there are passages (in the first edition) in the section on connections which entitle a man to have his loss made up out of my gain, in which he discusses real connections: Kames introduced them in the first edition thus (1st: 29): "If in the cases above mentioned, where there is scarce any personal connection, a relief in equity be given, there ought to be still less doubt about this relief in the following cases, where, to the most intimate connection betwixt loss and gain, there is superadded a personal connection not of the slightest kind." Second, some of the material was placed in the first edition in the first chapter of part II.

article dealing with situations where one who is not a gainer must indemnify one who is a loser. In the later edition, Kames rethinks the principles which lie behind the *actio negotiorum gestorum,* according to which a person who has voluntarily taken charge of another's affairs in his absence is to be recompensed for it. In the first edition, he rooted this obligation in "quasi-contract": assuming that the parties had accidentally failed to provide for the case by way of contract, the law gave them a remedy as if they had contracted (see Appendix, p. 487, Extract [1st: 34–35]). By the time of the second edition (2nd: 114–15), Kames had changed the argument to that followed also in the third (3rd: 1: 180–82; pp. 109–111 above), noting that "it seems a wide stretch in equity to give to a supposition the effects of a real contract." He now suggested that the claim for recompense "has a solid foundation in justice, and in human nature, without necessity of recurring to the strained supposition of a contract" (3rd: 1: 182n; p. 110 above). This was a highly significant step, for in taking it, Kames argued that the claim for recompense was one founded in notions of equity rather than in presumed contractual consent. Kames's change of view, from a "quasi-contractual" to a "restitutionary" view can be seen in two other passages in this chapter. The first is the passage (3rd: 1: 184; p. 112 above) where he discusses the case of the master of a ship, who wishes to recover from the owners of the goods shipped the sums he has paid as a ransom to get them back, even though the owners have obtained no benefit from his action, as the goods were later lost at sea. Whereas he had used contractual language in the first edition, in the second (2nd: 115) and third editions (3rd: 1: 184; p. 112 above), he simply noted that from the moment the transaction was finished, the owners became debtors to the master for the amount he had paid on their account, for he did not undertake the risk of the cargo. The second example (which follows immediately thereafter) concerns jettison, about which Kames makes the point that the cargo owner whose goods have been jettisoned at sea can claim a contribution from other cargo owners, as soon as any goods have been landed, even if these goods are later destroyed (though he cannot if all the goods are lost at sea subsequent to the jettison). Once again, the contractual language used in the first edition is dropped by the second.

There follows in each edition a chapter devoted to imperfections in deeds and covenants. The second and third editions devote long chapters in the first book to this topic, which begin with a discussion of contracting in general.[15] While there are some differences in the way the material is arranged in the chapter between the second and third editions,[16] Kames's major reorganization of the material took place between the first and second editions. For the first edition distributed the material later consolidated into one chapter across two separate chapters: chapter 3 of part I (on defects with respect to rights founded on will), which largely dealt with the problem of interpreting contracts and deeds when there were defects in the way in which they were written; and chapter 1 of part II (on injustices with respect to rights founded on will), where he dealt mainly with vitiating factors not recognized by common law, such as fraud, error, or oppression (for the introductory paragraph to this chapter, see Appendix, p. 494, Extract [1st: 77]).

In the first edition, in place of the discussion of contracting in general, Kames begins his chapter on defects in contracts with the argument that parties often make mistakes in writing down contracts, or fail to foresee events which might occur, and that equity fills this gap by "conjecturing what would have been the will of the parties had they foreseen the event" (1st: 40) (see Appendix, p. 488, Extract [1st: 39–40]). After discussing problems which arise when parties have expressed their will imperfectly, Kames turns to the problem of "defective will," dealing with cases where equity intervenes to accomplish the real ends of the parties. He then sets out a distinction between means and ends which he uses more extensively in the first edition than in the later ones. Kames argues that judges must distinguish between contracts where the performance stipulated is the ultimate end, and those where it is only a means to a further end. Equity cannot intervene in the former case, he says, but it may in the latter.[17] Since one of the tasks of equity is to make rights effectual, Kames argues that it should assist where the ultimate aim is to confer a right, even if the means expressed in the contract are imperfect.

15. The discussion of this is fuller and more nuanced in the third edition.

16. For instance, in the third edition, the introduction to this chapter ends with material on the *condictio ex poenitentia* (where Kames discusses whether a party who had entered into an engagement can change his mind before performance) which had separate sections devoted to it in the first (book 1, part 2, chap. 1, sect. 7) and second editions (book 1, part 1, chap. 4, sect. 7).

17. Kames explains that this is the principle behind the Roman distinction between contracts *stricti iuris* and *bonae fidei*.

Turning to discuss how the judge is to determine whether a right was intended to be conferred, Kames sets out an argument (omitted in the later editions) that where a deed is gratuitous, equity will not intervene to carry out what the granter would have intended but failed to express. Gratuitous deeds, he explains, can generate no *right* in justice; and since equity only intervenes on the ground of utility to prevent mischief, rather than to promote benefits, it has no ground to give relief here (see Appendix, p. 489, Extract [1st: 44–47]). He adds (1st: 51) that "a gratuitous deed, which has no foundation other than will merely, cannot be supported in any particular, except so far as will is actually interposed."[18] In the later editions, Kames changed his mind on the question of whether equity could assist in such cases. This can be seen from his later treatment of the case cited to support his views in the first edition: *Straiton* v. *Wight.* In the second edition (2nd: 149), the case was criticized on the ground that Kames now felt that equity *should* give a remedy in such cases. He had come to the view that equity could intervene (even in the case of a gratuitous deed) if the intention of the granter is clear. But in the third edition, Kames moved away from this position once more: the case was now invoked (3rd: 1: 258; p. 152 above) simply to show that equity will not supply a nonexistent will. As he now put it, where will is clearly expressed in a deed, it is not open to the courts to alter it. In effect, between the first and third editions, Kames sharpened his argument, making a general proposition that equity cannot alter a will clearly expressed in a deed or covenant. By 1778, his view was that where the deed makes clear what the right is, equity cannot look beyond the deed.

The means/ends distinction was also used in the first edition as a method to determine whether a term in a contract should be treated as a strict condition, which must be complied with, or whether equity could dispense with it and substitute another. This issue is discussed in both the chapters on defects and injustices regarding rights founded on will,[19] with the former dealing with cases where the words fall short of will, and the latter

18. This argument is restated later in the "Powers and Faculties" chapter of book 3: see Appendix, p. 516, Extract [1st: 255]. This paragraph is omitted when the same material is discussed at 3rd: 2: 288 (p. 390 above).

19. Kames's discussion of this issue in sect. 2 of the first chapter of part 2 is concerned with whether irritant clauses in deeds are to be regarded as strict conditions.

dealing with cases where they go beyond will (Appendix, p. 495, Extract [1st: 80–82]). Where terms are only inserted as means to accomplish a particular end, Kames suggests in 1760, they are not to be regarded as strict conditions. Kames warns that by overlooking the distinction between means and ends, one is liable to misapprehend the will of the granter:

> One in an overly view is apt to consider the means as ultimate, and consequently to admit of no other means, though these named by the granter prove deficient. But the granter's will is best ascertained from adverting to the end proposed by him; and if it appear, that the means named in the deed are chosen with no other view than to advance that end, it is the duty of the court of equity, where these prove deficient, to supply other means in order to fulfil the will of the granter. (1st: 53)

Kames gives the example of a sale of land, where the purchaser "by some accident" fails to pay the money which was due to be paid by a certain day. In such a case, he argues, equity can order specific performance of the contract of sale, and substitute another day for payment for that inserted in the agreement:

> A term specified for performance is not readily supposed to imply a condition: it is considered only as a means to bring about the end proposed; and when it proves ineffectual, it is the province of a court of equity to supply other means; that is, in the present case to name another day for performance. This is what the parties themselves would have done, had they foreseen the event. (1st: 48)

He gives other examples of the same issue, citing cases involving deeds granted by the Minister of Weem and Colonel Campbell, where the court interposed to make grants effective, after an insufficient number of trustees and referees had agreed to act. The court intervened, he suggests, because the appointment of these individuals was a means to effect the purpose of the grant, and not an end in itself.

The distinction between means and ends, which is so strongly emphasized in the first edition, becomes less pronounced as the editions progress. For instance, while in the second edition Kames includes the material on the Minister of Weem and Colonel Campbell in a section entitled "Where an unforeseen accident renders ineffectual the means provided in the deed or covenant to bring about the desired end" (2nd: 145), he makes the argument that the court should look at the parties' intent, rather than asking whether the term was a means or an end. In the third edition (3rd: 1: 205; p. 123 above), this material is placed in a section discussing how to proceed when words leave us uncertain about the will, where Kames again treats the question as one of discovering whether the parties intended to make a conditional bargain or not, without mentioning the distinction between means and ends.[20]

The distinction is also used as a more prominent explanatory tool in the first edition when Kames discusses how equity deals with mistakes. While each edition has a section dealing with deeds which fail to bring about the end for which they were made, the emphasis within those sections on the means/end distinction diminishes. In the first edition, the topic is introduced by a long discussion cast in terms of the distinction (see Appendix, p. 497, Extract [1st: 85–87]). In the second edition, the introductory part is shorter, but the distinction is still set out as the explanation of how equity can give relief where a contract does not answer the end proposed by it (Appendix, p. 526, Extract [2nd: 139–40]). In the third edition, the distinction is still made, but it is used more narrowly to explain why parties who enter unexecuted contracts under a mistake can rescind them. In the third edition, he is also more keen at this point to caution that parties cannot avoid contracts which turn out not to answer their private or secret ends.[21] By the third edition, his analysis had become more nuanced, with the means/ends distinction bearing less emphasis.

Between the second and third editions Kames also made modifications in his argument on engagements occasioned by error.[22] In the earlier edi-

20. The terminology of means and ends does not disappear. For instance, when discussing conditional bonds or grants (as where a young woman is granted money on condition of her marrying a suitable husband: 3rd: 1: 231ff.; pp. 136 ff. above), Kames explains the distinction between those conditions which are to be taken strictly and those which are not, by asking whether the stipulation was a means or an end in itself.

21. It is at this point in the third edition that he makes his criticism of Pufendorf (3rd: 1: 261). Kames makes the same point in the equivalent section of the first edition (1st: 88; p. 154 above), albeit later in the chapter, while in the second, the criticism of Pufendorf is placed in the general introduction to chapter 4 (2nd: 120).

22. This topic is covered in book 1, part 2, chap. 1, sect. 6 in the first edition; in book 1, part 1, chap. 4, sect. 10 in the second; and in book 1, part 1, chap. 4, sect. 6 of the third.

tions, Kames argues that there are two kinds of error. The first is where the parties are not in agreement about the subject matter of the contract, so that the error prevents consent arising. Since errors of this kind make the contract void at common law, there is (he says) "no occasion for the interposition of equity" (1st: 109). The second is where the error is one of motive: where although on the face of it, the parties have an agreement, one of the parties was mistaken about something which led him into the deed. Equity will intervene in such cases, Kames argues, but only where one party seeks to make a gain at the other's expense. He develops the argument by distinguishing between deeds and mutual contracts. Discussing the former, he says that where a deed is gratuitous, it will not be enforced if it was entered into under an error of motive; but where it was given for cause and is not gratuitous, it will be upheld. Discussing the latter (contracts), he argues that equity will relieve if the error is such as to undermine the end of the contract, rather than the means. This is because "[t]o make a covenant so unhappily as not to answer the purposed end, must always proceed from error" (1st: 111; see Appendix, p. 503, Extract [1st: 109–13]). The argument in the third edition is different. He begins by noting that errors as to motive are primarily found in deeds, rather than contracts; and argues that where a mistake led the granter to make the deed, equity will relieve, unless there were also other motives for the deed being granted. He then turns to discuss errors "in a deed or covenant after it is made," which he divides into two kinds: errors preventing consent (which allow the contract to be set aside), and errors as to quality (which do not). He then sets out to explain the distinction between these kinds of error.

Book 1 of each of the editions contains a short part devoted to nonpecuniary matters. In the third edition, this part is divided into two chapters: a long one devoted to the problem of how far a promise in favor of a third party is effectual, and a short one on immoral acts. In the first and second editions, the chapter on acts *contra bonos mores* was placed at the start of book 2, and ended with some material omitted in the third [see Appendix, p. 512, Extract [1st: 174–75]. Besides reorganizing this part,[23] between the first

---

23. In the first edition, when discussing this material (1st: 174), he does say of an act *contra bonos mores,* "It might, as a wrong not pecuniary, have found a place in the

and second editions, Kames also refined his presentation of the argument that promises for the benefit of third parties should be enforced, making it both simpler and clearer (for the first edition, see Appendix, p. 510, Extract [1st: 165]). Moreover, in one significant respect he altered his argument. In the first edition, Kames included passages which indicated that a third party beneficiary had no right to claim the promised performance, even after the promisee's death (see Appendix, p. 511, Extract [1st: 166], Extract [1st: 167–68]). This was a matter on which he had changed his mind by the second edition.

Much of book 3 on the application of equity to "several important subjects" is reproduced with little change across the editions. However, Kames does significantly alter the argument of the second chapter, on conventional penalties, in the third edition. As he points out, penal clauses in contracts—such as penal sums stipulated to be paid in case of late payment of a debt—may be mitigated in equity whenever the party's failure to perform is not clearly culpable, though the party in breach must indemnify the other from any damage suffered by the delay. In the first two editions, Kames takes a favorable view of such clauses. To begin with, he treats the term inserted in Scottish bonds for the payment of money, according to which the party in breach must pay an additional fifth part of the sum, not as a penalty proper, but as a "liquidation of that damage which the creditor may sustain by the debtor's failing to pay at the term covenanted" (2nd: 280). In his view, such contracts were not proper ones for equity to mitigate: the Court of Session had only done so in reaction to the exorbitant sums demanded in the past by money lenders. He next considers whether an innocent party should be wholly relieved from a conventional penalty. He tests this by asking whether relief should be given where a party fails to pay his debt on time because he is disputing it *bona fide* in a law suit. Kames's view is that relief should not be given against a penalty designed to secure the lender from having to pay costs. Although in ordinary cases, a litigating party can only be penalized with costs if he acts in bad faith, in matters of contract parties may stipulate for damages,

---

foregoing book; but as it makes a greater figure by its poisonous and undermining consequences, I chose it as proper for the front of the present book."

even for an innocent failure to perform. Hence, a lender may contract with a borrower for the latter to pay for any expense which the lender may incur in recovering his money. Kames sees this as perfectly just: otherwise, the lender may end up with no benefit from the loan. He concludes that penalties are incurred even for wholly innocent failures: being a matter of contract, the question of good faith is not relevant. Equity may give relief where the breach is not culpable, but in a way to indemnify the other party for costs.

In the third edition, the argument changes, with Kames being more critical of penal clauses. Arguing that equity will not intervene where a sum is inserted which corresponds "in any moderate degree to the damage that may ensue" (3rd 2: 155; p. 325 above), he notes critically that the Court of Session treats the "fifth part" term inserted in Scottish bonds as a liquidated sum, although in many cases (where the bond is for a high sum), it bears no relation to actual loss. In place of this, he argues that the court should introduce a rule limiting the penalty. Kames next proceeds to discuss the problem of the party who fails to pay a bond which he is disputing at law. In contrast to the earlier argument, he now says that "to extend against a *bona fide* defendant the penal clause in a bond, would be rigorous and unjust" (3rd: 2: 160; p. 327 above). Were a man to agree in a contract to pay any costs of suit incurred by his creditor, he now argues, would "be rejected by the court of session as exacted from a necessitous debtor by a rigorous and oppressive creditor." Finally, he modifies his argument with respect to costs: "Litigiosity must be evident to infer costs at common law; but the slightest fault, or even doubt, on the defendant's part, though far from amounting to litigiosity, will subject him to the modified penalty" (3rd: 2: 161; p. 328 above).

The rest of book 3 changes little across the editions, save for the long final chapter. In the first edition, Kames takes the view that the Court of Session only has jurisdiction regarding foreign matters over defendants actually in Scotland: as a result of a decision of June 1760 (*Hog* v. *Tenent*) he changed his view in the second and third editions. The third section of the chapter (dealing with the question of how the court was to deal with the movable property of foreigners in Scotland or Scots abroad) was also rewritten for the third edition. Where in the first two editions Kames explained the rules by a set of illustrative ex-amples (Appendix, p. 517, Extract [1st: 274–77]), in the third edition he set out a more theoretical distinction, between "permanent" and "transient" moveables, arguing that legal issues relating to the former class were deter-mined by the law of the country in which the property was situated, while in the latter they were determined according to the law of the proprietor's nationality.

TABLE OF CONTENTS
OF THE FIRST EDITION (1760)

The numbers in italics refer to corresponding material or passages in the third edition, indicating volume and page number.

BOOK I.

TABLE OF CONTENTS
OF THE SECOND EDITION (1767)

The numbers in italics refer to corresponding material or passages in the third edition, indicating volume and page number.

APPENDIX

Extracts from the First and Second Editions

EXTRACT [1st: iv–v]: "These more refined duties of the law of nature, making at present a great branch of equity, require to be explained with all possible accuracy; and, to give satisfaction I shall endeavour to trace them from their true source in human nature.

"The mind of man, limited in its capacity, cannot at once comprehend many objects; and a small proportion of what it can comprehend, suffices to exhaust the whole stock of benevolence that falls to the share of any individual. Disregarding what hath been taught by visionary philosophers, I must adhere to the principle laid down by all the practical writers on the laws of nature and nations, That it is our duty to abstain from injuring others, but that the doing good to those of our own species, merely as such, is not incumbent on us as a matter of strict duty. It is indeed evident, that universal benevolence, inculcated by some writers as a duty, would be extremely disproportioned to the limited capacity of man: his attention behoved to be distracted and his duty rendered impracticable, among an endless number and variety of objects.[1]

1. Kames's reference is to Samuel Clarke's *A Discourse Concerning the Unchangeable Obligations of Natural Religion and the Truth and Certainty of the Christian Revelation* (4th ed., London: James Knapton, 1716), p. 72 (1st ed. 1706). Kames had already come to the conclusion as a young man that Clarke's view was flawed. In 1723, he wrote a letter to Clarke, asking the latter to clarify the meaning of his text. In the letter, Henry Home set out three possible positions on the nature of duties owed to others. According to the first, certain rights were granted to every man by the laws of nature; and "every man is obleiged so to act with relation to his neighbour as not directly to doe him damage or which is the same thing disturb him in the exercise of his rights but on the other hand that he is not bound to advance his good." According to the second,

"Nature, or rather the God of nature, hath more wisely adjusted the duty of man to his limited capacity. Benevolence, it is true, is his duty; but then, the objects of his benevolence are limited in exact conformity to his nature. Distress never fails to beget compassion, which is a species of benevolence: and the exercise of compassion, by relieving the distressed, is acknowledged to be a duty. But, abstracting from distress, benevolence is not raised unless when we have a more strict connection with the person than merely that we are of the same species. Hence we may conclude with certainty, that the doing good to one of our own species, merely as such, never is a duty; for it is a law in our nature, that we are not bound in duty to perform any action to which we are not antecedently prompted by some natural principle.* The connections that excite benevolence differ widely in degree, from the most remote to the most intimate: and

----

"every man is positively bound to advance the good of others in all Cases, where it does not contradict his own good." According to the third, "every man must directly Chuse that which takeing all Circumstances will doe most good without Considering himself but as one of the infinite number whose good he's equally bound to advance; this last 'tis plaine destroyes all other rights and obligations to raise it self upon their ruins." Home thought that Clarke held one of the latter two views, but he was not quite sure which. He wrote, "I Cannot Certainly determine, whither your Sence be that he ought to doe all the good he Can provideing he doe himself no harm or if the Rule be absolute that he is under a positive obligation in Every Action, to do what is best in the whole, without Considering himself in any other view, but as a single particle of this whole." But in any event, Home was persuaded by neither of the latter two positions. Instead, "The first were I obliged to fix would be my Scheam and I have the Securest Side of the question, the presumption being for me, from the nature of rights 'tis indeed evident, that I'm bound to doe my neighbour no harm but if you carrie the point higher, and obleige me also to doe him good, yours must be the probation; for I'll never submit myself to greater burden than I see in duty that I'm bound, besides that if you Establish any of the other scheme of consequence you make all the Common Epithets, Generosity, Benevolence, Selfishness, Kindness &c meer Empty Sounds without any fixed Ideas for how can you recon that man Generous or benevolent who in doeing all the good he is capable of doing, does nothing beyond what he is directly bound to. Since no body is reconed Generous for paying his just debts, and the man who neglects this just duty is not properly named Selfish; but still after all, there's no direct demonstration; and if you adhere to your Rule lay'd down in page 72 you'l be so kind as to acquaint me what strictly is the meaning." National Archives of Scotland, GD24/1/548/1.

* See Essays on Morality and natural Religion, part 1. Ess[ay] 2 ch. 5 [Kames, *Essays on the Principles of Morality and Natural Religion,* chap. 5: "Of the Principles of Action."].

benevolence is excited in a just proportion to the degree of the connection. These connections, various and widely diffused, are at the same time fully sufficient to employ all the benevolence of which human nature is capable, and consequently to give ample scope to the duty of benevolence. The chief objects of benevolence, whether considered as a duty or a virtue only, are friends and relations. It is extended to neighbours at home, and countrymen abroad. Some are naturally so benevolent, as to bestow a share on persons of the same profession or calling, and even on those of the same name, though a mighty slender connection. And thus benevolence, successively exerted upon a series of objects, lessens gradually with the connection, till both become imperceptible." (Referred to at p. 20 n. 5 above.)

EXTRACT [1st: 34–35]: "It appears even at first view, that the connection must not be a little singular, which can produce so strong an effect, as to oblige a man who has not made a profit to diminish his stock by making up another's loss. This singular connection I shall proceed to explain. A man who, in pursuance of a mandate or commission, lays out his money for the service of another, has a good claim for retribution, whether the money be profitably expended or not. To found an action at common law, it is sufficient that the money is laid out according to order. But in human affairs certain circumstances and situations frequently occur that make a proper subject for a covenant; so proper indeed, that if there happen to be no covenant we are apt to ascribe the omission to some unforeseen accident. In cases of this nature, for which there is no remedy at common law, equity affords the same remedy in all respects that the common law gives where a covenant is actually made. The following is a proper example. A sudden call forces me abroad, without having time to regulate my affairs. They go into disorder in my absence, and a friend, in order to serve me, undertakes the management. Here nothing prevents a mandate or commission but want of opportunity; and it is justly supposed, that I would have gladly given the commission to my friend, had I known his good intentions towards me. Equity accordingly, fulfilling what would have been my will had the event been foreseen, holds the mandate as granted, and gives it the same actions on both sides that the common law gives in pursuance of a mandate. Cases accordingly of this nature, where the same relief is given that would be given upon an express covenant, are, in the Roman law, termed *Quasi-contractus*. This leads directly to the *actio negotiorum gestorum*. If I am profited by what my friend expends upon my affairs, he is entitled, according to the doctrine of the first article, to have his loss made up out of my gain. But what if, after bestowing his money and labour with the utmost precaution, the undertaking prove unsuccessful? What if, after laying out his money profitably, the benefit be lost to me by the casual destruction of the subject? It would not be just, that this friend who acted solely for my interest should run the risk. Equity therefore interposes and makes me liable, as the common law would do had I given a mandate or commission. This doctrine is laid down by Ulpian in clear terms: 'Is autem, qui negotiorum gestorum agit, non solum si effectum habuit negotium quod gessit, actione ita utetur: sed sufficit, si utiliter gessit, etsi effectum non habuit negotium. Et ideo, si insulam fulsit, vel servum aegrum curavit, etiamsi insula exusta est, vel servus obiit, aget negotiorum gestorum. Idque et Labeo probat.'[2] And I must observe, that utility joins with material justice in support of this doctrine. For is it not enough that a friend bestows his money and pains, without risking his money, even when laid out with the greatest prudence? Instead of inviting men to serve their friends in time of need, such risk would be a great discouragement." (Referred to at p. III n. I and p. 458 above.)

EXTRACT [1st: 39–40], the opening paragraph of book I, part I, chapter 3 (Defects in Common Law with respect to rights founded on Will): "To every covenant there belong certain capital articles that are rarely neglected: in a bargain and sale, for example, the price is seldom forgot. But it is not less rare to foresee and provide for every incident that may occur fulfilling a covenant. Further, when a covenant is taken down in writing, it is not always easy to avoid mistakes: articles sometimes are misapprehended, sometimes omitted. To remedy such errors, though they obviously require a remedy, belongs not to a court of common law. In such a court, the words of a covenant, or of any other deed, are the only rule for judging, because words are the only *legal* evidence of will. A defect of will cannot be

---

2. See translation in the text above, p. III, note *.

supplied, nor a mistake in writing rectified. Hence, with respect to matters of this kind, the necessity of a court of equity, which, authorized by the principle of justice, ventures to correct words by circumstances, and to supply omissions in will, by conjecturing what would have been the will of the parties had they foreseen the event. This, in law-language, is to judge according to the presumed or implied will of the parties: not that any will was interposed, but only that equity directs the same thing to be done, which it is probable the parties themselves would have directed, had their foresight reached so far.

"Words and writing are imperfect or erroneous, when they do not truly express the will of parties. Will itself is defective when any article is omitted that ought to have been under the consideration of parties. These two subjects, being distinct, must be handled separately." (Referred to at p. 459 above.)

EXTRACT [1st: 44–47], the opening of book I, part I, chap. 3, sect. II, "Defective Will": "Not many branches of law lie under greater obscurity than that which makes the subject of the present section. The instances are numerous where a court of equity hath interposed to supply defective covenants and deeds, in order to accomplish their end or purpose. Nor are instances fewer in number where this interposition has been refused. We are left in a labyrinth without a clue to guide us. A noted division of covenants in the Roman law, *viz. bonae fidei* and *stricti juris,* may possibly afford a clue. The former are such where equity can be applied to remedy defects and inequalities: the latter affording no place for equity, are judged by the common law. But what contracts are to be reckoned *bonae fidei,* and what *stricti juris,* the Roman writers are not agreed. Some of the commentators indeed give us lists or catalogues; but they pretend not to lay down any rule by which the one sort may be distinguished from the other. In applying equity to deeds and covenants, the slight and superficial notice that is generally taken of their purpose and intendment, is one great source of obscurity. This matter is not set in a clear light by the Roman writers, though several of them show great sagacity in evolving equitable principles. I shall endeavour to supply this defect in the clearest manner I am able. Every person who enters into a covenant, or executes a deed, has an event which he proposes to accomplish; and he

appoints certain things to be done in order to bring about the event. A
covenant therefore, or a deed, considered in its true light, is means concerted for accomplishing some end or purpose. The means thus concerted
are not always proportioned to the end proposed. It sometimes comes to
be discovered, that sometimes they go beyond the end, and sometimes
fall short of it. The former case comes in afterwards: the latter is our
present theme.

"To come at a general rule for determining when it is that a court of
equity may interpose to supply defective means, in order to fulfil a deed or
covenant, the following consideration is of importance. The chief province
of a court of equity is to make rights effectual, where the common law
gives no aid. The principle of justice demands this measure; and it would
be a gross defect in the law of any country to leave any valuable right without a remedy. Hence with respect to every sort of engagement, it follows
clearly, That wherever a right arises upon it to any person, justice directs
that the engagement be made effectual, if not by a court of common law,
at least by a court of equity. I give for illustration the following examples.
A mortgage or contract of wadset contains the usual clause for consigning
the money in case it be refused. The place of consignation is agreed on,
but the parties forget to name a consignator. In this case a court of equity
ought to name a consignator; for it would be unjust that the omission
should bar the proprietor from redeeming his land. Again, I deliver a cargo
of wheat, and refer the price to a third party, who refuses to determine.
The wheat in the mean time being consumed by the purchaser, justice
requires that the price be ascertained by a court of equity; for otherwise I
am forfeited of a sum to which I have a good claim.

"Upon this head of covenants, one would scarce think it necessary to
mention as a caveat, that a court of equity ought not to interpose till it be
first certain that there is a defect; for otherwise it may be in hazard of overturning express paction, and of creating a right beyond what was intended.
I give the following example. A sum of £120 was given with an apprentice;
and by the articles it was provided, that if the master died within a year,
£60 should be returned. The master being sick when the articles were
executed, and dying within three weeks, the bill was to have a greater sum
returned. And though the parties themselves had provided for this very

accident, yet it was decreed, in direct opposition to the covenant, that 100 guineas should be paid back.*

"With respect to a gratuitous deed, whether justice require the interposition of a court of equity to supply the want of means or articles, I proceed to examine. A gratuitous disponee, for example, has a right, so far as the will of the granter is interposed; and so far the deed is made effectual at common law. But with respect to an event not foreseen, and consequently not provided for in the deed by proper means or articles corresponding to such event, the disponee has no claim in justice. For in general, when a deed draws its obligatory force from the will merely of the granter, without any other cause, no right can be generated except so far as will is actually interposed. The doctrine will be sufficiently illustrated by the following example. A gratuitous bond executed by a minor being, being revoked and voided by the heir of the granter, the creditor insisted for an equivalent out of the moveables, upon the following ground, That the bond implied a legacy, which the minor could grant, as minority is no bar to the making a testament. It could not be doubted that the minor who granted a bond to be effectual against himself, would have given a legacy in place of it, had he foreseen the heir's challenge. But as the minor had not exerted any act of will with relation to this point, the court refused to interpose, or to transubstantiate the bond into a legacy.†

"Utility is the only other principle that can authorize the interposition of a court of equity in any matter of law; and if this principle tend not to

---

* 1 Vernon 460 [*Newton* v. *Rowse* (1687), reprinted in *The English Reports*, vol. 23, p. 586. This case is discussed in 3rd: 1: 239–40].

† Fountainhall, 15th December 1698, Straton contra Wight [M 10326. This case is discussed in the second edition (p. 149) in a section discussing means and ends, where Kames takes a different view of it: "In this case, as it appears to me, the *ratio decidendi* is taken from the common law, not from equity. One thing seems clear, that the minor intended in all events to bestow the sum named upon his friend the obligee; for if he was willing to bind himself personally to pay the sum, he could not have the least hesitation to bind his representatives by bequeathing it as a legacy. And if this be admitted, the consequence is fair, that the friend thereby acquired a right, which it was the duty of the court of session to make effectual, by sustaining a claim against the executor in the same manner as if the sum had been a legacy." However in the third edition (3rd: 1: 257–58; p. 152 above), he used the case to show that equity had no power to alter a man's will or supply a complete lack of will; a view he now appeared to endorse.]

give effect to a gratuitous deed, farther than the granter has actually interposed his will, it must be evident that such a deed is altogether beyond the reach of a court of equity. Gratuitous deeds are beneficial to society as exertions of kindness and generosity: but however beneficial, they are certainly not essential to society, which may subsist in vigour without them. Now it belongs to the legislature only, to enact regulations for advancing the positive good or happiness of society. A court of equity, acting on the principle of utility, is confined to the more humble province of preventing mischief. So far this court is useful, if not necessary. But hitherto, in Britain at least, its powers have not been farther extended; because it has appeared unnecessary to trust with it more ample powers.*

"But though means cannot be supplied in favour of a donee to give him a more beneficial right than is actually granted, yet undoubtedly his right may be limited or burdened in equity, so as to make it answer more perfectly the purposes of the donor. For gratitude binds the donee in conscience, to obey not only the donor's declared will, but even what would have been his will as to any incident had it been foreseen; and it belongs to a court of equity to inforce the duty of gratitude, as well as other natural duties that are neglected by the common law. The equitable obligation upon a tenant in tail to extinguish the annual burdens, is a proper example of this doctrine, as will be seen at the close of the present section.

"Upon the whole it appears, that the power of a court of equity, with respect to imperfect deeds or covenants, is regulated by the principle of justice; and that this court cannot interpose to supply the oversight of parties, unless to make right effectual. I now proceed to apply this rule to particular cases. With respect to covenants, in the first place, It is the current practice of the court of session to supply omitted articles that are necessary for compleating the ultimate purpose of the contracters; and the powers of the court here are so evidently founded on justice, that it would be losing time to multiply instances. I shall therefore confine myself to a few that appear somewhat curious. In a bargain of sale the price is referred to a third party. There is no performance on either side, and the referee dies suddenly without determining the price. Here there is no remedy at

* See book 1. chap. 2. at the beginning.

common law, because there is no price ascertained. But upon application of either party, can a court of equity ascertain the price, in order to make the bargain effectual? This question will depend upon the construction that is given to the bargain. If the reference be taken strictly as a condition, and that the parties intend not to be bound otherwise than by the judgment of the referee, equity, it is evident, cannot be applied; for it is a conditional bargain never purified. But if, on the other hand, it was the intention of the parties that the bargain should in all events be effectual, the reference to the third party must be held as a means only for accomplishing the end in view; and the failure of one means has no other effect than to make it necessary to employ others.³ Considering the bargain in the light last mentioned, it bestows a right upon each party, which ought to be made effectual. If the parties had foreseen that the referee might die without fixing the price, they would have provided a remedy; and justice calls upon a court of equity to supply the defect. In a word, wherever articles are concerted for accomplishing the purposed end, and are considered as means only, without being converted into a condition, a court of equity ought to supply other means if these prove insufficient." (Referred to at p. 460 above.)

EXTRACT [1st: 76–77], the opening to book 1, part 2: "In the introduction is explained the necessity of a court of equity to correct the injustice of common law, as well as to supply its defects. A court of common law, as there set furth, is governed by a few general rules established when law was in its infancy, and which at that time were deemed sufficient. But experience having discovered numberless cases to which these rules did not extend, and cases not fewer in number that behoved to be excepted from them, a court of equity became necessary. The necessity of supplying defects arises from a principle sacred in all well regulated societies, 'That wherever there is a right it ought to be made effectual.' The necessity of making exceptions and thereby correcting injustice, arises from another principle not less sacred, 'That there ought to be a remedy for every wrong, not even excepting what is committed by authority of law.' We have had occasion to see how imperfect the common law is, leaving

3. A similar example is used in 3rd: 1: 206; p. 123 above.

justice to shift frequently for itself, without any support. We are now to
enter upon a number of particulars, in which the common law exceeds
just bounds and unwarily authorises oppression and wrong. This proceeds
from the unavoidable imperfection of general rules; which never are so cautiously framed, as without exception to be rational or just in every case they
comprehend. A court of common law however cannot afford a remedy, because it is tied down to the letter of the law. The privilege of distinguishing
betwixt will interposed in general terms, and what could have been the will
of the legislature upon a singular case had it been foreseen, is reserved to
courts of equity; and a jurisdiction is bestowed upon such courts, to restrain
the operation of common law in every case where a rule extends beyond
its professed aim and purpose. We find daily instances of oppressive claims
clearly founded on a general rule of common law, applied to some singular
case out of the reason of the law. In every case of this kind, it is the duty
of a court of equity to interpose, by denying action upon such a claim. To
trust this power with some person, or some court, is evidently a matter of
necessity; for otherways wrong would be authorized without control. With
respect to another particular formerly mentioned, a court of common law
is equally imperfect, *viz* that it is bound to judge by the words even where
they differ from will. By this means, statutes are often extended beyond
the will and purpose of the legislature, and covenants beyond the will and
purpose of the contracters. The injustice thus occasioned cannot otherways
be redressed than by a court of equity." (Referred to at p. 454 above.)

EXTRACT [1st: 77], the opening paragraph of book 1, part 2, chap. 1 (Injustice of Common Law with respect to Rights founded on Will): "The common law with respect to deeds, covenants, and other acts of will, confines
its view to two circumstances. First, Whether will was actually interposed:
next, In what words it is declared. A writing may have the appearance
of an engagement without the reality. One through force or fear may be
compelled to utter certain words, or to subscribe a certain writing, without
intending mentally to be bound. This circumstance must weigh even in a
court of common law, because in reality there is no obligation. But once
admitting an obligation, a court of common law must interpose its authority to make it effectual. That it was brought about by fraud, by error,

or by oppression, will not be regarded; and as little that the articles covenanted go beyond the intention of parties, or that the words go beyond the articles that were really concerted. These and many other particulars concerning acts of will creative of right or obligation, are appropriated to a court of equity; and justice requires that due weight be laid upon each of them." (Referred to at p. 459 above.)

EXTRACT [1st: 80–82], the opening of book 1, part 2, chap. 1, sect. 2 (Where the Means concerted reach inadvertantly beyond the End proposed): "The doctrine concerning the nature of obligatory acts of will is explained above. Every man who makes a covenant or executes a deed, has an event in view which he proposes to accomplish by means of the covenant or deed. A covenant therefore and a deed are in reality means concerted for accomplishing some end or purpose. They are not however always proportioned to the end in view. They sometimes fall short of the end, and sometimes go beyond it. The former case is discussed, and the latter is the subject of the present section.

"I must premise, that the end proposed in every obligatory act of will, ought to be lawful, without which no countenance will be given to it in any court: for to make effectual an unlawful act, is inconsistent with the very nature of courts of law. Thus a bond granted by a woman, binding her to pay a sum if she should marry, is unlawful, as tending to bar procreation; and therefore will be rejected even by a court of common law. And the same fate will attend every obligation granted *ob turpem causam;* a bond, for example, granted to a woman as a bribe or temptation to commit fornication. So far there is no occasion for a court of equity.[4] But now suppose an obligation of this kind has been fulfilled by payment, a court of common law cannot sustain an action for recalling the money. Neither can the action be sustained in equity; for the person who pays is not less guilty than the person who receives payment, and in general, no action lies in equity more than at common law, to recall money paid voluntarily. The person who receives payment, may, it is true, be justly deprived of the money he has gained by an unlawful act: but the power of forfeiture is a

4. This material is reproduced in 3rd: 1: 262.

prerogative of the legislature, and is not trusted with any court. Hence the maxim of the Roman law, that *in turpi causa potior est conditio possidentis.*

"Supposing now the end proposed to be lawful; a court of common law makes no other enquiry but what acts of will were really exerted, which are made effectual without the least regard to consequences. A court of equity, more at liberty to follow the dictates [of] refined justice, considers every deed in its true light of a means employed to bring about some event; and in this light refuses to give force to it, farther than as conducive to the purposed event. In all matters whatever, as well as in matters of law, the end is the capital circumstance; and the means are regarded so far only as they contribute to the end. For a court then to put a deed or covenant in execution beyond the purposed end, involves the absurdity of preferring the means to the end, or of making that subordinate which is principal, and that principal which is subordinate. Such proceeding would be unjust as well as absurd. No man in conscience feels himself bound to perform any promise or covenant, further than as it contributes to the end or event for the accomplishing of which it was made. And it is inconsistent with the very nature of a court of equity, to compel a man to perform any act where he is not antecedently bound in conscience and duty.

"Irritant clauses in grants and other single deeds, produce frequently more severe consequences than are intended by the maker. There is a great variety of such clauses; but there is no occasion to be solicitous about distinguishing them from each other; for equity considering them all as means, gives no effect to any of them farther than as they contribute to make the end effectual. A noted irritancy is what is frequently contained in bonds of provision to young women, 'That the bond shall be void if she marry without consent of such and such persons.' This irritancy I have had occasion to discuss above;* and have endeavoured to make out, that whether expressed as a suspensive or resolutive condition, the bond is due, though the creditor marry without consent, provided she marry not below her rank. An irritancy of this kind, is conceived to be *in terrorem* only, and in order to be a compulsion upon the creditor to make a right choice. From which conception it clearly follows that if a right choice be made,

---

* Part 1. Ch. 3. Sect. 2.

the irritant clause has had its full effect; and to give it in the case the effect of a forfeiture, is going beyond the purpose of the granter, and the end intended by the irritancy. I have resumed the reasoning here, because, if I mistake not, it is applicable to every other irritancy. And with respect to the irritancy under consideration, I must observe, that it affords one of the rare examples where a court of equity ought to interpose, though without the aid of any general rule: for there evidently can be no standard of what is a suitable or insuitable match. But the severity of such irritancies, which are often innocently incurred, renders the interposition of equity necessary. At the same time, where the match is not actually disgraceful, there is little danger of arbitrary measures. The opinion of a court of equity, where the case is doubtful, will naturally lean to the milder side, by relieving from the forfeiture a young woman, who is sufficiently punished by an imprudent match, without adding to her distress, and depriving her of her fortune. Equity however, as mentioned in the place above cited, is not commonly carried to such refinement. It is not the practice to prolong the term where the condition is suspensive, or precedent, as termed in England." (Referred to at p. 461 above.)

EXTRACT [1st: 85–87], the opening of book 1, part 2, chap. 1, sect. 3 (Where the Means concerted tend not to bring about the purposed End or Event): "From considering an obligatory act of will as a means to an end, it clearly follows in reason, that its legal force and efficacy must depend upon the greater or less degree of its aptitude to bring about the proposed end. A covenant calculated in the most accurate manner and with perfect foresight to bring on the desired event, is binding in reason as well as in conscience. For what possible objection can there lie against performance? If a covenant in any article fall short of the desired event, the defect is supplied by a court of equity, and if it go beyond, the excess is restrained by the same court; acting in both cases to make the means correspond to the end, which in every act of will is the capital point. These particulars are discussed in the foregoing part of this work. But we have not yet exhausted all the consequences that follow from considering an obligatory act of will as a means to an end. It may be erroneously made, so as not to tend in any article to the end or event proposed by it. Or it may be made with a view to a certain event expected to happen, in place of which another event happens which was not expected. In cases of this nature there is no place for rectification. The deed must either be made effectual without regard to the end, or it must be voided altogether. A court of common law, regarding the words only, will make it effectual; which resolves into considering the deed as ultimate, and not, as it truly is, a means to an end. But justice teacheth a different doctrine, which will clearly appear from the following deduction. A rational man when he promises, when he contracts, or in general, when he acts, has some end in view which he purposes to accomplish. Sometimes the very thing one engages to do is the end proposed, as when a man grants a bond for payment of borrowed money. The payment covenanted is the end of the engagement; and when the payment is made, the engagement has its full effect, by accomplishing the end proposed by it. But, for the most part, the thing pactioned to be done, is considered as a means to some farther end; as where I buy a horse as a stallion. The contract is a means for acquiring the property of the horse, and the acquisition is the means for raising a breed of horses. Whether the thing a man immediately engages to perform, is to be deemed the ultimate end of the engagement, or a means only to a farther end, if not cleared by the words, must be gathered from the nature of the subject. And in all engagements this point is necessary to be ascertained; because the engaging to perform any act as a means, is evidently different from the engaging to perform it absolutely or as an end. In the latter case one is bound in reason as well as in conscience; for no more is demanded from him than what he agreed to perform with a full view of all consequences. But in the former, a man is not bound, if the thing he agreed to perform is discovered not to be a means to the end proposed. He agreed to the thing as a means only, not absolutely; and if the thing prove not to be a means, neither reason nor conscience binds him to perform; because this case is not comprehended in the engagement, or rather is excluded from it. I need go no farther than the foregoing example for illustration. The horse I bought as a stallion happens by some accident to be gelt before delivery. I am not bound to accept the horse, or pay the price; because I bought him not singly as a horse, but as a stallion in order to breed horses.

"With respect then to the cases that belong to the present section, we discover a new operation of equity. Hitherto its operation has been to support deeds and covenants, by adjusting them as means to the proposed end. But here the operation of equity is directly opposite, *viz.* To void deeds and covenants where they prove altogether ineffectual as means. Writers upon law, who find it sometimes difficult to trace matters to their true source, take an easy method for explaining this operation of equity. They suppose the engagement to be conditional; as if it were expressly provided, that it shall not bind unless it prove a means to the end proposed; and this supposition or fiction is termed an implied condition. But fictions in law are a very unsatisfactory method of solving difficulties.

"The most noted case that comes under this section, is where goods by some latent insufficiency answer not the purpose for which they are bought. Though the vender be in *bona fide,* yet the purchaser is relieved in equity from performance, because the bargain, being a means to an end, doth not answer the end proposed by it." (Referred to at p. 154 n. 2 and p. 462 above.)

EXTRACT [1st: 94–95]: "The same rule holds where the granter is alive, supposing only he to have put it out of his power to alter; for so long as the deed is under his own power, he has no occasion for an equitable relief. When an obligation is sought to be made effectual in an unexpected event, a court of equity denies its authority. The plaintiff is unjust in his demand; and this must furnish an objection to the defendant whoever he be, whether the granter or the heir of the granter. This rule with respect to the living shall be illustrated by several examples. A disposition of land granted by a man to his wife was ratified by the heir, who in the same deed bound himself to purge the incumbrances affecting the land, 'upon the view and in contemplation of succeeding to the rest of the estate,' as expressed in the deed of ratification. The heir being charged by the widow to purge incumbrances, the following reason of suspension was sustained, that the heir was excluded by an expired apprising of the whole estate, of which he was ignorant when he granted the ratification; and that this fact must liberate him from his obligation, to grant which he could have no other motive but his prospect of enjoying the estate.* Equity here justly re-

---

* Fountainhall, Dec. 19. 1684, Home Mar. 1685 Dutchess of Lauderdale *contra* Earl of Lauderdale [M 6379].

lieved from performance of an obligation in an event which was not fore-seen, and which would have been guarded against had it been foreseen.[5]

"No person can hesitate about the application of this rule to unforeseen events, which are brought about, not casually, but by the person in whose favours the deed is granted. A man having no male issue, settled his whole estate, real and personal, upon his eldest daughter, with the following pro-viso, That she should pay 10,000 merks to her two sisters. The disposition, being granted on death-bed, was challenged by these sisters, and voided as to the land-estate. The question ensued, Whether they who by their challenge got more than the 10,000 merks, had a claim for this sum over and above. They urged their father's express will. But it being answered, That having overturned their father's will, they could not claim upon it; their claim was dismissed.* Here was not only an unexpected event, which would have been guarded against had it been foreseen, but further, the event, repugnant to the will of the granter, was the operation of persons honoured by the deed, and their ingratitude justly barred them from tak-ing any benefit by it."[6] (Referred to at p. 146 n. 6 and p. 183 n. 30 above.)

EXTRACT [1st: 96], the concluding paragraphs of book 1, part 2, chap. 1, sect. 4 (Where Provision is made for an expected Event that never hap-pens): "Reflecting upon the foregoing doctrine, we perceive a remarkable difference betwixt a donation compleated by a transference of property, and a donation incompleated, which requires an action against the donor or heirs. In the former case, no unforeseen event will be sufficient to re-store the property to the donor. There is no principle of law or equity upon which such an action can be founded. In the latter case, an un-foreseen event makes it the duty of a court of equity to deny action, and consequently to render the donation ineffectual, unless the granter or his heir be so scrupulously moral, as of their own accord to fulfil it.

"Donations *mortis causa* are regulated by the same principle. A man having a near prospect of death, executes a deed in favour of a relation or friend. Contrary to expectation he recovers and survives the deed many

---

5. This material is reproduced in 2nd: 139.

* Stair, Feb. 1. 1671, Pringle contra Pringle [M 6374].

6. This material is reproduced in 2nd: 138.

years. It is no doubt effectual at common law; but the heirs of the granter are relieved in equity, because it was made with a view to an event that did not happen."[7] (Referred to at p. 146 n. 6 above.)

EXTRACT [1st: 97], the introduction to book I, part 2, chap. I, sect. 5, art. I (Deeds or Obligations procured from Persons weak and facile): "The practice of the court of session with relation to matters of this kind, has not hitherto been brought under any precise rules. The nature of the bargain, equal or unequal, must have a great influence; and yet this circumstance admits not any general rule. It is certainly the safest course to lean to the common law, and to refuse relief unless where the inequality is conspicuous. In this case, a court of equity, however reserved as to matters that are in a great measure arbitrary, cannot avoid lending a helping hand, where the gross inequality is occasioned by imbecillity on the one side and undue influence on the other." (Referred to at p. 456 above.)

EXTRACT [1st: 98]: "Many decisions have been given on this point that seem not to accord quite well together. I shall confine myself to a few, which may serve to illustrate the doctrine here inculcated. From a debtor proved to be weak and facile, dispositions being elicited at different times of valuable subjects, for security and payment of trifling patched up claims; and the disponee having at last obtained a total discharge of the reversion for an inconsiderable sum, the debtor at that time being much pinched in his circumstances; the court, viewing the facility and weakness of the debtor, and the great inequality of the bargain, judged these circumstances sufficient to presume undue influence on the part of the creditor, and therefore voided the discharge."* (Referred to at p. 456 above.)

EXTRACT [1st: 100–101], the beginning of book I, part 2, chap. I, sect. 5, art. II (An Obligation or Deed procured by Fraud): "All positive loss or damage that one suffers unjustly, whether by fraud or other means, is repaired in a court of common law. Fraud that occasions harm of a less

7. This material is reproduced in 2nd: 138–39.
* Feb. 13. 1729, Maitland *contra* Ferguson [M 4956, from Kames, *Dictionary*, vol. 1, p. 337].

direct kind is repaired in a court of equity.* With respect again to a covenant or single deed procured by fraud, redress cannot be obtained but in a court of equity. For, with respect to all engagements in general, a court of common law is not at liberty to take under consideration the inductive cause or motive: it is confined to one particular, viz. whether consent was or was not interposed. If there be no consent, the court must pronounce that there is no engagement: if consent was actually given, there exists an obligation to which the common law gives force by whatever means the consent was obtained. In old Rome accordingly, restitution against fraud was a branch of the Pretorian law. In England, all covins frauds and deceits, for which there is no remedy at common law, are and were always redressed in the court of chancery.† And the same thing no doubt obtains in Scotland.

"The bulk of the matters that come under this article are governed by the following principle of equity, That no man is suffered to take benefit by his own fraud. And upon authority of this principle, a court of equity not only refuses action for performance of an agreement brought about by fraud, but also, on application of the person defrauded, sets aside or voids such agreement. A few examples may be proper, and a few shall suffice. The following case regards the first branch, That of refusing action. A having failed in his trade, compounded with his creditors at so much per pound, to be paid at a time certain. Some of the creditors refusing to stand to the agreement, he brought his bill to compel a specific performance.‡ But it appearing that A, to draw in the rest of the creditors, had underhand made an agreement with some of them to pay their whole debts, though they were seemingly to accept of the composition, which was a deceit upon the rest of the creditors, the court would not decree the agreement, nor relieve the plaintiff, but dismissed his bill.§

"The following cases regard the second branch, That of voiding the deed. A bill of exchange fraudfully procured was set aside by a bill in

* Book i. Part i. Chap. i.

† Coke 4 Inst. 84 [Coke, 4 Institutes, p. 84].

‡ See Note, foot of page 48 [a note on p. 48 of the 1760 edition explaining specific performance].

§ 2 Vernon 71, Child contra Danbridge [1688; reprinted in The English Reports, vol. 23, p. 655].

chancery.* A policy of insurance was also set aside by a bill in chancery upon fraud.†

"What if a man have benefit by another's fraud to which he has no accession? In handling this point we must make a progress through different cases. The first is a mutual contract, which is always made effectual where the parties themselves are guilty of no wrong. Where fraud produces no inequality, it is nothing: and even supposing a great inequality, the principle of utility, for the sake of commerce, supports the contract.‡ Second, With respect to a gratuitous deed which makes the receiver *locupletior,* equity will not permit such deed to be made effectual where it is brought about by the fraud of a third party. 'Tis sufficient that a donation be made effectual by law when it proceeds from the deliberate will of the maker; but it can never contribute to the good of society in general, or to the satisfaction of individuals, to compel any man to fulfil a gratuitous promise which was drawn from him by imposition. Third, if property be transferred whether in pursuance of a mutual contract or of a donation, the acquirer cannot be deprived of his property though the transference was brought about by the fraud of a third party. For it is a general rule, That no man can be forfeited of his property but by his own consent or by his own fault. Thus a second disposition of land, though gratuitous, with the first infeftment, is preferred before the first disposition without infeftment, though for a valuable consideration. But if by such preference the gratuitous disponee be made *locupletior aliena jactura,* he may hold the land, but he must be subjected for the value to his party."§ (Referred to at p. 456 n. 11 above.)

EXTRACT [1st: 109–13], the beginning of book 1, part 2, chap. 1, sect. 6 (Relief afforded in Equity against an Engagement occasioned by Error):[8] "Error may be distinguished into two kinds. One prevents consent altogether; as for example, where the purchaser has one subject in view and the

---

* 2 Vernon 123 [*Dyer* v. *Tymewell* (1690), reprinted in *The English Reports,* vol. 23, p. 688].

† 2 Vernon 206 [*Whittingham* v. *Thornburgh* (1690), reprinted in *The English Reports,* vol. 23, p. 734].

‡ See Book I. Part 2. Chap. 1. Sect. 3.

§ Forbes, Jan. 24. 1706 Wilson *contra* Lord Saline [M 942].

8. The text of 2nd: 173–76 is largely the same: it is the start of book 1, part 1, chap. 4, sect. 10: "Where a deed or covenant is occasioned by error."

vender another. In this case there is no bargain; for the parties agree not in the same thing. This can only happen in covenants; and as no obligation can arise where there is no agreement, such a covenant, if it can be called so, is void by the common law; and there is no occasion for the interposition of equity. The other kind is where the error is not such as to prevent consent, but is a motive only for entering into an engagement. An error of this kind may happen in single deeds as well as in covenants; and as here will or consent is really interposed, the deed must be effectual at common law; and the question is, Whether, or how far, there ought to be a relief in equity on account of the error?

"A maxim above laid down* will pave the way to the solution of this question, *viz.* that one *certans de damno evitando* may lawfully take advantage of an error committed by another; but that justice forbids such advantage to be taken in order to make positive gain by it. From the investigation of this maxim in the place cited, it will appear that justice makes no distinction betwixt an error in fact and an error in law. One difference indeed there is, that an error in law is not so readily presumed as an error in fact.

"I shall begin with showing what influence an error has with relation to grants and other single deeds. Some are purely gratuitous, some are founded on an antecedent rational cause. Such cause must in all events support the deed, because justice will not permit the maker to seek restitution against a deed which it was rational to grant. And supposing him to be bound in conscience only, a court of equity will not void an honest deed, though occasioned by an erroneous motive. A rich man, for example, executes a bond in favour of an indigent relation, moved by an erroneous belief, that this relation had behaved gallantly in a battle where he was not even present. Equity will not relieve the granter against this deed, being in itself rational, and which at any rate is a matter of charity. The creditor, it is true, gains by the error: but then it cannot be said that he lays hold of this error to hurt the granter of the bond; because a man cannot be said to be hurt by doing an act of generosity or charity.

"Equity therefore relieves not from error, except with relation to deeds

---

* Part 1. Ch. 2. Sect. 2.

purely gratuitous; such as donations, legacies, &c. nor with relation to these, unless where the motive or impulsive cause of granting is erroneous. An error the discovery of which would not have totally prevented the deed, cannot at all be regarded. A gratuitous deed must be sustained in whole or voided in whole, because there is not here as in covenants any measure of equality or inequality. With respect then to a gratuitous deed the impulsive cause of which is erroneous, justice requires that the granter be relieved from performance. He feels himself not bound in conscience; and the grantee's conscience dictates to him, that he ought not to make profit by the granter's error. To this purpose Papinian. 'Falsam causam legato non obesse, verius est; quia ratio legandi legato non cohaeret. Sed plerumque doli exceptio locum habebit, si probetur alias legaturus non fuisse.'*

"The opinion here delivered points at a distinction to which attention ought to be given, because it has great influence in practice. In deeds merely gratuitous, the cause of granting specified in the writing, is not always the true impulsive cause. It is common to have a secret and a revealed will; and the ostensible cause mentioned in the deed, differs frequently from the real motive which remains in the breast of the granter. Now, if there be no error in the true impulsive cause, the deed evidently must be effectual, however erroneous the ostensible cause may be. Hence it appears, that Papinian's rule *Quod ratio legandi legato non cohaeret* applies to the ostensible cause only. And therefore the following texts of the *Corpus Juris* must be understood to refer to the common law; for they are certainly wrong in point of equity. 'Longe magis legato falsa causa adjecta, non nocet: veluti cum quis ita dixerit *Titio, quia me absente negotia mea curavit, stichum do, lego.* Vel ita, *Titio, quia patrocinio ejus capitali crimine liberatus sum, stichum do, lego.* Licet enim neque negotia testatoris unquam gesserit Titius, neque patrocinio ejus liberatus sit, legatum tamen valet. Sed si conditionaliter enunciata fuerit causa, aliud juris est: veluti hoc modo, *Titio, si negotia mea*

---

* l. 72. §6. De condicionibus et demonstrationibus et causis et modis eorum, quae in testamento scribuntur [On conditions, particularizations, explanations for, and modalities of provisions in wills, D 35.1.72.6: Watson iii: 194: "The truer view is that an incorrect motivation is no impediment to a legacy because the reason for a bequest is no part of the bequest; still the defense of bad faith will generally be applicable if it be established that the testator would not otherwise have made the legacy." This is quoted in the text above at p. 163].

curaverit, fundum meum do, lego.' Again, 'Quod autem juris est in falsa demonstratione, hoc vel magis est in falsa causa. Veluti ita, *Titio fundum do, quia negotia mea curavit.* Item, *Fundum Titius filius meus praecipito, quia frater ejus ex arca tot aureos sumpsit:* licet enim frater hujus pecuniam ex arca non sumpsit, utile legatum est.'[†] Where the cause specified in the deed appears to be the true impulsive cause, which seems to be supposed in the texts now cited, it cannot be doubted that a relief will be afforded in equity, provided it be made evident, that the grant owes its existence purely to error. Of this there is one remarkable instance in the Roman law, which is a fine illustration of the doctrine here inculcated. 'Pactumeius Androsthenes Pactumeiam Magnam filiam Pactumeii Magni ex asse heredem instituerat; eique patrem ejus substituerat. Pactumeio Magno occiso, et rumore perlato quasi filia quoque ejus mortua, mutavit testamentum, Noviumque Rufum heredem instituit, hac praefatione: *Quia heredes quos volui habere mihi, continere non potui, Novius Rufus heres esto.* Pactumeia magna supplicavit imperatores nostros; et, cognitione suscepta, licet modus institutione contineretur, quia falsus non solet obesse, tamen ex voluntate testantis putavit imperator ei subveniendum: igitur pronunciavit, *hereditatem ad Magnam pertinere, sed legata ex posteriore testamento eam praestare debere, proinde atque si in posterioribus tabulis ipsa fuisset heres scripta.'*[‡]

---

* §31. Instit. De legatis [On Legacies, Inst. 2.20.31: Birks & McLeod 85: "Still less does it matter if the testator discloses a false belief in the background. Take 'I give and bequeath Stichus to Titius because he managed my affairs in my absence' or 'I give and bequeath Stichus to Titius because by his advocacy I was acquitted of a capital charge.' Here the legacy is valid even if Titius never managed his affairs or secured his acquittal. It is different if it is put conditionally: 'I give and bequeath land to Titius, if it was he who managed my affairs in my absence.'" This passage is quoted in the text above at p. 164].

† l. 17. §2. De condicionibus et demonstrationibus et causis et modis eorum, quae in testamento scribuntur [On conditions, particularizations, explanations for, and modalities of provisions in wills, D 35.1.17.2: Watson iii: 184: "The law in respect of false particularization applies the more to a false explanation, for example, 'I give the estate to Titius because he looked after my affairs' or 'let my son Titius take the estate as a preferred gift because his brother abstracted so many gold pieces from the chest'; the legacy is valid, even though the brother did not take the money from the chest." This passage is quoted in the text above at p. 164].

‡ l. ult. De heredibus instituendis [On the institution of heirs, D 28.5.93: Watson ii: 850: "Pactumeius Androsthenes had instituted Pactumeia Magna, the daughter of

In this case two separate foundations of an equitable relief appear in a clear light. First, A settlement caused by error. Secondly, A provision made by a settlement for a figured event, not for that which really existed.* Justice therefore interposes against such a settlement; because to sustain it would be the same as disinheriting the favourite heir, contrary to the intention of the maker.

"With respect to legacies contained in the latter testament, against which no relief was granted, the opinion delivered appears well founded. For though the testator was determined by an erroneous motive, to make the testament so far as concerned Rufus the heir; there was no evidence nor presumption that he was determined by the same error to make the legacies.

"The doctrine of error with respect to mutual contracts will be found to coincide with a doctrine above laid down, *viz.* That a covenant is not binding in equity unless it serve as a means to bring about the end proposed by it.† To make a covenant so unhappily as not to answer the purposed end, must always proceed from error; and an error of this kind ought to relieve from performance, because no man feels himself bound in conscience to fulfil such an engagement. Any other error of less importance will not be regarded. I purchase, for example, a telescope, judging it to be mounted with silver; equity will not relieve me of the bargain though the mounting proves to be of a baser metal. The same of a watch, the case of which I take

---

Pactumeius Magnus, as heir in respect of his whole inheritance and had substituted her father to her. When Pactumeius Magnus had been killed and a rumour had reached him that Pactumeius Magnus's daughter also was dead, he changed his will and instituted Novius Rufus as heir, prefacing the institution as follows: 'Because the heirs whom I wished that I might have I could not have, let Novius Rufus be heir.' Pactumeia Magna petitioned our emperors and, having held a *cognitio* [that is, a judicial inquiry or cognizance], although a limitation was placed on the institution, because an erroneous [limitation] does not usually form an obstacle [to an institution], the emperor took the view that, nevertheless, having regard to the testator's wishes, she should be helped. Therefore, he gave judgment that the inheritance belonged to Magna but that she must pay the legacies given in the later will, just as if she herself had been appointed heir in the later will." This passage is quoted in the text above at 3rd: 1: 163].

* See Sect. 4 of the present chapter ["Where provision is made for an expected event that never happens"].

† Sect. 3 of the present chapter ["Where the Means concerted tend not to bring about the purposed End or Event"].

to be gold, though it be only silver gilt. The ornaments of an instrument or machine have no relation to use; and if the subject purchased answer its end, the chief view of the purchaser is obtained. The most that could be made of an error as to other circumstances, is to found a claim in equity for abating the price in order to make the bargain strictly equal; and this was done by the Roman law, which annulls every sale where the lesion or prejudice is *ultra duplum* [more than double].* But a claim of this nature, as prejudicial to commerce, is opposed by the principle of utility, and for that reason is rejected in most commercial countries.[†,9]

"This matter may be considered in a different light. No man is bound to fulfil a gratuitous deed, to grant which he was moved by an error. The same rule may be justly applied to covenants; and will bring out the conclusion that is laid down above. It will never be presumed, that a covenant which answers the end proposed by it is occasioned by error; and with respect to any other error, it will only be presumed, that the discovery would have produced a more equal bargain, but not have prevented it altogether.

"To illustrate the coincidence of the doctrine about error with that above set forth, which considers an engagement as a means to an end, I shall add a few words about transactions. A transaction putting an end to any matter in controversy or dispute, must be effectual. A deed will never be presumed to proceed from error, where there is a just or rational motive for making it. A transaction again must be effectual in equity, if it answer the end proposed by it, *viz.* to put an end to a law-suit, or any matter in controversy. On the other hand, if a man be moved to make a transaction upon a supposition of a claim which has no foundation, an error of this kind will undoubtedly entitle him to be relieved in equity. 'Si ex falsis instrumentis transactiones vel pactiones initae fuerint, quamvis jusjurandum de his interpositum sit, etiam civiliter falso revelato, eas retractari praecipimus; ita demum, ut si de pluribus causis vel capitulis eaedem pactiones seu transactiones initae fuerint, illa tantummodo causa vel pars retractetur, que ex falso instrumento composito convicta fuerint, aliis capitulis firmis

---

* l. 2. C. de rescindenda venditione [On the rescission of a sale, C 4.44.2: "A price is considered to be too small if half of the true price is not paid"].

† Sect. 3. of the present chapter.

9. The second half of this paragraph is largely reproduced in 3rd: 1: 281; pp. 165–66 above.

manentibus.'* Here the motive for making the transaction must have been erroneous. The transaction at the same time is not a means to the end proposed by it, which was to extinguish a doubtful claim; and here there was no claim.

"One indeed may be moved by error to make an unequal transaction, which would be corrected by equity did not utility stand in the way; for to extinguish law-suits and controversies, the great source of idleness and discord, is not advantageous to those only who deal in commerce, but to all. Upon this account, no inequality, however great, ought to be regarded in a transaction where there is no other cause for giving relief. An interposition, even in the strongest case, must give encouragement to law-suits; for if one obtain redress, others will hope for it who have not so good a claim. It will have still a worse effect by making judges arbitrary, who in such a case can have no general rule to direct their decrees." (Referred to at p. 162 n. 1 and p. 463 above.)

EXTRACT [1st: 114–15]: "In making effectual a purchase, three circumstances only are regarded by a court of common law, first, Whether the vender was proprietor; next, Whether his consent was interposed to transfer the subject to the purchaser; and last, Whether delivery was accordingly made. Yet many things may be figured out that ought to render ineffectual a purchase attended with these circumstances all of them. I give for an example a prior engagement to alien the subject to another. Stellionate is a crime punishable by statute: and yet, as I have had occasion to observe,† a purchaser is secure by the common law, even where he is *in mala fide* by having notice of the prior engagement. Such wrong is redressed in a court of equity; and it is redressed in the most natural and most compleat manner, by annulling the second purchase, and restoring the first purchaser to his former situation. This step in favour of the latter is just, being the proper reparation of the wrong done him; and it is not less just against the

* l. 42 C. de transactionibus [On negotiated settlements, C 2.4.42: "If negotiated settlements or agreements have been made as a result of forged documents, even though they are confirmed by oath, still we order that they be revoked when shown to be forged according to civil law; provided that if the settlements have been made with many provisions and heads, only that provision and part is to be revoked, which is shown to be concocted from forgeries, the other heads remaining valid"].

† Part i. Ch. i. Sect. i.

former, because to him the rule applies, that no man is suffered to take benefit by any wrong he himself commits. This rule is obviously agreeable to the principles of justice, and to the common sense of mankind. It holds accordingly in general, That though a second purchaser, whose title is first compleated, is at common law preferable to the first purchaser, yet the first purchaser will be preferred, if his right was known to the other before his purchase. This short-hand method of preferring the incompleat title, is in effect the same with voiding that which is compleat." (Referred to at p. 266 n. 12 above.)

EXTRACT [1st: 165], paragraphs from book 1, part 3, following material which in the third edition is placed in the introductory section to book 2, part 2]: "The example I shall give of a right not pecuniary, opens an extensive field; and I have chosen it in order to explain the famous Roman law maxim, *Alii per alium non acquiritur obligatio,* which, so far as I can judge, is but imperfectly handled by the writers on that law. A very simple case shall introduce the subject. I obtain a gratuitous promise from a stranger, to pay a sum to my friend or to build a house for him; and the question is, What is the legal effect of this promise with respect to myself and with respect to my friend? A promise made to me must create a right in me: but then, as I cannot qualify any pecuniary interest in having a sum paid to another, I have not an action at common law to enforce performance of this promise.

"With respect to my friend again, he, no doubt, hath a pecuniary interest to have the sum or to have the house. But as interest merely without right will not generate an action either at common law or in equity, the cardinal point is, Whether any right arise to my friend by this promise. From the very nature of a contract or promise, the parties are bound to each other and to no one else. It is their mutual dependance on performance that constitutes the obligation. I pledged my faith to the person with whom I contracted; and as he naturally relies on me for performance, my breach of faith to him is evidently a wrong. A person with whom I have no connection may have an interest that the contract be performed: but I did not pledge my faith to him, and for that reason am not bound to him.* Thus it appears, that the Roman

* See l. 11 De obligationibus et actionibus [On obligations and actions, D 44.7.11: Watson iv: 642], L. 38 §17 De verborum obligationibus [On verbal contracts, D 45.1.38.17:

maxim above mentioned, *Alii per alium non acquiritur obligatio,* arises from the very nature of a covenant." (Referred to at p. 277 n. 2 and p. 464 above.)

EXTRACT [1st: 166]: "But now let us vary one circumstance. The obligee dies without discharging or passing from the promise. Has the person to whom it was to be performed an action in that case? A promise, it is true, ought to be fulfilled: but then, a man is not bound to fulfil his promise, unless performance be exacted from him by the person to whom the promise was made. The person who was to reap the benefit, not being a party to the promise, cannot claim upon it, and I discover no other medium for a claim, in equity more than at common law." (Referred to at p. 278 n. 3 and p. 464 above.)

EXTRACT [1st: 167–68]: "But in the case above figured, if I die suddenly before delivery, what will become of the money? Has my heir a claim? has my friend a claim? or, if neither have, will the money be suffered to remain with the servant if he chuse not to execute the order given him? My heir evidently has no right to the money, because equity will not permit him to take by succession what is destined by me for another. Neither has he an action to compel performance, because, with respect to matter not pecuniary, he has only an equitable interest to have his own will performed, not mine. My friend again has no action upon the promise. Must it then be left entirely upon the servant's conscience to perform, or to retain the sum, if avarice prevail over conscience? By no means. Here is a sum of money in the servant's hands, to which he has no right, and which therefore he cannot retain without gross injustice. He is bound therefore to make delivery; and if my heir have no right, which I have endeavoured to show, the money must be delivered to my friend according to my destination. The subject *in medio,* not the promise, is here what founds the obligation and the action in equity for making it effectual. My servant, on the one hand, cannot hold the money, but ought to deliver it. My friend, on the other hand, has, by my will, an equitable claim to the money; and a court of equity will interpose to make his claim effectual. This case then of a

Watson iv: 655–56]. See also Kames, *Essays on the Principles of Morality and Natural Religion,* edit. 2 [1758], p. 88 [Liberty Fund ed., pp. 53–54].

rei interventus must be held an exception to the foregoing maxim *Alii per alium non acquiritur obligatio.* The following decisions rest evidently upon this foundation, Colvil, December 1591, Wood *contra* Moncur. Durie, 25. Spottswood (contract), 26. June 1634, Lord Renton *contra* Lady Aiton. Stair, June 8. 1676, Irvine *contra* Forbes.

"Supposing me now to die bankrupt, and that the sum in the servant's hand is claimed by my friend to whom it was destined, and by my creditors. Here equity which declared for my friend against my heir, declares for my creditors against my friend; according to the well known maxim *Quod nemo debet locupletari aliena jactura.*

"The last variation I shall suggest is, that the money was put by me in the servant's hand, to be delivered to one of my creditors for his payment. As it was all along in my power to recal the money before delivery to the creditor, it was undoubtedly mine at my death, and consequently made a part of my moveable estate. The creditor for whose payment the sum was destined, hath no doubt an equitable interest in it, but so have all my creditors; and therefore, in case of my bankruptcy, equity rules, that the money in question with my other effects be equally distributed among them. And this precisely was decreed, Jan. 4. 1744, Sir John Baird *contra* creditors of Murray." (Referred to at p. 279 n. 2 and p. 464 above.)

EXTRACT [1st: 174–75], similar to a passage in the second edition, p. 251: "A bond which appears from its narrative to be granted as a temptation to commit adultery or any other crime, will be reprobated even at common law, and though the cause be not mentioned in the bond itself, it will be rejected by a court of equity, if it appear from collateral evidence, that such was the cause of granting the bond. But as it is a duty, not a wrong, to provide for a bastard child, or to provide for a woman that the man has robbed of her chastity, a bond or settlement made for that purpose is effectual both in law and equity.*

"The Marquis of Annandale having for two years had criminal conversation with Harris his house-keeper, and having a child by her that afterwards died, gave her a bond of £. 4000 penalty, conditioned to pay her £. 2000

---

* Durie, June 25. 1642, Ross *contra* Robertson [M 9470].

within three months after his death. The bond being put in suit after the death of the Marquis, a bill was brought to be relieved against the bond, as being given *pro turpi causa*. The bill was dismissed, the bond being *praemium pudoris*. And this decree was affirmed by the house of Lords. A case was cited, where Mrs. Ord, a young lady of about fourteen years of age and entitled to £. 12,000 fortune, was seduced by Sir William Blacket, who settled on her £. 300 yearly for life: and the young lady had a decree for the £. 300 as *praemium pudicitiae*. A like case happened in the exchequer, where a man having debauched a young woman, and intending afterwards to trick her, settled on her £. 30 yearly for life out of an estate that was not his: the court decreed him to make the settlement good out of his own estate."* (Referred to at p. 288 n. 4 and p. 463 above.)

EXTRACT [1st: 194]: "But if there be no legal claim, there will be no extinction. My reasons are these. Supposing first a legal claim, the case must be considered in the following light. In the hand of the *bona fide* possessor is a sum claimable in strict law by the proprietor of the land, being the value of his rents consumed. This indeed comes to be a rigorous claim upon the *bona fide* possessor, who, considering these rents to be his own, applied them without scruple for maintaining himself and family. Equity therefore, correcting the rigor of common law, refuses to sustain this claim. But when the proprietor, instead of demanding the money to be paid to himself, insists only, that it shall operate so far as to extinguish the real incumbrances. Equity interposeth not against this demand, because the claim so restricted is not rigorous and unjust; and if equity interpose not the extinction must take place.

"If on the other hand there be no claim at common law for the value of the rents consumed, I cannot perceive any foundation for extinguishing the real debts belonging to the possessor. The man who levies rents and consumes the rents *bona fide,* is not liable to the proprietor more than if he had not intermedled. He has nothing in his hands that belongs to the proprietor; he is not in any respect debtor to the proprietor; and therefore the proprietor has no medium upon which to plead an extinction of the

---

* Abridg. Cases in Equity. Ch. 13. Sect. C. §6 [*Marchioness of Anandale* v. *Harris* (1725), 1 Eq. Cas. Abr. 87, reprinted in *The English Reports,* vol. 21, p. 898].

debts. Upon the former supposition, there is a fund in the hands of the *bona fide* possessor, which the judge can apply for payment of the debts: upon the present supposition there is no fund. But as it is made out above, that the *bona fide* possessor is not liable even at common law for the value of the rents he consumes, it is clear that his possession cannot have the effect to extinguish any real debts belonging to him, unless the following proposition can be maintained, That the very act of levying the rents extinguishes *ipso facto* these debts, without necessity of applying to a judge for his interposition." (Referred to at p. 321 n. 8 above.)

EXTRACT [1st: 205]: "On the other hand, an obligation for which an equivalent is given,[10] is in its nature perpetual and ought in all events to be fulfilled. Such must be presumed the intention of parties, in every engagement that has for its object the exchange of one thing for another, and is not purely an exercise of benevolence. An obligor accordingly who has received a valuable consideration, must, in all events, perform his part of the engagement, unless the contrary be stipulated. The obligee's death, in particular, before the term of payment, will not relieve him, though heirs be not named in the deed. The common law, it is true, affords not to the heir an action in this case more than where the obligation is gratuitous: but equity, supplying the defects of common law, affords an action in order to fulfil the rules of justice, which will not suffer the valuable consideration to remain with the obligor without performing the equivalent pactioned. Hence, with respect to the point under consideration, an obligation for a valuable consideration is directly opposite to that which is gratuitous." (Referred to at p. 329 n. 2 above.)

EXTRACT [1st: 209], similar to a passage in the second edition, pp. 288–89: "The third resembles a voluntary security; for it proceeds no farther than to give a security upon the debtor's funds, leaving the creditor to operate his payment by virtue of the security. This is the case of an adjudication during the legal, which impowers the creditor to draw his payment out of the debtor's rents, provided the tenants be willing to pay: if refractory. They may be compelled by a decree against them personally for their

---

10. The second edition (p. 285) has "for a valuable consideration."

rents. This decree, termed *a Decreet of Mails and Duties,* compleats the
security, by giving direct access to the debtor's tenants. A decree for making furthcoming sums of money due to the debtor is of the same nature.
It is a security only, not payment; and such a decree may be justly defined
a power given to the creditor to draw payment from the debtors of his
debtor. What follows to compleat the process may be done by private
consent. The person against whom the decree of forthcoming is obtained
ought to pay without further compulsion; and payment thus obtained
voluntarily, extinguishes the debt upon which the furthcoming is founded.
In a word, a decree of furthcoming obtained by my creditor against my
debtor, resembles in every circumstance an order by me upon my debtor,
to deliver the sum he owes me to my creditor for satisfying the debt I owe
him. A decree of furthcoming is a judicial order, having the same effect
with a voluntary order. Hence it clearly follows, that if my debtor, against
whom the decree of furthcoming is obtained, prove insolvent, the sum is
lost to me, not to my creditor. His security indeed is gone, but the debt
which was secured remains entire." (Referred to at p. 334 n. 3 above.)

EXTRACT [1st: 236–37]: "Upon what principle shall we rest the famous
case of Street and Mason, which is as follows? 'A disposition by a merchant to his infant son of his whole estate, without reserving his liferent
or a power to burden, was deemed fraudulent in order to cheat his correspondents, being foreign merchants, who had been in a course of dealing
with him before the alienation, and continued to deal with him after it
upon the faith that he was still proprietor. And their debts, though posterior to the disposition, were sustained to affect the said estate. Nor was it
respected that the infant's seisine was on record, which strangers are not
bound to know.'* This case comes not under the words of the statute 1621,
which are in favour of prior creditors only. It may be thought however a rational extension of the statute, to fulfil the purpose of the legislator against
fraud. A man who accepts a deed, fraudulently contrived against others, is
evidently accessory to the fraud of his author: and equity will not indulge

---

* Stair, July 2. 1673, Street and Jackson *contra* Mason [M 4914]. Stair, Dec. 4. 1673,
Reid *contra* Reid [M 4925].

an infant with a gain of which a person at full age would be deprived. Supposing only a few years to pass, the infant himself, understanding the vicious motive that procured him the estate, would be accessory to the fraud if he should pretend to take benefit by it." (Referred to at p. 102 n. * and p. 364 n. 21 above.)

EXTRACT [1st: 251], similar to a passage in the second edition, p. 330: "The cases above mentioned are governed by the rules of the common law; and as a *bona fide* purchase for a valuable consideration is the highest title of property, this title, if good at common law, will never be impugned in equity. For that reason, a power to burden, when it enters the lists against such a purchase, is confined within the strictest rules of law. A faculty to impose a personal burden, stands upon more advantageous ground: where a valuable consideration has been given, it is supported in equity beyond the bounds of common law. In particular, where the will of the person who reserves the faculty appears to be more extensive than the creative words, equity interposes to give the faculty its intended effect. Nay, even a defect in will is supplied, if from the circumstances it appear, that the maker would have interposed his will had his foresight reached so far. Thus in a gratuitous disposition of a land-estate a power reserved to burden the same with sums to a certain extent has evidently a valuable consideration; and yet this power will not at common law entitle the disponer to subject the disponee personally: but the disponee will be liable in equity, because it could not have been the intention of the disponer, reserving power over the land, to exclude himself from a power of burdening also the disponee; and therefore it must have been an oversight merely that power was not reserved to burden the disponee as well as the land." (Referred to at p. 384 n. 8 above.)

EXTRACT [1st: 255]: "How far in this matter the common law is subjected to the correction of equity we shall next proceed to enquire, after paving the way by settling some preliminary points. One point seems clear, that here, as well as in every other branch of the law, it is the duty of a court of equity to make the will of the granter effectual, without regarding the words where they happen to differ from the will.* But is a court of equity

* See Book 1. Part 1. Ch. 3. Sect 1.

also authorized to supply a defect in will, by sustaining the exercise of powers in cases not provided for, which it is probable the granter would have provided for had his foresight reached so far? With respect to covenants, especially where there is a *rei interventus,* such defects must be supplied by a court of equity in order to fulfil the rules of justice. But with respect to deeds deriving their obligatory force from the will solely of the granter, this extraordinary power can never be necessary, because upon such a deed no right can be founded except so far as will is actually interposed.* This doctrine being clearly applicable to the present subject, it follows clearly, that a court of equity cannot supply any such defect in will, and that its province is to make effectual what truly was the will of the maker. To ascertain that will, it is not indeed confined to the words of the deed; but may lay hold of other circumstances to supply what is defective in the words, or to clear what is dark or intricate." (Referred to at p. 390 n. 15 and p. 460 above.)

EXTRACT [1st: 268]: "In the last place, this court, with relation to foreign matters, has a jurisdiction over persons not so extensive as it has with relation to common law or equity. When it judges of foreign matters, the man who is to be made defendant must, I incline to think, be personally in Scotland; because I do not find that the extraordinary citation of absents at the market-cross of Edinburgh pier and the shore of Leith, has been extended to foreign matters. Nor doth analogy justify the extention. One extraordinary step to compleat an ordinary jurisdiction is natural; but it is harsh and unnatural to accumulate extraordinary remedies one upon another. Our propension is to enlarge an ordinary and accustomed jurisdiction, but to confine what is extraordinary within strict bounds. Thus if I bring an action against my countryman and fellow-traveller for payment of a sum I lent him at Rome, and even produce the bond in court, the action will not be sustained against him while he remains abroad. The jurisdiction of the court as to foreign matters ought to reach none but who are in Scotland at the time." (Referred to at p. 405 n. 3 above.)

EXTRACT [1st: 274–77], similar to passages in 2nd: 355–58: "Moveables as well as immoveables have a local situation; and it is a provision acknowl-

---

* Ibid. Sect. 2.

edged by all our lawyers, that Scotch moveables as well as Scotch land are regulated by our municipal law. Though an executor may be named by a nuncupative will in England, yet such will is never sustained to carry moveables in Scotland, because writ with us is an essential solemnity in the nomination of an executor.* In England again, a bastard enjoys the privilege of making a testament, which privilege is denied to a bastard here. And, therefore, notwithstanding a testament made by a bastard in England, his effects here were escheated to the crown.†

"The application of the foregoing rule to land is abundantly easy, in Europe at least where the marches of different kingdoms and territories are ascertained with precision. But the slight connection that moveables have with the place where they are found, makes it often a difficult problem to ascertain the country they belong to. And yet the solution of this problem is necessary with respect to many questions concerning them, such as the right of succession, the manner of transmission *inter vivos,* and from the dead to the living. All questions of this kind were regulated by the law of the country to which these moveables properly belong. For it will be evidently too precarious a rule, to consider them as belonging to the country where they happen to be, occasionally or accidentally. If a foreigner, for example, happen to die here with valuable moveables about him, it will not be thought reasonable that these moveables should be given to his next of kin according to the law of Scotland, when his next of kin according to the law of his own country are different, and when these next of kin will take the effects he left at home. The local situation of moveables is attended with such variety of circumstances that it is difficult to bring all of them under general rules, leading to correct and just decisions. It is necessary however to make an attempt; and the following rules may, I presume, exhaust the bulk of these circumstances.

"In the first place, moveables belonging to a Scotchman and locally in Scotland, are deemed Scotch effects, to be regulated by the law of Scotland. Nor will it vary the case that the proprietor happened to be occasionally abroad *non animo remanendi.* An assignment made by him there

---

* Stair, Gilmour, Newbyth, Jan. 19. 1665. Shaw *contra* Lewis [M 4494].

† Haddington, Feb. 1. 1611. Purves *contra* Chisholm [M 4494, from Kames, *Dictionary,* vol. 1, p. 320].

according to the *lex loci,* will not transfer these moveables to the assignee. But according to what is said above with respect to land, it will entitle the assignee to demand from the court of session that the moveables be adjudged to him; or to demand damages, unless the cedent be willing to grant a more formal assignment. Next, if the proprietor happen to die abroad, his succession will be regulated by the law of Scotland, as also the form of making up titles. The connection with his own country continues entire in the mind of every person, and all matters are determined in the same manner as if he had died at home. That this is the common sense of mankind is testified by good authority, *viz.* act 88. p. 1426, enjoining, 'That where a Scotchman dies abroad occasionally, *non animo remanendi,* his Scotch effects must be confirmed in Scotland.'[11]

"Moveables on the other hand occasionally in Scotland belonging to a foreigner, are held to be foreign effects, not regulated by the law of this country. The occasional connection with this country, yields to the more intimate connection with the proprietor who is a foreigner. For this reason, a foreign assignment of such moveables, formal according to the *lex loci,* will be sustained by the court of session acting as judges in foreign matters. And, for the same reason, an executor named by the proprietor will have a good claim to such moveables, provided he compleat his title *secundum consuetudinem loci.* And even though the proprietor here occasionally fall sick and die, the court of session will prefer those who are next of kin according to the law of his country; and if he be an Englishman, for example, will sustain letters of administration from the prerogative court[12] as the proper title. In like manner, if a Scotchman occasionally in England die there, the moveables he carried with him ought to be held Scotch moveables to be regulated by the law of Scotland. And the English judges, were they allowed to judge *secundum bonum & aequum,* without being fettered by their own municipal law, would certainly be of the same opinion. This article demands peculiar attention. Here is a situation of things not a little singular, a situation that obliges our judges to follow,

---

11. *APS* ii: 14: 1427, c. 8, De causis mercatorum extra regnum decedencium tractandis.

12. That is, the Prerogative Court of Canterbury: this was the highest ecclesiastical court in the province of Canterbury in England, which heard testamentary and matrimonial suits.

not their own law, not the *ius gentium,* but the municipal law of another country.

"In the third place, moveables locally in Scotland and originally belonging to a Scotchman, do not change their legal country, if I may use the expression, by being sold to a foreigner, or by being conveyed to him in the course of succession. A foreign assignment will not be a good title of property, nor will the foreign method of conveying effects from the dead to the living be held sufficient. The nomination of an executor by will is, it is true, an universal title effectual *jure gentium,* which therefore ought to be sustained everywhere: but letters of administration from the prerogative court of Canterbury, for example, will not be sustained here, even though granted to the next of kin. The powers of that court are confined within its own territory, and therefore the next of kin must be confirmed here.

"In the fourth place, as to moveables connected with an immoveable subject, such as the furniture of a house, the goods in a shop, or the stocking of a farm, the country of the principal determines that of the accessory, without regard to the proprietor, of whatever country he be. The connection here betwixt the moveables and the immoveable subject, prevails over their connection with the proprietor. And accordingly where the principal subject is in Scotland, these accessory moveables will, to all intents and purposes, be governed by the municipal law of Scotland. To illustrate this branch I put the following case. A family has been long in possession of two land-estates, one in England, one in Scotland, with two mansion-houses compleatly furnished, which are inhabited by turns. The proprietor dies without children, leaving a brother, and children of a deceased brother. This makes it a question of importance in the succession to his moveables, whether the law of England or of Scotland be the rule. In England, there is a representation in moveables as well as in land; and when a man dies, the children of a deceased brother or sister take a share of the moveables with the brothers and sisters alive. In Scotland, there is no representation in moveables. Will this question then depend on the accident of the proprietor's dying in England or in Scotland? This will hardly be admitted; for the mind is averse to make right depend on chance. And yet, abstracting from this accident, there is no reason to prefer the law of either country to that of the other. The result then must be, that the household-furniture in England, as English effects, be distributed among the next of kin according to the English law; and that the Scotch law be the rule with respect to the effects in Scotland.

"In the last place, with respect to a process as well as with respect to legal execution, no circumstance is regarded but loco-position merely, however occasional or accidental. A judge has authority over every person and every legal subject within his territory; and to whatever country goods may belong, the proprietor or a creditor must claim them from the court to which they are subjected for the time. No other judge can give authority to apprehend the possession, or to seize them by execution for payment of debt." (Referred to at p. 411 n. 1 and p. 466 above.)

EXTRACT [1st: 279–80]: "With respect to debts due here to foreigners, it is a question not less intricate than important, In what manner they are to be attached by execution, and from what court the execution must issue, whether from the court to which the creditor is subjected or from that of the debtor. In England, debts like other moveables are attached by the legal execution of *Fieri Facies,* similar to our poinding; and by this execution the *jus crediti* is transferred *funditus* from the original creditor to his creditor. At this rate it would seem that a *Fieri Facies* executed against the creditor in England, should, like an intimated assignment, be effectual against the debtor here, so as to make execution in this country unnecessary. This inference appears extremely plausible, but we must enquire whether it be solidly founded. Judicial powers, which are confined within a certain territory resemble not will or consent which operate everywhere with equal authority. A voluntary conveyance by a proprietor, or by a creditor, is an universal title that ought to be made effectual by judges in every country. And could law compel any man to make a conveyance, such conveyance would in justice be equivalent to a voluntary conveyance, to be effectual everywhere; because, supposing will to be interposed, it cannot hurt the deed that it proceeded from legal compulsion more than if it had been voluntary in the strictest sense. But it is not in the power of law to force the will; and therefore a conveyance by legal execution cannot be held a conveyance from the debtor. In order to supply the want of a voluntary conveyance to the creditor for payment of the debt due to him, all that can be done is for the judge to be the disponer; and this disposition he can make where the subject to be conveyed is under his power and authority. In our poinding, for example, the property of the goods is transferred to the poinder, not by the will of the debtor, but by the will and authority of the sheriff within whose territory the effects lie. But the sheriff cannot adjudge to the poinder the debtor's effects in any other territory because these are not subjected to his jurisdiction. The matter is clear as to moveable goods, and the same rule must hold as to debts. For if the judge cannot force the creditor to make a conveyance, all he can do by way of authority is to award execution against his debtor for payment of the debt upon which the execution proceeds. But this execution must be awarded by the judge within whose territory the debtor resides, for no other judge hath authority over him. Thus it is evident, that an English *Fieri Facies* is not a good title for demanding payment of a debt due in Scotland. And therefore, with respect to legal execution, it holds in general, that the judge of the territory within which the subjects are, or the debtor lives, must be applied to." (Referred to at p. 419 n. 7 above.)

EXTRACT [2nd: 92–93]: "The entailer's personal debts are not a burden upon the fruits, but only upon the heirs of entail personally; and therefore the foregoing medium for making the tenant in tail liable to relieve the heirs of entail of the current interest, fails here; and the question is, Whether there be any other medium subjecting him at common law? We must separate from this question, the division of burden between heir and executor. If a tenant in tail leave any moveable estate, it will no doubt be charged at common law with the arrears of interest, and with every moveable sum, principal or interest. But supposing that no moveable estate is left, and that the tenant in tail dies, leaving a land-estate of his own, descending to a different series of heirs who do not represent the entailer: in this case, the arrears of interest arising from the entailer's debts, must, with the principal, remain a debt upon the entailed estate at common law; unless it can be made out, that the tenant in tail became bound to relieve the heirs of entail of these arrears, in which case the arrears will be a charge upon his own estate." (Referred to at p. 85 n. 12 above.)

EXTRACT [2nd: 119]: "Every promise and covenant implies necessarily two persons: one who is bound, termed the *obligor;* and one to whom the obligation is directed, termed the *obligee.*

"That particular act of the will which binds us whether in promising or in contracting, is termed *consent.* And it is also that very act which makes a deed effectual; as will thus appear. A deed is of two kinds: one where the granter binds himself, as in a disposition, or in a charter; which being in effect a promise, is obviously binding upon him by his consent: the other kind is where the granter declares his will without being bound, as where by a deed he imposes burden upon his heir: it is the heir's consent which binds him in that case, a consent implied from his taking up the succession." (Referred to at p. 119 n. 3 above.)

EXTRACT [2nd: 130–31]: "To understand a deed or covenant to be no further effectual than as far as will is declared or expressed, is a lame and imperfect notion of these legal acts. Many deeds and covenants have effects that are not expressly provided for; which will thus appear. Every rational man who wills expressly to bestow a right, wills at the same time, though not expressly, to bestow every accessory or subordinate right that tends to make effectual the principal right; for he that wills the end, must be presumed to will the means proper to accomplish the end. But whatever a rational man wills, every man is presumed to will. And hence the foundation of what in law-language is termed *implied will;* that is, will presumed without being declared. And it is happy for man to be so constituted with respect to the faculty that binds him; for if in conscience he were only bound to the articles declared or expressed, deeds and covenants would often fall short of their purposed end; and, still worse, would often be the source of injustice.

"Before entering into the particulars that belong to this section, it must be premised in general, that every question concerning implied will is appropriate to a court of equity; because a court of common law regards not any act of will but what is expressed.

"Upon the principle mentioned, every lease or land, long or short, must necessarily imply a power to remove tenants, where the granter of the lease does not himself undertake to remove them; for to grant a lease intitling the lessee to enter to possession, and yet to with-hold from him the means of obtaining possession, is an absurdity of which no rational man can be guilty.

"A man who becomes bound to dispone a debt, will by implied consent be bound to convey every execution done upon it. And suppose he has granted the assignment without mentioning the execution, it is however understood to be convey'd by implied will.

"A disposition of an infeftment of annualrent mentioned only the real right, omitting a personal obligation that the debtor was under to pay the debt. The court judging that it was the intention of the parties to put the disponee in place of the disponer, without any view to benefit the debtor, sustained a personal action against the debtor at the instance of the disponee, in order to fulfil the said intention.* In a reduction *ex capite inhibitionis* at the instance of the assignee to a bond upon which an inhibition had been led, the court sustained the assignment as a title, though it neither mentioned the inhibition, nor had any general clause that could comprehend it. But it was understood to be the intention of the cedent to put the assignee in his place, without any view to relieve the debtor; and therefore his will to convey the inhibition along with the debt was implied.† The only scruple here is the conveying an inhibition or a personal obligation without writ. But where the principal subject is convey'd in a formal writ, it is not necessary that every accessory be expressed.

"When a man infefts his wife in land for security of her jointure payable in corn, it cannot be his intention, without any benefit to himself, to free his tenants from the obligation they are under to carry their farm-victual to the place of sale; and therefore his will is implied to convey to his wife this service of the tenants as a natural accessory to her right.‡

"The nicety in cases of this kind is, to determine from what circumstances will is to be implied. With respect to this point, peculiar attention ought to be given to the purposed end, and to what would have been

---

* Dury [Durie], 23d November 1627, Dunbar contra Williamson [M 570].

† Harcase, (Assignation), January 1682, Williamson contra Threapland [M 6306].

‡ Fountainhall, 29th July 1680, Countess-dowager of Errol contra the Earl [M 6550, from Kames, *Dictionary,* vol. 1, p. 440].

the will of the parties had the thing occurred to them. The superior of a feu-right, which was voidable *propter non solutum canonem,* disposes of the supe-riority for a valuable consideration; and the question is, Has the purchaser a title to insist in a reduction of the feu? It is an accessory of the superiority, but not so connected but that it may be easily disjoined. A reduction of this kind is severe punishment, which every one is not inclined to put in execution; and for that reason the conveyance of the privilege to the purchaser ought to be expressed, for it will not readily be implied.* If it would be wrong in a court of equity to imply a conveyance of any right or privilege without any rational presumption of the granter's will, it would be a still greater wrong to decree any thing contrary to the declared will; which, however, seems to have been done in the following case." (Referred to at p. 141 n. 1 above.)

EXTRACT [2nd: 136]: "I give an example that will be a key to the whole. An old bachelor, having no prospect of issue because he had no intention to marry, makes a settlement of his estate by disponing the same to a near relation, and to a certain series of heirs, reserving his own liferent, with a power to alter, he takes a different thought, marries, and dies suddenly, without altering his settlement, leaving his wife pregnant. A male child is born, and claims the estate. The settlement will be supported at common law, because the words are clear for the disponee. And as the granter's will is also for him in express terms, it is not obvious upon what principle a court of equity can interpose to overturn this settlement, without making a new will for a man who made none for himself. Yet, on the other hand, it would be a conclusion in law extremely harsh, to exheredate this favourite child, upon no better ground than a mere oversight of his father, and to inforce a settlement in an event which the maker would avoid with horror were he alive. The following argument promises to extricate us from this dilemma. The will of the maker in favour of the disponee, is not absolute to take place in all events; but only upon supposition of what he took for granted, that he was to have no issue. Therefore in the event that has happened the disponee cannot say that the will of the maker is for him:

* Haddington, 14th February 1612, Wedderburn contra Nisbet [M 6322, from Kames, *Dictionary,* vol. 1, p. 423].

consequently the settlement gives him no right. For the sake of illustration, it may be added, that there is no difference in substance between a limited will, such as that under consideration, and a will that is conditional; for the binding act of the will is equally qualified by both: the difference is with respect to evidence only; the same act of will that is said to be limited when the limitation is left to be gathered from circumstances, being termed *conditional* when the limitation is expressed and not left upon circumstances. For this reason, a limited will cannot create a more extensive right than a will that is conditional. This doctrine is by no means new, though put in a new dress; for what else is an implied condition so much talked of in the Roman law, but a limitation of will inferred from circumstances. Hence it follows, that the settlement under consideration is void in equity, for the same reason that it would be void even at common law, if the condition 'failing heirs of the granter's body' had been expressed.

"Another reason in equity concurs for voiding this settlement. The omission of the condition, 'failing heirs of the granter's body,' was plainly an oversight; and the disponee ought not in conscience to take advantage of that oversight *ad lucrum captandum.* This follows from the rule above laid down, That *in damno evitando* one may take advantage of an error, but not *in lucro captando.*

"But where the child died in a few months, the settlement was sustained; because the child was not hurt by the settlement."* (Referred to at p. 161 n. 2 above.)

EXTRACT [2nd: 139–40], the introductory section to book 1, part 1, chap. 4, sect. 4 (A deed or covenant considered as a means to an end): "When a deed is granted, or a covenant made, in order to bring about some event, the event as the end is chiefly in view, and the deed or contract is not effectual in conscience or in reason farther than as a mean to bring about the end. A deed or covenant calculated with perfect foresight to bring about the desired end, is binding in justice; for in that case there can be no pretext for with-holding performance: but if a deed or covenant, by ignorance or mistake, answer not the end for which it was made, a court

---

* Next of kin of Isabel Watt contra Isabel Jervie, July 30. 1760 [M 6401, from Kames, *Select Decisions,* p. 228].

of equity will not make it effectual. For considering it to be a mean, the objection against it is invincible, That no mean ought to be regarded but as far as it tends to accomplish the end. To think otherwise is to suppose the performance of the deed or covenant to be the ultimate end, and not the mean to the ultimate end." (Referred to at p. 154 n. 2 and p. 462 above.)

EXTRACT [2nd: 170], a passage placed in the second edition in the section on how far a deed void at common law is supported in equity, and following the discussion of cases included at 3rd: 1: 312 (p. 181 above): "In the cases mentioned, there are none who have occasion for the equitable relief but those only who are parties to the transaction. But in many cases third parties happen to be affected, of which take the following example. A younger brother serves heir to his father, and if infeft, the eldest having been so long abroad as to be reputed dead. He comes home, and claims the succession; which *ipso facto* voids the service and infeftment of the brother; because a service can have no legal effect without a right to be served. In the interim the younger brother has acted *bona fide* as proprietor: and many have been his transactions with third parties, who were also *in bona fide;* which transactions, being founded upon his title of property, are null and void, as flowing *a non habente potestatem.* Is there no relief in equity in a case of this nature, where the hardship on third parties is intolerable? One thing is clear, that the *bona fides* of the younger brother will secure him against a claim for the rents consumed. On the other hand, it is equally clear, that no sale made by him can be effectual, unless as far as necessary for payment of the family-debts; to which extent a sale may be supported in equity. The only general rule is, That equity will support every act of ordinary administration; but that acts of extraordinary administration will not be effectual, except such as being prudent and rational are beneficial to the righteous heir. Upon that rule the court proceeded in the famous case of Missinish, who being the only heir in being at the time, was admitted to serve, though there was a nearer heir in possibility, who afterward existed. Missinish, by his service and infeftment, was only a conditional proprietor, his right depending on the existence or non-existence of a nearer heir; and as a nearer heir came to existence, Missinish's right was null *a principio.* But he having sold land for the payment of the family-debts while there was yet no prospect of a nearer heir, the sale was supported by the court of session, upon evidence brought that it was *in rem versum* of the true heir." (Referred to at p. 181 n. 25 and p. 303 n. 4 above.)

EXTRACT [2nd: 172]: "That such a temporary sterility cannot afford a defence in equity against payment of the rent, will appear from the following considerations. *Primo,* A lease puts the lessee in place of the landlord as to profit and loss; the profit is his without limitation, and so ought the loss: *Cujus commodum ejus debet esse incommodum* is a rule in equity that holds with the greatest force in a lease where the lessee draws all the profit, if it should be ten times his rent, and on the other hand can never lose more than his rent. *Secundo,* There can be no equity in the defence after the lease is at an end. For at that rate the tenant has a fine game to play: if the sterility continue to the end of the lease, the tenant takes advantage of the equitable defence to get free of the rent; but if fruitfulness be restored, he takes advantage of the lease, and makes all the profit he can. The landlord by this means continues bound while the tenant is free, which is repugnant to all the rules of equity as well as of common law. *Tertio,* At any rate the tenant cannot pick out one or other sterile year to get free of that year's rent: if equity afford him any deduction, it must be upon calculation of the whole years of the lease; for if he be a gainer upon the whole, which is the present case, he has no claim in equity for any deduction." (Referred to at p. 193 n. 16 above.)

EXTRACT [2nd: 277–83]: "A stipulation of this kind constitutes properly an alternative obligation, putting it in the option of the obligor to perform the fact, or in place of it to pay the penal sum. And it must be observed, that this sum is improperly termed *a penalty;* for it is in reality a liquidation of the damages that the obligee suffers by want of performance; or rather a lump sum agreed on in place of damages. A sum thus stipulated, having nothing penal in its nature, is due in equity as well as at common law. Thus land being verbally set[13] to a tenant, under the following condition, That if he entered not he should pay a year's rent; the whole penalty was decreed, because the tenant entered not.*

13. This is a misprint: the first edition has "let."
* Durie, July 15, 1637. Skene [*contra* Anon. M 8401].

"The other kind of penalty is, where, beside performance of what is stipulated in the contract, the obligor is taken bound, if he fail of punctual performance, to pay a sum over and above: as, for example, the debtor becomes bound to pay the sum borrowed at a term specified; and, in order to inforce punctual performance, he becomes bound, if he suffer the term to elapse without payment, to pay an additional sum. Here, in case of failure, both articles must be fulfilled, the additional article as well as that which is principal; and therefore the additional article is more properly a penalty than that first mentioned, where the obligation is alternative.[14]

With respect to a penalty of this kind, it is clear, that a good defence against performance of what is principal, will relieve also from the penalty: but if there be no good defence, the penalty is due by agreement so soon as there is any failure in performance; and may be demanded at common law by an action *ex contractu*. Voet accordingly says, 'Committitur haec poenae stipulatio, si principalis obligatio, quae stipulatione penali firmata erat, impleta non sit, cum de jure implenda fuisset.'* And to prove this position he gives the authority of Paulus in the following words: 'Ad diem sub poena pecunia promissa, et ante diem mortuo promissore, committetur poena, licet non sit hereditas ejus adita.'† For here the death of the debtor before the term of payment afforded no legal defence to his heir; nor ought the creditor to suffer by that accident, *cui de jure implenda erat obligatio,* in the foregoing words of Voet.

"Whether and how far a court of equity will mitigate a penalty of this

---

14. In place of this paragraph, the first edition (p. 197) has the following: "A sum pactioned in case of failure, as where a man obliges himself to pay the sum borrowed with a certain sum over and above if he fail to pay at the term covenanted, is more properly a penalty, because it makes not an alternative obligation as a penalty of the other sort does. Both articles must be fulfilled, the penal article as well as that which is principal."

* §13. de verb. oblig. [Voet, *Commentarius ad Pandectas,* vol. 2, p. 898 (book XLV, tit. 1, sect. 13): "Such a stipulation for a penalty is brought into effect if the main obligation which had been confirmed by the penal stipulation has not been fulfilled, though it could lawfully have been fulfilled": translation from *The Selective Voet, Being the Commentary on the Pandects,* trans. P. Gane (Durban: Butterworths, 1957), vol. 6, p. 636].

† l. 77 Ibid. [D 45.1.77: Watson iv: 662: "Where money is promised on a certain day under penalty, the penalty is due even where the promisor dies before the day, although the inheritance is not yet accepted"].

kind comes next to be considered. What will first occur is, to distinguish culpable failure from what is innocent, and to afford relief in the latter case only. But a more accurate inspection will show this to be an Utopian thought, unsuited to practice. The extreme difficulty of making good this distinction by evidence, would render judges arbitrary, without attaining that refinement of justice which is intended by the distinction:[15] and therefore, it becomes necessary in practice to give relief to all without distinction, unless where it can be made clearly to appear that the failure is culpable.

"The next point is, How far equity will relieve. When an obligor who performs late demands to be relieved from the penal sum, justice requires that the obligee be indemnified of what damage he has sustained by the delay; according to an obvious rule in equity formerly mentioned, which the English lawyers express thus, 'He that demands equity must give equity.' And hence in this island it is the constant practice to decree the penalty to the extent of the damage; and this the obligee is intitled to, however innocent or involuntary the delay may have been. A debtor, for example, disappointed of money, fails to make payment at the term covenanted, which draws upon him a storm of execution: however innocent, he must pay the penalty restricted to the expence of execution; because the conventional penalty so far is not a punishment upon the debtor, but reparation to creditor; and so far it is due in equity as well as at common law. Take another example. A debtor suspends his bond *bona fide;* and the creditor, after discussing the suspension,[16] is satisfied to restrict his penalty to the costs of suit: the penalty thus restricted is not a penal claim, and therefore is due in equity as well as at common law. This example may be viewed in a different light: there must be error, at least, in every case where the obligor refuses to fulfil a just claim, however innocent he may be; and equity relieves from the effect of error, so far only as the person

---

15. The first edition (p. 198) proceeds with the following sentence: "That the innocent, at whatever time they perform, ought to be relieved, is clear: it is not supposable that a penal paction is intended against them; and supposing it so intended, they would still be relieved against a paction that is rigorous and oppressive. And if the innocent be relieved, so must the culpable; for the difficulty of carrying the distinction into practice makes it necessary, with very few exceptions, to give relief to all or none."

16. See glossary, "suspension."

who takes advantage of the error is *in lucro captando,* not where he is *in damno evitando.**

"An English double bond is an example of the second kind of conventional penalties. It was introduced originally to evade the common law of England, which prohibits the taking interest for money: and though that prohibition be no longer in force, the double bond continues in practice; being converted into a different use, *viz.* to compel punctual payment of the money lent. The penalty accordingly is due at common law if the covenanted term be allowed to elapse without payment: and this penal stipulation is in the practice of England governed by the rule of equity above laid down:"After the day of payment, the double sum becomes the legal debt; and there is no remedy against such penalty but by application to a court of equity, which relieves on payment of principal, interest, and costs."†,17

"In our bonds for payment of money, a clause is generally added binding the debtor 'to pay a fifth part more of liquidate expences in case of failzie.' This clause is commonly treated as intending a penalty of the kind last mentioned, contrived to inforce performance: but I think improperly; for the words plainly import a liquidation of that damage which the creditor may sustain by the debtor's failing to pay at the term covenanted. It is of the nature of a transaction *de re futura,*18 being a lump sum in place of all that can be demanded in case of future damage by the said failure. Lord Stair, talking of the court of session as a court of equity, considers the clause in the foregoing light. 'The court of session (says our author) modifies exorbitant penalties in bonds and contracts, even though they bear the name of liquidate expences with consent of parties, which necessitous debtors yield to. These the Lords retrench to the real expence and damage of the parties. Yet these clauses have this effect, that the Lords take slender probation of the true expence, and do not consider whether it be necessary or not, provided it exceed not the sum agreed on; whereas in other cases they allow no expence but what is necessary or profitable.'‡

* See p. 98 [= 3rd: 1: 36; p. 35 above].
† [M. Bacon,] *A New Abridgment of the Law,* vol. 3 [1740], p. 691.
17. This paragraph is reproduced (with slight variations) in 3rd: 2: 156–57.
18. "Concerning a future thing."
‡ Book 4. tit. 3. §1 [that is, sect. 2; Stair, *Institutions,* p. 813].

"Considering the foregoing clause as a transaction *de re futura,* it may be doubted, whether in any case it ought to be mitigated. On the one hand, whatever be the extent of the damage, the creditor by agreement can demand no more but the liquidated sum; and therefore on the other, it may be thought that he is intitled to this sum even where it exceeds his damage: *Cujus incommodum ejus debet esse commodum.* This argument is conclusive, supposing the transaction fair and equal, stipulating no greater sum than the damages ordinarily amount to. But it ought to be considered, that formerly money-lenders in Scotland were in condition to give law to those who borrow. Hence exorbitant sums as liquidate expences, which, being rigorous and oppressive, ought to be mitigated in equity. Upon that account, the lump sum for damages has been generally considered as a penalty; which in effect it is when exorbitant, and as such it shall hereafter be treated of.

"The only doubtful point touching this penalty, is to determine at what time and by what means it is incurred. If we adhere to the words of the clause, it is incurred by *failzie* in general, and consequently by every sort of failzie. But many good lawyers, moved with the hardship of subjecting an innocent person to a penalty, hold, that the penalty is not incurred except in the case of culpable failzie, and that this must be understood the meaning of the clause. They maintain accordingly, that when a debtor, in place of payment, enters into a law-suit, he is not liable for any part of the penalty, though restricted to the costs of the suit, if he have *probabilis causa litigandi.* They do not advert, as above laid down, that a conventional penalty restricted to the expence of execution or costs of suit, ceases in that case to be penal; and that the creditor, when such claim is made effectual to him, draws nothing but what he hath actually expended. But as this is a point of great importance in practice, it merits deliberate discussion; to which I proceed.

"In order to give satisfaction upon this subject, I must state a preliminary point, *viz.* What claim there is for costs of suit abstracting from a conventional penalty. A man who opposes a just claim, acts against law: but is he therefore bound to repair the damage he occasions to the pursuer? If he be litigious in any degree, he is bound; for though it may require a crime to subject a man to punishment, the slightest voluntary wrong or fault is a sufficient foundation for damages, even at common law. But it is a rule in municipal law, derived from the law of nature, 'That a man free from fault or blame is not liable to repair any hurt he occasions';* and therefore there is no foundation even at common law for subjecting to the costs of suit, or to any damage, a defendant who is *in bona fide.* Equity is still more averse from making an innocent person in any case liable to damages; for, considering that a man is a fallible being, his case would be deplorable were he bound to repair all the loss he may occasion by an involuntary wrong. What then shall we say of the act 144. parl. 1592, appointing, 'That damage, interest, and expences of plea, be admitted by all judges, and liquidated in the decree, whether condemnator or absolvitor'? If this regulation could ever be just, it must have been among a plain people, governed by a few simple rules of law, supposed to be universally known. Law, in its present state, is too intricate to admit a presumption that every person who goes against it is *in mala fide;* and yet, unless *mala fides* be presumed in every case, the regulation cannot be justified.[19]

"Taking it now for granted, that, abstracting from a paction, costs of suit cannot be claimed, otherwise than upon the medium of litigiosity, I proceed in my inquiry. And I begin with examining, whether it be lawful to stipulate damages upon the obligor's failure to perform, not even excepting an innocent failure. To bring this question near the eye, I put a plain case. A man is willing to lend his money at common interest; but insists, that if he be put to any expence in recovering payment, the borrower, who occasions this expence, shall be liable for it; and the borrower agrees to take the money upon that condition. Is this paction one of these oppressive provisions, against which the debtor will be relieved in equity? I cannot discover any injustice in this paction, nor any oppression. A paction of this nature, so far from being unjust or oppressive, appears naturally to be a natural consequence from the law against usury. Where a man is permitted to take what interest he can for his money, a high interest may be held sufficient to counterbalance what may be expended in recovering payment; but where the creditor is limited to a certain rate of interest, it

* See the chapter immediately foregoing.

19. This paragraph is reproduced (with slight variations) in 3rd: 2: 158; pp. 326–27 above.

seems intended by the legislature, that he should be in all events secure of that interest, without being forc'd to expend it, and perhaps more, upon recovering the very sum he lent. Where-ever this happens, the creditor, instead of the common rate of interest, receives no interest at all; and must be satisfied to receive back a sum, that, in effect, has all along been barren.

"An inquiry here into what is lawful, smooths the road in our present progress. If the paction above mentioned be lawful, we cannot hesitate in presuming that every creditor will take the advantage of it; and consequently that this paction must be implied in the penal clause contained in our bonds of borrowed money. To confine the meaning of this penal clause to a culpable failure, is truly to destroy the effect of it altogether; for a culpable failure subjects the debtor to damages at common law, independent of the clause. Nor can we doubt that the meaning of the clause is as above set forth, when we see the same meaning given to a penal clause in England and in old Rome.

"That the penalty in our bonds of borrowed money is incurred even by an innocent failure, appears, not only from the presumed will of the parties, but also from the inveterate practice of the court of session in mitigating these penalties, which would be against equity supposing the failure to be criminal or culpable.[20] I urge in the next place, that the failure of a debtor to pay at the term covenanted, must *in dubio* be held innocent till the contrary be proved. This is a legal privilege, common to a debtor with the rest of mankind. Hence it necessarily follows, that if the clause under consideration be confined to culpable failure, a charge of horning cannot

---

20. In the first edition (p. 202), this paragraph begins thus: "But I am not satisfied to ascertain the sense of the clause from the presumed will of the parties. I am able to show, that the sense I espouse is established by inveterate practice. I urge in the first place, that if culpable failzie be the meaning of the clause, the constant practice of the court of session, which mitigates a conventional penalty in certain circumstances, is destitute of all foundation in law. It is made out above, that a conventional penalty is not mitigated but under the colour of being innocent. A conventional penalty considered as culpable, cannot be mitigated in equity. Here then is an evident dilemma. If it be maintained, that a conventional penalty is not incurred unless the failure be culpable, it follows necessarily, that it never can in any case be mitigated. On the other hand, if it be admitted, as it must be, that the court of session can in some cases afford relief against a conventional penalty, it follows not less necessarily, that it is incurred by every sort of failure, innocent as well as culpable."

pass for the penalty, till it be proved in a process, that the failure is culpable. Here is a vexing dilemma: if culpable failure be the meaning of the clause, the practice of charging for the penalty so soon as the term of payment is past, must be given up as irregular and illegal, though acquiesced in for centuries without the least opposition: on the other hand, if it be admitted, as it must be, that this practice is agreeable to law, it follows necessarily, that a conventional penalty is incurred by innocent as well as by culpable failure.

"Add the following observation. Where a bond stipulating interest after the term of payment, is suspended and the letters are found orderly proceeded, after an intricate and doubtful litigation of many years, no lawyer ever dreamed that the suspender's *bona fides* will relieve him from interest. And yet it will puzzle the ablest lawyer to say, where the difference lies in this case between interest and costs of suit: if a plausible defence prevent the stipulated penalty from being incurred, it ought also to prevent the stipulated interest from being incurred. Both are due *ex contractu* upon the failure of payment; and if there be any reason for barring innocent failure in the paction for the penalty, there is the same reason for barring it in the paction for interest. If there be a difference, the penalty restricted to costs of suit is the more favourable claim: it is money out of the creditor's pocket, it is *damnum datum;* whereas the claim for interest is only *lucrum cessans.* With respect to the English double bond, this argument concludes beyond the possibility of cavil; the penal stipulation being the only foundation for claiming interest as well as claiming costs.

"Upon the whole, it shall now be taken for granted, that in a bond of borrowed money the penal sum is incurred by innocent as well as by culpable failure. In the latter case, supposing the *culpa* clearly proved, equity pleads not for a mitigation: in the former, equity requires a mitigation, as far as the stipulation is truly penal; that is, as far as the penal sum exceeds the damage occasioned to the creditor by the delay of payment. This mitigation arises necessarily from the rule above mentioned, 'He that demands equity must give equity.' And hence, in innocent failure, the practice is to mitigate the penalty to the costs of suit and to what other damage is clearly ascertained. This, at the same time, by putting the creditor in the same condition as if punctual payment had been made, fulfils all the intention he could fairly have in stipulating a penalty." (Referred to at p. 324 n. 3 above.)

Letter from Kames to Robert Dundas of Arniston, Lord President of the Court of Session, Including a Paper Entitled "Jurisdiction of the Court of Session as a Court of Equity"

Kames 16 Octr 1764

The want of a regulation to bring in Creditors pari passu upon a Bankrupt's moveables similar to what there is upon his Land, has long given me disquiet. An hour, a minute of priority is with us held a good cause of allotting to a Creditor his whole Debt, frequently to the utter ruin of others who in justice and equity are equally intitled to their payment. This is not only grossly unjust, but extremely inexpedient with respect to Commerce. An arrestment can be executed in a minute, and Creditors at a distance have no chance. Our London Correspondents are sensible of this, and the Credit of our dealers is much impaired by it. At any rate, it puts us under a great disadvantage in our commercial dealings with strangers who cannot be blamed for laying upon the price of their commodities, sufficient to ensure them against this risk.

It is well known to your Lordship what pains I have taken to have the act of sederunt renewed for Ranking Arresters pari passu in the case of Bankruptcy.[1] A scroll of a new act has long been before the court with improvements, and it has always amazed me to find such listlessness and languor among our Brethren about a matter of so great importance. The last time I had the honour to converse with your Lordship upon this subject, you seemed to approve of the new Plan, but you doubted of the powers of the Court to make such an act. I hoped for an opportunity to

A copy of this manuscript, from the Dundas of Arniston Papers, is held in the National Archives of Scotland: Mfm RH4/15/2. It is reproduced here with the kind permission of Mrs. Althea Dundas-Bekker.

1. *AS* 478: 10th August 1754, Act of sederunt anent poindings and arrestments.

satisfy your Lordship viva voce that we had power. But finding this to be in vain during the Session, it struck me lately to put my thoughts in writing for a leisure hour in the vacation. The inclosed paper includes contains my thoughts upon this subject; and your Lordship will observe that I place my argument upon the nobile officium[2] of the Court, by no means upon the power given to the Lords of Session to make rules, statutes, and ordinances with relation to their manners and order of proceeding; which obviously relates to forms only.

If your Lordship upon a serious perusal of the inclosed paper, be of opinion that the Court has power to renew the act of sederunt, we shall go on with alacrity to do a public service to our Country; being confident that if your Lordship show any warmness for the act, not one of our Brethren will stand out. On the other hand, tho I should be so misfortunate as to have your opinion against me, I shall gain however so much by this attempt as no longer to be disquieted about what I shall then find to be impracticable. But I hope better things from your Lordship's enlightened understanding. You can have no hesitation about the justice and expedience of the act; and I would gladly flatter myself you will now have as little about our powers.

> Your Lordship's
> ffaithful and Obedient Servant
> Henry Home

---

2. The "noble office": on this concept, see the Editor's Introduction.

Jurisdiction of the Court of Session
as a Court of Equity

The jurisdiction of the Court of Session as a Court of common law, concerns property and whatever may be termed pecuniary interest. Other matters are distributed among different Courts. But as such distribution cannot be accurate, articles emerged from time to time that fall not properly under the jurisdiction of any Court. To supply this defect, an extraordinary or equitable jurisdiction is attributed to the sovereign and supreme civil Court with respect to causes that belong not to any other Court; and this equitable jurisdiction is founded upon a noble principle, that there ought to be no wrong without a remedy. It is so well known in our practice as to have a name appropriated to it, being termed the nobile officium of the Court of Session. The Court of Chancery in England enjoys the same priviledge. Every wrong is redressed in the Court of Chancery, where a different remedy is not provided by common Law or by statute. And hence it is, that the jurisdiction of this Court, confined originally within narrow bounds, has been gradually enlarged over a boundless variety of affairs.

In Scotland as well as in other civilized Countries, the King and Council was originally the only Court that had power to remedy defects or redress unjustice in Courts of common Law. To this extraordinary or equitable Jurisdiction the Court of Session naturally succeeded, as being the supreme Court in Civil matters. It may at first sight seem surprising, that no mention is made of this Jurisdiction in any regulation concerning the Court of Session. The thing was not thought of, and possibly was not intended: the necessity however of such a Jurisdiction brought it to an establishment. It is curious to observe the wavering of the Court of Session about their powers, before this matter came to be perfectly understood, of which I shall give one instance. In the [year] 1582 they ventured a bold step, exceeding the powers of any Court, and that was to make an act of sederunt authorising a charge of Horning upon a liquid debt, an extraordinary remedy that undoubtedly required the authority of the legislature itself. And yet ten years thereafter viz Nov. 1592 they made an act of sederunt declaring "that in time coming they will judge and decide upon clauses irritant contained in contracts, Tacks, Infeftments, Bonds, and obligations, precisely according to the words and meaning of the same";[1] which in effect was declaring themselves a Court of common Law, not of Equity. But the mistake was discovered in time: the act of sederunt wore out of use; and now for more than a Century, the Court of Session has acted as a Court of Equity as well as of common Law.[2]

By the abolition of the Privy Council in Scotland, many injuries appropriated to that Court without a word of appropriating them to any other Court. The Legislature surely did not intend that these injuries should pass with impunity. The intention must have been to transfer them to the Court of Session.

By virtue of this extraordinary or equitable jurisdiction, it belongs to the Court of Session, first to supply defects in common Law, which are manifold, and next, to correct or mitigate the rigour and injustice of common Law occasioned by confining Courts of common Law to strict rules which they have no power to soften. These branches come both of them under the name of Equity; and are the same that were assumed by the Roman Praetor from necessity without any express authority. l: 7. §1 De justitia et jure.[3]

It would fill a volume to enumerate the various cases where the nobile officium of the Court of Session has been exerted to supply defects in common Law and to mitigate its rigour or unjustice. A few instances shall be selected. The common Law is wonderfully defective with respect to execution. It's apprising is confined to land rights, and so is the adjudication that is put in place of it by the Act 72.[4] There is no method at com-

1. *AS* 19.

2. Cf. *Principles of Equity*, above, p. 32.

3. On Justice and Law, D 1.1.7.1: Watson i: 2: "Praetorian law is that which in the public interest the praetors have introduced in aid or supplementation or correction of the *jus civile* (civil law)."

4. Act 19, parl. 1672; *APS* viii: 93: 1672, c. 45, Act concerning Adjudications [Adjudications Act 1672].

mon Law for attacking a reversion, a Bond secluding Executors, a sum of money with which a Disposition is burdened &c. But as it would be gross unjustice to with-hold from Creditors any effects that can be converted into money for their payment, an Adjudication was early contrived by the sovereign Court for carrying subjects of this kind; and there was as great necessity for an Adjudication in implement and for a declaratory Adjudication, Diligences unknown at common Law. The citation at the market cross of Edinburgh Pier and Shoar of Leith, is one illustrious instance of a defect in common Law supplyed by the Court of Session; for the common Law both of England and Scotland reaches no man but while he continues within it's territorial jurisdiction.

The same nobile officium is extended to supply deffect in statute Law. The priviledge of selling the Predecessor's Estate is by the act 1695[5] confined to heirs apparent; But ex paritate rationis[6] is extended by the Court of Session to heirs entered cum beneficio[7] The Act 62 Parliament 1661[8] Declaring apprisings purchased by an apparent heir to be redeemable within two years, has almost, in every one of it's circumstances been extended beyond the words, in order to complete the remedy intended by the Legislature.* The positive prescription, confined to land rights by the Act 1617,[9] is extended to tacks, rights to tythes &c.

Next with respect to mitigating the rigour or unjustice of common Law. The act of sederunt 28 of ffebruary 1662[10] was made to prevent the unjust advantage that Creditors at hand have to sweep away the moveable effects of their defunct Debtor; and the remedy given is to bring in pari passu those who do Diligence within six months. Upon the same principle

5. *APS* ix: 427: 1695, c. 39, Act for obviating the frauds of appearand heirs.

6. "By a parity of reason."

7. That is, *cum beneficio inventarii:* "with the benefit of an inventory"; for which see glossary, "benefit of inventory."

8. *APS* vii: 317: 1661, c. 344, Act for ordering the payment of debts betwixt creditor and debtor [Diligence Act 1661].

* See Kames, *Dictionary* vol. 1 page 359 [section entitled "Redemption of apprising from apparent heirs"].

9. Act 12, parl. 1617; *APS* iv: 543: 1617, c. 12, Anent prescriptioun of heretable rights [Prescription Act 1617].

10. *AS* 82: Act anent executors-creditors.

Adjudications and apprisings within year and day are ranked pari passu by statute.

With respect to bankruptcy the common Law is extremely defective; for without the least respect to the circumstances of Bankruptcy, it sustains every Deed whoever may be the granter, provided only the property be in him to enable him to make the Deed; and thus the utmost latitude is given for defrauding Creditors. Justice and Equity dictate a very different rule, which is that a man being bound to all his personal Creditors equally, he ought in a state of insolvency to distribute his effects fairly and equally among them; because to pay one his whole debt is so far diminishing the fund that ought to go to others. Conscience dictates this conduct, and no man can have peace of mind who transgresses this rule. No Creditor on the other hand can be innocent, who knowing the Bankruptcy takes more than his proportion: if he takes more by the Bankrupt's deed, he is accessory to the Bankrupt's fraud; and if he attempt to take more by legal Diligence and so far to deprive his fellow Creditors of their proportion, he ought not to be countenanced by a Court of Equity.

This is the moral and equitable foundation of the Act of Sederunt 1754,[11] Ranking arresters pari passu in the case of Bankruptcy. The same moral and equitable foundation ought to be a prevailing motive for renewing this temporary act with proper improvements. And that the Court of Session has power to make this act cannot be doubted, supposing only what is clear from the whole history of our Law, that they have power to supply the defects of common Law, and to mitigate it's vigour and injustice.

11. *AS* 478.

GLOSSARY

absolvitor: a decree or decision in favor of the defendant.

accessory obligations: obligations which "cannot subsist by themselves, but are accessions to, or make part of, other obligations to which they are interposed": Erskine, *Institute,* vol. 2, p. 469 (book III, tit. 3, sect. 60).

accresce: *see* accretion.

accretion: the perfection of a defective title by some act of the party who conveyed an imperfect title to the current holder: that is, when A, who has conveyed to B, has an imperfect title, which is later perfected, this "accresces to" and perfects B's title.

actio de in rem verso: an action for money applied to the defendant's advantage (*in rem versum:* turned to his account); to reverse an unjust enrichment (Roman law).

actio in factum (an action in regard to the fact): an action in Roman law granted by the praetor when no standard action was available.

actio negotiorum gestorum: In Roman law, where one person voluntarily undertook the management (*gestio*) of another person's affairs (*negotia*), he became liable for any damage done to the property by his fraudulent or culpable conduct and was bound to return any proceeds made from the property while in his hands. At the same time, he was entitled to be compensated for any expenses he had reasonably incurred in the management,

Unless I have indicated otherwise, the terms in the glossary relate to the law of Scotland. I am grateful to Professor John Cairns and Professor Mark Godfrey, who have helped my by answering queries on some technical terms of Scots law; responsibility for any remaining errors is mine alone.

even if his efforts to preserve the property proved unsuccessful. In Roman law, the "direct" *actio negotiorum gestorum* was the action brought against the *gestor* or manager to recover proceeds or to obtain damages; while the "contrary" *actio negotiorum gestorum contraria* was used by the *gestor* to recover his expenses. Kames uses the former phrase when speaking of the *gestor's* right to compensation.

action of mails and duties: *see* mails and duties.

action on the case/trespass on the case: a common law action in England, originating in the fourteenth century, to provide a general remedy for nonforcible wrongs.

act of sederunt: a rule made by the judges of the Court of Session, usually regulating the forms of proceedings to be used in actions.

ad factum praestandum (for the performance of a certain act). Obligations *ad facta praestanda* are obligations (imposed by the court) to perform the act; for specific performance.

adjudication: a process used to attach heritable property, to allow a creditor to take a debtor's land to satisfy a debt owed to a creditor. The Adjudications Act 1672 (*APS* viii: 93) introduced two kinds of adjudication. "Special" adjudication was the process whereby the Court of Session would "adjudge" from the debtor so much of his land to be transferred to the creditor in satisfaction of his debt as was commensurate with the debt due and charges, along with an extra fifth as compensation for the trouble to the creditor in having to take land for payment instead of money. The debtor could redeem his lands within five years. The process of "general" adjudication allowed a creditor, in case the debtor refused to renounce his possession or ratify the court's decree, to adjudge all his land to the creditor. In this case, the debtor could redeem within ten years.

adjudication in implement: the procedure used when a party selling heritable property (the grantor) fails to fulfill his obligation to convey a complete title to the grantee. In this process, the grantee asks that, in "implement" of the grantor's obligation, the property in question should be "adjudged" from the grantor and declared to belong to the grantee.

advocation: a form of process by which cases are removed from inferior to superior courts in Scotland, either to review the decision of the inferior court or to continue the process in the Court of Session.

annualrent: interest on money. *See also* annualrent-right.

annualrent-right: a yearly rent of land, granted to a lender by deed as security for a loan. Such grants were redeemable on repayment of the loan.

apparency: the period of time before an heir-apparent has decided to take up or renounce his succession.

apparent heir: the heir to an estate, who has the right to enter into the succession, but who has not yet completed his title to his ancestor's estate, and who must decide within a year and a day whether to take up or renounce the succession.

apprising: the diligence (execution against a debtor) used for transferring land to a creditor in satisfaction of the owner's debt. Under this procedure, the debtor's land was transferred to his creditor in satisfaction of the debt, if he did not have sufficient moveable property to pay the debt, subject to a debtor's power (given by the Diligence Act 1469 (*APS* ii: 96) to redeem the land on repayment of the debt within seven years. By the early seventeenth century, the practice had been established that creditors were allowed to take possession of the land, taking the rents and profits from it, with the land itself continuing to belong to the debtor unless he repaid within seven years. The Diligence Act 1621 (*APS* iv: 609) provided that the creditor had to repay such rents and profits as exceeded the interest on his debt. Since the system still allowed for large estates to be lost for the nonpayment of small debts, the system was reformed by the Adjudications Act 1672 (*APS* viii: 93), which introduced a new procedure of adjudication [q.v.].

arrestment and forthcoming: *Arrestment* is the attaching of a debtor's property in the hands of a third person: that is, a legal process ordering that the goods or debts "arrested" be kept in the same state until the arrested has been paid or given security. All moveable property belonging to a debtor, including debts owing to him, are subjects which can be arrested. *Forthcoming* is the action used to make the property attached available to the arrester.

The action of forthcoming is brought against the arrestee (the person hold-ing the goods) and the "common debtor," that is, the party owing a debt to both the arrester and arrestee. See Kames's discussion in vol. 2, pp. 173–74.

assoilzie: to absolve.

astruct: to establish.

attach: to seize under legal authority.

author: the person from whom the property is purchased, in contrast to "ancestor," from whom property is inherited.

backbond: an instrument which qualifies another unqualified instrument.

bailie: a municipal office or magistrate in Scotland, equivalent to an En-glish alderman.

base infeftment: infeftment [s.v.] of land to be held under the grantor, rather than directly under his superior; subinfeudation.

beneficium competentiae (the privilege of competency): the right of the debtor, who assigns his property to his creditors, to be ordered to pay only as much as he reasonably can, leaving him enough to live on (Scots and Roman law).

benefit of inventory: where an heir doubted whether his ancestor's estate was sufficient to satisfy his debts, he was allowed by the 1695 Act for obvi-ating the frauds of appearand heirs (*APS* ix: 427) to enter within a day and a year of his ancestor's death *cum beneficio inventarii* (with the benefit of an inventory), the effect of which was that he would not be liable beyond the value of the estate. Previous to this act, the heir became liable to all the debts of his ancestor by his entry to the land. The doctrine of the benefit of inventory was adapted from the Roman law: C. 6.30.22.

bond in judgment: in England, debtors could confess an action against them, either by giving a warrant of attorney or by a *cognovit actionem* (he has confessed the action).

bond of corroboration: a written obligation, creating an additional per-sonal obligation in respect of an existing bond, which it confirms. It was used to confirm an earlier bond given for a debt, granted either by the person giving the bond of corroboration or by another person, such as his ancestor. "The bond of corroboration is used where the interest has been allowed to run into arrear, in order to accumulate the whole into a new principal sum bearing interest; or it is used where an additional security is to be given, or where the obligation is to be renewed by the heir of the debtor": Robert Bell, *A System of the Forms of Deeds Used in Scotland*, 2 vols. (Edinburgh: Guthrie, 1797–99), vol. 2, pp. 153–54.

bond of provision: a deed granted by a father, granting a provision for his children.

bond secluding executors: under the 1661 Act concerning heritable and moveable bonds (*APS* vii: 230) obligations bearing interest descended to executors; but the act excepted bonds which excluded (or secluded) executors, where the bond passed to the heirs. See further Erskine, *Institute,* vol. 1, p. 172 (book II, tit. 2, sect. 12).

by and attour: over and above, in addition to.

caption: process used in Scotland for imprisonment for debt. Imprisonment for debt "proceeds upon letters of horning [s.v.] and caption, issued from the Court of Session, either upon a judgment of that Court, pronounced in an action; or on a decree of registration by consent, or under the statute relative to bills; or on a decree given in supplement of the judgment of an inferior court": George Joseph Bell, *Commentaries on the Laws of Scotland,* 2nd ed. (Edinburgh: Archibald Constable & Co, 1810), p. 10.

catholic creditor: a creditor whose debt is secured over several subjects belonging to the debtor.

caution: security.

cautioner: surety.

cedent: a person who assigns property to another; assignor.

certans de damno evitando: striving to avoid a loss.

certans de lucro captando: striving to make a profit; attempting to obtain an advantage.

certiorari: a prerogative writ used in England to remove cases into the Court of King's Bench.

cess: a land tax on the produce and rent of real property, originally imposed in Scotland in 1652.

cessio bonorum (surrender of goods): Using this procedure, "a bankrupt in prison giving up his whole estate to his creditors upon oath, may apply to the Court of Session for liberation": N. Bailey, *An Universal Etymological Dictionary,* 28th ed. (Edinburgh: Neill, 1800).

cessio in jure: a transfer in law. In Roman law, *in jure cessio* was a means of transferring ownership by means of a fictitious suit in the form of a *rei vindicatio* [s.v.].

chalder: a unit of measure of capacity made up of sixteen "bolls."

citation: the procedure by an officer of the court that calls on a party to appear in court, to answer an action or to testify.

collateral heir-male: A male heir, not in a direct line of descent from the deceased, but in a diverging line of descent.

compensation: the provision in Scots law whereby mutual debts can be extinguished by setting one off against the other. Under legislation passed in 1592 (*APS* iii: 573, c. 61), a defendant could plead any debt he was owed by the pursuer by way of exception or defense before a decree was given; though he could not raise it by way of suspension [s.v.] or reduction [s.v.] after decree.

composition: the acceptance of a smaller sum in payment of a larger sum, usually by the creditors of a bankrupt.

composition to a superior: the payment made by a purchaser to obtain an entry into the land held of the superior.

condemnator: a decision against the defendant; condemnatory.

condictio: a personal action in Roman law used to demand the return of something, including money (from *condicere,* to demand back).

conditional institute: An "institute" is the person entitled to take up possession of heritable property as the immediate disponee of the granter. Where the institution of that person was made conditional on certain events, it was a "conditional institute."

condition precedent: an act or event specified in a contract or grant, which must be performed or occur before any rights conferred in the contract or grant can vest.

condition resolutive: a condition which brings a right or obligation to an end if a specified event occurs.

condition suspensive: a condition which suspends the coming into force of a right or obligation until such time as the condition is fulfilled.

confirmation: the confirmation of the creditor of the deceased debtor as executor-creditor (s.v.).

conjunct and confident person: someone related by blood and connected by interest; or (under the Bankruptcy Act 1621, *APS* iv: 615) someone to whom an alienation of property is made by an insolvent person without cause.

conjunct rights: right taken jointly. Between husband and wife, where rights were taken "in conjunct fee and liferent [s.v], and the heirs of their body," the husband was taken to be the sole owner of the fee and the wife a liferenter: see Erskine, *Institute,* vol. 2, p. 560 (book III, tit. 8, s. 36).

conquest: property rights obtained by acquisition (such as purchase), rather than by inheritance. Scottish marriage contracts often contained provisions settling the "conquest" acquired during the marriage on the issue of the marriage. Cf. Erskine, *Institute,* vol. 2, p. 564: "By conquest is understood the estate which the father shall acquire during the marriage" (book III, tit. 8, sect. 43).

consideration: the reason or cause of entering into a contract or granting a deed. In English law, all contracts not entered into by deed required evidence of consideration (either a detriment to the person who was promised something under the contract or a benefit to the person making the promise) in order to be considered valid. In Scots law, a deed granted for a gratuitous consideration (that is, with nothing in exchange) was valid.

consignator: A person authorized to accept the delivery of money from a debtor, where the creditor refuses to accept it.

constituent: the principal who appoints an agent.

constitute/constitution: to determine or establish a debt in court. A decree which ascertains the extent of a debt is a decree of constitution.

corpora of moveable property: tangible moveable goods, in contrast to intangible ones, such as obligations to pay debt.

Corpus Juris Civilis: the body of Roman law enacted under Emperor Justinian, comprising the *Digest, Code,* and *Institutes,* and including the later *Novellae Constitutiones.*

curator: guardian.

curator bonorum or *curator bonis:* the administrator of the estate of an insolvent debtor.

curtesy: a tenancy (both in Scotland and England) by which a surviving husband was a tenant for his life (or liferenter, in Scots law) of heritable estates held by his wife. It was a tenancy "by the curtesy of England" (William Blackstone, *Commentaries on the Laws of England* [Oxford: Clarendon Press, 1765–69], vol. 2, p. 126) or "by the courtesy or curiality of Scotland" (Stair, *Institutions,* p. 450, book II, tit. 6, sect. 19).

debita fructuum: a debt chargeable on the fruits of the land, as opposed to *debita fundi,* debts chargeable on the land itself.

decern: to decree.

declarator, or declaratory actions: actions where the pursuer seeks to have a right judicially declared, but without making any claim on a defendant.

declaratory adjudication: a procedure, developed in the mid-eighteenth century, to make effective the rights of beneficiaries of landed property held in trust in Scotland. By this procedure, the court could decree the trust at an end and order the feudal superior to grant charters to infeft [see infeftment] the beneficiary.

decree: final judgment.

decreet-arbitral: the decision of an arbiter.

devise over: make provision in a will for the property to pass to another person in case of failure of the intended devisee.

diligence: execution against debtors.

discuss a suspension: to hear and determine an order of the court suspending execution of judgment. The party seeking a suspension of the execution (the "suspender") and the original claimant (the "charger") give their reasons in court. In Bankton's words (*Institute,* vol. 3, p. 10: book IV, tit. xxxviii, sect 10), "if both suspension and charge are produced, and appearance is made for both parties, the charger repeats his charge, and the suspender his reasons of suspension, and the charger his answers; and if the reasons are sustained, the letters [of caption, q.v.] are suspended, either Simply, which is an absolute extinguishment of the debt; or till a certain event, according to the import of the reasons. If the reasons of suspension are repelled, the letters and charge are found Orderly proceeded, *i.e.* execution upon the decree, or other ground of debt suspended, will be allowed, and the suspender anew decreed in payment of the sums charged for, and frequently in damages and the full costs of suit."

discussion (benefit of): the right of a surety to require the creditor to take proceedings to obtain payment from the principal debtor before seeking payment from the surety. Adapted in Scots law from the Roman law *beneficium ordinis* (privilege of order).

disposition: a unilateral deed by which property is transferred.

distraint/distress: the seizure of a chattel from someone who has failed to perform an obligation owed to the person seizing, done to procure performance of the obligation; most commonly done in cases of nonpayment of rent (English law).

donatar: one to whom a donation has been made, usually of escheated land.

double bond: a "double bond," or "conditional bond," was a sealed bond granted by a debtor, which obliged him to pay a penal sum if he did not fulfill a condition in the bond whose performance rendered the obligation void. The usual practice in the eighteenth century was for borrowers to grant a bond for double the sum borrowed, with a condition that the bond would be void if he repaid the sum actually borrowed by a certain date. The Court of Chancery gave relief against penalties, requiring the debtor only to pay the sum really due; and legislation in the late seventeenth and early eighteenth centuries enacted that the common law would also only require the debtor to pay the sum really due (English law).

dower: a widow's right to a life-interest in one-third of the land held in fee by the husband (English Law).

duplie: in Scottish legal pleading, a defender's rejoinder to the pursuer's reply.

dyvour: a bankrupt, who made cession of all his goods in favor of his creditors and who was required to wear "the dyvour's habit"—a yellow hat or bonnet—and to sit on a pillory near the market cross of Edinburgh.

ease: a reduction or remission of an amount of service due.

effeir: to fall by right; to appertain.

ejectment (*ejectio firmae*): a method to try title to land in English law, developed in the sixteenth and seventeenth centuries. The action of ejectment was a tort action (which was simpler than the older real actions) in which a person claiming to have been wrongfully ejected from his land sought to recover possession. The nominal parties in the suit were fictitious ("John Doe" and "Richard Roe"), so that no physical ejectment took place.

elegit: a writ of execution used in England on a judgment for debt or damages. Under this writ, a plaintiff obtained the defendant's chattels to satisfy the debt. If they were insufficient, he was entitled to take half of the profits from the defendant's land until the debt was satisfied.

entail: an estate held under a settlement which limited the inheritance to a particular line of succession (known in English law as an estate-tail). In order to preserve family estates intact, settlements were drawn up to prevent the settlor's heirs from disposing of the estates or altering the line of succession. In Scotland, entails (or tailzies) were regulated by the Entail Act 1685 (*APS* viii: 477).

equity of redemption: the right of the mortgagor or pledgor to redeem his property, on discharging the liability secured by the mortgage or pledge.

The phrase referred in particular to the English Court of Chancery's use of its equitable power to allow the mortgagor to redeem, even after the time for payment had passed. However, the Court of Session also gave relief against irritant clauses in wadsets [s.v.]. As Bankton put it, "There are infinite other cases, where the court of session gives relief in equity, when, in strict law, there seems to be none; as in redemption of wadsets limited to a precise term, after which the lands are deemed irredeemable: this court allows the equity of redemption, notwithstanding the irritancy incurred": Bankton, *Institute,* vol. 2, pp. 516–17.

estate at will: a tenancy which is terminable at will and has no fixed period of duration.

estate-tail: *see* entail.

exceptio doli: a defense or plea of fraud (Roman law).

exception: a form of defence to an action. In Roman law, an *exceptio* was a plea by the defendant alleging facts or legal provisions to deny the claim.

execution: putting into effect a court order. In Scots law, it also refers to the document which attests that the officer has carried this out.

executor-creditor: a person who in order to recover a debt in legal proceedings has himself confirmed as executor in respect of some items only of the deceased's assets.

executor-dative: an executor named by the court.

executor-nominate: an executor nominated by the deceased.

ex parte: proceedings in which only one side is heard.

extract of a decree: a written instrument signed by a court official (an "extract") containing a statement of a decree. "To extract" is to procure the instrument.

extra territorium: beyond the territory (of a jurisdiction).

factor: an agent.

factor fee: a fee paid to a factor.

failzie: failure, or nonperformance.

fee, feu: unit of land held by feudal tenure; a heritable estate held by a vassal (feu-vassal or feuar) in return for a token annual payment, in commutation of the military service due under the feudal system to the superior. Distinguished in Scotland from land held in "liferent" [s.v.].

fee simple: the highest form of interest in land available in the English feudal system of land tenure; granted to the tenant and his heirs forever, it lasts as long as the tenant has heirs.

feme covert: married woman (English law).

feu: *see* fee.

feu duties: annual duties payable in money or in kind, in respect of land held by feudal holding.

feuer/feuar: vassal; one who holds a feu.

feu-right: the right to the feu duties payable in respect of land held by feudal tenure.

fiar: the owner of a fee, or the person in whom property in an estate is vested, in respect of which a liferent has been created. The fiar is contrasted with the "liferenter" [s.v.].

fine: a method of conveying land in England, abolished in 1833, taking the form of a fictitious personal action between the parties—in which the grantee of the land claimed to have been deforced of the land by the grantor—ending in a legal compromise, or "final concord." Since the grantor admitted that the lands are already those of the grantee, there was no need for a "livery of seisin" (a formal ceremonial transferring of the land).

formulae: model pleas developed in Rome by the praetor, authorizing the judge to find for the plaintiff if certain facts were proved.

forthcoming: *see under* arrestment.

glebe: lands belonging to the church.

heir of provision: one who succeeds by virtue of a provision in a settlement.

heirs-portioners: co-heirs; females succeeding jointly to a heritage for which there is no male heir.

heritable property: property which descends to the heir in "heritage," including all immoveable property (land).

heritable debt: debts secured on land which pass to the heir.

heritor: landowner.

holographic will: a will handwritten by the testator.

horning: the denunciation of a person as an outlaw. *See also* letters of horning.

in aemulationem vicini: (in envy of the neighbor). In Scots law, this phrase referred to the use of land in a way intentionally injurious to one's neighbor. The phrase (taken from medieval civilian writers who developed the *ius commune* tradition) was used to express the principle that one should not exercise a legitimate right with the sole aim of annoying one's neighbor, or "purely out of envy." See Bankton, *Institute,* vol. 1, p. 252 (book I, tit. 10, sect. 40).

infeftment: the act of transferring ownership of an estate in land; the act of giving symbolic possession of land or other heritable property.

infeftment of annualrent: a real burden on the land, taking the form of the grant of an "annualrent-right" [q.v.].

inhibition: A form of diligence [q.v.] against a debtor prohibiting him from burdening or disposing of heritable property to the prejudice of a creditor.

in mala fide: in bad faith.

in rem versum: to the enrichment [of someone] (turned to his account).

institute: the person to whom an estate is first given in a settlement. *See also* conditional institute.

instruct: to confirm by evidence.

interdiction: a system of restraint provided for those who are liable to imposition. These were of two types: "voluntary" interdictions, where a person aware of his vulnerability voluntarily imposed a restraint on himself (usually by bond), obliging himself to do nothing which might affect his estate without the consent of a person or persons named in the grant, who were known as "interdictors." "Judicial" interdictions were imposed by the Court of Session, usually at the request of a close kinsman of the person restrained.

interdictor: *see* interdiction.

interlocutor: judgment.

inter vivos: between living people.

intimation: formal notice given (for example, via a notarial instrument) by an assignee to the debtor of the assignment, necessary for the complete transfer of the right assigned.

in totum: in its entirety.

intromission: the act of dealing with another person's property.

investiture: the act by which a transfer of the right to land is effected, by means of a charter and instrument of sasine (that is, the act of giving legal possession of feudal property), duly registered.

irritancy: the forfeiture of a right in consequence of failure to observe duties imposed by law or agreement. It could occur by force of law (legal irritancy), as where a feu [q.v] was forfeited for nonpayment of the feu-duty for two years, or where a lease was forfeited if the tenant was two years in arrear of rent (see further the act of sederunt of 14 December 1756 [*AS* 503], setting out the acts for which a lease could be forfeited). It could also occur for breaches of contractual stipulations (conventional irritancy).

irritant clauses: clauses in a deed specifying that if the holder performs an act specifically prohibited by the deed, the deed shall be voided.

jointure: a provision in a marriage settlement for land to be settled on the husband and wife jointly for the life of the survivor. This was done to permit the widow to remain the tenant of the land during her life, and was given in lieu of the widow's common law right to dower (a life interest in one-third of her late husband's land).

jure gentium: by the law of nations.

legal: the period of time allowed to the person whose land is in the process of adjudication [q.v], within which the money owed may be paid and the land freed of the adjudication.

letters of horning: letters issued on a warrant from the Court of Session, following a decree by a court directing messengers-at-arms to charge the person against whom the letters are issued to comply with the order in the letter, usually to pay a debt. Such letters charge the debtor named to pay, on pain of being regarded as a rebel (being "put to the horn").

lex commissoria in pignoribus: agreements for strict foreclosure of pledges. The term applied to a clause inserted in a contract of pledge, stating that the pledge should be forfeited if the demand was not paid at the time agreed. It was outlawed by Emperor Constantine in A.D. 326: C. 8.34.3 (Roman law).

liferent: the right to use and enjoy the property of another (the fiar, q.v.) during one's life.

liferenter: the person in possession of an estate, by virtue of a liferent right.

liferent-locality: the liferent created in marriage contracts in favor of a wife: "locality" is an appropriation of certain lands to the wife in liferent.

litigious: *see* render litigious.

loco facti impraestabilis succedit damnum et interesse: "damages and interest follow in place of something which cannot be performed."

locupletior: enriched.

mails and duties, action of: an action for the rents of an estate (from *mails and duties,* the rents of an estate, whether in cash or grain). It could be used by a proprietor, or by one claiming the right to the property, or as a form of execution against a debtor by which a heritable creditor procured the rents of the property to be paid directly to him.

march: boundary of land.

meliorations: improvements to property made by tenants or liferenters [q.v.]. Scots law had various rules on the ability of the tenant or liferenter to be compensated for such spending from the landlord. According to Bankton, *Institute,* vol. 1, p. 213 (book I, tit. viii, sect. 15), "if the *bona fide* possessor has made improvements or repairs, he must compensate these with the rents, and cannot bring the expence as a charge upon the proprietor; except in so far as the rents fall short, and that, by such meliorations, the value of the subject is increased. In this case he will be allowed to retain possession till he is refunded his expence, if it is less than the value of the improvement; or otherwise, in the option of the owner, the value of the improved rent, after allowance of the rents received."

mora: delay; normally a claimant's delay in asserting a right or claim, to the prejudice of the defender.

mortification: giving property for religious or charitable purposes.

moveable bond: a "simple bond" for the repayment of borrowed money; in contrast to a "heritable bond," a bond for a sum of money to which is joined a conveyance of land or heritable property to be held as security for the debt.

moveables: all kinds of property, whether corporeal or incorporeal, which do not descend to an heir in heritage.

multure: a toll paid to the proprietor of a mill in return for grinding corn; it is paid from a proportion of the grain ground.

narrative: recital in a deed, setting for the cause of its being granted.

nemo debet locupletari aliena jactura: "no one should be enriched at another's expense."

notour bankrupt: (notorious) bankrupt.

nuncupative will: an unwritten will.

pari passu (by equal step): that is, proportionally, without preference.

personal property: property in things other than land or things attached to land.

poinding: taking the debtor's moveables by way of execution.

poinding the ground: to take goods on land in virtue of a real burden [s.v.] imposed on the land.

porteur: payee of a bill of exchange.

postponed creditor: a creditor whose claims rank behind those of another (preferable) creditor.

praetor: an annually appointed magistrate in the Roman Republic, who was responsible for civil law and who had control over the formulary system of Roman civil litigation. Each praetor could issue a new edict for his year in office, setting out what actions he would countenance; this led to the development of a body of "praetorian law."

precept: a warrant, or authority granted.

precept of sasine: an order from a feudal superior to give infeftment [q.v.] of certain lands to his vassal. "Sasine" is the act of giving legal possession of feudal property.

preferable creditor: the creditor with a right to priority of payment.

preferable debts: debts with a right to priority of payment over other debts.

preference: priority of payment given to one creditor over another.

prescription: the acquisition or loss of rights through use or nonuse over a defined period of time. Introduced by the Prescription Act 1617 (*APS* iv: 543), "positive prescription" is the acquisition of property rights through the possession of the right for an unbroken period of forty years. A "negative prescription" is the loss of a right through its nonexercise for the whole period of prescription.

procurator: legal representative or attorney.

procurator-fiscal: the prosecutor in Scottish inferior courts, representing the Lord Advocate.

procuratory: a mandate or commission granted by one person to act for another.

procuratory *in rem suam:* an authority given to another to act "in his own affairs"; the assignee was authorized by the creditor to sue the debtor in his own name.

procuratory of resignation: a written mandate given by a vassal, authorizing his feu [q.v.] to be returned to his superior, to be granted out to a new vassal.

progress of titles: series of title deeds which constitute the holder's title to lands. Bankton, *Institute,* vol. 1, p. 546 (book II, tit. iii, sect. 35): "All rights to be holden of the granter are original rights; because a new fee is thereby constituted; but rights to singular successors, to be holden of the grantor's superior, by confirmation or resignation, are rights by progress."

purify: fulfill or discharge the condition attaching to a conditional obligation.

pursuer: plaintiff or claimant.

ranking and sale: a process whereby the heritable property of an insolvent was sold and the proceeds distributed among his creditors.

real burdens: *see* real debts.

real debt or real burden (*debitum fundi*): an obligation laid on lands to pay money, declared in a deed naming the creditor, the lands affected, and the amount of the burden. Bankton, *Institute,* vol. 1, p. 652 (book II, tit. v, sect. 18): "To explain a little farther real debts or burthens, termed *Debita fundi,* the ground is properly the debtor in those, it being therewith affected, and such debts a real Lien thereon, to use the term in the English law . . . *Debitum fundi,* therefore, as above is a yearly profit or duty out of the ground, as bygone feu-duties, annuities, or other real debts affecting it."

real property: any property in land or in things attached to land.

reclaiming petition: a process to submit the decisions of the Lords Ordinary of the Court of Session to review by the Inner House of the court (or to submit decisions of the Inner House itself to review).

recovery: a method of conveying land in England (abolished in 1833), taking the form of a feigned or collusive real action between the parties, in which the grantee successfully "recovered" the land.

redargue: disprove or refute.

reduce: to set aside.

reduction: legal action to set aside a deed.

reduction on the head of deathbed: in Scots law, the "law of deathbed" provided that an heir in heritage could reduce [q.v.] all voluntary deeds granted to his prejudice by his predecessor within sixty days of his death, provided he was then suffering from the illness of which he later died. It was based on a presumption that the granter would not have been of sound mind.

reduction upon minority and lesion: the setting aside a deed granted by a minor (or his tutor) on the ground that it is "to his lesion," that is, to his damage.

registrable bond: a written obligation, acknowledging the receipt of money and binding the debtor to repay with interest at a certain time. It included a penalty for late payment and ended with a consent to registration, allowing the creditor to obtain immediate execution of judgment against the debtor on failure of payment. Cf. H. Home, Lord Kames, *Historical Law-Tracts,* 2 vols. (Edinburgh: A. Kincaid and J. Bell, 1776), i: 106–7.

rei vindicatio: an action by the owner of a thing to recover it (Roman law).

relaxation: letters (or a warrant) issued by the Court of Session under the signet whereby a debtor was "relaxed" from personal diligence (that is, execution of judgment), either by the consent of the creditor or because of an error in the proceedings.

relict: widow.

render litigious: a legal prohibition of the alienation of property, in order to defeat an action or execution which has commenced but not been completed.

repeat/repetition: repayment of money which was not owed.

residuary legatee: the person designated to receive the residue of the deceased's estate.

reverser: the proprietor of land who has granted a wadset [s.v.] of the land, and who has the right to recover the land (or the right of *reversion*) on repayment of the money advanced to him.

single escheat: the forfeiture to the crown of moveable estate. Until 1748, such forfeiture was suffered by those who had been denounced for nonpayment or nonperformance of a civil obligation (as well as those who had committed criminal offences). This civil forfeiture was abolished by 20 Geo. II c. 50.

singular successors: those who acquire property otherwise than by succession on the death of the owner; for example, purchasers.

special charge: general and special "charges to enter heir" were the foundation of proceedings against an heir for a debt, consisting of writs ordering the heir to enter as heir to his predecessor within forty days, with a certification that if he failed to do so, the creditor could have an action against him as if he had done so. Where a general charge was used, no summons could be issued for the debt until after a year, when the heir might renounce the succession; where the special charge was used (relating "specially" to particular heritable property), adjudication against the property could be had after forty days. According to Erskine (*Institute,* vol. 1, p. 383: book II, tit. 12, sect. 12), "A special charge fully supplies the want of a service; it states the heir, *fictione iuris* [by a legal fiction] in the right of the subjects to which he is charged to enter, and consequently makes those subjects liable to the same execution at the suit of the creditor, as if the heir had entered to them, and been infeft upon his service. A general charge is, on the other hand, intended barely for fixing the representation of the heir, or subjecting him to that debt which was formerly due by his ancestor; but does not establish in him the right of such heritable subjects as are carried by a general service, so as they may be affected by the creditor's diligence."

spuilzie: taking another person's moveable goods out of his possession against his will. An action of spuilzie is a civil action to remedy this wrong. Erskine, *Institute,* vol. 2, p. 526 (book III, tit. 7, sect. 16): "Spuilzie is the taking away or intermeddling with moveable goods in the possession of another, without either the consent of that other, or the order of law. When a spuilzie is committed, action lies against the delinquent, not only for restoring to the former possessor the goods or their value, but for all the profits he might have made of these goods, had it not been for the spuilzie. These profits are estimated by the pursuer's own oath, and get the name of *violent,* because they are due in no other case than that of violence or wrong."

style: model form of deed or document.

substitutes in an entail: those heirs who succeed in case of failure of the person granted the estate in tail.

suit and service to the manor: English manors had courts-baron, which were both customary courts, dealing with copyhold estates (and in which copyholders had to attend the court), and also courts of common law, in which freeholders who held land of the lord had the duty to attend, giving "suit and service": see Blackstone, *Commentaries*, vol. 3, p. 33.

superior: the granter of heritable property, held by grantees (vassals) for the payment of feu-duties and other services stipulated in the grant.

suspension: the process by which execution on a sentence or decree is stayed until a final decision has been made by the supreme court.

tabellion: a notary (France).

tack: a lease. "A tack is a location or contract, whereby the use of any thing is set to the tacksman for a certain hire": Sir George Mackenzie, *The Institutions of the Law of Scotland* (Edinburgh: John Reid, 1684), part II, tit. 6, p. 133.

tacksman: leaseholder.

tailzie: entail (grant of land to a prescribed set of heirs in succession).

teind: tithe collected for the maintenance of the Scottish Kirk.

tercer: the holder of a terce, a liferent [q.v.] given to a widow, of one-third of the heritage of which her husband died infeft [q.v.].

thirlage: a servitude enjoyed by mill owners; possessors of lands subject to the servitude were bound to grind their grain at a particular mill.

tocher: dowry or marriage portion.

transaction: an agreement between parties to settle a disputed claim.

trespass on the case: *see* action on the case.

tutor-at-law: If there is no tutor nominated by the father (tutor-nominate), a tutor-at-law takes his place. The tutor-at-law acquires his position by law and is the nearest male over the age of twenty-five, on the father's side.

tutor *sine quo non:* a tutor whose consent is indispensable.

wadset: Scottish equivalent to English mortgage: the conveyance of land in pledge for a loan (or in satisfaction of an obligation), with a reserved power in the debtor to redeem the land on payment of the sum lent. The lender is termed the wadsetter, the borrower the reverser [q.v.]. Under a "proper wadset," the wadsetter enjoyed all the profits of the land in lieu of interest for the loan; under an "improper wadset," he had to account to the borrower for any surplus received above the interest.

warrandice: an obligation on a party conveying a right to land or goods to ensure that the right is effectual and binding him to indemnify the grantee in case it is not; a warranty. "By our law, in sale of *goods* and *lands*, where no warrandice is exprest, absolute warrandice is implied, *viz.* That the seller has good right to the same . . . and further, as to goods, that they labour under no latent insufficiency": Bankton, *Institute*, vol. I, p. 424 (book I, tit. xix, sect. 8).

waste: permanent harm to real property caused by the tenant, for which legal liability was incurred.

BIBLIOGRAPHY

Works Cited or Alluded to by Kames

The Acts of Sederunt of the Lords of Council and Session, from the 15th of January 1553 to the 11th of July 1790. Edinburgh: Elphinstone Balfour, 1790. Cited as *AS* in the text.

The Acts of the Parliament of Scotland. Edited by T. Thomson and C. Innes. 13 vols. Edinburgh, 1814–75. Cited as *APS* in the text.

Bacon, Francis. *De Augmentis Scientiarum.* In vol. 1 of *The Works of Francis Bacon.* 4 vols. London: A. Millar, 1740. Cited as Bacon, *Works*, vol. 1, in the text.

Bacon, Matthew. *A New Abridgment of the Law.* 5 vols. London: Nutt and Gosling for Lintot, 1736–66.

Balfour, Sir James, of Pittendreich. *Practicks, or a System of the More Ancient Law of Scotland.* 2 vols. Edinburgh: A. Kincaid and A. Donaldson, 1754. Facsimile reprint, edited by P. G. B. McNeill, Edinburgh: Stair Society, 1962. Cited as Balfour, *Practicks,* in the text.

Bankton, Andrew McDouall, Lord. *An Institute of the Laws of Scotland in Civil Rights.* 3 vols. Edinburgh: Fleming for Kincaid & Donaldson, 1751–53. Facsimile reprint, Edinburgh: Stair Society, 1993–95. Cited as Bankton, *Institute,* in the text.

Bruce, Alexander. *The Decisions of the Lords of Council and Session, in most cases of importance, for the months of November and December 1714, and January, February, June and July 1715.* Edinburgh: James McEuen, 1720. Cited as Bruce in the text.

Cases Argued and Adjudged in the High Court of Chancery Published from the Manuscripts of Thomas Vernon. 2 vols. Dublin: Watts, 1726–29. Cited as Vernon in the text.

565

Cases Argued and Decreed in the High Court of Chancery. 2nd ed. London: Atkyns for Walthoe, 1707. Cited as 1 Chancery Cases in the text.

Clarke, Samuel. *A Discourse Concerning the Unchangeable Obligations of Natural Religion and the Truth and Certainty of the Christian Revelation.* 4th ed., London: James Knapton, 1716.

Codex Iustinianus (The Code of Justinian). Edited by Paul Krueger. Berlin: Weidmann, 1877. Cited as C in the text.

Coke, Edward, Sir. *The First Part of the Institutes of the Laws of England, or a Commentary on Littleton.* London: G. Kearsley and G. Robinson, 1775. Cited as Coke, *1 Institutes,* in the text.

———. *The Fourth Part of the Institutes of the Laws of England, Concerning the Jurisdiction of Courts.* London: Flesher for Lee and Pakeman, 1644. Cited as Coke, *4 Institutes,* in the text.

———. *The Second Part of the Institutes of the Lawes of England.* London: M. Flesher and R. Young, 1642. Cited as Coke, *2 Institutes,* in the text.

A Collection of Decisions of the Lords of Council and Session in two parts. The first contains decisions from July 1661 to July 1666. Observ'd by Sir John Gilmour of Craigmiller. Edinburgh: John Vallange, 1701. Cited as Gilmour in the text.

[Colquitt, Anthony]. *Modern Cases, or Select Cases Adjudged in the Courts of Kings Bench, Chancery, Common-pleas, and Exchequer since the Restauration of His Majesty King Charles II.* London: T. Basset, J. Wright, R. Chiswell, and S. Heyrick, 1682.

Cooper, Anthony Ashley, Earl of Shaftesbury, *A Letter Concerning Enthusiasm.* London: J. Morphew, 1711.

———. *Soliloquy: or, Advice to an Author.* London: J. Morphew, 1710.

Cooper, T. M., ed. *Regiam Majestatem.* Edinburgh: Stair Society 11 (1947).

Decisions of the Court of Session, Collected by Sir Roger Hog of Harcase . . . from 1681 to 1691. Edinburgh: G. Hamilton and J. Gilmour, 1757. Cited as Harcase in the text.

Decisions of the Court of Session from 1698 to 1718, Collected by the Right Honourable Sir Hew Dalrymple. Edinburgh: G. Hamilton and J. Balfour, 1758. Cited as Dalrymple in the text.

Decisions of the Court of Session, from the Year 1738 to the Year 1752. Collected and Digested into the Form of a Dictionary. By Sir James Fergusson of Kilkerran. Edinburgh: J. Bell and W. Creech, 1775. Cited as Kilkerran in the text.

The Decisions of the Lords of Council and Session from June 6th 1678 to July 12th 1712. Collected by Sir John Lauder of Fountainhall. 2 vols. Edinburgh: G. Hamilton and J. Balfour, 1759–61. Cited as Fountainhall in the text.

Duck, Arthur. *De usu et authoritate juris civili Romanorum in dominiis principum Christianorum.* London: Richard Hodgkinson, 1653.

Durie, Sir Alexander Gibson of. *The Decisions of the Lords of Council and Session . . . from July 1621 to July 1642.* Edinburgh: George Mosman, 1690. Cited in the text as Durie.

Elchies, Patrick Grant of. *Decisions of the Court of Session from the Year 1733 to the Year 1754.* Edited by W. M. Morison. 2 vols. Edinburgh: Printed for the Editor, 1813.

Erskine, John. *An Institute of the Law of Scotland.* 2 vols. Edinburgh: John Bell, 1773. Cited as Erskine, *Institute,* in the text.

Falconer, David. *The Decisions of the Court of Session. From the Month of November 1744.* 2 vols. Edinburgh: W. & T. Ruddimans. Cited as Falconer in the text.

Finch, Thomas, ed. *Precedents in Chancery: Being a Collection of Cases Argued and Adjudged in the High Court of Chancery from the Year 1689 to 1722.* 2nd ed. London: H. Lintot, 1747.

Forbes, William. *A Journal of the Session. Containing the Decisions of the Lords of Council and Session . . . from February 1705 till November 1713.* Edinburgh: for the author, 1713. Cited as Forbes in the text.

Foster, Michael, Sir. *A Report of Some Proceedings on the Commission of Oyer and Terminer and Gaol Delivery for the Trial of the Rebels in the Year 1746 in the County of Surry, and of Other Crown Cases to which are added Discourses upon a few Branches of the Crown Law.* Oxford: Clarendon Press, 1762.

A General Abridgment of Cases in Equity. 4th ed. 2 vols. London: Lintot, 1756. Cited as Eq. Cas. Abr. in the text.

Hale, Matthew. *The History of the Pleas of the Crown.* 2 vols. London: Nutt and Gosling, 1736.

[Halhed, Nathaniel Brassey]. *A Code of Gentoo Laws, or Ordinations of the Pundits, from a Persian Translation.* London, 1776.

Justinian. *The Digest of Justinian.* Edited by Theodor Mommsen and Paul Krueger; English translation edited by Alan Watson. 4 vols. Philadelphia: University of Pennsylvania Press, 1985. Cited as D or Watson in the text.

―――. *Justinian's Institutes.* Translated and edited by Peter Birks and Grant McLeod. London: Duckworth, 1987. Cited as Inst or Birks & McLeod in the text.

Kames, Henry Home, Lord. *Decisions of the Court of Session, from its first institution to the present time. Abridged and digested under heads in the form of a dictionary.* 2 vols. Edinburgh: Richard Watkins, Alexander Kincaid, and Robert Fleming, 1741. Cited as Kames, *Dictionary,* in the text.

————. *Elucidations Respecting the Common and Statute Law of Scotland.* Edinburgh: William Creech, 1777.

————. *Essays on the Principles of Morality and Natural Religion.* 2nd ed. London: C. Hitch & L. Hawes, R. & J. Dodsley, J. Rivington & J. Fletcher, and J. Richardson, 1758; Indianapolis: Liberty Fund, 2005.

————. *Essays upon Several Subjects Concerning British Antiquities.* Edinburgh: A. Kincaid, 1747.

————. *Historical Law-Tracts.* 2 vols. Edinburgh: Millar, Kincaid and Bell, 1758.

————. *Remarkable Decisions of the Court of Session from 1716 to 1728.* Edinburgh: T. Ruddiman, 1728 (cited as Home in the text); 2nd ed. Edinburgh: Bell & Bradfute, 1790 (cited as Kames, *Remarkable Decisions* i, in the text).

————. *Remarkable Decisions of the Court of Session from 1730 to 1752.* Edinburgh: A. Kincaid and J. Bell, 1766; 2d ed. Edinburgh: Bell & Bradfute, 1799. Cited as Kames, *Remarkable Decisions* ii, in the text.

————. *Select Decisions of the Court of Session, from the Year 1752 to the Year 1768.* Collected by a member of the Court. Edinburgh: John Bell, 1780; 2nd ed., Edinburgh: Bell and Bradfute, 1799 (cited as Kames, *Select Decisions,* ii, in the text).

————. *Sketches of the History of Man.* 2nd ed. 4 vols. Edinburgh: Strahan, Cadell, and Creech, 1778; Indianapolis: Liberty Fund, 2007.

————. *The Statute Law of Scotland Abridged.* Edinburgh: A. Kincaid and A. Donaldson, 1757.

Kilkerran, Sir James Fergusson of. *Decisions of the Court of Session from the Year 1738 to the Year 1752.* Edinburgh: J. Bell and W. Creech, 1775.

Locke, John. *An Essay Concerning Human Understanding.* 15th ed. 2 vols. London: D. Browne et al., 1760.

Mackenzie, George, Sir. *Observations upon the 18th Act of the 23d Parliament of King James the Sixth against Dispositions Made in Defraud of Creditors &c.* In vol. 2 of *The Works of That Eminent and Learned Lawyer Sir George Mackenzie of Rosehaugh.* 2 vols. Edinburgh: James Watson, 1716–22.

Mascardus, Josephus. *De probationibus.* 3 vols. Frankfurt am Main: E. Kempffer, 1619.

Morison, William Maxwell. *The Decisions of the Court of Session from its institution until the separation of the Court into two divisions in the year 1808, digested under proper heads in the form of a dictionary.* 42 vols. Edinburgh: Archibald Constable & Co., 1811. Cited as M in the text.

Pufendorf, Samuel von. *Of the Law of Nature and Nations.* Translated by B. Kennet. Oxford, 1703.

Reid, Thomas. *An Inquiry into the Human Mind, on Principles of Common Sense.* Edinburgh: Millar, Kincaid & Bell, 1764.

Richardson, H. G., and G. O. Sayles, eds. *Fleta.* London: Selden Society 72 (1953). London: Quaritch, 1955.

Rousseau, Jean-Jacques. *Émile, ou de l'éducation.* 4 vols. Frankfurt, 1762.

———. *Lettres de deux amans habitans d'une petite ville au pied des Alpes.* [*La Nouvelle Heloïse*]. Amsterdam: Rey, 1761.

Salkeld, William. *Reports of Cases Adjudg'd in the Court of King's Bench.* London: Nutt & Gosling for Walthoe, 1717. Cited as Salkeld in the text.

The Second Part of Cases Argued and Decreed in the High Court of Chancery continued from the 30th Year of King Charles II to the 4th Year of King James II. London: Atkyns for Walthoe, 1701. Cited as 2 Chancery Cases in the text.

Shower, Bartholomew, Sir. *Cases in Parliament Resolved and Adjudged, upon petitions and writs of error.* London: A. & J. Churchill, 1698.

Siderfin, Thomas. *Les reports des divers special cases argue & adjudge en le Court del Bank le Roy.* 2nd ed. 2 vols. London: Nutt for Keble, Browne, Ward, Mears and Browne, 1714. Cited as Sid. in the text.

Some Doubts and Questions in the law, especially of Scotland. As also, some decisions of the Lords of Council and Session: collected and observ'd by Sir John Nisbet of Dirleton. Edinburgh: G. Mosman, 1698. Cited as Dirleton in the text.

Stair, James Dalrymple, Viscount of. *The Decisions of the Lords of Council & Session in the Most Important Cases debate before them, with the Acts of Sederunt.* Edinburgh: Andrew Anderson, 1683–87.

———. *The Institutions of the Law of Scotland.* Edited by David M. Walker. Edinburgh and Glasgow: University Presses of Edinburgh and Glasgow, 1981. Cited as Stair, *Institutions,* in the text.

van den Sande, Johan. *Decisiones Frisicae; sive rerum in suprema frisiorum curia judicatarum libri quinque.* Amsterdam: T. Myls, 1698.

Vinnius, A. *In quatuor libros Institutionum imperialum commentarius.* Edited by J. G. Heineccius. Leiden: Joannes van der Linden, 1726.

Voet, Johannes. *Commentarius ad Pandectas.* 2 vols. The Hague: Anthony van Dole, 1734.

Secondary Sources

Ford, J. D. *Law and Opinion in Scotland during the Seventeenth Century.* Oxford: Hart Publishing, 2007.

Helo, A. "The Historicity of Morality: Necessity and Necessary Agents in the Ethics of Lord Kames." *History of European Ideas* 27 (2001): 239–55.

Koyanagi, K. "Civilization and History in Lord Kames and William Robertson." In *The Rise of Political Economy in the Scottish Enlightenment,* edited by Tatsuya Sakamoto and Hideo Tanaka, 150–61. Routledge Studies in the History of Economics, 56. London: Routledge, 2003.

Lehmann, W. C. *Henry Home, Lord Kames and the Scottish Enlightenment: A Study in National Character and in the History of Ideas.* The Hague: Martinus Nijhoff, 1971.

———. "The Historical Approach in the Juridical Writings of Lord Kames." *Juridical Review* 9 (1964): 17–38.

Lieberman, D. *The Province of Legislation Determined: Legal Theory in Eighteenth-Century Britain.* Cambridge: Cambridge University Press, 1989.

Lobban, M. "The Ambition of Lord Kames's Equity." In *Law and History,* edited by A. D. E. Lewis and M. Lobban, 97–121. Current Legal Issues 6. Oxford: Oxford University Press, 2004.

Manolescu, B. I. "Kames Legal Career and Writings as Precedents for *Elements of Criticism.*" *Rhetorica* 23 (2005): 239–59.

McGuinness, A. E. *Henry Home, Lord Kames.* New York: Twayne, 1970.

Rahmatian, A. "The Property Theory of Lord Kames." *International Journal of Law in Context* 2 (2006): 177–205.

Reid, K., and R. Zimmermann, eds. *A History of Private Law in Scotland.* 2 vols. Oxford: Oxford University Press, 2000.

Ross, Ian Simpson. *Lord Kames and the Scotland of His Day.* Oxford: Clarendon Press, 1972.

———. "The Natural Theology of Lord Kames." In *The Scottish Enlightenment: Essays in Reinterpretation,* edited by Paul Wood, 335–50. Rochester, N.Y.: University of Rochester Press, 2000.

Ross, T. "Copyright and the Invention of Tradition." *Eighteenth-Century Studies* 26 (Autumn 1992): 1–27.

Walker, D. M. *A Legal History of Scotland.* Vol. 5, *The Eighteenth Century.* Edinburgh: T. & T. Clark, 1998.

INDEX

A. against B., 7 Dec. 1686 [M 6298], 74n5

A. against B., 9 Feb. 1676 [M 9505], 34n*

Abercromby, Dr. William, contra Earl of Peterborough, 13 July 1745 [M 4894 and 16429], 61–62

Abercromby contra Graham, 18 Jan. 1717 [M 4112], 387n†

Aberdeen, Alexander, contra Robert Aberdeen, 13 Dec. 1757 [M 6598], 151n*

Aberdeen, Earl of, contra Trustees of Blair (Earl of Aberdeen contra Creditors of Lowis of Merchiston and Scot of Blair), 3 Feb. 1736 [M 1208], 377n*

Abney v. Kendal (1663), 266n†

abridgment of lawsuits, 297–300

absent persons, covenants or promises in favor of, 275–87, 510–12

absolute warrandice, 108–9, 167, 170, 173, 174, 564

absolvitor, 327, 429, 533, 543

abuse of rights (acting *in aemulationem vicini*), doctrine of, 46–47, 456, 555

accessories, criminal, 66, 268

accessory obligations, 142–43, 523–24, 543

accretion, 136n6, 543

actio de in rem verso, 94, 543

actio in factum, 93, 543

actio in rem versum, 94n10, 106, 303, 319*n*a, 528, 543, 555

actio negotiorum gestorum, xxv, 22n7, 30, 34, 110–11, 435, 458, 488, 543–44

actiones in factum, 93

action of mails and duties, 215n19, 248, 251–52, 321, 333, 445, 515, 557

action on the case, 422, 544

actio quanti minoris, 159–60

actio redhibitoria (redhibitory action), 159–60, 435

Actor sequitur forum rei, 417

acts before answer, xix*n*25

acts *contra bona mores*, 25–26, 463–64

acts *contra utilitatem publicam*, 295, 297

acts *ob turpen causam*, 155

acts of litiscontestation, xix*n*25

acts of sederunt, xix, xxi, 544

Acts of the Parliament of Scotland (Thomson and Innes, 1814–75), xxviii, xxxiii. *See also specific statutes*

adjudication: declaratory adjudications, 251, 252, 440, 541, 550; defined, 544; in implement, xx*n*31, 251, 541, 544; original index entry, 436; *pluris petitio*, 258–68

Adjudications Act 1672 (Scotland), 247, 540

adultery, xlix, 155, 272, 436, 512

advocation, 292, 294, 297, 545

Aikenhead contra Durham, 24 June 1703 [M 14701], 394n‡

Airth, Laird of, contra Laird of ———, 11 March 1612 [M 8938], 391n‡

This book is set in Adobe Garamond, a modern adaptation by Robert Slimbach of the typeface originally cut around 1540 by the French typographer and printer Claude Garamond. The Garamond face, with its small lowercase height and restrained contrast between thick and thin strokes, is a classic "old-style" face and has long been one of the most influential and widely used typefaces.

Printed on paper that is acid-free and meets the requirements of the American National Standard for Permanence of Paper for Printed Library Materials, z39.48-1992. ∞

Book design by Louise OFarrell
Gainesville, Florida
Typography by Graphic Composition, Inc.
Bogart, Georgia
Printed and bound by Worzalla Publishing Company
Stevens Point, Wisconsin